Major Problems in the History of the American South

MAJOR PROBLEMS IN AMERICAN HISTORY SERIES

GENERAL EDITOR

THOMAS G. PATERSON

Major Problems in the History of the American South

Volume II: The New South

DOCUMENTS AND ESSAYS

THIRD EDITION

EDITED BY

SALLY G. McMILLEN

DAVIDSON COLLEGE

ELIZABETH HAYES TURNER

UNIVERSITY OF NORTH TEXAS

PAUL D. ESCOTT

WAKE FOREST UNIVERSITY

DAVID R. GOLDFIELD

UNIVERSITY OF NORTH CAROLINA, CHARLOTTE

Australia • Brazil • Japan • Korea • Mexico • Singapore • Spain • United Kingdom • United States

Major Problems in the History of the American South, Volume II: The New South, Third Edition

Sally G. McMillen, Elizabeth Hayes Turner, Paul D. Escott, David R. Goldfield

Senior Publisher: Suzanne Jeans

Acquisitions Editor: Jeffrey Greene

Development Editor: Terri Wise

Editorial Assistant: Patrick Roach

Senior Marketing Manager: Katherine Bates

Marketing Coordinator: Lorreen Pelletier

Marketing Program Manager: Caitlin Green

Content Project Management: PreMediaGlobal

Senior Art Director: Cate Rickard Barr

Senior Print Buyer: Sandee Milewski

Rights Acquisition Specialist: Jennifer Meyer Dare

Cover Designer: Gary Ragaglia, Metro Design

Cover Image: Stephen Morgan Etnier (1903–1984)
Georgetown, South Carolina, 1934
Oil on canvas, 28 x 36 inches
Photo courtesy of The Charleston Renaissance Gallery, Charleston, SC

Compositor: PreMediaGlobal

Library of Congress Control Number: 2011934200

ISBN-13: 978-0-547-22833-4

ISBN-10: 0-547-22833-3

Wadsworth
20 Channel Center Street
Boston, MA 02210
USA

Cengage Learning is a leading provider of customized learning solutions with office locations around the globe, including Singapore, the United Kingdom, Australia, Mexico, Brazil, and Japan. Locate your local office at **international.cengage.com/region**.

Cengage Learning products are represented in Canada by Nelson Education, Ltd.

For your course and learning solutions, visit **www.cengage.com**

Purchase any of our products at your local college store or at our preferred online store **www.cengagebrain.com**.

Instructors: Please visit **login.cengage.com** and log in to access instructor-specific resources.

Printed in the United States of America
1 2 3 4 5 6 7 15 14 13 12 11

Contents

Preface

Historian David M. Potter once wrote that the South has been "a kind of Sphinx on the American land." Nothing in the two volumes of *Major Problems in the History of the American South* will challenge that description of a great American enigma. The documents and essays in these volumes demonstrate that the search to know what the South was and what it is remains at the core of southern history.

William Faulkner observed that in the South the past is not dead; it is not even past. Some students of southern history may well recognize this statement to be true; others will decide the South has moved beyond its past, becoming more like the rest of the nation. Or perhaps, as some people conclude, the rest of the nation has become more like the South. In any case, today the South is less a geographical entity than a state of mind, offering a panorama of almost bewildering diversity. Writers and historians have yet to agree on what makes the region's culture and history different from the rest of the nation. For all who have sought to discover its essence, the challenge has been in the pursuit and in the insights that come from what the scholar Fred Hobson has called "the southern rage to explain." We hope the selections in this book will encourage readers to pursue that quest to understand the South's past.

Both volumes I and II include recent scholarship published after 1999 when the second editions appeared, as well as classic essays that continue to withstand the test of time. It is hoped that these documents and essays will continue to make evident the incredible richness and variety of southern history. These two volumes follow the same general format as other volumes in the *Major Problems in American History* series. Each chapter begins with a brief introduction to its topic, followed first by documentary readings and then by essays that illuminate the central theme. Headnotes that place the readings in historical and interpretive perspective introduce each chapter's primary sources and essays. A "Further Reading" section, suggesting important books and articles for those who wish to explore the subject in more depth, closes each chapter.

Like the first and second editions of *Major Problems in the History of the American South*, this revised Volume II on the New South follows a mostly chronological tour of southern history, from the challenge and dislocations of Reconstruction to the rise of the Republican Party in the South. This volume concludes by sharing essays on southerners' cultural expressions while exposing concern over environmental issues that have influenced the modern-day South. The documents selected evoke the atmosphere, personal experiences, and events of the time.

In preparing the new edition, we consulted with professors who teach southern history and drew on our own approach to teaching the subject. As a result, we have added a new chapter on historical memory and have collapsed two chapters on Progressivism into one. Chapter 1 includes two new essays, one by historian C. Vann Woodward, who argues that what makes the South distinctive is simply its history, which he views from three distinct points of view. The other essay by sociologist, John Shelton Reed, also finds three completely different variations on the South, alluding to agriculture, industry, and popular culture. Chapter 2 features the new historiographical emphasis on violence in the overthrow of Reconstruction with an essay by Hannah Rosen. Chapter 4 focuses primarily on textile mills in the South, with photographs by Lewis W. Hine and a new article by Bryant Simon, who shifts the discussion toward the politics of mill workers. Chapter 5 centers mainly on the Populists and introduces Charles Postel's essay on race and the disfranchisement process stemming from the Populist movement. Chapter 6, "The Intimidation Factor," a term borrowed from Leon F. Litwack, includes his new essay on segregation as well as a new article by Steven Hahn on the origins of disfranchisement and black resistance. Mark Twain makes an appearance through "The United States of Lyncherdom," an essay published only after his death. Religion receives its own chapter with more emphasis on race, lynching, and politics in relationship to southern religion. Mark A. Noll and Donald G. Mathews add new perspectives on these topics.

The newest chapter in Volume II, "Southern Memory and History," includes essays by David R. Goldfield and W. Fitzhugh Brundage, who seek to remind readers that a collective Lost Cause memory among southern whites was countered through the decades by an equally important, although comparatively underfunded, emancipationist memory kept alive by southern African Americans. The newest study, by Micki McElya of the movement for a national Mammy monument, suggests that memorials to the faithful slave continued to be strong in public memory well into the 1920s. Chapter 9, "Progressivism in the Age of Jim Crow," is supported by a new essay on women and voting by Lorraine Gates Schuyler. Chapter 10 introduces James C. Cobb's interpretive essay on the Southern Renaissance as a rebuttal to the New South Creed. Chapter 11 on the New Deal and World War II brings forth two new articles by New Deal specialists Anthony J. Badger, who argues that the New Deal brought little change to the region, and Patricia Sullivan, who sees openings in the racial wall due to New Deal policies. These are supported by new documents—letters from women supplicants and memories of Virginia Foster Durr with evidence of the bi-racial nature of the Southern Conference for Human Welfare. The focus of Chapter 12, "Race Relations and Freedom Struggles," turns toward the challenges faced by students, nine of whom integrated all-white Central High School in Little Rock, Arkansas. Elizabeth Jacoway's new essay portrays with sickening detail the psychological torture Minnijean Brown endured as she became the target of white supremacists' daily attacks. Barbara Ransby's new essay describes Ella Baker's role in the birth of the Mississippi Freedom Democratic Party and its challenge to the established Regular Democratic Party in Mississippi. Both essays are supported by newly added primary documents, including an account by Melba Pattillo Beals, photographs, and recollections by Anne Moody. Chapter 13, "The Recent South and Its Culture Wars," is heavily influenced by the shift toward right-wing politics and its impact on the region and the nation. Dan T. Carter, Matthew D. Lassiter and Kevin M. Kruse, and Marjorie Julian Spruill bring new information to light regarding the rise of George Wallace, white flight to southern suburbs, and the assaults by Mississippi women and men on the feminist movement.

The final chapter, "The South in America," recognizes the enormous influence the region presents to the nation. The South is not a monolith, as historians, sociologists, political scientists, and journalists have noted. There are many Souths, and each one—an environmental South, a musical and cultural South, and a South prone to disasters with huge national repercussions—has had its effect on the nation. Newcomers to this edition, Pete Daniel, Jack Temple Kirby, and John Egerton, all contribute to the final conversation on the South's most recent history, its impact on national processes, and its future as a viable and growing region. Once called the haunted South, the lynching-bee South, and the nation's number one economic problem, the "New" New South is presented here with many of its problems and much of its significant transformation.

In choosing the essays, we have provided historical perspective on some of the major issues southerners confronted and have included provocative interpretations of those key issues. Nothing could be more illustrative of the competing views of southerners themselves than in the evocation of collective memory. In Chapter 8, images depicting somber Lost Cause warrior Robert E. Lee in bronze and stone contrast sharply with an ebullient Juneteenth emancipation celebration where no glorifying statues may be found. Equally divergent are the essays in this chapter that analyze how southerners remembered their pasts from differing perspectives of race and gender. In both the documents and the essays, a variety of viewpoints are represented, inviting readers to reach their own conclusions about major interpretative problems in southern history.

Many friends and colleagues contributed to these volumes: For help with the third edition of Volume Two, we want to thank Charles Bittner, *The Nation;* Bradley Bond, University of Southern Mississippi; Gregg Cantrell, Texas Christian University; Cita Cook, recently retired from the University of West Georgia; Glenda Gilmore, Yale University; Angela Hornsby-Gutting, University of Mississippi; William A. Link, University of Florida; Todd Moye, University of North Texas; Michael Perman, University of Illinois at Chicago; Randy Sparks, Tulane University; Jennifer Wallach, University of North Texas; and Marjorie Spruill Wheeler, University of South Carolina. Several graduate students from the University of North Texas helped at various stages of the project. We thank

Greg Ball, Jared Donnelly, Simone De Santiago Ramos, Lisa Fox, and Jessica Brannon-Wranosky.

The following instructors provided detailed and extremely helpful written reviews: Dan Dupre, University of North Carolina at Charlotte; Caroline Emmons, Hampden-Sydney College; Jonathan Kasparek, University of Wisconsin, Waukesha; Scott Nelson, College of William & Mary; and Richard Straw, Radford University. We are grateful to our editor, Jeff Greene, who shepherded this project from the beginning and who even made visits to the campus at UNT. In addition we thank Terri Wise for her editing role, keeping us on track throughout the latter stages of the process. We wish to thank the Department of History, University of North Texas for its support during the research stage of this project, and The William P. Clements Center for Southwest Studies at Southern Methodist University for a Clements Fellowship, which allowed time to clear the desk and finish the project.

Without the unlimited support and patience of our families, this project would not have been completed. This volume is dedicated to our children and grandchildren–all twelve of them–and to our students who continue to remind us that the history of the South is a complex and fascinating subject.

S. M.

E. H. T.

P. E.

D. G.

CHAPTER 1

The Historians' South

Historian Michael O'Brien noted that "no man's South is the same as another's." Although there is general agreement that the South is (or at least was, at some time) distinct from other regions of the United States, there is no consensus on either the nature or the duration of that difference. Definitions of the South have stressed everything from the obvious (for example, climate and white supremacy) to the obscure (the geographical line below which grits replace hash browns).

Part of the problem is that there are many Souths. Those who lived in the South Carolina lowcountry were different in terms of ethnicity, accent, ideology, occupation, religion, music, and language from the people of the southern Appalachians. Distinctions exist within states—lowcountry versus upcountry, Piedmont versus coastal plains, and Delta versus piney woods. Then there are great differences between the southern states east and west of the Mississippi River. These disparities have led some to contend that the South is more a state of mind than a geographical region.

Yet some thing or things draw these disparate areas together, and observers since the earliest settlements have tried to identify what constitutes "the South." The task is more than a mere intellectual exercise. As with the study of any ethnic group, distinction helps to define identity. And the study of the South has helped to define our national identity as well. The South has often served as a counterpoint, both good and bad, to the rest of the country. In learning what is special about the South and how it became that way, we are learning about our national culture as well.

ESSAYS

Four scholars offer different views of the South. W. J. Cash's *The Mind of the South* is among the most eloquent and forceful statements of southern identity, though the Charlotte journalist's emphasis on the continuity of southern history has provoked sharp responses from other historians, including the late C. Vann Woodward of Yale University. The first two essays present Cash's and Woodward's differing views. Defining southern distinctiveness is a major academic industry. John B. Boles, professor of history at Rice University and editor of the *Journal of Southern History,* notes the complex task of identifying the South's distinct character and how individuals continue to try to rediscover and embrace its uniqueness. Finally, John Shelton Reed, professor emeritus of sociology at the University of North Carolina, wrote the program for the 1996 Summer Olympics held in Atlanta and in it tried to explain the South's unique character.

The Continuity of Southern History

W. J. CASH

There exists among us by ordinary—both North and South—a profound conviction that the South is another land, sharply differentiated from the rest of the American nation, and exhibiting within itself a remarkable homogeneity.

As to what its singularity may consist in, there is, of course, much conflict of opinion, and especially between Northerner and Southerner. But that it is different and that it is solid—on these things nearly everybody is agreed. Now and then, to be sure, there have arisen people, usually journalists or professors, to tell us that it is all a figment of the imagination, that the South really exists only as a geographical division of the United States and is distinguishable from New England or the Middle West only by such matters as the greater heat and the presence of a larger body of Negroes. Nobody, however, has ever taken them seriously. And rightly.

For the popular conviction is indubitably accurate: the South is, in Allen Tate's phrase, "Uncle Sam's other province." And when Carl Carmer said of Alabama that "The Congo is not more different from Massachusetts or Kansas or California," he fashioned a hyperbole which is applicable in one measure or another to the entire section.

This is not to suggest that the land does not display an enormous diversity within its borders. Anyone may see that it does simply by riding along any of the great new motor roads which spread across it—through brisk towns with tall white buildings in Nebraska Gothic; through smart suburbs, with their faces newly washed; through industrial and Negro slums, medieval in dirt and squalor and wretchedness, in all but redeeming beauty; past sleepy old hamlets and wide fields and black men singing their sad songs in the cotton, past log cabin and high grave houses, past hill and swamp and plain.... The distance from Charleston to Birmingham is in some respects measurable only in sidereal terms, as is the distance from the Great Smokies to Lake Pontchartrain. And Howard Odum has demonstrated that the economic and social difference between the Southeastern and Southwestern states is so great and growing that they have begun to deserve to be treated, for many purposes, as separate regions.

Nevertheless, if it can be said there are many Souths, the fact remains that there is also one South. That is to say, it is easy to trace throughout the region (roughly delimited by the boundaries of the former Confederate States of

America, but shading over into some of the border states, notably Kentucky, also) a fairly definite mental pattern, associated with a fairly definite social pattern—a complex of established relationships and habits of thought, sentiments, prejudices, standards and values, and associations of ideas, which, if it is not common strictly to every group of white people in the South, is still common in one appreciable measure or another, and in some part or another, to all but relatively negligible ones.

It is no product of Cloud-Cuckoo-Town, of course, but proceeds from the common American heritage, and many of its elements are readily recognizable as being simply variations on the primary American theme. To imagine it existing outside this continent would be quite impossible. But for all that, the peculiar history of the South has so greatly modified it from the general American norm that, when viewed as a whole, it decisively justifies the notion that the country is—not quite a nation within a nation, but the next thing to it.

To understand it, it is necessary to know the story of its development. And the best way to begin that story, I think, is by disabusing our minds of two correlated legends—those of the Old and the New Souths.

What the Old South of the legend in its classical form was like is more or less familiar to everyone. It was a sort of stage piece out of the eighteenth century, wherein gesturing gentlemen move soft-spokenly against a background of rose gardens and dueling grounds, through always gallant deeds, and lovely ladies, in farthingales, never for a moment lost that exquisite remoteness which has been the dream of all men and the possession of none. Its social pattern was manorial, its civilization that of the Cavalier, its ruling class an aristocracy coextensive with the planter group—men often entitled to quarter the royal arms of St. George and St. Andrew on their shields, and in every case descended from the old gentlefolk who for many centuries had made up the ruling classes of Europe.

They dwelt in large and stately mansions, preferably white and with columns and Grecian entablature. Their estates were feudal baronies, their slaves quite too numerous ever to be counted, and their social life a thing of Old World splendor and delicacy. What had really happened here, indeed, was that the gentlemanly idea, driven from England by Cromwell, had taken refuge in the South and fashioned for itself a world to its heart's desire: a world singularly polished and mellow and poised, wholly dominated by ideals of honor and chivalry and *noblesse*—all those sentiments and values and habits of action which used to be, especially in Walter Scott, invariably assigned to the gentleman born and the Cavalier.

Beneath these was a vague race lumped together indiscriminately as the poor whites—very often, in fact, as the "white-trash." These people belonged in the main to a physically inferior type, having sprung for the most part from the convict servants, redemptioners, and debtors of old Virginia and Georgia, with a sprinkling of the most unsuccessful sort of European peasants and farm laborers and the dregs of the European town slums. And so, of course, the gulf between them and the master classes was impassable, and their ideas and feelings did not enter into the makeup of the prevailing Southern civilization.

But in the legend of the New South the Old South is supposed to have been destroyed by the Civil War and the thirty years that followed it, to have been swept both socially and mentally into the limbo of things that were and are not, to give place to a society which has been rapidly and increasingly industrialized and modernized both in body and in mind—which now, indeed, save for a few quaint survivals and gentle sentimentalities and a few shocking and inexplicable brutalities such as lynching, is almost as industrialized and modernized in its outlook as the North. Such an idea is obviously inconsistent with the general assumption of the South's great difference, but paradox is the essence of popular thinking, and millions—even in the South itself—placidly believe in both notions.

These legends, however, bear little relation to reality. There was an Old South, to be sure, but it was another thing than this. And there is a New South. Industrialization and commercialization have greatly modified the land, including its ideology.... Nevertheless, the extent of the change and of the break between the Old South that was and the South of our time has been vastly exaggerated. The South, one might say, is a tree with many age rings, with its limbs and trunk bent and twisted by all the winds of the years, but with its tap root in the Old South. Or, better still, it is like one of those churches one sees in England. The facade and towers, the windows and clerestory, all the exterior and superstructure are late Gothic of one sort or another, but look into its nave, its aisles, and its choir and you find the old mighty Norman arches of the twelfth century. And if you look into its crypt, you may even find stones cut by Saxon, brick made by Roman hands.

The mind of the section, that is, is continuous with the past. And its primary form is determined not nearly so much by industry as by the purely agricultural conditions of that past. So far from being modernized, in many ways it has actually always marched away, as to this day it continues to do, from the present toward the past.

The Search for Southern Identity

C. VANN WOODWARD

The time is coming, if indeed it has not already arrived, when the Southerner will begin to ask himself whether there is really any longer very much point in calling himself a Southerner....

The South is ... in the midst of an economic and social revolution that has by no means run its course, and it will not be possible to measure its results for a long time to come. This revolution has already leveled many of the old monuments of regional distinctiveness and may end eventually by erasing the very consciousness of a distinctive tradition along with the will to sustain it. The sustaining will and consciousness are also under the additional strain of a moral

C. Vann Woodward, "The Search for Southern Identity," in *The Burden of Southern History* (Baton Rouge: Louisiana State University Press, 1993). Reprinted by permission of Louisiana State University Press.

indictment against a discredited part of the tradition, an indictment more uncompromising than any since abolitionist times.

The Southerner may not have been very happy about many of those old monuments of regional distinctiveness that are now disappearing. He may, in fact, have deplored the existence of some—the one-horse farmer, one-crop agriculture, one-party politics, the sharecropper, the poll tax, the white primary, the Jim Crow car, the lynching bee. It would take a blind sentimentalist to mourn their passing. But until the day before yesterday there they stood, indisputable proof that the South was different. Now that they are vanished or on their way toward vanishing, we are suddenly aware of the vacant place they have left in the landscape and of our habit of depending upon them in final resort as landmarks of regional identification. To establish identity by reference to our faults was always simplest, for whatever their reservations about our virtues, our critics were never reluctant to concede us our vices and shortcomings.

It is not that the present South has any conspicuous lack of faults, but that its faults are growing less conspicuous and therefore less useful for purposes of regional identification. They are increasingly the faults of other parts of the country, standard American faults, shall we say. Many of them have only recently been acquired—could, in fact, only recently be afforded. For the great changes that are altering the cultural landscape of the South almost beyond recognition are not simply negative changes, the disappearance of the familiar. There are also positive changes, the appearance of the strikingly new.

The symbol of innovation is inescapable. The roar and groan and dust of it greet one on the outskirts of every Southern city. That symbol is the bulldozer, and for lack of a better name this might be called the Bulldozer Revolution. The great machine with the lowered blade symbolizes the revolution in several respects: in its favorite area of operation, the area where city meets country; in its relentless speed; in its supreme disregard for obstacles, its heedless methods; in what it demolishes and in what it builds. It is the advance agent of the metropolis. It encroaches upon rural life to expand urban life. It demolishes the old to make way for the new....

According to nearly all of the indices, so the economists find, economic growth of the South in recent years greatly exceeds the rate maintained in the North and East. The fact is the South is going through economic expansion and reorganization that the North and East completed a generation or more ago. But the process is taking place far more rapidly than it did in the North. Among all the many periods of change in the history of the South it is impossible to find one of such concentration and such substantive impact. The period of Reconstruction might appear a likely rival for this distinction, but that revolution was largely limited to changes in legal status and the ownership of property. The people remained pretty much where they were and continued to make their living in much the same way. All indications are that the bulldozer will leave a deeper mark upon the land than did the carpetbagger.

It is the conclusion of two Southern sociologists, John M. Maclachlan and Joe S. Floyd, Jr., that the present drive toward uniformity "with national demographic, economic, and cultural norms might well hasten the day when the South, once perhaps the most distinctively 'different' American region, will have become in most such matters virtually indistinguishable from the other urban-industrial areas of the nation."

The threat of becoming "indistinguishable," of being submerged under a national steamroller, has haunted the mind of the South for a long time. Some have seen it as a menace to regional identity and the survival of a Southern heritage....

The traditionalist who has watched the Bulldozer Revolution plow under cherished old values of individualism, localism, family, clan, and rural folk culture has felt helpless and frustrated against the mighty and imponderable agents of change. Industrialism, urbanism, unionism, and big government conferred or promised too many coveted benefits. They divided the people and won support in the South, so that it was impossible to rally unified opposition to them.

The race issue was different. Advocates and agents of change could be denounced as outsiders, intruders, meddlers. Historic memories of resistance and cherished constitutional principles could be invoked. Racial prejudices, aggressions, and jealousies could be stirred to rally massive popular support. And with this dearly bought unity, which he could not rally on other issues, the frustrated traditionalist might at last take his stand for the defense of all the defiled, traduced, and neglected values of the traditional order. What then is the prospect of the Phillipsian "cardinal test" as a bulwark against change? Will it hold fast where other defenses have failed?

Recent history furnishes some of the answers. Since the last World War old racial attitudes that appeared more venerable and immovable than any other have exhibited a flexibility that no one would have predicted. One by one, in astonishingly rapid succession, many landmarks of racial discrimination and segregation have disappeared, and old barriers have been breached. Many remain, of course—perhaps more than have been breached—and distinctively Southern racial attitudes will linger for a long time. Increasingly the South is aware of its isolation in these attitudes, however, and is in defense of the institutions that embody them. They have fallen rapidly into discredit and under condemnation from the rest of the country and the rest of the world.

Once more the South finds itself with a morally discredited Peculiar Institution on its hands. The last time this happened, about a century ago, the South's defensive reaction was to identify its whole cause with the one institution that was most vulnerable and to make loyalty to an ephemeral aspect which it had once led in condemning the cardinal test of loyalty to the whole tradition. Southerners who rejected the test were therefore forced to reject the whole heritage. In many cases, if they were vocal in their rejection, they were compelled to leave the South entirely and return only at their peril. Unity was thus temporarily achieved, but with the collapse of the Peculiar Institution the whole tradition was jeopardized and discredited for having been so completely identified with the part abandoned.

Historical experience with the first Peculiar Institution ought strongly to discourage comparable experiments with the second. If Southernism is allowed to become identified with a last ditch defense of segregation, it will increasingly lose its appeal among the younger generation. Many will be tempted to reject their entire regional identification, even the name "Southern," in order to dissociate themselves from the one discredited aspect. If agrarianism has proved to be a second lost cause, segregation is a likely prospect for a third.

With the crumbling of so many defenses in the present, the South has tended to substitute myths about the past. Every self-conscious group of any size fabricates myths about its past: about its origins, its mission, its righteousness, its benevolence, its general superiority. But few groups in the New World have had their myths subjected to such destructive analysis as those of the South have undergone in recent years. While some Southern historians have contributed to the mythmaking, others have been among the leading iconoclasts, and their attacks have spared few of the South's cherished myths.

The Cavalier Legend as the myth of origin was one of the earlier victims. The Plantation Legend of ante bellum grace and elegance has not been left wholly intact. The pleasant image of a benevolent and paternalistic slavery system as a school for civilizing savages has suffered damage that is probably beyond repair. Even the consoling security of Reconstruction as the common historic grievance, the infallible mystique of unity, has been rendered somewhat less secure by detached investigation. And finally, rude hands have been laid upon the hallowed memory of the Redeemers who did in the Carpetbaggers, and doubt has been cast upon the antiquity of segregation folkways. These faded historical myths have become weak material for buttressing Southern defenses, for time has dealt as roughly with them as with agrarianism and racism....

Since the cultural landscape of his native region is being altered almost beyond recognition by a cyclone of social change, the Southerner may come to feel as uprooted as the immigrant. Bereft of his myths, his peculiar institutions, even his familiar regional vices, he may well reject or forget his regional identification as completely as the immigrant.

Is there nothing about the South that is immune from the disintegrating effect of nationalism and the pressure for conformity? Is there not something that has not changed? There is only one thing that I can think of, and that is its history. By that I do not mean a Southern brand of Shintoism, the worship of ancestors. Nor do I mean written history and its interpretation, popular and mythical, or professional and scholarly, which have changed often and will change again. I mean rather the collective experience of the Southern people. It is in just this respect that the South remains the most distinctive region of the country. In their unique historic experience as Americans the Southerners should not only be able to find the basis for continuity of their heritage but also make contributions that balance and complement the experience of the rest of the nation.

At this point the risks of our enterprise multiply. They are the risks of spawning new myths in place of the old. Awareness of them demands that we redouble precautions and look more cautiously than ever at generalizations.

To start with a safe one, it can be assumed that one of the most conspicuous traits of American life has been its economic abundance. From early colonial days the fabulous riches of America have been compared with the scarcity and want of less favored lands. Immense differentials in economic welfare and living standards between the United States and other countries still prevail. In an illuminating book called *People of Plenty*, David Potter persuasively advances the thesis that the most distinguishing traits of national character have been fundamentally shaped by the abundance of the American living standard....

The South at times has shared this national experience and, in very recent years, has enjoyed more than a taste of it. But the history of the South includes a long and quite un-American experience with poverty. So recently as 1938, in fact, the South was characterized by the President as "The Nation's Economic Problem No. 1." And the problem was poverty, not plenty. It was a poverty emphasized by wide regional discrepancies in living standard, per capita wealth, per capita income, and the good things that money buys, such as education, health, protection, and the many luxuries that go to make up the celebrated American Standard of Living. This striking differential was no temporary misfortune of the great depression but a continuous and conspicuous feature of Southern experience since the early years of the Civil War. During the last half of the nineteenth and the first half of the twentieth centuries, when technology was multiplying American abundance with unprecedented rapidity, the South lagged far behind. In 1880 the per capita wealth of the South, based on estimated true valuation of property, was $376 as compared with $1,186 per capita in the states outside the South. In the same year the per capita wealth of the South was 27 per cent of that of the Northeastern states. That was just about the same ratio contemporaneously existing between the per capita wealth of Russia and that of Germany.

Generations of scarcity and want constitute one of the distinctive historical experiences of the Southern people, an experience too deeply embedded in their memory to be wiped out by a business boom and too deep not to admit of some uneasiness at being characterized historically as a "People of Plenty." That they should have been for so long a time a "People of Poverty" in a land of plenty is one mark of enduring cultural distinctiveness. In a nation known around the world for the hedonistic ethic of the American Standard of Living, the Southern heritage of scarcity remains distinctive.

A closely related corollary of the uniquely American experience of abundance is the equally unique American experience of success. During the Second World War Professor Arthur M. Schlesinger made an interesting attempt to define the national character, which he brought to a close with the conclusion that the American character "is bottomed upon the profound conviction that nothing in the world is beyond its power to accomplish." In this he gave expression to one of the great American legends, the legend of success and invincibility. It is a legend with a foundation in fact, for much can be adduced from the American record to support it and explain why it has flourished....

Almost every major collective effort, even those thwarted temporarily, succeeded in the end. American history *is* a success story. Why should such a nation not have a "profound conviction that nothing in the world is beyond its power to accomplish"?...

This is but one among several American legends in which the South can participate only vicariously or in part. Again the Southern heritage is distinctive. For Southern history, unlike American, includes large components of frustration, failure, and defeat. It includes not only an overwhelming military defeat but long decades of defeat in the provinces of economic, social, and political life. Such a heritage affords the Southern people no basis for the delusion that there is nothing whatever that is beyond their power to accomplish. They have had it forcibly and repeatedly borne in upon them that this is not the case. Since their experience in this respect is more common among the general run of mankind than that of their fellow Americans, it would seem to be a part of their heritage worth cherishing.

American opulence and American success have combined to foster and encourage another legend of early origin, the legend of American innocence. According to this legend Americans achieved a sort of regeneration of sinful man by coming out of the wicked Old World and removing to an untarnished new one. By doing so they shook off the wretched evils of feudalism and broke free from tyranny, monarchism, aristocracy, and privilege—all those institutions which, in the hopeful philosophy of the Enlightenment, accounted for all, or nearly all, the evil in the world. The absence of these Old World ills in America, as well as the freedom from much of the injustice and oppression associated with them, encouraged a singular moral complacency in the American mind. The self-image implanted in Americans was one of innocence as compared with less fortunate people of the Old World. They were a chosen people and their land a Utopia on the make. Alexis de Tocqueville's patience was tried by this complacency of the American. "If I applaud the freedom which its inhabitants enjoy, he answers, 'Freedom is a fine thing, but few nations are worthy to enjoy it....'"

How much room was there in the tortured conscience of the South for this national self-image of innocence and moral complacency? Southerners have repeated the American rhetoric of self admiration and sung the perfection of American institutions ever since the Declaration of Independence. But for half that time they lived intimately with a great social evil and the other half with its aftermath. It was an evil that was even condemned and abandoned by the Old World, to which America's moral superiority was supposedly an article of faith. Much of the South's intellectual energy went into a desperate effort to convince the world that its peculiar evil was actually a "positive good," but it failed even to convince itself. It writhed in the torments of its own conscience until it plunged into catastrophe to escape. The South's preoccupation was with guilt, not with innocence, with the reality of evil, not with the dream of perfection. Its experience in this respect, as in several others, was on the whole a thoroughly un-American one.

An age-long experience with human bondage and its evils and later with emancipation and its shortcomings did not dispose the South very favorably toward such popular American ideas as the doctrine of human perfectibility, the belief that every evil has a cure, and the notion that every human problem has a solution. For these reasons the utopian schemes and the gospel of progress that flourished above the Mason and Dixon Line never found very wide acceptance below the Potomac during the nineteenth century. In that most optimistic of centuries in the most optimistic part of the world, the South remained basically pessimistic in its social outlook and its moral philosophy. The experience of evil and the experience of tragedy are parts of the Southern heritage that are as difficult to reconcile with the American legend of innocence and social felicity as the experience of poverty and defeat are to reconcile with the legends of abundance and success....

The most reassuring prospect for the survival of the South's distinctive heritage is the magnificent body of literature produced by its writers in the last three decades—the very years when the outward traits of regional distinctiveness were crumbling. The Southern literary renaissance has placed its writers in the vanguard of national letters and assured that their works will be read as long as American literature is remembered. The distinguishing feature of the Southern school, according to Allen Tate, is "the peculiar historical consciousness of the Southern writer." He defines the literary renaissance as "a literature conscious of the past in the present." The themes that have inspired the major writers have not been the flattering myths nor the romantic dreams of the South's past. Disdaining the polemics of defense and justification, they have turned instead to the somber realities of hardship and defeat and evil and "the problems of the human heart in conflict with itself." In so doing they have brought to realization for the first time the powerful literary potentials of the South's tragic experience and heritage. Such comfort as they offer lies, in the words of William Faulkner, in reminding us of "the courage and honor and hope and pride and compassion and pity and sacrifice" with which man has endured.

After Faulkner, [Thomas] Wolfe, [Robert Penn] Warren, and [Eudora] Welty no literate Southerner could remain unaware of his heritage or doubt its enduring value. After this outpouring it would seem more difficult than ever to deny a Southern identity, to be "merely American." To deny it would be to deny our history. And it would also be to deny to America participation in a heritage and a dimension of historical experience that America very much needs, a heritage that is far more closely in line with the common lot of mankind than the national legends of opulence and success and innocence. The South once thought of itself as a "peculiar people," set apart by its eccentricities, but in many ways modern America better deserves that description.

The South was American a long time before it was Southern in any self-conscious or distinctive way. It remains more American by far than anything else, and has all along. After all, it fell [to] the lot of one Southerner from Virginia to define America. The definition he wrote in 1776 voiced aspirations that were rooted in his native region before the nation was born. The modern Southerner should be secure enough in his national identity to escape the compulsion of less secure minorities to embrace uncritically all the myths of nationalism. He should be secure enough also not to deny a regional heritage because it is at variance with national myth. It is a heritage that should prove of enduring worth to him as well as to his country.

The Difficulty of Consensus on the South

JOHN B. BOLES

Any prospective reader of a book of essays on the modern South might expect a certain consensus of viewpoints, a commonly accepted definition of the region,

John B. Boles, "The Dixie Difference," introduction to *Dixie Dateline* (Houston: Rice University Studies, 1983). Reprinted by permission of John Boles.

even a general agreement about the South's past, if not its future.... No single conclusion, no mutually accepted point of view emerges. What the South is, whether it is persisting as a distinct region or vanishing into a great homogenous American culture, or whether that "loss" should be applauded, regretted, or prevented by some intellectual cardiopulmonary contraption, remains a riddle that different individuals answer differently. It has always been so with the South. Everyone has a ready image of the region, but the closer one comes to examine the South, the more the differences merge into similarities, and vice versa. Like a giant sphinx on the American land—as one historian called it—Dixie beckons investigators even as it resists explication. Therein of course lies its attraction.

The South is both American and something different, at times a mirror or magnifier of national traits and at other times a counterculture. That difference has been good, bad, and indefinable, but it has long been felt.... The South still challenges those who try to separate image from reality, stereotype from myth. Accepting the difficulty of consensus, wary of simple truths, adventurous readers will find here hard thinking, suggestive analysis, but ultimately no single key to understanding the South. And that makes the whole endeavor not futile but exciting. The southern character is too complex for easy answers, and southerners—at least the publishing kind—enjoy the perennial search for southern identity.

For at least two centuries Americans have recognized a distinctive South, and perhaps there is no more enduring regional image in the American mind than that of a Dixie different from the rest of the nation. In a famous letter to the Marquis de Chastellux, dated September 2, 1785, Thomas Jefferson compared the characteristics of northerners and southerners by listing their traits in parallel columns:

In the North they are	In the South they are
cool	fiery
sober	voluptuary
laborious	indolent
persevering	unsteady
independant [*sic*]	independant [*sic*]
jealous of their own liberties, and just to those of others	zealous for their own liberties, but trampling on those of others
interested	generous
chicaning	candid
superstitious and hypocritical in their religion	without attachment or pretensions to any religion but that of the heart

Jefferson was so certain that these traits conformed to geographical setting that he wrote: "An observing traveller, without aid of the quadrant, may always know his latitude by the character of the people among whom he finds himself."

Jefferson ascribed the South's peculiarities to "that warmth of their climate," a judgment echoed almost a century and a half later by U. B. Phillips of Yale

University. Georgia-born Phillips, the first great southern historian, commenced his classic account of the Old South with the sentence, "Let us begin by discussing the weather, for that has been the chief agency in making the South distinctive." We are less concerned here with the role of climate or the accuracy of Jefferson's classification than with the underlying assumption of southern distinctiveness. That idea grew slowly. Historians still debate when the South emerged as a self-consciously separate section, perceived as such also by the nation as a whole. Taking their cue from Jefferson and pronouncements made by delegates from several southern states during and shortly after the chaos of the American Revolution, some historians argue that the "South"—as distinct from the geographically southern colonies—existed as early as 1776, set apart even then by slavery.

Historians of course are no more likely to agree than are economists or theologians. Few scholars accept this early a date for the existence of full-blown southern identity. Instead, most view the long generation following the Treaty of Paris (1783) as the high-water-mark of southern Americanism, when southerners were at the liberal forefront of national decisionmaking and in fact controlled four of the first five presidential administrations. Washington, Jefferson, Madison, and Monroe were nation-builders, not dismantlers of the Union. For many twentieth-century southern liberals, these founding fathers represented the true South, the Great South, before slavery interests and John C. Calhoun led the region down the seductive path of sectionalism, then secession, Civil War, and Reconstruction, to sharecropping and colonial status within the nation.

There is a pleasing symmetry to this view, for it allows one to think of the history of southernness as a kind of long aberration, ended perhaps in 1976 when southerner Jimmy Carter became president. The great break occurred sometime between the War of 1812—when even John C. Calhoun was a fiercely nationalistic "war hawk"—and the early 1830s, by which time the nullification crisis in the South and the rise of modern antislavery activities in the North called forth a militant southern sectionalism. Perhaps the pivotal year was 1819, when the debate over the admission of Missouri as a state raised the critical question of the expansion of slavery. In that year also the deep economic depression—the Panic of 1819—highlighted profound economic differences between North and South. In retrospect it seems that a southern recognition of divergent values, contrasting social and economic systems, and an emerging distinctive culture began that eventful year, a full century and a half after the slavery-plantation system had developed.

Once the perception arose that the South had a unique destiny, events were interpreted to prove the perception. Old realities were observed in a new light. Many contemporaries saw the divisive issues and dilemmas of the next four decades as springing from the essential dichotomy between North and South. From this perspective the Civil War became necessary, even irrepressible, for a southern nation had arisen with manifold interests so different that continued union was impossible. Thus the Civil War, the apex of southern separateness, appears almost predetermined, with the long and often arduous century afterwards being merely the slow process by which the South was brought back into the Union, first legally in 1876, then politically in 1976, and not quite yet economically.

In this sense of the South's finally rejoining the nation, some commentators heralded Jimmy Carter's election to the presidency as ending the region's long sojourn as a separate province. How appropriate it seemed, on the nation's 200th birthday, for the great sectional rapprochement to occur. Yet those who thought that the nation was finally done with things distinctly southern were ill-prepared for the next few years. Punsters quickly labeled the Carter-Mondale team "Grits and Fritz," and Jimmy's brother Billy added a new dimension to the stereotype of the Good Ole Boy. With toe-tapping country music in the White House and recipes for catfish in the *New York Times*, southern fried chic seemed to suit the national taste. The subtitle of John Egerton's book, *The Southernization of America*, was perhaps more appropriate than its title, *The Americanization of Dixie*. The upshot of the matter was the question, with the South becoming more like the North, or vice versa, was there validity any more to the hoary concept of the distinctive South? Journalists vied with sociologists and historians to describe the death of Dixie. Their efforts proved premature.

Of course even an attempt to eulogize the South implies the assumption of regional distinctiveness, and the origin of that assumption lies intertwined with much of American history. For two centuries Americans North and South have felt a need to define the Dixie difference. In the antebellum days of slavery and plantations the South's economy and its labor system differentiated it from the rest of the nation, but southerners, feeling defensive about their peculiar institution and not a little guilty, sought to apotheosize their society. Real regional differences were exaggerated and elaborated upon. Like whistling in the dark to dispel fears and doubts, southerners tried, largely successfully, to persuade themselves that theirs was a higher form of civilization than the frenzied, industrial North. According to the plantation legend, the South produced gentlemen rather than vulgar businessmen; a leisurely life of manners and lofty thoughts rather than a hurried, pell-mell struggle for ever-higher profits; a working class of contented slaves, not sullen, unruly factory laborers. Thus the myth of the Old South emerged, but not entirely because it soothed southern consciences. Many northern intellectuals, dismayed by the social changes being wrought by the incipient Industrial Revolution, helped create the plantation legend and then used it to criticize the changing North. The Old South of moonlight and magnolias, of carefree hospitality and happy-go-lucky Sambos, served both regions as myths usually do, relieving social tensions and reconciling conflicting values.

During the generation before the Civil War both North and South conspired to create an image of the South, an illusion that never bore close resemblance to reality. For their contrasting needs Americans in the two regions constructed self-serving portraits of the Old South, an exotic, romantic "touched-up" portrait with the diversity, the conflict, the frontier aspects of the South removed. In the aftermath of Appomattox, white southerners, suffering a depression of both morale and money, sought to recoup some of their pride by romanticizing the Old South with a vengeance, constructing a never-never land of mess, magnolias, mansions, and mammies. Many southern clergy found meaning in Confederate defeat by arguing that God was thereby testing the South for a higher purpose, the reformation of the nation along the lines of evangelical Protestantism. Southern traditions were united with biblical themes to produce a religion of the Lost Cause, a faith that practically equated the heritage of Dixie with Holy Scripture.

Following Reconstruction, secular advocates of an urban, industrial "New South" of profits and progress helped sell their program, legitimate themselves as southern, and assuage vague guilt feelings about imitating the Yankees by piously glorifying the Old South. Joel Chandler Harris, for example, wrote booster editorials by day and Uncle Remus stories by night, seemingly without noticing the conflict. Ever since, students have labored under the heavy burden of myth and contradiction. In fact, much historical scholarship in the twentieth century has been an attempt to demythologize the popular notions of southern history. The list of myths debunked is long—the Lazy South, the Romantic South, the Cavalier South, the New South. Historians point out again and again, for example, that the large majority of southern whites in 1860 did not own slaves; that Reconstruction was not a "blackout of honest government"; that slaves were not happy Sambos; that Sunbelt notions to the contrary, the South is still the nation's poorest region. But the myths live on. Now historians are turning their attention to the function of myths, how they have helped shape southern history by forging unity, offering rationales for action, providing a common goal.

After acknowledging the prevalence of several mythical Souths and then trying to analyze the reality behind the facade, one quickly realizes that more riddles abound. Even defining the South quickly transcends geography to become a problem in cultural and intellectual history. Simple geography brings difficulties. The Mason-Dixon Line does not suffice as a boundary between North and South, for such a division would assign Delaware to the South. If we were to consider the former Confederate states as delimiting the South, we would be excluding Maryland and Kentucky, two important slave states, as well as Missouri. Some expansive Sunbelt theoreticians would lump the Southeast along with New Mexico, Arizona, and much of California and call the broad swath of geography "the southern rim," meanwhile searching in vain for parallels between southern California and South Carolina. In this century migrations of southerners northward and northerners southward have blurred the boundaries. Much of southern Illinois and Indiana have a southern cast, as do sections of Detroit; and Bakersfield, California, is a southern enclave in the West. The Virginia suburbs of Washington, D. C., the coastal areas of the Florida peninsula, and the cosmopolitan suburbs of Houston and Atlanta have been so penetrated by persons of northern birth as to lead to a proliferation of delicatessens and the easy availability—even home delivery—of the *New York Times*. Where does the South begin and end?

To make matters worse, any geographical concept of the South conveys the false impression of homogeneity. Expressions such as "the Solid South" have created the image of a monolithic region, a huge, warm, culturally flat region of slow-talking people who prefer grits with breakfast and their pork barbecued. Yet within the South there is variety of every kind: geological, climatic, cultural, ethnic. Even the favored styles of barbecue differ. The piedmont and mountain areas of Virginia, North Carolina, and Tennessee are as different from the coastal plains of Louisiana as Savannah is from Dallas. The Texas Germans and Czechs, the Louisiana Cajuns, and the North Carolina Moravians are people very different from the First Families of Virginia (the FFVs) and the aristocracies of Charleston and New Orleans. The mountain folk of the Appalachian valleys share little with Texas wildcatters or Georgia blacks. Yet all are southerners. One of the important roles of myth has been to create an illusion of unity out of this diversity. Similarly, students of the region, seeking to impose order on a crazy-quilt topic, have labored mightily to find a central theme of southern history with which to comprehend the whole. In many ways the search for a central theme has been the central theme of southern history; that quest now has added urgency because of the perception that the South is slowly, before our very eyes, disappearing as a definable entity.

Despite the historical uses and convenience of myths and stereotypes in characterizing or describing the region, most students of the South accept the truth that there really is something different about Dixie. From Jefferson's day the climate has frequently been interpreted as having played a major role in making the South distinctive. According to this view, a long growing season allowed the South to satisfy world demand for tobacco and cotton. The successful introduction of these crops led in turn to the rise of the broad-acred plantation system with its need for cheap labor, a need ultimately met by Negro slavery. Here then were the essential ingredients of southern history: a rural, agricultural region dominated by large planters, with a suppressed racial minority on the bottom. In tangible, measurable ways, the antebellum South was different from the antebellum North. From this fact emerged images of the romantic Old South, as well as the idea, expressed best in 1928 by U. B. Phillips, that the essence of southernism was "a common resolve indomitably maintained" that the South "shall be and remain a white man's country." Whether "expressed with the frenzy of a demagogue or maintained with a patrician's quietude," this was, according to Phillips, "the cardinal test of a Southerner and the central theme of Southern history." The myth of a planter aristocracy, the theme of an agrarian republic, the identification of the South with gracious living or white domination or rural-dominated Bible-Belt religion or one-party politics—all have evolved from the old assumption that environment shaped events.

The economy and society that were made possible and produced by the climate gave rise to a people who possessed certain characteristics, and many observers have shifted their attention away from the immediate consequences of climate and focused on those acquired human traits that seem to define southerners. Rather than its crops, it is its people and their character that distinguish the region. Because geography fails, we turn to defining the South as a region possessing a unique folk culture, or having experienced a history very unlike the rest of the nation. The South becomes a way of living, a sense of belonging, a state of mind. W. J. Cash's great book, *The Mind of the South*, is the classic of this genre, although in his emphasis on southerners' feeling instead of thinking, on their simple hedonism mixed with a rigid Puritanical streak, Cash came close to arguing that the South did not have a mind. Southerners, it seems, *are* more violent, more religious, more conservative, more fatalistic than nonsoutherners. Thinking does affect behavior. Statistics show that the southern death rate from tornadoes, for example, is significantly higher than elsewhere, and the best explanation is that southerners ignore warnings and neglect to build storm cellars in the belief that if your time has come, you can't escape, and if your time has not come, then why bother with precaution. Southerners also speak differently, whether with a Georgia drawl or an East Texas twang, and have an infatuation with words, a tendency to express themselves not in straightforward analytical prose but with detailed, richly textured stories.... The love affair with talk may explain the world-renowned outpouring of southern fiction, as well as the disproportionate number and influence of southern journalists and historians—people who, after all, mainly tell stories. Even that most southern of music, labeled "country," is peculiarly concerned with the stories that unfold in the lyrics.

In recent decades the quest to understand southern distinctiveness has produced more emphasis on the human dimension. David Potter, a Georgia-born historian who taught at Rice, Yale, and Stanford universities, argued that southern identity inhered in what he called a unique folk culture. In this folk society a sense of belonging, a relatedness of people to people and people to land, persisted amidst a national culture that was increasingly urban and technological. This identification with place and family seemed to be particularly true among rural southerners, and the South remained largely rural until after World War II. The urban areas in the South today are still peopled mostly by rural folk who have migrated to the cities in search of jobs. They have brought with them their tastes in food, music, sports, and religion. In subtle ways they have changed the cities, and certainly their urban residence has changed their expectations, even if it has not rendered them completely urbane. During the decade of the 1970s, Dixie was the only region of the nation in which urban growth outpaced rural growth. The rising generation of city-born southerners will determine whether the South can survive urbanization and remain recognizably southern. If southernness is merely an artifact of rurality, then it will soon be gone with the winds of change and growth. Sociological data shows, however, that educated, urban southerners continue to attend church far more regularly than their counterparts nationally and identify themselves with their homeplaces with greater intensity than northerners—an indication that southern values will persist in the cities.

Realizing that the bulldozer revolution of urban sprawl and industrialization would eventually end the South's rural isolation, and that the Supreme Court's desegregation decision in *Brown* v. *Board of Education of Topeka* in 1954 would ultimately end the white South's intransigence on race, C. Vann Woodward sought the essence of southernness in the region's peculiar historical experience. According to Woodward, what had made the South different was not its relative absence of cities, its agrarian traditions, its inordinate concern with race, or its political practices, but rather the way it had been treated by time itself.

Writing a generation ago, Woodward contrasted the nation's history of prosperity—being the people of plenty—with the South's long travail of poverty, stretching from the rise of sharecropping to the trough of the Great Depression, when President Franklin D. Roosevelt called the region the nation's number one economic problem. Moreover, although no nation in all history had succeeded like the United States, winning all its wars and spreading its banner from sea to shining sea, the South had failed, and failed utterly, in its one great attempt to have a separate national destiny. And while the nation—born in liberty, protector of the Union, and emancipator of the slaves—basked in innocence, the South had to live with the guilt of slavery and secession bearing heavily on its soul. Thus, Woodward concluded, in a nation marked by success, prosperity, and innocence, the South was set apart by its failure, poverty, and guilt. That collective experience, shared by all southerners, gave them a sense of identity, a common heritage apart from the national norm. The South's history, a past that was not dead, defined the southern character. A sense of tragedy, a recognition of frailty and limits to endeavor marked the regional psyche. Because the southern experience has been more akin to the world experience than the northern experience has been, southern literature both fictional and historical attracts an enormous audience abroad. Moreover, two quintessential southern musical forms, jazz and country, enjoy a global acceptance. The southern encounter with history has ironically produced an intensely localistic people with universal dilemmas and international appeal.

Of course, in the years since Woodward made his influential analysis, the nation has undergone a series of shocks. In the aftermath of Vietnam, Watergate, and the discovery of poverty in the land of plenty—what Michael Harrington called "The Other America"—the national experience no longer seems so different from that of the South. And with the South solving its racial problems arguably more satisfactorily than the North, with Sunbelt prosperity narrowing the regional income gap, and with a recent southern president, one might even argue that the regions have flip-flopped. Such of course is not the case, but southerners now feel much freer of that scorn once directed their way, and are finding "Snowbelt" envy much more gratifying.

The southern folk culture that has experienced a history unlike the rest of the United States is in many ways biracial. In the South blacks and whites have lived together, cheek by jowl, for more than three hundred years. Nothing and no one in the South has escaped the mutual influences of the two races. Black values and styles have helped shape the white culture, and vice versa, to such an extent that today it is impossible to separate the strands. Southerners are truly both the white and black inhabitants of the region. Hearing Elvis Presley borrow from black vocal traditions or Charlie Pride singing Hank Williams, or eating southern home cooking, or listening to southern preachers or gospel singers, who can deny that we truly are one at the same time that we are two people?

But the question remains: where is and what is the South today? Efforts to reappraise the South seem to proliferate shortly after every period of change. At the end of the 1950s, Arkansas journalist Harry Ashmore wrote a perceptive book entitled *An Epitaph for Dixie*, but historian Francis B. Simkins of Virginia countered with *The Everlasting South*. Parallel titles could be supplied down to the present, with concern ever being raised about *The Americanization of Dixie*, then laid aside with reflections on *The Enduring South*. As change erodes the characteristics that were once thought to define the South—poverty, rurality, educational and "cultural" backwardness, segregation, Democratic hegemony—the South's separate existence seems threatened. With that threat of loss, writers of every sort start examining the region, hunting for surviving fossils of the past or subtle new forms of southern identity, and lo, that very concern with self-identity betrays a very southern habit of wanting to know who you are and from whence you came. That concern with family, with place, with "relatedness" that so epitomizes the southerner produces a spate of regional analysis and nostalgia and, yes, even pious self-congratulation that keeps the South alive. Whether one assumes that there is still a tangible essence that sets the region apart or that one must, in the face of modernization and homogenization, "Dixiefy Dixie" ... to keep the image alive artificially, the search for southern identity has continued for at least two centuries and shows no signs of faltering or concluding.

With the South, as with much else, a great deal lies in the eye of the beholder. High technology, interstate highways, and industrial growth may threaten one vision of the South, but recorded country music, fast food outlets for fried chicken and biscuits and sausage, C-B radios in eighteen-wheelers crackling with good-ole-boy talk from their drivers, and the working poor who have moved from the fields to the factories keep alive memories of the past. Southern speech patterns and that signal form of ethnic identification, gastronomic preferences, show sure signs of resisting change. While the architecture and form of southern cities appear as standardized as American cities elsewhere, ... in human terms the texture of life in them reveals surprising continuity with the rural past. Yet popular images often lag behind changing reality, and the myth of southern distinctiveness may ultimately be more tenacious, and more significant, than actuality. Perceptive journalists ... can document that southern universities are more than holding their own and subscribing to national standards for research, tenure, and curricula. Yet a "manual" like *The Insiders' Guide to the Colleges* (1971) stereotypically includes most southern universities under the category "Hard Playin', Hard Drinkin', Hard Lovin' Southern Schools." How do myth, perception, and reality merge in the popular mind? The acceptance of diversity, real or imagined, can make a real difference. As long as southerners believe in, fear, or desire a regional identity, or worry about whether one exists, there will be a South. What that South is, precisely speaking, no one can say.

And surely few will not admit that the loss of many "southern characteristics" is a great blessing. The South's long heritage of spirit-breaking poverty, of ignorance and religious prejudice, of savage racism and brutal violence, of irrelevant politics and undemocratic control, took a heavy toll on all southerners. To the extent that *that* South has died, humanity has triumphed. Better schools and improved job opportunities have freed thousands from poverty and given them immeasurably better lives. While city dwellers acknowledge a twinge of nostalgia for life back on the farm, the higher pay, greater scope of entertainment, and educational and medical advantages of urban life keep them in town. Even so, many still identify with their rural homeplaces and intend to retire and be buried there. For the huge majority of southerners, black and white, the South today is certainly a much better place to live than it was a generation ago. The beneficial changes in race relations alone represent a fundamental reshaping of the social, cultural, and political landscape, and give promise of improving relations in the future. The tide of black migration has turned back toward the South, and southern blacks are finding new purpose and meaning in their original American homeland. Even today one is surprised, driving into Montgomery from Atlanta, to see overhead the large green interstate sign proclaiming the "Martin Luther King, Jr., Expressway," but what could be a better symbol of the changing South?

In one sense this whole endeavor of defining and making predictions about the continuity of southernness has an abstract, ersatz quality about it. Most southerners take their sense of regional identity for granted even if they cannot articulate its nature. Perhaps one even has to be a southerner to know really what it is. For southerners, after all, grew up with a perception of differentness that had its roots in that long-ago time when slavery gave a concreteness that has since evaporated to the idea of separate cultures. That folk memory of distinction, imbibed with their mothers' milk, predisposes southerners to assume their distinctiveness, even when tangible evidence is wanting. And for generations, except when threatened by or contrasted to outsiders, the search for regional self-identity was what kept novelists and historians and journalists in business; the folk simply were southerners. The magnitude of the change in recent years, however, has brought urgency, a sense of potential loss, not only to aspiring authors but to average persons who can instinctively sense that they are drifting away from their old world. Often loss brings reflection and renewed appreciation, and exactly that seems to be happening with southernness.

People are suddenly eating homestyle cooking and saying "y'all," purposely being southern as a personal statement of identity. People are no longer ashamed to be southerners. A perception that the South might be disappearing in a cultural sense has led to a discovery of its importance in personal and national terms. Ninety years ago the census revealed that the American frontier was closed; three years later a great historian discovered "The Significance of the Frontier." … [S]omething similar might be happening in the South's largest and most rapidly changing city. Houston's phenomenal growth in population and prosperity has changed its motto from the "Magnolia City" to the "Urban West." A new culture is emerging, neither completely southern nor western. But as Houston becomes less like the Texas of old, with its heritage of openness and individuality, native Houstonians (and transplanted rural Texans) eagerly try to recapture that old ethic. Cowboy chic began not as a movie gimmick but as a grassroots attempt to recapture and hold on to a way of life and a mythical identity that was rapidly disappearing. Moreover, the thousands of mobile Americans from California, Michigan, and New York who have moved to Houston—rootless searchers for economic opportunity and advancement—seize upon the cowboy image in an attempt to legitimate their residence and show that they "belong." While the western cowboy seems to have conquered the southern cavalier in Texas, partly because of the more favorable popular associations of the cowpoke with freedom and "good" and partly because the cowpuncher is a more national hero, Houston's cowboy renaissance may suggest the future of southernness.

As the South disappears in demographic, economic, and political terms, there seems to be a corresponding effort to rediscover and revivify at least certain components of the southern way of life. Opinion molders sense the popular concern, and thus symposia, books, clothing, musical fads, and even college curricula—witness the proliferation of "southern institutes"—speak to that concern. In a very real sense, southerners did not exist until about 1819, when they began to perceive themselves as an identifiable group. The underlying socioeconomic factors that gave substance to the perception existed for more than a century before the perception arose. Self-identification as "southern" was the essence of southernness, and that perception has acquired a life of its own, in large part independent of material reality. Southernness is now almost an intellectual construct, "the flesh made word," .... Having a distinctiveness to lose makes possible a recognition of loss, and that triggers a process of retrospection and nostalgia that bodes well to keep the South alive and thriving. The South will continue to exist, if only by an act of the will. After all, ... they aren't having symposia in Phoenix to discuss the everlasting West.

The Three Souths

JOHN SHELTON REED

You're in the American South now, a proud region with a distinctive history and culture.

A place that echoes with names like Thomas Jefferson and Robert E. Lee, Scarlett O'Hara and Uncle Remus, Martin Luther King and William Faulkner, Billy Graham, Mahalia Jackson, Muhammad Ali, Elvis Presley. Home of the country blues and country music, bluegrass and Dixieland jazz, gospel music and rock and roll. Where menus offer both down-home biscuits and gravy and uptown shrimp and grits. Where churches preach against "cigarettes, whiskey, and wild, wild women" (all Southern products) and American football is a religion.

You're in the region that leads the nation in job creation, the most industrialized part of the country, a place of shining skyscrapers, sprawling suburbs, and boundless optimism. You're in a region where problems of rural poverty still defy easy solution, where many still live in the shadow of the plantation.

You're in the only part of America that ever fought the Stars and Stripes, the only one to suffer military defeat and occupation. You're in the region that now supplies the largest proportionate share of America's soldiers and wears its American patriotism most conspicuously.

You're in the part of America where slavery lasted longest and died hardest, where a system of virtual apartheid prevailed for decades, where only yesterday "white supremacy" was preached as a positive good. You're in a region that is now attracting black migrants by the hundreds of thousands, where schools are less segregated and more blacks hold public office than anywhere else in the country.

You're in what used to be called "the Solid South"—solid in support of the Democratic party and opposition to the party of Lincoln, the Union, and Reconstruction. You're in a region that cast most of its votes in 1992 against a Democratic ticket from Arkansas and Tennessee, and now dominates the leadership of the national Republican party.

You're in a region renowned for Southern hospitality, for its ladies and gentlemen, for its courtesy and gracious living; a region with the nation's highest rate of church membership—and its highest homicide rate. A place whose name has evoked moonlight and magnolias, pellagra and poll taxes, now home to the Cable News Network and Compaq Computer.

You're below the Mason-Dixon Line. In the Cotton Kingdom, the Old Confederacy, Dixie. In the Bible Belt, the Sahara of Bozart. In the New South, the Sunbelt, the Southeast. In "Uncle Sam's other province." You're in a land of contradictions.

Welcome to the South. Confusing, ain't it?

One source of confusion is that the phrase "the South" refers to at least three different regions. They overlap one another and all sometimes go by that same name, but their origins, their defining features, their prospects, and even their boundaries are quite distinct.

The old South—call it "Dixie"—came into being with the spread of cotton agriculture and slavery in the early 1800s. This South was an agricultural region, and after 1865 it was a *poor* agricultural region, with unique racial and economic problems. It lasted well into this century and some aspects of it still survive here and there, but it's less of a reality each decade, and in most respects it will soon be of interest only to historians.

Emerging as we watch, however, is a quite different South that we can call (for reasons we will get to) the "Southeast." This is a vibrant, dynamic, industrial region, a magnet for migration and investment from other parts of the nation and increasingly from abroad. It is a metropolitan region, its cities linked by innumerable ties of commerce and communication. It is in fact a *nation* in every sense but the political.

At the same time, there is an enduring *cultural* South, set off from the rest of the United States by its people's distinctive ways of doing things. This South is defined by things like religion, cuisine, family life, manners, musical styles, sports, and recreation—all of the idioms and imponderables that make a population a people—and this is the South that evokes the pride and enlists the loyalties of Southerners.

In Atlanta, you're in all three of these Souths at once. Let's try to sort them out.

"Let us begin by discussing the weather," wrote the distinguished historian Ulrich B. Phillips in 1929, "for that has been the chief agency in making the South distinctive." You have undoubtedly noticed that the South can be hot and humid. Some vegetable life loves that—a fact with fateful consequences.

In particular, much of the South is suited for the cultivation of cotton, and for nearly a century Southerners grew that crop everywhere they *could* grow it: everywhere with two hundred or more frost-free days, annual precipitation of twenty-three inches or more, and soil that wasn't swamp. This created a peculiar region, defined in the early 1800s by plantation agriculture and slavery and distinguished ever since by the consequences of those institutions.

This is Dixie, the land of cotton, where (as Abe Lincoln's favorite Confederate song observed) old times are not forgotten. Even today a band of rural counties with substantial black populations traces the old cotton belt in a long arc from southeastern Virginia down and across to eastern Texas, with arms reaching north and south through the bottomlands along the Mississippi River. The cotton South is the *Deep* South: many "Southern" characteristics and phenomena have been concentrated here; some have been found *only* here.

Alabama calls itself "the heart of Dixie," but the real core of the Cotton Kingdom is probably the Mississippi Delta south of Memphis, "the most Southern place on earth"—if what you mean by Southern has to do with plantations, the blues, and the civil-rights movement.

For decades this was seen as what the South was all about, and rightly so.

This was the South that went to war in 1861, when South Carolina, "the cradle of secession," left the Union, joined by six other Deep South states that shared its commitment to the future of plantation agriculture and slavery. (Only later, and with some reluctance, did the states of the upper South add their stars to the Confederate flag.)

This was the South celebrated at Atlanta's great Cotton States and International Exposition of 1895. That the most memorable speech at that exposition was by Booker T. Washington of Tuskegee Institute reminds us that this was also the heartland of racial segregation.

For nearly a century after Reconstruction this was the political "Solid South," where whites didn't vote Republican and blacks didn't vote at all. In the 1930s its continuing poverty led President Franklin Roosevelt to call it "the nation's number-one economic problem."

During and after World War I millions fled Dixie, in one of the great mass migrations of human history, seeking opportunity in the North and West. In the 1960s this was the setting for the stirring events of the civil-rights movement, events that captured the attention of the world....

Urbanization, industrialization, and the civil-rights movement's successful assault on racial segregation have changed the South's economy and politics beyond recognition. The last fifty years have seen the emergence of a very different South. It occupies much of the same territory as Dixie, but that shouldn't blind us to the fact that it is an entirely new development—indeed, in many respects an entirely different region. Almost every unfavorable statistic that used to define the South has shown dramatic change.

Perhaps most striking have been the changes in Southern race relations. Only a generation ago the South's system of racial segregation was fixed in law, seemingly for all time; yet almost overnight it was dismantled by federal legislation and court decisions. With half of America's black population, the South elects two-thirds of the nation's black officeholders, and although black incomes in the South are still lower than white, they are approaching parity with black incomes elsewhere in the U.S.

Economic and demographic statistics have also shown startling improvement. As late as the 1930s per capita income in the South was half of that elsewhere in the United States. Personal income is still lower in the South (only Virginia and Florida are above the national average), but the remaining difference is small enough that it is largely offset by a lower cost of living.

Two out of three Southerners are now urban or suburban folk, and even most rural Southerners work in industry. The agricultural labor force has dropped from half of the total to under 5 percent, and Southern agriculture has increasingly become "agribusiness." (One telling statistic: 10 percent of the 1950 cotton crop was picked by machine; in 1970 the figure was 90 percent.) As the South has moved from agriculture to industry, its birth rate has declined; indeed, since the mid-1950s it has been slightly *lower* than the U.S. average.

The industrial development of the South is continuing. In the 1990s eight of the top ten states in the growth of manufacturing plants were in the South. In 1992–1994 over half the nation's new jobs and ten of the top thirteen states in jobs added per hundred thousand population were Southern (the top three were North Carolina, Mississippi, and Kentucky).

Even in automobile manufacturing, the classic heavy industry, the South has been coming on strong since the 1980s. Tennessee now has Nissan and Saturn plants, Kentucky has Toyota, South Carolina BMW, and Alabama Mercedes-Benz. All told, these factories represent a $7 billion investment to create some twenty thousand well-paid jobs.

Foreign investment is increasingly important. There are forty-six German-owned companies in Spartanburg County, South Carolina, alone: the nearby section of Interstate 95 is known locally as "the Autobahn." One out of every eleven South Carolinians now works for a foreign-owned company, nearly twice the U.S. average.

Interregional migration now flows *into* the South, not out of it, as the South's booming economy slows out-migration and attracts migrants from other regions. Shortly after 1960 more whites began moving to the South than were leaving it; a decade later, the same was true for blacks. Now more than one of every eight residents of the South was born outside it. In consequence, the South's population has increased rapidly. New York has now been replaced by Texas as the second most populous state....

When the South seceded in 1861, Karl Marx said scornfully of the Confederacy that it was not a nation at all, just a battle cry. He meant that the new country had no industrial base, no transportation network, no national press, no obvious capital city to tie it all together—none of what a *real* nation has to make it go. And Marx was right: one of the Confederacy's many problems was that it was trying to build these institutions while fighting for its very existence, and it never entirely succeeded.

But now there are dozens of regional publications, scores of regional trade and professional associations, hundreds of regional corporations. There is a sense—Marx's sense—in which the South is more of a nation now than when it was politically independent.

And Atlanta is its capital. Here is where regional trade associations have their annual conventions, where regional corporations are likely to be headquartered, where national corporations have their regional offices. Here is where the Southern correspondents of television networks and national publications are clustered. The *Wall Street Journal's* Atlanta office now publishes a regional supplement, and the *Journal-Constitution* is the nearest thing the South has to a national newspaper. Atlanta is at the center of the South's transportation grid as well: its airport is the second-busiest in the U.S., giving rise to the Southern joke that even if you're going to hell you'll have to change planes in Atlanta.

This is the South of the future. Call it the "Southeast." This region barely existed before World War II, but it is all around us now. And it seems to be unstoppable, as its booming economy and surging population are translated into political power (primarily through the medium of the Republican party, Dixie's old adversary).

But there is a reason to call it the South*east*. This is a smaller region than Dixie.

We can see plainly now a development that regional sociologists were predicting fifty years ago: Atlanta is not the capital of *all* of the historic South. The post-agricultural South has split down the middle into a southeastern region centered on Atlanta and a southwestern one that is essentially greater Texas. Dallas and Houston don't report to Atlanta the way Charlotte and Nashville and Jacksonville do. The western South has its own regional institutions, its own magazines and corporate headquarters, even its own edition of the *Wall Street Journal*.

To complicate matters still further, most of Virginia is now tied into the economy of the mid-Atlantic states to its north, much of Kentucky now looks to the Midwest, and Miami is becoming the de facto capital of a Caribbean region all its own.

So there is an old, agricultural South that is fading and a new, industrial South that is coming apart at the seams. Put that way, is there any reason, anymore, to talk about the South as *the South?*...

From the start the South has been the home of peoples whose intertwined cultures have set them off from other Americans. And where the economic and political story has been largely one of conflict, division, and separation, the tale of the cultural South is one of blending, sharing, mutual influence—and of continuing unity and distinctiveness.

Start with the fact that the South was settled primarily from Great Britain (especially from its "Celtic fringe" of Scotland, Ireland, and Wales) and from West Africa. To be sure, the native Indians made early and lasting contributions. It is impossible to ignore the French influence in Louisiana—and who would want to? Germans were an early and important presence in Texas and in Virginia's Shenandoah Valley. There are noticeable concentrations of Greeks in Florida, Chinese in Mississippi, and so forth. Acknowledge all that.

Still, Southern culture has been largely a matter of African Americans and Protestant whites of British descent borrowing from each other, imitating each other, shaping one another's attitudes, tastes, and values in ways both obvious and subtle. Black and white Southerners have created distinct but related cultures that are usually recognizable variations on a shared *Southern* culture. In the process, together, they have made the South a great seedbed—possibly *the* great seedbed—of distinctively American culture, inventing and exporting everything from Coca-Cola to rock and roll.

Here is where cultural differences persist in America. If you're looking for how the South is different these days, don't look at what people do from nine to five on weekdays. During those hours Southerners now do pretty much the same things everyone else does. Look instead at what people do in the evenings, on Saturday night, Sunday morning, and weekend afternoons. Look at tastes and cultural patterns that don't simply reflect how people make their livings, or how good a living they make. Look at things that are passed on from generation to generation within families, things that people take with them when they move on geographically, or move up economically. Look at things like manners, religion, cuisine, sports, and music.

When you do, you find a cultural South that is bigger than the Cotton Kingdom, one that encompasses both the Southeast and the Southwest (if not South Florida). Southern values and habits and practices are found in the Appalachian and Ozark Mountains, in Texas and Oklahoma, in a great many areas marginal to the plantation South but settled by Southerners. Mapping cultural patterns makes it easy to figure out who settled most of Kentucky and Missouri, as well as the southern parts of Illinois, Indiana, and Ohio. Indeed, many of the same features can be found in scattered enclaves of Southern migrants throughout the U.S.—among Michigan auto workers, Southern blacks in Chicago and Harlem, or the children and grandchildren of Okies in California.

In nearly all of the South, for example, religious life is dominated by evangelical Protestant denominations (which makes the South unique not just in the U.S. but in the world). A religious Solid South preceded the political one and seems to be outlasting it, because in this respect the South is perhaps becoming even *more* different from the rest of the country. Almost nine out of ten Southerners are Protestant, more than half of those are Baptists, and the region is more Baptist now than it was in 1900.

And the South's fastest-growing denominations are even more unusual. Consider the Church of God in Christ, for instance, a black pentecostal group with its origins in the Mississippi Delta. At COGIC's centenary in 1997 it claimed some four million members, making it perhaps the least well known of America's major religious groups.

The religious life of the Southern highlands and the Southwest is every bit as Southern as that of the Deep South. Early on, evangelical Protestants established their dominance in the Southern backcountry; as Southerners moved on to the west and south, they took their religion with them. Not many people live in West Texas, but those who do are likely to be Baptist or Methodist or Church of Christ. The mountain South, too, is virtually indistinguishable from the rest of the region.

And when it comes to Southern music, the mountains and the Southwest are right at the heart of things. Although black musicians in the Deep South gave us jazz and the blues, the white songwriters and performers of country music mostly hail from a fertile crescent extending from the mountains of Southwest Virginia through Kentucky and Tennessee to Arkansas, Oklahoma, and Texas. (Nashville's role in country music is well known, but the country-music center of Branson, Missouri—in the Ozarks just across the Arkansas line—has recently become second only to Las Vegas as a destination for American tourists.) And when black music from the Deep South met white music from the Southern uplands, in and around Memphis, rock and roll was born.

Both country music and traditional black music reveal in their lyrics another persisting cultural trait: a propensity for several sorts of violence. The FBI's crime statistics show that this is not just talk. The South has had a higher homicide rate than the rest of the U.S. for as long as reliable records have been kept, and the mountains and Southwest share fully in this pattern. But Southern violence is not random (it tends to be the kind of vengeance those songs are about) and it is usually directed outward (the South has the nation's lowest suicide rates).

Southerners have also displayed relatively conservative family and sexrole attitudes. These differences have surfaced in the legal system: Southern states were slow to enact women's suffrage; most never did ratify the Equal Rights Amendment; until recently few had state laws against sex discrimination. Although Southern women have actually been more likely than other American women to work outside the home (they have needed the money more), most often they have worked in "women's jobs"—as textile operatives or domestic servants, for example—and the percentage of women who work in predominantly male occupations remains lower in the South than elsewhere.

Some of these Southern characteristics go back to the early days of Dixie, if not to the British Isles and African savannahs from which so many of the South's people came. Many were mentioned by travelers in the antebellum South. But other regional folkways are of quite recent origin.

Occasionally Southerners have just appropriated pastimes invented somewhere else. American football, for instance, had its origins in New England, and it was not until Alabama beat Washington in the 1926 Rose Bowl that Americans were persuaded that Southerners could play the game competitively. Now, of course, the South provides far more than its share of players in the National Football League, and the tailgate party has become a Southern institution.

More often, however, new differences have emerged as Southerners have used their new resources and opportunities to express traditional values and tastes in new ways. Country music draws on old musical styles, but it took its modern form only after radio and the phonograph turned isolated rural folk into a mass audience. Similarly, stock-car racing reflects a historic admiration for daring and grace under pressure, but it appeared only after the whiskey distillers of the upland South met the automobile.

Notice that the persistence of the cultural South does not require that Southerners stay poor and rural. Indeed, poor folks can't afford some of its trappings: new Southern phenomena from high-tech competitive bass fishing to *Southern Living* magazine require technology, affluence, and mobility that simply did not exist in the South even a half-century ago.

No, mass society has made some inroads, but Southerners still do many things differently—and they keep inventing new ways to do things differently. In the past quarter-century the culture of the South has begun to adapt to migration into the region by unprecedented numbers of Northerners, Hispanics, and Asians. How these newcomers will be assimilated and how they will enrich the culture of the South are interesting questions, but *that* they will seems hardly in doubt. The cultural South has always shown remarkable resilience, and it will probably continue to do so.

The South is no longer defined by an economic system that exports raw materials and surplus population, while generating a variety of social and economic problems for itself. Some aspects of Dixie still linger, and a few of its legacies (notably a substantial black population) will be with us for the foreseeable future. But that South is largely—well, gone with the wind. And, for the most part, good riddance.

The South is now, more than ever, defined by its commercial and industrial economy, by the network of institutions that have emerged to serve it, and by the ever-increasing number of people who have an interest in making sure that it continues to exist. Here, however, the brute facts of distance and diversity conspire to reduce the South to a southeastern core, with the Southwest and South Florida and various borderlands taking their natural place with other regions or as regions in their own right.

But the South has always been and still is set apart by its people. Whatever else it has been or is becoming, the South is the homeland of people who think of themselves as Southerners. Some have even suggested that Southerners ought to be viewed as an American ethnic group, like Italian or Polish Americans, a people with a sense of group identity based on a shared history and a common culture. This is what W. J. Cash had in mind when he wrote in *The Mind of the South* that the South is "not quite a nation within a nation, but the next thing to it."

Geographers have come up with scores of criteria for locating the South, mapping everything from the kudzu vine to where people name their businesses "Southern" this and "Southern" that. But maybe the best way to define the South is with what Hamilton Horton calls the "Hell, yes!" line: you know you are in the South if that's what people say when you ask if they are Southerners.

FURTHER READING

John B. Boles, *The South through Time: A History of an American Region* (1983).

W. J. Cash, *The Mind of the South* (1941).

James C. Cobb, *The Most Southern Place on Earth: The Mississippi Delta and the Roots of Regional Identity* (1992).

Albert E. Cowdrey, *This Land, This South: An Environmental History* (1983).

Carl Degler, *Place over Time: The Continuity of Southern Distinctiveness* (1977).

Paul D. Escott, ed., *W. J. Cash and the Minds of the South* (1992).

Larry J. Griffin and Don H. Doyle, eds., *The South as an American Problem* (1995).

Florence King, *Southern Ladies and Gentlemen* (1975).

Jack Temple Kirby, *Mockingbird Song: Ecological Landscapes of the South* (2006).

Bill C. Malone, *Southern Music, American Music* (1979).

John Shelton Reed, *One South: An Ethnic Approach to Regional Culture* (1982).

Francis Butler Simkins, *The Everlasting South* (1963).

William R. Taylor, *Cavalier and Yankee: The Old South and American National Character* (1961).

Charles Reagan Wilson, et al. eds., *The New Encyclopedia of Southern Culture* (2006–2011).

C. Vann Woodward, *The Burden of Southern History*, 3rd ed. (1993).

Howard Zinn, *The Southern Mystique* (1964).

CHAPTER 2

Reconstructing the South

The United States, in the aftermath of the Civil War, faced difficult dislocations. Northerners had sacrificed an estimated 360,000 men to the War Between the States; southerners lost 258, 000 men. In addition the South suffered enormous economic losses that would impede its recovery for decades after the war. In the aftermath of this bloody conflict Congress struggled with problems it had never before encountered. The most important political question facing the nation was how to bring the southern states back into the Union. President Abraham Lincoln urged Congress to consider his plan that would allow former rebel states to return to the nation after 10 percent of southern voters from the 1860 election swore allegiance to the United States. Congress considered this too lenient and offered a counter proposal that a majority of southern voters swear allegiance. This bill was pocket vetoed by President Lincoln shortly before his death. His successor, President Andrew Johnson drew up a plan whereby states would be admitted to the Union after ratifying the Thirteenth Amendment. Congress, which took an eight-month recess just after Johnson came into office, returned to Capitol Hill in December 1865. Under presidential Reconstruction a few southern states elected representatives to Congress; most of them were ex-Confederates, including Vice President of the CSA Alexander H. Stephens of Georgia. Congressmen were shocked to find former rebel leaders in their midst and sent the southern representatives packing. They then worked on a new plan for restoring southern states to the Union. After the Republican party won a giant victory in the 1866 elections, Congress acted to rescind Johnson's plan and institute measures that would disfranchise former Confederate leaders, uphold black civil rights, and reform southern state governments. After two southern cities erupted into race riots in 1866, and with the institution of Black Codes in southern states, Congress passed the Military Reconstruction Act of 1867 and put southern states under Union occupation. Congress demanded that the nation ratify the Fourteenth and Fifteenth Amendments, granting citizenship to freedpeople (with disfranchisement for Confederate supporters) and voting rights to black men. Then the southern states could write new constitutions, form new state governments, and send representatives to Congress.

If bringing the southern states back into the Union was the nation's number one political problem, its most important social issue was how to help four million ex-slaves move into freedom to become part of the body politic and the economic life of the nation. African Americans endured the greatest changes in the war's aftermath, moving from slavery to freedom, wage earning, and citizenship. Starting in 1867, freedpeople took advantage of Reconstruction reforms and exercised their rights of peaceable assembly – emancipation day celebrations, parades, and militia drills—as well as voting and holding office. Congress created a Freedmen's Bureau in 1865 to help whites and blacks in transition after the war. It provided needed relief, schools, and aid in advancing free labor. Most white southerners, however, resented black political influence and potential economic independence, and they worked to end Reconstruction reforms. The Republican party, starting with President Ulysses S. Grant, moved away from its progressive agenda for African Americans when Congress decided to pardon ex-Confederates, allowing them voting and office holding privileges. Meanwhile, scandals and corruption plagued the party, and in 1873 the nation suffered its first postwar depression. Distracted by political problems of their own, Republicans abandoned their pledge to protect the rights of black southerners by removing federal troops from the South in the Compromise of 1877. Violence, generated in part by the Ku Klux Klan, had already spread throughout the South against white Republicans and black voters. By 1880, Redemption, the return of white power to the South, was complete and Reconstruction came to an end.

At one time, historians echoed the assessment of Reconstruction prevailing among white southerners: that Reconstruction had been a disastrous episode in which unscrupulous northern carpetbaggers, aided by traitorous scalawags and unqualified blacks, seized power in southern governments and inaugurated an orgy of corruption, robbery, and misrule. But the civil rights movement and new historical research since 1960 have led to a revision of this once standard interpretation. While noting the importance of many white southerners' opposition to racial and other changes, revisionist studies have presented a much more balanced assessment of the role of Reconstruction. They have investigated the political debates in Washington, the administrations of Johnson and Grant, the meaning of Radical Reconstruction, the developing violence and racism in the South, and the return to Democratic rule in the 1870s. How did Congress address the problem of returning the southern states to the Union? How did Congress address the problem of granting civil rights and economic opportunities to freed-people? What did Congress require of the former Confederate states during Reconstruction? What policies did Republican governments follow? What was the response of white southerners? How did ex-slaves create new lives for themselves and their families? What impact did the Ku Klux Klan and other terrorist organizations have on the end to Reconstruction?

DOCUMENTS

When the war ended in 1865 southern state legislatures, filled with ex-Confederates, passed laws to define the rights of freedpeople. The Mississippi Black Code, seen in Document 1, represents an example of the limited way that whites understood civil rights after emancipation. Freedpeople expected full rights as promised by the U.S. Constitution. The Mississippi legislature with this code seemed to want to return to slavery. Black Codes were rescinded during Reconstruction after 1867, but for two years, blacks lived with a limited form of freedom. Congress's involvement in the postwar Reconstruction is summarized in the next three Reconstruction Amendments—13 (emancipation), 14 (defined citizenship), 15 (black male voting rights). These were passed and ratified in part because southern state governments had returned ex-Confederates to office and state legislatures had enacted Black Codes, restricting the freedom of ex-slaves. In Document 3, we see a report from J. R. Johnson, a Freedmen's Bureau superintendent. He quotes a corporal in the U.S. Colored Troops, who tied the hopes and happiness of millions of freedpeople to civil rights. Legal marriage was a right that had been denied slaves but was granted after emancipation. They saw marriage as the foundation of all their rights because it allowed them to establish households independent of white interference or intrusion by state courts. In the turbulent years just after the war, courts bound out or apprenticed black children, especially of single mothers, to former masters who were eager to get them back under conditions that resembled slavery. Courts were less likely to take black children away from married couples who could support them. The Military Reconstruction Act of 1867, Document 4, is Congress's answer to white southern intrasigence in the face of reform. Two race riots that ignited New Orleans and Memphis in 1866, continued suppression of black rights, and talk of sustained rebellion led the Radical Republicans to pass a far reaching law that would order U.S. troops to the South to protect black voter rights and "suppress insurrection, disorder, and violence...." Once freedmen had been granted the right to vote under the Military Reconstruction Act, they flocked to the polls and took their places on juries and in elected and appointed offices. Document 5, demonstrates through cartoons the newly won rights to vote, hold office, or serve on juries. These drawings show the contrast between the stereotypical African American and white southerner as they appeared to the northern press in 1867. The first image suggests a sinister outcome for black voters. At other times northern newspapers showed the dignity, responsibility, and gravity of the political changes that came over the South during Reconstruction as seen in the succeeding images. In Document 6, we see southern whites respond to Reconstruction governments with vehement published protests. The last document adumbrates the effectiveness of the Ku Klux Klan and its violence against black and white Republican voters.

1. Mississippi Legislates Black Codes, 1865

An Act to Confer Civil Rights on Freedmen, and for other Purposes

Section 1. All freedmen ... may sue and be sued, implead and be impleaded, in all the courts of law and equity of this State, and may acquire personal property ... and may dispose of the same in the same manner and to the same extent that white persons may: *Provided,* That the provisions of this section shall not be so construed as to allow any freedman ... to rent or lease any lands or tenements except in incorporated cities or towns, in which places the corporate authorities shall control the same.

Laws of the State of Mississippi, Passed at Regular Session of the Mississippi Legislature, held in Jackson, October, November, and December, 1865 (Jackson, 1866), pp. 82–93, 165–67.

Section 2. All freedmen … may intermarry with each other, in the same manner and under the same regulations that are provided by law for white persons….

Section 3. All freedmen … who do now and have herebefore lived and cohabited together as husband and wife shall be taken and held in law as legally married, … and it shall not be lawful for any freedman … to intermarry with any white person; nor for any person to intermarry with any freedman, free negro or mulatto; and any person who shall so intermarry shall be deemed guilty of felony, and on conviction thereof shall be confined in the State penitentiary for life.

Section 4. In addition to cases in which freedmen … are now by law competent witnesses, freedmen … shall be competent in civil cases, when a party or parties to the suit, either plaintiff or plaintiffs, defendant or defendants; also in cases where freedmen … are either plaintiff or plaintiffs, defendant or defendants. They shall also be competent witnesses in all criminal prosecutions where the crime charged is alleged to have been committed by a white person upon or against the person or property of a freedman, free negro or mulatto: *Provided,* that in all cases said witnesses shall be examined in open court … and shall … be subject to the rules and tests of the common law as to competency and credibility.

Section 5. Every freedman … shall, on the second Monday of January, one thousand eight hundred and sixty-six, and annually thereafter, have a lawful home or employment, and shall have written evidence thereof….

Section 6. All contracts for labor made with freedmen … for a longer period than one month shall be in writing, and a duplicate, attested and read to said freedman … by a beat, city or county officer, or two disinterested white persons of the county in which the labor is to be performed … and if the laborer shall quit the service of the employer before the expiration of his term of service, without good cause, he shall forfeit his wages for that year up to the time of quitting.

Section 7. … Every civil officer shall, and every person may, arrest and carry back to his or her legal employer any freedman … who shall have quit the service of his or her employer before the expiration of his or her term of service without good cause; and said officer and person shall be entitled to receive for arresting and carrying back every deserting employee aforesaid the sum of five dollars, and ten cents per mile from the place of arrest to the place of delivery; and the same shall be paid by the employer, and held as a set-off for so much against the wages of said deserting employee: *Provided,* … either party shall have the right of appeal to the county court….

An Act to Regulate the Relation of Master and Apprentice, as Relates to Freedmen, Free Negroes, and Mulattoes

Section 1. … It shall be the duty of all … civil officers of the several counties in this State, to report to the probate courts of their respective counties semi-annually, … all freedmen, free negroes, and mulattoes, under the age of eighteen, in their respective counties, beats or districts, who are orphans, or whose parent or parents have not the means or who refuse to provide for and support said minors; ... it shall be the duty of said probate court to order the clerk of said court to apprentice said minors to some competent and suitable person ... *Provided,* that the former owner of said minors shall have the preference when, in the opinion of the court, he or she shall be a suitable person for that purpose.... If any apprentice shall leave the employment of his or her master or mistress, without his or her consent, said master or mistress may pursue and recapture said apprentice, and bring him or her before any justice of the peace of the county, whose duty it shall be to remand said apprentice to the service of his or her master or mistress....

An Act to Amend the Vagrant Laws of the State

Section 1. *Be it enacted* ... That all rogues and vagabonds, idle and dissipated persons, beggars, jugglers, or persons practicing unlawful games or plays, runaways, common drunkards, common night-walkers, pilferers, lewd, wanton, or lascivious persons, in speech or behavior, common railers and brawlers, persons who neglect their calling or employment, misspend what they earn, or do not provide for the support of themselves or their families, or dependents ... shall be deemed and considered vagrants ... and upon conviction thereof shall be fined not exceeding one hundred dollars, with all accruing costs, and be imprisoned at the discretion of the court, not exceeding ten days.

Section 2. ... All freedmen ... in this State, over the age of eighteen years, found on the second Monday in January, 1866, or thereafter, with no lawful employment or business, or found unlawfully assembling themselves together, either in the day or night time, and all white persons so assembling themselves with freedmen ... on terms of equality, or living in adultery or fornication with a freed woman, free negro or mulatto, shall be deemed vagrants, and on conviction thereof shall be fined in a sum not exceeding, in the case of a freedman ... fifty dollars, and a white man two hundred dollars, and imprisoned at the discretion of the court, the free negro not exceeding ten days, and the white man not exceeding six months....

Penal Laws of Mississippi

Section 1. *Be it enacted,* ... That no freedman, free negro or mulatto, not in the military service of the United States government, and not licensed so to do by the board of police of his or her county, shall keep or carry fire-arms of any kind, or any ammunition, dirk or bowie knife, and on conviction thereof in the county court shall be punished by fine, not exceeding ten dollars, and pay the costs of such proceedings, and all such arms or ammunition shall be forfeited to the informer....

Section 5. ...If any freedman ... convicted of any of the misdemeanors provided against in this act, shall fail or refuse for the space of five days, after conviction, to pay the fine and costs imposed, such person shall be hired out by the sheriff or other officer ... to any white person who will pay said fine and all costs, and take said convict for the shortest time.

2. The Nation Ratifies Three Reconstruction Amendments: 13, 14, and 15

Amendment XIII [Adopted 1865]

Section 1. Neither slavery nor involuntary servitude, except as a punishment for crime whereof the party shall have been duly convicted, shall exist within the United States, or any place subject to their jurisdiction.

Section 2. Congress shall have power to enforce this article by appropriate legislation.

Amendment XIV [Adopted 1868]

Section 1. All persons born or naturalized in the United States, and subject to the jurisdiction thereof, are citizens of the United States and of the State wherein they reside. No State shall make or enforce any law which shall abridge the privileges or immunities of citizens of the United States; nor shall any State deprive any person of life, liberty, or property, without due process of law; nor deny to any person within its jurisdiction the equal protection of the laws.

Section 2. Representatives shall be apportioned among the several States according to their respective numbers, counting the whole number of persons in each State, excluding Indians not taxed. But when the right to vote at any election for the choice of Electors for President and Vice-President of the United States, Representatives in Congress, the executive and judicial officers of a State, or the members of the legislature thereof, is denied to any of the male inhabitants of such State, being twenty-one years of age and citizens of the United States, or in any way abridged, except for participation in rebellion, or other crime, the basis of representation therein shall be reduced in the proportion which the number of such male citizens shall bear to the whole number of male citizens twenty-one years of age in such State.

Section 3. No person shall be a Senator or Representative in Congress, or Elector of President and Vice-President, or hold any office, civil or military, under the United States, or under any State, who, having previously taken an oath, as a member of Congress, or as an officer of the United States, or as a member of any State legislature, or as an executive or judicial officer of any State, to support the Constitution of the United States, shall have engaged in insurrection or rebellion against the same, or given aid or comfort to the enemies thereof. Congress may, by a vote of two-thirds of each house, remove such disability.

Section 4. The validity of the public debt of the United States, authorized by law; including debts incurred for payment of pensions and bounties for services in suppressing insurrection or rebellion, shall not be questioned. But neither the United States nor any State shall assume or pay any debt or obligation incurred in aid of insurrection or rebellion against the United States, or any claim for the

These are Constitutional Amendments 13, 14, and 15.

loss of emancipation of any slave; but all such debts, obligations, and claims shall be held illegal and void.

Section 5. The Congress shall have power to enforce, by appropriate legislation, the provisions of this article.

Amendment XV [Adopted 1870]

Section 1. The right of citizens of the United States to vote shall not be denied or abridged by the United States or by any State on account of race, color, or previous condition of servitude.

Section 2. The Congress shall have power to enforce this article by appropriate legislation.

3. J. R. Johnson Preaches on Marriage Covenants and Legal Rights, 1866

Freedmen's Village, Va. June 1st 1866.

Dear Col: I have the honor to report to you concerning my efforts as Supt. of Marriages in 5th Dist Va. from April 25th, to May 31st, (inclusive) 1866....

On the evening of April 25th, I preached on the subject of Marriage to the soldiers at Fort Corcoran, 107. U.S.C.I. co. A & co E. Capt. Goff of co. A. and commander of the Fort, was present, and assisted me, by reading the Circular on Marriage, explaining it—and adding earnest remarks, which exerted much influence on the minds of the soldiers. I record for him my *thanks* for such timely, and efficient assistance. I addressed the soldiers at that Fort several other times, on the same theme: these occasions included two Sabbath evenings. At the close of service on one of those evenings—Corporal Murray (of co A), said:—

"Fellow Soldiers:—

I praise God for this day! I have long been praying for it. The Marriage Covenant is at the foundation of all our rights. In slavery we could not have *legalised* marriage: *now* we have it. Let us conduct ourselves worthy of such a blessing—and all the people will respect us—God will bless us, and we shall be established as a people." His character is such, that every word had power.

I have preached & lectured, or *talked* publicly five times at Freedmens Village. From Apr 26 to May 30th, gave fifteen certificates: six to soldiers of 107 USCI Fort Corcoran; three to 107. Vienna Fairfax county—one-107 Freedmens Village—one 107 Alx——; and four couples of citizens, all of Alexandria co. Nearly three weeks of sickness prevented me from accomplishing more. Yesterday, 31st of May, we gave seventy nine certificates in Freedmens Village. We have much more to do. Rev R S Laws, Rev D A. Miles & lady teachers, much help me. Spent last Sabbath with Capt Ross, of Vienna & the way is open for work in that region. Yours

J. R. Johnson

From Ira Berlin and Leslie Rowland, eds., *Families and Freedom: A Documentary History of African American Kinship in the Civil War Era* (New York: New Press, 1997), pp. 168, 170.

4. Congress Passes The Military Reconstruction Act, 1867

Whereas no legal State governments or adequate protection for life or property now exists in the rebel States of Virginia, North Carolina, South Carolina, Georgia, Mississippi, Alabama, Louisiana, Florida, Texas, and Arkansas; and whereas it is necessary that peace and good order should be enforced in said States until loyalty and republican State governments can be legally established: Therefore

Be it enacted, ... That said rebel States shall be divided into military districts and made subject to the military authority of the United States ...

Section 2. ... It shall be the duty of the President to assign to the command of each of said districts an officer of the army, not below the rank of brigadier general, and to detail a sufficient military force to enable such officer to perform his duties and enforce his authority within the district to which he is assigned.

Section 3. ... It shall be the duty of each officer assigned as aforesaid to protect all persons in their rights of persons and property, to suppress insurrection, disorder, and violence, and to punish, or cause to be punished, all disturbers of the public peace and criminals, and to this end he may allow local civil tribunals to take jurisdiction of and to try offenders, or, when in his judgment it may be necessary for the trial of offenders, he shall have power to organize military commissions or tribunals for that purpose; and all interference under color of State authority with the exercise of military authority under this act shall be null and void....

Section 5. ... When the people of any one of said rebel States shall have formed a constitution of government in conformity with the Constitution of the United States in all respects, framed by a convention of delegates elected by the male citizens of said State twenty-one years old and upward, of whatever race, color, or previous condition, ... and when such constitution shall provide that the elective franchise shall be enjoyed by all such persons as have the qualifications herein stated for electors of delegates, and when such constitution shall be ratified by a majority of the persons voting on the question of ratification who are qualified as electors of delegates, and when such constitution shall have been submitted to Congress for examination and approval, and Congress shall have approved the same, and when said State, by a vote of its legislature elected under said constitution, shall have adopted the amendment to the Constitution of the United States, proposed by the thirty-ninth Congress, and known as article fourteen, and when said article shall have become a part of the Constitution of the United States, said State shall be declared entitled to representation in

This document can be found in the United States of America Statutes at Large, Volume 13, pp. 428–29.

Congress, and senators and representatives shall be admitted therefrom on their taking oaths prescribed by law, and then and thereafter the preceding sections of this act shall be inoperative in said State: *Provided,* That no person excluded from the privilege of holding office by said proposed amendment to the Constitution of the United States shall be eligible to election as a member of the convention to frame a constitution for any of said rebel States, nor shall any such person vote for members of such convention.

Section 6. ... Until the people of said rebel States shall be by law admitted to representation in the Congress of the United States, any civil governments which may exist therein shall be deemed provisional only, and in all respects subject to the paramount authority of the United States at any time to abolish, modify or control, or supersede the same; and in all elections to any office under such provisional governments all persons shall be entitled to vote, and none others, who are entitled to vote under the provisions of the fifth section of this act; and no person shall be eligible to any office under any such provisional governments who would be disqualified from holding office under the provisions of the third article of said constitutional amendment.

5. The Northern Press Views the Enfranchisement of Freedmen, 1867

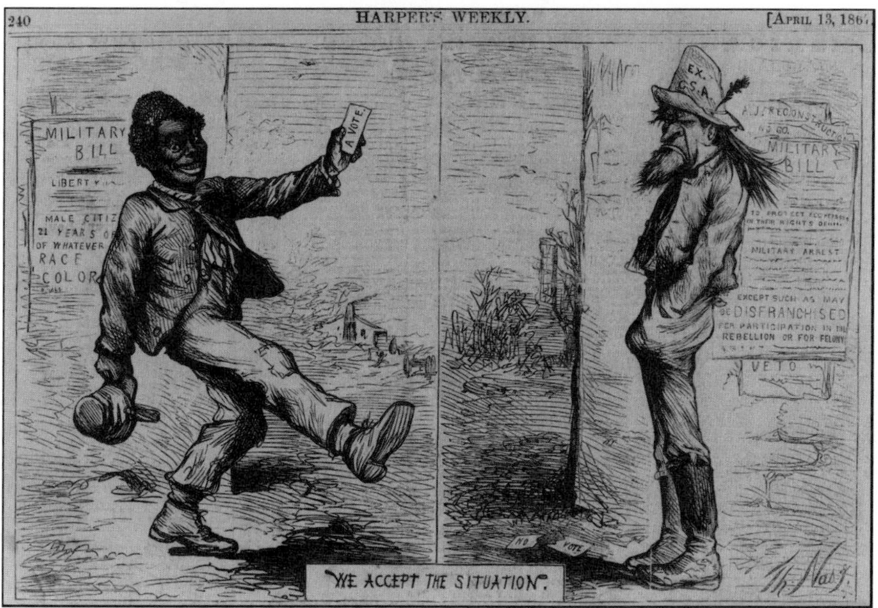

"We Accept the Situation" by Thomas Nast. *Harper's Weekly*, April 13, 1867. (Library of Congress)

"The First Vote, 1867" by A. R. Waud. *Harper's Weekly*, November 16, 1867. (Library of Congress)

"A Jury of Whites and Blacks," by James E. Taylor. *Frank Leslie's Illustrated Newspaper*, November 30, 1867. (Library of Congress)

6. A Southern Newspaper Denounces Reconstruction, 1869

That the State has been cursed and almost ruined by a class of "carpet bag" vultures from the North, aided by degenerate and too often corrupt natives, is patent to anybody who opens his eyes. We have not been slow to tell the people of the villainies that have been perpetrated and are yet being perpetrated, day and night, by the present State government, at the expense and injury of the people, black and white. We intend to continue to do so regardless of cost or consequences.

Our firm conviction is that the people will not tolerate these villainies a great while longer; the day of reckoning cometh, and it will be terrible. The "carpet bagger" race will then hurry off to some other field of spoils and laugh at the calamity of their dupes and co-workers in iniquity; but the *native* culprit must answer at the bar of public opinion, and in many cases at the bar of the Court for high crimes. We tell the native scalawags that the day is not far distant, when the thin vail that now hides their crimes from public gaze will be withdrawn, and they will be exposed to the scorn and indignation of an outraged people. Yes, and that small class of our people who claim to be good and true men, who, for the sake of a little gain, have *secretly* colluded with the bad wretches who have plundered and impoverished the people without mercy, they, too, will be exposed. Yes, we repeat, the day will be mercilessly exposed. And such perpetration or crime will thenceforth be a *stench* in the nostrils of all decent men, white and black. Everybody will bate them, mock and hiss at them as they pass by. The Penitentiary fraud will be exposed, the Railroad frauds will be exposed; it will yet be known how much money was used to corrupt the members of the Legislature, who used it, who paid it, and where it came from; it will yet be known how many warrants have been made on the Treasury not authorized by law. We have the best of reasons for saying that the passage of the Railroad acts cost the State tens and hundreds of thousands of dollars. The people will yet ferret out those who so recklessly and criminally spent the treasure of the people. Yes, gentlemen, the day of reckoning will come. Mark what we say! Let every man watch how he connects himself even innocently with those who have so outraged the State and the people.

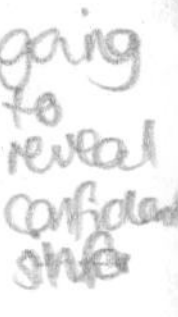

7. Congress Hears Testimony on the Ku Klux Klan, 1871

Ben Hill on the Klan

Question. You have not studied this organization?

Answer. I have only investigated a few cases for the purpose of ascertaining who were the guilty offenders. One reason for investigating the few cases was

---

This document originally appeared in the *Raleigh Daily Sentinel,* August 6, 1869, page 2 under the title, "The Day of Reckoning Will Come."

This document can be found as part of the United States of America's Congress' testimony taken by the Joint Select Committee to inquire into the Condition of Affairs: Georgia, volume I, p. 308; volume II, pp. 770–71.

upon the attempt to reconstruct Georgia some time ago, and these Ku-Klux outrages were made to bear very, very heavily against even Union parties [who opposed returning Georgia to military rule]. I wanted to know if that was the case, and if so, I wanted the people to put down the Ku-Klux....

Question. Can you state any particulars you may have heard in reference to the attack on [Jourdan] Ware?

Answer. Yes, sir; I can state what I heard. A body of about twenty-five or thirty disguised men went one night and met him upon the road. (I think this was the case of Jourdan Ware.) I am not certain that they went to his house. I believe they met him on the road, somewhere or other, and demanded of him his arms and his watch. I believe he gave up his arms, and they shot him upon his refusal to surrender the watch, and he died a day or two afterward.

Question. Did you ever hear that there was any accusation of his having done anything wrong?

Answer. No, sir; I think not, except I believe I did hear that there was some complaint of his impudence, or something of that sort.

Question. We hear from a great many witnesses about the "impudence" of negroes. What is considered in your section of the country "impudence" on the part of a negro?

Answer. Well, it is considered impudence for a negro not to be polite to a white man—not to pull off his hat and bow and scrape to a white man, as was always done formerly.

Question. Do the white people generally expect or require now that kind of submissive deportment on the part of the negroes that they did while the negroes were slaves?

Answer. I do not think they do as a general thing; a great many do.

Question. Are there many white people who do require it?

Answer. Yes, sir; I think there are a great many who do require it, and are not satisfied unless the negroes do it.

Question. Suppose that a negro man has been working for a white man, and they have some difference or dispute in relation to wages, will your people generally allow a negro man to stand up and assert his rights in the same way and in the same language which they would allow to a white man without objection?

Answer. O, no sir, that is not expected at all.

Question. If the colored man does stand up and assert his rights in language which would be considered pardonable and allowable in a white man, that is considered "impudence" in a negro?

Answer. Yes, sir; gross impudence.

Question. Is that species of "impudence" on the part of the negro considered a sufficient excuse by many of your people for chastising a negro, or "dealing with him?"

Answer. Well, some think so....

Question. In your judgment, from what you have seen and heard, is there something of a political character about this organization?

Answer. I think it is entirely political.

Question. What makes you think so?

Answer. Because the parties who are maltreated by these men are generally republicans. I have never known a democrat to be assaulted....

Question. Give the committee your judgment in relation to the object with which this organization has been gotten up. What do its members intend to attain by it?

Answer. Well, sir, my opinion is that the first object of the institution of the Ku-Klux, or these disguised bands, was to cripple any effect that might be produced by Loyal Leagues. That is my opinion—that this organization was an offset to the Loyal Leagues.

Question. But the Ku-Klux organization kept on increasing after the Loyal Leagues were disbanded?

Answer. Yes, sir.

Question. What, in your opinion, is the object of keeping up the Ku-Klux organization and operating it as they do? What do they intend to produce or effect by it?

Answer. My opinion is, that the purpose was to break down the reconstruction acts; that they were dissatisfied with negro suffrage and the reconstruction measures and everybody that was in favor of them.

Question. Do you think this organization was intended to neutralize the votes of the negroes after suffrage had been extended to them?

Answer. Yes, sir, I think so.

Question. How? By intimidating them?

Answer. Any way. Yes, sir, by intimidation.

Question. Making them afraid to exercise the right of suffrage?

Answer. Yes, sir.

Question. Do you believe that the organization and its operations have, in fact, produced that effect?

Answer. I think they have to some extent.

Question. What is the state of feeling which has been produced among the colored people by this armed, disguised organization, and the acts they have committed?

Answer. Well, in my section of the country, the colored people, generally, are afraid now, and have been for some time, to turn out at an election. They are afraid to say much, or to have anything to do with public affairs. I own a plantation on Coosa River, upon which I have, perhaps, about 40 negroes, and some of them have been pretty badly alarmed, afraid to say much. Some have lain out in the woods, afraid to stay at home.

ESSAYS

In the first essay, Professor Eric Foner delineates with care the role that African Americans played in reconstructing the South, through Union Leagues and through political and economic leadership. He points to their civic aspirations, which included voting, the right to hold office, full citizenship, and equal rights under the law. Over 2,000 African Americans held offices of every kind all over the South; some came from the North to escape northern racism and to experience the opportunities afforded by Reconstruction in the South. Voting rights and office holding by African Americans were among the most fervently desired and the most urgently needed in order to protect the status of freedpeople, but it was just such rights that white southerners feared would destroy their political hegemony. The result of white resistance to Reconstruction governments was often violence and intimidation, especially as federal troops began to be called out of the South. Foner ends his essay by recounting the rise of a region-wide Ku Klux Klan that intimidated black voters and white Republicans into giving up their political aspirations. Foner argues that even in the North, where "corrupt election procedures, political chicanery … were hardly unknown" violence on the level found in the South in 1870s did not exist. Republicans, Foner notes, usually used conciliatory tactics to foster stability. This approach did not work in the South. Reconstruction ended with terror, extraordinary bloodshed, murder, and mayhem. Hannah Rosen, in this gendered interpretation of Reconstruction-era violence reveals how night raids by the Ku Klux Klan and the raping of women by white men, was used to intimidate free blacks. These actions had a terrifying impact on black families, but Rosen also argues that freedpeople reported the transgressions, using the law to affirm their citizenship rights. In both essays, the authors attribute the cause of the decline of Reconstruction governments to the designs of white supremacists who insisted on regaining power and diminishing African Americans' rights by whatever method they could.

Black Activism and the Rise of the Ku Klux Klan

ERIC FONER

In 1867, politics emerged as the principal focus of black aspirations. In that annus mirabilis, the impending demise of the structure of civil authority opened the door for political mobilization to sweep across the black belt. Itinerant lecturers, black and white, brought the Republican message into the heart of the rural South. A black Baptist minister calling himself Professor J. W. Toer journeyed through parts of Georgia and Florida with a "magic lantern" exhibiting "the progress of reconstruction.… He has a scene, which he calls 'before the proclamation,' another 'after the proclamation' and then '22nd Regt. U. S. C[olored] T[roops] Duncan's Brigade'." Voting registrars instructed freedmen in American history and government and "the individual benefits of citizenship." In Monroe County, Alabama, where no black political meeting had occurred before 1867, freedmen crowded around the speaker shouting, "God bless you," "Bless God for this." Throughout the South, planters complained of blacks neglecting their labor. Once a week during the summer of 1867, "the negroes from the entire county" quit work and flocked to Waco, Texas, for political rallies. In Alabama,

---

Excerpt from *Reconstruction: America's Unfinished Revolution 1863–1877* by Eric Foner.

"they stop at any time and go off to Greensboro" for the same purpose. On August 1, Richmond's tobacco factories were forced to close because so many black laborers attended the Republican state convention.

So great was the enthusiasm that, as one ex-slave minister later wrote, "Politics got in our midst and our revival or religious work for a while began to wane." The offices of the black-controlled St. Landry (Louisiana) *Progress*, where several hundred freedmen gathered each Sunday to hear the weekly issue read aloud, temporarily displaced the church as a community meeting place. More typically, the church, and indeed every other black institution, became politicized. Every AME [African Methodist Episcopal] preacher in Georgia was said to be actively engaged in Republican organizing, and political materials were read aloud at "churches, societies, leagues, clubs, balls, picnics, and all other gatherings." One plantation manager summed up the situation: "You never saw a people more excited on the subject of politics than are the negroes of the south. They are perfectly wild."

The meteoric rise of the Union League reflected and channeled this political mobilization. Having originated as a middle-class patriotic club in the Civil War North, the league now emerged as the political voice of impoverished freedmen. Even before 1867, local Union Leagues had sprung up among blacks in some parts of the South, and the order had spread rapidly during and after the war among Unionist whites in the Southern hill country. Now, as freedmen poured into the league, "the negro question" disrupted some upcountry branches, leading many white members to withdraw altogether or retreat into segregated branches. Many local leagues, however, achieved a remarkable degree of interracial harmony. In North Carolina, one racially mixed league composed of freedmen, white Unionists, and Confederate Army deserters, met "in old fields, or in some out of the way house, and elect candidates to be received into their body."

By the end of 1867, it seemed, virtually every black voter in the South had enrolled in the Union League or some equivalent local political organization. Although the league's national leadership urged that meetings be held in "a commodious and pleasant room," this often proved impossible; branches convened in black churches, schools, and homes, and also, when necessary, in woods or fields. Usually, a Bible, a copy of the Declaration of Independence, and an anvil or some other emblem of labor lay on a table, a minister opened the meeting with a prayer, new members took an initiation oath, and pledges followed to uphold the Republican party and the principle of equal rights, and "to stick to one another." Armed black sentinels—"a thing unheard of in South Carolina history," according to one alarmed white—guarded many meetings. Indeed, informal self-defense organizations sprang up around the leagues, and reports of blacks drilling with weapons, sometimes under men with self-appointed "military titles," aroused considerable white apprehension.

The leagues' main function, however, was political education. "We just went there," explained an illiterate North Carolina black member, "and we talked a little; made speeches on one question and another." Republican newspapers were read aloud, issues of the day debated, candidates nominated for office, and banners with slogans like "Colored Troops Fought Nobly" prepared for rallies, parades, and barbecues. One racially mixed North Carolina league on various occasions discussed the organization of a July 4 celebration, cooperation with the Heroes of America (itself experiencing a revival among wartime Unionists in 1867), and questions like disenfranchisement, debtor relief, and public education likely to arise at the state's constitutional convention. A York County, South Carolina, league "frequently read and discussed" the Black Code, a reminder of injustices in the days of Presidential Reconstruction.

The detailed minute book of the Union League of Maryville, Tennessee, a mountain community with a long-standing antislavery tradition, offers a rare glimpse of the league's inner workings. It records frequent discussions of such issues as the national debt and the impeachment of President Johnson, as well as broader questions: "Is the education of the Female as important as that of the male?" "Should students pay corporation tax?" "Should East Tennessee be a separate state?" Although composed largely of white loyalists—mainly small farmers, agricultural laborers, and town businessmen, many of them Union Army veterans—and located in a county only one-tenth black, the Maryville league chose a number of black officers, called upon Tennessee to send at least one black to Congress, and in 1868 nominated a black justice of the peace and four black city commissioners, all of whom won election.

The local leagues' multifaceted activities, however, far transcended electoral politics. Often growing out of the institutions blacks had created in 1865 and 1866, they promoted the building of schools and churches and collected funds "to see to the sick." League members drafted petitions protesting the exclusion of blacks from local juries and demanding the arrest of white criminals. In one instance, in Bullock County, Alabama, they organized their own "negro government" with a code of laws, sheriff, and courts. (The army imprisoned its leader, former slave George Shorter.)...

This hothouse atmosphere of political mobilization made possible a vast expansion of the black political leadership (mostly, it will be recalled, freeborn urban mulattoes) that had emerged between 1864 and 1867. Some, like the Charleston free blacks who fanned out into the black belt spreading Republican doctrine and organizing Union Leagues, did have years of political activism behind them. Others were among the more than eighty "colored itinerant lecturers" financed by the Republican Congressional Committee—men like William U. Saunders, a Baltimore barber and Union Army veteran, James Lynch, who left the editorship of the *Christian Recorder* to organize Republican meetings in Mississippi, and even James H. Jones, former "body servant" of Jefferson Davis. Of the black speakers who crisscrossed the South in 1867 and 1868, Lynch was widely regarded as the greatest orator. "Fluent and graceful, he stirred the audience as no other man did or could do," and his eloquence held gatherings of 3,000 freedmen or more spellbound for hours at a time.

Not a few of the blacks who plunged into politics in 1867 had been born or raised in the North. Even in South Carolina, with its well-established native leadership, Northern blacks assumed a conspicuous role. One white participant in the state's first Republican convention, "astonished" by "the amount of intelligence and ability shown by the colored men;" singled out Ohio-born

William N. Viney, a young veteran (he was twenty-five in 1867) who had purchased land in the low country and, after the passage of the Reconstruction Act, organized political meetings throughout the region at his own expense. Many Northern blacks, like Viney, had come south with the army; others had served with the Freedmen's Bureau, or as teachers and ministers employed by black churches and Northern missionary societies. Still others were black veterans of the Northern antislavery crusade, fugitive slaves returning home, or the children of well-to-do Southern free blacks who had been sent north for the education (often at Oberlin College) and economic opportunities denied them at home. Reconstruction was one of the few times in American history that the South offered black men of talent and ambition not only the prospect of serving their race, but greater possibilities for personal advancement than existed in the North. And as long as it survived, the southward migration continued. As late as 1875, twenty-two year old D. B. Colton came to South Carolina from Ohio and promptly won a position as election manager. As a consequence, Northern black communities were drained of men of political ambition and of lawyers and other professionals. Having known discrimination in the North—Jonathan C. Gibbs had been "refused admittance to eighteen colleges" before finding a place at Dartmouth—black migrants carried with them a determination that Reconstruction must sweep away racial distinctions in every aspect of American life.

Even more remarkable than the prominence of Northern blacks was the rapid emergence of indigenous leadership in the black belt. Here, where few free blacks had lived before the war, and political mobilization had proceeded extremely unevenly before 1867, local leaders tended to be ex-slaves of modest circumstances who had never before "had the privilege" of expressing political opinions "in public." Many were teachers, preachers, or individuals who possessed other skills of use to the community. Former slave Thomas Allen, a Union League organizer who would soon win election to the Georgia legislature, was a propertyless Baptist preacher, shoemaker, and farmer. But what established him as a leader was literacy: "In my county the colored people came to me for instructions, and I gave them the best instructions I could. I took the New York Tribune and other papers, and in that way I found out a great deal, and I told them whatever I thought was right." In occupation, the largest number of local activists appear to have been artisans. Comprising 5 percent or less of the rural black population, artisans were men whose skill and independence set them apart from ordinary laborers, but who remained deeply embedded in the life of the freedmen's community. Many had already established their prominence as slaves, like Emanuel Fortune, whose son, editor T. Thomas Fortune, later recalled: "It was natural for [him] to take the leadership in any independent movement of the Negroes. During and before the Civil War he had commanded his time as a tanner and expert shoe and bootmaker. In such life as the slaves were allowed and in church work, he took the leader's part." The Union League catapulted others into positions of importance. James T. Alston, an Alabama shoemaker and musician and the former slave of Confederate Gen. Cullen A. Battle, had "a stronger influence over the minds of the colored men in Macon county" than any other individual, a standing he attributed to the commission he received in 1867 to organize a local Union League.

And there were other men, respected for personal qualities—good sense, oratorical ability, having served in the army, or, like South Carolina Republican organizer Alfred Wright, being "an active person in my principles." Calvin Rogers, a Florida black constable, was described by another freedman as "a thorough-going man; he was a stump speaker, and tried to excite the colored people to do the right thing.... He would work for a man and make him pay him." Such attributes seemed more important in 1867 than education or political experience. "You can teach me the law," wrote one black Texan, "but you cannot [teach] me what justice is." Nor, in a region that erected nearly insuperable barriers against black achievement, did high social status appear necessary for political distinction. "All colored people of this country understand," a black writer later noted, "that what a man does, is no indication of what he is."

In Union Leagues, Republican gatherings, and impromptu local meetings, ordinary blacks in 1867 and 1868 staked their claim to equal citizenship in the American republic. Like Northern blacks schooled in the Great Tradition of protest, and the urban freemen who had dominated the state conventions of 1865 and 1866, former slaves identified themselves with the heritage of the Declaration of Independence, and insisted America live up to its professed ideals. In insistent language far removed from the conciliatory tones of 1865, an Alabama convention affirmed its understanding of equal citizenship:

> We claim exactly *the same rights, privileges and immunities as are enjoyed by white men*—we ask nothing more and will be content with nothing less.... The law no longer knows white nor black, but simply men, and consequently we are entitled to ride in public conveyances, hold office, sit on juries and do everything else which we have in the past been prevented from doing solely on the ground of color....

Violence ... had been endemic in large parts of the South since 1865. But the advent of Radical Reconstruction stimulated its further expansion. By 1870, the Ku Klux Klan and kindred organizations like the Knights of the White Camelia and the White Brotherhood had become deeply entrenched in nearly every Southern state. One should not think of the Klan, even in its heyday, as possessing a well-organized structure or clearly defined regional leadership. Acts of violence were generally committed by local groups on their own initiative. But the unity of purpose and common tactics of these local organizations makes it possible to generalize about their goals and impact, and the challenge they posed to the survival of Reconstruction. In effect, the Klan was a military force serving the interests of the Democratic party, the planter class, and all those who desired the restoration of white supremacy. Its purposes were political, but political in the broadest sense, for it sought to affect power relations, both public and private, throughout Southern society. It aimed to reverse the interlocking changes sweeping over the South during Reconstruction: to destroy the Republican party's infrastructure, undermine the Reconstruction state, reestablish control of the black labor force, and restore racial subordination in every aspect of Southern life....

By and large, Klan activity was concentrated in Piedmont counties where blacks comprised a minority or small majority of the population and the two parties were evenly divided. But no simple formula can explain the pattern of terror that engulfed parts of the South while leaving others relatively unscathed.  Georgia's Klan was most active in a cluster of black belt and Piedmont cotton counties east and southeast of Atlanta, and in a group of white-majority counties in the northwestern part of the state. Unknown in the overwhelmingly black South Carolina and Georgia lowcountry, the organization flourished in the western Alabama plantation belt. Scattered across the South lay counties particularly notorious for rampant brutality. Carpetbagger Judge Albion W. Tourgée counted twelve murders, nine rapes, fourteen cases of arson, and over 700 beatings (including the whipping of a woman 103 years of age) in his judicial district in North Carolina's central Piedmont. An even more extensive "reign of terror" engulfed Jackson, a plantation county in Florida's panhandle. "That is where Satan has his seat," remarked a black clergyman; all told over 150 persons were killed, among them black leaders and Jewish merchant Samuel Fleischman, resented for his Republican views and reputation for dealing fairly with black customers.

Nowhere did the Klan become more deeply entrenched than in a group of Piedmont South Carolina counties where medium-sized farms predominated and the races were about equal in number. An outbreak of terror followed the October 1870 elections, in which Republicans retained a tenuous hold on power in the region. Possibly the most massive Klan action anywhere in the South was the January 1871 assault on the Union county jail by 500 masked men, which resulted in the lynching of eight black prisoners. Hundreds of Republicans were whipped and saw their farm property destroyed in Spartanburg, a largely white county with a Democratic majority. Here, the victims included a considerable number of scalawags and wartime Unionists, among them Dr. John Winsmith, a member of "the old land aristocracy of the place" wounded by Klansmen in March 1871. In York County, nearly the entire white male population joined the Klan, and committed at least eleven murders and hundreds of whippings; by February 1871 thousands of blacks had taken to the woods each night to avoid assault. The victims included a black militia leader, found hanging from a tree in March with a note pinned to his breast, "Jim Williams on his big muster," and Elias Hill, a self-educated black teacher, minister, and "leader amongst his people." Even by the standards of the postwar South, the whipping of Hill was barbaric: A dwarflike cripple with limbs "drawn up and withered away with pain," he had mistakenly believed "my pitiful condition would save me." Hill had already been organizing local blacks to leave the region in search of the "peaceful living, free schools, and rich land" denied them in York County. Not long after his beating, together with some sixty black families, he set sail for Liberia.

Contemporary Democrats, echoed by subsequent scholars, often attributed the Klan's sadistic campaign of terror to the fears and prejudices of poorer whites. (More elevated Southerners, one historian contends, could never have committed these "horrible crimes.") The evidence, however, will not sustain such an interpretation. It is true that in some upcountry counties, the Klan drove blacks from land desired by impoverished white farmers and occasionally attacked planters who employed freedmen instead of white tenants. Sometimes, violence exacerbated local labor shortages by causing freedmen to flee the area, leading planters to seek an end to Klan activities. Usually, however, the Klan crossed class lines. If ordinary farmers and laborers constituted the bulk of the membership, and energetic "young bloods" were more likely to conduct midnight raids than middle-aged planters and lawyers, "respectable citizens" chose the targets and often participated in the brutality.

Klansmen generally wore disguises—a typical costume consisted of a long, flowing white robe and hood, capped by horns—and sometimes claimed to be ghosts of Confederate soldiers so, as they claimed, to frighten superstitious blacks. Few freedmen took such nonsense seriously. "Old man, we are just from hell and on our way back," a group of Klansmen told one ex-slave. "If I had been there," he replied, "I would not want to go back." Victims, moreover, frequently recognized their assailants. "Dick Hinds had on a disguise," remarked an Alabama freedmen who saw his son brutally "cut to pieces with a knife." "I knew him. Me and him was raised together." And often, unmasked men committed the violence. The group that attacked the home of Mississippi scalawag Robert Flournoy, whose newspaper had denounced the Klan as "a body of midnight prowlers, robbers, and assassins," included both poor men and property holders, "as respectable as anybody we had there." Among his sixty-five Klan assailants, Abram Colby identified men "not worth the bread they eat," but also some of the "first-class men in our town," including a lawyer and a physician.

Personal experience led blacks to blame the South's "aristocratic classes" for violence and with good reason, for the Klan's leadership included planters, merchants, lawyers, and even ministers. "The most respectable citizens are engaged in it," reported a Georgia Freedmen's Bureau agent, "if there can be any respectability about such people." Editors Josiah Turner of the Raleigh *Sentinel,* Ryland Randolph of the Tuscaloosa *Monitor* (who years later recalled administering whippings "in the regular *ante bellum style*"), and Isaac W. Avery of the Atlanta *Constitution* were prominent Klansmen, along with John B. Gordon, Georgia's Democratic candidate for governor in 1868. When the Knights of the White Camelia initiated Samuel Chester in Arkansas, the pastor of his church administered the oath and the participants included Presbyterian deacons and elders "and every important member of the community." In Jackson County, Florida, the "general ring-leader of badness … the generalissimo of Ku-Klux" was a wealthy merchant; elsewhere in the black belt, planters seem to have controlled the organization. Even in the upcountry, "the very best citizens" directed the violence. "Young men of the respectable farming class" composed the Klan's rank and file in western North Carolina, but its leaders were more substantial—former legislator Plato Durham, attorney Leroy McAfee (whose nephew, Thomas Dixon, later garbed the violence in romantic mythology in his novel *The Clansman*), and editor Randolph A. Shotwell. As the Rutherford *Star* remarked, the Klan was "not a gang of *poor trash,* as the leading Democrats would have us believe, but men of property … respectable citizens." …

Violence had a profound effect on Reconstruction politics. For the Klan devastated the Republican organization in many local communities. By 1871, the party in numerous locales was "scattered and beaten and run out." "They have no leaders up there—no leaders," a freedman lamented of Union County, South Carolina. No party, North or South, commented [Missippi Governor] Adelbert Ames, could see hundreds of its "best and most reliable workers" murdered and still "retain its vigor." Indeed, the black community was more vulnerable to the destruction of its political infrastructure by violence than the white. Local leaders played such a variety of roles in schools, churches, and fraternal organizations that the killing or exiling of one man affected many institutions at once. And for a largely illiterate constituency, in which political information circulated orally rather than through newspapers or pamphlets, local leaders were bridges to the larger world of politics, indispensable sources of political intelligence and guidance. Republican officials, black and white, epitomized the revolution that seemed to have put the bottom rail on top. Their murder or exile inevitably had a demoralizing impact upon their communities.

The violence of 1869–71 etched the Klan permanently in the folk memory of the black community. "What cullud person dat can't 'membahs dem, if he lived dat day?" an elderly Texas freedman asked six decades later. The issue of protecion transcended all divisions within the black community, uniting rich and poor, free and freed, in calls for drastic governmental action to restore order. To blacks, indeed, the violence seemed an irrefutable denial of the white South's much-trumpeted claims to superior morality and higher civilization. "Pray tell me," asked Robert B. Elliott, "who is the barbarian here?"

More immediately, violence underscored yet again the "abnormal" quality of Reconstruction politics. Before the war, Democrats and Whigs had combated fiercely throughout the South, but neither party, as Virginia Radical James Hunnicutt pointed out, advised its supporters "to drive out, to starve and to perish" its political opponents. Corrupt election procedures, political chicanery, and even extralegal attempts to oust the opposition party from office were hardly unknown in the North, but not pervasive political violence. "I never knew such things in Maine," commented an Alabama carpetbagger. "Republicans and Democrats were tolerated there." Democracy, it has been said, functions best when politics does not directly mirror deep social division, and each side can accept the victory of the other because both share many values and defeat does not imply "a fatal surrender of ... vital interests." This was the situation in the North, where, an Alabama Republican observed, "it matters not who is elected." But too much was at stake in Reconstruction for "normal politics" to prevail. As one scalawag pointed out, while Northern political contests focused on "finances, individual capacity, and the like, our contest here is for life, for the right to earn our bread ... for a decent and respectful consideration as human beings and members of society."

Most of all, violence raised in its starkest form the question of legitimacy that haunted the Reconstruction state. Reconstruction, concluded Klan victim Dr. John Winsmith, ought to begin over again: "I consider a government which does not protect its citizens an utter failure." Indeed, as a former Confederate officer shrewdly observed, it was precisely the Klan's objective "to defy the reconstructed State Governments, to treat them with contempt, and show that they have no real existence." The effective exercise of power, of course, can command respect if not spontaneous loyalty. But only in a few instances had Republican governments found the will to exert this kind of force. Only through "decided action," wrote an Alabama scalawag, could "the state ... protect its citizens and vindicate its own authority and *right to be*." Yet while their opponents acted as if conducting a revolution, Republicans typically sought stability through conciliation.

Terror in the Heart of Freedom

HANNAH ROSEN

Late in May 1871, eleven disguised men rode up to a cabin on a plantation in Gwinnett County, Georgia. After tying up their horses about 100 yards away, they approached the house yelling, "Open the door." A former slave named Hampton Mitchell was inside with his wife, his son-in-law, and his wife's father. Before anyone inside the house was able to get to the door, the men outside had forced it open. Mitchell recognized three of the intruders, despite their masks, as white men from the area. After grabbing Mitchell's gun, these men ordered him to kneel beside the cabin's threshold. "Hampton, is this your house?" the intruders demanded. "Yes, sir," Mitchell replied. They repeated the question, "Is this your house?" and Mitchell repeated his reply. Then, with Mitchell remaining on his knees in the doorway, guarded and intermittently struck by two of the men, others forced members of his family to come out of the house one at a time. First, they called to his son-in-law and "gave him a severe whipping." Next, they beat Mitchell's wife with their guns. And last, they ordered his father-in-law to come outside, beat him, sent him back into the house, and then called him out and beat him again. Finally, they ordered Mitchell to go inside and close the door.

Former slaves living throughout the South in the years following emancipation would have recognized this scene. The years of Reconstruction saw extensive campaigns of vigilante terror, making this one of the most violent eras in U.S. history. Bands of white men roamed the rural areas of the South, attacking African Americans in their homes. From groups known as "bushwhackers" or "jayhawkers" during the war, to local vigilante gangs of returned Confederate soldiers just after southern surrender, to men in costume claiming membership in the Ku Klux Klan during congressional Reconstruction, intrusions in the night by companies of hostile white men were experienced by many and feared by most former slaves. Although freedpeople made distinctions between these groups, they also labeled them all "night riders" and perceived in all of them conspiracies of terror with similar overall practices, objectives, and effects. Former slaves understood attacks by any of these vigilante gangs as violent efforts to crush their newly won rights and to limit the meaning of their freedom.

Freedpeople went to great lengths to report night riders' actions to officials and to seek redress, leaving extensive documentation of violence in the records of the Freedmen's Bureau, of state and federal prosecutions of Klan members, and of an 1871 congressional investigation into Klan activity that conducted hearings in Washington, D.C., North Carolina, South Carolina, Georgia, Alabama, Mississippi, and Florida. These records reveal consistent patterns of violence across the South as well as local and individual variations. Forcing Hampton Mitchell to identify the site where he and his family were attacked as his domain—and thereby mocking his power within it—may have been unique. However, testimony suggests that night rider violence during Reconstruction often operated through similar kinds of performance. These attacks were not brief encounters.... [I]ntrusions in the night lasted at times for hours and involved prolonged interaction and dialogue between assailants and victims. Through this interaction and dialogue, through their words and actions, assailants staged meanings for race that contested the rights and identities claimed by African Americans in freedom. These scenes drew on gendered imagery to represent blackness as subordination and vice and whiteness as authority and power. In this way, assailants invented and communicated a fantasy post-Civil War world wherein white men's power approximated that before the war, thereby erasing military defeat and reclaiming the political privileges of whiteness bestowed by the system of slavery even on nonslaveholding white men. And the stage for acting out these scenes charged with race and gender symbolism was most often the homes of former slaves.

Certainly, this violence had concrete political motives and material effects. These motives were frequently explicit, and the effects were traumatic and often deadly. White gangs directed violence at agents of the radical social transformations that followed emancipation, particularly those people who most visibly exercised, promoted, or enabled the citizenship of former slaves. Common targets were black Union soldiers, black teachers, and black preachers. Freedpeople involved in labor disputes or able to purchase land coveted by local whites could also anticipate being the victims of a nighttime attack. Assailants undermined the independence of freedpeople by seizing their land or stealing their means of support and self-defense, such as weapons, food, cash, clothing, and other valuables. They interfered with collective action by preventing nighttime travel and assembly of African Americans. And when black men gained the right to vote in 1868, organized night riding moved directly onto the terrain of electoral politics, targeting Republican leaders, Union League members, black men suspected of voting Republican, and the families of these men. Night rider violence was, in fact, so seemingly instrumental and so explicitly targeted for political ends that it is difficult to resist reducing its meaning entirely to its apparent functions. Yet this violence also took striking forms seemingly unrelated to function that were consistent across a wide region and over several years. Most saliently, this politically targeted and instrumental violence was suffused with imagery of gender and sexuality beyond anything necessitated by the explicit political ends of its assailants. The gendered nature of night riding, in turn, raises questions about understanding this violence as a mere instrument of force. It was also a complex rhetoric of power and a stage for the formation and contestation of racial and gender meanings, identities, and hierarchies....

Night rider violence can be read as a type of performance, a theatrical form of political expression that drew on gender to resignify race and to undermine African American citizenship. The symbolism enacted through violence conveyed assailants' visions for a hierarchical racial order for southern society despite emancipation and formal legal equality. From the perspective of their creators, these brutal scenes righted a world turned upside down. In scenes such as the attack on Hampton Mitchell's house, white men acted out the impossibility of black men demonstrating the same kinds of mastery over their households, their property, and the security of their family members that white men claimed powerfully linked to popular constructions of white manhood and of citizenship. In other scenes, particularly those involving sexual insult, assault, and rape, white men also rejected black women's potential identities as honorable wives and daughters, caring for and protected within their families. Instead, assailants' words and actions positioned black women and men outside proper domestic relationships and inside realms of the illicit, transgressive, and criminal....

The Domestic Stage of Political Violence

A form of night riding also emerged out of the conditions of war. Commonly called "bushwhackers" or "jayhawkers," groups of Confederate deserters formed armed guerrilla gangs that operated essentially as bandits in the rural outreaches of various southern states, requisitioning or stealing provisions from local residents and governing communities through fear or co-optation. After the war, these gangs continued to operate in some locales as alternative governments or "regulators" who resisted Union military authority and sought to restore antebellum social relations. They commonly disarmed black Union soldiers returning from battle and attacked former slaves who refused to continue working for their former owners. These men, too, were "night riders" who commonly represented their violence against freedpeople as punishment for some alleged infraction against a "law" they had established and sought to enforce....

Similar resistance to an independent domestic life among former slaves shaped activities of later Reconstruction-era gangs, who would over time operate increasingly under the rubric of the Ku Klux Klan. In southern mythology, this organization is represented as having had innocuous beginnings in a secret club formed by six young white men in Pulaski, Tennessee, in the early summer of 1866.... These men were allegedly bored ex-Confederate soldiers seeking amusement. Amusement was supposedly found in, among other things, dressing as ghosts and setting out to frighten former slaves. This story is repeated in numerous historical accounts of the Klan, and the role of the six men in Pulaski in founding an entity they named the Klan seems certain. However, it is doubtful that these men had no expectation that their amusement would be politically useful or would include violence. Over the next year, numerous other "clubs" calling themselves the Ku Klux Klan appeared throughout middle and west Tennessee. The fact that the Klan spread here first may be connected to the fact that Tennessee was the first state to extend suffrage to black men (in a statute passed in February 1867) and the only southern state to do so before the Reconstruction Acts. Within less than a year of the founding of the infamous social club, leading Tennessee conservatives held meetings seeking a statewide organization to harness Klan tactics for electoral purposes, lending the Klan its first widespread legitimacy with elites.

By 1868, after the Reconstruction Acts imposed black male suffrage on the other ten southern states, the order's secrecy and menacing rituals and reputation became useful to conservative leaders throughout the South as a means resisting Republican political dominance. There is evidence of efforts by these leaders to coordinate organization across state boundaries and to establish governance and rules for the Klan. It is almost certain, though, that these self-designated leaders had little contact with most white men calling themselves Klansmen and acting as regulators in their local communities. County-wide organization existed in some areas, with command hierarchies and co-ordination across different local "camps" that met to discuss targets, plan missions, and dispense and receive orders. Former members of local Klans in North Carolina testified to being called into neighboring areas to act on behalf of other camps in local conflicts. But this sort of coordination was far from universal. Some local "Klans" operated on whim and placed few restraints on whom and how they attacked. Other groups of men with no connection or affiliation with a county, let alone regionwide, Klan used the name "KuKlux" when identification with a larger and foreboding power proved useful to them in local conflicts with freedpeople. That various rituals and gimmicks associated with the Klan were widespread suggests some region-wide communication, but it is also likely that many men simply mimicked what they read in the newspaper or learned through rumor and word of mouth.

The most useful innovation offered to would-be night riders by the emergence of the Klan was the element of disguise. Some of the more elaborate theatrics of the Klan intended to create an aura of mystery and superhuman power—posting cryptic notes using bizarre and apparently coded language at the offices of local newspapers, posing as ghosts of dead Confederate soldiers, or creating the illusion of an ability to drink enormous quantities of water by hiding tubes and buckets underneath the robes commonly used as Klan costumes—were prevalent in the early years but were dropped quickly, no doubt because they were both labor intensive and unconvincing. But disguises and the anonymity they provided continued to be useful. Not only did masking their faces, clothing, and even horses assist men in escaping identification and retribution under the law for their acts. The fact that it was anonymous "KuKlux" who patrolled the night, as opposed to the grocer, mechanic, hired hand, local sheriff, or plantation owner well known to the community, produced the sensation among assailants, at least, and perhaps the image for victims of something more ominous and powerful than local residents. Anonymity suggested an omnipotent and omnipresent force of white men whose numbers and specific identities were unknown and who had knowledge of black people's affairs, labor arrangements, and political activities.

This aspect of Klan violence was recognized by freedpeople and incorporated into their modes of resistance. Freedpeople often scrutinized shoes, coats, stature, gait, or voice seeking ways to deny Klansmen the protection and power of anonymity, and victims even occasionally tore off disguises in the midst of attacks. Identification of horses, too, could be used to undermine Klansmen's disguise. Two freedwomen whipped by Klansmen in their South Capitalize Carolina home identified—and then reported—their assailants by searching town the next morning for the horses seen at their house the night before. The women reportedly followed the horses with their riders back to the men's residences and thereby learned who their attackers were. Freedpeople also contested the Klan's self-fashioned image of omnipotence. A freedman in Madison, Georgia, stated boldly to a white neighbor that "they call themselves Ku-Klux, but they are just disguised white men."

Another practice common to Klansmen was borrowed from earlier forms of night riding: during violent attacks assailants often articulated to victims rationales for why they or their family members were being hurt. In this way violence was represented as punishment or retribution for violation of a code of conduct that corresponded to antebellum racial hierarchy. Victims were told they were made to suffer for their or a relative's role in the Union Army, for refusing to labor for a particular planter, for insubordination to a white person, for membership in a Union League, or for voting for a Republican candidate. The actions for which freedpeople were allegedly punished represented the exercise of choice that accompanied freedom and citizenship. Expressing these rationales as integral parts of an act of violence allowed assailants to stage their own supposed governing authority and to produce and enforce a type of "law" in which the exercise of citizenship by former slaves was forbidden. This "law" governing social organization and particularly matters of race operated outside and against the existing state (though at times assailants were, in fact, local law enforcement officials). Often the supposed charges stemmed from a real event or conflict. At other times, rationales were pretexts, infuriating in their inaccuracy to the victims of violence.... Whether their content was accurate or false, rationales became part of the ritual of violence itself; they offered functional meaning to the acts committed and attributed to Klansmen extralegal governing power....

Catching victims off guard, in bed, and at night may have served practical ends, reducing avenues for escape and time to plan resistance. But the consistent pattern of attacking freedpeople in, and by dragging them from, their homes also carried enormous symbolic significance. The practice speaks to the gendered political culture of assailants. A home was the space and symbol for white southern men of their identities and powers as men. It was the world in which they were constituted as patriarchs and masters, where they exercised domestic authority that, in turn, was widely represented as justifying their claim to citizenship and political power. It was the source of their economic self-sufficiency, where, in most cases, they and their family and, in some cases, their slaves produced their livelihood and thus their independence. Important identities of southern white women also emerged from homes and the relations and activities contained within them, such as those of wife, mother, or daughter. Slaves, by contrast, had been forcibly incorporated into the households of white slave-owners and subjected to the constant interruption or severing of what domestic ties and arrangements they had been able to construct. Their lack of homes and of official recognition of patriarchal or other domestic relationships distinguished slaves from "freemen" and "freewomen," as whites often identified themselves. By attacking African Americans' homes, night riders attacked not only African American economic independence but also a key signifier of freedom and equal citizenship....

Nonetheless, to former slaves, homes and the relations nurtured within them were profound manifestations of personal liberty, as well as the means through which their economic subsistence was now secured. Slavery had simultaneously destroyed families—as slaveholders had the power to separate families at will—and strengthened their cultural importance as institutions that sustained slaves through the difficulties of bondage. Historians have demonstrated how the centrality of family relationships to slaves was evident upon emancipation, as freedpeople went to great lengths to reunite with family members from whom they had been separated under slavery, to assert parental rights over their children in opposition to apprenticeship, and to legitimate their marriage vows. The comments of an army chaplain for a regiment of black Union soldiers in Little Rock, Arkansas, in February 1865 were common: "Weddings, just now, are very popular, and abundant among the Colored People. They have just learned, of the Special Order No' 15 of Gen Thomas by which, they may not only be lawfully married, but have their Marriage Certificates, *Recorded*; in a *book furnished by the Government.* This is most desirable". Officially recorded marriages meant state recognition and legitimation of former slaves' unions and, thus, of their rights and identities as wives, husbands, and parents. This chaplain added at the end of the letter on freedpeople's enthusiasm for marriage, "The Colord Peopl here, generally consider, this war not only their *exodus*, from bondage; but the road, to Responsibility; Competency; and an honorable Citizenship." This represents the white chaplain's views more than those of former slaves, but it suggests a general understanding of marriage and secure domestic relationships as a right and practice of citizenship....

When Klansmen asked Hampton Mitchell, "Is this your house?" they were, in fact, contesting his claim to it and asserting to him and his family that freedom did not mean that former slaves could now claim the right to privacy, autonomy, and authority within the boundaries of a home. Instead, the intruders enacted their own authority to rule over the members of the Mitchell household. Thus, rather than autonomous realms of black patriarchal power, freedpeople's homes were to continue to be penetrable at any and all moments by the power of white men. Neither were private black domains to constitute independence and the rights of citizenship. When white men attacked freedpeople's private identities as husbands and wives, they were also attacking their worthiness for public rights as citizens. The fact that white opposition to African American freedom and citizenship was expressed through attacks on gender identities embedded within domestic domains shaped the kind of violence that freedpeople suffered. Eli Barnes, a leading black Republican in his home county of Hancock, Georgia, told the congressional investigating committee, "It has got to be quite a common thing to hear a man say, 'They rode around my house last night, and they played the mischief there; my wife was molested, my daughter badly treated, and they played the wild generally with my family.'"...

The Performance of Rape

Sexual violence was frequent enough during the postwar years for Essic Harris, a black man reporting the rape of a neighboring freedwoman by Klansmen in North Carolina, to say, "That has been very common ... it has got to be an old saying by now." Harris also noted, though, "They say that if the women tell anything about it, they will kill them." It is indeed safe to assume that many women who suffered sexual violence at the hands of night riders did not report it to officials for fear of retaliation. (Rape has been a notoriously under-reported crime under any circumstance, for this and other reasons.) It is also likely that many rapes that victims and witnesses did wish to report nonetheless do not appear in the historical record. The documentation of rape in this period was conditioned by factors beyond freedpeople's readiness to testify. Whether or not a freedwoman or a friend or family member who decided to report a rape could do so depended on her or his access to a Freedmen's Bureau agent, federal prosecutor, or congressional hearing. Bureau offices and federal hearings were located in cities and towns, while the ... majority of night rider violence occurred in rural areas of the South. Thus most victims had to have both time and means to travel in order to record their testimony. Whether or not testimony was preserved in federal records depended further on the competency of federal officials, especially if testimony was given to a local agent who, working in a makeshift office and without adequate staff or, in some cases, unsympathetic to freedpeple's concerns, might easily misplace or fail to file an affidavit. These factors make it impossible to calculate how many women were raped by white men during Reconstruction-era political violence.

Yet, despite threats of retaliation and obstacles to having one's words recorded and preserved, many women did manage to testify about these crimes before federal officials, as did family members who were present, neighbors who learned of rape after the fact, or even people who knew of it only as rumor, and their testimony can be found in federal archives. The research for this chapter ... turned up stories concerning forty-five different women who suffered rape or other forms of sexual attack by white men between 1865 and 1871. The testimony documenting each case varies greatly in degree of detail and in the proximity of the witness to the actual event. The form of sexual violence documented varies too, from rape or its attempt, threat, or simulation, to sexually charged humiliation, insulting solicitation, and beatings following refusals to have sex. In conjunction with comments such a Harris's, the stories discussed here—most likely only a small portion of the rapes that actually occurred during Reconstruction—reveal a pattern of violence of which freedpeople were acutely aware and which added to their trepidation, no doubt, whenever they entered into a conflict with white men....

In Sumner County, a night rider crudely propositioned and threatened with rape Patsy Duvall.... Patsy and her husband, Jim Duvall, reported to the Freedmen's Bureau that at the end of June 1866 they were visited in the night by two white men who were looking for their neighbor, Jim Warren. The men ordered Jim Duvall to direct them to Warren's home. Patsy recounted her hostile exchange with one of these men, whom she recognized as Richard Pentle: "I said to him that it would be a pity to kill Jim Warren from his children, when he answered back saying he would have his pistol and his God damned scalp after." The men did find Jim Warren, brought him back to just outside the Duvall house, and shot and killed him within ear-shot of Patsy. In his affidavit, Jim Duvall reported that after killing Jim Warren, "the one who shot him came in to my house and stayed some time; Both then left and when leaving, told me not to leave or have report made." Patsy's affidavit explained what Jim's did not: that while Pentle "stayed some time" in their house, he sought to coerce Patsy to submit to sexual intercourse with him. "Pentle came into the house and said he got Jim Warren's pistol and his scalp too," Patsy testified, "and that if he did not get connection with me he would also kill my husband." Patsy had invoked Jim Warren's responsibilities as a father to protest Pentle's intention to take his life. Pentle retaliated by forcing his way into her home and staging her incapacity to be a chaste and respectable wife. The fact that Jim Duvall omitted this aspect of Pentle's actions from his affidavit could indicate an attempt to avoid reliving before the Freedmen's Bureau the pain he felt at the indignity his wife suffered and the shame he felt at being positioned in a script in which he failed to act as his wife's protector. It was, in fact, Patsy who acted to protect her husband's life and her own. According to her report, she refused Pentle's demand and insisted that he would not hurt her husband either: "I said I would not do it, and that I thought he would not kill him, (my husband), for I thought he had done enough."

In the same county in Tennessee, on the night of September 4, 1866, three white men came to the home of Ed Link and challenged him to protect his family while simultaneously making it impossible for him to do so. The white men demanded that Link tell them "how many girls I had in the family." Link informed the men that he had five daughters, the eldest eighteen years old. Link later told Captain Walsh of the choice with which these men then presented him: "They asked me which I would rather do, to go out to the woods myself, or let my girls go." It seems that Link ran out of the back of the house in search of a weapon but did not get far before he was shot and wounded by one of the intruders. This man apparently already had Link's daughter Elmira by the arm. The silence in the affidavit on anything further happening to Elmira suggests two possibilities: that the man let her go when he ran after

Link to shoot him, or that Link could not bring himself to testify to the fact that his daughter was raped....

Constructing black homes and communities as spaces for white men's pleasure framed other incidents of rape. In late December 1870, in Chatham County, North Carolina, a gang of white men intruded into a "settlement" of freedpeople living and working on the land of a white man named Mr. Finch. The intruders barged into several of the houses in the settlement and took weapons from the residents, activities suggesting that the invaders were on a political mission. But they were also dressed in a variety of disguises, and some were wearing women's clothing, indicating an impromptu dress-up and even the anticipation of a raucous "good time" violating proper social roles, much like carnival. This attitude was reflected in their actions. A freedman from the settlement told the congressional committee investigating Klan violence that in one house they "ate something there," and "some of them played a fiddle and danced awhile." They then moved on to a house where four freedwomen lived together with male relatives, called one of the women out of the house, and raped her. Earlier that same month, in Madison County, Alabama, a gang calling themselves "Ku-Klux" found a dance going on in freedman Wiley Strong's house. Strong described what happened to a local Freedmen's Bureau agent, who in turn reported it to the congressional committee: "The negroes were having a little dance at the house, and these men rushed in on them. Some of the men, I understood, resisted them, and they drove them out, and then ravished ... two women." Both of these sexual attacks occurred in counties where numerous whippings and widespread gun theft by night riders had been reported. Violent campaigns of this sort, then, also involved carnival-like revelry in which white men engaged in rowdy behavior and redefined black homes as dance halls, saloons, and brothels....

Another case highlights how night riders' forcing black women to become spectacles of indecency might have been a direct response to freedpeople organizing their family lives in ways previously reserved for whites. Aury Jeter lived with her husband, Columbus, in Douglass County, Georgia, where he had contracted to work on the land of a white man named Morris. The Jeters' relationship with Morris was strained from the beginning. Morris objected to the fact that the couple, devout Baptists, attended a church that was twelve miles from his land, saying he did not want them away for long periods of time. He also opposed Aury teaching freedpeople to read in their house during the day and Columbus giving lessons at night. Morris confronted Columbus in a manner suggesting that the fact that Aury was not working as a field laborer also contributed to the contention between them. Columbus recounted their exchange: "Your wife, the damned bitch, is teaching a colored school.' I said, 'I work for her and maintain her; why should she not teach school? the laws of the country permit it.'" Morris then cursed Aury again, calling her "the damned nigger." Columbus objected to Morris's verbal abuse of his wife, responding, "Don't curse any," which led Morris to draw his knife. Columbus defended himself with a stick, and the fight that ensued ended with the Jeters leaving Morris's land.

The family settled as laborers on another white man's land. One week later, they were awakened in the night by orders to open their door. Columbus scurried up their chimney before a group of white men burst into the house. These men beat Aury over the head, yanked her by the hair, and put a pistol to her chest as they demanded to know where her husband was. When she finally revealed his hiding place, the intruders fired shots up the chimney and pulled Columbus down. They then dragged both husband and wife from the house and whipped them. Aury reported that one of the men also "exposed me.... They turned my clothes up to my waist." That this gesture was intended to humiliate Aury by treating her indecently is suggested by the objection of one of the men. "One of them went up and said that I had told the truth and should be let alone; he said it was ridiculous to treat me in that way." Another comment made to Columbus while the assailants were beating him is also suggestive: "Now Columbus, do you think a colored man is as good as a white man?" Columbus's efforts to support his wife while she engaged in something other than field labor and then to defend himself when assaulted by Morris were read by these assailants as challenges to their identities and superiority as white men. In retaliation, Aury, who represented herself as Columbus's wife, a Christian woman, and a teacher, was made to suffer the indignity of being made into a "show," as Mary Brown described it, a spectacle of sexual dishonor and humiliation....

When three Klansmen raped Harriet Simril in York County, South Carolina, they claimed she was being punished for her husband's political participation. This rape occurred in the midst of what was perhaps the most extensive Klan campaign against black men's voting during Reconstruction. After the Republicans carried the county in the 1870 state elections, freedpeople living in the countryside surrounding the town of Yorkville suffered almost nightly Klan violence for months. When night riders first visited Simril's home, they whipped her husband, Sam, demanding that he "join the Democratic ticket." After this, Sam joined many black men in the area trying to evade further nighttime attacks by sleeping in the woods. Colonel Lewis Merrill, the commander of federal troops sent to York County to try to quell the violence, estimated that four-fifths of the county's black male residents did not feel safe sleeping at home. Though some women, too, slept in the woods, Harriet chose at first to stay at home in the Clay Hill section of the county. She subsequently described to a federal court prosecuting suspected Klan members what she suffered during a second Klan visit to her house: "They came after my old man and I told them he wasn't there. They searched about in the house a long time. They were spitting in my face and throwing dirt in my eyes.... After awhile, they took me out of doors and told me all they wanted was my old man to join the Democratic ticket. After they got me out of doors, they dragged me into the road and ravished me out there." Assailants told Simril, as they had told Childs, that they raped her as a means of attacking her husband or of punishing her husband for challenging white men's dominance....

Night rider sexual violence during Reconstruction was in some ways, then, a brutal form of political expression. Violence served as a both verbal and corporeal language revealing the gendered political culture through which white southerners contested the changes in social relations resulting from emancipation and articulated their visions for the postemancipation meaning of race. But Reconstruction was also a rare historical moment when freed-people had access to federal arenas in which to record black women's experiences of rape. By testifying to sexual assaults as violation and by constructing white men coercing sex with black women as rape, freedwomen and freedmen challenged the hierarchical meanings for race, and particularly the assertion of a denigrated blackness and virtuous whiteness, conveyed by assailants' actions. They therein fought to establish a meaningful citizenship. To be a potential victim of rape in the eyes of the law was also to be recognized as a citizen, and, ... freedwomen claimed this status and its attendant rights.

FURTHER READING

Eric Anderson and Alfred A. Moss Jr., *The Facts of Reconstruction: Essays in Honor of John Hope Franklin* (1992).

Peter W. Bardaglio, *Reconstructing the Household: Famlies, Sex, and the Law in the Nineteenth Century South* (1995).

Michael Les Benedict, *A Compromise of Principle: Congressional Republicans and Reconstruction, 1863–1869* (1974).

———, *The Impeachment and Trial of Andrew Johnson* (1973).

Nancy Bercaw, *Gendered Freedoms: Race, Rights, and the Politics of Household in the Delta, 1861–1875* (2003).

Ira Berlin et al., *Slaves No More: Three Essays on Emancipation and the Civil War* (1992).

Carol R. Bleser, *The Promised Land: The History of the South Carolina Land Commission, 1869–1890* (1969).

Orville Vernon Burton, *In My Father's House Are Many Mansions: Family and Community in Edgefield, South Carolina* (1985).

Randolph B. Campbell, *Grassroots Reconstruction in Texas, 1865–1880* (1997).

Dan T. Carter, *When the War Was Over: The Failure of Self-Reconstruction in the South, 1865–1867* (1985).

Jane Turner Censer, *The Reconstruction of White Southern Womanhood, 1865–1895* (2003).

Paul Cimbala, *Under the Guardianship of the Nation: The Freedman's Bureau and the Reconstruction of Georgia, 1865–1870* (1997).

Richard N. Current, *Those Terrible Carpetbaggers* (1988).

David Donald, *The Politics of Reconstruction, 1863–1867* (1965).

Edmund L. Drago, *Black Politicians and Reconstruction in Georgia: A Splended Future* (1982).

W. E. B. Du Bois, *Black Reconstruction* (1935).

Laura Edwards, *Gendered Strife and Confusion: The Political Culture of Reconstruction* (1997).

Paul D. Escott, *Many Excellent People: Power and Privilege in North Carolina, 1850–1900* (1985).

Barbara Jeanne Fields, *Slavery and Freedom on the Middle Ground: Maryland during the Nineteenth Century* (1985).

Michael W. Fitzgerald, *The Union League Movement in the Deep South: Politics and Agricultural Change during Reconstruction* (1989).

———, *Urban Emancipation: Popular Politics in Reconstruction Mobile, 1860–1890* (2002).

Eric Foner, *Reconstruction: America's Unfinished Revolution, 1863–1877* (1988).

———, *Freedom's Lawmakers: A Directory of Black Officeholders during Reconstruction* (1993).

William Gillette, *Retreat from Reconstruction, 1869–1879* (1979).

Matthew Pratt Guterl, *American Mediterranean: Southern Slaveholders in the Age of Emancipation* (2008).

Steven Hahn, *A Nation Under Our Feet: Black Political Struggles in the Rural South from Slavery to the Great Migration* (2003).

William C. Harris, *Day of the Carpetbagger: Republican Reconstruction in Mississippi* (1979).

Thomas Holt, *Black over White: Negro Political Leadership in South Carolina during Reconstruction* (1977).

Elizabeth Jacoway, *Yankee Missionaries in the South* (1979).

Jacqueline Jones, *Soldiers of Light and Love: Northern Teachers and Georgia Blacks, 1865–1873* (1985).

LeeAnna Keith, *Colfax Massacre: The Untold Story of Black Power, White Terror, and the Death of Reconstruction* (2009).

Peter Kolchin, *First Freedom: The Responses of Alabama's Blacks to Emancipation and Reconstruction* (1972).

J. Morgan Kousser and James M. McPherson, eds., *Region, Race, and Reconstruction: Essays in Honor of C. Vann Woodward* (1982).

Nicholas Lemann, *Redemption: The Last Battle of the Civil War* (2006).

Leon F. Litwack, *Been in the Storm So Long: The Emergence of Black Freedom in the South* (1979).

Edward Magdol, *A Right to the Land: Essays on the Freedmen's Community* (1977).

Jay R. Mandle, *Not Slave, Not Free: The African-American Experience since the Civil War* (1992).

Carl H. Moneyhon, *Texas after the Civil War: The Struggle of Reconstruction* (2004).

Robert C. Morris, *Reading, 'Riting, and Reconstruction: The Education of Freedmen in the South 1861–1870* (1981).

Donald G. Nieman, ed., *Freedom, Racism, and Reconstruction: Collected Writings of Lawanda Cox* (1997).

Susan Eva O'Donovan, *Becoming Free in the Cotton South* (2007).

Otto H. Olsen, ed., *Reconstruction and Redemption in the South* (1980).

Claude F. Oubre, *Forty Acres and a Mule: The Freedmen's Bureau and Blackland Ownership* (1978).

Michael Perman, *Reunion without Compromise: The South and Reconstruction, 1865–1868* (1973).

———, *The Road to Redemption: Southern Politics, 1869–1879* (1984).

Lawrence N. Powell, *New Masters: Northern Planters during the Civil War and Reconstruction* (1980).

George C. Rable, *But There Was No Peace: The Role of Violence in the Politics of Reconstruction* (1984).

James L. Roark, *Masters without Slaves: Southern Planters in the Civil War and Reconstruction* (1977).

Willie Lee Rose, *Rehearsal for Reconstruction: The Port Royal Experiment* (1964).

Hannah Rosen, *Terror in the Heart of Freedom: Citizenship, Sexual Violence, and the Meaning of Race in the Postemancipation South* (2009).

Julie Saville, *The Work of Reconstruction: From Slave to Wage Laborer in South Carolina, 1860–1870* (1994).

Leslie A. Schwalm, *A Hard Fight for We: Women's Transition from Slavery to Freedom in South Carolina* (1997).

Rebecca J. Scott, *Degrees of Freedom: Louisiana and Cuba after Slavery* (2008).

Kenneth M. Stampp, *The Era of Reconstruction, 1865–1877* (1965).

Mark Wahlgren Summers, *A Dangerous Stir: Fear, Paranoia, and the Making of Reconstruction* (2009).

———, *Railroads, Reconstruction, and the Gospel of Prosperity* (1984).

Albion W. Tourgee, *A Fool's Errand* (1879).

Allen W. Trelease, *White Terror: The Ku Klux Klan Conspiracy and Southern Reconstruction* (1971).

Ted Tunnell, *Crucible of Reconstruction: War, Radicalism, and Race in Louisiana, 1862–1877* (1984).

Charles Vincent, *Black Legislators in Louisiana During Reconstruction* (1976).

Xi Wang, *The Trial of Democracy: Black Suffrage and Northern Republicans, 1860–1910* (1997).

Vernon L. Wharton, *The Negro in Mississippi, 1865–1890* (1947).

LeeAnn Whites, *The Civil War as a Crisis in Gender: Augusta, Georgia, 1860–1890* (1995).

Jonathan Wiener, *Social Origins of the New South: Alabama, 1860–1885* (1978).

Sarah Woolfolk Wiggins, *The Scalawag in Alabama Politics, 1865–1881* (1977).

CHAPTER 3

Land and Labor in the New South

After the Civil War, southerners turned once again to the land. Fields, pastures, streams, and woods remained much as they had always been, except in areas devastated by the war, but the relationship of people to land changed with the demise of slavery. White planters had expected freedpeople to stay on the plantations, work the cotton fields in gangs, live in slave cabins, and accept "discipline" from white supervisors. Planters sought to implement this system but without success. Then they tried yearly contracts, with payment to laborers at the end of the year, but that satisfied neither party. African Americans yearned for independence, ownership of land, and the opportunity to become economically self-sufficient. The reality of postwar economics was this: White landowners needed labor, freedpeople without land needed work, and the South was a cash poor region where few landowners had money for wages. Thus a new system of tenant farming and sharecropping emerged and was fully in place by 1880. Economist Gavin Wright wrote that "Sharecropping was a balance between the freedman's desire for autonomy and the employer's interest in extracting work." This system lasted until well into the twentieth century.

To accommodate freedpeople's desires for independence, white landowners divided their lands into smaller units—perhaps 20 to 40 acres. They built houses or cabins, often provided fertilizer, seeds, plows, mules, and some furnishings in exchange for one-half of the crop. Those sharecroppers who owned tools and animals could use the land in exchange for a share of the crop—usually a third of their corn and a fourth of their cotton. Black families won the semi-independence they sought, but the system led to economic vulnerability for croppers. When families needed to buy food, clothing, or supplies, and they had no cash, they often used credit to purchase these goods at the local store, owned in many cases by the landlord or a furnishing merchant. Sharecroppers could mortgage their future crops and sign a crop-lien agreement, but the interest rates were often as high as 50 percent. The so-called crop-lien system was dangerous because it could put a family in debt for years, leading to debt peonage. As long as sharecroppers owed money, state laws prevented them from leaving the land, and they continued year after year to try and work off the debt. The crop-lien, debt peonage system also led to fraud; illiterate sharecroppers could not check the books kept by the store owners. In any case, it was considered an affront to question a white man about his bookkeeping. The system gave African Americans almost zero negotiating power, and it led to poverty, not only for freedpeople and their progeny but also for the region. The results were tragically disappointing. By 1880, per capita income for southerners was one-third that of the rest of the nation.

All scholars agree that there was one other fundamental, underlying reason for poor returns in agriculture and that was a worldwide decline in cotton prices. Demand was growing much more slowly than it had between 1800 and 1860, and the South's booming production led only to depressed prices. Then why did the South maintain its heavy reliance on cotton? The answer lies in the sharecropping and furnishing systems, which locked landowners and farm workers into the production of one of the South's few cash crops, and it kept blacks in an economically subordinate position in southern society.

What was sharecropping and how did it develop? What role did merchants, landowners, and laborers play in the sharecropping system? Did it benefit sharecroppers and tenant farmers, or did it lead to abuses? What role did race play in the system? Historians still ponder these questions because they relate to larger issues concerning the South's overall economic health. How did the region's economy fare under this system, and to what extent was the system responsible for the South's slower economic recovery after the Civil War?

DOCUMENTS

In Document 1 former slave owner William Grimes, who owned land along the Tar River in North Carolina, wrote this sharecrop contract in 1882, parceling out the land to poor white and black families in return for a share of the crop, mainly cotton. It is typical of innumerable contracts made in the South in the last decades of the nineteenth century and well into the twentieth. Document 2 is an agricultural lien, or "crop lien," which gave assurance to the landowner that his expenses for "furnishing" the cropper with food, seed, fertilizer, or supplies would be repaid. The crop lien customarily accompanied any sharecropping agreement. (This document also pledged the cropper's real and personal property as collateral for the loan.) In Document 3, Nate Shaw, whose real name was Ned Cobb (1885–1973), was a black sharecropper in Alabama. He describes some of his experiences with the sharecropping system and recounts its special dangers to black families, given pervasive racism in the South. Note the important role Mrs. Cobb played in defending their interests. Document 4 provides a different and more positive view of sharecropping by William Alexander Percy, a white Mississippian who in the 1930s became the head of a large landowning family. In Document 5, William A. Owens, who later became a professor of English at Columbia University, describes his life as a white boy and the rhythms of life on a tenant farm in East Texas. Tenant farmers were able to rent land for the entire year if they paid in advance. The benefit of renting land instead of sharecropping was that tenant farmers kept all the profits from their crops. Fatherless, Owens credits the family's survival to the energy and resourcefulness of his mother and grandmother. Finally, tenant farmers and farm laborers increasingly found themselves left out of any New South prosperity, as their comments to the North Carolina Bureau on Various Subjects in Document 6 plainly show.

1. William Grimes Writes a Sharecropping Contract, 1882

A Sharecrop Contract, 1882

To every one applying to rent land upon shares, the following conditions must be read, and agreed to. To every 30 and 35 acres, I agree to furnish the team, plow, and farming implements ... and I do not agree to furnish a cart to every cropper. The croppers are to have half of the cotton, corn, and fodder (and peas and pumpkins and potatoes if any are planted) if the following conditions are complied with, but-if not- they are to have only two-fifths (2/5). Croppers are to have no part or interest in the cotton seed raised from the crop planted and worked by them. No vine crops of any description, that is, no watermelons, muskmelons, ... squashes or anything of that kind, except peas and pumpkins, and potatoes, are to be planted in the cotton or corn. All must work under my direction. All plantation work to be done by the croppers. My part of the crop to be housed by them, and the fodder and oats to be hauled and put in the house. All the cotton must be topped about 1st August. If any cropper fails from any cause to save all the fodder from his crop, I am to have enough fodder to make it equal to one-half of the whole if the whole amount of fodder had been saved.

For every mule or horse furnished by me there must be 1000 good sized rails ... hauled, and the fence repaired as far as they will go, the fence to be torn down and put up from the bottom if I so direct. All croppers to haul rails and work on fence whenever I may order. Rails to be split when I may say. Each cropper to clean out every ditch in his crop, and where a ditch runs between two croppers, the cleaning out of that ditch is to be divided equally between them. Every ditch bank in the crop must be shrubbed down and cleaned off before the crop is planted and must be cut down every time the land is worked with his hoe and when the crop is "laid by," the ditch banks must be left clean of bushes, weeds, and seeds. The cleaning out of all ditches must be done by the first of October. The rails must be split and the fence repaired before corn is planted.

Each cropper must keep in good repair all bridges in his crop or over ditches that he has to clean out and when a bridge needs repairing that is outside of all their crops, then any one that I call on must repair it.

Fence jams to be done as ditch banks. If any cotton is planted on the land outside of the plantation fence, I am to have three-fourths of all the cotton made in those patches, that is to say, no cotton must be planted by croppers in their home patches.

All croppers must clean out stable and fill them with straw, and haul straw in front of stable whenever I direct. All the cotton must be manured, and enough fertilizer must be brought to manure each crop highly, the croppers to pay for

---

Grimes Family Papers (#3357), 1882. Held in the Southern Historical Collection University of North Carolina, Chapel Hill.

one-half of all manure bought, the quantity to be purchased for each crop must be left to me.

No cropper is to work off the plantation when there is any work to be done on the land he has rented, or when his work is needed by me or other croppers....

Road field is to be planted from the very edge of the ditch to the fence, and all the land to be planted close up to the ditches and fences. No stock of any kind belonging to croppers to run in the plantation after crops are gathered.

If the fence should be blown down, or if trees should fall on the fence outside of the land planted by any of the croppers, any one or all that I may call upon must put it up and repair it.

Every cropper must feed or have fed, the team he works, Saturday nights, Sundays, and every morning before going to work, beginning to feed his team (morning, noon, and night every day in the week) on the day he rents and feeding it to including the 31st day of December. If any cropper shall from any cause fail to repair his fence as far as 1000 rails will go, or shall fail to clean out any part of his ditches, or shall fail to leave his ditch banks, any part of them, well shrubbed and clean when his crop is laid by, or shall fail to clean out stables, fill them up and haul straw in front of them whenever he is told, he shall have only two-fifths (2/5) of the cotton, corn, fodder, peas, and pumpkins made on the land he cultivates.

If any cropper shall fail to feed his team Saturday nights, all day Sunday and all the rest of the week, morning/noon, and night, for every time he so fails he must pay me five cents.

No corn or cotton stalks must be burned, but must be cut down, cut up and plowed in. Nothing must be burned off the land except when it is impossible to plow it in.

Every cropper must be responsible for all gear and farming implements placed in his hands, and if not returned must be paid for unless it is worn out by use.

Croppers must sow & plow in oats and haul them to the crib, but must have no part of them. Nothing to be sold from their crops, nor fodder nor corn to be carried out of the fields until my rent is all paid, and all amounts they owe me and for which I am responsible are paid in full.

I am to gin & pack all the cotton and charge every cropper an eighteenth of his part, the cropper to furnish his part of the bagging, ties, & twine.

The sale of every cropper's part of the cotton to be made by me when and where I choose to sell, and after deducting all they owe me and all sums that I may be responsible for on their accounts, to pay them their half of the net proceeds. Work of every description, particularly the work on fences and ditches, to be done to my satisfaction, and must be done over until I am satisfied that it is done as it should be.

No wood to burn, nor light wood, nor poles, nor timber for boards, nor wood for any purpose whatever must be gotten above the house occupied by Henry Beasley—nor must any trees be cut down nor any wood used for any purpose, except for firewood, without my permission.

2. Alonzo T. Mial and A. Robert Medlin Sign A Crop Lien, 1876

No. 123.—Lien Bond secured by Real and Personal Property.

STATE OF NORTH CAROLINA,

Wake County.

Articles of Agreement, Between *Alonzo T. Mial* of said County and State, of the first part, and *A. Robert Medlin* of the County and State aforesaid, of the second part, to secure an Agricultural Lien according to an Act of General Assembly of North Carolina, entitled "An Act to secure advances for Agricultural purposes":

Whereas, the said *A. R. Medlin* being engaged in the cultivation of the soil, and being without the necessary means to cultivate his crop, *The Said A. T. Mial* has agreed to furnish goods and supplies to the said *A. R. Medlin* to an amount not to exceed *One Hundred and fifty* Dollars, to enable him to cultivate and harvest his crops for the year 1876.

And in consideration thereof, the said *A. R. Medlin* doth hereby give and convey to the said *A. T. Mial* a LIEN upon all of his crops grown in said County in said year, on the lands described as follows: *The land of A. R. Medlin adjoining the lands of Nelson D. Pain Samuel Bunch & others.*

And further, in Consideration thereof, the said *A. R. Medlin* for One Dollar in hand paid, the receipt of which is hereby acknowledged, have bargained and sold, and by these presents do bargain, sell and convey unto the said *A. T. Mial his* heirs and assigns forever, the following described Real and Personal Property to-wit: *All of his Stock horses, Cattle Sheep and Hogs—Carts and Wagons House hold and kitchen furnishings.* To Have and to Hold the above described premises, together with the appurtenances thereof, and the above described personal property, to the said *A. T. Mial his* heirs and assigns.

The above to be null and void should the amount found to be due on account of said advancements be discharged on or before the *1st* day of *November* 1876: otherwise the said *A. T. Mial his* executors, administrators or assigns, are hereby authorized and empowered to seize the crops and Personal Property aforesaid, and sell the same, together with the above Real Estate, for cash, after first advertising the same for fifteen days, and the proceeds thereof apply to the discharge of this Lein, together with the cost and expenses of making such sale, and the surplus to be paid to the said *A. R. Medlin,* or his legal representatives.

IN WITNESS WHEREOF, The said parties have hereunto set their hands and seals this *29th* day of *February,* 1876.

his
A. Robert X *Medlin*, [seal]
mark

Witness: *L. D. Goodloe* [signed] *A. T. Mial* [signed], [seal]

A lien bond between A. Robert Medlin and Alonzo T. Mial: 1876. All italicized words were handwritten in the original. This document is from the Alonzo T. and Millard Mial Papers, North Carolina Division of Archives and History.

3. Nate Shaw Recounts His Story of Farming in Alabama (c. 1910), 1971

I didn't make two good bales of cotton the first year I stayed with Mr. Curtis. Sorry land, scarce fertilizer, Mr. Curtis not puttin out, riskin much on me and I a workin little old fool, too. I knowed how to plow—catch the mule out the lot, white man's mule, bridle him, go out there and set my plow the way I wanted—I knowed how to do it. Bout a bale and a half was what I made.

The second year he went out there and rented some piney wood land from Mr. Lemuel Tucker, sixteen acres bout a half mile from his plantation and he put me on it. Well, it was kind of thin but it was a king over Mr. Curtis's land. I worked it all in cotton; what little corn I had I planted on Mr. Curtis's place. Well, I made six pretty good bales of cotton out there for Mr. Curtis and myself. When I got done gatherin, wound up, by havin to buy a little stuff from Mr. Curtis at the start, in 1907—it sort of pulled the blinds over my eyes. It took all them six bales of cotton to pay Mr. Curtis. In the place of prosperin I was on a standstill. Second year I was married it took all I made on Mr. Tucker's place, by Mr. Curtis havin rented it from Mr. Tucker for me, to pay up 1908's debts and also 1907's debts—as I say, by me buyin a right smart to start me off to housekeepin, cleaned me. I had not a dollar left out of the cotton. And also, Mr. Curtis come in just before I moved off his place—I was determined to pay him and leave him straight; in fact, I reckon I just had to do it because he'd a requested it of me, moving from his place, clean up and leave myself clear of him.

Mr. Curtis had Mr. Buck Thompson to furnish me groceries. Mr. Curtis knowed all of what Mr. Thompson was lettin me have; kept a book on me. See, he was standin for everything Mr. Thompson gived me; he paid Mr. Thompson and I paid him—the deal worked that way—out of my crop. So he made somethin off my grocery bill besides gettin half my crop when the time come.

Took part of my corn to pay him. He come to my crib, him and Mr. Calvin Culpepper come together to my crib and got my corn, so much of it. And what I had he got the best of it, to finish payin him on top of them six bales of cotton.

Then I moved to Mr. Gus Ames', 1908. Mr. Ames' land was a little better than Mr. Curtis's, but it was poor. Worked his pet land hisself and whatever he made off me, why, that was a bounty for him. I didn't make enough there to help me.

Hannah was dissatisfied at it, too. We talked it over and our talk was this: we knew that we weren't accumulatin nothin, but the farmin affairs was my business, I had to stand up to em as a man. And she didn't worry me bout how we was doin—she knowed it weren't my fault. We was just both dissatisfied. So, we taken it under consideration and went on and she was stickin right with me. She didn't work my heart out in the deal. I wanted to work in a way to please her

---

and satisfy her. She had a book learnin, she was checkin with me at every stand. She was valuable to me and I knowed it. And I was eager to get in a position where I could take care of her and our children better than my daddy taken care of his wives and children.

Mr. Curtis and Mr. Ames both, they'd show me my land I had to work and furnish me—far as fertilize to work that crop, they'd furnish me what *they* wanted to; didn't leave it up to me. That's what hurt—they'd furnish me the amount of fertilize they wanted regardless to what I wanted. I quickly seed, startin off with Mr. Curtis in 1907, it weren't goin to be enough. First year I worked for him and the last year too he didn't allow me to use over twenty-two hundred pounds of guano—it come in two-hundred-pound sacks then—that's all he'd back me up for all the land I worked, cotton and corn. It was enough to start with but not enough to do any more. Really, I oughta been usin twice that amount. Told him, too, but he said, "Well, at the present time and system, Nate, you can't risk too much."

I knowed I oughta used more fertilize to make a better crop—if you puts nothin in you gets nothin, all the way through. It's nonsense what they gived me—Mr. Curtis and Mr. Ames, too—but I was a poor colored man, young man too, and I had to go by their orders. It wasn't that I was ignorant of what I had to do, just, "Can't take too much risk, can't take too much risk." ... But you had to do what the white man said, livin here in this country. And if you made enough to pay him, that was all he cared for; just make enough to pay him what you owed him and anything he made over that, why, he was collectin on his risk. In my condition, and the way I see it for everybody, if you don't make enough to have some left you aint done nothin, except givin the other fellow your labor. That crop out there goin to prosper enough for him to get his and get what I owe him; he's makin his profit but he aint goin to let me rise. If he'd treat me right and treat my crop right, I'd make more and he'd get more—and a heap of times he'd get it all! That white man gettin all he lookin for, all he put out in the spring, gettin it all back in the fall. But what am I gettin for my labor? I aint gettin nothin. I learnt that right quick: it's easy to understand if a man will look at it....

If you want to sell your cotton at once, you take it to the market, carry it to the Apafalya cotton market and they'll sample it. Cotton buyin man cuts a slug in the side of your bale, reaches in there and pulls the first of it out the way and get him a handful, just clawin in there. He'll look over that sample, grade that cotton—that's his job. What kind of grade do it make? You don't know until he tells you. If it's short staple, the devil, your price is cut on that cotton. Color matters too, and the way it was ginned—some gins cuts up the cotton, ruins the staple.

They had names for the cotton grades—grade this, or grade that or grade the other. Didn't do no good to argue with the man if you didn't agree with the grade. Thing for you to do if he graded your cotton, examined it and gived you a low bid, take it to the next man.

Much of it is a humbug just like everything else, this gradin business. Some of em don't pay you what that cotton's worth a pound. They want long staple, clean cotton: the cleaner and the prettier it is and the nearer it comes to the specification of the staple they lookin for, the more they'll offer you. Generally, it's a top limit to that price and that's what they call the price cotton is bringin that year. If it's forty-cent cotton or six-cent cotton, it don't depend much on *your* cotton. It's a market price and it's set before you ever try to sell your cotton, and it's set probably before you gin your cotton and before you gather it or grow it or even plant your seed.

You take that cotton and carry it around to the cotton buyers. You might walk in that market buildin to a certain cotton buyer and he'll take your sample and look it over, look it over, give it a pull or two and he just might if he's very anxious for cotton, offer you a good price for it. But if he's in no hurry to buy your cotton and he gives you a price you don't like you can go to another buyer.

Heap of em buyin that cotton to speculate; he got plenty of money, wants to make more money, he buyin that cotton for himself and he don't care what company buys it from him. Maybe he might be buyin for a speculatin company, a company what does business in speculation. Or he might be buyin for a company that uses that cotton. Or if he can handle the matter, he buys for two companies.

Niggers' cotton didn't class like a white man's cotton with a heap of em. Used to be, when I was dealin with them folks in Apafalya, some of em you could have called em crooks if you wanted to; they acted in a way to bear that name, definitely. Give a white man more for his cotton than they do you.

I've had white men to meet me on the streets with a cotton sample in my hand, say, "Hello, Nate, you sellin cotton today?" White men, farmers like myself, private men; some of em was poor white men.

I'd tell em, "Yes, sir, I'm tryin. I can't look like get what my cotton's worth."

"What you been offered?"

"Well, Mr. So-and-so—"

"O, I see here such-and-such a one offered you so-and-so-and-so—"

Heap of times the scaper that I offered to sell him my cotton had a knack of puttin his bid on the paper that the cotton was wrapped up in. I didn't want him to do that. The next man would see how much this one bid me and he wouldn't go above it.

And so, I'd have my cotton weighed and I'd go up and down the street with my sample. Meet a white man, farmin man like myself, on the street; he'd see what I been offered for my sample—the buyer's marks would be on the wrapper—or I'd tell him. And he'd take that sample, unwrap it, look at it; he'd say, "Nate, I can beat you with your own cotton, I can get more for it than that."

Aint that enough to put your boots on! The same sample. He'd say, "Let me take your sample and go around in your place. I can beat what they offered you."

Take that cotton and go right to the man that had his bid on it and he'd raise it; right behind where I was, had been, and get a better bid on it. I've gived a white man my sample right there on the streets of Apafalya; he'd go off and come back. Sometime he'd say, "Well, Nate, I helped you a little on it but I couldn't help you much."

And sometime he'd get a good raise on it with another fellow out yonder. He'd bring my sample back to me with a bid on it. "Well, Nate, I knowed I could help you on that cotton."

That was happenin all through my farmin years: from the time I stayed on the Curtis place, and when I moved to the Ames place and when I lived with Mr. Reeve, and when I moved down on Sitimachas Creek with Mr. Tucker, and when I lived up there at Two Forks on the Stark place, and when I moved down on the Pollard place and stayed there nine years. Colored man's cotton weren't worth as much as a white man's cotton less'n it come to the buyer in the white man's hands. But the colored man's labor—that was worth more to the white man than the labor of his own color because it cost him less and he got just as much for his money....

I come up to my house one day—I was out checkin on my fences—and my wife told me there was a card in the mailbox tellin me to come to the bank in Apafalya and sign papers on my place. I said, "If I go, any way I go, you goin with me." See, she had book learnin and she could read and write. So I told her, "Well, we'll go to Apafalya this evenin, right after dark."

She was right down with me. Sometimes she'd say, "Darlin, you know what's best to do. But you can't decide *what* to do until you knows every side of the proposition. And bein that you can't read and write, it's profitable for us all for you to make me your partner."

I told her, one day, and many a time, "I'm married to you. And I think my best business should be in your hands. If anybody knows the ins and outs of it, you the one to know. But so far as workin in the field, I aint never had a high opinion of that and I intend to always be that way. Your business is at the house, mine's out in the field."

She was a girl that her mother would put all her business in her hands—her mother couldn't read and write. You could drop any sort of paper in front of Hannah and she could pick it up and read it like a top. She was pretty far advanced in education. She wasn't a graduate but she understood anything and could talk it off, too. She was, in a way of speakin, the *eyes* and I was the mouthpiece.

So, when I went there to sign them papers, I told her, "You goin with me."

I wanted her to read them papers to me; I knowed they weren't goin to do it. All I had to do was sign, but I wanted to know what I was signin.

Watson had taken over the place from the federal government and it was him I had to sign with. My wife and I jumped in the car and went right on to Apafalya. Got there and walked in—weren't nobody there in the bank but Mr. Grace and Mr. Watson. O good God, the doors flew right open and I broke out; I couldn't help it, I got red hot. I was signin—called it signin papers on that place. I knowed what I was signin before I signed; that's what brought the devil up.

"Hi, hello, Nate."

"Hello, Nate."

"How do you do, Mr. Watson, Mr. Grace."

Said, "Well, you come here to sign your papers, didn't you?"

I said, "Yes sirs, that's why I'm here."

Pushed it through the window for me to sign. My wife was standin right there and I just handed it to her. That's when I found out the devil was in the concern; that kept crossin my mind all the time and that kept me, to a great extent, from signin any notes at all with Watson.

Hannah turned away, stepped off a step or two, whipped that paper right over in a jiffy. She come back with it and touched me on my arm. I listened to her. She said, "Darlin, that paper covers everything you got: your mules, wagon, all your tools and your cows and hogs and everything you got's on that paper."

Good God, when she told me that I hollered. I just pushed the paper back to em through the bars. I said, "I won't sign that paper, noway under the sun it could be fixed like it is."

I'd expected to come there that night and sign papers on the land—Watson knowed what I had—not reach out and take my mules, my wagon, my hogs, my cows, on that paper. And if I'd a signed it like they was preparin me to do, I could have lost it all. Just be late payin on the land and they would take everything I had. I had sense enough through my wife to see what they was tryin to do to me. Woooooooooo, I meant to buck it.

I said, "Aint that land sufficient to stand for itself and not none of my personal property on it? I can't carry it nowhere."

Tried to saddle everything I had. Right there I burst like a butterbean in the sun. I wouldn't sign that note for Jesus Christ. I just stuck that paper back through them bars—I knowed the type of him. I felt a fire in my heart; told my wife, "Let's go."

If I couldn't do better I was goin to move away from there. Soon as I told my wife, "Let's go," and got nearly to the door, "Come back, come back, Nate, we can change the paper; come back, come back, we can change it."

I just say now I was a fool—I went back. They changed that paper to suit me and I signed it. It just spoke for the land then. So I signed to buy the place from Mr. Watson and if I couldn't make the payments all they could do was take it back....

4. William Alexander Percy Views Sharecropping, 1941

I have no love of the land and few, if any, pioneer virtues, but when Trail Lake became mine after Father's death, I must confess I was proud of it. I could reach it in three quarters of an hour. It was a model place: well drained, crossed by concrete roads, with good screened houses, a modern gin, artesian-well water, a high state of cultivation, a Negro school, a foolish number of churches, abundant crops, gardens and peach trees, quantities of hogs, chickens, and cows, and all the mules and tractors and equipment any place that size needed.

Father had operated it under the same contract that Fafar used on the Percy Place. The Negroes seemed to like it and I certainly did. I happen to believe that profit-sharing is the most moral system under which human beings can work together and I am convinced that if it were accepted in principle by capital and labor, our industrial troubles would largely cease. So on Trail Lake I continue to be partners with the sons of ex-slaves and to share fifty-fifty with them as my grandfather and Father had done.

In 1936 a young man with a passion for facts roved in from the University of North Carolina and asked to be allowed to inspect Trail Lake for the summer. He was Mr. Raymond McClinton, one of Doctor Odum's boys, and the result of his sojourn was a thesis entitled "A Social-Economic Analysis of a Mississippi Delta Plantation." That's coming pretty stout if you spend much of your time trying to forget facts and are stone-deaf to statistics. But some of his findings were of interest even to me, largely I suspect because they illustrated how Fafar's partnership-contract works in the modern world. In 1936, the year Mr. McClinton chose for his study, the crop was fair, the price average (about twelve cents), and the taxes higher than usual. Now for some of his facts:

Trail Lake has a net acreage of 3,343.12 acres of which 1,833.66 are planted in cotton, 50.59 are given to pasture, 52.44 to gardens, and the rest to corn and hay. The place is worked by 149 families of Negroes (589 individuals) and in 1936 yielded 1,542 bales of cotton. One hundred and twenty-four of the families work under Fafar's old contract, and twenty-five, who own their stock and equipment, under a similar contract which differs from the other only in giving three-fourths instead of one-half of the yield to the tenant. The plantation paid in taxes of all kinds $20,459.99, a bit better than $6.00 per acre; in payrolls for plantation work $12,584.66—nearly $4.00 an acre. These payrolls went to the Negroes on the place. The 124 families without stock of their own made a gross average income of $491.90 and a net average income of $437.64. I have lost Mr. McClinton's calculation of how many days of work a plantation worker puts in per year, but my own calculation is a maximum of 150 days. There is nothing to do from ginning time, about October the first, to planting time, about March the fifteenth, and nothing to do on rainy days, of which we have many.

These figures, as I read them, show that during an average year the 124 families working on Trail Lake for 150 days make each $437.64 clear, besides having free water and fuel, free garden plot and pasturage, a monthly credit for six months to cover food and clothing, a credit for doctor's bills and medicine, and a house to live in. The Negroes who receive this cash and these benefits are simple unskilled laborers. I wonder what other unskilled labor for so little receives so much. Plantations do not close down during the year and there's no firing, because partners can't fire one another. Our plantation system seems to me to offer as humane, just, self-respecting, and cheerful a method of earning a living as human beings are likely to devise. I watch the limber-jointed, oily-black, well-fed, decently clothed peasants on Trail Lake and feel sorry for the telephone girls, the clerks in chain stores, the office help, the unskilled laborers everywhere—not only for their poor and fixed wage but for their slave routine, their joyless habits of work, and their insecurity....

Share-cropping is one of the best systems ever devised to give security and a chance for profit to the simple and the unskilled. It has but one drawback—it must be administered by human beings to whom it offers an unusual opportunity to rob without detection or punishment. The failure is not in the system itself, but in not living up to the contractual obligations of the system—the failure is in human nature. The Negro is no more on an equality with the white man in plantation matters than in any other dealings between the two. The white planter may charge an exorbitant rate of interest, he may allow the share-cropper less than the market price received for his cotton, he may cheat him in a thousand different ways, and the Negro's redress is merely theoretical. If the white planter happens to be a crook, the share-cropper system on that plantation is bad for Negroes, as any other system would be. They are prey for the dishonest and temptation for the honest. If the Delta planters were mostly cheats, the results of the share-cropper system would be as grievous as reported. But, strange as it may seem to the sainted East, we have quite a sprinkling of decent folk down our way.

Property is a form of power. Some people regard it as an opportunity for profit, some as a trust; in the former it breeds hubris, in the latter, noblesse oblige. The landed gentry of Fafar's time were of an ancient lineage and in a sober God-fearing tradition. Today many have thought to acquire membership in that older caste by acquiring land, naked land, without those ancestral hereditaments of virtue which change dirt into a way of life. On the plantation where there is stealing from the Negro you will generally find the owner to be a little fellow operating, as the saying goes, "on a shoe-string," or a nouveau riche, or a landlord on the make, tempted to take more than his share because of the mortgage that makes his title and his morals insecure. These, in their pathetic ambition to imitate what they do not understand, acquire power and use it for profit; for them the share-cropper system affords a golden opportunity rarely passed up.

5. William A. Owens Describes Tenant Farm Life in 1906

My mother was then in a family of women who had lost most of their men: her grandmother, born Missouri Ann Cleaver, who lived on the Pin Hook road between the graveyard and the store; her mother, Alice Chennault, who had married off her two daughters and was "living around"; her mother's sister, Ellen Victoria, Aunt Vick; her mother's half-sister, Elizabeth Penelope Haigood, who lived across Little Pine Creek on the Novice road. All her life she had seen these women doing the work of men—plowing, cutting wood, feeding stock. In the beginning of winter she had to take up the work of a man and do what she could for the children....

My grandmother ... came to live with her, to help with the children and to keep house while my mother went to the field. She had raised a family without a man. So could any woman who wanted badly enough to hold her children together. At the time she was a tall raw-boned woman of fifty and, as the people said of her, "as stout as e'er a man." The strongest daughter of the stronger Missouri Ann, she had survived the hard times of the Civil War, the walk from Camden, Arkansas, to Blossom Prairie, the hardships of making a living at Pin Hook. She had buried a husband and a son. It was time for her to take a rest, but rest had to be farther along the road....

In Pin Hook, November is often wet and gray but rarely wintry. Monroe and Dewey could go to school, barefoot because there was no money for shoes that year. In December and January they would have to miss some days when blue northers swept down and left ice on the ruts in the road, but they were pushed to get as much learning as they could while they could. To give them the chance, my mother cut and hauled wood to keep fires going in the fireplace and cookstove. At night she helped them with their lessons in front of the fire.

Three months of schooling and then they had to stop. By the first warm days of February plowing had to start and Monroe had to be a hand in the field. They hitched Old Maud, the bay mare, to a kelly turning plow and began to flatbreak the land my father had plowed the year before, taking it a square at a time, first for corn and then for cotton. Hour after hour my mother went, holding the plow in the ground, guiding the mare with rope lines looped over her shoulders. When she was too tired to manage both, Monroe held the lines. It was backbreaking, heartbreaking work, going as they did from first light till first dark. Breaking the land was only the beginning. Planting and cultivating still had to come....

By the middle of March the garden had to be started and the hens set. New shoots of poke and dandelion and peppergrass were beginning to show along the rail fences and turnrows. My grandmother took on the jobs of garden and chickens, and picking "sallet" greens. The older children could trail after her. I had to be taken to the field, to lie on a quilt on the ground.

All that spring I spent my days in the field, sleeping, waking, crying when I was hungry or needed changing. When I was big enough to crawl, my mother tied me to a stake to keep me from going off into the woods where there were snakes and scorpions and long blue santafees with yellow stingered legs. Where the rows were long, she tied me in the middle of the field. When she was plowing and Monroe planting, she staked me between them, where one or the other could keep an eye on me.

My toys were the dirt, and a stick to dig the dirt. No one could live closer to the earth than I did. I dug the sand, I rolled in it, I covered myself with it. Before my first year had passed I had eaten the peck of dirt everyone, Pin Hook people said, is entitled to. I had learned the feel, the smell, the taste of earth.

That year and later I learned, hardly knowing I was learning it, how farm life is shaped by the land and the seasons—by what will grow and the days or weeks or months of growing time—of making the best of sun and rain and seed in the earth. In Pin Hook, corn had to be planted in late February or early March, the time of sandstorms out west. There were days when the sky was overcast with a cloud of red dust, and the sun shone through a muddy red. Corn planted then was in the ground on time. Corn planted later might twist and burn and never tassel in the drouth of late July and August. Cotton planting had to wait till the ground was warm. All in the month of May it had to be planted, plowed, chopped, to make it ready for fast growing in the hot moist days of June. Farming was going right for anybody who could say, "I found me a cotton bloom Fourth of July." In the heat of summer, crops had to be "laid by" with a last running of the Georgia stock down the middles. Once they were through laying by, Pin Hookers could rest a little before gathering time.

Gathering time came and my mother began to take heart. The crop was light, but she had made a crop. The land had not been lost; the children were still all together. My mother knew that she could go on. She could gather this year's crop. She could plant the next. She could see that the children got to school when they were not in the field.

Gathering corn came first, each trip down the field with the wagon taking a swath five rows wide. My mother took two rows on one side, Monroe took two on the other. The other children "carried the down row," the row of stalks knocked down by the wagon. I rode in the front of the wagon, with boards between me and the pile of pale yellow shucks.

Cotton picking came next. Grown-ups and older children dragged long canvas sacks down the middles, picking two rows at a time, their fingers working down the stalks, pulling out the white lint, leaving yellow burrs among the green leaves. The smaller children picked in flour sacks, and cried when the points of cotton burrs pricked their fingers. I rode on my mother's sack, or slept on a pile of cotton in the wagon.

Potato digging had to come before frost, while the sand was still warm and dry. The diggers had to work close to the earth. First the rows were turned up with a kelly turning plow. Then the diggers went on their hands and knees, grabbling in the earth with their fingers. It was a job for children. They could crawl and roll in the dirt as much as they liked. In moments of rest they could build sand houses and tunnels over their bare feet.

On the farm, sights and smells go with the seasons, and I learned them the first year, with each following year only a relearning: the green of young corn, the white of cotton blossoms slowly turning pink, the burnt brown of grass under an August sun; the sweetness of corn in silk and tassel, the dryness of dust in a cotton middle, the new-clothes smell of cotton lint when the face is pressed down into it.

The year passed. I was one year old, my father one year in the grave. Work had been hard, but there was enough to live on: milk and cornbread, sweet potatoes and black-eyed peas. Cotton money had to go for doctor bills and medicine. Times were bad, but they could be worse. Next year they would be better. At night they could be truly thankful when, after the Bible reading, they knelt beside hickory-bottomed chairs for the prayers they made themselves.

"If our health holds out," my mother and grandmother said.

6. Tenants and Farmers Assess the New South, 1887–1889

Extracts from Letters to the Bureau on Various Subjects from Tenants and Farm Laborers in the Different Counties of the State

1887

A. R.—There is general depression and hard times and almost broken spirits among the tenant farmers. There are many things that contribute somewhat to this bad state of things but the one great cause is the outrageous per cent. charged for supplies bought on credit; it is sapping the life of North Carolina.

F. M. S.—The poor cannot clothe their children decently enough for a school room because of the exorbitant rate of interest they are charged for supplies; they are obliged to pay whatever the merchants charge. This is a most pressing evil and should be stopped by law or it will soon swallow us body and soul.

T. D. H.—Some think they pay only 25 or 30 per cent. for what they buy on crop liens, but if they will figure it out, they will see it is 100 to 200 per cent. per annum on the amount they buy over cash prices. There would be an over supply of labor if they would work. Negroes with some education will not work on the farm if they can help it. They have a keener desire for education than the whites and attend school much better.

W. J. M.—I think the present depressed condition of the farming interest is largely due to the mortgage system in buying supplies. There is no chance for improvement where this system is in operation.

J. M. B.—There is no man and no county that can long exist on 50 per cent. charged on everything eaten by farmers; unless a remedy is found the county will be ruined very soon.

O. E.—There ought to be a law passed forbidding any man planting more than ten acres in cotton to the horse.

J. S. M.—The condition of the farmers is bad and will get no better until we adopt some system and unite in our efforts to better ourselves and stop looking to others to help us; we must depend upon ourselves. When we become united we can get all the legislation we need; not till then.

J. L. H.—Merchants require a mortgage on whatever property tenant has, besides the crop. They are more strict this year than ever before. There were many that could not pay out last year. Tenants pay an advance of at least 25 per cent. on the average.

J. H. R.—The system of buying on time and using guano has broken up many farmers, and has driven so many to the towns to seek employment that

---

This document is taken from the First Annual Report of the Bureau of Labor Statistics of the State of North Carolina, W. N. Jones, Commissioner (Raleigh: Josephus Daniels, State Printer and Binder, Presses of Edwards and Broughton, 1887), and Third Annual Report of the Bureau of Labor Statistics of the State of North Carolina for the Year 1889, John C. Scarborough, Commissioner (Raleigh: Josephus Daniels, State Printer and Binder, Presses of Edwards & Broughton, 1890).

wages have been greatly reduced. If this state of things continues it will soon put all the land in the hands of a few men and ruin all classes.

F. W. R.—Attendance at school ought to be enforced by law; the schools are now usually taught in winter when the child of the poor man is poorly clad and hence unable to attend; in summer they must work, and so they do not attend school. This should not be so—we must get out of this condition or we shall go backward as a people and State.

S. A. H.—Many whites do not send their children to school for want of proper clothes. The people are in a bad condition and most of their lands are mortgaged, in most cases too irredeemably. I see no hope for the county to get better unless the government comes to their help and lends them money at 1 per cent. to redeem their land and gives them twenty years to pay out. Wages have decreased on farms owing I believe to the tariff.

S. S.—We farmers work very hard, but get in no better condition. Evidently there is something wrong. The towns flourish, while in the country, where the producing element is, the people get worse off. We do not mind the work—were raised to it—but would like to get something for it.

W. H. B.—The mortgage system is working its deadly way into this county, and making sad havoc where its tempting offers are once entered into. Alas! one never gets out from its magic embrace until he dies out or is sold out. I wish this ruinous law could be repealed, and with it the homestead law, which is the father of the mortgage system.

L. P.—The trouble in this county is the awful time prices that we have to pay the merchants, not less than 50 per cent. The price of labor is low and it should be higher, but the farmer can't afford to pay even present prices, because the high per cent. keeps him down. The homestead law should be repealed and then the lien law and the high time prices would have to go.

P. H. H.—The poor tenant and farm laborers and in many cases land-owners, are in a bad condition, mostly on account of the heavy per cent. charged by merchants for supplies.

J. E. D.—Labor is down; so is the farmer. The merchant is the prosperous man now. Half of the farms are mortgaged to the commission merchants, who charge 50 per cent. above cash prices. Half of the farmers of this county are bound to merchants by the mortgage system.

1889

Remarks.—In my opinion, the greatest evil with the farmers here is, that the land-owners will rent their lands and hire their teams to tenants, and furnish provisions; the consequence is, the tenant gets so far in debt to the landlord that, before the crop is laid by, the tenant gets dissatisfied and fails to work the crop as it ought to be, and, therefore, raises bad crops and the land is left in bad condition. If the landlord would hire the labor, his land would be in better condition and labor would be better also.

Remarks.—The year in this section was not favorable to farming. Spring late. The heavy rain-fall in June and July injured the general crop badly, particularly cotton. The sweet-potato crop not good—too much rain. Had a killing frost on the nights of October 5 and 6, which did considerable damage.

Remarks.—I will name a few evils the farmer has to contend with, viz: The price of everything produced by the farmer is fixed by the merchant, or purchaser, as well as everything bought by the farmer, and high rates for transportation on railroads. The first evil mentioned can be overcome by the farmers paying cash for what they purchase, and cooperation. The second should be overcome by proper legislation—a Railroad Commission Bill.

Remarks.—The mortgage system, with the consequent high prices exacted for supplies, and the one-crop (cotton) system hangs like an incubus about this people and have well-nigh ruined them financially. The system of working the public roads now in vogue with us is very unsatisfactory with us, not to say unjust. Capital or property and labor should both be taxed to keep up the public highways. My idea would be to value an able-bodied man, with nothing but his head, say at $500 or $1,000 each, as the exigencies of the case might demand, and then require every $500 or $1,000 worth of capital or property to contribute a like amount, either in labor or its equivalent in money. I have given this matter much thought and this strikes me as the most equitable and feasible plan. Our public school system in this part of the State is very inefficient.

Remarks.—Time was in this vicinity nearly every farmer not only supported himself and family from the products of the farm, but had something to spare as well. That time has passed away, I fear, forever. Then very little cotton was raised, and the farmers looked well to grain crops, horses, cattle, hogs and sheep. There was not much opulence, but much of substantial independence. Now, instead of being a year before, they are a year, at least behind, and, toil as they may, too many of them at the close of the year, when the books are opened, find the balance-sheet against them, "though every nerve was strained." The mortgage system, which hangs like a pall of death over many an honest, hard-working man, will ruin any business interest in this country. No farmer can borrow money, or buy on crop-time, at an advance of from thirty to fifty per cent. No farmer can farm successfully without some money; the present rates offered him amounts to prohibition. I cannot, in the brief space allowed, recount many of the ills now affecting us, or make any suggestion in the palliation of them. To be brief, farmers are very much dispirited at the outlook, while they have worked harder for the last two years than at any time within my knowledge.

ESSAYS

In the first essay, historian Jonathan M. Wiener explores the relationship between class structure and economic development in the South. He begins by discussing class conflict and the plantation system during the early years of Reconstruction and argues that the South's labor system was essentially different from that of the North. He explains that the system of "bound labor" was applicable to both renters and sharecroppers who were held on the land by five types of laws passed by southern state legislatures to "restrict the free market in labor." Detrimental to the South's overall economy and destructive to human incentive, especially to freedpeople, one might well ask, how did African Americans survive? Sharon Ann Holt answers this in her essay by closely observing the multifaceted methods small farmers used to supplement their incomes and alleviate the negative effects of sharecropping. Although pervasive racism and class prejudice continued to create economic inequities, a family's maintenance often depended on the creative use of the household economy, wage earning, and farming skills.

Bound Labor in Southern Agriculture

JONATHAN M. WIENER

The social history of the immediate postwar period ... indicates that [southern] planters reached different conclusions about what constituted economic rationality. They believed that the most profitable course was to maintain the plantation as a centralized unit of production. By using supervised gang laborers who were paid wages and incorporated into the organizational structure of the antebellum plantation, the planters hoped to preserve economies of scale and centralized management....

Planters organized to limit the free market in labor and to force freedmen to work on plantation gangs, sought to enlist the Freedmen's Bureau in the same effort, and worked in the state legislatures to establish repressive laws. Some turned to terror—to the Ku Klux Klan—to force blacks to labor in plantation gangs. Planters throughout the South in the years immediately following the war organized to limit competition among themselves. At a typical meeting in the fall of 1867, planters in Sumter County, Alabama, unanimously resolved that "concert of action" was "indispensable" in hiring labor. Thus, all would offer the same terms to the freedmen, and none would "employ any laborer discharged for violation of contracts." Other planters held similar meetings in places like Sumter, South Carolina, and Amite County, Mississippi, followed by statewide meetings of planter representatives. The report of the Freedmen's Bureau in 1866 complained of the planters' "community of action," and the Joint Congressional Committee on Reconstruction heard evidence on the same phenomenon. As one planter explained the strategy to John Trowbridge in 1866, "The nigger is going to be made a serf, sure as you live. It won't need any law for that. Planters will have an understanding among themselves: 'You won't hire my niggers, and I won't hire yours,' then what's left for them? They're attached to the soil, and we're as much their masters as ever." Planters went beyond these informal organizations and used state power to enforce the interests of their class and prevent those individualists among them who desired to engage in market

From Jonathan M. Wiener, "Class Structure and Economic Development in the American South, 1865–1955," from *American Historical Review* (October 1979). Reprinted by permission of the author.

economics. "Enticement" acts passed in every Southern state immediately after the war made it a crime to "hire away, or induce to leave the service of another," any laborer "by offering higher wages or in any other way whatsoever." The criminal defined by this law was not the black who left his plantation, but the planter who sought a free market in labor....

Louisiana law ... made it a crime to "feed, harbor, or secrete any person who leaves his or her employer," and enticement laws in most states provided that farm laborers hired away by better offers could be forcibly returned to the original employers. Vagrancy acts were even more extreme efforts to control the mobility of labor. The definition of vagrancy usually included "stubborn servants ..., a laborer or servant who loiters away his time, or refuses to comply with any contract ... without just cause." Planters could thus enlist local courts in keeping "their" laborers on their plantations.

The planters' bitter opposition to the presence of the Freedmen's Bureau did not stop them from seeking to enlist the bureau's agents in an effort to tie blacks to the land. Planters put intense and calculated social pressure on the Union representatives in their midst. As early as 1864, a War Department report warned that officials in charge of the freedmen were "received into the houses of the planters and treated with a certain consideration," so that, under the "influences" that the planters brought to bear, officials often ("without becoming fully conscious of it") became "the employers' instrument of great injustice and ill-treatment toward ... colored laborers." A black-belt newspaper explained in 1866 that Union officials who were "gentlemen" were "received ito the best families ... on probation" but those who kept "company with Negroes ... could not get into society." When the Freedmen's Bureau opened an office in the Alabama black belt, "the white people ... determined to win their good will," according to Walter L. Fleming. "There were 'stag' dinners and feasts, and the eternal friendship of the officers, with a few exceptions, was won." Fleming gave more credit to the persuasive power of stag dinners with planters than the feasts probably deserved, but he was undoubtedly correct in describing the planters' intentions as well as the effect of their efforts: some agents of the Freedmen's Bureau helped planters get freedmen to work on terms agreed to by planter organizations and often sided with planters in disputes with freedmen.

Finally, some planters restricted blacks' freedom to move by resorting to terror. Historians concerned with the politics of Reconstruction have overlooked the extent to which the Klan in the black belt was an instrument of the planter class for the control of labor. Planters played a major role in organizing and directing Klan activities there; and Klan terror contributed to the repression of black labor, primarily by threatening those who contemplated emigration. As early as 1866, masked bands "punished Negroes whose landlords had complained of them." According to the Congressional testimony of one planter, when blacks "got together once to emigrate ..., disguised men went to them and told them that if they undertook it they would be killed," in order to keep "the country from being deprived of their labor." In the words of a black belt lawyer, the Klan was "intended principally for the negroes who failed to work." And Allen

W. Trelease has shown that the Klan pursued blacks who "violat[ed] ... labor contracts by running away."

Despite the planters' use of informal organization, formal law, the Freedmen's Bureau, and the Klan, they failed to preserve the plantation as a centralized unit cultivated by gangs of wage laborers. To understand this failure, it is necessary to look beyond the abstract logic of the market and focus on the relatively concrete process of class conflict between planters and freedmen. Rational as the planters' effort was, preservation of the centralized plantation confronted an insurmountable obstacle: the freedmen's refusal to agree to it. Their widespread resistance to working for wages in gangs, which appears in the sources as a "shortage of labor," played a crucial role in the reorganization of agriculture after the war. Such shortages were reported throughout the plantation South in the immediate postwar years. Robert Somers, who visited the South in 1871 and wrote a book about his experiences, titled his chapter on the Alabama black belt "Despair of the Planters for Labor." Reports by the Freedmen's Bureau and the Boston textile firm of Loring and Atkinson concurred. The freedmen's idea of a rational system of production differed from that of the planters; the blacks hungered for land. Eugene Genovese has quoted a plantation mistress's description of a typical situation at the war's end: "our most trusted servant ... claims the plantation as his own." The Joint Congressional Committee on Reconstruction noted the freedmen's fierce "passion ... to own land," and the Montgomery *Advertiser* agreed that blacks were "ravenous for land." The freedmen made their claim on the basis of a kind of labor theory of value; as a "Colored Convention" proclaimed in Montgomery in May 1867, "the property" that the planters held was "nearly all earned by the sweat of our brows, not theirs." And an exslave wrote in 1864, "we wants land—dis bery land dat is rich wid de sweat ob we face and de blood ob we back."

By creating a "shortage of labor," the freedmen defeated the planters' efforts to preserve the plantation as a single, large-scale unit worked by gangs. Increasingly in 1867 and 1868, planters divided their plantations into small plots and assigned each to a single family. In establishing decentralized family sharecropping as the prevailing organization of cotton production after the war, the planters made a major concession to the freedmen and their resistance to the slavelike gang system. The Selma *Southern Argus*, one of the most articulate and insightful voices of the planter class, admitted this explicitly: sharecropping was "an unwilling concession to the freedman's desire to become a proprietor ..., not a voluntary association from similarity of aims and interests." Thus, class conflict shaped the form of the postwar plantation more than did purely economic forces operating according to the logic of the free market....

The North's economy depended on the market mechanism to allocate "free" labor; capitalists competed for labor and laborers were free, at least in theory, to move in response to better offers. This was the "classic capitalist" route to industrial society. Until the Great Depression of the 1930s, planters in the postwar South used more directly coercive methods of labor allocation and control. These restrictions on the South's labor market distinguished the planter from the Northern bourgeois, turned the sharecropper into a kind of "bound" laborer, and made the development of postwar Southern capitalism qualitatively different from the Northern pattern.

To argue that Northern agricultural laborers enjoyed freedoms denied to their Southern counterparts is not to say that the capitalist development of the North eliminated exploitation, oppression, or poverty. But their characteristic forms were different in kind from those under which Southern sharecroppers labored. The typical laborer in the "bonanza" wheat farms of the Northern plains was a migrant wage worker who was oppressed not by peonage but by seasonal unemployment and the need to travel great distances over the course of the year. The terms of disparagement for these workers—"tramps," "bums," "riffraff"—precisely described their mobility, their absence of ties to the land. In other areas of the North, agricultural laborers worked primarily as "hired hands" on family farms and received wages by the month or, during the harvest season, by the day. Farm labor took other forms in the truck gardens of the East and on the great farms of California's central valley. Studies of tenancy in the Midwest contain no evidence that debt peonage was widespread. Northern farm laborers were "forced to be free," the fate of labor wherever agriculture develops in classic capitalist fashion.

The most important institution in the South's system of bound labor was debt peonage. Pete Daniel's work on this central element in postwar Southern history is indispensable. Tenants began each season unable to finance the year's crop and had to seek credit from their landlords or the local merchants, who required that the tenant remain until the debt was paid, however many seasons that took. Hard-working tenants could be made to stay by exaggerating their indebtedness through dishonest bookkeeping; undesirable ones could be ordered to move on, with their debts transferred to a new landlord. The movement of tenants among landlords preserved the system's repressive nature as long as the debt moved with the tenant, as typically it did. Movement alone does not, therefore, disprove the existence of debt peonage. Its extent is difficult to measure precisely; no doubt it varied along with economic cycles. Most contemporaries and historians describe it as a characteristic feature of cotton agriculture in the postwar South, and one study has found that 80 percent of the sharecroppers in Alabama had an indebtedness of more than one year's standing.

Debt peonage was not limited to sharecroppers; nor were they necessarily more exploited and oppressed by the labor-repressive system than were cash renters, usually regarded as one step up the socioeconomic ladder. During the 1890s, when cotton prices reached their low point for the century, renting replaced sharecropping at an astonishing rate. Higgs, for one, has taken this shift to rental labor as a sign of progress, "a response to the growth in the number of experienced black farmers to whom landlords were willing to grant such contracts." An alternative interpretation is more plausible: the economic collapse during that decade made it more profitable for landlords to collect rent instead of a share of the cotton crop from their tenants. Landlords, therefore, responded to the depression by forcing their tenants to assume the full extent of the risk, a risk in which the planters had previously shared. Landlords could still require tenants to obtain credit from them, thereby earning interest and tying their renters to the land by debt peonage until another season, when cotton might become profitable once again; then renters could be turned back into sharecroppers.

The actions of the planter class during the Mississippi River flood of 1927 are revealing. High water covered fifty miles on each side of the channel, submerging the delta plantation district and driving four hundred thousand black tenants from their homes. The planters believed, according to William Alexander Percy, one of their leaders, that "the dispersal of our labor was a longer evil ... than a flood." They insisted that laborers not be permitted to leave the region so that the tenants could be returned to the plantations when the waters receded. The Red Cross and the National Guard operated refugee camps and helped the planters by acceding to their demand that the camps be "closed"—fenced and locked—so that the blacks could not get out and labor recruiters from other areas could not get in. The governor of Mississippi himself denounced labor recruiters who offered employment elsewhere to victims of the flood. Planters argued that, since labor contracts had already been signed for the 1927 season and since advances had been made to tenants, blacks had to go back and work after the flood, even though it became clear that the waters would not recede quickly enough to permit any planting. The Red Cross distributed emergency supplies not to the blacks inside the locked camps but to the local planters, some of whom billed their tenants after passing on the supplies, creating further indebtedness. The NAACP [National Association for the Advancement of Colored People] denounced the "peonage" practiced in refugee "concentration camps," but the planters succeeded in preventing blacks from leaving the region and in tightening the bonds that tied the tenants to their landlords.

The regional apparatus of involuntary servitude that prevailed between Reconstruction and World War II extended well beyond debt peonage; it also consisted of five different kinds of laws, all of which worked to restrict the free market in labor: enticement statutes, which made it a crime for one planter to hire laborers employed by another; emigrant agent laws, which severely restricted the activities of out-of-state labor recruiters; contract enforcement statutes, which made it a criminal offense for tenants to break contracts with landlords; vagrancy statutes, drawn broadly enough to permit landlords to enlist the aid of local courts to keep laborers at work; and the criminal surety system, backed up by the system of convict labor, which permitted convicts to serve their sentences laboring for private employers. Enticement acts were revived in eight out of ten Southern states after Reconstruction and survived with amendments into the mid-twentieth century. An Alabama statute from 1920 outlawed even attempted enticement. Like the enticement laws, emigrant agent acts were intended to control competition among white employers rather than to punish workers who moved. They sought to prevent the activities of out-of-state labor recruiters by levying prohibitive license fees. In the Carolinas, the license cost one thousand dollars per county, with a penalty for unlicensed recruiting of up to five thousand dollars or two years in prison. Six states of the Deep South passed such laws between 1877 and 1912, and three more did so between 1916 and 1929.

Other laws limited the freedom of laborers to move. Vagrancy acts forced workers to sign labor contracts. Penalties and apparently enforcement as well increased between 1890 and 1910 in response to the rise of agrarian insurgency. Georgia's law of 1895 provided for a fine of one thousand dollars or six to twelve months on the chain gang for those found without employment. The vagrancy acts permitted sheriffs to function as labor recruiters for planters, rounding up "vagrants" at times of labor shortage. Additional laws upheld labor contracts. Late in the nineteenth century six states passed "contract enforcement" and "false pretenses" statutes, which held that a worker's unjustified failure to work constituted "*prima facie* evidence of the intent to injure or defraud the employer." An Alabama law of 1903 did not permit the defendant to rebut testimony about his intentions. Under "criminal surety" laws, employers were permitted to pay the fines of individuals convicted under contract enforcement or vagrancy proceedings; the convict had to work for that employer until his earnings repaid the fine. Thus a laborer whose work displeased his landlord could not only be convicted of a crime but also be compelled by the court to labor for the same employer. The alternative for convicts was the chain gang, and almost anything was preferable to its brutality. A distinctly Southern institution, it was reserved primarily for convicts who refused to sign criminal surety contracts or who were unable to get any landlord to pay their fine and hire them.

Thus, the Southern states established a net of laws to limit the mobility of labor. Vagrancy acts forced workers to sign labor contracts; contract enforcement and false pretenses laws prevented them from leaving. If they left nevertheless, the criminal surety system could return them to the employer, who was backed by the threat of the chain gang. Enticement and emigrant agent statutes prevented another employer from seeking their labor. In the North a laborer whose work displeased his employer could be fired; in the South he could be convicted of a criminal offense. This web of restrictive legislation distinguished the South's labor system from that of the classically capitalist North.

How successful were these laws? It is difficult to tell. William Cohen has suggested that one measure is the extent of their litigation in higher courts, an expensive and time-consuming practice—undertaken, presumably, only if enforcement were of great importance. The Alabama criminal surety law came before the state supreme court at least sixteen times between 1883 and 1914, and the Georgia contract enforcement law was litigated in appellate courts on eighty different occasions between 1903 and 1921. These cases suggest fairly extensive reliance on the law to repress labor, for those argued in the appellate courts were only the tip of the iceberg. The mere threat of prosecution usually sufficed to bring about the desired result; and, since only a handful of sharecroppers had the resources to appeal a conviction, planters, sheriffs, and local judges had virtually a free hand. Informal practice extended the law; extralegal and illegal acts were often undertaken to accomplish the same ends. In September 1901 local officials in the Mississippi black belt rounded up "idlers and vagrants" and drove them "into the cotton fields," where the farmers were "crying for labor." In February 1904 police in Newton, Georgia, made "wholesale arrests of idle Negroes ... to scare them back to the farms from which they emanated." In 1908 the steamer *America* docked at a Natchez wharf, seeking to recruit black laborers. White businessmen established a local committee, whose methods according to one Southern reporter were "so emphatic that the negroes concluded to abandon their idea of leaving."

Legal and illegal efforts to restrict the mobility of labor in the South did not, of course, completely succeed; they only made it difficult. But the planter class did not require that every laborer be tied to his landlord, only that most, too frightened to leave, remain in order to preserve the low-wage, labor-intensive system of production. The most resourceful, energetic, and determined were always able to escape from their landlords and from the region, and more did so each year—but not because the planters made no effort to stop them. The typical departure occurred under cover of darkness, with family and neighbors sworn to secrecy. Large-scale black migrations from the South took place only twice between Reconstruction and the Depression: the "Kansas Fever" exodus of 1879–80 [a large migration of blacks to Kansas and other midwestern states] and the migration during World War I. Aside from these two movements, the migration rate from Southern states was significantly lower than that from other areas of the country, another measure of the success of repressive law and regional practice.

Freedpeople Working for Themselves

SHARON ANN HOLT

In early June of 1880, Mr. E. G. Butler stopped at the home of Thomas Sanford in Oxford, North Carolina. A thriving town of almost 1,400 people, Oxford was the seat of Granville County and the marketing center of a bustling trade in bright leaf tobacco. Butler's call was on business, his business as the county's federal census enumerator. In addition to his wife and children, Thomas Sanford included in the record of his household two servants, Ottawa Lee, a black man, and Nancy Lee, a mulatto woman. He guessed their ages to be about fifty and forty years respectively.

Several days later Butler unknowingly entered the home of those very same Lees and counted them a second time in his census tally. Speaking for themselves, Nancy and Ottawa Lee revealed rather different lives than Thomas Sanford had described. They noted that they were husband and wife, a connection not recorded in the first enumeration. Mr. Lee was thirty-six, not fifty, and Mrs. Lee was twenty-six, not forty. The couple shared their home with Mrs. Lee's widowed sister, Ann Norman, who worked as a washerwoman. And, while acknowledging that they were both domestic servants by trade, the Lees informed Butler that they also owned two acres of land, worth about $150.

Sharon Ann Holt, "Making Freedom Pay: Freedpeople Working for Themselves, North Carolina, 1865–1900," *Journal of Southern History*, LX, No. 2 (May 1994), pp. 229–62. The notes for this piece have been omitted.

The bureaucratic accident of double-counting has preserved two versions of the lives of Ottawa and Nancy Lee, and the differences between the two accounts are eloquent. The first enumeration includes only the portion of their lives that fell within Thomas Sanford's domain.... The Lees were residents of Sanford's home only part of the time; they also kept a household of their own, which they shared with a wage-earning sister. When the Lees were counted as dependents of Thomas Sanford, the structure of the enumeration highlighted a difference in their skin color and made their marriage invisible. The enumeration taken under their own roof recorded their marriage and failed to distinguish their color. Most important, in Sanford's household the Lees are listed only as servants, while in their own they appear both as servants and as landowners.

While Butler's mistake may have slightly distorted his population count, it actually brings economic reality sharply into focus. Butler's record reveals that the Lees lived two lives within one; while they worked as wage-earning servants in the Sanford household, they led another life as a family of small proprietors. Their economic livelihood encompassed not only wages from Thomas Sanford but also Ann Norman's earnings and the produce of a small family farm.

Freedpeople like the Lees generated resources for themselves from manifold activities within their households in arrangements that whites like Sanford scarcely knew existed. Major historical studies of the postbellum period have tended to reproduce the priorities of the census, bypassing evidence of small-scale household production and building their analyses of freedpeople's lives around the economic dependency associated with wage labor and various forms of tenancy....

It is not surprising that historians and economists have riveted on tenancy and left household production largely unstudied, because the significance of the household labor of freedpeople is far from obvious. Nothing about the activity in freedpeople's homes signals that this is labor that deserves special attention. Slaves, too, had raised chickens, hunted game, tended small food crops, and produced textiles, as had poor southern white farmers and, indeed, rural householders almost everywhere. What seems to distinguish freedpeople from both their enslaved parents and their white farming neighbors is their confinement in tenant farming, not their competence in household production. The very nature of household work further compounds the temptation to disregard it; most of the primary produce of the household economy is immediately consumed, making its tracks almost undetectable. Assuming that freedpeople's household work was as ephemeral in value as it was in substance, economic historians have seen the world largely as Thomas Sanford saw it—a place where freedpeople worked for whites, period.

Two aspects of the lives of freedpeople, however, combine to direct attention to the work they did for themselves in the household economy. The first is the postemancipation reduction in field labor, recorded in the countless complaints made to newspapers and government officials by frustrated southern labor managers unable to get a sufficiency of hands into the fields. The second is the achievement of the emancipated slaves in laying the foundation for black-controlled community life by establishing schools and churches and purchasing farms. That these developments occurred at the same time and that each was a direct result of emancipation raises several questions. Where had the "missing" labor gone? Whence came the resources to build these new communities? And could the household economy be the link between the two phenomena?

The household economy was one of two means that freedpeople used to generate resources. The other, most often, was some form of tenant farming, which, by the terms of their contracts with employers, demanded the weekday labor of adult males. The household economy was a miscellany of productive activities that consumed the days, nights, and weekends of every other member of the household and the after-hours labor of adult males. This two-sided economy was a complex structure that defies conventional characterizations.

The two parts of freedpeople's economic lives cannot properly be contrasted under such rubrics as *public* versus *private, cash* versus *non-cash*, or *women's work* versus *men's work*. Both household production and contract work were public in the sense that their existence was known and their merchandise was traded openly; trade in both sectors involved cash as well as goods; and women and men of both races participated in both domains. Nor can the two kinds of economic activity properly be designated *primary* and *secondary*, a hierarchy that replicates the landlord's perspective. Though the household economy produced much less in total value each year than contract work, it could hardly have been of secondary concern to freedpeople, since it was virtually their only source of discretionary income.

Moreover, the two types of work were more entangled than a hierarchical distinction suggests: household production coexisted with and was linked vitally to the structure of farm tenancy. Tenants gained access to houses and to land for gardens by contracting with planters. Planters, in turn, boosted their profits by keeping tenant shares low and rations short, leaving tenant families to sustain themselves through gardening and home manufacturing. Without a contract, moreover, freedpeople, and especially freedmen, risked harassment and arrest under vagrancy statutes. Contract-based farming for a landlord cleared the way socially, as well as providing the physical location, for the home-based economy to operate, while household production partially indemnified landlords against the disintegration of a severely exploited labor force.

The most meaningful distinction between home-based and contract-based production turns on differences of power and control. The surplus from the household economy was available to freedpeople to spend as they pleased, while the fruits of contract work were not—at once a modest and a momentous difference. Landlords controlled the way contract work was paid for, providing, in return for labor, fixed items, like the use of a house, regular allotments of food, and occasional clothing. Any wages due over and above the value of these allowances were generally paid by a note from the landlord, often good only for specific provisions and redeemable only at the local store. Tenants had to have houses, food, clothing, and store goods; contract work was valuable because it provided them. But because landlords controlled the timing, the substance, and the method of payment for contract work, freedpeople could only rarely use their contract wages for the independent work of community building. The rewards of household production, meager though they were, came to freedpeople directly. Such cash and produce, controlled by freedpeople themselves, could be applied to the creation of schools and churches and to the purchase of farms....

The term *household economy* does not describe a physical geography of production so much as a social and economic geography that reflects the flow of resources into and out of households. Conceptually, the freedpeople's household economy begins where landlord entitlement ends.

Household production included house-bound activities like manufacturing baskets, shoes, hats, and clothing for use or sale. Hauling, gardening, hunting, and foraging must also be reckoned within the household economy, though they took place outside the home itself. Moreover, to reveal fully the ways that households functioned as centers of resource production, the definition of the household economy must also include waged work by women, children, and the old, as well as after-hours or off-season wage-earning by men. Though wage-earning is conventionally considered the antithesis of household production, among the freedpeople wages functioned in precisely the same way as activities like truck farming or raising chickens. If wives and children earned wages, then they did so at the expense of other productive work for their families, and the proceeds of their outside labor were as a matter of course turned over to the family exchequer. Occasional wage-earning by all family members was one among many productive strategies that farm families exercised on their own behalf. Because wages flowed into the family and remained there for the family to control, wage-earning should be considered with, not apart from, other modes of home production.

Though household production was nested intimately within the structure of plantation economics, few planters or merchants recognized that it generated surpluses for tenants themselves. Their ignorance was no accident. Black tenants purposefully concealed their economic achievements from whites, and in this regard the small sale and perishability of household production served their purposes exactly. Household production was not lucrative enough to attract the attention of the landlords and merchants who directed the contract work of tenants.... The absence of white supervision, besides being a good in itself, allowed black households to conceal the extent of their independent activity and the degree of autonomy that it underwrote.

However common and personally gratifying freedpeople's modest independent income may have been, such small capital would remain of trifling historical importance except for its significant effect on the society beyond individual households. The impact of freedpeople's household production on community development depended not only on their small savings but also on their successful use of credit. Judicious use of certain kinds of credit made their small surpluses large enough to provide meaningful support to schools, churches, and family farms. Credit thus became an important bridge, though a rickety and dangerous one, between household production and community uplift.

Credit presented a different face to the freedpeople than it did to poor whites, though in fact property ownership, rather than race itself, was the decisive factor in shaping the meaning of credit. Since credit could boost the power of their meager household surpluses, freedpeople, and especially the landless, could approach credit as an opportunity for accumulation and advancement. Those, white or black, who already owned small farms tried to protect their hold on land and possessions by avoiding indebtedness. They mobilized household production less to accumulate new goods than to prevent staple crop production and market relations (including credit) from overwhelming their relative self-sufficiency. In short, the propertied of both races saw loss and entanglement in credit, while the propertyless saw a potential opportunity. Analysis of how the freedpeople borrowed, therefore, ties the small-scale operations of the household economy to credit and land distribution, the large shaping forces of the postbellum economy.

Household production by freedpeople, then, was neither the miscellany of meaningless chores it seems at first glance nor a romantic routine of friendly barter in quilts and cheese. It was a major enterprise on a minor scale, providing crucial evidence of what freedpeople did for themselves, and of how their goals and efforts shaped the economic life of the South as a whole. The former slaves found in the home economy a productive venture that could help them—at the margins—not only to cope with but also to alter the conditions of their lives. Household production soaked up the labor that former masters longed to see in the fields, and it provided the fuel to develop and fulfill the individual and community aspirations of the emancipated slaves....

Labor power was the freedpeople's greatest resource, and home-based production allowed them to employ everyone in the household to the fullest extent. Household production occupied the very young and the very old as well as employing adults in their prime; disabled members made significant contributions alongside the more able-bodied. Freedpeople drew on productive skills that they had developed as slaves as well as on the new opportunities that freedom made possible. As they had under slavery, families gardened and foraged, they chopped and hauled, they spun and sewed, and they saved by doing without. Freedom offered the chance to earn wages, to send members off to seek distant, seasonal employment, and to raise and sell staple crops on their own behalf.

Each person's particular contribution was conditioned by age, gender, overall ability, and immediate need. Children contributed heavily to work around the house. If they were not watching infant siblings, young children might carry water to workers in the fields, forage for and trade berries and wild eggs, tend the family garden, or collect kindling. Joseph Adams, farming in Goldsborough, North Carolina, in the 1870s, speculated that his garden vegetables—probably raised by his children—might have enabled him to save three or four dollars each month. Adams does not say who took care of the family garden, but he does note that his wife cooked out for a local family and that he himself had only half of every other Saturday off, during which time he tended a patch of cotton and corn. With both adults working away from the home, it seems likely that it was the children who brought the family fresh vegetables. Children might also card cotton, piece quilts, and help their mother or an older sister wind yarn. In the mid-1870s, nine-year-old Elizabeth Johnson stayed up late helping her grandmother make quilts and rose early to hawk produce from her grandfather's garden. Children were available to run errands into town or carry messages to neighbors. Children contributed to millinery, draying, and other income-producing enterprises; through their foraging, which they often combined with play, they also provided food for the family table.

As they grew older, boys might begin to hunt and fish with their fathers, or help with wood cutting or hauling for pay if the family owned a wagon. William Scott recalled that "when we farmed share cr[o]p dey took all we made. In de fall we would have to split cord wood to live through de winter." Girls, too, sometimes hunted or hauled; more often, they did domestic work. They might sew dresses, apply ribbons to hats, weave baskets, or candle eggs until well past dark. Most of these tasks continued as children grew. After about age ten, field labor was added to the list. As an alternative to farm labor, older girls might go out to work in the homes of nearby whites. Older boys, if fortunate, might learn a trade; more often they, too, chose between domestic service and farm labor.

If young household members worked hard, so did the elder ones. Age and infirmity by themselves rarely ended a person's working life. Sarah Louise Augustus reported that her grandmother, a former slave named Sarah McDonald, worked until her death of pneumonia at age 110. The elder Sarah was, by her granddaughter's account, an accomplished and experienced nurse. At 110 years of age, she commuted about sixty miles by train between her home in Fayetteville, North Carolina, and a nursing job for a family in Raleigh. When she missed a connecting train one rainy night, she sat in the station all night in wet clothing, took sick the next day, and died. Sarah McDonald's story was echoed in the reports of other former slaves who worked for wages into their nineties and beyond....

Activities performed inside the home did not exhaust a family's productive capacity. While children and elders worked in or around the house as much as possible, adults in their prime ventured farther afield to earn wages and grow staple crops. James E. O'Hara, a prominent Edgecombe County black man who served in the United States Congress from 1883 to 1887, counted "three or four hundred colored men" heading south each spring to work until fall in the turpentine fields, presumably leaving their families behind to tend the crops. Margaret Thornton, a former slave raised in Harnett County, North Carolina, earned wages year-round as a nurse and laundress, despite her husband's protests. Five years old at emancipation, she explained, "I wus brung up ter nurse an' I'se did my share of dat.... I has nursed 'bout two thousand babies I reckins. I has nursed gran'maws an' den dere gran'chiles." Her account suggests that her mother may also have nursed and passed on the skill to Margaret. Mrs. Thornton commented on the relationship of her nursing to the income of her whole family: "Tom [her husband] never did want me ter work hard while he wus able ter work, but I nursed babies off an' on all de time he lived[.] When he wus in his death sickness he uster cry case I had ter take in washin'. Since he's daid I nurses mostly, but sometimes I ain't able ter do nothin'." Despite her husband's wish to support the family by his own work, the Thorntons found it necessary for

Margaret to earn as well. This arrangement may have been more satisfactory to Margaret Thornton than to Tom. Her work clearly created a network of connections that spanned several generations in satisfied families. Those families may even have helped her support herself or provided charity to her after her husband's death.

Harvest time brought the highest wage rates of any part of the year, offering a bonanza to families who could send family members into the fields to pick.... With laborers' wages around ten dollars per month, these harvest earnings [$6-$11] represented a genuine windfall. Wage-earning, like the rest of household production, could be year-round or occasional, and there were opportunities for men and women alike. Each household evaluated its needs and skills in an effort to formulate at least an adequate, if not an optimal, mix of productive activities.

Besides earning wages picking other people's crops, freedpeople also grew staples on a small scale for themselves. Joseph Adams, whose family had a vegetable garden and whose wife cooked for a local family, tended a "patch" of cotton in addition to his tenant field. Mattie Curtis grew cotton in Franklin County, North Carolina. She supported her family with the proceeds of her cotton crops and eventually bought and cleared fifteen acres. Curtis anticipated hostility toward her success, however, which made her wary; when she carried her first bale to town and failed to locate the cotton market, she gave up and went home rather than ask directions, fearing to reveal that the cotton, and the income it would produce, belonged solely to her....

Awareness of how the freedpeople's household economy worked leads almost ineluctably to a further question: how did freedpeople use the resources they amassed? Household production can be considered critical to the advancement of freedpeople only if the resources developed within it did more than meet a family's basic needs for food and shelter. There is evidence that fulfillment of the desires that animated the freedpeople after emancipation—for religious autonomy, for literacy, and for farms of their own—depended heavily on household production. Freedpeople did indeed use resources drawn from the household economy to staff, house, and endow their churches; to build, equip, and sustain primary schools; and to purchase, pay taxes on, and sustain their farms.

Before emancipation, some communities of slaves had been able to create independent, often clandestine, religious institutions, and one of their first projects as freedpeople was to bring those assemblies out of hiding. Congregations commonly began by building a rudimentary sanctuary for worship along with a Sabbath school for educating both children and adults. Deeds recorded in Granville County indicate that black congregations often paid market price or higher for the plots they bought for their churches. New Corinth Baptist Church purchased its one-acre lot from a member for ten dollars, about the price of an acre of good farmland. The trustees of Flat Creek Baptist Church paid twenty-five dollars for their one-acre building site. Blue Wing Grove Church, an exception to the pattern, acquired one acre for one dollar from two members, C. A. and Louisa B. Tuck, "in consideration of [their] love and respect for religious and educational advantages." In Promised Land, South Carolina, Elizabeth Rauh Bethel records that "in 1875 James Fields [freedman and local community leader] sold one acre of his land to the Mt. Zion African Methodist Episcopal Trustees for forty dollars. In 1882 Wells Gray [another leading citizen of the town] sold two acres of his land to the Crossroads Baptist Church Board of Deacons for thirty-two dollars."...

Freedpeople built and rebuilt their churches several times as the size and means of congregations expanded. The congregation of Huntsville Baptist Church, another Granville County institution, began meeting in a brush arbor in the 1830s and then built a log church after emancipation; the log structure was replaced in turn by a clapboard building. Finally, in the 1920s, the congregation built the sturdy brick sanctuary that stands today. St. Paul's AME church in Rockingham County, North Carolina, kept a record of one of its building-fund drives, and the record illustrates the importance of small contributions from the congregation in the repeated building and rebuilding of a sanctuary. The members of St. Paul's had built their first edifice in 1878, and probably another one after that. In 1909 church members set out once again to raise funds to build a new sanctuary. The ledger kept during that fund drive indicates that the drive lasted nearly a year and a half and raised somewhat less than $100, mostly in pledges from church members of one, two, and five dollars. The ledger also records contributions from churchwomen of money and of apples, oranges, and cakes, the food designed presumably for a fund-raising dinner. Some of the revenue came from a species of beauty contest wherein the young woman who collected the most cash in tribute to her beauty was declared the winner, and all proceeds went to the building fund. With that money, supplemented by donations of labor, wood, and homemade vestments, the congregation ultimately assembled a small, clapboard church with a bell tower. It stood until 1987, when the abandoned structure finally collapsed in a storm.

Efforts like those made at Huntsville Baptist and St. Paul's AME were repeated across the postbellum South as black congregations built and rebuilt their sanctuaries, expanding and upgrading them as the means of the assembly would permit. Fund-raising was a permanent aspect of church life; when the money was not required for building, the collections underwrote salaries, bought supplies, and provided charity. Each contribution was small, and indeed, the total was small—it was enough largely because it had to be. Church members' households could not produce any more.

As much as freedpeople helped their churches, they did even more for their schools. Freedpeople's schools and churches, at first, were often one and the same. The minister and his family might be the only literate members of a rural black community, and they were expected to teach as well as preach. Moreover, one-half to two-thirds of all pupils reported to be in school between 1866 and 1870 attended Sabbath schools rather than day or night schools.

Much was expected of schooling in the postbellum South, by both freedfolk and philanthropists, and perhaps for that reason school development is the most thoroughly documented private effort of the period. Many instances of critical support provided by the freedpeople are in the records; however, the importance of their work for schools has received scant attention. To support missionary schools, freedpeople paid tuition, purchased lots, and built school buildings, though often of the most rough-and-ready sort. They paid, housed, and fed missionary teachers, and they raised or contributed funds for such essentials as books, slates, maps, and heating stoves. Older students helped in the overcrowded classrooms by serving as assistant teachers, hearing the recitations of pupils just inferior to themselves in skill. Alongside the schooling sponsored on their behalf by missionaries, white churches, and northern philanthropists, freedpeople ran their own schools, independent of assistance.

The Freedmen's Bureau sent John W. Alvord, the bureau's newly appointed school superintendent, on a fact-finding tour of the defeated Confederacy in the summer of 1865. Only months after emancipation and a year or more before northern teachers arrived in force, Alvord estimated that over 500 black-run schools were already in operation. This number grew, and in his second report, dated July 1866, Alvord noted to his superior that "we estimated in January [1866] that the entire educational census of the bureau was 125,000 pupils. We now, with increased means of information and greater assurance of certainty, estimate that, beyond the 90,778 pupils as officially reported, there are, including the above irregular and Sabbath schools, with colored soldiers and individuals who are learning at home, one hundred and fifty thousand (150,000) freedmen and their children [studying their books]." Many independent schools continued to operate long after missionary teachers had arrived, especially in remote areas where it was too dangerous for northerners to venture. As late as 1869, when the missionaries had been active in the field for several years, James W. Hood, North Carolina's State Superintendent of Colored Schools, found that 41 percent of the state's black pupils were being taught in private, independent schools.... A number of so-called missionary or Freedmen's Bureau schools were in fact independent schools that the philanthropic societies simply absorbed.... Freedpeople in Warrenton wrote to officers of the AMA, offering to pay a teacher $10 a month, provide a home and schoolhouse, and fill the school with eighty to ninety scholars. AMA teacher David Dickson reported from outside Fayetteville, North Carolina, that "the building which we have for schools is now rented and we have collected $26.50 for rent, wood, &c this month." In Fayetteville proper, freedpeople had purchased a lot for $140, built a school with $3,800 from the freedmen's Bureau and the AMA, furnished the building with another $400 gift, and funded $200 worth of improvements out of their own pockets.

Freedpeople's support did not end once a school had opened; it was used to provide food, firewood, and funds to further the work of the teachers.... Freedpeople also worked to reconstruct and refine the drafty, ramshackle school buildings in which AMA teachers met their classes. In Beaufort during the winter of 1866, "the thrifty portion" of the local community pledged $212 and the time of their best carpenters to erect a solid, draft-free building. In Smithville the teacher collected $22.50 from the pupils, most of which was spent on a stove, with a bit left over to purchase books and slates. David Dickson's pupils outside Fayetteville paid for "fuel, lights, and books" and offered to pay for an assistant if Dickson required one.

As late as 1876, four years after the opening of public schools in North Carolina, freedpeople continued to subsidize the education supposedly provided to them by the state. In Raleigh, parents pledged to pay ten cents a week to keep the local school open after state appropriations ran out. Another AMA school in Raleigh, which met in the sanctuary of Long Church, reported a successful "exhibition and concert on Thursday ... for the purpose of raising some money to pay for repairs of church." Besides repairing their sanctuary/schoolroom, the pupils at Long Church routinely contributed "about enough for light and fuel." Indeed, the contributions continued for at least a generation. In the early twentieth century, 7 percent of black schoolchildren still met in crude log schoolhouses and 44 percent of them were still sitting on homemade benches.

To speak of the work of missionary, Freedmen's Bureau, or even public schools in the South after the war without explicit acknowledgment of freedpeople's own contributions obscures the commitment and resourcefulness of the many black communities that created and sustained these schools. The very first schools were already joint enterprises, not gifts, and long after schooling officially became the responsibility of state governments, black schools continued to draw deeply at the well of their [pupils'] resources. The support offered to the schools—labor, firewood, food, and bits of cash—[was] precisely the type of goods most readily generated within the household economy.

Building and supporting their churches and schools did not exhaust the freedpeople's means nor fulfill all their dreams. There was still the hope of owning a farm, a dream long cherished and suddenly, thanks to freedom, just barely within reach. When freedmen all over the South met in conventions in 1865 and 1866 to draft memorials to their state constitutional conventions, the liberty to worship, the opportunity to learn, and a legal guarantee of equal rights stood at the top of their lists of desiderata. Right behind, and in their minds necessary to all the rest, was protection of their right to own property. Freedpeople wanted farms of their own, believing that farm ownership was essential to their long-term prosperity. As hope for the redistribution of Confederate properties receded, freedpeople began acquiring land directly. Household production played as crucial a role, though a different one, in this process as it did in the support of churches and schools. The proceeds of household production alone were too small to purchase farm acreage, but borrowing could make the proceeds larger. Freedpeople's savings became seed money in the risky business of southern credit, with home production as a kind of mortgage insurance. The mixture of household production and credit, with an occasional stroke of good luck, could help a family gain and keep a farm....

Freedpeople found their opening not in the widely used and justly reviled annual crop lien but in a less rigid instrument, the short-term chattel mortgage. Chattel mortgages were by no means free of risk, since creditors usually demanded collateral worth much more than the loan amount. Just as store owners built their high interest rates into the prices of their wares, so creditors built their risk calculations into the amount of collateral that they demanded. However, for any individual black farmer making the choice between the high cost of lien-based credit and the high cost of chattel-based credit, the chattels held one important advantage. Chattel mortgages were much more flexible than annual liens in time, terms, and collateral.... Under a chattel mortgage, the period of borrowing could be as short as a week or a month, and lenders accepted livestock, farm equipment, and household goods as collateral in addition to crops. Chattel mortgages, in other words, allowed freedpeople to borrow against home production, which they could control, rather than against future crops, which they could not. Though freedpeople commonly used the annual lien to support their planting and harvesting operations, the rest of their economic lives, including buying and selling land, equipment, and livestock, depended upon the credit available through chattel mortgages. The flexible terms of chattel mortgage credit played to the strengths of the household economy, making household production essential to the successful manipulation of chattel loans. At the price of some risk, small infusions of credit greased the slow machinery of accumulation, while the value of goods produced in the household helped indemnify the family against possible loss.

Those who sought to buy land had first to acquire mortgageable goods. The need for and terms of chattel mortgage credit tended to oblige freedpeople to follow a common pattern of accumulation of goods preceding land purchase, and this pattern can be discerned in census and tax records. Families usually began with the acquisition of chickens, which were the cheapest livestock available and the only farm animals not subject to taxation. Chickens provided eggs, meat, and feathers, all goods that could be sold, traded, or consumed in place of store-bought goods. Properly managed, chickens could rather quickly generate the dollar or two needed to purchase a pair of pigs. Like chickens, pigs were directly productive, representing both pork and piglets. With good fortune, pigs and chickens together might soon underwrite the purchase of a cow, which represented the first major threshold of accumulation. John O. Kelly, a freedman from Raleigh, explained the link between owning a cow and escaping tenancy to the Senate investigating committee in 1879. "There are not many who are going to live but if they have got a cow and such things as that." Kelly assured the senators that "they will do business for themselves." Any family able to save enough to buy a cow would be tempted to try to purchase an acre of land and move off the tenant farm....

In the complex economic life of North Carolina's freedpeople, all signs point to the center, to the household as a critical turbine of production. Operating from within their own households, freedpeople tried every kind of productive activity that might generate resources they could use, from humble efforts to raise potatoes to extensive and carefully organized forays into staple crop agriculture. They fought for control over their own labor, limiting the claims of landlords to the time of women and children and fighting off their landlords' attempts to fasten extra work on adult males. The resources they scratched together in this variegated process became the seeds of larger communal endeavors as well as the foundation of private family hopes. Schools were kept open and teachers supported with food, wages, stoves, and supplies by the families of their pupils. Churches were respectably housed and Sunday schools provided with books and slates because the community dug into its pockets to provide. For a family seeking a farm on which to stake its future, the care and management of chickens, pigs, cows, and credit became the milestones on their road. Moreover, because household production was by its very nature modest in scale and unremarkable in content, these projects could proceed right under the collective nose of a society that was openly hostile to black aspirations. Within the restrictions imposed by tenancy, poverty, and persecution, freedpeople found ways to shape their own future. Household production provided what the freedpeople required—a way to accumulate a surplus, a way to push desperation just far enough away from the door to make room for hope, to provide reasons for effort, and to deliver the resources needed for the uplift of the community.

FURTHER READING

Charles S. Aiken, *The Cotton Plantation South since the Civil War* (1998).

Armando C. Alonzo, *Tejano Legacy: Rancheros and Settlers in South Texas, 1734–1900* (1997).

Pete Daniel, *The Shadow of Slavery: Peonage in the South, 1901–1969* (1972).

Ronald L. F. Davis, *Good and Faithful Labor: From Slavery to Sharecropping in the Natchez District, 1880–1890* (1982).

Stephen J. DeCanio, *Agriculture in the Postbellum South: The Economics of Production and Supply* (1974).

Charles L. Flynn Jr., *White Land, Black Labor: Caste and Class in Late Nineteenth-Century Georgia* (1983).

Eric Foner, *Nothing but Freedom: Emancipation and its Legacy* (1983).

Thavolia Glymph and John J. Kushma, eds., *Essays on the Postbellum Southern Economy* (1985).

Robert Higgs, *Competition and Coercion: Blacks in the American Economy* (1977).

Sharon Ann Holt, *Making Freedom Pay: North Carolina Freedpeople Working for Themselves, 1865–1900* (2000).

Samuel C. Hyde, ed., *Plain Folk of the South Revisited* (1997).

Gerald D. Jaynes, *Branches without Roots: Genesis of the Black Working Class in the American South, 1862–1882* (1986).

Jacqueline Jones, *Labor of Love, Labor of Sorrow: Black Women, Work, and the Family from Slavery to the Present* (1985).

Jay Mandle, *Not Slave, Not Free: The African American Economic Experience since the Civil War* (1992).

———, *The Roots of Black Poverty: The Southern Plantation Economy after the Civil War* (1978).

Daniel A. Novak, *The Wheel of Servitude: Black Forced Labor after Slavery* (1978).

William Alexander Percy, *Lanterns on the Levee: Recollections of a Planter's Son* (1941).

Peter J. Rachleff, *Black Labor in the South: Richmond, Virginia, 1865–1890* (1984).

Roger L. Ransom and Richard Sutch, *One Kind of Freedom: The Economic Consequences of Emancipation* (1977).

Lawrence D. Rice, *The Negro in Texas, 1874–1900* (1967).

Theodore Rosengarten, *All God's Dangers: The Life of Nate Shaw* (1974).

Edward Royce, *The Origins of Southern Sharecropping* (1993).

Thad Sitton and Dan K. Utley, *From Can See to Can't: Texas Cotton Farmers on the Southern Prairies* (1997).

Michael Wayne, *The Reshaping of Plantation Society: The Natchez District, 1860–1880* (1983).

Kyle G. Wilkison, *Yeomen, Sharecroppers, and Socialists: Plain Folk Protest in Texas, 1870–1914* (2009).

Harold Woodman, *King Cotton and His Retainers: Financing & Marketing the Cotton Crop of the South, 1800–1925* (1968).

Gavin Wright, *Old South, New South: Revolutions in the Southern Economy since the Civil War* (1986).

———, *The Political Economy of the Cotton South: Households, Markets, and Wealth in the Nineteenth Century* (1978).

CHAPTER 4

Mills, Workers, and the Myth of a New South

After the Civil War, southern leaders publicly recognized the need for what they had formerly foresworn: industry in the South. Following Reconstruction a vision appeared of a New South invigorated by industrial and economic progress. Advocates of this New South, such as Henry W. Grady, managing editor for the Atlanta Constitution, *urged southerners to change their traditional ways and imitate the victorious Yankees in habits of thrift, labor, and industry.*

By 1900 the South had apparently changed. A southern textile industry, replete with factories and mill villages, had reached sizable proportions in the Piedmont of Virginia, the Carolinas, Georgia, and Alabama. Nearly 100,000 men, women, and children worked at below national average wages to turn out mostly cotton and some wool cloth, hosiery, thread, and bagging. Southern boosters thought of the cotton mill movement as a crusade that would revolutionize the region's economy and bring about a true New South. Grady, for example, sought praise from the nation's leading businessmen and confidently awaited "the verdict of the world." Broadus Mitchell recalled that when mills opened, investors took great risks, but they gave employment to the "necessitous masses of poor whites." The early mills were touted as philanthropic entities, offering work to yeomen families whose marginal farms yielded few profits and whose children faced an insecure future. Mill owners and capitalists, Mitchell argued, had succeeded in bringing a great "moral movement to help the lower classes" that would increase the productivity of the plain folk, advance the region, and become the symbol of the New South. It was true that textile mills in the Piedmont area of the South grew exponentially. In 1890 the total number of spindles reached nearly 4 million, the workers nearly 100,000, and the number of bales used to make cloth nearly 1.5 million. By 1900 there were 400 mills in operation, and by 1910 southern mills outnumbered those in northern states. In the early years, the investment dividends were high (investors earned between 18 and 25 percent a year), but workers' wages were extremely low, averaging about 12 cents a day for 9 to 12 hours of labor.

Other industries also attracted workers, although salaries were low and conditions dangerous: Coal mining in Appalachia and in northern Alabama accompanied the development of iron and steel plants. South-wide railroads, lumber and logcutting operations, and cigarette and chewing tobacco companies expanded. Finally, after 1901 the discovery of huge oil reserves in Texas brought wildcatters, roughnecks, and eventually national oil companies to the South, making Houston the region's largest city.

Had southerners changed along with increasing industrialization? New South advocates promised a better life for industrial workers. Was it better? Who benefited from this New South—factory owners, investors, farmers, workers, labor unions? How did mill workers respond to the "habits of industry" imposed on them by factory owners? How were race and gender relations affected during this period of industrial growth? How were labor grievances settled? And finally, what role did politics play in the lives of the mill workers?

DOCUMENTS

One of the foremost exponents of the New South was Atlanta newspaper editor Henry W. Grady who spoke before northern audiences and boasted that in the aftermath of the war the South was changing. Northerners, he said, could trust southern capitalists with loans and purchase orders and could rely on its social policies, especially regarding African Americans. The excerpts from two of Grady's speeches in Document 1 cover some of his major ideas and suggest the tone of the New South myth (of a prosperous industrialized region). The notion that enthusiasm for textile development grew into a public-spirited, community movement was enshrined in the historical writings of Broadus Mitchell, seen here in Document 2. Those who worked in the South's factories, however, had a different view of their benefits. When asked about their conditions by a North Carolina state agency, the Bureau of Labor Statistics, mill workers identified many areas of dissatisfaction, noted in Document 3. Hopes for industrial prosperity animated Warren C. Coleman, a black entrepreneur. In Document 4, he calls on others of his race to support his plans for a cotton mill run by African Americans. In Document 5, photographer Lewis W. Hine, a progressive reformer who despised child labor and worked for the National Child Labor Committee, sometimes disguised himself to gain entry to mills and photograph children at work. In the first image, Hine photographed a girl who looked to be about six years old and noted, "A little spinner in the Mollahan Mills, Newberry, S.C. She was tending her 'sides' like a veteran, but after I took the photo, the overseer came up and said in an apologetic tone that was pathetic, 'She just happened in.' Then a moment later he repeated the information. The mills appear to be full of youngsters that 'just happened in,' or 'are helping sister.' Dec. 3, 08." Hine notes on the second photograph taken at Bibb Mill No. 1, Macon, Georgia, "Many youngsters here. Some boys were so small they had to climb up on the spinning frame to mend the broken threads and put back the empty bobbins." Bertha Miller of Thomasville, in North Carolina (Document 6), describes her upbringing on a farm and her transition to mill factory work at the young age of 11. Note the realities of mill work for young women before 1915. Document 7, a map of the textile mills in the Piedmont and Alabama, shows the greatest concentration of mills in North Carolina and indicates the importance of the industry to the southeastern states.

1. Henry W. Grady Boasts about the New South, 1886, 1889

From Speech Before Boston's Bay State Club, 1889

I attended a funeral once in Pickens county in my State.... This funeral was peculiarly sad. It was a poor "one gallus" fellow, whose breeches struck him under the armpits and hit him at the other end about the knee—he didn't believe in *decollete* clothes. They buried him in the midst of a marble quarry: they cut through solid marble to make his grave; and yet a little tombstone they put above him was from Vermont. They buried him in the heart of a pine forest, and yet the pine coffin was imported from Cincinnati. They buried him within touch of an iron mine, and yet the nails in his coffin and the iron in the shovel that dug his grave were imported from Pittsburg. They buried him by the side of the best sheep-grazing country on the earth, and yet the wool in the coffin bands and the coffin bands themselves were brought from the North. The South didn't furnish a thing on earth for that funeral but the corpse and the hole in the ground. There they put him away and the clods rattled down on his coffin, and they buried him in a New York coat and a Boston pair of shoes and a pair of breeches from Chicago and a shirt from Cincinnati, leaving him nothing to carry into the next world with him to remind him of the country in which he lived, and for which he fought for four years, but the chill of blood in his veins and the marrow in his bones.

Now we have improved on that. We have got the biggest marble-cutting establishment on earth within a hundred yards of that grave. We have got a half-dozen woolen mills right around it, and iron mines, and iron furnaces, and iron factories. We are coming to meet you. We are going to take a noble revenge, as my friend, Mr. Carnegie, said last night, by invading every inch of your territory with iron, as you invaded ours twenty-nine years ago.

From Grady's Speech, "The New South," Delivered to the New England Club in New York, 1886

We have established thrift in city and country. We have fallen in love with work. We have restored comfort to homes from which culture and elegance never departed. We have let economy take root and spread among us as rank as the crabgrass which sprung from Sherman's cavalry camps, until we are ready to lay odds on the Georgia Yankee as he manufactures relics of the battlefield in

---

These speeches can be found in Joel Chandler Harris' *Life of Henry W. Grady* (New York: Cassel Publishing Company, 1890).

a one-story shanty and squeezes pure olive oil out of his cotton seed, against any down-easter that ever swapped wooden nutmegs for flannel sausage in the valleys of Vermont. Above all, we know that we have achieved in these "piping times of peace" a fuller independence for the South than that which our fathers sought to win in the forum by their eloquence or compel in the field by their swords.

It is a rare privilege, sir, to have had part, however humble, in this work. Never was nobler duty confided to human hands than the uplifting and upbuilding of the prostrate and bleeding South—misguided, perhaps, but beautiful in her suffering, and honest, brave and generous always. In the record of her social, industrial and political illustration we await with confidence the verdict of the world.

But what of the negro? Have we solved the problem he presents or progressed in honor and equity toward solution? Let the record speak to the point. No section shows a more prosperous laboring population than the negroes of the South, none in fuller sympathy with the employing and land-owning class. He shares our school fund, has the fullest protection of our laws and the friendship of our people. Self-interest, as well as honor, demand that he should have this. Our future, our very existence depend upon our working out this problem in full and exact justice. We understand that when Lincoln signed the emancipation proclamation, your victory was assured, for he then committed you to the cause of human liberty, against which the arms of man cannot prevail—while those of our statesmen who trusted to make slavery the corner-stone of the Confederacy doomed us to defeat as far as they could, committing us to a cause that reason could not defend or the sword maintain in sight of advancing civilization.

Had Mr. Toombs said, which he did not say, "that he would call the roll of his slaves at the foot of Bunker Hill," he would have been foolish, for he might have known that whenever slavery became entangled in war it must perish, and that the chattel in human flesh ended forever in New England when your fathers—not to be blamed for parting with what didn't pay—sold their slaves to our fathers—not to be praised for knowing a paying thing when they saw it. The relations of the southern people with the negro are close and cordial. We remember with what fidelity for four years he guarded our defenseless women and children, whose husbands and fathers were fighting against his freedom. To his eternal credit be it said that whenever he struck a blow for his own liberty he fought in open battle, and when at last he raised his black and humble hands that the shackles might be struck off, those hands were innocent of wrong against his helpless charges, and worthy to be taken in loving grasp by every man who honors loyalty and devotion. Ruffians have maltreated him, rascals have misled him, philanthropists established a bank for him, but the South, with the North, protests against injustice to this simple and sincere people. To liberty and enfranchisement is as far as law can carry the negro. The rest must be left to conscience and common sense. It must be left to those among whom his lot is cast, with whom he is indissolubly connected, and whose prosperity depends upon their possessing his intelligent sympathy and confidence. Faith has been kept with him, in spite of calumnious assertions to the contrary by those who assume to speak for us or by frank opponents. Faith will be kept with him in the future, if the South holds her reason and integrity....

The old South rested everything on slavery and agriculture, unconscious that these could neither give nor maintain healthy growth. The new South presents a perfect democracy, the oligarchs leading in the popular movement—a social system compact and closely knitted, less splendid on the surface, but stronger at the core—a hundred farms for every plantation, fifty homes for every palace—and a diversified industry that meets the complex need of this complex age.

The new South is enamored of her new work. Her soul is stirred with the breath of a new life. The light of a grander day is falling fair on her face. She is thrilling with the consciousness of growing power and prosperity. As she stands upright, full-statured and equal among the people of the earth, breathing the keen air and looking out upon the expanded horizon, she understands that her emancipation came because through the inscrutable wisdom of God her honest purpose was crossed, and her brave armies were beaten.

2. Broadus Mitchell Explains the Myth of the "Cotton Mill Campaign," 1921

Notices of ceremonies held when a mill commenced operation convey sometimes touchingly the pride of a community in the plant and the public character of the enterprise. Townspeople were like children with a very precious new toy; newspapers described the arrangement of the machinery in the factory with the keenest interest.

The potency of associative effort, so marked in Southern cotton mill building in this period, overcame timidity that might have been prompted by a frank and individual canvass of attending economic facilities. "The mill at Albemarle, North Carolina, had its origin in the desire of the Efirds to have a mill at the town. Whether there existed real advantages or not, the people would make it appear that there were advantages for that particular location. Many mills were located at places where there was the spirit for them, rather than where they would be, economically, most successful." A Marylander knowing the industry thoroughly said there was little community interest in his State, but that "down South the community interest was very strong. Every little town wanted a mill. If it couldn't get a big one, it would take a small one; if not a sheeting, then a spinning mill."

Broadus Mitchell, *The Rise of Cotton Mills in the South*, pp. 129–132; 134–135.

"A good deal of patriotism developed," said a not impressionable mill man, "and every town would vie with others in building mills. Some people took stock and sold it at a discount when it was apparent that the mill would be operated. They were willing to give so much to secure the mill for the town." There is no stronger indication of the different spirit characterizing the building of mills in the eighties as contrasted with earlier periods than the fact that after 1880 many plants were located within the corporate limits of towns and cities. In the earlier enterprises community spirit had not counted, and even the mills of the seventies, such as Piedmont, were taken to the water powers. Eager discussion as to the comparative advantages of water and steam power marked this transition. From being an excuse for the town, the cotton mill came to be erected to invigorate a place that was languishing. It has been said that at least half the South Carolina mills were community enterprises. Later, when the commercial spirit was more pronounced, factories were built just outside the corporation to escape town taxes.

In the case of some investors with whom assistance to the town was an indirect motive, the creation of a payroll, putting more money in circulation, was the causal stimulus. An editorial recommended the Charleston Manufacturing Company "as a means of enlarging the common income.... The employment given to hundreds of persons ... will increase the value of house-property at once. They who earn nothing can't spend much. It was calculated last year that every $228 invested in cotton manufactures in South Carolina supported one person.... It is evident that the building of half-a-dozen cotton factories would revolutionize Charleston. Two or three million dollars additional poured annually into the pockets of the shopkeepers ... would make them think that the commercial millennium had come.

To give employment to the necessitous masses of poor whites, for the sake of the people themselves, was an object animating the minds of many mill builders. One does not have to go outside the ranks of cotton manufacturers to find denials of this, but a study of the facts shows how frequent and normal was the philanthropic incentive....

No undertaking was born more emphatically in the impulse to furnish work than the Salisbury Cotton Mills. All the circumstances of the founding of this factory were singularly in keeping with the philanthropic prompting. The town of Salisbury, North Carolina, in 1887 had done nothing to recover from the war. It was full of saloons, wretched, unkempt. It happened that an evangelistic campaign was conducted; Mr. Pearson, remembered as a lean, intense Tennesseean, preached powerfully. A tabernacle was erected for the meeting, which lasted a month and, being undenominational, drew from the whole town and countryside. The evangelist declared that the great morality in Salisbury was to go to work, and that corruption, idleness and misery could not be dispelled until the poor people were given an opportunity to become productive. The establishment of a cotton mill would be the most Christian act his hearers could perform. "He gave Salisbury a moral dredging which made the people feel their responsibilities as they had not before, and made them do something for these folks. There had been little talk of manufacturing before Pearson came; there had been some tobacco factories in the town, but they had failed. The Salisbury Cotton Mills grew out of a moral movement to help the lower classes, largely inspired by this campaign. Without the moral issue, the financial interest would have come out in the long run, but the moral considerations brought the matter to a focus."

3. Mill Workers Comment on the New South, 1887, 1889

Superintendent Cotton Mill—Ten hours are enough for a day's work, where children are worked from twelve years old and up, and I think the mills of this section are willing to it, if all would adopt it. I think there should be a law making all run 60 hours per week, and compelling parents to send their children to school. I work 11½ hours per day, at $75 per month. Have four in family and one at school. Live in my own house.

Employee—There are about 225 to 250 hands engaged at different classes of work in this mill, about 100 of them children—many of them very small children, under 12 years of age. Wages are about as good here as at any mill in the State and I think better than at many of them, the only trouble about wages is that they are not paid in cash—trade checks are issued with which employees are expected to buy what they need at the company's store, which is not right. The same system is practised I am told, at the most of the cotton mills in the State, but that does not make it right and just. The tobacco factories in this town pay the cash every week. Any man who has ever tried it knows there is a great difference in buying with cash. This, with the long hours required for a day's work, (12 hours) is the only cause for complaint; the officers are kind and close attention to work and sobriety and morality is required of all who work here.

Employee—I work in the cotton mills. They employ men, women and children—many children who are too small to work, they should be at school; the parents are more to blame than are the mill-owners. The hands in the mills in this section are doing very well, and if they only received their pay weekly in cash instead of "trade checks," and store accounts they would not complain if they were paid in cash and were allowed to buy for cash where they pleased, it would be much better. Ten hours are enough for a day's work. I believe the mills here would be willing to it if there was a law making all conform to it. I believe compulsory education would be a benefit too.

Employee—This mill runs day and night. The day hands commence work at 6 o'clock in the morning and run tell 7 o'clock at night. They stop at 12 o'clock for dinner and ring the bell at 12:30 o'clock. I contend that the hands are in actual motion 13 hours per day. The trade check system is used here, and is not as good as cash, at this place nor any other place. If the hands trade their checks to any other firm, and they present them for cash, this firm demands a discount of 10 per cent. The best trade check used in this county is not worth over 75 per cent. Some of the checks used in this county are almost worthless. This long-hour system is destroying the health of all the young women who

---

This document can be found in the First Annual Report of the Bureau of Labor Statistics of the State of North Carolina, W. N. Jones, Commissioner, 1887, and the Third Annual Report of the Bureau of Labor Statistics of the State of North Carolina, John C. Scarborough, Commissioner, 1889.

work in the mills. The employment of children in the mills at low wages keeps a great many men out of employment. Our Legislature should do something in regard the long-hour system and trade checks, and compel employers to pay cash for labor; then, you see, competition in trade would take place, and we could save some of our earnings, which would enable us to have night schools and improve our condition much in the way of education.

4. A Black Entrepreneur Builds a Cotton Mill, 1896

Please allow me to call the attention of the public to the fact that a movement is on foot to erect a cotton mill at Concord to be operated by colored labor. The colored citizens of the United States have had no opportunity to utilize their talents along this line. Since North Carolina has fairly and justly won for herself in the Centennial at the World Fair at Chicago and at the Atlanta Exposition the honored name of being "the foremost of the States," she will further evidence the fact if she is the first to have a cotton mill to be operated principally by the colored people. We are proud of the spirit and energy of the white people in encouraging and assisting the enterprise and will our colored people not catch the spark of the new industrial life and take advantage of this unprecedented opportunity to engage in the enterprise that will prove to the world our ability as operatives in the mills thereby solving the great problem "can the Negroes be employed in cotton mills to any advantage?" And now that the opportunity is before us, experience alone will determine the question and it behooves us to better ourselves and do something, and as one man ... [make] the effort that is to win for us a name and place us before the world as industrious and enterprising citizens.

Don't think for a moment that this desireable and enviable position can be obtained by merely a few of our people, but on the other hand, it will require the united effort of the race. Then when the people of the white race who are our friends clearly see that we are surely coming, they will "come over into Macedonia and help us." The enterprise will be just what we make of it. There is nothing to gain but everything to lose by allowing the enterprise to prove a failure.

In case of a failure, it will be due to mere neglect. If it proves a success, it will be to the honor and glory of the race. If racial weakness is set forth, it will only strengthen the sentiment already expressed about us. We can see the finger of Providence directing our cause, for we believe that God helps only those who help themselves. If we show no desire to succeed in this, and in all the enterprises designed for the industrial and financial development of the race, then it can be proven that our Liberty is a failure. We cannot afford to be idle or lukewarm in this matter. There is too much connected with it that would not let our

---

conscience rest if we did not make the effort to carry out the plan. Can there be any among us who do not wish to see the moral, intellectual, religious and industrial character of our people elevated to a higher and broader plan[e] of civilization and true usefulness? There is no middle ground. We are either going forward or backward. The watchword is onward and upward, and if we ever expect to attain the heights of industrial usefulness, we must fall in line and march shoulder to shoulder in one solid phalanx along the road that leads to fortune and fame.

When we grasp the opportunities offered for the betterment of our condition, we are performing the great task which will at last determine our future position in the ranks of the great nations of the world. The markets of Madagascar, Zanzibar and other tropical regions where there are millions of inhabitants are open for all goods that can be produced in the mills.

Let us not be discouraged but move onward with the enterprise, with that spirit and determination that makes all things possible for those who strive in real earnest.

5. Lewis W. Hine Photographs Children Working in the Mills, 1908, 1909

The Little Spinner, Newberry, South Carolina, by Lewis W. Hine, 1908. (Library of Congress)

↳ sad? - or not? cameras took a long time to process - most relaxed face

↳ dirty floor

Lewis W. Hine, *Doffers at the Bibb Mill No. 1*, Macon, Georgia, 1909. (Library of Congress)

6. Bertha Miller Recalls Her Days as a Cotton Mill Girl (1915), 1984

I was born in Randolph County ninety years ago. I wanted to be a farmer. Yeah, but I didn't get to be one. I was raised on a farm and I like a farm. I'd rather plow than do any other kind of work I've ever done in my life. We rented our land, we didn't own it, but we had all we wanted to tend. We raised corn, wheat, barley, tobacco, and enough cotton to make quilts and stuff like that. That was the best living I ever did, was living on a farm. We'd go possum hunting, rabbit hunting, cut wood together, work on the farm, and me and my daddy, we'd plow. I remember old Doc Phillips come walking by one day. Doc Phillips brought me in this world and all my young-uns too. We lived side by side down in the country. So that day he come walking by and I was plowing corn. He stopped there at the house and hollered for me to come in the house. He said, "You're going to get killed on that thing." And I said, "No I ain't. I reckon I got enough sense to plow." I wasn't nothing but a youngun then.

Reprinted from Victoria Byerly, *Hard Times Cotton Mill Girls: Personal Histories of Womanhood and Poverty in the South*. Copyright © 1986 by Cornell University. Used by permission of the publisher, Cornell University Press.

My grandpap used to live with us. He made coffins. He lived with us for years, then he went back to his little home in the country and that's where he died. My daddy, he was a hard worker. I remember he got sick after we come to town. He worked down at the cotton mill for several years until he got down, plumb down, and wanted to go back home to the farm. That's where he died. My mother was a little old bitty thing, weighed about ninety pounds. She was a good Christian woman. When we moved here from the country, she went out there at the cotton mill and went to work. We all did.

I was so little for my age that at three years old, old Doc Phillips told my mother, he said, "Lou, give Pug,"—he always called me Pug—"a chew of tobacco." That was going to make me grow. So Ma cut me off a little chew of tobacco and I just chomped on it. First thing I knew my head started going around maybe ninety miles an hour and oh I was sick. I just laid down on the porch and vomited like a dog. I thought I was going to vomit my insides out. But I kept tasting it along and finally one day I said, "Give me a dip of snuff, maybe it won't make me sick." But it did. Still I kept dipping it a little longer 'til I got to where I dipped it regular. Then I started to grow. When I worked in the mill, just about all the girls in there dipped snuff. They dipped to keep the lint out of their throats. You never saw a woman smoking cigarettes back then. The awfullest looking sight I ever saw was a woman smoking a cigarette. I thought, Lord help.

I was eleven years old when I went to work in the mill. They learnt me to knit. Well, I was so little that they had to build me a box to get up on to put the sock in the machine. I worked in the hosiery mill for a long time and, well, then we moved back to the country. But me and my sister Molly finally went back up

Bertha Miller, *right,* with a friend, about 1915. (Reprinted from Victoria Byerly, *Hard Times Cotton Mill Girls: Personal Histories of Womanhood and Poverty in the South,* Copyright © 1986 Cornell University. Used by permission of the publisher, Cornell University Press.)

there in 1910 and I went to work in the silk mill. Molly went to work in the hosiery mill. I come over here in 1912 and boarded with Green Davis and Lou. They kept four other mill girls besides me. We all worked in the Amazon Cotton Mill. When we weren't working in the mill, there wasn't nothing much to do only sit around there and laugh and talk. Us girls, we'd wash our clothes and stuff like that. That's all there was to do. There weren't no place to go. We'd go to the show every once in a while, but it was so far to walk to town. Still, we had a good time. Mrs. Welch lived beside of us and she had three girls. We'd all get together and sing and go on. Me, Berthie, Nan, and all of us, we'd get in one room and we'd sing religious songs and laugh and talk. We'd have a good time and enjoyed ourselves right there in the house. Weren't allowed to go nowhere. Didn't get out and frolic around at night. We'd just sit right there at home and talk about what we was going to do when we got old enough to get married and all such things as that. We worked twelve hours a day for fifty cents. When paydays come around, I drawed three dollars. That was for six days a week, seventy-two hours. I remember I lacked fifty cents having enough to pay my board.

7. Map of the Piedmont Textile Mills, 1931

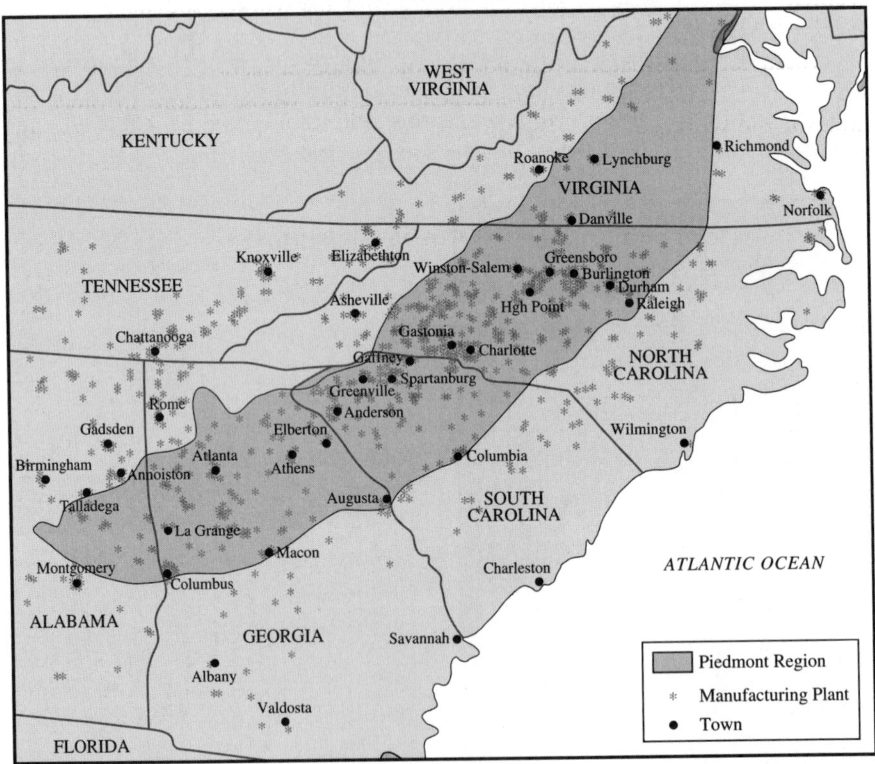

Location of Textile Mills, 1931.

SOURCE: Adapted from B. F. Lemerl. *The Cotton Textile Industry of the Southarn Appertion Piedmont.* (Cengage Learning)

ESSAYS

Historian C. Vann Woodward began the scholarly reevaluation of the New South with his seminal book *Origins of the New South, 1877–1913*, published in 1951. In the first selection, Woodward examines the "cotton mill campaign" and argues that the textile mill crusade, rather than serving as philanthropy to poor farmers, exploited the laborers and profited the owners. He also maintains that ownership was in the hands of elite southerners who were not connected to the antebellum planters but rather represented a new rising entrepreneurial class. The second article, by a team of researchers from the University of North Carolina, explores the lives of mill workers using their own testimony and documents. Taking the perspective of the workers rather than the mill owners, this article explodes the myth of southern labor's docility. The authors argue that workers created a community atmosphere out of the mill owners' paternalism, and the workers emerge from these interviews as much less unwitting victims than participants, however circumscribed, in their own destinies. The final essay, by Bryant Simon, uses a gender construct to argue that South Carolina mill hands felt emasculated by the system of paternalism offered by mill owners, by "the growing assertiveness of women," and by "African American progress." Male workers sought redemption at the polls where they had considerable strength as a voting bloc. They generally voted for gubernatorial candidate Cole Blease, a racist demogogue whose speeches promoted mill worker independence but whose actions in office did little for the workers. Why, Simon asks, would textile workers remain devoted to Blease?

The Rise of Southern Industry

C. VANN WOODWARD

The dramatic elements in the rise of the Southern cotton mill gave the movement something of the character of a "crusade." The successful competition with New England, the South's old political rival, the popular slogan, "bring the factories to the fields," and the organized publicity that attended every advance, have combined to enshrine the cotton mill in a somewhat exalted place in Southern history. Burdened with emotional significance, the mill has been made a symbol of the New South, its origins, and its promise of salvation. Facts that embarrass this interpretation of cotton-mill history have been somewhat neglected.

Rising in the Old Order, the cotton mills of the South showed a rather remarkable tenacity and even prosperity in the troubled decades that followed secession. Of the three leading cotton-manufacturing states of the South, North Carolina doubled the value of her output between 1860 and 1880, Georgia

---

Reprinted by permission of the Louisiana State University Press from *Origins of the New South 1877–1913* by C. Vann Woodward, pp. 131–135, 153–155.

tripled her ante-bellum record, and South Carolina quadrupled hers. These gains continued right through the supposedly blighting years of Reconstruction. The case of a large Augusta mill was by no means unique. Running some 30,000 spindles and 1,000 looms, this mill paid cash dividends averaging 14.5 per cent a year during the seventeen years following 1865 and laid aside a surplus of about $350,000. These and other facts call into serious question the tradition of dating the beginning of the cotton-mill development of the South from 1880.

In the eighties the rate of cotton-mill expansion was simply accelerated, but it was accelerated to a speed never attained in earlier years, a pace vastly exceeding the rate of growth outside the South. In his report on the cotton-textile industry in the Census of 1890, Edward Stanwood wrote that "the extraordinary rate of growth in the south" during the eighties was "the most important" aspect of the period. In 1900 he was even more emphatic, saying that "The growth of the industry in the South is the one great fact in its history during the past ten years." The number of mills in the South mounted from 161 in 1880 to 239 in 1890, and to 400 in 1900—an increase of 48.4 per cent in the eighties and 67.4 in the nineties. This, as compared with a national increase of 19.7 and 7.5 per cent in the two decades, and an apparent decrease in New England. A great number of the new mills, moreover, were equipped with more up-to-date machinery than the mills of the old textile regions. The first factory operated entirely by electricity was located in the South, and many improvements first found their way into the country through that region. The increase in the number of mills reveals only a fraction of the expansion. In the four leading states of North and South Carolina, Georgia, and Alabama—in which virtually all the increase took place—the average number of spindles per mill increased from 3,553 in 1880 to 10,651 in 1900. In total number of spindles the same states rose from 422,807 in 1880 to 1,195,256 in 1890, a gain of 182.7 per cent; and in the next decade the total mounted to 3,791,654 or an additional increase of 217 per cent in the nineties. Between 1880 and 1900 the total number of operatives in all Southern mills rose from 16,741 to 97,559; the number of bales consumed, from 182,349 to 1,479,006; the capital invested, from $17,375,897 to $124,596,874. Not untypical of the relative rate of expansion was the increase in capital invested in cotton manufactures, which, between 1890 and 1900 amounted to 131.4 per cent in the South as compared with 12.1 per cent in New England.

Both the historians and the promoters of the cotton-mill campaign have held that the movement was motivated by "moral incitement" and became "a form of civic piety" in the South. While the incentives common to most industrialization were admittedly present, "the moral considerations brought the matter to a focus." The cotton-mill executives were "thinking for the whole people." The extent of this motivation should be carefully explored, but it is well to point out first that in the early years of the movement, according to the census report of 1900, "the return upon investment in Southern cotton mills has greatly exceeded that upon factories in the North." In 1882 an average of 22 per cent profit was received on investments in Southern mills, under good and bad management—and there was much of the latter. There were failures as well as successes among the new mills. But profits of 30 to 75 per cent were not unheard of in those years.

As important as these inducements undoubtedly were, they cannot account for the public zeal that, in the Carolinas, Georgia, and Alabama, converted an economic development into a civic crusade inspired with a vision of social salvation. Not only did this process occur in cities like Charleston, Atlanta, and Charlotte, with their efficient chambers of commerce, big newspapers, and Northern visitors and settlers, but even more typically in isolated Piedmont towns. Old market villages of a few hundred citizens that had drowsed from one Saturday to the next since the eighteenth century, were suddenly aflame with the mill fever and "a passion for rehabilitation." Stock was often subscribed in small holdings. Among the professions from which early mill executives were called, Broadus Mitchell lists lawyers, bankers, farmers, merchants, teachers, preachers, doctors, and public officials. City dailies and country weeklies devoted columns to the crusade and itinerant evangelists added the theme to their repertoire. With a headlong zeal not uncharacteristic of the region in war as in peace, the Southeast embraced the cotton mill. "Even machinery was wrapped with idealism and devotion," according to one account.

Much was made by mill promoters of the philanthropic motive of giving "employment to the necessitous masses of poor whites." Undoubtedly this motive was sincere in some cases. Its force, however, is somewhat diminished by evidence submitted by the promoters themselves. Francis W. Dawson of Charleston, one of the most forceful propagandists for cotton mills, wrote in 1880 that employment in the mills subjects the poor whites "to elevating social influences, encourages them to seek education, and improves them in every conceivable respect." In the same editorial he stated that in South Carolina there were at that time "2,296 operatives, upon whom 7,913 persons are dependent for support. The amount paid out in wages monthly is $38,034." The average worker and dependent thus enjoyed an income of a little over twelve cents a day. In the same article Dawson estimated that the profits of these factories "ranged from 18 to 25½ per cent a year ... under the most unfavorable circumstances." The profit motive did not necessarily preclude the philanthropic motive, but it does seem to have outweighed it in some instances.

The question of the relative proportion of Southern and Northern capital in the Southern cotton mills is hedged with difficulties. Acknowledging the importance of Northern investment in Georgia and in areas of other states, authorities are in substantial agreement that after the seventies and before the depression years of the nineties, when Northern capital moved southward in quantities, the initiative lay with the South, and the chief source of capital was local. One writer finds "no evidence of any cotton mill established in North Carolina by Northern interests before 1895." This could not be said of any other mill state. A widespread practice was to raise only part of the required capital locally and then issue a large percentage of the stock of a new mill to Northern textile machinery and commission firms. Dependence upon these absentee firms, which often charged exorbitant rates of interest and employed injurious marketing practices, resulted in milking off a sizable proportion of profits....

Within the little islands of industrialism scattered through the region, including the old towns as well as the new, was rising a new middle-class society. It drew some recruits from the old planter class, but in spirit as well as in outer aspect it was essentially new, strikingly resembling the same class in Midwestern and Northeastern cities. Richmond, former capital of the Confederacy, observed the social revolution within its walls with complacency: "We find a new race of rich people have been gradually springing up among us, who owe their wealth to successful trade and especially to manufactures.... [They] are taking the leading place not only in our political and financial affairs, but are pressing to the front for social recognition.... 'The almighty dollar' is fast becoming a power here, and he who commands the most money holds the strongest hand."...

The facts of the record would not seem to warrant the contention that "whereas in England many from the middle class became captains of industry, here [in the South] the characteristic leadership proceeded from the aristocracy." According to this interpretation, the English industrialists were "small men who struck it lucky," whereas the Southern mill men were "gentlemen." A study of the background of 254 industrialists in the South of this period reveals that "about eighty per cent came of nonslave-owning parentage." Out of a total of 300 studied only 13 per cent were of Northern birth. Professor John Spencer Bassett, the historian, who took a peculiar delight in the rise of the new and the decline of the old ruling class, wrote that "The rise of the middle class has been the most notable thing connected with the white population of the South since the war.... Everywhere trade and manufacturing is almost entirely in the hands of men who are sprung from the non-planter class, and ... the professions seem to be going the same way." As for the old planters, a decadent class, Bassett thought, "They have rarely held their own with others, and most frequently they have been in the upper ranks of those who serve rather than those who direct business.... But the captains of industry ... are men who were never connected with the planter class." A shrewd New England observer corroborated the Southerner's view when he wrote in 1890: "now, like a mighty apparition across the southern horizon, has arisen this hope or portent of the South,—the Third Estate,—to challenge the authority of the old ruling class." He advised his section against "exclusive observation of the old conflict of races" in the South. "For the coming decade, the place to watch the South is in this movement of the rising Third Estate. What it demands and what it can achieve in political, social, and industrial affairs ... on these things will depend the fate of this important section of our country for years to come."

Mark Twain on a Southern junket in the eighties was brought face to face with these men of the New South: "Brisk men, energetic of movement and speech; the dollar their god, how to get it their religion." Somewhat awkwardly, but with great show of self-assurance, this new man adjusted to his shoulders the mantle of leadership that had descended from the planter. Some considerable alteration was found necessary: less pride and more "push," for example. Punctilio was sacrificed to the exigencies of "bustle," and arrogance was found to be impracticable in the pursuit of the main chance.

The Lives and Labors of the Cotton Mill People

JACQUELYN DOWD HALL, ROBERT KORSTAD,

AND JAMES L. LELOUDIS II

Textile mills built the new South. Beginning in the 1880s, business and professional men tied their hopes for prosperity to the whirring of spindles and the beating of looms. Small-town boosterism supplied the rhetoric of the mill-building campaign, but the impoverishment of farmers was industrialization's driving force. The post–Civil War rise of sharecropping, tenantry, and the crop lien ensnared freedmen, then eroded yeoman society. Farmers of both races fought for survival by clinging to subsistence strategies and habits of sharing even as they planted cash crops and succumbed to tenantry. Meanwhile, merchants who had accumulated capital through the crop lien invested in cotton mills. As the industry took off in an era of intensifying segregation, blacks were relegated to the land, and white farmers turned to yet another strategy for coping with economic change. They had sold their cotton to the merchant; now they supplied him with the human commodity needed to run his mills. This home-grown industry was soon attracting outside capital and underselling northern competitors. By the end of the Great Depression, the Southeast replaced New England as the world's leading producer of cotton cloth, and the industrializing Piedmont replaced the rural Coastal Plain as pacesetter for the region....

Nothing better symbolized the new industrial order than the mill villages that dotted the Piedmont landscape. Individual families and small groups of local investors built and owned most of the early mills. Run by water wheels, factories flanked the streams that fell rapidly from the mountains toward the Coastal Plain. Of necessity, owners provided housing where none had been before. But the setting, scale, and structure of the mill village reflected rural expectations as well as practical considerations. Typically, a three-story brick mill, a company store, and a superintendent's house were clustered at one end of the village. Three- and four-room frame houses, owned by the company but built in a vernacular style familiar in the countryside, stood on lots that offered individual garden space, often supplemented by communal pastures and hog pens. A church, a company store, and a modest schoolhouse completed the scene. By 1910 steam power and electricity had freed the mills from their dependence on water power, and factories sprang up on the outskirts of towns along the route of the Southern Railway. Nevertheless, the urban mill village retained its original rural design. Company-owned villages survived in part because they fostered management control. Unincorporated "mill hills" that surrounded towns such as Charlotte and Burlington, North Carolina, and Greenville, South Carolina, enabled owners to avoid taxes and excluded workers from municipal government. But the mill village also reflected the workers' heritage and served their needs.

Jacquelyn Dowd Hall, Robert Korstad, and James L. Leloudis II, "Cotton Mill People: Work, Community, and Protest in the Textile South, 1880–1940," *American Historical Review* 91 (April 1986), pp. 245–286. Reprinted by permission of the authors.

Like the design of the mill village, the family labor system helped smooth the path from field to factory. On farms women and children had always provided essential labor, and mill owners took advantage of these traditional roles. They promoted factory work as a refuge for impoverished women and children from the countryside, hired family units rather than individuals, and required the labor of at least one worker per room as a condition for residence in a mill-owned house. But this labor system also dovetailed with family strategies. The first to arrive in the mills were those least essential to farming and most vulnerable to the hazards of commercial agriculture: widows, female heads of households, single women, and itinerant laborers. By the turn of the century, families headed by men also lost their hold on the land. Turning to the mills, they sought not a "family wage" that would enable a man to support his dependents but an arena in which parents and children could work together as they had always done.

The deployment of family labor also helped maintain permeable boundaries between farm and mill. The people we interviewed moved with remarkable ease from farming to mill work and back again or split their family's time between the two. James Pharis's father raised tobacco in the Leaksville-Spray area of North Carolina until most of his six children were old enough to obtain mill jobs. The family moved to a mill village in the 1890s because the elder Pharis "felt that all we had to do when we come to town was to reach up and pull the money off of the trees." From the farm Pharis saved his most valuable possession: his team of horses. While the children worked in the mill, he raised vegetables on a plot of rented ground and used his team to do "hauling around for people." Betty Davidson's landowning parents came up with the novel solution of sharing a pair of looms. "My father would run the looms in the wintertime," Davidson remembered, "and go to and from work by horseback. And in the summertime, when he was farming, my mother run the looms, and she stayed in town because she couldn't ride the horse. Then, on the weekends, she would come home."

This ability to move from farming to factory work—or combine the two—postponed a sharp break with rural life. It also gave mill workers a firm sense of alternative identity and leverage against a boss's demands. Lee Workman recalled his father's steadfast independence. In 1918 the superintendent of a nearby cotton mill came to the Workmans' farm in search of workers to help him meet the demand for cloth during World War I. The elder Workman sold his mules and cow but, contrary to the superintendent's advice, held on to his land. Each spring he returned to shoe his neighbors' horses, repair their wagons and plows, and fashion the cradles they used to harvest grain. "He'd tell the superintendent, 'You can just get somebody else, because I'm going back to make cradles for my friends.' Then he'd come back in the wintertime and work in the mill." This type of freedom did not sit well with the mill superintendent, but the elder Workman had the upper hand. "'Well,' he told them, 'if you don't want to do that, I'll move back to the country and take the family.'"

Although Lee Workman's father periodically retreated to the farm, his sons and daughters, along with thousands of others, eventually came to the mills to stay. There they confronted an authority more intrusive than anything country folk had experienced before. In Bynum, North Carolina, the mill owner supervised the Sunday School and kept tabs on residents' private lives. "If you stubbed your toe they'd fire you. They'd fire them here for not putting out the light late at night. Old Mr. Bynum used to go around over the hill at nine o'clock and see who was up. And, if you were up, he'd knock on the door and tell you to cut the lights out and get into bed." Along with surveillance came entanglement with the company store. Mill hands all too familiar with the crop lien once again found themselves in endless debt. Don Faucette's father often talked about it. "Said if you worked at the mill they'd just take your wages and put it in the company store and you didn't get nothing. For years and years they didn't get no money, just working for the house they lived in and what they got at the company store. They just kept them in the hole all the time."

The mill village undeniably served management's interests, but it also nurtured a unique workers' culture. When Piedmont farmers left the land and took a cotton mill job, they did not abandon old habits and customs. Instead, they fashioned familiar ways of thinking and acting into a distinctively new way of life. This adaptation occurred at no single moment in time; rather, it evolved, shaped and reshaped by successive waves of migrations off the farm as well as the movement of workers from mill to mill. Village life was based on family ties. Kinship networks facilitated migration to the mill and continued to play a powerful integrative role. Children of the first generation off the land married newcomers of the second and third, linking households into broad networks of obligation, responsibility, and concern. For many couples, marriage evolved out of friendships formed while growing up in the village. One married worker recalled, "We knowed each other from childhood. Just raised up together, you might say. All lived here on the hill, you see, that's how we met."...

Cooperation provided a buffer against misery and want at a time when state welfare services were limited and industrialists often refused to assume responsibility for job-related sickness and injury. It bound people together and reduced their dependence on the mill owners' charity. When someone fell ill, neighbors were quick to give the stricken family a "pounding." "They'd all get together and help. They'd cook food and carry it to them—all kinds of food—fruits, vegetables, canned goods." Villagers also aided sick neighbors by taking up a "love offering" in the mill....

Community solidarity did not come without a price. Neighborliness could shade into policing; it could repress as well as sustain. Divorced women and children born out of wedlock might be ostracized, and kinship ties could give mill supervisors an intelligence network that reached into every corner of the village. Alice Evitt of Charlotte remarked that "people then couldn't do like they do now. They was talked about. My daddy would never allow us to be with people that was talked about. This was the nicest mill hill I ever lived on. If anybody done anything wrong and you reported them, they had to move."...

Given such tensions, we were struck by how little ambivalence surfaced in descriptions of mill village life. Recollections of factory work were something else again, but the village—red mud and all—was remembered with affection. The reasons are not hard to find. A commitment to family and friends represented a realistic appraisal of working people's prospects in the late nineteenth- and early twentieth-century South. Only after World War II, with the expansion of service industries, did the Piedmont offer alternatives to low-wage factory work to more than a lucky few. Until then, casting one's lot with others offered more promise and certainly more security than the slim hope of individual gain. To be sure, mill people understood the power of money; they struggled against dependency and claimed an economic competence as their due. Nevertheless, they had "their own ideas … about what constitute[d] the 'good life.'" Communal values, embodied in everyday behavior, distanced mill folk from the acquisitiveness that characterized middle-class life in New South towns.

This is not to say that mill village culture destroyed individuality. On the contrary, it conferred status and dignity that the workplace could seldom afford. Although mill ways encouraged group welfare at the expense of personal ambition, they did support individual accomplishment of a different sort. The practice of medicine provides one example, music another.

Folk medicine formed an important part of workers' "live-at-home" culture. Until well into the twentieth century, mill hands simply could not afford medical fees; besides, they viewed doctors with distrust and fear. In emergencies, the village turned to its own specialists. Among the earliest of these in Bynum was Louise Jones's mother, Madlena Riggsbee. "She was what you'd say was a midwife. She could just hold up under anything. Unless they were bound and compelled to have the doctor, they'd usually get her to go." In the 1920s and 1930s, the company retained the services of a physician, paid for with funds withheld from workers' checks. But in the eyes of the villagers, he was a partner—indeed a junior partner—to Ida Jane Smith, a healer and midwife who was one of the most respected figures in the community. "Lord, she was a good woman," Carrie Gerringer recalled. "She knowed more about younguns than any doctor."

If the midwife was the most prestigious member of the female community, the musician held that place among men. String bands had been a mainstay of country gatherings, and they multiplied in the mill villages where musicians lived closer together and had more occasions to play. Mastery of an instrument brought a man fame as the local "banjo king" or expert guitar picker. Musicians sometimes played simply for their own enjoyment. Paul Faucette and a small group of friends and kinfolk used "to get together on the porch on Saturday night and just have a big time." On other occasions, they performed for house dances and community celebrations. Harvey Ellington remembered that on Saturday night "you'd have a dance in somebody's house—they'd take the beds and all out, and then we'd just play." The dance might end before midnight, but the musicians' performance often continued into the morning. "We'd be going home and decide we didn't want to go to bed. So we'd take the fiddle and the guitar and the banjo and stop at the corner and harmonize—do what they call serenade. The people would raise their windows and listen. That's the best sounding music, wake up at night and hear somebody playing."

Special talents won Harvey Ellington and Madlena Riggsbee places of honor in their neighbors' memories. But most villagers never achieved such distinction. They lived in quiet anonymity, often guided and strengthened by religious faith. Most textile workers were evangelical Protestants, and many worshipped in churches built and financed by factory owners. On one level, these churches proved helpful, maybe even essential, to the mills. Like their counterparts in other industrializing societies, they inculcated the moral and social discipline demanded by factory life. Still, there was another side to evangelical religion, one that empowered the weak, bound them together, and brought them close to God. At springtime revivals, faith turned to ecstasy. "People got happy and they shouted. They'd sing and hug each other—men and women both." When the Holy Spirit moved individuals to confessions of sin, the entire body of worshippers joined in thanksgiving for God's saving grace.

The physical and social geography of the mill village, then, was less a product of owners' designs than a compromise between capitalist organization and workers' needs. For a more clear-cut embodiment of the manufacturers' will, we must look to the factory. The ornate facades of nineteenth-century textile mills reflected their builders' ambitions and the orderly world they hoped to create. The mill that still stands at Glencoe is an excellent example. Situated only a few hundred yards from the clapboard houses that make up the village, the mill is a three-story structure complete with "stair tower, corbelled cornice, quoined stucco corners, and heavily stuccoed window labels." In contrast to the vernacular form of the village, the architecture of the factory, modeled on that of New England's urban mills, was highly self-conscious, formal, and refined.

At Glencoe, and in mills throughout the Piedmont, manufacturers endeavored to shape the southern yeomanry into a tractable industrial workforce. Workers' attitudes toward factory labor, like those toward village life, owed much to the cycles and traditions of the countryside. Owners, on the other hand, sought to substitute for cooperation and task orientation a labor system controlled from the top down and paced by the regular rhythms of the machine. Barring adverse market conditions, work in the mills varied little from day to day and season to season. Workers rose early in the morning, still tired from the day before, and readied themselves for more of the same. For ten, eleven, and twelve hours they walked, stretched, leaned, and pulled at their machines. Noise, heat, and humidity engulfed them. The lint that settled on their hair and skin marked them as mill workers to the outside world. The cotton dust that silently entered their lungs could also kill them.

Owners enforced this new pattern of labor with the assistance of a small coterie of supervisors. As a rule, manufacturers delegated responsibility for organizing work and disciplining the help to a superintendent and his overseers and second hands. A second hand in a pre–World War I mill recalled, "You had the cotton, the machinery, and the people, and you were supposed to get out the production. How you did it was pretty much up to you; it was production management was interested in and not how you got it." Under these circumstances, supervision was a highly personal affair; there were as many different approaches to its problems as there were second hands and overseers. As one observer explained, "There was nothing that could be identified as a general pattern of supervisory practice."

At times, discipline could be harsh, erratic, and arbitrary. This was particularly true before 1905, when most workers in southern mills were women and children. Even supervisors writing in the *Southern Textile Bulletin* admitted that "some overseers, second hands, and section men have a disposition to abuse the help. Whoop, holler, curse, and jerk the children around." James Pharis remembered that "you used to work for the supervisor because you were scared. I seen a time when I'd walk across the road to keep from meeting my supervisor. They was the hat-stomping kind. If you done anything, they'd throw their hat on the floor and stomp it and raise hell."

In the absence of either state regulation or trade unions, management's power seemed limitless, but there were, in fact, social and structural constraints. Although manufacturers relinquished day-to-day authority to underlings, they were ever-present figures, touring the mill, making decisions on wages and production quotas, and checking up on the help. These visits were, in part, attempts to maintain the appearance of paternalism and inspire hard work and company loyalty. At the same time, they divided power in the mill. Workers had direct access to the owner and sometimes saw him as a buffer between themselves and supervisors, a "force that could bring an arbitrary and unreasonable [overseer] back into line." Mack Duncan recalled that in the early years "most all the mill owners seemed like they had a little milk of human kindness about them, but some of the people they hired didn't. Some of the managers didn't have that. They were bad to exploit people." Under these circumstances, the commands of an overseer were always subject to review. Workers felt free to complain about unjust treatment, and owners, eager to keep up production, sometimes reversed their lieutenants' orders. Federal labor investigators reported in 1910 that "when an employee is dissatisfied about mill conditions he may obtain a hearing from the chief officer of the mill ... and present his side of the case. Not infrequently when complaints are thus made, the overseer is overruled and the operative upheld."

Authority on the shop floor was further complicated by social relations in the mill village. Before the introduction of industrial engineers and college-trained foremen in the 1920s and 1930s, most supervisors worked their way up through the ranks....

A personal style of labor management posed but one obstacle to the imposition of strict discipline. Mill owners also faced the limitations of existing technology. The small size of most mills before World War I made it difficult to coordinate production in a way that kept all hands constantly at work....

Mill owners and workers alike had to accommodate themselves to a work environment not entirely of their own choosing. Factory labor did not allow the independence and flexibility of labor on the farm, but neither did it meet the standards of rigor and regularity desired by owners. An informal compromise governed the shop floor. "We worked longer then in the mill than they do now," explained Naomi Trammell, "and made less, too. But we didn't work hard. I done all my playing in the mill."...

World War I marked a turning point in the development of the southern textile industry. Stimulated by wartime demand, new mills sprang up, old ones operated around the clock, wages rose, and profits soared. But, when peace came, overexpanded businesses went into a tailspin. The situation worsened when tariff policies and the advent of textile manufacturing in other parts of the world cut into the southern industry's lucrative foreign markets. A sudden change in clothing styles added to manufacturers' troubles. Young women in the 1920s hiked their skirts six inches above the ankle, then all the way to the knee, causing consternation among their elders and panic in the textile industry. All in all, the depression that hit the rest of the country in 1929 began for textile manufacturers in the immediate postwar years.

Mill officials greeted the armistice with a rollback of workers' wages. But, to the owners' surprise, mill hands refused to abandon small but cherished advances in their standard of living. When wage cuts were announced in 1919, thousands of workers joined the American Federation of Labor's United Textile Workers (UTW). "They are in deadly earnest," reported the Raleigh *News and Observer*, "and almost religiously serious in their belief in the union." Manufacturers were equally determined not to employ union members, and in many cases they simply shut their factory gates to all workers. As the conflict dragged on, threats of violence mounted. Armed strikers patrolled the mill villages, intent on enforcing community and union solidarity. Manufacturers eventually agreed to a settlement but insisted that "the adjustment ... shall not be construed as a recognition by the mills of collective bargaining." Similar confrontations occurred throughout the Piedmont until 1921, when a severe business downturn crippled union locals and gave management the upper hand. But workers had made their message clear: mill owners would no longer be able to shore up profits simply by cutting wages.

The impasse created in 1921 by hard times and workers' protests set the stage for a new era of corporate consolidation. As smaller firms went bankrupt, more aggressive competitors gobbled them up. J. Spencer Love, who took over faltering mills in Alamance County and eventually built Burlington Mills into the world's largest textile enterprise, set the pace. Love's generation led the region to ascendancy in the production of synthetics and helped effect a permanent shift of cotton manufacturing from New England to the Piedmont. These "progressive mill men" also set out to find new solutions to problems of profitability and labor control. The methods they adopted aimed at altering the structure of work and breaking the bonds between supervisors and the mill village community. But their freedom of action depended on a ballooning labor supply....

In 1927 resistance to management tactics by individuals and small groups gave way to labor conflict on an unprecedented scale. The battle opened in Henderson, North Carolina, where workers struck for restoration of a bonus withdrawn three years before. Then on March 12, 1929, young women in a German-owned rayon plant in Elizabethton, Tennessee, touched off a strike wave that spread quickly into the Carolinas. The involvement of the communist-led National Textile Workers Union and the shooting deaths, first of the police chief and then of Ella May Wiggins, the strikers' balladeer, brought Gastonia, North Carolina, a special notoriety. But the carnage was even worse in nearby Marion, where deputies opened fire on demonstrators, wounding twenty-five and killing six. In 1930, revolt hit the massive Dan River Mill in Virginia—a model of welfare capitalism.

Responding to these workers' initiatives, the UTW tried to remedy its neglect of southern labor. Most energetic was the American Federation of Hosiery Workers, an autonomous UTW affiliate, represented by Alfred Hoffman, an intrepid organizer who popped up in virtually every trouble spot until his militancy landed him in a Marion jail. But even Hoffman usually arrived after the fact, and a number of the less well known but more successful walkouts ran their course with no official union involvement at all. In 1929, thousands of South Carolina workers formed their own relief committees, held mass meetings, and negotiated modifications in the stretch-out—all without help from the UTW. Similarly, in 1932, in High Point, North Carolina, hosiery workers sparked sympathy strikes at textile mills and furniture plants and used automobile caravans to spread walkouts to nearby towns. Fearing a "revolution on our hands," officials conceded most of the workers' demands.

Whether independently organized or union led, each walkout was shaped by local circumstances. But more important than the differences were the experiences strikers shared. In community after community, mill folk turned habits of mutuality and self-help to novel ends. Union relief funds were paltry at best, and survival depended on neighborly sharing. Many of the Marion strikers "had a good garden, and they'd divide their gardens with people that didn't have any." Those who held back found themselves donating anyway. Sam Finley remembered frying chickens for hungry picketers—supplied by a boy who could "get a chicken off the roost and leave the feathers." Baseball games, picnics, and barbecues buoyed spirits and fostered solidarity. As in the routines of daily life, women workers were essential to this mobilization of community resources. "The women done as much as the men," Lillie Price asserted. "They always do in everything."...

In these ways, workers fashioned a language of resistance from established cultural forms. But the young people who led the protests had also come of age in a society different from the one their parents had known. Most had grown up in the mill villages or moved as children from the countryside. They did not see themselves as temporary sojourners, ready to beat a retreat to the land, or as displaced farmers for whom "it was heaven to draw a payday, however small." Their identities had been formed in the mill village; they had cast their fate with the mills.

Mills, Workers, and the Myth of a New South

BRYANT SIMON

Like Will Thompson, Joe Childers was a white millworker. A newspaper reporter described him as a "respectable laboring man" with a "good reputation." On the night of March 27, 1912, Childers met Joe Brinson and Frank Whisonant, both African Americans, near the train station in the tiny up-country town of Blacksburg, South Carolina, The meeting proved tragic.

What happened that night among Childers, Brinson, and Whisonant will never be known. Depending on who told the story, Childers either asked Brinson and Whisonant to get him a pint—or a quart—of whiskey or the two African

From *A Fabric of Defeat: The Politics of South Carolina Millhands, 1810–1948* by Bryant Simon.

Americans badgered the innocent white man until he finally agreed to buy liquor from them. The three men got drunk. According to Childers, Brinson and Whisonant ordered him to drink all of the whiskey. Fearing for his safety, he drank as much as he could as fast as he could, but he could not drain the bottle. As Childers guzzled the rust-colored rotgut—or maybe it was clear white lightning—Brinson and Whisonant taunted him; when he did not finish, they grew quarrelsome. They forced him into a cemetery and made him take off his clothes. N. W. Hardin, a local attorney, recounted what he heard happened next: "They [Brinson and Whisonant] drew their pistols, cocked them and told Childers to open his mouth, and keep it open, that if he closed it, he would be shot on the spot." Then, in Hardin's version, Brinson made Childers perform oral sex on Whisonant.

Following this consensual or coerced sexual act, or what the press dubbed the "unmentionable act"—the phrase commonly used to talk about the rape or alleged rape of a white woman by an African American man—Childers "escaped." He ran straight to the police. The law officers quickly apprehended Brinson and Whisonant and charged them with selling liquor, highway robbery, carrying a concealed weapon, assault with a deadly weapon, and sodomy. The local magistrate fined the two men twenty dollars each. Some thought that the penalty, which was roughly the equivalent of three weeks' wages for a textile worker, was too lenient. Regardless, Brinson and Whisonant had no money and went to jail.

The next morning E. D. Johnson of Blacksburg got up early and walked to the well in the center of the town square. Johnson discovered that the rope used to pull up the water bucket was missing. Puzzled, he looked around; his eyes eventually stopped at the sturdy stone and brick jail. The front door was knocked down. Johnson peered inside and saw a broken padlock and an open cell. He must have known what had happened. He ran to tell the mayor. It did not take the men long to find the missing rope and the missing prisoners.

"The job," wrote a reporter, "had been done in a most workman-like manner." Brinson and Whisonant's cold, stiff bodies dangled from the rafters of the blacksmith shop located just behind the jail. Bound hand and foot, both victims had been gagged, one with cotton, the other with rope. The killers had not wanted them to scream.

Word of the lynching spread through the area, but the crime did not bring together, in the words of a student of southern vigilantism, Arthur Raper, "plantation owners and white tenants, mill owners and textile workers." Instead, the killings stirred discord. "Law and order," worried the editor of the *Gaffney Ledger*, "has been flaunted" as "passions [have become] inflamed and reason dethroned." "Every good citizen," he was certain, "deplored the crime." The newsman, however, had no sympathy for the dead. "Those were two bad negroes who were lynched in Blacksburg," he conceded. "But," he added, "those who outraged them became worse whites."

No one publicly named the "worse whites." Many people, especially in Blacksburg, speculated that a mob—totaling as many as a dozen or as few as six men—drove into town or rode in on horseback from the mill villages of Gaffney, Cherokee Falls, Hickory Grove, and King's Mountain. Others insisted that the killers were from Blacksburg. Though questions about where the murderers resided lingered, there was little doubt about what they did for a living. "My idea," wrote N. W. Hardin, "is that as Childers was a factory operative, the lynching was done by the operatives of the surrounding mills, trying to take care of their class." If millworkers committed the crime, townspeople were sure where the larger blame for the murders lay. "Some of the d – d fools are already saying," reported Hardin, "this is Bleasism." The *Gaffney Ledger* echoed this view. "If a majority of the people of South Carolina want Blease and Bleasism," the editor wrote of the lynching, "they will have it in spite of those who desire law and order."

Bleasism was the term used to designate the political uprising of first-generation South Carolina millworkers. This electoral surge took its name from its standard-bearer, Coleman Livingston Blease. "Coley," as his loyal backers called him, had occupied the governor's office for more than a year and was gearing up for his reelection drive when Brinson and Whisonant were killed. Although Blease did not play any role in the murders, commentators who linked him to the disorder in Blacksburg were, at least in part, right. Blease's racially charged, antireform campaigns and his irreverent leadership style inflamed many of the

A lynching in the South Carolina upcountry sometime before World War I. According to John Hammond Moore, in *Carnival of Blood: Dueling, Lynching, and Murder in South Carolina, 1880–1920*, this picture probably depicts the lynching of Joe Brinson and Frank Whisonant in Blacksburg, March 1912. (Historical Center of York County, York, South Carolina)

same cultural, economic, and sexual anxieties that ultimately led some working-class white men to lynch African American men.

Despite the homoerotic overtones of the meeting at the railway station, the killers must have decided that Childers was "innocent," that he had been "raped," and that the crime symbolized more than one shocking evening in a cemetery. The imagined rape of the millworker Joe Childers may have represented in microcosm the assaults on white manhood posed by industrialization. Even more than the rape of a white woman, the rape of this white man by another man graphically represented male millworkers' deepest fears of emasculation. That the perpetrators were African Americans magnified the offense. The alleged sexual attack not only erased the color line but also placed an African American man "on top," in a position of power over a white man. A few male textile workers appear to have made a connection between how the "rape" of Childers feminized him and how industrialization stripped them of control over their own labor and that of their families, and thus their manhood. Some southern white wage-earning men apparently felt that industrialization could potentially place them in the position of a woman: vulnerable and dependent, powerless at home and in public.

By murdering Joe Brinson and Frank Whisonant, the killers tried to reassert their manhood. The same fierce determination to uphold white supremacy and patriarchy that led to the Blacksburg lynching propelled Cole Blease's election campaigns. The same sexual and psychological fears that drew the lynch mob to the jail that spring night in 1912 brought many more men to the polls a few months later to vote for Blease. Middle-class South Carolinians—professionals and members of the emerging commercial elite—also connected the lynching in Cherokee County with Blease's political success. They argued that both stemmed from the collapse of "law and order" in the mill villages and together demonstrated the need for reform.

The anxieties that fueled Bleasism and triggered the Blacksburg lynching were not confined to South Carolina or, for that matter, to the American South. Across the United States and indeed the globe, the reconfiguration of productive landscapes—the shift from fields to factories—jarred gender relations. Industrialization triggered an almost-universal crisis of male identity. In South Carolina, the crisis of masculinity among first-generation millhands aggravated race and gender relations and eventually spilled over into politics, splitting the state along class lines....

By the time Blease started to campaign for office in 1906, more than 80 percent of South Carolina's textile mills were located in the upcountry, half in Greenville, Spartanburg, and Anderson counties alone. The modernization of the state's economy produced "unbalanced growth."...

While the South Carolina Constitution imposed limits on Palmetto State democracy, it also gave the Democratic Party—the only party that mattered, after Reconstruction—the right to determine who could and could not vote in its all-important primary. After a long debate, state Democrats in the 1890s decided to extend the suffrage to all white men over the age of twenty-one, regardless of wealth or education. The constitutional poll tax, moreover, applied only to the rather meaningless general election. As a result of these rules and the racial composition of the textile workforce, the expanding mill population possessed considerable electoral strength. By 1915 nearly one out of every seven Palmetto State Democrats lived in a mill village. Affirming at the same time the ideal of herrenvolk democracy, that is, of white political equality, the state's emerging political culture also provided poor whites with a powerful ideological lever. Despite constitutional checks on democracy, this myth defined citizenship by race and implicitly put forth the idea that all white men were equal. In the years to come, white millworkers repeatedly demanded that elites honor the tenets of herrenvolk democracy by treating them with the respect and dignity that equal citizens deserved....

Cole Blease himself recognized the electoral harvest to be reaped in the textile communities. As soon as Blease turned away from a career in law to one in politics, he focused his attention on the mill hills around his hometown of Newberry. He spent afternoons and evenings in front of company stores and at nearby roadhouses, and he joined the clubs, fraternal organizations, and brotherhoods that textile workers belonged to. Sometime early in this century it was said, and no one disputed it, that Blease knew more millhands by name than anyone else in the state. He turned this familiarity into votes. In 1890 he was elected to represent Newberry County in the South Carolina General Assembly. Twice, in 1910 and 1912, Blease triumphed in the governor's race. On a number of other occasions he won enough votes to earn a spot in statewide second primaries or runoff elections. In most of these contests, millhands made up the bulk of his support.

Male textile workers did not just cast their ballots for Blease, they were fiercely devoted to him. When he went up to the mill hills, poking fun at elites, issuing chilling warnings about black rapists, and slamming "Yankee-ridden" unions, overflow crowds greeted him with "tornado[es] of shrieks, yells, and whistles." Mill people named their children after Blease, hung his picture over their mantels, and wrote songs and poems about him. "If you want a good chicken," an upcountry bard was heard to say, "fry him in grease. If you want a good governor get Cole Blease." When a reporter asked a textile worker why he supported Blease, the man snapped, "I know I ain't goin' to vote for no aristocrat." Another millhand once hollered, "Coley, I'd vote fer you even if you was to steal my mule tonight."

Millworkers' allegiance to Cole Blease has long baffled historians. Because he promoted white supremacy, derided national unions, rejected child labor restrictions, and lambasted compulsory school legislation, scholars have accused him of being "a feather-legged demagogue" with "no program for the benefit of the factory workers." Historians have contended that the reform policies Blease opposed would have saved workers from the misery and poverty of the mill village, but they did not care. They preferred a politician who spouted off about race to one who promoted reform. How, historians have wondered, could such perplexing behavior be explained? Ignorance and false consciousness were the answers most often given. Spellbound by Coley's saber-rattling rhetoric, this argument goes, uneducated millhands turned their backs on their natural class interests and a logical alliance with African American laborers and farmers, voting instead with their hateful, racist hearts....

Yet as the Blacksburg lynching indicated, there were still other issues behind workers' support for Cole Blease's antireform agenda. By reexamining Bleasism, this time through the overlapping lenses of sexuality, gender, race, and class, some of these other factors can be seen. Race, it becomes clear, was not the only issue that mattered to first-generation South Carolina textile workers; neither were notions of traditional independence nor the passions of antimodernism.

As the grisly Blacksburg lynching suggests, the attitudes of male workers combined concerns about race, class, and gender. They reflected private fears about declining parental authority as well as public qualms about the actions of elected officials and self-appointed reformers. To male millhands, politics was about power—in other words, about patriarchy and suffrage, economic autonomy and white supremacy. The public and private were closely linked, never really as far apart for workers as they have been for historians. First generation South Carolina industrial workers were certainly committed to independence, ... but to most white men this meant more than living unencumbered by the modernizing state. Instead, their concepts of independence mixed together shifting ideas about citizenship, race, economic autonomy, and masculinity....

Mill village life challenged long-standing male conceptions of independence. Tending looms and operating carding machines stripped men of control of their time and labor. The boss in the rural household now worked to the relentless rhythms of the machines and the angry bark of the foreman. Some even compared the factory regime to slavery. "They are trying to treat the help more like slaves than free people," protested T. V. Blair of Pelzer. S. E. Arthur of Langley added: "We do not have more showing than the negroes in slavery time." Millhands deployed the metaphor of slavery to protest against the nature of mill work and to articulate their fears about their growing dependence on the will of others. Without control over their own labor, male workers must have worried that it now would be difficult for them to impose their authority over others.

Wages, if they had been high enough to support the entire family, might have provided some men with a sense of compensation for their dwindling control. But few mill men earned enough to feed and clothe their families. Under these conditions, children and wives were compelled to take up what southern millhands revealingly labeled "public work"—that is, paid labor. Though fathers often disciplined their children on the shop floor, scolding those who misbehaved and pushing slackers to work harder, they no doubt knew that the real source of authority was the foreman and the mill owner, men who were more powerful than they were. Male millhands familiar with the dynamics of the shop floor also knew that some supervisors used their power over hiring and firing to intimidate female workers sexually, which only heightened the anxieties of fathers and husbands. Yet these men also understood that if they accused the supervisors of harassing their wives and daughters, they risked losing their own jobs, and an unemployed worker was even less of a man than an underpaid one.

The participation of dependents in the paid labor force realigned the balance of power within the family. Feeling enfranchised by their contributions to the household economy, working wives and children periodically challenged their husbands and fathers over the dispensation of their wages. Sons and daughters, in particular, often demanded the right to spend at least a portion of their earnings on whatever they wanted. How they spent their wages was also an issue. Across the urban South in the first decades of the twentieth century, young workers, especially women, shaped a new heterosexual aesthetic. Makeup, bobbed hair, and shorter skirts were evidence of this trend. A refraction of the new city sensibilities quickly reached the mill hills. Some young mill women purchased the latest styles, went out with their friends, male and female, on Saturday nights, and skipped church on Sundays. Much more than their cousins back on the farm, young millworkers expressed themselves as independent, autonomous individuals who were culturally at odds with their parents....

For first-generation white male workers, assaults on their independence and manhood seemed to be coming from every direction. Each millhand dealt with the confusion of industrialization, low wages, waning parental authority, the growing assertiveness of women, middle-class hostility, and African American progress in his own way. Some workers gave up on the mill and returned to the countryside. Others drank too much, and a few probably deserted their families. A small number took out their frustrations on their wives and children. Violence was not confined to households; during the first two decades of the twentieth century millhands, along with white men and a few women from every part of town, assembled in lynch mobs. They killed African Americans who, they believed, wanted to wipe away the color line and undermine white masculinity. Others spoke out for shorter working hours and higher pay, and a few joined trade unions and went on strike. Many, armed as they were with the vote, turned to politics—or, perhaps more accurately, politicians turned to them. The most famous of these politicians was Cole Blease.

In a nearly biennial ritual between 1906 and 1916, textile workers went to the polls and voted for Cole Blease as a solid bloc. Blease brought male millhands out on election day in record numbers because he had honed a political message that expressed their gathering resentments. He spoke to their concerns and frustrations in ways that made sense to them.... Like the Blacksburg lynching, Blease's rhetoric represented a window into millhands' outlooks. The candidate's words both revealed and shaped a complicated and volatile constellation of ideas about race, class, gender, sexuality, and state power....

The stump was where Blease stood out. Turning politics into vaudeville, he put on the best show in town except perhaps for the annual tent meeting. Strutting across the podium, waving his arms, pointing his finger, shouting and whispering, he played the master of ceremonies, comedian, old friend, and preacher all wrapped into one. He berated, mocked, and belittled his opponents. Low-country planters, middle-class South Carolinians, and reformers, not factory owners, caught the brunt of Blease's verbal blitzes.

Unimpressed by their sizable bank accounts, college degrees, big words, or claims of selflessness, Blease dismissed the reformers as "intellectuals," "fool theorists," "wise-looking old fossils," and members of the "holier than thou crowd." Grinning and winking, he regularly made light of the rule of law—that cardinal tenet of bourgeois ideology—by admitting to drinking bootlegged whiskey every now and then. Each time that he made this confession, Blease noted, his opponents said that he was a threat to law and order. But, according to the candidate, they were hypocrites. "Why, I saw men up here last summer," Blease said, his voice thick with sarcasm, during his 1913 inaugural address, "hollering, 'Law and Order,' yelling for 'Law and Order,' and 'We must redeem South Carolina.'... I saw some of those same people down here at the State Fair drinking liquor and mixing it with coca-cola and betting on horses." "Who," Blease chuckled, "is going to redeem them?"

When Blease was not poking fun at his opponents, he battered them with male bravado. They were, he blazed, unmanly "cowards," "belly crawlers," "pap-suckers," "nigger lovers," "molly-coddles," and "very small m[e]n." Blease was especially dismissive of women reformers and suffragists. He accused them of neglecting their homes and children so they could run around the state "'doing society,' playing cards for prizes, etc." A supporter complained that female reformers wanted "to give us their dresses for our pants." Blease agreed. He opposed woman suffrage, hinting that the right to vote and enter the public sphere might unsex women....

Blease offered white laborers more than antiaristocratic rhetoric. Understanding their frustrations, he vowed to uphold the privileges of race. Pledging his allegiance to the idea of a white man's democracy, he battled to make sure that all white males over the age of twenty-one could continue to vote in the Democratic primary regardless of their background or income. He also endorsed legislation to bar African Americans from textile mills, despite the fact that by 1910 almost no mills would hire blacks for jobs inside the factories. To make sure that people knew exactly where he stood on the issues of employment and race, as one of his first acts as governor he fired every black notary in the state. Although Blease favored passing new laws to bolster white supremacy, he opposed virtually all other state action.

Blease's fight against laws for compulsory education was a case in point. These measures would have required all children under the age of fourteen, or sixteen, to attend school. Reformers talked glowingly about the social benefits of the classroom for working-class children. Blease scoffed at the humanitarian depiction of these educational statutes, portraying them instead as part of a broad campaign to control mill people's private lives. Nature, he argued, determined that fathers and mothers, not the government, should oversee families. Cotton mill people, he continued, "should be left alone ... and allowed to manage their own affairs.... Compulsory education means disrupting the home, for it dethrones the authority of the parents and would place paid agents in control of the children which would destroy family government." On another occasion he declared of a compulsory school bill, "Of course I am opposed ... it [the bill] comes ... from some narrow-minded bigot who has made a failure in raising his own children ... and now wants to attempt to raise somebody else's."... Blease's hostility toward compulsory schooling did not mean that he opposed public education. Indeed, in 1914 he called for higher pay for teachers, more male instructors, improved libraries, longer school terms, and more "books, especially histories, by southern authors for southern children."

Even more than compulsory education, progressive plans to mandate medical inspections of mill children infuriated Blease. Proponents insisted that such examinations would compensate for "the oversight of the child's environment" and would correct deformities that were easily correctable but had been left unattended to by ignorant parents. Blease asserted that such a scheme highlighted the reformers' arrogance and their tendency to treat male textile workers as less than men. "Do you not think," he asked lawmakers, "that every man in this State is able to care and has love enough for his children to care for and protect them? … Have all the people and all classes of the people become imbeciles and children that the Legislature at every turn must pass acts creating guardianships? … Do you wish to … force every poor man to bow down to the whims of all the professions?"

For Blease, sex—that is to say, deviant sexuality—linked the emerging middle class of the New South to the debauched aristocracy. He asked what doctors would do with the information they gathered from their studies of mill children. Would they publicize their findings? If a mill girl suffered from an embarrassing ailment, would they broadcast the news and turn the examination into yet another humiliating ritual for working people? "Do not say," Blease warned, "that every young girl in the State … without her consent, must be forced to be examined and her physical condition certified by her physician to some school teacher, to be heralded around as public property." The most dangerous aspect of the law, he insinuated, was that it would make it easier for morally lax men to sexually abuse poor white women. Some "male physicians," a correspondent wrote to Blease in 1914, "boast openly that they can seduce their female patients." One even kept a diary, a supporter told the governor, of his sexual exploits with working-class girls.… In a final horrific charade of politically opportunistic logic, Blease wondered aloud about doctor's assistants, "third parties," and "negro janitors." Would physicians, he asked, permit the "unmentionable crime"—the virtual rape of a white woman—by allowing voyeuristic black men to watch the medical inspections of mill girls?

Once again, Blease turned the bourgeois conception of the world on its head. Reformers viewed medical examinations as a tool for creating a modern New South. In the minds of the middle classes, doctors were asexual individuals, pillars of the community, and architects of a more orderly universe. Blease laughed at these flattering characterizations. To him, doctors perhaps more than others had the capacity for evil. Under the guise of morality, they undermined morality by defiling innocent working-class women. By vigorously opposing the medical inspection bill, Blease positioned himself as the millworkers' defender of decency, masculine honor, and white womanly virtue.

Blease tied his assaults on elites and reformers and his appeals to white workers together with the threads of race, class, and gender. He accused the reformers of trying to place the "cotton mill men … on the same basis as a free negro." Laws that dictated who could vote and who could not and told mill parents when their children had to go to school and when they must stay at home violated the principles of independence, white equality, and patriarchal authority. Only blacks, minors, and women, Blease maintained, should have their behavior so rigidly regulated. To put white men in the same category was to turn the natural order of the world upside down.

"I am no enemy of the negro but I believe in keeping him in his place at all times," Blease often remarked.... Blease's world was immutable. He opposed spending white tax dollars on black schools. Educating a black person would simply "ruin a good field hand, and make a bad convict." Blease insisted that black immorality was natural and that black men had to be watched at all times. "I tell you that it is not all quiet in South Carolina," he cautioned. In his imagination, "the black ape and baboon" lurked in the shadows waiting for the opportunity to rape a white woman. If this crime did take place, or even if there was a hint of an African American crossing the sexual color line, lynching was the only answer. Not to lynch would only make black men more brazen. To Blease, then, those who joined the lynch mobs were not disorderly or lawless; they were manly and moral. Those who questioned the principles of white equality across class and economic lines and the need for lynching were, like aristocrats and doctors, effete and dangerous, and had to be stopped....

When white men joined lynch mobs and cheered Blease's ritual dances, they attempted to assert their power not only over African Americans but also over their own homes and families. As Jacquelyn Dowd Hall and Gail Bederman have argued, "by constructing black men as 'natural' rapists and by resolutely and bravely avenging the (alleged) rape of pure white womanhood, Southern white men constructed themselves as ideal men: 'patriarchs, avengers, righteous protectors.'" Blease spoke to the multiple meanings of lynching. In the summer of 1913 a supporter informed the governor of an alleged rape of a white woman in Laurens. "The brute," he explained, was captured and "tried before an honest jury." "It was not a mob," he assured the state's chief executive, "but a crowd of determined men anxious to have justice meted out to one never more deserving of its fruits." "You did like men and defended your neighbors and put their black bodies under ground," Blease congratulated the members of the Laurens County lynch mob, which included "many of the 'cotton mill boys,'" some of whom were apparently angry about the hiring of African Americans for "white" jobs. The governor praised these criminals as well for "their defense of the white womanhood of our state—our mothers and our sisters."

The Blacksburg lynching of Joe Brinson and Frank Whisonant took place fifteen months before the murder in Laurens. Both events demonstrated that sexual tensions, class issues, and vigilante justice were always intertwined in the New South. In each case, millworkers defended their manhood and their whiteness under the cover of darkness. In Blacksburg, some people believed that local blacks lay in wait to ravage not only white women but also white men like Joe Childers. These same men must have worried about the fate of white womanhood, white manhood, and white supremacy if white men could not even protect themselves from black sexual predators. Male laborers in Blacksburg and Laurens emphatically answered these doubts. They asserted their masculinity by murdering three black men for allegedly sexually humiliating a white man and a white woman and thus all white people. In the anxious world of the industrializing New South, interracial sexual contact of any kind—even a homosexual act—that became public knowledge could easily threaten white independence and white manhood. Although Blease did not dance for, or even condone, every lynching—and he did not comment on events in Blacksburg—he understood why some poor white men executed black men, and these white men repaid him for his understanding with their votes.

Only some whites regarded Blease in this way. In the early twentieth century, white South Carolinians were divided on questions of race, class, gender, and even lynching. These divisions became politicized and eventually fractured the electorate into two rival camps: Bleasites and anti-Bleasites. Blease's message sounded different to each audience. Middle-class residents detected nothing of substance in his critique of society; they heard only the dissonant chords of demagoguery, disorder, and lawlessness. Male millworkers, on the other hand, interpreted Blease's rhetoric and actions as a defense of their manhood against the forces of industrialization and the reform agenda of the progressives. By voicing laborers' discontent and abusing those who demeaned them, Blease provided workers with a way to strike out at their perceived oppressors. Casting their ballots for Cole Blease, textile workers pressed their claims of patriarchal privilege and equality with all white men and asserted in the strongest language available to them that the economic and socially mighty did not control everything. "Even though Coley don't ever do a durn thing for us poor fellows," explained an Aiken laborer, "he does at least promise us somethin', and that's more than any of the others do."...

FURTHER READING

Edward L. Ayers, *The Promise of the New South: Life after Reconstruction* (1992).

Dwight B. Billings Jr., *Planters and the Making of a "New South": Class, Politics and Development in North Carolina, 1865–1900* (1979).

Orville V. Burton and Robert C. McMath, eds., *Toward a New South?: Studies in Post-Civil War Southern Communities* (1982).

David L. Carlton, *Mill and Town in South Carolina, 1880–1920* (1982).

James C. Cobb, "Beyond Planters and Industrialists: A New Perspective on the New South," *Journal of Southern History 54* (February 1988), 45–68.

———, *Industrialization and Southern Society, 1877–1984* (1984).

Don H. Doyle, *New Men, New Cities, New South: Atlanta, Nashville, Charleston, Mobile, 1860–1910* (1990).

Paul D. Escott, *Many Excellent People: Power and Privilege in North Carolina, 1850–1900* (1985).

Walter J. Fraser Jr. and Winfred B. Moore Jr., eds., *From Old South to New: Essays on the Transitional South* (1981).

Neil Foley, *The White Scourge: Mexicans, Blacks, and Poor Whites in Texas Cotton Culture* (1997).

Paul M. Gaston, *The New South Creed: A Study in Southern Mythmaking* (1970).

David R. Goldfield, *Cotton Fields and Skyscrapers: Southern City and Region, 1607–1980* (1982).

Steven Hahn, *The Roots of Southern Populism: Yeoman Farmers and the Transformation of the Georgia Upcountry, 1850–1890* (1983).

Dolores E. Janiewski, *Sisterhood Denied: Race, Gender, and Class in a New South Community* (1985).

Daniel Letwin, *The Challenge of Interracial Unionism: Alabama Coal Miners, 1878–1921* (1997).

Melton A. McLaurin, *The Knights of Labor in the South* (1978).

———, *Paternalism and Protest: Southern Cotton Mill Workers and Organized Labor, 1875–1905* (1971).

Broadus Mitchell, *The Rise of Cotton Mills in the South* (1921).

Sydney Nathans, *The Quest for Progress: The Way We Lived in North Carolina, 1870–1920* (1983).

I. A. Newby, *Plain Folk in the New South: Social Change and Cultural Persistence* (1989).

Stephen H. Norwood, "Bogalusa Burning: The War Against Biracial Unionism in the Deep South, 1919," *Journal of Southern History* 63 (August 1997), 591–628.

Gail W. O'Brien, *The Legal Fraternity and the Making of a New South Community, 1848–1882* (1986).

Harold L. Platt, *City Building in the New South: The Growth of Public Services in Houston, Texas, 1830–1910* (1982).

Howard Rabinowitz, *The First New South, 1865–1920* (1992).

———, *Race Relations in the Urban South, 1865–1890* (1978).

Crandall A. Shifflett, *Patronage and Poverty in the Tobacco South: Louisa County, Virginia, 1860–1900* (1982).

Laurence Shore, *Southern Capitalists: The Ideological Leadership of an Elite, 1832–1885* (1986).

Bryant Simon, *A Fabric of Defeat: The Politics of South Carolina Millhands, 1910–1948* (1998).

John F. Stover, *The Railroads of the South, 1865–1900* (1955).

Nannie M. Tilley, *The Bright-Tobacco Industry, 1860–1929* (1948).

Allen Tullis, *Habits of Industry: White Culture and the Transformation of the Carolina Piedmont* (1989).

G. C. Waldrep III, *Southern Workers and the Search for Community: Spartanburg County, South Carolina* (2000).

Peter Wallenstein, *From Slave South to New South: Public Policy in Nineteenth-Century Georgia* (1987).

David E. Whisnant, *All That Is Native and Fine: The Politics of Culture in an American Region* (1983).

Jonathan M. Wiener, *Social Origins of the New South: Alabama, 1860–1885* (1978).

C. Vann Woodward, *Origins of the New South, 1877–1913* (1951).

Annette Wright, "The Aftermath of the General Textile Strike: Managers and the Workplace at Burlington Mills," *Journal of Southern History* 60 (February 1994), 81–112.

Robert H. Zieger, ed., *Southern Labor in Transition, 1940–1995* (1997).

CHAPTER 5

The Southern Populist Movement

At the close of Reconstruction in 1877, white southern men, many of them former Confederates, regained the right to vote in state and national elections, ran for office, and resumed control of the state assemblies; every southern state had a Democratic majority by 1886. The result was an era of political domination known as Redemption; its followers were called Redeemers, Bourbons, or Conservatives. They created a solidly Democratic South, or the "Solid South." Southern state legislatures rewrote their constitutions, instituted low taxes, and provided minimal government services. Development of industry at the expense of workers' needs stole the attention of most politicians, who remained comparatively unresponsive to farmers, industrial laborers, and African Americans. There were episodic attempts to overthrow the Redeemers: the Virginia Readjusters, the Greenbackers, and the Knights of Labor had enthusiastic followings but no success. Finally by the late 1880s, harsh economic conditions—worldwide overproduction of cotton, falling prices for farm products, the crop lien and sharecropping systems, scarcity of capital, and abuses of the convict leasing system accompanied by a sense of political impotence—led to a massive political upheaval called the Populist movement. It had begun with the Grange, a farmers' educational and social organization, and continued with the rise of the National Farmers' Alliance, the Colored National Farmers' Alliance, and, eventually, the Southern Alliance. Finally, in 1892 the movement culminated in the creation of the People's party, a third party that produced one of the nation's most progressive political platforms and attracted millions of voting followers.

The Populists demanded far-reaching changes in the national economic and political systems; they advocated institution of income taxes, a subtreasury plan that would pay farmers to store their non-perishable produce until prices increased, public ownership of utilities and railroads, a government-backed system to protect savings accounts, an increase in the amount of money in circulation including coinage of silver, an eight-hour workday, the secret ballot, state initiatives and referenda, and the direct election of U.S. senators. These ideas frightened both bankers and leaders of the New South's budding industries. Even more alarming to southern Democratic party leaders was the threat of biracial political solidarity engendered by the Populist movement. Finding the Democratic party unsupportive, the Populists began courting the votes of black southerners. This step brought racial issues to center stage, and as a result the battles over Populism in the South involved not only economic questions but also an alleged threat to white supremacy and fears of a return to "black rule."

How did the South become the "Solid South"? Who benefited from Conservatives' gains? Were the Populists radicals or would-be capitalists seeking needed economic reforms? Why did their movement create such deep divisions in southern society? Why did Populism ultimately fail? What were the consequences for farmers, laborers, and African Americans in the South?

DOCUMENTS

Farmers' Alliances provided men, women, and children isolated on farms with opportunities for social contact as well as political strategizing. Document 1, a series of letters from Texas women to the *Southern Mercury,* describes Alliance encampments where recreation followed politics. Talk of political reform led to discussions of women's rights and gender roles as seen from the perspective of farm women. A wellspring of Populist strength was the suffering and frustration of thousands of southern farmers, many of whom were in debt and had lost or feared losing their land. Their pent-up anger is conveyed in Document 2, containing selections from letters of North Carolina farmers to a state agency explaining the reasons for farmers' poor conditions. The political demands and program of the Farmers' Alliances (predecessor to the Populist party) are summarized in the Ocala platform, Document 3. Note its proposal for a subtreasury system and changes in the nation's money supply. In Document 4, Georgia's Tom Watson, the most prominent Populist leader in the South, describes the problems of southern farmers in an article in the *Arena,* a national magazine. He urges the formation of a political party that can speak to the interests of both black and white voters. His strategy for relief calls for political cooperation across racial lines, but his article provides clues to the extent and limit of racial tolerance among Populists. In 1894, just before the congressional elections, Populists hoped to win victories in several southern states. Depicted in Document 5 as the two ugly stepsisters, the Republicans and the Democrats run from the threatening storm of southern Populist gains. Document 6 reveals a Populist speaker's maneuvering around the racial issue in 1898, when the Populists were in decline and the Democrats' white supremacy campaign in North Carolina was gaining ground.

1. Texas Alliance Women Write to the *Southern Mercury*, 1888

An Alliance Encampment

July 31, 1888. Americus, Marion County. Mrs. V. A. Taylor.

EDITOR MERCURY: Variety is the spice of life so I concluded this time to send you a short letter describing the events of last Saturday, viewed through the spectacles of an Alliance picnicker (to wit, myself).

From *Women in the Texas Populist Movement: Letters to the Southern Mercury*, edited by M. K. Barthelme. Published by Texas A&M University Press, 1997. Used by permission.

First there was the hurry and bustle of the morning's packing provisions, placing baskets and children in the wagon so as to consume as little space as possible for we must take in friends on the way until we are pretty thoroughly jammed. No inconvenience I assure you however for our sub-Alliance which had been invited to join the Lasater Alliance in a day of general boom, fun and frolic must be well represented, hence the cram in all available vehicles. A drive of eight miles over rough roads, under a blazing sun did not in the least damp the ardor and enthusiasm and we arrived there with keen zest for the enjoyments of the day, meeting old friends and forming of new acquaintances under the auspices of being united in fraternal love.

I look upon this Alliance movement as the most potent abettor of Christianity that was ever originated, but hold! I am not going to moralize just now. The program of the day was first music; second, essay on the principles, aims and possibilities of the Alliance, by your scribe; third, lecture by Bro. Macready who was sent to us by Dr. [C.W] Macune; and I have only to say if the Dr. is as successful in running that Exchange as he is in getting hold of good material for speeches, it is bound to succeed; fourth, dinner, and that in quality and quantity all that could be desired. After dinner, music, then as he expressed it a sort of "fill up the time talk" by Bro. D. R. Hale, but let me whisper in your ear that those are the kind of "fill up talks" it pays one to listen to. His happy hits and telling anecdotes fill us with mirth and enjoyment while his unlimited zeal fires us with enthusiasm for the cause. Next, short speeches from the candidates for county office and there seemed to be less palaver this year than ever before. I believe that class of office-seeker is becoming extinct or do not dare to show themselves among Alliance people.

Toward the end, I allowed certain side issues, viz. music and dancing, to divert my attention from the graver questions of the day, but I had an excuse. I took my little ones where for the first time they might behold displays of the terpsichorean art; not that I cared to witness, oh no (?) but like school teachers and preachers who have to carry the little ones to circuses and menageries, sacrificed my wishes in order to please and interest the children.

The sinking sun reminded us of the weary miles we had to plod upon our home-ward way and bidding goodbye to friends departed with the kindest of feelings in our hearts, our loyalty to the Alliance strengthened.

Defending the Woman's Sphere

July 31, 1888. Bexar County. Corn Bread.

EDITOR MERCURY: I have seen so much said about "woman's rights" I thought I would beg admittance to you, dear paper, to say a few words. Although I have not been one of you, yet I feel a deep interest in all you do; for does not a vow which is made before the high heavens bind us? We are the housewives, the makers of the home, and the home makes the nation. It puts me all out of patience to hear some of the ladies talk about their "woman's rights." How can any true wife and mother walk up to the polls on election day amid a crowd of gaping men, perhaps some of them drunk and some of them using slang. I don't mean all when I say some. You have no right to do such a thing, dear ladies, that is your husbands' and brothers' and fathers' business, not yours. Then you must know that if you are to be a man's equal in these things you must help to make the living. My husband is a farmer and I think I would much rather be a housewife than be a "woman's rights" woman: not that I do not believe in us all having our rights; if you only knew it, we have more rights than a man has, "the housewife makes the home and the home makes the nation."

Dear ladies, are you not the counselor of all your household? Do you not know why your husbands object to your going to the polls? It is because as a masculine woman you are no longer the dear little girl whom he promised to love, honor and cherish. Be contented as we are and make the home pure (if the men can't make the laws so) and stand by them. The ladies had better keep out of politics.

First Mention of Frances Willard, Advocate of Temperance and Suffrage; First Letter from Ann Other

May 31, 1888. Ennis, Texas. Ann Other.

WHERE SHALL WE LOOK FOR HELP?

EDITOR MERCURY: As we are searching for facts on this subject, and I sincerely believe that none of us are writing for argument's sake, let us look candidly on the matter and sift each point, and try to give fair and unprejudiced opinion on the arguments.... Now, sister Rebeca *[sic]*,...

You class the decline of patriotism with the rise of the popularity of universal suffrage and "woman neglecting her duty in her proper sphere." Now will someone kindly tell me what is her proper sphere? I have always heard the expression, but have failed to locate it by any series of studies I have taken up. I am obliged to conclude it is whatever the state of society dictates to her.

Men have intruded and wrestled from her what were formerly her legitimate occupations. And her present effort is only to recover a useful sphere in life by those who have become weary for others to do that which God intended she should do for herself.

Women used to be our bakers, brewers, dry-salters, butter-makers, cooks, dressmakers, cheese-makers, confectioners, jam and jelly makers, pickle makers, soap makers, spinners, weavers, sock makers, lace makers, embroiders, and midwives. Thus crowded out of her old fields of labor by men's intrusion and invention, she must either accept a life of idleness, and be satisfied with such as her brothers see proper to give her, or she must demand a more useful and energetic life....

Have you not seen Frances E. Willard's address before the senate committee? For fear you have not, I will quote a little from it: "I suppose these honorable gentlemen think that we women want the earth, when we only want one half of it. Our brethren have encroached upon the sphere of women. They have very definitely marked out that sphere and then they have proceeded with their incursions by the power of invention, so that we women, full of vigor and full of desire to be active and useful and to react upon the world around us, finding our industries largely gone, have been obliged to seek out new territory and to preempt from the sphere of our brothers, as it was popularly supposed to be, some of the territory that they have hitherto considered their own. So we think it will be very desirable indeed that you should let us lend a hand in their affairs of government." It is said that if women are given the right to vote, it will prevent their being womanly; how it is a sentiment of chivalry in some good men that hinders them from giving us the ballot. They think we should not be lacking in womanliness of character, which we most certainly wish to preserve but we believe that history proves they have retained that womanliness, and if we can only make men believe that, the ballot will just come along sailing like a ship with the wind beating every sail.

2. Farmers Describe the Crisis, 1890s

Remarks.—The average farmer in our county, under existing circumstances, cannot make much money over his living. Wages are low, but on account of the scarcity of money the farmer can't afford to give better wages. I think that we need—that the times imperatively demand—a greater volume of circulating currency. I am nearly eighty-four years old and have seen such a great scarcity of money but twice; when Andrew Jackson vetoed the National Bank bill and during the great negro speculation; but those depressions did not last so long.

Remarks.—Owing to the low price of products the farmers are behindhand. We think the trouble lies in our financial system. With a better system of finance than we have, and with the push and energy that our farmers have, they would certainly overcome all their troubles in a few years. But there will have to be changes in the policy of our National Government before we get much relief. The Farmers' Alliance is doing a grand work on this line.

Remarks.—The farmers in my vicinity are much rejoiced at the result of their labor for 1890. Cotton crops are especially good, but, as the results of bad legislation, the cotton, in many instances, will have to be sold for less than the cost of production, caused principally by an insufficient circulation of money to purchase the agricultural products....

Remarks.—The cotton crop is above an average; it is the best that has been made in this township since I have been farming (or in ten years). I think the greatest evil that exists in this county is the high rate of interest. It is that that makes the poor poorer and the rich richer. We have to pay eight per cent. per annum and a premium of ten per cent. in advance, making eighteen per cent. per annum. The average farmer is poorer than he was ten years ago, and

---

These documents can be found in the Fourth Annual Report of the Bureau of Labor Statistics of the State of North Carolina, John C. Scarborough, Commissioner, 1890: the Fifth Annual Report of the Bureau of Labor Statistics of the State of North Carolina, John C. Scarborough, Commissioner 1891; and in the Tenth Annual Report of the Bureau of Labor Statistics of the State of North Carolina, B. R. Lacy, Commissioner, 1896.

getting poorer every year. I think the next Legislature ought to fix the rate of interest at about five or six per cent., and make it a misdemeanor to charge any more.

Remarks.—The present debts heavily oppress the people. In fact many are forced to give a mortgage or crop lien at the beginning of the year. We have reached a crisis when many cannot run a farm without first pledging it as security for supplies. Do away with the National Banks and abolish all trusts and combines with the abolition of the tariff, and give us the Sub-Treasury Bill; it would afford much relief....

Remarks.—...Our people are not only not prosperous, but are growing poorer as the years go by. Not a man in all my knowledge is making a dollar to lay up for the future or to enlarge his operations. With farmer and mechanic it is a *pull for life.* Farm laborers get poor wages, because the farmer owning the land and hiring labor is not in condition to pay good wages, and laborers are, for the same reason, not regularly employed, but are strolling over the country a large part of the time looking for work. Scarcely any progress is made on farms, and for these reasons the negroes, who constitute the bulk of our farm laborers, are being driven, from necessity, to leave the State in large numbers. This is to our hurt. If hands could be employed regularly the year round it would be to the great advantage of farmers and laborers. With all this, I think there are not so many mortgages given now as for the past few years.

What is to become of the country under these conditions I cannot imagine. Farming is the great "king-wheel" which moves every other branch of business when it moves easily and prosperously. Without success and prosperity in farming, no prosperity can come to other business in our section of this country....

Remarks.—Farming pays in this country; but, on account of high interest and scarcity of money, it pays the wrong man. We are oppressed with debt, time prices and high interest. These hinder business of every kind. Manufactured articles are kept up to usual prices, while the products of farm labor drop lower every year. The need of more money in circulation is felt by the farmers all over the country....

Remarks.—Times here are very close in money matters. Sometimes they are higher, at others lower. I could not sell anything for cash at present. The money men have closed in on us farmers again. I believe in money being worth its value, but I do not believe in it being shut off entirely. What is this done for? Only to make slaves of the farmers. How is this to be remedied—free silver? I think so. Is it to reduce the homestead exemption? I think so. Has it been any benefit to the farmer? I think not. Do our leaders legislate more for the sake of party than for the good of the country? I think the majority do. Is the farmer as honorable as anybody else? I think he is. God made all men equal.

Remarks.—High interest on money is one of our drawbacks. It oppresses the person who borrows it. Great bodies of land owned by one man or company of men is a drawback to our county. Manufacturing ought to be the moneyed men's object, and not the oppression of agriculture. It is demoralizing to the people to take what belongs to man as a gift from God and force men to be tenants or slaves on the soil of a free country. High taxes, big salaries to our county, State and national officers are also demoralizing. Low wages, low prices for produce, and high prices for manufactured goods, handled by many speculators before they reach the consumers, are demoralizing. We want direct trade from the manufacturer to the consumer at the present prices of our produce. More money is needful to make our produce high. Plant peas for manure, sown one to two bushels per acre, and mow down the hay for stock.

Remarks.—... Tobacco is our money crop, and since our products are priced before we plant, the future is quite gloomy. Before the American Tobacco Trust was organized we got much better prices, as we raise bright tobacco in this section; but now the price is just half. Farmers are gloomy, and making no money. We hope to see the time when trusts and futures are to be no more. Money is scarce at this time in this section. I have answered the question as near right as I can, trusting you may be successful in helping us.

DEAR SIR:—These are extra hard times. I have been an employer of labor for many years, and never before saw such hard times. I am still giving full time, full employment, and full pay, but the Lord only knows how long it can last. As to what would be best for our working people, I hardly know what to say. If all could have constant work, that would be a splendid help. Thousands are idle, not of their own choice, but they just can't help themselves. I had rather belong to a country where everybody had work, and everybody *had to* work, than have it as it is. Call it socialism or what you please. Damn a country where there is nobody prosperous but the bond-holder and the money-lender. I want all prosperous—*give all work,* and money enough in circulation to pay for it.

Respectfully,

J. S. RAGSDALE.

DEAR SIR:—Owing to legislation in favor of monopolies our lands are gradually slipping from the hands of the wealth-producing classes and going into the hands of the few. I do not believe God ever intended that a few should own the earth, but that each should have a home. But we cannot take the lands from the rich and give to the poor; no, but let us have legislation to limit a man's freehold, and all that he may own over and above that the law limits him to levy a special tax, something of the nature of an income tax, on it. By this means we could have a revenue for our State that would enable us to educate the children of the State. Three-fourths of our population are tenants, and are not able to buy land at present prices; they are the men who create the wealth and pay the taxes. Let us have legislation that will do justice to all, protect all, and that will bless us as a nation.

Respectfully,

J. A. WILSON.

3. Farmers Create the Ocala Platform, 1890

Proceedings of the Supreme Council of the National Farmers' Alliance and Industrial Union

1. a. We demand the abolition of national banks.

b. We demand that the government shall establish sub-treasuries or depositories in the several states, which shall loan money direct to the people at a low rate of interest, not to exceed two per cent per annum, on nonperishable farm products, and also upon real estate, with proper limitations upon the quantity of land and amount of money.

c. We demand that the amount of the circulating medium be speedily increased to not less than $50 per capita.

2. We demand that Congress shall pass such laws as will effectually prevent the dealing in futures of all agricultural and mechanical productions; providing a stringent system of procedure in trials that will secure the prompt conviction, and imposing such penalties as shall secure the most perfect compliance with the law.

3. We condemn the silver bill recently passed by Congress, and demand in lieu thereof the free and unlimited coinage of silver.

4. We demand the passage of laws prohibiting alien ownership of land, and that Congress take prompt action to devise some plan to obtain all lands now owned by aliens and foreign syndicates; and that all lands now held by railroads and other corporations in excess of such as is actually used and needed by them be reclaimed by the government and held for actual settlers only.

5. Believing in the doctrine of equal rights to all and special privileges to none, we demand—

a. That our national legislation shall be so framed in the future as not to build up one industry at the expense of another.

b. We further demand a removal of the existing heavy tariff tax from the necessities of life, that the poor of our land must have.

c. We further demand a just and equitable system of graduated tax on incomes.

d. We believe that the money of the country should be kept as much as possible in the hands of the people, and hence we demand that all national and state revenues shall be limited to the necessary expenses of the government economically and honestly administered.

6. We demand the most rigid, honest, and just state and national government control and supervision of the means of public communication and transportation, and if this control and supervision does not remove the abuse now existing, we demand the government ownership of such means of communication and transportation.

7. We demand that the Congress of the United States submit an amendment to the Constitution providing for the election of United States Senators by direct vote of the people of each state.

This document can be found in Henry Steele Commager, *Documents of American History*, 4/e, vol. II. pp. 142–143.

4. Tom Watson Devises a Strategy for Biracial Cooperation, 1892

Having given this subject much anxious thought, my opinion is that the future happiness of the two races will never be assured until the political motives which drive them asunder, into two distinct and hostile factions, can be removed. There must be a new policy inaugurated, whose purpose is to allay the passions and prejudices of race conflict, and which makes its appeal to the sober sense and honest judgment of the citizen regardless of his color.

To the success of this policy two things are indispensable—a common necessity acting upon both races, and a common benefit assured to both—without injury or humiliation to either.

The white people of the South will never support the Republican Party. This much is certain. The black people of the South will never support the Democratic Party. This is equally certain.

Hence, at the very beginning, we are met by the necessity of new political alliances. As long as the whites remain solidly Democratic, the blacks will remain solidly Republican.

As long as there was no choice, except as between the Democrats and the Republicans, the situation of the two races was bound to be one of antagonism. The Republican Party represented everything which was hateful to the whites; the Democratic Party, everything which was hateful to the blacks.

Therefore a new party was absolutely necessary. It has come, and it is doing its work with marvellous rapidity.

Why does a Southern Democrat leave his party and come to ours?

Because his industrial condition is pitiably bad; because he struggles against a system of laws which have almost filled him with despair; because he is told that he is without clothing because he produces too much cotton, and without food because corn is too plentiful; because he sees everybody growing rich off the products of labor except the laborer; because the millionnaires who manage the Democratic Party have contemptuously ignored his plea for a redress of grievances and have nothing to say to him beyond the cheerful advice to "work harder and live closer."

Why has this man joined the PEOPLE'S PARTY? Because the same grievances have been presented to the Republicans by the farmer of the West, and the millionnaires who control that party have replied to the petition with the soothing counsel that the Republican farmer of the West should "work more and talk less."

Therefore, if he were confined to a choice between the two old parties, the question would merely be (on these issues) whether the pot were larger than the kettle—the color of both being precisely the same.

The key to the new political movement called the People's Party has been that the Democratic farmer was as ready to leave the Democratic ranks as the Republican farmer was to leave the Republican ranks....

This document can be found in Thomas E. Watson, "The Negro Question in the South," *Arena*, 1892, vol. VI, p. 548.

The very same principle governs the race question in the South. The two races can never act together permanently, harmoniously, beneficially, till each race demonstrates to the other a readiness to leave old party affiliations and to form new ones, based upon the profound conviction that, in acting together, both races are seeking new laws which will benefit both. On no other basis under heaven can the "Negro Question" be solved.

Now, suppose that the colored man were educated upon these questions just as the whites have been; suppose he were shown that his poverty and distress came from the same sources as ours; suppose we should convince him that our platform principles assure him an escape from the ills he now suffers, and guarantee him the fair measure of prosperity his labor entitles him to receive,—would he not act just as the white Democrat who joined us did? Would he not abandon a party which ignores him as a farmer and laborer; which offers him no benefits of an equal and just financial system; which promises him no relief from oppressive taxation; which assures him of no legislation which will enable him to obtain a fair price for his produce?

Granting to him the same selfishness common to us all; granting him the intelligence to know what is best for him and the desire to attain it, why would he not act from that motive just as the white farmer has done?

That he would do so, is as certain as any future event can be made. Gratitude may fail; so may sympathy and friendship and generosity and patriotism; but in the long run, self-interest *always* controls. Let it once appear plainly that it is to the interest of a colored man to vote with the white man, and he will do it. Let it plainly appear that it is to the interest of the white man that the vote of the Negro should supplement his own, and the question of having that ballot freely cast and fairly counted, becomes vital to the *white man*. He will see that it is done....

Let the colored laborer realize that our platform gives him a better guaranty for political independence; for a fair return for his work; a better chance to buy a home and keep it; a better chance to educate his children and see them profitably employed; a better chance to have public life freed from race collisions; a better chance for every citizen to be considered as a *citizen* regardless of color in the making and enforcing of laws,—let all this be fully realized, and the race question at the South will have settled itself through the evolution of a political movement in which both whites and blacks recognize their surest way out of wretchedness into comfort and independence....

The conclusion, then, seems to me to be this: the crushing burdens which now oppress both races in the South will cause each to make an effort to cast them off. They will see a similarity of cause and a similarity of remedy. They will recognize that each should help the other in the work of repealing bad laws and enacting good ones. They will become political allies, and neither can injure the other without weakening both. It will be to the interest of both that each should have justice. And on these broad lines of mutual interest, mutual forbearance, and mutual support the present will be made the stepping-stone to future peace and prosperity.

5. Populists "Got 'em on the Run," 1894

Anthony Weekly Bulletin (Kansas), November 2, 1894. http://history.missouristate.edu/wrmiller/populism/pcartoon/pcartoon31.htm. (Kansas State Historical Society)

6. A Populist Speaker Responds, 1898

[In 1896 the Democrats] said "silver! silver! silver!" and on every breeze and every lip it was silver from every Democratic tongue. They ran that campaign on National issues. Why don't they do it again? Silver is just as urgent an issue now as it was then, certainly so far as Congressmen are concerned. No, they go back to their old cry and say "the white metal and the white man," but they don't say much about the white metal. You can pick up Democratic papers and there is nothing about silver or William J. Bryan in them. They have left it off, and it is just "nigger! nigger! nigger!" forevermore. That is all the politics the

"Dr. Thompson's Great Speech" taken from the Torrance-Banks Family Papers, Special Collections, Atkins Library, The University of North Carolina at Charlotte.

Democratic party has in the State now; it is all they had prior to 1896, and they took silver up then because they saw the rank and file of their party would leave them and come to the Peoples Party if they did otherwise. Is there a prominent Democrat here who does not believe that? Why, he knows I am telling the living truth; they all know I am telling the truth....

I saw yesterday morning the Raleigh News and Observer. It had a cartoon in it—a picture you know, of Jim young "a negro politician in Raleigh bossing things at the Blind Asylum" in the city of Raleigh. The Democratic party dares not go before the people of North Carolina on any issue of politics and state its belief upon these issues. It therefore howls "nigger." What has Jim Young got to do with the blind institution in the city of Raleigh? Is he on the board? Not at all. There is not a negro on any institutional board in North Carolina except [institutions] for neg[r]oes, and has not been for a matter of some months, with the single exception of a colored man by the name of Peace on the board of penitentiary directors. In the name of common sense and human suffering, is there no question in North Carolina but the question of "negro?" Is that all; and will the Democratic party persist in it and insult the intelligence of men and make light of the poverty of the people by injecting this as the one issue in their campaign?...

And that is not all. Let's look a little further. You have heard Democrats talk about the town of Greenville having a negro policeman. Well, let's see. There is one there. How did he get there? The town has four colored and two white councilmen. Two of the colored councilmen proposed to elect Mr. Cherry, a white Republican policeman, if Mr. Blow, the Democratic County Chairman, Mr. Jarvis' law partner, and Mr. Brown, the other white co[u]ncilman would vote with them. Blow and Brown refused to do it, so the four negroes voted together and elected a negro. Who is responsible for the negro's election? Blow could have prevented it. They could have prevented it if they had wanted to, but they did not want to prevent it. They wanted it for campaign thunder. Well, was that anything out of the way for them to have a negro policeman in the town of Greenville? As far back as 1878, when the town was Democratic, they always elected William Hamahan a negro, for one policeman, and a white man for the other, and in the case of big crowds, when they had to appoint special policemen, they always appointed as many negroes as whites....

You remember the campaign of 1876 was largely upon the issue of "nigger." It was then the cry of negro equality. Now it is the cry of "negro domination." I state here that the Democratic party does not desire to rid itself of the negro in politics. When the Democratic party in North Carolina removes the negro from politics in North Carolina, the Democratic party goes out of existance in North Carolina. If they had desired to get rid of the negro as a disturbing factor in North Carolina, they acquired the power of 1876, when, contrary to all of their professions upon the stump, and their denunciations of the Republican party for putting negroes in office in North Carolina, they proceeded to elect negro magistrates in New Hanover, in Craven and in other counties in the State. They had it in their power to remove the negro from politics from that day until 1895, and yet they left him for the purpose of future campaigns. When they fail of the negro issue in North Carolina, what issue will the Democratic party have?

Why, when Peg-leg Williams in the days of negro exodus was carrying thousands of negroes out of the State of North Carolina, it was a Democratic legislature that rose up and passed a law stopping the business under a penalty of a thousand dollars. I have heard it said that our friend Captain Kitchen felt so outraged at the lessening of the negro population in the county of Halifax that he assaulted poor old Peg-leg Williams who was carrying his thousands further South.

I continue this charge against the Democratic party. It has always howled the nigger, and yet it has given the negro office when it could, notwithstanding its howl....

[Democrats] are the men in North Carolina who have their quiet conferences with negroes, and openly in their public prints say to the negroes, "you do a majority of the voting; therefore you are entitled to a majority of the offices of your party; demand them!" I read this advice in a paper published over here in Dunn, in the same issue of which I found also an appeal for the formation of white supremacy clubs to beat back the waves of negro domination.

What hypocrits these Democrats be. It is astonishing to me that God Himself lets them live. It is a wonder he does not start out and blast them for their hypocrisy.

ESSAYS

In the first essay, Edward L. Ayers shows the difficulties inherent in maintaining cooperation between the black and white Farmers' Alliances and the subsequent challenge presented by the issue of race in forming the Populist party. He injects a positive note, however, by suggesting that race relations during hard economic times could be fluid, allowing for political alliances based on class rather than on race. In the end, the Populist party, he writes, was constructed on ideals of economic opportunity and American democracy. Charles Postel, in the second essay, argues that the experiment in biracial cooperation gave some hope to millions of black voters but ultimately failed in the arena of race relations. The Populists' attitude toward ethnic whites, Mexican Americans, and Native Americans was more open minded, but with regard to the Chinese, they favored exclusion laws. White Populists were tolerant of black farmers' alliances and knew that they could not win against the Democrats without black support, but ultimately they turned away from future cooperative alliances and actually stood at the heart of the movement toward disfranchisement and segregation of African Americans.

Alliances and Populists

EDWARD L. AYERS

The Farmers' Alliance could not avoid the tensions, promises, and dilemmas of the New South....

During the winter of 1891–92, as everyone waited to see what would happen in a long-anticipated convention of reform groups in St. Louis in February, some of the incongruities and impossibilities began to be resolved. Farmers who thought the Alliance had no business even thinking of a third party rushed back to the Democrats. Farmers who considered the subtreasury unconstitutional, too expensive, or politically dangerous dropped out of the Alliance. Farmers who had joined in the hopes of immediate help in the marketplace left as the cooperatives failed. Politicians who had joined the Alliance in the easy days of the late 1880s, when the order asked little of its members, returned to their old party as the stakes got higher.

Those Alliancemen who remained through all these trials made a stronger commitment to the Alliance. Even as the formal Alliance organization lost members in 1891 and 1892, men who had not joined the original movement found themselves attracted by the possibility of a new political party in the South. Even farmers too independent, poor, cheap, isolated, or cynical to join the Farmers' Alliance could and did become excited by the possibilities of a third party in the South. Farmers who lacked the interest or the means to participate in cooperative stores, weekly meetings, theoretical debates, or mass picnics might be engaged by the different sort of emotions and commitments created by an overtly political party. Even men who had originally seen little appeal in the Alliance might well be disgusted at the way the Democrats bullied the opposition in local elections, legislative halls, and newspaper columns in 1891 and 1892. As the Alliance and the Democrats broke into open warfare, many voting farmers watched with mounting interest and excitement.

Black men, balancing an especially precarious set of aspirations and fears, sought to define their place in the movement as well. The Colored Farmers' Alliance had built a formidable organization in the late 1880s with little help from the white Alliance. In the St. Louis convention of 1889 the black Alliance had met separately, though the white Alliance had officially acknowledged the black order by exchanging visitors to committee meetings. The awkward maneuvers between the races continued at the Ocala, Florida, convention of 1890, where the Colored Alliance again held a separate but simultaneous meeting. The black Alliancemen suggested to the whites that representatives of the two organizations create a confederation "for purposes of mutual protection, cooperation, and assistance." The white leaders eagerly agreed and both sides "heartily endorsed" a pledge to work together for "common citizenship ... commercial equality and legal justice."

It was hard for black people to know which way to turn in the summer of 1891. Over the last year, the white Alliance had publicly professed its support for the Colored Alliance, had funded some of the white organizers of the movement, and had denounced the race-baiting tactics of the Democrats. This show of support gave black farmers confidence in the Alliance, for the white Republican allies of black voters appeared as ready as always to desert their black compatriots at the first opportunity. On the other hand the black and white Alliances did not agree on political matters of key importance to blacks, such as the Lodge elections bill and black office-holding. Just as important, black and white Alliancemen tended to occupy antagonistic positions in the Southern economy, the positions of tenant and landowner. Even a group filled with determination to overcome racial barriers as a matter of principle could not have reconciled those conflicts. The white Farmers' Alliance did not have that conviction.

To top it all off, blacks in the Colored Alliance differed deeply among themselves as well. The tensions, internal and external, erupted in the early fall of 1891 when some within the Colored Farmers' Alliance sought to use its newfound strength to tackle the most pressing problem facing its membership. Over the preceding years the amount paid to cotton pickers had declined. R. M. Humphrey the white general superintendent of the Colored Alliance, suggested that the pickers go on strike on September 6 until planters agreed to pay a dollar a day instead of the prevailing rate of 50 cents. Humphrey claimed that 1,100,000 pickers throughout the South had sworn to strike if called. Other leaders of the Colored Alliance, black men, argued against the plan. In Atlanta, E. S. Richardson, the superintendent in Georgia, argued that "this was not the purpose of our organization; that we were banded together for the purpose of educating ourselves and cooperating with the white people, for the betterment of the colored people, and such a step as this would be fatal." Whites agreed: Leonidas Polk argued that the demand for higher wages was "a great mistake on the part of our colored friends at this time. With cotton selling at 7 and 8 cents, there is not profit in it." The *Progressive Farmer* urged white Alliancemen to leave their cotton unpicked rather than cave in to the black demands.

Many in the Colored Alliance seemed eager to take some concrete action despite these admonitions, and Humphrey allowed his call for a strike to stand, organizing the "Cotton Pickers' League" to lead the effort. A group of black men attempted to begin a strike in East Texas but a planter summarily fired them and announced the conflict "immediately settled." The strike flared up again, though, a week later and several hundred miles away. It was led by Ben Patterson, a thirty-year-old black man from Memphis who traveled to Lee County, Arkansas, to organize the pickers. He won more than 25 men to his side, several of whom combed the area trying to win more converts to the cause. When black workers on one plantation got into a fight with the strikers, two non-strikers were killed. While a posse went out in search of Patterson and his allies, a white plantation manager was killed and strikers burned a cotton gin. Eventually 15 black men died and another six were imprisoned. The white Alliance immediately sought to dissociate itself from the strike and distanced itself from R. M. Humphrey. The Colored Farmers' Alliance fell into sharp decline....

The beginning of 1892 confronted the Farmers' Alliance with an extraordinarily complicated set of circumstances. The order was losing members every day and remaining cooperatives faced imminent failure. The two most important leaders, Leonidas Polk and C. W. Macune, fell into open disagreement and distrust over tactics and leadership. The Colored Farmers' Alliance had challenged the basic class and racial relations of the rural South, only to be crushed. Democrats and Republicans who had been cautiously receptive to the movement in years past now denounced the movement as a threat to the white South, the black South, the national economy, the national party system, property, democracy, and freedom.

Yet Alliancemen could find reasons for optimism as the order approached the St. Louis convention in February of 1892. Many farmers who had been resistant to the Alliance before now seemed deeply interested in a third-party effort; perhaps an election year was just what the order needed to bring it new life. The People's Party had coalesced the previous year in Cincinnati and many expected the St. Louis convention to witness the merging of the Farmers' Alliance with the nation's other insurgent groups; Terence V. Powderly of the Knights of Labor was in attendance, as was Frances Willard of the Women's Christian Temperance Union. Everything seemed to depend on the movement of the Southern Alliance into a third party, and Leonidas Polk immediately removed any doubts in his opening remarks to the convention: "The time has arrived for the great West, the great South and the great Northwest, to link their hands and hearts together and march to the ballot box and take possession of the government, restore it to the principles of our fathers, and run it in the interest of the people."

In Washington, the two major parties struggled in an especially tumultuous political arena. The control of Congress won by the Republicans in 1888 had soon proven to be a burden for the party. Labeled by their opponents the "Billion Dollar Congress," Republican lawmakers had enacted virtually everything for which they had campaigned. To the great majority of white Southerners each law was anathema or disappointment: the Lodge "force bill," the highest tariff in American history, increased pensions for Union veterans, a bill that would siphon money from the embarrassingly bloated treasury into black schools in the South, a largely ineffectual compromise on the financial system.

Voters elsewhere in the nation were disappointed with the Republican Congress as well, and the Democrats regained control of the House in 1890. With a Republican President and Senate on one side and a Democratic House on the other, the national government accomplished little as the economic condition of the country deteriorated and dissident parties gathered strength. The Democrats could barely wait for the 1892 presidential election. Grover Cleveland began to plan for another run for the White House and it soon became apparent that he would win his party's nomination. The party made no sign of trying to conciliate the Alliance and its demands....

The People's Party—or "Populists," as they came to be called by their opponents and then by themselves—tried to mobilize their forces using the tactics of the Farmers' Alliance. Tom Watson's *People's Party Paper* urged its readers on, conveying an image of the party as a healthy, family-oriented, religious, sane alternative to the bluster of the Democrats. Populists such as Watson spoke in a self-consciously straightforward language that tried to cut through the thick tangle of emotion, memory, self-interest, race pride, and fear that tied white Southern men to the Democrats. Sometimes the voice was intimate, the voice of one friend to another. "Stand by your principles and vote for Sally and the babies," Watson urged in the spring of 1892. "What is 'party' to you?"

The Democrats, though, had tradition and "common sense" on their side. From the viewpoint of regular party men, the Populists were misfits, men who could not hope to win the game if they played by the regular rules of politics. Confronted with the third-party challenge, Democrats suddenly discovered that the perpetually detested Republicans were really not so bad after all—and the Republicans suddenly found a soft spot in their hearts for the Democrats as well. "We are sure there are too many honest Republicans and Democrats to allow this crowd to get there just yet," a Republican upcountry Tennessee paper assured its readers about the Populists. To the Democrats and Republicans, the third party (the demeaning label most frequently used by the Populists' opponents) seemed to want something for nothing. Doggerel in the Atlanta *Constitution* put these words in the mouths of the Populists: "Rah for labor! Smash your neighbor! Ring out the old—Ring in the gold and silver, too! Whiskey free for you and me; Milk and honey. Fiat money; Inflammation and damnation." "Poor, pitiful, sinful cranks!" one Democratic paper commented in mock sympathy for the Populists and their lack of sophistication. "Not one of them were ever inside a bank, and know as little as to how they are managed as a hog does about the holy writ of God."

The national elections of 1892 offered real opportunities and real dangers for the Populists. Events in Washington and the South pushed the party ahead—perhaps faster than it was ready to run. Cleveland's nomination at the head of the Democrats despite his well-known advocacy of the gold standard and the national convention's failure to adopt the Farmers' Alliance platform drove many undecided Democrats into the Populist rush. The Republicans' recent billion-dollar Congress and force bill prevented disenchanted Democrats who might have thought of moving into the Republican party from doing so. Meanwhile, the Southern cotton economy continued to decline. On the other hand, the death of Polk left no one at the head of the national Populist organization to give the movement direction. The Farmer's Alliance deteriorated and Populist policies developed no farther. No one came forward with "some better system" than the subtreasury, and yet that idea, without the nourishment provided by a vital Farmers' Alliance organization, seemed to atrophy. One situation offered both opportunity and danger: despite the attrition of the black vote by legal disfranchisement in several Southern states, a majority of Southern blacks still voted in the late 1880s and early 1890s. Neither white Democrats nor white Populists could afford to ignore the black voters.

Because the arrogance and greed of white Republicans had eroded the bonds between black voters and the party of Lincoln, in the early 1890s black leaders made it known that they would consider switching their allegiance to a party that would grant them a fairer deal. Moreover, the increase in the numbers of propertied blacks in towns and in the country in the 1880s created voters who might be more independent and who might have influence among their compatriots. All these contingencies made the already heated conflict between Democrats and Populists even hotter. There were many precincts, counties, and congressional districts where black votes might swing the election.

White Populist leaders set the tone of any interracial negotiations. While black voters and leaders could respond in a variety of ways to white invitations or threats, they could not publicly initiate interracial politics. White Democrats, for their part, had already staked out their positions, had already struck their deals; they could not appear to be scared or intimidated into making new public overtures to black voters. Populist leaders, on the other hand, were starting from scratch. They had to make their positions on race known and they often experimented to find a rhetoric and a strategy that would permit them to win black votes without losing white ones. As a result, tactics varied widely. Populist candidates in Alabama, Louisiana, Virginia, North Carolina, and Texas, while using the same behind-the-scenes techniques of winning black votes that the Democrats used, made few public statements about black rights and opportunities. Although influential blacks worked among black voters, attended conventions as delegates, and spoke from the same platforms, the Populist press of those states published few accounts of interracial cooperation and said little about the implications of the third-party crusade for black citizens in the 1892 campaign. It was to no white candidate's interest to profess anything in public that could be construed as racial heresy and to no black leader's interest to heighten racial conflict. It was to everyone's interest to be on the winning side, however, and winning often required clandestine dealing. In most states in 1892 the racial struggle surrounding Populism remained a quiet and desperate sort of hand-to-hand combat.

In Georgia, though, the Populists publicly confronted the political meaning of race in the New South in 1892. Tom Watson was both temperamentally inclined and strategically impelled to articulate what others refused to say. Watson had been elected to Congress in 1890 as an outspoken Alliance man from Georgia's Tenth District, running as the Democratic representative of rural counties against the entrenched power of the Democrats in the cotton-mill city of Augusta. The same savagely honest language that got Watson elected kept him in the forefront of the farmers' movement and on the front page of the state's newspapers. An early convert to the third-party strategy after Ocala, Watson clashed so repeatedly with the Georgia Democratic party that he considered himself, with cause, "the worst abused, worst disparaged, worst 'cussed' man in Georgia." In Washington, Watson became the most active and aggressive Populist legislator in the House, introducing bill after bill to keep the demands of Ocala before the nation. He published a book about the Populist challenge whose subtitle was *Not a Revolt; It Is a Revolution,* a book the Democrats attacked on the floor of Congress with blistering criticism.

So when Tom Watson came back to Georgia to campaign for reelection in the spring of 1892, he was the focus of great attention. Crowds lined the railroad track beyond the bounds of his district, and when he got home farmers carried him on their shoulders to a stage. An enormously popular speaker and soon sole owner of the *People's Party Paper,* Watson was never at a loss for an opportunity or a desire to make his opinions known. His opponent, James C. C. Black, seemed the embodiment of the town-based Democrats: a lawyer, a Confederate veteran, and a Baptist deacon. He argued that "it is un-American and un-Christian, arraigning one class against another," that he was "a friend of all classes," and that the farmer's economic troubles were "exaggerated." The campaign was brutal. Watson fumed when Populist [presidential] candidate James Weaver was driven from Georgia by Democratic mobs, and he warned that the intimidation was only a foreshadowing of what was to come in the fall elections....

In the midst of this important campaign, Watson wrestled with the role of race in Southern politics. Both in his speeches and in the columns of his newspaper, Watson discussed what many thought should not be discussed. His appeal to blacks was relatively simple. "There is no reason why the black man should not understand that the law that hurts me, as a farmer, hurts him, as a farmer; that the same law that hurts me, as a cropper, hurts you, as a cropper; that the same law that hurts me, as a mechanic, hurts you, as a mechanic." His guiding idea was that "self interest rules," and that as long as white and black Populists each followed their own—congruent—self-interest, they could work together. As long as blacks were on Watson's side, he would help preserve their vote.

Other Georgia Populists were willing to join him. "Why is it that the Democrats are hallooing negro supremacy so persistently?" a man who signed himself "Hayseeder" wrote to the *People's Party Paper* from Burke County, Georgia. "Are they not citizens of the State, holding the same rights under the law that the white man does? If so, isn't it better to give them representation in the convention [as the Populists did in the Georgia State Convention in 1892], that they may know for whom they are voting, thereby getting them to vote with the white people at home than to ignore them till the day of election and then try to buy or force them to vote, thereby driving them into the Republican party?" The correspondent asked these questions because he was "no politician, but simply an old hayseeder, who was born under a Democratic roof, rocked in a Democratic cradle, sung to sleep with a Democratic lullaby, and have always voted with the Democratic party, but finding, in my humble judgment, that the party had drifted from the landmarks of its founders."....

Such pronouncements were indeed remarkable in the New South. Just a few months earlier, no white would have thought of saying them. The political exigencies of the Populist revolt put good orthodox white men in the position where the racial injustice of their society suddenly appeared to them as injustice. When it was *their* allies attacked and threatened, *their* voters bullied and bought, *their* morality challenged, suddenly things appeared different than when only white Republicans were implicated. The very fact that such language could surface so quickly in the New South is one more indication of the fluidity of the political world and of race relations. We should not be too quick to write off such statements as self-serving campaign tactics or as the idiosyncratic rantings of isolated men. Populist speakers stood on platforms in front of hundreds of hard-drinking, fired-up white men and said these things, stood on platforms alongside black men and said these things. In the context of 1892, they were brave things to say.

There were other things said on those platforms, though, things that were also a part of the white Populist view of blacks. In the same speech where Watson talked of the self-interest that should unite blacks and whites, he also made very clear what he did not mean. "They say I am an advocate of social equality between the whites and the blacks. THAT IS AN ABSOLUTE FALSEHOOD, and the man who utter[s] it, knows it. I have done no such thing, and you colored men know it as well as the men who formulated the slander." The *People's Party Paper* made a point of including the responses of blacks in the audience as a sort of chorus, showing that black men recognized the wisdom of Watson's words. "It is best for your race and my race that we dwell apart in our private affairs. [Many voices among the colored: 'That's so, boss.'] It is best for you to go to your churches, and I will go to mine; it is best that you send your children to your colored school, and I'll send my children to mine; you invite your colored friends to your home, and I'll invite my friends to mine. [A voice from a colored man: 'Now you're talking sense,' and murmurs of approval all through the audience.]" What Watson did not want blacks to do was to vote Republican "just because you are black. In other words, you ought not to go one way just because the whites went the other, but that each race should study these questions, and try to do the right thing by each other." Watson, in other words, wanted blacks to support Populist economic policies but not to expect anything besides economic unity....

It should not be surprising that black voters approached the Populists cautiously. Even a black man who joined Watson on the speakers' stand during the heat of the 1892 campaign gave an extremely wary endorsement of the third-party cause....

It was dangerous for a black man to say more. One of Watson's most assiduous allies was a young black minister, H. S. Doyle. Despite many threats of assassination, Doyle made 63 speeches for Watson. As the campaign drew to a close, Doyle received threats of a lynching. He went to Watson for help, and Watson sent out a call to gather supporters to help protect his black ally. Two thousand men appeared, heavily armed, after hearing rumors that Watson himself was in danger; they stayed for two nights. Watson announced at the courthouse "that the humblest white or black man that wants to talk our doctrine shall do it, and the man doesn't live who shall touch a hair of his head, without fighting every man in the people's party." "Watson has gone mad," a Democratic paper warned. Although the two thousand would not have rushed to save the black man alone, the event took on a momentum and racial meaning of its own. White men, after all, had rallied to support a leader who had boldly breached the wall between the races....

The 1892 elections unleashed tensions and conflicts that had been building for years....

It was hard in 1892 to know just who voted for the Populists, and historians ever since have been trying to untangle that mystery. Class or race interests, already complex, became even more so when refracted through the political system. Southern politics in the age of Populism, despite the apparent simplicities of black versus white, town versus countryside, and rich versus poor, were extraordinarily intricate. A close look at the way voting returns meshed with economic and demographic conditions may reveal patterns not immediately apparent from correspondence and newspaper accounts.

Since there were not enough town folk to outnumber the angry farmers, the question has to be why some farmers voted for the Populists while others did not. The starting place is clear: in most states, especially those of the lower South where the Populists were strongest, the higher the percentage of blacks in a county, the less likely Populists were to win. The most obvious reason for this pattern is that the possibilities for fraud, intimidation, persuasion, and violence directed at black men were much greater in the Black Belt than elsewhere. Voting returns from the Black Belt cannot be accepted at face value for reasons that congressional inquiries and outraged Populist editorials made all too clear.

A large black presence in a county, though, had effects other than the mere opportunity for manipulation by Democrats. Black Belt counties possessed a social and political order quite different from that of other counties in their states. First of all, many whites in heavily black counties tended to be better off because they owned land that black tenants worked for them; these landlords, who often lived in town and were closely tied to the merchant elite, were too satisfied with the status quo to listen to the Populists. Just as important, poorer white men in heavily black counties had fewer opportunites to build autonomous parties and groups. Those whites were often tenants or customers of richer men, often bound by ties of debt, obligation, or gratitude to the bulwarks of the Democratic party. The poorer whites also tended to belong to the same churches and sometimes to the same families as their wealthier neighbors. There were many social and economic reasons, then, for tenants and small farmers in the Black Belt to shun the Populists.

There were political reasons as well. Despite class differences, whites in the Black Belt often felt compelled to maintain political unity, whether by consensus or by force, against the black majority. Blacks, after all, had held political power fifteen or twenty years earlier in those counties and had struggled to maintain a living Republican party in the years since. Those Republicans were often anxious to cut a deal with the Populists to help dislodge the Democrats; they had the power of numbers and organization among black voters to offer the insurgents, and in dozens of counties such coalitions won in the early 1890s. It did not seem inconceivable that black and white Republicans could regain some of their old power if white Democrats let down their guard, if a version of the force bill were enacted, if the Democrats lost the presidency.

As incongruous as it may appear, too, considerable numbers of black men, with varying degrees of willingness and enthusiasm, voted for the Democrats in Black Belt counties. As white Republicans in the nation, state, and county increasingly banded against their black compatriots, it began to seem that black voters might do just as well to forge political alliances with the powerful whites in their own districts. In the short run, the Democrats had far more to offer blacks than did the third party. A Georgia Populist bitterly complained in the wake of the 1892 elections that though the whites in his county voted for the new party, "the negroes voted with the opposition, with some few exceptions. What the promise to have their names on the jury list did not bring into the fold of the 'dear old Democratic party,' the lavish use of 'red-eye' and money did." A black man might well decide that his appearance on a jury in the next session of his county court, or even hard cash in his pocket, was worth more than a hypothetical subtreasury plan that must have seemed far away.

Although a heavily black electorate strengthened the hands of the Democrats, a heavily white electorate was no guarantee of Populist success. In Kentucky, Tennessee, Virginia, and North Carolina, the Populists did best in counties where blacks made up a considerable part of the population and won virtually no support in the almost entirely white mountain districts. White mountain Republicans, long persuaded that the Democrats were a drag on progress—just as the Populists charged—turned to their own party for relief. The same kind of social and economic ties that bound Democratic whites to one another in the Black Belt bound Republican whites to one another in the mountains. As a result, the Populists won few votes in Appalachia even though white farmers there faced none of the racial constraints on their voting confronted by potential white Populists in the Black Belt.

In Georgia and Alabama, on the other hand, upcountry whites proved to be some of the strongest supporters of the Populists. Most Georgia and Alabama upcountry whites—unlike their counterparts in the upper South—had been neither staunch antebellum Whigs nor wartime Unionists and had not been willing to go over to the Republicans after the war. On the other hand, their interests often conflicted with the Democratic powers in Montgomery and Atlanta as well as with the Democratic rings in their county seats, and throughout the 1870s and 1880s the farmers of the Georgia and Alabama upcountry had experimented with ways to exert their own political voice without deserting to the Republicans. Those regions had been strongholds of independent and Greenback movements and were willing to listen to other dissident voices. They listened to the Populists when they arrived on the scene.

Even the strongest statistical likelihood, of course, could be circumvented by a persuasive speaker, the influence of friends, effective organizing, or a particularly obnoxious Democratic employer. Even the most powerful tendencies could be overridden by a powerful personality, as when Tom Watson led his heavily black Georgia Tenth District into the forefront of the Populist movement. Such leaders were scarce, though, and if the Populist movement as a whole were to succeed it would have to win in counties without cities and without heavy black majorities. An examination of those predominantly white rural counties in the five most successful states for the Populists—Georgia, Alabama, North Carolina, Arkansas, and Texas—reveals a strong pattern. Populist votes tended to increase in counties where the concentration on cotton was strong but where the land was poor or relatively unimproved.

That does not mean that there was a simple or straightforward connection between the misery cotton caused and Populist voting. Populism was strongest in counties where white farmers still owned the land they farmed, not in counties where the crop lien had stripped land from former owners. Populism does not seem to have been a product of particularly isolated or backward rural counties. The presence or absence of railroads made little difference, and the cumulative size of village population counted for little in every state except North Carolina—where Populist votes actually increased as town population increased. Stores did tend to be dispersed in Populist counties, which probably reflected a lack of towns. Populist votes tended to be few where manufacturing was present, though the relationship was weak.

Populism, in other words, grew in counties that had seen the arrival of the new order's railroads, stores, and villages but not its larger towns and mills. The Populists tended to be cotton farmers who worked their own land, though it was land that produced only with reluctance. Living in counties that were predominantly white but had no strong Republican presence, these farmers felt they could, indeed must, break with the Democrats.

The Populists, judging from their words and their backgrounds, wanted a fair shot at making a decent living as it was being defined in the Gilded Age. There is little evidence that Populist voters wanted to return to the "hog and hominy" days of their fathers, abandon railroads, or withdraw from the market. The state with the largest Populist presence of all, Texas, attracted men who took anything but a cautious approach to their economic lives. They had risked everything to move to the farming frontier and were determined that their risks would not be in vain. They were farmers, with all the ideological, social, political, and economic connotations of that word—not small businessmen or petty capitalists—and they wanted a fair place in market relations as producers and as consumers. The Populists' language rang with disdain for monopoly capitalism and monopoly politics, for Populists saw both as recent perversions of a political economy that could have been democratic and equitable. The Populists did not urge that their communities return to the way things used to be. Instead, they insisted that the new order be brought into alignment with the ideals of American democracy and fair capitalism.

Such a vision had radical implications in late nineteenth-century America. Far from being conservative, it sought to change the way the government and the economy operated. The Populist campaign revealed the radical component always latent in mainstream American ideals: a persistent and unmet hunger for vital democracy, a constant chafing at the injustices of large-scale capitalism. Those ideals, usually held in suspension by a relatively widespread prosperity and by a wide and expanding suffrage, could, given the right conditions, coalesce into powerful and trenchant critiques of the status quo. The raw material for such critiques lay all around the farmers, in the messages of Christian equality they heard in their churches, in the messages of the Declaration of Independence they heard at political rallies, in the ideals of just and open market relations they knew from Jefferson and Franklin. Amidst the many injustices of the New South and in the context of the Farmers' Alliance and Populist party, these ideals worked their way to the surface....

There was really no bright side to 1896 for the Southern Populists. The momentum built up over the preceding decade dissipated as the movement flew in many directions at once. Even those who believed in the cause with all their hearts could see that the party had suffered a crushing blow with Bryan's defeat and the party's loss of unanimity. "Our party, as a party, does not exist any more," Watson admitted. "Fusion has well nigh killed it. The sentiment is still there, but confidence is gone."

The year of 1896 marked a turning point in Southern politics. A Republican President once again held the White House, espousing doctrines that few white Southerners supported; the Republicans controlled the House, Senate, and presidency for the next fourteen years. The Democrats at home had been badly shaken, discredited by their weakness and by their flagrant injustices at the polls. Many townsmen, manufacturers, and workers lost faith in the old guard Democrats even though they were unwilling to vote for the Populists. The Populists had lost their sense of separate identity but had attained none of their goals. Southern politics churned under the surface.

Populists and the Shaping of a New Racial Order

CHARLES POSTEL

The formation of the People's party posed a racial dilemma. In the early 1890s, African Americans still clung to the right to vote in much of the South. Their choices, however, were growing increasingly narrow. The Republican party had lost its former strength in the South, and what remained often adopted "lily-white" policies of racial exclusion. At the same time, the Democratic party offered the black community small concessions in exchange for votes, with the understanding that blacks would acquiesce to the Democratic doctrines of white supremacy. For the new People's party to have any chance of success at the polls it had to attract a section of the black vote without undermining its support among white farmers. This was a politically difficult and dangerous undertaking for the emerging People's party across the South. In Texas the task largely rested on the able shoulders of John B. Rayner.

Rayner's trajectory was similar to that of other Populist leaders. Born in 1850, he was the son of U.S. Congressman Kenneth Rayner, whose North Carolina plantation fell on hard times after the Civil War. John studied the classics, labored in county politics, and eventually moved to Calvert, Texas, where he taught school.... In 1892 Rayner joined the People's party. With his gift for public speaking, he gained renown as he campaigned across the remote country districts of eastern Texas. By 1895 he served on the party's state executive committee. Soon thereafter, as the Populist fires cooled, he devoted his attention to farmers' technical education....

But something separated Rayner from the other leaders of Texas Populism. He was born chattel, his mother the slave property of his father. Despite his light complexion he lived on the black side of the American color line. This reality influenced his Populist vision. Although Rayner and other black Populists shared with white Populists a common set of assumptions about social progress, they had their own preoccupations and emphasized a distinct set of Populist ideas. Black Populists looked to the movement with limited expectations. Whereas white Populists hoped for a broad reordering of the nation's economic and political priorities, black Populists often focused on immediate life-and-death issues of legal justice and political rights. Whereas white Populists pursued racial uplift with the confidence of innate superiority, blacks pursued racial improvement with the bitterness of having all other paths closed by the debilitating combination of extreme poverty and the restrictions imposed by white power. In the multiplicity of Populist thought the racial chasm produced two Populisms, black and white....

White Populists understood that they lived in a "white man's country." American society, however, refused to divide neatly along the color line. Farm reformers grappled with who was white, who was not, and what to do about it. Did German immigrants belong in the Farmers' Alliance with the native-born and English-speaking farmers, or should they be shunned as aliens? The Chinese carried the double burden of being nonwhite and alien, yet what about the farmers' needs for their labor? Were Mexican farmers nonwhite, or simply unfortunate captives of a nonprogressive culture and religion? Did Native Americans make for good Alliance members, or did progress require their imprisonment upon reservations? White Populists shared concerns of this type with much of the rest of Anglo-America and, like other Anglo-Americans, their ideas about race ran the spectrum from relative tolerance to lynch-mob oppression and forced exclusion.

Populism emerged at a time of dramatic innovations in American race relations: the Chinese Exclusion Act of 1882, Jim Crow laws, and then the disfranchisement of black voters. Contemplating the ominous changes in the racial order, John Rayner observed that "the momentum of our progress calls for sudden innovations and many upheavals and convulsions in sociological affairs." He had a point. The separate but equal system of American apartheid arrived on the wings of progress. True, the "moss-backed" economic conservatives also took part. But the self-styled progressives of the New South movement bore special responsibility. Mainly comprising urban business-men, lawyers, educators, and editors, the New South movement sought to renovate and modernize southern life. In line with the widely accepted assumptions of the day, they viewed white supremacy as scientific and modern. And separation of the races formed an essential part of the New South doctrine of progressive development....

For different reasons, African Americans also adopted elements of the New South doctrine on racial matters.... The same ideas echoed in Booker T. Washington's famous address to the 1895 Atlanta Exposition. "In all things that are purely social," he reassured the white South and the nation, "we can be as separate as the fingers, yet one as the hand in all things essential to mutual progress," Many blacks resigned themselves to segregation as a means of survival. For black Populists like John Rayner, separate racial development also opened possibilities for racial uplift.

The Populists saw themselves as shaping the modern society of the future—a future in which racial separateness would be further institutionalized and defined. The Farmers' Alliance laid a foundation by spreading the principle of racial distance as it organized across rural America. The subsequent entry of the Alliance movement into third-party politics led to politically driven experiments in biracial cooperation. For a brief moment, white and black Populists succeeded in finding patches of common political ground. But even at the height of cooperation, white and black Populists often pursued separate goals. The color line held. Historians have stressed that the reform movement had few choices given the weight of the white supremacist tradition in the American South and the virulence of the backlash against any and all challenges to this tradition. The reformers, however, were not mere victims of an intractable tradition. From the strivings of the Farmers' Alliance through the campaigns of the People's party, the Populists played an active part in shaping the racial order that proved such an immovable political object.

The white Farmers' Alliance was a driving force behind the new Jim Crow segregation laws adopted across the South in the 1890s....

The Farmers' Alliance provided a powerful rural constituency for the new [segregation] laws. In a typical resolution, a local Alliance in Franklinton, North Carolina, voted in favor of adopting a new railroad law "with separate cars for white and colored." An Alliance newspaper in North Carolina ridiculed black objections to separate railroad cars as only confirming their necessity. Jim Crow legislation also merged with demands for reform. "When it comes to making a separate car for the negroes to ride in," explained a young Texas woman and member of the Farmers' Alliance, the demand for public control of the railroads would ensure that white farmers "would have our own way" in segregating them. Starting in 1890, white farm reformers would have their way as Alliance-backed "farmers' legislatures" in Georgia, Louisiana, and other states initiated "separate accommodation" laws on the railroads....

As the farm reform movement "went into politics," the white Alliance leadership adopted a more conciliatory policy toward the Colored Alliance. When in December of 1890 the supreme council of the white Farmers' Alliance held their annual meeting in Ocala, Florida, the Colored Alliance held its national council in Ocala at the same time. As their mutual exclusion rules dictated, they did not attend each other's sessions, but representatives from the white Alliance visited the black hotel to meet with their black counterparts. The result was a succinct statement by the white Alliance on racial matters. "We recommend and urge," read the Ocala resolution, "that equal facilities, educational, commercial and political, be demanded for colored and white Alliance men alike, competency considered, and that a free ballot and a fair count be insisted upon and had for colored and white alike, by every true Alliance man in America."

The wording of the Ocala resolution may have seemed generous at the time. Over the course of the ensuing decade it grew increasingly apparent that the same promise of "equal facilities" justified profoundly unequal schools, train cars, and public services. Similarly, the rhetoric of a clean ballot would provide a pretext for stripping blacks of their voting rights. At the time, however, the national meeting at Ocala offered promise—or so superintendent Richard Humphrey reported it to the Colored Alliance membership. By recognizing "common citizenship," "commercial equality," and "common protection of all," the Alliance movement was on the road to racial justice and harmony. Humphrey predicted that Ocala would "be known in future ages as the burial of race conflict, and finally of race prejudice."

It was not to be. Before the year was out conflict and prejudice scuttled further cooperation between the black and white Alliances....

The Farmers' Alliance defined itself as an association of "white" persons and denied membership to persons identified as being of African ancestry. When it came to other groups of questionable whiteness or American pedigree, however, drawing the color line often proved more complicated. Most members of the Farmers' Alliance thought of themselves as of "Anglo-Saxon stock," had roots in the Protestant churches, spoke English, and were American born. They often treated Catholic and non-English-speaking farmers with indifference or even hostility. Despite cultural barriers, a number of immigrant farmers joined the Alliance movement. Robert Schilling of Milwaukee, for example, edited the *National Reformer,* a German-language newspaper that adhered to Alliance doctrine.

Several communities of Bohemian farmers in central Texas similarly looked to the Alliance as "the savior of the rural workers." They published a reform newspaper, *Roinik,* and organized into a series of suballiances near Caldwell, Texas. Charles Macune credited a Bohemian suballiance with a pioneering boycott of merchants that became an important tactic in Alliance business efforts. Yet Texas farmers wrote to the *Southern Mercury* protesting that "we want neither Bohemians nor Chinamen" in the state. When the Bohemian suballiances criticized the *Mercury* for printing such inflammatory statements, the editors rebuked them with the advice that although they may be bona fide members of the Alliance, they needed to make themselves "less Bohemian and more American."

In the West, communities of Mexican farmers also joined the Alliance. Several Mexican suballiances in New Mexico petitioned for membership. White Alliance members reported that, notwithstanding their Catholic "bondage," Mexican farmers could be "enlightened through the Alliance" to embrace "progress and reform." Despite white Populist rhetoric about "drunken and renegade Indians," farmers of the Chickasaw Nation in the Indian Territory also joined the Alliance. The North Carolina Alliance enrolled Cherokee and Croatan Indians, but only if they were "of pure Indian blood and not less than half white." In other words, for a tribe member to be eligible for membership he had to have mainly white ancestry and, according to the one-drop rule, no black ancestry. Recognizing the complexity of such restrictions, the Farmers' Alliance allowed each state a degree of discretion as to the complexion of its members, with the proviso that "none but white men shall be elected as delegates to the Supreme Council."

While the Alliance color line stretched and bent around the meanings of whiteness and Americanness, it pulled taut against the Chinese. In eastern Texas and Mississippi large plantation owners had experimented with the importation of Chinese field workers, inflaming anti-Chinese attitudes....

White solidarity vis-à-vis the Chinese extended beyond the West Coast. In his 1888 speech at the Texas State Fair, Henry Grady welcomed the "exclusion of the Chinese [as] the first step in the revolution" that would solidify white brotherhood. White supremacy was not a sectional issue, he explained to the Texas farmers. "It speaks wherever the Anglo-Saxon touches an alien race. It has just spoken in universally approved legislation in excluding the Chinamen from our gates." Grady's anti-Chinese appeal received praise from the editors of the *Southern Mercury*. Tom Watson's *People's Party Paper* demanded strict enforcement of exclusion laws against Chinese "moral and social lepers," and Mary Lease similarly warned of a "tide of Mongols." A small number of reformers, especially those interested in Asian religions, accepted the idea that the Chinese were part of the human moral family. But from Illinois to Texas and Georgia to California, the farmers' movement largely embraced the vision of a "white man's country" purged of "Asiatic labor."...

Populism conceived of itself as the party of law, order, and due process. Progress required clean government and replacing the Democratic old guard of "bulldozing," corruption, and violence. Populist and Democratic practice often proved dismally similar when it came to the treatment of black citizens. Even so, African Americans paid close attention to the smallest shades of difference given their lack of options and the perils they faced. As W. H. Warwick, the superintendent of the Virginia Colored Alliance, put it, blacks were "ready to act with any party that will go to work to remedy the evils" of ballot stuffing and lynch mobs. This sentiment goes a long way to explain the motives of blacks who threw in their lot with the People's party in the face of considerable personal risks of white retribution. Black Populism represented the narrow hope that the new party might indeed deliver on its promise of law-based government and due process.

Such a hope brought John B. Rayner into the Populist fold. He joined the Texas People's party in 1892 and quickly gained a reputation as the "silver tongued orator of the colored race." The Texas party had other black officials, including Melvin Wade of Dallas, R. H. Hayes of Fort Worth, and C. M. Ferguson of Houston. Rayner, however, was the most prominent. He was also the least urban as he made his home and political base in the remote and desolate farm districts of east Texas. By profession—like so many white Populists—he worked as a schoolteacher and occasionally as a Baptist minister. Unlike many of his white counterparts, he had only a secondary interest in the economic problems of agricultural reform. His commitments were primarily political. He viewed Populism as a means to a political end whereby a person such as himself might obtain the legal and political standing that he was denied for most of his adult life.

As a young man Rayner looked forward to his prospects in post–Civil War North Carolina. With the assistance of his white father, he received a classical education in Raleigh before he moved to rural Edgecombe County to seek his fortune. The county offered an ambitious young black man political possibilities, for it had a Republican administration and a two-thirds black majority. For several years he held the appointed position of constable of the grand jury of the superior court. In 1875 he won election as a township magistrate. By this time, however, the Democrats busily prepared to drive out black officeholders and "redeem" the state for white supremacy. Toward this end the Redeemers rewrote the state constitution to restrict local self-government and make the office of magistrate an appointed rather than elected position. The Democrats viewed the presence of black judicial officials as a particular insult to the white race. The Redeemer government closed all doors to Rayner, despite his education, his experience, and his electoral support.

The wrongs of Redemption proved a defining experience in Rayner's life. He never forgot or forgave. "The civilization that teaches me to think, and then limits my aspiration," he would later note, "will asphixicate itself with the mephitic breath of its own intolerance." As his biographer Gregg Cantrell points out, Rayner and many blacks of his generation who experienced Reconstruction spent their adult lives trying to regain what they had lost. A first step was to leave the shattered expectations behind and join the black exodus out of North Carolina for a new start in Texas.

Rayner settled in the east Texas county of Robertson, a county of large cotton plantations with black tenants, sharecroppers, and laborers accounting for almost half the population. He tended to stay out of the political fray as he grew increasingly disillusioned with the Republican party. The "lily-white" Republicans, he observed, appealed only to "complexional prejudices, blue veins, straight hair and business sentiments." Black Republicans, meanwhile, had been reduced to political impotence, what he contemptuously described as "hotel flunkies, barbers, dude school teachers, ignorant preachers, saloon waiters." Of course, Rayner himself was a schoolteacher and a preacher. Those were the professions open to an educated black man. But he was also the son of a U.S. congressman and had once held positions of authority. He believed in power, not sentiment.... "The only rights we negroes will ever enjoy," he counseled, "will be rights the southern white man gives us."

Rayner looked to powerful whites, especially those willing to recognize the worth of a man such as himself, as the best hope. "The superior man," he believed, "is he who makes a righteous use of power." The Populists, in his calculations, were white people of that type. His fellow black Populist Melvin Wade, with his experience in the Knights of Labor, demanded and expected that the People's party would provide equal treatment, "work[ing] a black and white horse in the same field." Rayner, on the other hand, had few illusions about Populism as a vehicle for racial equality. He did, however, hope that the third party would have the power to overthrow Democratic rule. And toward this end he made common cause with wealthy and influential whites who otherwise shared little with their black neighbors. He made a working alliance with E. S. Peters, a Robertson County planter who owned several thousand acres of cotton lands and was the president of the Texas branch of the American Cotton Growers Association. Rayner and Peters, along with another wealthy planter, led the work of the county's Populists.

White Populists in Texas knew that without the black vote the third party was lost. People's party meetings often included black men and they occasionally elected black delegates to party conventions. For a man of Rayner's ambition the

People's party allowed him to tour the state speaking to black and white audiences, setting up new Populist clubs in his wake, and rising to the party's highest councils. Such biracial politics, however, did not translate into challenging the principles of segregation or white supremacy. The People's party in Texas rarely disrupted the white monopoly of officeholding and black Populists made no claims on statewide office. Even such an effective campaigner as Rayner did not run as a candidate.

Rayner focused his political energies on electing Populist judges and sheriffs at the county level. The People's party, he believed, represented law and order—ideals to which he had been committed since his days as a magistrate in North Carolina. Before the public he stressed the importance of obedience to the law for the uplift of the black race. In part this was designed to placate white audiences. It also conformed to his notion that the cultivation of the law-abiding duties of citizenship was essential for racial progress. Moreover, as he saw it, the worst enemies of progress were lawless white mobs and corrupt and ignorant officers and jurors. Hence the imperative to put "the best white citizens" in the jurors' box. At the same time, blacks had to be part of the legal process. "The man who is not allowed to help enforce the law can not reverence the law," he reasoned. "Therefore all educated worthy tax paying Negroes, feel that they have a legal and moral right to serve as jurors and help enforce the law."

Rayner considered the jury question essential. He hoped that seating black jurors in cases involving black defendants would provide a minimal safeguard against the widespread practice of convicting blacks on trumped-up charges and delivering them to the abuses of the convict-lease system. The People's party proposed reforms in the convict labor laws and made occasional promises to place blacks on juries. White Populists also voiced opposition to mob violence and lynching. But the practical distinction between white Populists and white Democrats often remained submerged under the politics of white supremacy....

In his private papers John Rayner criticized race prejudice as "the Devil's race track." He resented white claims of superiority and the obstacles to black political and economic opportunities. At the same time, he was wary of "utopian" challenges to the racial system. The failure of white Populists to challenge the "Negro" signs in the railroad cars troubled black Populists like Melvin Wade. Rayner, on the other hand, made peace with the separate but equal doctrine as it corresponded to his own understanding of racial difference. Like most late nineteenth-century Americans, he accepted the idea that race was an essential and natural marker of human characteristics. The separation of public facilities by race only reaffirmed this notion.

Rayner also saw in the separate but equal doctrine possibilities for positive good as seen by his contribution to the platform of the Texas People's party. He helped shape two measures of particular interest to blacks when he served on the platform committee at the 1894 state convention in Waco. The first called for state accommodations for the insane "without discrimination in color." The second demanded more funds for both white and black schools, but with the significant proviso that the segregated schools would also have racially separate administrations, whereby "each race shall have its own trustees and control its own schools." Separate administrations for segregated institutions would provide careers for educated and talented blacks. Rayner himself would later seek the post of superintendent of the state Colored Blind Asylum. But more broadly he believed that a more complete separation would open the way for the free progress of both blacks and whites....

White Populists viewed racial separatism as a positive good and "social equality" as a definite evil. "We have no advocates of social equality with the darkey," a North Carolina Populist explained. "There is not a cartload of white men in the State that would tolerate such an idea a moment, and the negroes don't want it." At the same time, white Populists could and did appeal for black and white unity based on common interests. As Henry Grady told the farmers at Dallas, creating a new racial order meant that the white man had to lead the black man "to confess that his interests and the interests of the [white] people of the South are identical." On the same principles the Populists made experiments to win black votes by emphasizing a shared economic interest. In Grimes County, Texas, blacks were a majority of the population, and winning a portion of the black vote was essential to Populist political strategy....

Charles C. Post, the chairman of the Georgia Populist party, explained the racial politics of cotton prices before an audience in Battle Creek, Michigan, where concerns about the plight of the former slaves were kept alive by old abolitionist sentiments. According to Post, "The best thing they could do for [blacks] was to turn in and help the People's party ... bring cotton up to where we could afford to pay a nigger more than fifty cents a day without ourselves coming out in debt to the merchant to do it." Better farm prices would help white farmers to settle accounts with the merchants and thereby improve the life of their black tenants and laborers. In political reality, the logic that blacks should go to the ballot box to help white farmers to secure higher prices implied a leap of faith, a leap that black voters were reluctant to take....

[T]he Populist challenge to Democratic rule in the South held much significance for race relations. In translating the ideology of white supremacy into practice, the evidence suggests that both parties included more and less virulent white supremacists. Although the Populists occasionally showed a practical caution compared to the fanatical racial campaigns of the Democrats, the significance of Populism did not lie in possible shadings in a common master race ideology and practice. Rather it lay in the Populist role in reviving political competition. The Populists, no less than the Democrats, represented white supremacy, as did the "lily-white" Republicans. But when the Populists engaged in political combat with the Democrats—especially when this combat made for alliances with a Republican party that continued to have a significant African American constituency—cracks opened in the walls of racial oppression.

Party competition mattered. It gave black political activists opportunities to speak and organize. It also compelled all three parties to address issues of concern to potential black voters, including "an honest count," legal due process, and school funding. As long as blacks still had the franchise, party competition at times required negotiations with the black community. But in no case did these negotiations call into question the basic assumptions of the New South racial outlook. The Democrat James Hogg displayed personal courage when he sought murder charges for the ringleaders of the Paris, Texas, lynch mob that burned alive Henry Smith. The Populists Tom Watson and Marion Butler of North Carolina also showed bravery: Watson by protecting Seb Doyle from a Democratic mob, and Butler in his defense of black voting rights. But Hogg, Watson, Butler, and the other southern white members of their parties never articulated a challenge to white supremacy and segregation.

Black Populism, on the other hand, contained a covert element of subversion. The public pronouncements of the Colored Alliance, and particularly those of its white superintendents, reassured the white South that its members acquiesced in the separate but equal doctrines of white supremacy. But black members such as the Reverend J. L. Moore of Florida clearly understood this as a stratagem, as a means toward black progress and a new trial of strength out of which educated and prosperous African Americans "will come to the top" and "come to stay." For his part, John Rayner embraced much of the New South racial creed, but rejected its permanence. He believed that even in the confines of segregation and white supremacy, by taking part in politics blacks could pursue racial uplift and transcend the system of "racial egoism."

At great personal risk, Moore, Rayner, and other African Americans seized on the possibilities opened up by divisions within the white supremacist camp. In their hopes for schools and a better life they organized the Colored Alliance in the face of white neglect and hostility. In an expression of faith in the political process, they exploited interparty competition to press demands for education, legal justice, and political rights. Not only the black Populists but also a much larger number of black Republicans (and an overlooked number of black Democrats) bore the brunt of the white supremacist campaigns of intimidation, beatings, and murder. But by the turn of the century, Jim Crow statutes, disfranchisement amendments, and the powerful reassertion of nationalistic white solidarity largely dashed black hopes. It is impossible to separate the Populists from this brave new world of race relations....

FURTHER READING

A. M. Arnett, *The Populist Movement in Georgia* (1922).

Donna A. Barnes, *Farmers in Rebellion: The Rise and Fall of the Southern Farmers Alliance and People's Party in Texas* (1984).

Victoria E. Bynum, *The Long Shadow of the Civil War: Southern Dissent and Its Legacies* (2010).

Gregg Cantrell, *Kenneth and John B. Rayner and the Limits of Southern Dissent* (1993).

Jeffrey J. Crow and Robert F. Durden, *Maverick Republican in the Old North State: A Political Biography of Daniel L. Russell* (1977).

Charles Crowe, "Tom Watson, Populists, and Blacks Reconsidered," *Journal of Negro History* 55 (April 1970), 99–116.

Robert F. Durden, *The Climax of Populism: The Election of 1896* (1965).

J. Wayne Flynt, *Dixie's Forgotten People: The South's Poor Whites* (1971, 2004).

Gerald H. Gaither, *Blacks and the Populist Revolt: Ballots and Bigotry in the New South* (1977).

Lawrence Goodwyn, *Democratic Promise: The Populist Moment in America* (1976).

Dewey Grantham, *The Life & Death of the Solid South: A Political History* (1988).

James R. Green, *Grass-roots Socialism: Radical Movements in the Southwest, 1895–1943* (1978).

Sheldon Hackney, *Populism to Progressivism in Alabama* (1969).

Steven Hahn, *The Roots of Southern Populism: Yeoman Farmers and the Transformation of the Georgia Upcountry, 1850–1890* (1983).

William Ivy Hair, *Bourbonism and Agrarian Protest: Louisiana Politics, 1877–1900* (1969).

Roger L. Hart, *Redeemers, Bourbons, and Populists: Tennessee, 1870–1896* (1975).

John D. Hicks, *The Populist Revolt: A History of the Farmers' Alliance and the People's Party* (1931).

Richard Hofstadter, *The Age of Reform: From Bryan to F.D.R.* (1955).

William F. Holmes, "The Southern Farmers' Alliance and the Jute Cartel," *Journal of Southern History* 60 (February 1994), 59–80.

Paul Horton, "Testing the Limits of Class Politics in Postbellum Alabama: Agrarian Radicalism in Lawrence County," *Journal of Southern History* 61 (1991), 63–84.

Michael Kazin, *The Populist Persuasion: An American History* (1995).

J. Morgan Kousser, *The Shaping of Southern Politics: Suffrage Restriction and the Establishment of the One-Party South, 1880–1910* (1974).

Robert C. McMath, *American Populism: A Social History* (1993).

———, *Populist Vanguard: A History of the Southern Farmers' Alliance* (1975).

James Tice Moore, "Redeemers Reconsidered: Change and Continuity in the Democratic South, 1870–1900," *Journal of Southern History* 44 (August 1978), 357–378.

Stuart Noblin, *Leonidas Lafayette Polk: Agrarian Crusader* (1949).

Bruce Palmer, *"Man Over Money": The Southern Populist Critique of American Capitalism* (1980).

Norman Pollack, *The Populist Response to Industrial America* (1962).

Michael Schwartz, *Radical Protest and Social Structure: The Southern Farmers' Alliance and Cotton Tenancy, 1880–1890* (1976).

Barton C. Shaw, *The Wool-Hat Boys: Georgia's Populist Party* (1984).

James Turner, "Understanding the Populists," *Journal of American History* 67 (September 1980), 354–373.

Samuel Webb, *Two-Party Politics in the One-Party South: Alabama's Hill Country, 1874–1920* (1997).

C. Vann Woodward, *Origins of the New South, 1877–1913* (1951).

———, *Tom Watson: Agrarian Rebel* (1938).

CHAPTER 6

The Intimidation Effect: Disfranchisement, Segregation, and Violence

In the South, the struggle for political leadership had dramatic consequences. During the 1890s the Populists had entertained the idea of black and white voters following their economic interests as a voting bloc. After the defeat of the Populists, however, conservative Democrats in state legislatures passed restrictive laws designed to discourage black and white political unity. The result was disfranchisement and the imposition of segregation. Black southerners (along with some poorer whites) lost many of the political rights they had gained during Reconstruction. In addition, a legally mandated system of cradle-to-grave segregation imposed on southern blacks the stigma of inferiority. If this did not send a clear message to African Americans, then lynching and race riots would. By 1900, Jim Crow had come to roost in the South.

Clearly, this institutionalization of white supremacy was in some ways a culmination of racist trends that had been developing since emancipation or even before. But it also marked a drastic change in the legal, political, and social status of African Americans. Black men had voted since 1867; they held office and continued to do so, albeit in fewer numbers, until the 1890s. African Americans had not been legally barred from many areas of southern life. Separation by race before Jim Crow laws were passed, for example in schools and churches, was a matter of custom in each locality. Blacks and whites often lived in the same neighborhoods, rode street cars together, and worked alongside of each other in industries such as coal mining and steel making. Most states did not enact segregation laws until after 1896, when the U.S. Supreme Court in Plessy *v.* Ferguson *ruled that "separate but equal" was constitutional. Equal provision for African Americans was not enforced and the exclusion of blacks from "white" institutions—universities, professions, juries, hospitals, neighborhoods, and unions, in addition to lodgings, restaurants, libraires, swimming pools, parks, and playgrounds—was only the most visible manifestation of segregation. Behind these indignities was the reality that the police powers of the state maintained the laws of segregation, giving sanction to the notion that southerners must live within an unalterable caste society. The other side of this equation was that the police powers of the state would do little or nothing to protect African Americans from lynchings, rapes, and race riots.*

The causes of disfranchisement, segregation, and violence are complex and therefore have generated considerable historical debate. What could be the connection between Populism and segregation? What role did the politics of the 1890s play in advancing disfranchisement and segregation, and what role did gender play? Which decade saw the greatest number of lynchings and why? Did segregation have any influence on the gradual decline of lynching? How did the federal government aid in advancing segregation? How did white southerners respond to disfranchisement and segregation? How did African Americans respond to the rising tide of racism, attempts to impede their voting rights, and the imposition of Jim Crow laws?

DOCUMENTS

In Document 1, the actual incidence of lynching is charted by region, by state, and by year. Causes for lynching, as described by protester Ida B. Wells in Document 2, changed over time, but the rape of a white woman by a black man was often considered the most justifiable reason for violence. In her newspaper, the *Free Speech,* Wells documented that lynchings were more often motivated by economic jealousy. She raised the ire of white citizens in Memphis in 1892 when she suggested that many so-called rapes were in fact voluntary romantic alliances between a white woman and a black man. The legal formulas for disfranchisement—literacy tests, poll taxes, and grandfather clauses (used to benefit otherwise unqualified whites)—are illustrated by excerpts from a North Carolina statute in Document 3. Although institutional and political power had swung against them, black leaders protested vigorously, as shown by the remarks of Robert Smalls, a black delegate to South Carolina's 1895 constitutional convention, in Document 4. By the end of the century, white supremacists villified black males, especially as threats to white womanhood, as shown in Document 5 via excerpts from the *Raleigh News and Observer.* By the turn of the century, Mark Twain, America's loving critic, shows his deep disdain for the southern appetite for lynching. He wrote the essay in Document 6 in reaction to a lynching in his home state of Missouri. The essay was published in 1923, 13 years after his death. Sarcastic as the essay may seem, Twain was deadly serious about the horror of lynching. The consequence of violent rhetoric was violent action. In Document 7, Walter White, who grew up in Atlanta but later became executive director of the National Association for the Advancement of Colored People, describes how he was affected by the Atlanta race riot of 1906. Document 8, a shortened version of the Alabama Literacy Test, was still used to qualify or disqualify potential voters until passage of the 1965 Voting Rights Act. If you were living in Alabama in 1964, could you pass the test and vote?

1. Lynching in the United States, 1882–1930

TABLE 1 Number of Persons Lynched, by Region and by Race for Five-Year Periods, 1889–1928

Years	South	Non-South	Black	White	Totals
1889–1893	705	134	579	260	839
1894–1898	680	94	544	230	774
1899–1903	492	51	455	88	543
1904–1908	362	19	354	27	381
1909–1913	347	15	326	36	362
1914–1918	311	14	264	61	325
1919–1923	287	14	273	28	301
1924–1928	95	5	91	9	100

SOURCE: Compiled from data in NAACP, *Thirty Years of Lynching* (New York: NAACP, 1919) and *Supplements* (1919–1928). Southern states are Alabama, Arkansas, Florida, Georgia, Kentucky, Louisiana, Mississippi, Missouri, North Carolina, Oklahoma, South Carolina, Tennessee, Texas, Virginia, West Virginia—the fifteen states in which the ASWPL was active.

TABLE 2 Number of Persons Lynched, by States, 1882–1930

State	Whites	Blacks	Total
Alabama	46	296	342
Arizona	35	1	36
Arkansas	64	230	294
California	42	4	46
Colorado	70	6	76
Connecticut	0	0	0
Delaware	0	1	1
Florida	25	241	266
Georgia	34	474	508
Idaho	16	6	22
Illinois	15	16	31
Indiana	33	19	52
Iowa	19	1	20
Kansas	34	18	52
Kentucky	62	151	213
Louisiana	60	328	388

(*Continued*)

From *Revolt Against Chivalry: Jessie Daniel Ames and the Women's Campaign Against Lynching* by Jacquelyn Dowd Hall.

TABLE 2 Number of Persons Lynched, by States, 1882–1930 (Continued)

State	Whites	Blacks	Total
Maine	0	0	0
Maryland	3	27	30
Massachusetts	0	0	0
Michigan	4	4	8
Minnesota	6	3	9
Mississippi	45	500	545
Missouri	53	63	116
Montana	91	2	93
Nebraska	55	5	60
Nevada	12	0	12
New Hampshire	0	0	0
New Jersey	0	1	1
New Mexico	39	4	43
New York	1	1	2
North Carolina	14	85	99
North Dakota	12	2	14
Ohio	9	13	22
Oklahoma	116	44	160
Oregon	22	3	25
Pennsylvania	1	5	6
Rhode Island	0	0	0
South Carolina	5	154	159
South Dakota	34	0	34
Tennessee	44	196	240
Texas	143	349	492
Utah	6	3	9
Vermont	0	0	0
Virginia	16	88	104
Washington	30	0	30
West Virginia	15	35	50
Wisconsin	6	0	6
Wyoming	38	7	45
Total	1,375	3,386	4,761

SOURCE: Monroe Work, ed., *The Negro Year Book: An Annual Encyclopedia of the Negro, 1931–1932* (Tuskegee: Negro Year Book Publishing Co., 1931), p. 293.

2. Ida B. Wells Reports the Horrors of Lynching in the South, 1892

From 1865 to 1872, hundreds of colored men and women were mercilessly murdered and the almost invariable reason assigned was that they met their death by being alleged participants in an insurrection or riot. But this story at last wore itself out. No insurrection ever materialized; no Negro rioter was ever apprehended and proven guilty, and no dynamite ever recorded the black man's protest against oppression and wrong. It was too much to ask thoughtful people to believe this transparent story, and the southern white people at last made up their minds that some other excuse must be had.

Then came the second excuse, which had its birth during the turbulent times of reconstruction. By an amendment to the Constitution the Negro was given the right of franchise, and, theoretically at least, his ballot became his invaluable emblem of citizenship. In a government "of the people, for the people, and by the people," the Negro's vote became an important factor in all matters of state and national politics. But this did not last long. The southern white man would not consider that the Negro had any right which a white man was bound to respect, and the idea of a republican form of government in the southern states grew into general contempt. It was maintained that "This is a white man's government," and regardless of numbers the white man should rule. "No Negro domination" became the new legend on the sanguinary banner of the sunny South, and under it rode the Ku Klux Klan, the Regulators, and the lawless mobs, which for any cause chose to murder one man or a dozen as suited their purpose best. It was a long, gory campaign; the blood chills and the heart almost loses faith in Christianity when one thinks of Yazoo, Hamburg, Edgefield, Copiah, and the countless massacres of defenseless Negroes, whose only crime was the attempt to exercise their right to vote.

But it was a bootless strife for colored people. The government which had made the Negro a citizen found itself unable to protect him. It gave him the right to vote, but denied him the protection which should have maintained that right. Scourged from his home; hunted through the swamps; hung by midnight raiders, and openly murdered in the light of day, the Negro clung to his right of franchise with a heroism which would have wrung admiration from the hearts of savages. He believed that in that small white ballot there was a subtle something which stood for manhood as well as citizenship, and thousands of brave black men went to their graves, exemplifying the one by dying for the other.

The white man's victory soon became complete by fraud, violence, intimidation and murder. The franchise vouchsafed to the Negro grew to be a "barren

---

From *Southern Horrors* by Royster, Bedford/St. Martin's Press, 1996.

ideality," and regardless of numbers, the colored people found themselves voiceless in the councils of those whose duty it was to rule. With no longer the fear of "Negro Domination" before their eyes, the white man's second excuse became valueless. With the Southern governments all subverted and the Negro actually eliminated from all participation in state and national elections, there could be no longer an excuse for killing Negroes to prevent "Negro Domination."

Brutality still continued; Negroes were whipped, scourged, exiled, shot and hung whenever and wherever it pleased the white man so to treat them, and as the civilized world with increasing persistency held the white people of the South to account for its outlawry, the murderers invented the third excuse—that Negroes had to be killed to avenge their assaults upon women. There could be framed no possible excuse more harmful to the Negro and more unanswerable if true in its sufficiency for the white man.

Humanity abhors the assailant of womanhood, and this charge upon the Negro at once placed him beyond the pale of human sympathy. With such unanimity, earnestness and apparent candor was this charge made and reiterated that the world has accepted the story that the Negro is a monster which the Southern white man has painted him. And to-day, the Christian world feels, that while lynching is a crime, and lawlessness and anarchy the certain precursors of a nation's fall, it can not by word or deed, extend sympathy or help to a race of outlaws, who might mistake their plea for justice and deem it an excuse for their continued wrongs....

If the Southern people in defense of their lawlessness, would tell the truth and admit that colored men and women are lynched for almost any offense, from murder to a misdemeanor, there would not now be the necessity for this defense. But when they intentionally, maliciously and constantly belie the record and bolster up these falsehoods by the words of legislators, preachers, governors and bishops, then the Negro must give to the world his side of the awful story.

A word as to the charge itself. In considering the third reason assigned by the Southern white people for the butchery of blacks, the question must be asked, what the white man means when he charges the black man with rape. Does he mean the crime which the statutes of the civilized states describe as such? Not by any means. With the Southern white man, any mesalliance existing between a white woman and a colored man is a sufficient foundation for the charge of rape. The Southern white man says that it is impossible for a voluntary alliance to exist between a white woman and a colored man, and therefore, the fact of an alliance is a proof of force. In numerous instances where colored men have been lynched on the charge of rape, it was positively known at the time of lynching, and indisputably proven after the victim's death, that the relationship sustained between the man and woman was voluntary and clandestine, and that in no court of law could even the charge of assault have been successfully maintained.

It was for the assertion of this fact, in the defense of her own race, that the writer hereof became an exile; her property destroyed and her return to her home forbidden under penalty of death, for writing [an] editorial [stating this] which was printed in her paper, the *Free Speech*, in Memphis, Tenn., May 21, 1892.

3. Literacy Test and Poll Tax in North Carolina, 1899

(Sec. 4.) Every person presenting himself for registration shall be able to read and write any section of the constitution in the English language and before he shall be entitled to vote he shall have paid on or before the first day of March of the year in which he proposes to vote his poll tax as prescribed by law for the previous year. Poll taxes shall be a lien only on assessed property and no process shall issue to enforce the collection of the same except against assessed property.

(Sec. 5.) No male person who was on January one, eighteen hundred and sixty-seven, or at any time prior thereto entitled to vote under the laws of any state in the United States wherein he then resided, and no lineal descendant of any such person, shall be denied the right to register and vote at any election in this state by reason of his failure to possess the educational qualification prescribed in section four of this article: *Provided*, he shall have registered in accordance with the terms of this section prior to December one, nineteen hundred and eight. The general assembly shall provide for a permanent record of all persons who register under this section on or before November first, nineteen hundred and eight: and all such persons shall be entitled to register and vote in all elections by the people in this state unless disqualified under section two of this article: *Provided*, such persons shall have paid their poll tax as requ[i]red by law.

4. Black Leaders Fight Disfranchisement, 1895

General Smalls' Speech

Gen. Robert Smalls who is known everywhere as South Carolina's "gullah statesman," then took the floor. He said: ...

I was born and raised in South Carolina, and today I live on the very spot on which I was born, and I expect to remain here as long as the great God allows me to live, and I will ask no one else to let me remain. I love the State as much as any member of this convention, because it is the garden spot of the south.

This document can be found in the Public Laws of North Carolina, 1899, Chapter 218.

The speech of General Robert Smalls of South Carolina can be found in *The Columbia State*, October 27, 1895.

Mr. President, this convention has been called for no other purpose than the disfranchisement of the negro. Be careful, and bear in mind that the elections which are to take place early next month in very many of the States are watching the action of this convention, especially on the suffrage question. Remember that the negro was not brought here of his own accord. I found my reference to a history in the congressional library in Washington ... that he says that in 1619, in the month of June, a Dutch man-of-war landed at Jamestown, Va., with 15 sons of Africa aboard, at the time Miles Kendall was deputy governor of Virginia. He refused to allow the vessel to be anchored in any of her harbors. But he found out after his order had been sent out that the vessel was without provisions, and the crew was in a starving condition. He countermanded his order, and supplied the vessel with the needed provisions in exchange for 14 negroes. It was then that the seed of slavery was planted in the land. So you see we did not come here of our own accord; we were brought here in a Dutch vessel, and we have been here ever since. The Dutch are here, and are now paying a very large tax, and are controlling the business of Charleston today. They are not to blame, and are not being blamed.

We served our masters faithfully, and willingly, and as we were made to do for 244 years. In the last war you left them home. You went to the war, fought, and come back home, shattered to pieces, worn out, one-legged, and found your wife and family being properly cared for by the negroes you left behind. Why should you now seek to disfranchise a race that has been so true to you?...

Since reconstruction times 53,000 negroes have been killed in the south, and not more than three white men have been convicted and hung for these crimes. I want you to be mindful of the fact that the good people of the north are watching this convention upon this subject. I hope you will make a Constitution that will stand the test. I hope that we may be able to say when our work is done that we have made as good a Constitution as the one we are doing away with.

The negroes are paying taxes in the south on $263,000,000 worth of property. In South Carolina, according to the census, the negroes pay tax on $12,500,000 worth of property. That was in 1890. You voted down without discussion, merely by a vote to lay on the table, a proposition for a simple property and educational qualification. What do you want? You tried the infamous eight-box [required poorly educated voters to place ballots correctly in eight separate ballot boxes, one for each office] and registration laws until they were worn to such a thinness that they could stand neither the test of the law nor of public opinion. In behalf of the 600,000 negroes in the State and the 132,000 negro voters all that I demand is that a fair and honest election law be passed. We care not what the qualifications imposed are, all that we ask is that they be fair and honest, and honorable, and with these provisos we will stand or fall by it. You have 102,000 white men over 21 years of age, 13,000 of these cannot read nor write. You dare not disfranchise them, and you know that the man who proposes it will never be elected to another office in the State of South Carolina. But whatever Mr. [Ben] Tillman can do, he can make nothing worse than the infamous eight-box law, and I have no praise for the Conservatives, for they gave the people that law. Fifty-eight thousand negroes cannot read nor write. This leaves a majority of 14,000 white men who can read and write over the same class of negroes in this State. We are willing to accept a scheme that provides that no man who cannot read nor write can vote, if you dare pass it. How can you expect an ordinary man to "understand and explain" any section of the Constitution, to correspond to the interpretation put upon it by the manager of election, when by a very recent decision of the supreme court, composed of the most learned men in the State, two of them put one construction upon a section, and the other justice put an entirely different construction upon it. To embody such a provision in the election law would be to mean that every white man would interpret it aright and every negro would interpret it wrong. I appeal to the gentleman from Edgefield to realize that he is not making a law for one set of men. Some morning you may wake up to find that the bone and sinew of your country is gone. The negro is needed in the cotton fields and in the low country rice fields, and if you impose too hard conditions upon the negro in this State there will be nothing else for him to do but to leave. What then will you do about your phosphate works? No one but a negro can work them; the mines that pay the interest on your State debt. I tell you the negro is the bone and sinew of your country and you cannot do without him. I do not believe you want to get rid of the negro, else why did you impose a high tax on immigration agents who might come here to get him to leave?

Now, Mr. President we should not talk one thing and mean another. We should not deceive ourselves. Let us make a Constitution that is fair, honest and just. Let us make a Constitution for all the people, one we will be proud of and our children will receive with delight.

5. Democrats Fight Back: The White-Supremacy Campaign, 1898

The Duty of White Men Today

No man who loves his State can read the daily occurrences of crime in North Carolina where the negro is the aggressor without trembling for the future of the State. There have been more assaults upon white women by negro brutes in one year and a half of Republican rule than in twenty years of Democratic rule. There have been more insults to white girls, more wrongs to white men, more lawlessness and more crime committed by negroes in North Carolina during the last twenty months than during the previous twenty years.

Taken from the *News and Observer* of Raleigh, North Carolina, September 22, 1898, p. 4.

The Fusion Candidate for the Senate in Edge-combe County.

"The Fusion Candidate for the Senate in Edgecombe County." Cartoon. *News and Observer* (Raleigh, N.C.), 22 September 1898. The North Carolina Election of 1898. North Carolina Collection, University of North Carolina at Chapel Hill.

More Negro Scoundrelism

Black Beasts Attempt to Outrage the
Young Daughter of a Respectable Farmer.

Her Father Swears to It
Attacked on the Public Highway in
Brunswick County While Returning
From Sunday-School—Her Screams
Saved Her From a Fate Worse Than Death.

(*Wilmington Star*)

Joseph Gore is an honest and respectable farmer of the county of Brunswick—poor in this world's goods, but esteemed by his neighbors. He has a wife and

These items originally appeared in the *Raleigh North Carolina News and Observer—Cartoon*. September 22, 1898, p. 1; "More Negro Scoundrelism" September 23, 1898, p. 1.

children, and there is a church and Sunday school near his home which are attended by his family. But he lives in a township where the negroes outnumber the whites more than three to one. This, coupled with the fact, no doubt, that Brunswick county is under Republican-fusion rule, emboldened two beastly negroes to make an attempt to outrage a young girl on the public road, as narrated in the following affidavit.

State of North Carolina,

County of Brunswick.

Personally appeared before me, Geo. H. Bellamy, a Justice of the Peace for Town Creek Township, Brunswick County, Joseph Gore, who being duly sworn, states: "Some days ago my daughter, aged 15 years, was returning from Sunday school, accompanied by her little brother, aged 12 years, about 3 o'clock in the afternoon. When about a quarter of a mile from home, two negro boys, aged about 16 to 18 years, ran after my daughter, with their coats turned over their heads to conceal their identity, and attempted to take hold of her, and doubtless would have placed their unholy hands on her person; and had it not been for her screams, would have doubtless accomplished their purpose. This was done in Town Creek Township, in broad daylight. The villains have not yet been detected.

(Signed.) "Joseph Gore."

Signed and sworn to before me, this 19th day of September, A.D., 1898.
Geo. H. Bellamy, J. P.

"The Vampire that Hovers Over North Carolina." Cartoon. *News and Observer* (Raleigh, N.C.), 27 September 1898. The North Carolina Election of 1898. North Carolina Collection, University of North Carolina at Chapel Hill.

White men of Brunswick County, can you stand that? Is there one left in the borders of your county who will not now vote against every candidate who consorts with negroes, and who is dependent on them for election? Has it come to this, that your daughters cannot attend church or Sunday school without having a body-guard to protect them from the lustful black brutes who roam through your county?

Rise in your might, white men of Brunswick. Assert your manhood. Go to the polls and help stamp out the last vestige of Republican-populist-negro fusion.

6. Mark Twain Writes "The United States of Lyncherdom," 1901

I

And so Missouri has fallen, that great state! Certain of her children have joined the lynchers, and the smirch is upon the rest of us. That handful of her children have given us a character and labeled us with a name, and to the dwellers in the four quarters of the earth we are "lynchers," now, and ever shall be. For the world will not stop and think—it never does, it is not its way; its way is to generalize from a single sample. It will not say, "Those Missourians have been busy eighty years in building an honorable good name for themselves; these hundred lynchers down in the corner of the state are not real Missourians, they are renegades." No, that truth will not enter its mind; it will generalize from the one or two misleading samples and say, "The Missourians are lynchers."...

II

Oh, Missouri!

The tragedy occurred near Pierce City, down in the southwestern corner of the state. On a Sunday afternoon a young white woman who had started alone from church was found murdered.... Although it was a region of churches and schools the people rose, lynched three negroes—two of them very aged ones—burned out five negro households, and drove thirty negro families into the woods.

I do not dwell upon the provocation which moved the people to these crimes, for that has nothing to do with the matter; the only question is, does the assassin *take the law into his own hands?* .... The Pierce City people had bitter provocation—indeed, as revealed by certain of the particulars, the bitterest of all provocations—but no matter, they took the law into their own hands, when by the terms of their statutes their victim would certainly hang if the law had been allowed to take its course, for there are but few negroes in that region and they are without authority and without influence in over-awing juries.

Why has lynching, with various barbaric accompaniments, become a favorite regulator in cases of "the usual crime" in several parts of the country? Is it

---

"The United States of Lyncherdom," In *Europe and Elsewhere*, pp. 239-49. By Mark Twain. Ed. By Albert Bigelow Paine. New York: Harper & brothers, 1923.

because men think a lurid and terrible punishment a more forcible object lesson and a more effective deterrent than a sober and colorless hanging done privately in a jail would be? Surely sane men do not think that. Even the average child should know better. It should know that any strange and much-talked-of event is always followed by imitations, the world being so well supplied with excitable people who only need a little stirring up to make them lose what is left of their heads and do things which they would not have thought of ordinarily.... The child should also know that by a law of our make, communities, as well as individuals, are imitators; and that a much-talked-of lynching will infallibly produce other lynchings here and there and yonder, and that in time these will breed a mania, a fashion; a fashion which will spread wide and wider, year by year, covering state after state, as with an advancing disease. Lynching has reached Colorado, it has reached California, it has reached Indiana—and now Missouri!...

It has been supposed ... that the people at a lynching enjoy the spectacle and are glad of a chance to see it. It cannot be true; all experience is against it. The people in the South are made like the people in the North—the vast majority of whom are right-hearted and compassionate, and would be cruelly pained by such a spectacle—and *would attend it,* and let on to be pleased with it, if the public approval seemed to require it....

It is thought ... that a lynching crowd enjoys a lynching. It certainly is not true; it is impossible of belief. It is freely asserted—you have seen it in print many times of late—that the lynching impulse has been misinterpreted; that it is act the outcome of a spirit of revenge, but of a "mere atrocious hunger *to look upon human suffering.*"...

Why does a crowd of the same kind of people in Texas, Colorado, Indiana, stand by, smitten to the heart and miserable, and by ostentatious outward signs pretend to enjoy a lynching? Why does it lift no hand or voice in protest? Only because it would be unpopular to do it, I think; each man is afraid of his neighbor's disapproval—a thing which, to the general run of the race, is more dreaded than wounds and death. When there is to be a lynching the people hitch up and come miles to see it, bringing their wives and children. Really to see it? No—they come only because they are afraid to stay at home, lest it be noticed and offensively commented upon. We may believe this, for we all know how we feel about such spectacles—also, how we would act under the like pressure. We are not any better nor any braver than anybody else, and we must not try to creep out of it.

A Savonarola [fifteenth-century religious reformer] can quell and scatter a mob of lynchers with a mere glance of his eye.... For no mob has any sand in the presence of a man known to be splendidly brave. Besides, a lynching mob would like to be scattered, for of a certainty there are never ten men in it who would not prefer to be somewhere else—and would be, if they but had the courage to go. When I was a boy I saw a brave gentleman deride and insult a mob and drive it away; and afterward, in Nevada, I saw a noted desperado make two hundred men sit still, with the house burning under them, until he gave them permission to retire....

Then perhaps the remedy for lynchings comes to this: station a brave man in each affected community to encourage, support, and bring to light the deep disapproval of lynching hidden in the secret places of its heart—for it is there, beyond question. Then those communities will find something better to imitate—of course, being human, they must imitate something. Where shall these brave men be found? That is indeed a difficulty; there are not three hundred of them in the earth. If merely *physically* brave men would do, then it were easy; they could be furnished by the cargo....

No, upon reflection, the scheme will not work. There are not enough morally brave men in stock. We are out of moral-courage material; we are in a condition of profound poverty....

In the meantime, there is another plan. Let us import American missionaries from China, and send them into the lynching field. With 1,500 of them out there converting two Chinamen apiece per annum against an uphill birth rate of 33,000 pagans per day, it will take upward of a million years to make the conversions balance the output and bring the Christianizing of the country in sight to the naked eye; therefore, if we can offer our missionaries as rich a field at home at lighter expense and quite satisfactory in the matter of danger, why shouldn't they find it fair and right to come back and give us a trial? The Chinese are universally conceded to be excellent people, honest, honorable, industrious, trustworthy, kind-hearted, and all that—leave them alone, they are plenty good enough just as they are; and besides, almost every convert runs a risk of catching our civilization. We ought to be careful. We ought to think twice before we encourage a risk like that; for, once civilized, *China can never be uncivilized again.* We have not been thinking of that. Very well, we ought to think of it now. Our missionaries will find that we have a field for them—and not only for the 1,500, but for 15,011. Let them look at the following telegram and see if they have anything in China that is more appetizing. It is from Texas:

> The negro was taken to a tree and swung in the air. Wood and fodder were piled beneath his body and a hot fire was made. *Then it was suggested that the man ought not to die too quickly, and he was let down to the ground while a party went to Dexter, about two miles distant, to procure coal oil.* This was thrown on the flame and the work completed.

We implore them [missionaries] to come back and help us in our need. Patriotism imposes this duty on them. Our country is worse off than China; they are our countrymen, their motherland supplicates their aid in this her hour of deep distress.... O kind missionary, O compassionate missionary, leave China! come home and convert these Christians! ...

7. Walter White Remembers the Atlanta Race Riot, 1906

There were nine light-skinned Negroes in my family: mother, father, five sisters, an older brother, George, and myself. The house in which I discovered what it meant to be a Negro was located on Houston Street, three blocks from the

From *A Man Called White: The Autobiography of Walter White* (Athens: University of Georgia Press, 1995, 1948), pp. 5–12. Reprinted in edited form by permission of Jane White Viazzi.

Candler Building, Atlanta's first skyscraper, which bore the name of the ex–drug clerk who had become a millionaire from the sale of Coca-Cola. Below us lived none but Negroes; toward town all but a very few were white. Ours was an eight room, two-story frame house which stood out in its surroundings not because of its opulence but by contrast with the drabness and unpaintedness of the other dwellings in a deteriorating neighborhood.

Only Father kept his house painted, the picket fence repaired, the board fence separating our place from those on either side white-washed, the grass neatly trimmed, and flower beds abloom.... This spic-and-spanness became increasingly apparent as the rest of the neighborhood became more down-at-heel, and resulted, as we were to learn, in sullen envy among some of our white neighbors. It was the violent expression of that resentment against a Negro family neater than themselves which set the pattern of our lives.

On a day in September 1906, when I was thirteen, we were taught that there is no isolation from life....

I had read the inflammatory headlines in the *Atlanta News* and the more restrained ones in the *Atlanta Constitution* which reported alleged rapes and other crimes committed by Negroes. But these were so standard and familiar that they made—as I look back on it now—little impression. The stories were more frequent, however, and consisted of eight-column streamers instead of the usual two- or four-column ones.

Father was a mail collector. His tour of duty was from three to eleven P.M. He made his rounds in a little cart into which one climbed from a step in the rear. I used to drive the cart for him from two until seven, leaving him at the point nearest our home on Houston Street, to return home either for study or sleep.... Father told me as we made the rounds that ominous rumors of a race riot that night were sweeping the town. But I was too young that morning to understand the background of the riot. I became much older during the next thirty-six hours....

One of the most bitter political campaigns of that bloody era was reaching its climax. Hoke Smith—that amazing contradiction of courageous and intelligent opposition to the South's economic ills and at the same time advocacy of ruthless suppression of the Negro—was a candidate that year for the governorship. His opponent was Clark Howell, editor of the *Atlanta Constitution,* which boasted with justification that it "covers Dixie like the dew." Howell and his supporters held firm authority over the state Democratic machine despite the long and bitter fight Hoke Smith had made on Howell in the columns of the rival *Atlanta Journal.*

Hoke Smith had fought for legislation to ban child labor and railroad rate discriminations. He had denounced the corrupt practices of the railroads and the state railway commission, which, he charged, was as much owned and run by northern absentee landlords as were the railroads themselves. He had fought for direct primaries to nominate senators and other candidates by popular vote, for a corrupt practices act, for an elective railway commission, and for state ownership of railroads—issues which were destined to be still fought for nearly four decades later by Ellis Arnall. For these reforms he was hailed throughout the nation as a genuine progressive along with La Follette of Wisconsin and Folk of Missouri.

To overcome the power of the regular Democratic organization, Hoke Smith sought to heal the feud of long standing between himself and the powerful ex-radical Populist, Thomas E. Watson. Tom Watson was the strangest mixture of contradictions which rotten-borough politics of the South had ever produced. He was the brilliant leader of an agrarian movement in the South which, in alliance with the agrarian West, threatened for a time the industrial and financial power of the East....

Watson ran for president in 1904 and 1908, both times with abysmal failure. His defeats soured him to the point of vicious acrimony. He turned from his ideal of interracial decency to one of virulent hatred and denunciation of the "nigger." He thus became a natural ally for Hoke Smith in the gubernatorial election in Georgia in 1906.

The two rabble-rousers stumped the state screaming, "Nigger, nigger, nigger!" Some white farmers still believed Watson's abandoned doctrine that the interests of Negro and white farmers and industrial workers were identical. They feared that Watson's and Smith's new scheme to disfranchise Negro voters would lead to disfranchisement of poor whites. Tom Watson was sent to trade on his past reputation to reassure them that such was not the case and that their own interests were best served by now hating "niggers."

Watson's oratory had been especially effective among the cotton mill workers and other poor whites in and near Atlanta. The *Atlanta Journal* on August 1, 1906, in heavy type, all capital letters, printed an incendiary appeal to race prejudice backing up Watson and Smith....

Fuel was added to the fire by a dramatization of Thomas Dixon's novel *The Clansman* in Atlanta. (This was later made by David Wark Griffith into *The Birth of a Nation,* and did more than anything else to make successful the revival of the Ku Klux Klan.) The late Ray Stannard Baker, telling the story of the Atlanta riot in *Along the Color Line,* characterized Dixon's fiction and its effect on Atlanta and the South as "incendiary and cruel." No more apt or accurate description could have been chosen.

During the afternoon preceding the riot little bands of sullen, evil-looking men talked excitedly on street corners all over downtown Atlanta. Around seven o'clock my father and I were driving toward a mail box at the corner of Peachtree and Houston Streets when there came from near-by Pryor Street a roar the like of which I had never heard before, but which sent a sensation of mingled fear and excitement coursing through my body. I asked permission of Father to go and see what the trouble was. He bluntly ordered me to stay in the cart. A little later we drove down Atlanta's main business thoroughfare, Peachtree Street. Again we heard the terrifying cries, this time near at hand and coming toward us. We saw a lame Negro bootblack from Herndon's barber shop pathetically trying to outrun a mob of whites. Less than a hundred yards from us the chase ended. We saw clubs and fists descending to the accompaniment of savage shouting and cursing. Suddenly a voice cried, "There goes another nigger!" Its work done, the mob went after new prey. The body with the withered foot lay dead in a pool of blood on the street.

Father's apprehension and mine steadily increased during the evening, although the fact that our skins were white kept us from attack. Another circumstance favored us—the mob had not yet grown violent enough to attack United States government property. But I could see Father's relief when he punched the time clock at eleven P.M. and got into the cart to go home. He wanted to go the back way down Forsyth Street, but I begged him, in my childish excitement and ignorance, to drive down Marietta to Five Points, the heart of Atlanta's business district, where the crowds were densest and the yells loudest. No sooner had we turned into Marietta Street, however, than we saw careening toward us an undertaker's barouche. Crouched in the rear of the vehicle were three Negroes clinging to the sides of the carriage as it lunged and swerved. On the driver's seat crouched a white man, the reins held taut in his left hand. A huge whip was gripped in his right. Alternately he lashed the horses and, without looking backward, swung the whip in savage swoops in the faces of members of the mob as they lunged at the carriage determined to seize the three Negroes.

There was no time for us to get out of its path, so sudden and swift was the appearance of the vehicle. The hub cap of the right rear wheel of the barouche hit the right side of our much lighter wagon. Father and I instinctively threw our weight and kept the cart from turning completely over. Our mare was a Texas mustang which, frightened by the sudden blow, lunged in the air as Father clung to the reins. Good fortune was with us. The cart settled back on its four wheels as Father said in a voice which brooked no dissent, "We are going home the back way and not down Marietta."

But again on Pryor Street we heard the cry of the mob. Close to us and in our direction ran a stout and elderly woman who cooked at a downtown white hotel. Fifty yards behind, a mob which filled the street from curb to curb was closing in. Father handed the reins to me and, though he was of slight stature, reached down and lifted the woman into the cart. I did not need to be told to lash the mare to the fastest speed she could muster.

The church bells tolled the next morning for Sunday service. But no one in Atlanta believed for a moment that the hatred and lust for blood had been appeased. Like skulls on a cannibal's hut the hats and caps of victims of the mob of the night before had been hung on the iron hooks of telegraph poles. None could tell whether each hat represented a dead Negro. But we knew that some of those who had worn the hats would never again wear any.

Late in the afternoon friends of my father's came to warn of more trouble that night....

We turned out the lights early, as did all our neighbors. No one removed his clothes or thought of sleep. Apprehension was tangible. We could almost touch its cold and clammy surface. Toward midnight the unnatural quiet was broken by a roar that grew steadily in volume. Even today I grow tense in remembering it.

Father told Mother to take my sisters, the youngest of them only six, to the rear of the house, which offered more protection from stones and bullets. My brother George was away, so Father and I, the only males in the house, took our places at the front windows of the parlor. The windows opened on a porch along the front side of the house, which in turn gave onto a narrow lawn that sloped down to the street and a picket fence. There was a crash as Negroes smashed the street lamp at the corner of Houston and Piedmont Avenue down the street. In a very few minutes the vanguard of the mob, some of them bearing torches, appeared. A voice which we recognized as that of the son of the grocer with whom we had traded for many years yelled, "That's where that nigger mail carrier lives! Let's burn it down! It's too nice for a nigger to live in!" In the eerie light Father turned his drawn face toward me. In a voice as quiet as though he were asking me to pass him the sugar at the breakfast table, he said, "Son, don't shoot until the first man puts his foot on the lawn and then—don't you miss!"

In the flickering light the mob swayed, paused, and began to flow toward us. In that instant there opened up within me a great awareness; I knew then who I was. I was a Negro, a human being with an invisible pigmentation which marked me a person to be hunted, hanged, abused, discriminated against, kept in poverty and ignorance, in order that those whose skin was white would have readily at hand a proof of their superiority, a proof patent and inclusive, accessible to the moron and the idiot as well as to the wise man and the genius. No matter how low a white man fell, he could always hold fast to the smug conviction that he was superior to two-thirds of the world's population, for those two-thirds were not white....

The mob moved toward the lawn. I tried to aim my gun, wondering what it would feel like to kill a man. Suddenly there was a volley of shots. The mob hesitated, stopped. Some friends of my father's had barricaded themselves in a two-story brick building just below our house. It was they who had fired. Some of the mobsmen, still bloodthirsty, shouted, "Let's go get the nigger." Others, afraid now for their safety, held back. Our friends, noting the hesitation, fired another volley. The mob broke and retreated up Houston Street.

In the quiet that followed I put my gun aside and tried to relax. But a tension different from anything I had ever known possessed me. I was gripped by the knowledge of my identity, and in the depths of my soul I was vaguely aware that I was glad of it.

8. Alabama Continues Its Literacy Test until 1965

1965 Alabama Literacy Test

There are 68 questions.

For this document a sampling of questions was taken with answers included.

1. Which of the following is a right guaranteed by the Bill of Rights?

____**Public Education**

____**Employment**

____**Trial by Jury**

____**Voting**

http://www.ccle.fourh.umn.edu/literacy.pdf

8. When the Constitution was approved by the original colonies, how many states had to ratify it in order for it to be in effect?______________

____

15. If a vacancy occurs in the U.S. Senate, the state must hold an election, but meanwhile the place may be filled by a temporary appointment made by____

19. Who passes laws dealing with piracy?________________________

____

23. Name two levels of government which can levy taxes:____________

____

28. The electoral vote for President is counted in the presence of two bodies. Name them:_____________________________________

30. Of the original 13 states, the one with the largest representation in the first Congress was ______________________________________

36. Congress passes laws regulating cases which are included in those over which the U.S. Supreme Court has________________ jurisdiction.

42. The only laws which can be passed to apply to an area in a federal arsenal are those passed by________________________ provided consent for the purchase of the land is given by the____________________.

47. If election of the President becomes the duty of the U.S. House of Representatives and it fails to act, who becomes President and when?______________________________________

52. Name two of the purposes of the U.S. Constitution._______________

____

57. If an effort to impeach the President of the U.S. is made, who presides at the trial? ____

64. If the two houses of Congress cannot agree on adjournment, who sets the time? ____

68. Any power and rights not given to the U.S. or prohibited to the states by the U.S. Constitution are specified as belonging to whom?____

Answers to Alabama Literacy Test

1. Trial by jury only
8. Nine
15. The governor
19. Congress
23. State and local

28. House of Representatives, Senate
30. Virginia
36. Co-appellate
42. Congress; state legislatures
47. The Vice President, until the House acts
52. (Preamble statements) "to form a more perfect union, establish justice, insure domestic tranquility, provide for the common defense, promote the general welfare, and secure the blessings of liberty to ourselves and our posterity."
57. The Chief Justice of the Supreme Court
64. The President
68. The states; the people

ESSAYS

In the first essay, Steven Hahn speaks to the systematic process by which whites disfranchised African American voters, using residency requirements, complicated registration requirements, poll taxes, and literacy tests. The success of the disfranchisement of blacks in Mississippi can be seen in the numbers; registered black voters dropped from "190,000 in 1890 to a mere 8,615 in 1892." While blacks resisted, there was no help from the Republican party or the U.S. Supreme Court, which upheld literacy tests in *Williams* v. *Mississippi* in 1898. Leon Litwack continues the history of discrimination with a discussion of segregation and the rationale behind it. Whereas Hahn argues that white fears of black political power brought about disfranchisement, Litwack suggests that fears of social equality pushed white legislatures to enact segregation laws. The thought of white women seated next to black men on trains or street cars brought a frightening (to whites) specter of intimate contact or amalgamation. In reality, however, black political and economic success caused more worry from white supremacists than did black poverty or lack of education. A successful boxer such as Jack Johnson defied the rules of segregation, married white women, and lived freely. He was a hero to African Americans, but most whites hated him, and with the power to legislate segregation, they enacted laws forbidding interracial marriage.

Black Political Struggles

STEVEN HAHN

The removal of African Americans, by constitutional means, from the southern body politic may be seen as the capstone of a lengthy offensive by which white employers and property owners attempted to construct a postemancipation regime of domination and subordination. Beginning with the "black codes"

"The Valley and the Shadows," reprinted by permission of the publisher from *A Nation Under Our Feet: Black Political Struggles In The Rural South* by Steven Hahn, pp. 441–451, Cambridge, Mass.: The Belknap Press of Harvard University Press, Copyright © 2003 by the President and Fellows of Harvard College.

and related legislation enacted under the auspices of Johnsonian Reconstruction, the offensive resumed, albeit unevenly and haphazardly, after the toppling of Republican governments. The most rapid and enduring advances came in the area of labor relations, as post-Reconstruction legislatures and state courts moved to sort out the complexities of the staple-crop economy....

But there occurred, as well, a protracted and, in the end, successful attack on the standing of African Americans in the official arenas of southern politics. The attack had two phases. The first commenced with Redemption in a widespread though uncoordinated manner. Its principal aim was to weaken black power, place obstacles in the way of black electoral participation, and wrest control of the balloting process. As best as the circumstances of state politics and federal tolerance would allow, this could entail the initiation of poll taxes, the gerrymandering of legislative and judicial districts, the encumbrance of registration requirements, the introduction of complicated voting procedures, and, most important, the centralization of state government authority over the selection of local election judges, which enabled white Democrats to organize polling venues and count ballots as they thought necessary. Henceforth, poor and illiterate voters would face significant hurdles, black and dissident candidates for office would have more trouble winning elections, and Democrats would enjoy a legally sanctioned position from which to intimidate opponents and commit fraud. Still, in the late 1880s momentum grew for an even more radical and permanent solution, for "some scheme," as one proponent put it, that "would effectually remove from the sphere of politics in the state the ignorant and unpatriotic negro."...

There can, however, be little doubt that the mobilizations and assertions of African Americans across a broad front of political activity in the late 1880s and early 1890s had provoked renewed concerns. The organization of black workers in the cotton and sugar fields, the reinvigoration of black Republicanism in states like Mississippi, Arkansas, and Tennessee, and the early Populist gestures toward biracialism together suggested that white Democrats had not stabilized the political order through statutory and fraudulent means, and that the infrastructures of black politics remained very much intact. In many places, the same grassroots networks and leaders facilitated the work of the Colored Alliance or Knights of Labor *and* the Republican party. As a consequence, constituencies of support—especially among sections of the white elite—began to cohere around the need for more sweeping constitutional revisions. Their rallying cry was "Negro domination": the threat, not so much of direct black power over whites, as of continuing black influence on electoral politics and governance and the openings for insurgent agitation that it made possible. "The question with regard to the colored 'citizens' of South Carolina," the conservative *Charleston News and Courier* pronounced, "is not how to keep them from being elected to office, but how to keep them from voting for other men, white or colored, who are candidates for office and can command their vote."

These provocations were clearly at work in Mississippi, where pressure for black suffrage restriction and other constitutional reforms had been blocked since Redemption by conservatives in the black-majority river counties who, owing to fusion arrangements and advantages in legislative apportionment, believed that the "negro problem" was largely under control. Then, a rapid succession of events in 1888–1889 appears to have shaken their confidence. The national Republican party won control of the presidency and both houses of Congress for the first time since Reconstruction and seemed poised to reimpose federal supervision of southern elections. A "conference of colored men," termed the "largest gathering of its kind ever assembled" in Mississippi, met in Jackson and denounced the violent suppression of the black vote. The black-dominated state Republican party then briefly fielded a full ticket for the first time in years and condemned the hypocrisy of Democrats who howled "Negro domination" but depended on black numbers to exercise disproportionate power in Mississippi and the nation. In Leflore County, Colored Alliance activism evinced a militancy and solidarity that drove white planters to brutal paramilitarism. Within months, a bill providing for a state constitutional convention was racing through the legislature and received the endorsement of the governor; within a year, the convention was in session, the first to gather in the former Confederate states in more than a decade.

There was wide agreement among the delegates, all but four of whom were Democrats and all but one of whom was white, as to the convention's chief object. It was "to devise measures" that would provide "a home government under the control of the white people" and take the blacks "out of politics." But at least two formidable obstacles lay in their path. The measures devised had to be "consistent with the Constitution of the United States," which in the Fifteenth Amendment prohibited denying the "right to vote" on the "grounds of race, color, or previous condition of servitude." And they had to be acceptable to rival party factions: to conservative big planters from the Delta who wished to protect their prerogatives, and to representatives of small planters and farmers from white-majority counties who wished to increase their power and feared that imposing qualifications on the suffrage might injure them.... Mississippi had toughened registration requirements in 1876, and the Tennessee legislature had just enacted poll-tax, secret-ballot, and registration laws. In fact, lines of communication with Tennessee had already been opened when the Mississippi convention assembled.

Even so, the delegates hardly seemed sure about how they might "secure a white majority." For a time, they explored proposals to enlarge the white electorate rather than diminish the black one, and they spent more than two weeks debating a plan for modified female suffrage, reflecting currents in the national woman suffrage movement and anticipating the political logic and discourse of the developing southern variant. But in the end, they legislated "against [the black man's] habits and weaknesses." They used registrars and registration, once the vehicles of black enfranchisement, as the vehicles of black exclusion, and crafted a package of provisions that exploited African-American poverty, illiteracy, and geographical mobility. Thus to qualify, a prospective voter would have to live in the state for two years and the election district for one, to register at least four months before an election, to pay a poll tax of two dollars by February 1 in each of two years preceding an election (a particularly onerous cumulative impost), and "to read" or "to understand" or to "give a reasonable interpretation" of "any section of the [state] constitution" (what was known as an "understanding clause"). The registrar was consequently armed with immense discretionary authority, both to dismiss potentially qualified black voters and, at least in theory, to admit potentially unqualified white voters. So immense was the registrar's discretionary authority that some white Mississippians who favored black disfranchisement nonetheless feared the potential for "fraud," "subterfuge," and "dissatisfaction."

Not even the most enthusiastic of the signatories could claim that Mississippi's new constitution and its franchise provisions represented a groundswell of white popular support. Few white voters bothered to participate in the selection of delegates, and the final document was not submitted for ratification. But the "plan" devised and the dramatic results so rapidly attained (the number of registered black voters plummeted from nearly 190,000 in 1890 to a mere 8,615 in 1892) made it an irresistible model for Democrats in other southern states. Not surprisingly, South Carolina, which closely resembled Mississippi in having a black majority and a weak tradition of white insurgency, held the next convention (1895). In neither state did Populism make much of a showing. Elsewhere, the tenor of political conflict or the scale of political opposition was greater, and the necessary backing for either constitutional conventions (in Louisiana, Alabama, and Virginia) or constitutional amendments (North Carolina, Texas, and Georgia) could not be obtained until very late in the decade or very early in the next century. Nonetheless, the "Mississippi plan," with some variation, was widely embraced.

Although white support for constitutional suffrage restrictions was subdued nearly everywhere in the former Confederacy (only North Carolina, Alabama, and Georgia had referenda, and the turnout was uniformly low), there was a striking absence of significant protest or resistance. The impulse for disfranchisement clearly came from Democratic party leaders, or from leaders of Democratic party factions, who lived in counties or districts with substantial black populations.... Democrats might fight over the wisdom and effects of particular measures but not over the goal of obliterating the black electorate. Yet what of the insurgents [Populists] who depended on the votes of humble whites and blacks and whose political prospects would surely suffer too? The record testifies to the limits of their radicalism and the unraveling of their biracialism. For while they rarely joined the charge to disfranchisement, neither did they mount much of a defense against it. The Populist *Dallas Southern Mercury* did denounce the poll tax in the midst of the campaign of 1896, noting that in Mississippi and South Carolina the "poor man, white and black, has been legislated clear out of the right to vote," but many in the rank and file eventually defected. Georgia Populist Tom Watson would become a powerful advocate of black disfranchisement and North Carolina Populist Marion Butler, who worried about the consequences of a proposed constitutional amendment, instead suggested a ban on black officeholding before leading his party into official silence. Ex-Readjuster governor William E. Cameron, who once proposed carrying "Africa" into his "war" against the Funders, played a prominent role in Virginia's constitutional convention of 1901–1902, condemning "negro suffrage as a cancer upon the body politic."

In many states, Democratic intimidation and paramilitarism—the White Man's Union in Texas or the Red Shirt movement of 1898–1900 in North Carolina were conspicuous examples—became part and parcel of the disfranchisement campaign and clearly encouraged white complicity or defeatism. One searches in vain for any strong public voices against the white supremacist storm. The only exceptions were to be found among the intended victims. Acutely aware of the gathering momentum and ferocity of the offensive against them, African Americans struggled to find some way to stem it: to find an ally, a strategy, a means of influencing the discussion and debate. Anger and indignation were widespread, and activity may be detected on a number of fronts. But the murderous atmosphere in much of the country-side, which already had claimed the lives of young militants through lynchings and political repression, produced caution and gave the initiative over to those black leaders most ready to reach an accommodation with whites.

With little hope of derailing the drive for disfranchisement, these black leaders often looked to mitigate the results by aligning with white conservatives, accepting educational or property qualifications, and asking that the qualifications be enacted and enforced in a color-blind fashion....

African Americans in South Carolina mounted a more substantial and vocal campaign—through the auspices of black ministers and the Republican party—to influence their constitutional convention's proceedings. They succeeded in electing six of the 160 delegates, all from the low country and all well-versed in state and local politics, none more so than William Whipper and Robert Smalls, who had been at it since the earliest days of Reconstruction. In the face of Governor Benjamin Tillman's fulminations about fraud, corruption, and "Negro domination," they defended their claims as rightful citizens, their contributions to the nation's freedom and independence, and their record of governance. Blacks, delegate Thomas E. Miller lectured, "displayed greater conservative force, appreciation for good laws, knowledge for the worth of financial legislation, regard for the rights of his fellow citizens in relation to property and aptitude for honest financial state legislation than has ever been shown by any other people." "We were eight years in power," he said pridefully. "We had built school houses, established charitable institutions, built and maintained the penitentiary system ... rebuilt the bridges and reestablished the ferries. In short we had reconstructed the state and placed it on the road to prosperity." Robert Smalls boldly submitted to the suffrage committee the provisions from the radical constitution of 1868, and together, the black delegates attacked the convention's franchise scheme as an "act of feudal barbarism," an example of "class legislation," and a "nullification of the fifteenth amendment," taunting the Tillmanites for their hypocrisies. Yet they too ended up proposing literacy and property requirements, offering, as delegate James Wigg pronounced, "the supremacy of law, of intelligence and property" as an alternative to "white supremacy and white degradation." ...

In Alabama, Booker T. Washington tried several strategies, including the initiation of a court suit, to influence events. In the spring of 1901, he called a meeting of "representative colored men" and signed their petition to the sitting state convention, which, in supplicating cadences, asked that "the Negro ... have some humble share in choosing those who shall rule over him." "We beg of your honorable body to keep in mind," the petitioners pleaded, "that as a race, we did not force ourselves upon you," that "we have gotten habits of industry, the English language, and the Christian religion, and at the same time we have tried, in a humble way, to render valuable service to the white man." Admitting that "immediately after the war we made mistakes," they insisted that "we have learned our lesson" and are "not seeking to rule the white man." One of their number soon believed that it might be possible, with clever political manuevers, to register "at least 60000 Negro voters." "I am of the conviction," he told Washington, "that one thing for the Negroes to do is to meet the enemy with the olive branch and beat them at their own game."

This was very much the fear of some disfranchisers: that African Americans would respond to the constitutional challenges by organizing in their "lodges and other secret societies" and "even at the churches and Sunday schools" to pay their poll taxes and ready themselves to "'answer' every question put to them" by the registrar. Fretting about the need for tighter and more efficient measures, a delegate to the Virginia constitutional convention confided that "Our *negroes more* intelligent, *more money,* & more exposed to *northern inspiration,*" and thus the "chances of being attacked were greater than in Miss. or S.C." Perhaps not. "The only effect of an educational qualification for suffrage," the *Aberdeen Examiner* warned Mississippi's convention delegates in September 1890, "would be to drive thousands of negro men to school." And in the Delta, at least, "night schools for negro men" were reported as being established later that fall.... Statewide, the number of registered black voters grew from a scant 8,615 in 1892 to 18,170 in 1899.

Where newly revised constitutions or constitutional amendments were submitted to the voters for ratification, efforts were made to defeat them. In Edgecombe County, North Carolina, a Democratic newspaper complained in July 1900 that blacks were "not only applying promptly to register, but they usually go to the registrar well schooled" by "the white fusionists and the local negro bosses." The *Weekly Press,* published in Mobile, Alabama, urged blacks to "fight the new constitution at the polls, and, if defeated there, carry the matter to the U.S. Supreme Court." In Georgia, blacks organized a suffrage league in 1908 with the same hope of stimulating a grassroots campaign of registration and opposition. These undertakings and agitations were reflective of widespread discontent both with the disfranchisement movement and with the willingness of some blacks leaders to accommodate it....

But in truth, there was little that either mobilization or accommodation could achieve, because the few allies that African Americans might have had either retreated or disappeared. During the 1890s, the U.S. Congress repealed all of the federal election laws. The Supreme Court (controlled by northern Republicans) upheld the southern approach to disfranchisement. New secret ballot laws and prior poll tax statutes already discouraged black voting. White Populists increasingly fled from any association with biracialism. And Democratic terrorists struck where necessary in the rural districts. By the early twentieth century throughout the former Confederate South, the black electorate had been reduced to a tiny fraction, the Republican party rendered virtually insignificant, and the Democrats, by means of black disfranchisement and the white primary, left to fight among themselves over how to rule their states and localities. The "one-party" Democratic South had been constructed, and the process of imposing official racial separation in public life was duly accelerated.

Wherever one stood, it was apparent that a moment of immense historical importance had arrived, that one historical era had come to a close and another had been ushered in. "To disfranchise the Negro," a black newspaper correspondent in South Carolina judged at the time of that state's constitutional convention, "is the last act in the bloody drama of intimidation to conquer the southern Negro." In the Alabama black belt, Ned Cobb, who "was a boy [when] I watched em disfranchise the Negro from votin" but still "old enough to look at folks and hear the talk," made the same point with more poignancy. He could remember a time when "they'd always go up ... to the Chapel Ridge beat, white and colored, to vote," when "the white man would let him vote, wanted him to vote," would "travel around, workin for who they wanted and get the nigger's decision about who they was going to vote for." Cobb understood that votes would be bought, that the white man would be "runnin all about the settlement buyin the niggers' votes," giving "him meat, flour, sugar, coffee, anything the nigger wanted," but he seemed to recognize that even in this relationship, power could be operating on both sides. Yet although Cobb "never did hear my daddy" say anything "bout losin the vote," he believed "with all my heart he knowed what it meant." As Cobb "growed to more knowledge," he came to think "that was as bad a thing as ever happened—to disfranchise the nigger." It was like "tellin him he didn't have a right to his thoughts. He just weren't counted to be no more than a dog." The white guardians of Virginia history put it another way. For them, the new constitution of 1902—with its extended residency requirement, cumulative poll tax, and complex "escape" clauses for whites—marked the true end of Reconstruction.

Trouble in Mind

LEON F. LITWACK

Even as the states restricted the vote, affecting most blacks and some whites, they acted to reassure whites of all classes of their racial superiority. "The quarter of a century that has passed since the war," a New Orleans newspaper editorialized, "has not diminished in the slightest degree the determination of the whites to prevent any such dangerous doctrine as social equality, even in the mildest form...." Even as a resident of Biloxi, Mississippi, voiced his satisfaction with the results of disfranchisement, he noted that it had "solved the race problem [only] so far as politics is concerned." Based on such sentiments, deeply rooted in the white psyche, the efforts to separate the races, to quarantine and marginalize black Southerners, extended beyond the polling places to every aspect of day-to-day life where blacks and whites came into contact with each other....

Racial segregation was hardly a new phenomenon. Before the Civil War, when slavery had fixed the status of most blacks, no need was felt for statutory measures segregating the races. The restrictive Black Codes, along with the few segregation laws passed by the first postwar governments, did not survive Reconstruction. What replaced them, however, was not racial integration but an informal code of exclusion and discrimination. Even the Radical legislatures in which blacks played a prominent role made no concerted effort to force integration on unwilling and resisting whites, especially in the public schools; constitutional or legislative provisions mandating integration were almost impossible to enforce. The determination of blacks to improve their position during and after Reconstruction revolved largely around efforts to secure accommodations that equaled those afforded whites. Custom, habit, and etiquette, then, defined the social relations between the races and enforced separation in many areas of southern life. Whatever the Negro's legal rights, an English traveler noted in Richmond in 1866, he knows "how far he may go, and where he must stop" and that "habits are not changed by paper laws."

But in the 1890s whites perceived in the behavior of "uppity" (and invariably younger) blacks a growing threat or indifference to the prevailing customs, habits, and etiquette. Over the next two decades, white Southerners would construct in response an imposing and extensive system of legal mechanisms designed to institutionalize the already familiar and customary subordination of black men and women. Between 1890 and 1915, state after state wrote the prevailing racial customs and habits into the statute books. Jim Crow came to the South in an expanded and more rigid form, partly in response to fears of a new generation of blacks unschooled in racial etiquette and to growing doubts that this generation could be trusted to stay in its place without legal force. If the old Negro knew his "place," the New Negro evidently did not. "The white people began to begrudge these niggers their running around and doing just as they chose," recalled Sam Gadsden, a black South Carolinian born in 1882. "That's all there is to segregation, that caused the whole thing. The white people couldn't master these niggers any more so they took up the task of intimidating them."

What made the laws increasingly urgent was the refusal of blacks to keep to their place. In the late nineteenth century, economic and social changes swept through the South, introducing new sites and sources of potential racial contact and conflict; at the same time, white women in increasing numbers moved into the public arena and workplace. Both races availed themselves of the expanding means of rail transportation, with middle-class blacks in particular asserting their independence and social position. Refusing to be confined to the second-class or "smoking" car, they purchased tickets in the first-class or "ladies" car, much to the consternation of whites who resented these "impudent" assertions of social equality. In response to white complaints, conductors expelled blacks from the first-class seats they had purchased, resulting in disruptive incidents and litigation.

Segregation, even more than disfranchisement, came to be linked to white fears of social equality. The railroad and the streetcar became early arenas of confrontation, precisely because in no other area of public life (except the polling place) did blacks and whites come together on such an equal footing. "In their homes and in ordinary employment," as one observer noted, "they meet as master and servant; but in the street cars they touch as free citizens, each paying for the right to ride, the white not in a place of command, the Negro without an obligation of servitude. Street car relationships are, therefore, symbolic of the new conditions." In daily travel, the proximity of the races was likely to be much closer, more intimate, more productive of evil, as a New Orleans newspaper suggested: "A man that would be horrified at the idea of his wife or daughter seated by the side of a burly negro in the parlor of a hotel or at a restaurant cannot see her occupying a crowded seat in a car next to a negro without the same feeling of disgust." An English visitor heard the Jim Crow car defended not only as a necessary means to keep the peace but "on the ground of the special aversion which ... the negro male excites in the white woman."...

To resolve this growing problem, state after state, beginning in the 1880s, responded by designating cars for whites and blacks, in many instances making the "smoking" or second-class car the only car available to black passengers. The same assertiveness by blacks on the urban streetcars and trolleys, including the refusal to sit in separate sections or to give up seats to whites, prompted municipalities to take similar action. In Jacksonville, Florida, for example, the city council enacted a separate streetcar ordinance after reports of disturbances on the cars and growing complaints from whites about "the attitude" of black passengers.

Some municipalities prescribed separate cars; most settled on partitions that separated the races on the same car, with blacks relegated to the rear seats. On boarding a streetcar in Atlanta, for example, the passenger would see over each door a sign reading

> White People Will Seat From Front of Car Toward
> the Back and Colored People from Rear Toward Front

With some exceptions, that became the standard arrangement. In Birmingham, blacks sat in the front section, and attempts to reverse the order clashed with custom. "After all," one white resident noted, "it is not important which end of the car is given to the nigger. The main point is that he must sit where he is told."...

The new railway stations in Birmingham, Atlanta, Charleston, and Jacksonville impressed visitors with their spaciousness and impressive architecture. Each station also had its separate entrances, waiting rooms, and ticket offices marked "For White Passengers" and "For Colored Passengers." The rod separating the white section from the black section, unlike the screens in streetcars, as one visitor noted, was neither provisional nor movable "but fixed as the foundations of the building." Throughout the South, segregation was extended to waiting rooms, most often confining blacks to smaller and cramped quarters....

Although blacks had previously experienced segregation in various forms, the thoroughness of Jim Crow made it strikingly different. What the white South did was to segregate the races by law and enforced custom in practically every conceivable situation in which whites and blacks might come into social contact: from public transportation to public parks, from the workplace to hospitals, asylums, and orphanages, from the homes for the aged, the blind, deaf, and dumb, to the prisons, from saloons to churches. Not only were the races to be kept apart in hospitals (including a special section for black infants requiring medical attention), but some denied admission to blacks altogether. Laws or custom also required that black and white nurses tend only the sick of their own race. By 1885, most states had already legally mandated separate schools. Where intermarriage and cohabitation had not been outlawed, states quickly moved to place such restrictions in law.

The signs "White Only" and "Colored" (or "Negroes") would henceforth punctuate the southern landscape, appearing over the entrances to parks, theaters, boardinghouses, waiting rooms, toilets, and water fountains. Movie houses were becoming increasingly popular, and Jim Crow demanded not only separate ticket windows and entrances but also separate seating, usually in the balcony—what came to be known as the "buzzard roost" or "nigger heaven." And blacks came to learn that in places where they were permitted to mix with whites—stores, post offices, and banks, for example—they would need to wait until all the whites had been served. Special rules also restricted blacks when shopping in white stores, forbidding women, for example, from trying on dresses, hats, and shoes before purchasing them.

The rapid industrialization of the South introduced another set of problems, increasing racial tensions in places employing both races. Where whites and blacks worked in the same factories, the law would now mandate segregation wherever feasible. The code adopted in South Carolina, for example, prohibited textile factories from permitting black and white laborers to work together in the same room, or to use the same entrances, pay windows, exits, doorways, or stairways at the same time, or the same "lavatories, toilets, drinking water buckets, pails, cups, dippers or glasses" at any time. Under certain conditions, such as an emergency, the code permitted black firemen, floor scrubbers, and repairmen to associate with white laborers.

Separation of the races often meant the total exclusion of black men and women from certain facilities. The expansion of recreation in the late nineteenth century mandated exclusion of blacks from most amusement parks, roller skating rinks, bowling alleys, swimming pools, and tennis courts. It was not uncommon to find a sign at the entrance to a public park reading "Negroes and Dogs Not Allowed." Excluding blacks from parks deprived them not only of a recreational area but of free public entertainment. "Think of it," a black visitor to Atlanta informed a friend in New York, "Negroes not allowed in some of the parks here, to listen to [a] band which plays here on Sundays." Some communities admitted blacks to parks on certain days, designated a portion for their use, or made arrangements for separate parks.

With few exceptions, municipal libraries were reserved for the exclusive use of whites. Between 1900 and 1910, some public libraries extended limited service—that is, blacks were still denied access to the reading room or the privilege of browsing in the stacks, but they might in some instances borrow books for home use. Rather than make any such provisions in the main library, some cities chose to establish separate branches to serve black patrons. But for whites who feared educated blacks, barring them from libraries altogether made eminently good sense....

The legislation of Jim Crow affected all classes and ages, and it tended to be thorough, far-reaching, even imaginative: from separate public school textbooks for black and white children and Jim Crow Bibles on which to swear in black witnesses in court, to separate telephone booths, separate windows in the banks for black and white depositors, and Jim Crow elevators in office buildings, one for whites and one for blacks and freight. New Orleans went so far as to adopt an ordinance segregating black and white prostitutes; Atlanta confined them to separate blocks, while a Nashville brothel settled for a plan by which black prostitutes were placed in the basement and white prostitutes on the ground and upper floors. In Atlanta, the art school that had used black models needed no law to dispense with their employment.

Even as the laws decreed that black babies would enter the world in separate facilities, so blacks would occupy separate places at the end of their lives. The ways in which Jim Crow made its mark on the ritual of death could assume bizarre dimensions. Will Mathis, a convicted white felon, appealed to a judge that he be hanged at a different hour than Orlando Lester, a black man, and from a different set of gallows. The same plea was made by a white Tennessean convicted of the brutal murder of his wife. After he objected to going to the gallows with three black men, the authorities agreed to hang them first. Custom, if not ordinances, dictated that blacks and whites be buried in separate cemeteries. "If a colored person was to be buried among the whites," one observer noted sarcastically in Alabama, "the latter would all rise from their graves in indignation. How they tolerate the 'niggers' in heaven is a mystery, unless the mansions there are provided with kitchens and stables."...

Law and custom interacted to keep blacks in their place, and it would be the responsibility of blacks to learn how to adapt to these conditions as a way of life. That required a knowledge not only of local customs and laws but also of the way these might differ from place to place. "Every town had its own mores, its own unwritten restrictions," a black educator recalled. "The trick was to find out from local [black] people what the 'rules' were."

Perhaps the most revealing aspects of Jim Crow were the exceptions made for black domestic workers. If a black servant, for example, accompanied a white child into a railroad coach or into a park reserved for whites, that was perfectly acceptable, since the association did not imply an equal relationship. "Everything was all right," a Georgia house servant revealed, "so long as I was in the white man's part of the street car or in the white man's coach as a servant—a slave—but as soon as I did not present myself as a menial, and the relationship of master and servant was abolished by my not having the white children with me, I would be forthwith assigned to the 'nigger' seats or the 'colored people's coach.'" The same exception applied to black servants overseeing white children in public parks that barred blacks. Some of the parks bore signs reading "No Negroes Allowed on These Grounds Except as Servants." A black teacher ventured into a restricted park in Charleston in the company of a white friend and fellow teacher and precipitated no objections. "Of course," she noted, "every one thought I was her maid."...

The demands made by Jim Crow worked their way into the daily routines of black men and women. Pauli Murray remembered all too vividly the signs and how they had "screamed" at her from every direction: "For White Only," "For Colored Only," "White Ladies," "Colored Women," "White," "Colored." The signs instructed blacks as to where they could legally walk, sit, rest, eat, drink, and entertain themselves. But if the signs were new to the South, the custom of segregating the races was not, only its legalization and the intensity with which the old customs were now enforced and expanded. Experiencing these strictures on movement and presence constituted the initiation of a new generation into the meaning of blackness and freedom in the post-Reconstruction South....

The workings of Jim Crow often seemed downright ludicrous. But blacks had no choice but to tolerate it, even as they mocked—among themselves—its absurdities, contradictions, and obscenities. It took little time for Jim Crow practices to become a standard item in black folklore and humor. Perhaps the only way to fathom the depths of white desperation and absurdity in keeping themselves apart from blacks was to subject white actions and rationales to the ridicule they deserved. One story told of a white deacon in Mississippi entering his church only to find a Negro. "Boy," he called out, "what you doin' in here? Don't you know this is a white church?" The black quickly explained, "Boss, I only just got sent here to mop up the floor." The response—and more importantly the manner in which it was rendered—reassured the deacon. "Well, that's all right then. But don't let me catch you prayin'." Still another story involved the elderly black man who managed to talk his way out of a traffic citation by telling the judge, "Lord, boss. I sho' thought them green lights was for the white folks and the red lights was for us cullud folks." The absurdities of race etiquette also became a target in black humor. A white woman, referring to her black servant, told her son, "I and John will look after the chickens." Her son, in the sixth grade, corrected her, "Mother, the grammar says it must be *John and I,*" to which his mother immediately responded, "Grammar or no grammar, boy, I won't put any Negro ahead of me."...

Like so many of the segregation statutes enacted in the 1890s and the early twentieth century, a law enacted by Louisiana in 1890 forbade any railroad passenger to enter "a coach or compartment to which by race he does not belong." Homer Plessy, a light-skinned black, claiming the statute violated his rights under the Thirteenth and Fourteenth Amendments, chose to challenge it in court. After purchasing a first-class ticket on the East Louisiana Railway from New Orleans to Covington, he took a vacant seat in a whites-only car. Not heeding the demand that he leave that car, Plessy was forcibly ejected and placed in the parish jail of New Orleans.

In *Plessy* v. *Ferguson,* the U.S. Supreme Court in 1896, by an overwhelming 8 to 1 vote, rejected Plessy's appeal and found no problem with accommodations that were "equal but separate." The majority opinion embraced popular views on race. "Social prejudices," wrote Justice Henry B. Brown for the majority, may not be "overcome by legislation," and legislative bodies were "powerless to eradicate racial instincts." Rejecting the idea that "the enforced separation of the two races stamps the colored race with a badge of inferiority," Justice Brown observed, "If this be so, it is not by reason of anything found in the act, but solely because the colored race chooses to put that construction upon it." Equal rights, in any event, did not require "an enforced commingling of the two races," and any effort to force such commingling would only exacerbate race relations. "If one race be inferior to the other socially, the Constitution of the United States cannot put them upon the same plane." The doctrine of white supremacy could not have been enunciated more clearly. Ironically, the lone dissent came from John Marshall Harlan, a southern justice and son of a slaveowner. By permitting the states to regulate civil rights "solely upon the basis of race," he argued, the Court had deprived black men and women of equal protection before the law. It would require another fifty-eight years for a majority of the Supreme Court to agree.

The decision in *Plessy* v. *Ferguson* was less than dramatic in its impact. For most black Southerners, it simply underscored what they already knew from personal experience—that the quality of their lives and freedom depended on the whims, will, and toleration of a majority of whites in their locality or state. The Court's decision, along with the elaborate structure of Jim Crow, remained in force for more than half a century, as did the reality of separate and unequal treatment. The train compartment reserved for blacks came to symbolize that reality. "[I]n every instance and without recourse," a white southern critic observed, it was "the most uncomfortable, uncleanest, and unsafest place."...

Where and how black men and women drew the line between accommodation and submission would be part of their legacy. Adopting a variety of responses, often intricate and not always easily ascertainable, they tried to circumvent the system and maintain their self-respect. For some, it was nothing less than a matter of common courtesy, an insistence that white people recognize them as visible and mature men and women. A Tennessee woman had no desire to "mess with" white folks. But, as she insisted, "when the white folks steps in this house, especially the men, I demand respect. I always says, 'Won't you rest your hat?' Yes-sir, just as I feel." Still another black woman, an elderly domestic, often walked the streets, muttering to herself, "I ain't nobody's aunt. They call me aunt, and I ain't nobody's aunt."

Reflecting some years later over the predicament southern blacks confronted in the early twentieth century, Ralph Ellison thought Richard Wright's generation had three choices available to them: "They could accept the role created for them by the whites and perpetually resolve the resulting conflicts through the hope and emotional catharsis of Negro religion; they could repress their dislike of Jim Crow social relations while striving for a middle way of respectability, becoming—consciously or unconsciously—the accomplices of the whites in oppressing their brothers; or they could reject the situation, adopt a criminal attitude, and carry on an unceasing psychological scrimmage with the whites, which often flared forth into physical violence."...

In real life, as in lore and song, the few who chose open defiance forfeited their lives for their contempt of authority. And black men and women reacted to them, much as they did to the legendary outlaws, with a certain ambivalence, an admiration of some of their exploits mixed with doubts about the ultimate meaning of those exploits. As a child in Mississippi, Richard Wright watched with awe black men who sneered at the customs and taboos, who cursed and violated the laws, who rode the Jim Crow streetcars without paying and sat where they pleased, who mimicked the antics of white folks and conspired to get what they wanted out of them, and who were happiest when they had outwitted their foes and saddest when they brooded over the impossibility of ever becoming free. All of these men, Wright confessed, left "a marked impression" on him, some of them because he had wanted to emulate their actions. But eventually, Wright observed, they paid a terrible price for their feats. "They were shot, hanged, maimed, lynched, and generally hounded until they were either dead or their spirits broken."

In an age of "bad niggers," many whites and blacks thought the boxer Jack Johnson the "baddest" of them all, suggesting how "bad" or "ba-ad" took on some strikingly different meanings in white and black communities. To blacks, Johnson became a folk legend; to whites, a reminder of the uppity, menacing, lustful black male they had come to fear. Born in Galveston in 1878, he worked at a variety of jobs while acquiring and honing his boxing skills. He shocked the sports world in 1908 when he defeated Tommy Burns, a white man, to become the first black world's heavyweight boxing champion, and the way he did it provoked even more consternation. Johnson not only defeated Burns, he taunted and humiliated him in the ring. One story making the rounds in black communities related how the two fighters met in the center of the ring for the referee's instructions. After eyeing his opponent, Burns is said to have warned him, "Boy, I'm gonna whip you good. I was *born* with boxing gloves on." Jack Johnson smiled and replied, "I have news for you, white man. You're about to die the same way!" Apocryphal or not, the story summed up the match. A black newspaper in Richmond headlined the event in bold type, "A Southern Negro Is Heavyweight Champion of the World," and it thought "no event in forty years has given more genuine satisfaction to the colored people of this country."

The burden of being "the hope of the white race" fell on Jim Jeffries, a former champion persuaded to come out of retirement despite his vow never to step into a ring with a black man. Billed as "the fight of the century," the Johnson-Jeffries bout attracted national attention....

When Johnson entered the ring, a brass band played and some twenty thousand rabidly partisan Jeffries fans sang the popular hit "All Coons Look Alike to Me." They did not sing for very long. Johnson demolished the heavily favored and previously unbeaten Jeffries. And, as in the Burns fight, he did so with a derisive smile and a taunting commentary that few whites or blacks could ever shake from their memory. "Come on now, Mr. Jeff. Let me see what you got," Johnson reportedly shouted. "Do something, man. This is for the champ*peenship*.... I can go on like this all afternoon, Mr. Jeff." Jeffries could not, and he suffered a devastating and humiliating defeat—as did, many acknowledged (or boasted), the entire white race.

To blacks, Jack Johnson's feats took on added symbolic importance. Even if some identified with him surreptitiously, so as not to provoke whites, Johnson gave them an outlet. When he brought a white man to his knees, humbling and humiliating him in the process, he brought the entire white race to its knees, acting out the frustrations and bitterness of tens of thousands of blacks based on a lifetime of insults and betrayals. It was a rare triumph in an era of devastating and often humiliating setbacks.

News of Johnson's spectacular victory spread rapidly. Ten-year-old Louis Armstrong was on his way to pick up the newspapers he delivered when he encountered a crowd of black youths running toward him on Canal Street in New Orleans. "You better get started, black boy," one of them said, pulling him along. "Jack Johnson has just knocked out Jim Jeffries. The white boys are sore about it and they're going to take it out on us." Richard Wright recalled Jack Johnson as one of a number of topics one should not raise in the presence of southern white men. Fourteen-year-old Benjamin Mays remembered "vividly" the impact of the fight and the need to avoid discussing the subject with whites. "White men in my county could not take it. A few Negroes were beaten up because a Negro had beaten a white man in far-away Nevada."

Overjoyed, blacks in some places dropped their masks, if momentarily, to give full voice to an impressive racial triumph. Dismayed whites reacted to Johnson's beating up on Jeffries by beating up indiscriminately on blacks in their vicinity. Racial skirmishes, sometimes violent riots, broke out in every southern state and in much of the country. A Richmond black newspaper advised its readers that "a colored man who imagines himself Jack Johnson, will get an awful beating." And a white newspaper in the same city, in warning blacks not to be misled, expressed concern that "all over the country a simple-minded race is getting into its head a false pride, a foolish impression, a disastrous ambition."...

The rage of white America centered on more than the reality of a black heavyweight champion. No sooner had whites suffered through Jeffries's humiliation in the ring than they had to watch Jack Johnson embrace his wife. She was white. "Jack Johnson committed two grave blunders as far as whites were concerned," Benjamin Mays recalled: "He beat up a white man and he was socializing with a white woman—both deadly sins in 1908." But Johnson was no ordinary black man. He did not know his place, he refused to acknowledge racial barriers. Violating nearly every racial code and custom, making no effort to mask his feelings, he flaunted his lifestyle, his fashionable clothes, his expensive jewelry, his shaved head, his fast automobiles, and the white women he escorted and, in three instances, married.

The stories of his prowess, in and out of the ring, entered fully into black folklore. The veracity of these tales made little difference; blacks perceived them as true, and for good reason. After Johnson's spectacular achievements in the ring, they could believe anything of him....

When the motion picture *Birth of a Nation* took the country by storm in 1915, the audience focused much of its attention on the black villain, Silas Lynch, who summed up the Black Peril in his impudence, venality, and lust for white women. Johnson had much the same effect on white America, and his boxing achievements and lifestyle resulted in a host of bills restricting and punishing interracial marriage. Congress outlawed the importation and interstate transportation of films or other visual representations of prizefights. "No man descended from the old Saxon race," one congressman declared, "can look upon that kind of contest without abhorrence and disgust."

But to working-class blacks, in particular, Jack Johnson remained a "ba-ad" man who commanded enormous admiration. No other black person in their memory had displayed so impressively the ability to outwit, outthink, and outfight white folks. The myth of white invincibility had been shattered, at least for a moment....

FURTHER READING

Theodore W. Allen, *The Invention of the White Race: The Origin of Racial Oppression* (1998).

Armando C. Alonzo, *Tejano Legacy: Rancheros and Settlers in South Texas, 1734–1900* (1998).

Eric Anderson, *Race and Politics in North Carolina, 1872–1901* (1981).

James D. Anderson, *The Education of Blacks in the South, 1860–1935* (1988).

Elizabeth Rauh Bethel, *Promiseland: A Century of Life in a Negro Community* (1981).

John W. Blassingame, *Black New Orleans, 1860–1880* (1973).

David Brown and Clive Webb, *Race in the American South: From Slavery to Civil Rights* (2007).

W. Fitzhugh Brundage, *Lynching in the New South: Georgia and Virginia, 1880–1930* (1993).

———, ed., *Under Sentence of Death: Lynching in the South* (1997).

John W. Cell, *The Highest Stage of White Supremacy: The Origins of Segregation in South Africa and the American South* (1982).

Jane Dailey, *The Age of Jim Crow* (2008).

Helen G. Edmonds, *The Negro and Fusion Politics in North Carolina, 1894–1901* (1951).

Neil Foley, *The White Scourge: Mexicans, Blacks, and Poor Whites in Texas Cotton Culture* (1997).

George Fredrickson, *The Black Image in the White Mind: the Debate on Afro-American Character and Destiny, 1817–1914* (1971).

Willard B. Gatewood, *Aristocrats of Color: The Black Elite, 1880–1920* (1990).

Glenda Gilmore, *Gender and Jim Crow: Women and the Politics of White Supremacy in North Carolina, 1896–1920* (1996).

Kenneth W. Goings, *Mammy and Uncle Mose: Black Collectibles and American Stereotyping* (1994).

John W. Graves, *Town and Country: Race Relations in an Urban-Rural Context* (1990).

Janette Greenwood, *Bittersweet Legacy: The Black and White "Better" Classes in Charlotte* (1994).

Steven Hahn, *A Nation Under Our Feet: Black Political Struggles in the Rural South from Slavery to the Great Migration* (2003).

Grace Hale, *Making Whiteness: The Culture of Segregation in the South* (1998).

Louis R. Harlan, *Booker T. Washington: The Making of a Black Leader, 1856–1901* (1972).

Stephen Kantrowitz, *Ben Tillman and the Reconstruction of White Supremacy* (2000).

Robert C. Kenzer, *Enterprising Southerners: Black Economic Success in North Carolina, 1865–1915* (1997).

J. Morgan Kousser, *The Shaping of Southern Politics: Suffrage Restriction and the Establishment of the One-Party South, 1880–1910* (1974).

Suzanne Lebsock, *A Murder in Virginia: Southern Justice on Trial* (2003).

Leon Litwack, *Trouble in Mind: Black Southerners in the Age of Jim Crow* (1998).

Gordon B. McKinney, *Southern Mountain Republicans, 1865–1900* (1978).

Neil R. McMillen, *Dark Journey: Black Mississippians in the Age of Jim Crow* (1989).

August Meier, *Negro Thought in America, 1880–1915* (1963).

Michele Mitchell, *Righteous Propagation: African Americans and the Politics of Racial Destiny* (2004).

Pauli Murray, *Proud Shoes: The Story of an American Family* (1956, 1978).

Sydney Nathans, *The Quest for Progress: The Way We Lived in North Carolina, 1870–1920* (1983).

Cynthia Neverdon-Morton, *Afro-American Women of the South and the Advancement of the Race, 1895–1925* (1989).

Robert J. Norrell, *The House I Live In: Race in the American Century* (2005).

———, *Up from History: The Life of Booker T. Washington* (2009).

Nell Irvin Painter, *Exodusters: Black Migration to Kansas after Reconstruction* (1977).

———, *The History of White People* (2010).

Howard N. Rabinowitz, *Race Relations in the Urban South, 1865–1890* (1978).

Mark Schultz, *The Rural Face of White Supremacy: Beyond Jim Crow* (2005).

Mark M. Smith, *How Race Is Made: Slavery, Segregation, and the Senses* (2006).

Diane M. Sommerville. *Rape and Race in the Nineteenth-Century South* (2004).

Donald Spivey, *Schooling for the New Slavery: Black Industrial Education, 1868–1915* (1978).

Mildred Thompson, *Ida B. Wells-Barnett: An Exploratory Study of an American Black Woman, 1893–1930* (1990).

George Brown Tindall, *South Carolina Negroes, 1877–1900* (1952).

Vernon Lane Wharton, *The Negro in Mississippi, 1865–1890* (1947).

Shane White and Graham White, *Stylin': African American Expressive Culture* (1998).

Joel Williamson, ed. *The Crucible of Race: Black/White Relations in the American South since Emancipation* (1984).

———, *The Origins of Segregation* (1968).

Amy Louise Wood, *Lynching and Spectacle: Witnessing Racial Violence in America, 1890–1940* (2009).

C. Vann Woodward, *Origins of the New South, 1877–1913* (1951).

———, *The Strange Career of Jim Crow*, 3rd rev. ed. (1974).

CHAPTER 7

Southern Religion

Religion remains one of the major characteristics of southern identity. Evangelical Protestantism became central to the perspectives of both black and white southerners, though they responded to its theology in different ways. In the postwar era, many white southerners, despondent over defeat and convinced of God's displeasure, sought solace in evangelical Protestantism, where the focus remained on hoped-for redemption, personally and regionally. African Americans formed evangelical churches, which served to unite, protect, support, and educate freedpeople in a sacramental and social institution. In towns and cities, black churches offered respite from racial discrimination and often provided a base for social protest. African American ministers emerged as powerful leaders who urged their congregations to persevere—and even to protest.

Evangelical Christianity's enthusiastic, joyful style of worship and distinctive preaching; its emphasis on conversion, salvation, and love; its focus on the individual's personal relationship with God; its insistence on funding missions and spreading the gospel; its fascination with sin, the eradication of "sinful vices," and God's punishment for sinners; its soulful music; its reluctance to engage in social reform; and its preference for large-scale revivals all contributed to a distinctive and unique religious culture in the South. So dominant was this evangelical culture that one may forget that the South was also home to mainstream Protestant and Roman Catholic churches as well as Jewish synagogues.

After the 1890s, many churchmen and churchwomen supported social reforms and considered themselves progressive. The roots of child labor reform, welfare, and even civil rights may be found in the South's religiosity. But the region's distinctive evangelical style remains in place, as evidenced by the fact that many of the region's televangelists have been southern. The South is still considered the most religious section of the nation.

How can the region's history help explain this? What has been the relationship between southern religion and segregation or between southern religion and reform? Is southern religion a force for inspiring change—or for sanctifying the status quo?

DOCUMENTS

Evangelical theology is not all of a piece; there are disparate black and white interpretations and numerous differences among the denominations. In black and white sacred music, the past figured significantly, but in contrasting ways. Negro spirituals from the slavery era often had double meanings, as indicated in "Steal Away to Jesus" in Document 1. Hymns in white churches after the Civil War sanctified the Lost Cause, as the 1901 variation on "When the Roll Is Called Up Yonder" in Document 1 reveals. In Document 2, black activist W. E. B. Du Bois reflects on the pervasiveness of religion in the life of African Americans. In Document 3 William A. Owens recounts his childhood memories of summer revivals and baptisms in a muddy pond in East Texas. After a long season of planting, hoeing, and worrying, farm families flocked to see preachers bring them "back into fold" and assure them of salvation if they accepted Jesus. In Document 4, an image printed in *Crisis*, the official publication of the National Association for the Advancement of Colored people (NAACP), suggests a correlation between the crucifixion of Jesus and the lynching of blacks. The ideas in this image are echoed in Donald Mathews's essay, "The Southern Rite of Human Sacrifice." The Southern Sociological Congress was a major organizational response to the progressive movement in the South. It was founded in Nashville in 1912 and was dedicated to coordinating social reform efforts. The 1914 meeting in Memphis took as its theme "The Solid South for a Better Nation," and one excerpt written by Rabbi Emmanuel Sternheim from the conference proceedings explains his vision of the church's mission. Presented here as Document 5, the rabbi's teachings reveal the strong clerical influence on progressive reform as well as progressives' interest in improving race relations. In Document 6, Lillian Smith, well-known author and civil rights advocate, recalls from her book *Killers of the Dream* the lessons that southern religion imparted to her, which contrast sharply with those remembered by Owens.

1. Southerners Cherish Two Hymns

"Steal Away to Jesus," a Negro Spiritual, N.D.

Chorus

Steal away, steal away, steal away to Jesus!
Steal away, steal away home,
I ain't got long to stay here.
Steal away, steal away, steal away to Jesus!
Steal away, steal away home,
I ain't got long to stay here.

My Lord, He calls me.
He calls me by the thunder,
The trumpet sounds within-a my soul,
I ain't got long to stay here.

First song can be found in James Weldon Johnson, ed., *The Book of Negro American Spirituals* (New York: Viking Press, 1925), pp. 114–117. Second song can be found in Robert H. Coleman ed., *The Modern Hymnal: Standard Hymns and Gospel Songs: New and Old for General Use in All Services* (Nashville: Broadman Press, 1926), p. 366.

Chorus

Green trees a bending, po' sinner stand a-trembling,
The trumpet sounds within-a my soul,
I ain't got long to stay here,
Oh, Lord I ain't got long to stay here.

"When the Roll Is Called Up Yonder," 1901

When this time with us shall be no more and final taps shall sound,
And the Death's last cruel battle shall be fought;
When the good of all the armies shall tent on yonder camping ground,
When the roll is called up yonder, let's be there.

On that mistless, lonely morning when the saved of Christ shall rise,
In the Father's many-mansioned home to share;
Where our Lee and Jackson call us to their homes beyond the skies,
When the roll is called up yonder, let's be there.

If all's not well with thee, my comrades, for thy entrance at the gate,
Haste thy calling and election to prepare;
You will find that precious peace, sweet peace,
When the roll is called up yonder, let's be there.

2. W. E. B. Du Bois Reflects on the Faith of the Fathers, 1903

It was out in the country, far from home, far from my foster home, on a dark Sunday night. The road wandered from our rambling log-house up the stony bed of a creek, past wheat and corn, until we could hear dimly across the fields a rhythmic cadence of song,—soft, thrilling, powerful, that swelled and died sorrowfully in our ears. I was a country school-teacher then, fresh from the East, and had never seen a Southern Negro revival. To be sure, we in Berkshire were not perhaps as stiff and formal as they in Suffolk of olden time; yet we were very quiet and subdued, and I know not what would have happened those clear Sabbath mornings had some one punctuated the sermon with a wild scream, or interrupted the long prayer with a loud Amen! And so most striking to me, as I approached the village and the little plain church perched aloft, was the air of intense excitement that possessed that mass of black folk. A sort of suppressed terror hung in the air and seemed to seize us,—a pythian madness, a demoniac possession, that lent terrible reality to song and word. The black and massive form of the preacher swayed and quivered as the words crowded to his lips and flew at us in singular eloquence. The people moaned and fluttered, and then the gaunt-cheeked brown woman beside me suddenly leaped straight into the air and shrieked like a lost soul, while round about came wail and groan and outcry, and a scene of human passion such as I had never conceived before.

W. E. B. DuBois on the Faith of the Fathers, 1903.

Those who have not thus witnessed the frenzy of a Negro revival in the untouched backwoods of the South can but dimly realize the religious feeling of the slave; as described, such scenes appear grotesque and funny, but as seen they are awful. Three things characterized this religion of the slave,—the Preacher, the Music, and the Frenzy. The Preacher is the most unique personality developed by the Negro on American soil. A leader, a politician, an orator, a "boss," an intriguer, an idealist—all these he is, and ever, too, the centre of a group of men, now twenty, now a thousand in number. The combination of a certain adroitness with deep-seated earnestness, of tact with consummate ability, gave him his preëminence, and helps him maintain it. The type, of course, varies according to time and place, from the West Indies in the sixteenth century to New England in the nineteenth, and from the Mississippi bottoms to cities like New Orleans or New York.

The Music of Negro religion is that plaintive rhythmic melody, with its touching minor cadences, which, despite caricature and defilement, still remains the most original and beautiful expression of human life and longing yet born on American soil. Sprung from the African forests, where its counterpart can still be heard, it was adapted, changed, and intensified by the tragic soul-life of the slave, until, under the stress of law and whip, it became the one true expression of a people's sorrow, despair, and hope.

Finally the Frenzy or "Shouting," when the Spirit of the Lord passed by, and, seizing the devotee, made him mad with supernatural joy, was the last essential of Negro religion and the one more devoutly believed in than all the rest. It varied in expression from the silent rapt countenance or the low murmur and moan to the mad abandon of physical fervor,—the stamping, shrieking, and shouting, the rushing to and fro and wild waving of arms, the weeping and laughing, the vision and the trance. All this is nothing new in the world, but old as religion, as Delphi and Endor. And so firm a hold did it have on the Negro, that many generations firmly believed that without this visible manifestation of the God there could be no true communion with the Invisible....

The Negro church of to-day is the social centre of Negro life in the United States, and the most characteristic expression of African character. Take a typical church in a small Virginian town: it is the "First Baptist"—a roomy brick edifice seating five hundred or more persons, tastefully finished in Georgia pine, with a carpet, a small organ, and stained-glass windows. Underneath is a large assembly room with benches. This building is the central club-house of a community of a thousand or more Negroes. Various organizations meet here,—the church proper, the Sunday-school, two or three insurance societies, women's societies, secret societies, and mass meetings of various kinds. Entertainments, suppers, and lectures are held beside the five or six regular weekly religious services. Considerable sums of money are collected and expended here, employment is found for the idle, strangers are introduced, news is disseminated and charity distributed. At the same time this social, intellectual, and economic centre is a religious centre of great power. Depravity, Sin, Redemption, Heaven, Hell, and Damnation are preached twice a Sunday with much fervor, and revivals take place every year after the crops are laid by; and few indeed of the community have the hardihood to withstand conversion. Back of this more formal religion, the Church often stands as a real conserver of morals, a strengthener of family life, and the final authority on what is Good and Right.

Thus one can see in the Negro church to-day, reproduced in microcosm, all that great world from which the Negro is cut off by color-prejudice and social condition....

Such churches are really governments of men, and consequently a little investigation reveals the curious fact that, in the South, at least, practically every American Negro is a church member. Some, to be sure, are not regularly enrolled, and a few do not habitually attend services; but, practically, a proscribed people must have a social centre, and that centre for this people is the Negro church. The census of 1890 showed nearly twenty-four thousand Negro churches in the country, with a total enrolled membership of over two and a half millions, or ten actual church members to every twenty-eight persons, and in some Southern States one in every two persons. Besides these there is the large number who, while not enrolled as members, attend and take part in many of the activities of the church. There is an organized Negro church for every sixty black families in the nation, and in some States for every forty families, owning, on an average, a thousand dollars' worth of property each, or nearly twenty-six million dollars in all.

3. William A. Owens Remembers a Revival and Baptism in Texas, c. 1910

Revival time came at the Novice Church in late August—still in the heat and drouth of dog days. Word of the meeting was passed up and down the road: Old Brother Cummings would do the preaching, and only at night. It was too hot and dusty for people to come out in the middle of the day, and the men could not take enough time off from work to build a brush arbor. Benches from the church could be brought out and left out. The organ could be carried out and back every night....

By the next night it looked like a baptizing all right. When Brother Cummings gave the call for sinners to come to the mourner's bench, grown men and women went and knelt close together, praying out loud, not to be converted but to be brought back into the fold. They were the ones who had strayed, the backsliders, brought back now by fear and the song the people were singing:

Come home, come home,
Ye who are weary come home.
Softly and tenderly Jesus is calling,
Calling, "Oh, sinner, come home."

It was a night of tears and prayers, of clapping hands and shouting when a sinner on his knees before Brother Cummings said he was ready to turn his back on the past and look to a new Promised Land.

It did not end for us when we left the church. Our wagon was like another meeting place with songs and prayers and talk of the need to be converted and then baptized. Converting had to come first—with a public confession. Without it, baptism was a blasphemy, a sin that could not be pardoned.

William A. Owens, *This Stubborn Soil: A Frontier Beyond* (New York: Nick Lyons Books, 1999) pp. 171, 175–78. Reprinted by permission.

The next night, when the call to the mourner's bench came, [his brother] Dewey got up and went, leaving a bench full of boys behind him, going to the bench where the deacons waited to put their arms around him and talk to him. He was tall and awkward and shy, and they did not have to work on him long till he was ready to ask for the right hand of fellowship. When he did, on his knees before Brother Cummings, my mother clapped her hands and cried. One of her sons was ready for the baptism.

Then they worked harder on [his brother] Monroe, the deacons going back to the bench where he sat to talk with him and pray with him. He listened to them, staring straight ahead, not showing how he felt, only holding back when they tried to start him toward the mourner's bench. Night after night they tried, but they never got him to go.

At the same time they were working on a man who lived up the road from us, a cocky little man who always had a joke and a laugh. At every revival meeting for years the preachers and deacons had worked on him, but he held back, "hardhearted, stiff-necked," Brother Cummings said in a prayer made only for him, "without a hope of seeing the Redeemer face to face." Then one night he went to the mourner's bench, and the preacher, the deacons, the sisters, and brethren went with him, to kneel over him, to cry and pray over him, and fan him with palm-leaf fans, and to sing over him in tear-wet voices, "Come home, come home, Ye who are weary come home." And then, "Almost persuaded now to believe; Almost persuaded Christ to receive." When they were tired and hoarse and wet with sweat he came through, still kneeling, with his hands up, reaching for Brother Cummings' hands. The singing and praying stopped. People leaned against each other and wept that the long hard fight was over, that one they had counted for lost would be washed clean.

The baptizing was after dinner on Sunday in a pool in a cow pasture, a hole of yellow water with cow tracks in the mud at the edge. The people had to leave their wagons at the road, crawl through a barbed-wire fence, and walk across dried grass to the pool. The men to be baptized wore white shirts and dark pants. The women wore loose white dresses with skirts down to their ankles. To keep their skirts from floating up in the water, they had tied them down below the knees so the steps they took were short, hobbled.

They gathered at the side of the pool for songs, prayers, and a sermon. Then it was time for the baptizing. The people were singing.

> Oh, think of the home over there
> Beyond the portals of light
> Where the saints all immortal and fair
> Are robed in their garments of white.

Brother Cummings, in his dull black suit and white shirt, took off his shoes at the edge of the water and waded in till his gray beard was just touching. Two of the deacons came to the edge of the water and waited.

From the women's side two sisters came with a girl between them leaning heavily on their arms. The singing went on.

> Over there, over there,
> Oh, think of the home over there....

They took her to the deacons, who took firm grips on her arms and moved her slowly out to the preacher. She stopped, clasped her hands on her breast, and looked up to the hot blue sky. He gripped her hands with his left hand and put his right behind her neck.

Over there, over there, over there,
Oh, think of the home over there....

Still gripping her with his left hand, Brother Cummings lifted his right and said in a loud voice:

"I baptize you in the name of the Father, the Son, and the Holy Ghost."

With his right hand behind her neck he lowered her out of sight in the water and raised her again. With water and tears running down her face, she came out of the pool and, met by the women, wrapped in a quilt, went behind the singers, who had again come to "Oh, think of the home over there."

One by one the women were led down, some of them hard to hold in their happiness, some of them shaking, scared at going into deep water. They were led out again and, in a group across the pasture and road to the church, to put on dry clothes, powder their faces, and comb their hair.

The men came next, wading in slowly, quietly, without help from the deacons, and stood in line, with bowed heads waiting to step up to Brother Cummings, to hear the words, to feel the water cover them. The greatest convert of them all was in the line but he did not bow his head. He stood stiff-necked as ever—maybe as hardhearted. Baptizing would be easier, everyone knew, if he would be a little limp-legged.

His time came and he stepped forward with his clasped hands pulled tight against his chest and his head up. Brother Cummings gripped his hands and said the words to end the fight hard won: "I baptize you in the name of the Father, the Son, and the Holy Ghost." Then he tried to push his head down, but the man pushed back. Brother Cummings took a new grip and got him under water up to his chin. A tin snuffbox popped out of his shirt pocket and floated on the water. With a look of sadness for this proof of sin, Brother Cummings grabbed the box and flung it out to the dry grass. Some of the people laughed, some looked on in anger, a few sighed. They knew it would not be easy for him to give up his sinful ways. Brother Cummings got another grip and pushed harder. He twisted and turned, but went down, not out of sight but far enough for Brother Cummings to say a loud "Amen."

The baptism was soon over, but not the talk about it. Some said he would have to be put down deeper than that to wash away his sins. Some said only the devil himself could have kept him from going under, Brother Cummings pushing as hard as he was. There were other questions: Had he been baptized? Could he go to heaven no more baptized than that? Would he be kept from sinning next time crapshooting came around?

On our way home in the wagon Dewey had nothing to say about the baptizing, but my mother spoke to the rest of us:

"I won't be happy till I see the last one of you come up out of that watery grave."

4. *Crisis* Magazine Presents the Image of Jesus Christ in Georgia, 1911

Cengage Learning wishes to thank the Crisis Publishing Co., Inc., the publisher of the magazine of the National Association for the Advancement of Colored People, for the use of the image first published in the December 1911 issue of *The Crisis*.

5. Rabbi Emmanuel Sternheim Explains the Mission of the Church, 1914

The Social Mission of the Church to City Life

RABBI EMMANUEL STERNHEIM, GREENVILLE, MISS.

True religion insists on human service, and this is the end toward which the real development of religion should be in the present suborned. One of the signs of the times is a new consciousness of others' needs. All men agree that there are rights which have not been recognized and duties which have not been performed. The desire to serve is forcing men to new and sometimes to strange

---

"Jesus Christ in Georgia," *Crisis* (December 1911), 70.

This document can be found in James E. McCulloch, ed., *Battling for Social Betterment: Southern Sociological Congress, Memphis, Tennessee, May 6–10, 1914* (Nashville: Southern Sociological Congress, 1914), p. 9.

activities, but nevertheless the desire to determine the relation of the individual to the community is a universal one.

Busy with our trade, and surrounded with the signs of wealth, we, like Jacob have been met by the angel of our forgotten brother. It is of the struggle of this angel, in the concerted effort to find what we must do for other's needs, that shall make of us princes of God, and enable us to remember that "the rich and poor meet together; the Lord is the maker of them all."...

I propose to devote myself to two or three specific duties of the Church about which there is usually some dispute.

The first claim I make is, that it is the duty of the Church to enter into the work of municipal government. There are arguments pro and con about this, but it seems to me to be axiomatic that the minister is a citizen and a man before he is a parson and he cannot be refused the rights of a citizen; but I am not keen on pressing the point, for my argument is to be that it is a comparatively unimportant thing whether the minister sits on the municipal board or not, but it is an essential to righteous city government that the united voices of the churches of the city shall speak through its personnel the demand for a godly and God-fearing administration....

Anticipating much the same objection and giving to it much the same reply, I am going to be sufficiently controversial to advocate the extension of the duty of the church to the domain of education. With a very complete and long experience of the evils of the infusion of religious differences into education, I am nevertheless anxious about the growth of a paramount utilitarian and materialistic education system....

By virtue of the position of the Church in regard to guidance, it should so cooperate with every educational effort in the city that every teacher in the city may thank God and take courage.

The last point with which I shall deal is the duty of the Church with regard to recreation....

What I am advocating here, however, is not so much the erection of the institutional church to which, of course, there can be no objection in the light of the principles enunciated in this address, but rather a conception of the duty of the Church in the fostering and the encouragement of every possible form of clean and wholesome amusement within the city limits....

Finally, it must be the conception of the Church that it is its function to stand for every effort to beautify the city. In the simple yet majestic words of Browning

> If you get simple beauty and naught else,
> You get about the best thing God invents.

In an ideal city all these things will be. The mission of the Church to the city is to make it ideal, and therefore all these things must be. In an ideal city none will be very rich and none will be very poor; knowledge and good will will join together to every child the best education; to render every house and street as healthy as the healthiest hillside in the world; to provide the most comfortable hospital for every one who is sick and to have at hand a friend for every one in trouble.

In our ideal city art will grow out of common life, undisturbed by contrasts of wealth and poverty. The people will have pleasure in their work and leisure to admire what is beautiful.

6. Lillian Smith Writes About God and Guilt, 1949

Our first lesson about God made the deepest impression on us. We were told that He loved us, and then we were told that He would burn us in everlasting flames of hell if we displeased Him. We were told we should love Him for He gives us everything good that we have, and then we were told we should fear Him because He has the power to do evil to us whenever He cares to. We learned from this part of the lesson another: that "people," like God and parents, can love you and hate you at the same time; and though they may love you, if you displease them they may do you great injury; hence being loved by them does not give you protection from being harmed by them. We learned that They (parents) have a "right" to act in this way because God does, and that They in a sense represent God, in the family.

Sometimes, when we felt weakened by anxieties that we had no words for, and battered by impulses impossible to act out, we tried to believe that God was responsible for this miserable state of affairs and one should not be too angry with parents. At least we thought this as we grew older and it helped some of us make a far more harmonious adjustment to our parents than to God.

As the years passed, God became the mighty protagonist of ambivalence although we had not heard the word. He loomed before us as the awesome example of one who injures, even destroys, in the name of "good" those whom He loves, and does it because He has the "right" to. We tried to think of Him as our best friend because we were told that He was. Weak with fear, we told ourselves that when you break the rules you "should be punished" by Him or your parents. But a doubt, an earthy animal shrewdness, whispered that anyone who would harm us was also our enemy. Yet these whispers we dared not say aloud, or clearly to ourselves, for we feared we might drop dead if we did. Even a wispy thought or two loaded us down with unbearable guilt. As we grew older and began to value reason and knowledge and compassion, we were told that He was wise and all-loving; yet He seemed from Old Testament stories to be full of whimsies and terrifying impulses and definitely not One whom a child could talk to and expect to receive an understanding reply from.

He was Authority. And we bowed before His power with that pinched quietness of children, stoically resigning ourselves to this Force as it was interpreted by the grown folks.

But life seemed a lost battle to many of us only after we learned the lesson on the Unpardonable Sin. Then it was that man's fate, our fate certainly, was sealed. According to this lesson, received mainly at revival meetings but graven on our hearts by our parents' refusal to deny it, God forgave, if we prayed hard and piteously enough, all sins but one. This one sin "against the Holy Ghost" He would never forgive. Committing it, one lived forever among the damned. What this sin was, what the "Holy Ghost" was, no one seemed to know. Or perhaps even grown folks dared not say it aloud. But the implication was—and this was made plain—that if you did not tread softly you would commit it; the best way was never to question anything but always accept what you were told.

Love and punishment ... redemption and the unpardonable sin.... He who would not harm a sparrow would burn little children in everlasting flames.... It added up to a terrible poetry and we learned each line by heart.

ESSAYS

In the first essay, historian Paul Harvey writes about black and white southern Baptists, the largest group among evangelical Protestants in the South. He argues that static concepts of evangelical individualism conceal the actual "diversity of southern religious life." He advocates understanding the central role that evangelicalism played in creating "redemption" for white Baptists and "liberation" for black Baptists. In "The Southern Rite of Human Sacrifice," Donald G. Mathews touches on one of the most disturbing questions regarding southern culture: What is the connection between southern religion and violence? How could white southerners who claimed to be the most religious in the nation commit the greatest number of horrific tortures and lynchings against African Americans? He answers this by examining white evangelical perceptions of God's vengeance in contrast to views of black Christians who saw in lynchings a direct connection to Jesus as victim. In their eyes "Christ had become black." In the third essay, historian Mark A. Noll argues that white evangelical Protestant traditions had always influenced American politics, especially when terms such as *redemption* were used by southern Democrats to regain power in their region and the Bible was used to help create laws of segregation. In this segment of his book, *God and Race in American Politics*, Noll also points out that it was evangelical Protestantism among African Americans that transformed "American political life" and provided a critical foundation for the modern civil rights movement.

Redeeming the South

PAUL HARVEY

Southern historians have searched for a central theme to bring together the difficult contradictions of the southern past—in particular, the paradox of slavery and freedom. Scholarship on religion in the American South, however, has engaged in little argument on the topic. The central theme of southern religious history in scholarly works remains the rise of evangelicalism, symbolized in the term "Bible Belt" and expressed institutionally in the numerical and cultural dominance of Baptist and Methodist churches. According to this view, the focused moment of salvation has constituted the bedrock of southern religious belief

From *Redeeming the South: Religious Cultures and Racial Identities Among Southern Baptists, 1865–1925* by Paul Harvey.

and practice. This evangelical individualism stifled any social ethic, leaving southern churches captive to racism and a dogmatic literalist theology.

Musicians and novelists of the South have recognized the centrality of evangelical Protestantism in a region "haunted by God." William Faulkner, hardly renowned for adherence to evangelical morality, nevertheless acknowledged how he "assimilated" the regional religious tradition, how he "took that in without even knowing it. It's just there. It has nothing to do with how much I might believe or disbelieve—it's just there."

But an overly simple and static use of the concept of evangelicalism hides the diversity of southern religious life. Thomas Dixon Sr. was a conservative Baptist minister in North Carolina. His son Thomas Dixon Jr. also pastored in Baptist churches but branched off into Shakespearean theater and authored the novels *The Leopard's Spots* and *The Clansman*, graphic classics of the popular culture of American racism. The later adaptation of these works into "Birth of a Nation," the 1915 technological wonder of the film world, provided Dixon (and director D. W. Griffith) with a canvas painted with grotesque white supremacist visions of a unified nation. Yet the junior Dixon also served as an advocate of the social gospel, a movement anathematized by many southern evangelicals. His brother, Amzi Clarence Dixon, helped to organize the emerging Fundamentalist movement of the early twentieth century and abhorred Thomas's popular works of fiction as much as Thomas poked fun at Amzi's stuffy theology. The Dixon family of North Carolina illuminates some of the diverse varieties of southern evangelicalism.

In the 1890s, many southern Baptist parishioners heard weekly homilies espousing conformity to a private, domestic evangelicalism and warning of the dangers of radical ideologies such as Populism. At the same time, rural congregants might hear fiery sermons that condemned the plutocrats and "social parasites" of the era. Rural Baptists of the era typically met in a one-room structure in the countryside in congregations of one hundred or fewer, heard a part-time bivocational minister at monthly meetings, and concentrated their religious expression on overcoming sin and achieving salvation. Meanwhile, inside the impressive structure of the First Baptist Church of Atlanta, a congregation of several hundred experienced an ordered and decorous service. The concept of southern evangelicalism thus explains everything and nothing at the same time.

The static use of this paradigm also obscures the dynamic function of black churches in the postbellum era. Booker T. Washington, a black Baptist layperson, found himself appointed as the designated race spokesman after his famous "Atlanta Compromise" speech in 1895, in which he had advised black Americans to "cast down" their buckets where they were—the South. In the minds of white listeners he seemed to accept second-class citizenship for African Americans. Washington found many supporters within the National Baptist Convention, an organization created in the same year of Washington's speech. But the black Baptist church also nourished figures such as Sutton Griggs, a minister, educator, and novelist from Texas who formulated an early form of Afrocentrism, and Nannie Burroughs, a woman who lashed out unflinchingly at racial hypocrisies while fiercely defending middle-class ideals and the rights of African Americans to aspire to them. After Reconstruction these churches rarely challenged the southern racial order in an overt way, providing instead a means of survival for a beleaguered community. This response in itself constituted a rebuke to a southern social order that mercilessly attacked the essential humanity of black people.

The growth of Baptist churches from small outposts of radically democratic plain-folk religion in the mid-eighteenth century into conservative and culturally dominant institutions in the twentieth century illustrates one of the most impressive evolutions of American religious and southern cultural history.... By 1910, about 40 percent of white churchgoers and 60 percent of black churchgoers in the South were Baptists. Most of these nearly five million southern Baptists worshiped in churches associated with the Southern Baptist Convention (white) or the National Baptist Convention (black). In the twentieth century, the Southern Baptist Convention (SBC) became the largest Protestant denomination in America, while the National Baptist Convention (NBC) grew to be the largest black religious organization in the world. Both conventions expanded their influence into outside areas, but until the 1920s the great majority of constituent churches for both groups remained in the South. Churches not affiliated with the SBC or NBC usually were connected to Primitive Baptist groups, who rejected larger denominational structures and mission endeavors. Primitive Baptists, concentrated in Appalachia and in up-country regions of the South, made up just over 10 percent of Baptists. Numerous other groups—Regulars, Old Regulars, Independent, Two-Seeds-in-the-Spirit, and so on—made up a rich tapestry of Baptists in Appalachia. Their religious expressions, lovingly described in Deborah McCauley's work, *Appalachian Mountain Religion*, made up an alternative subculture from the mainstream Baptist expressions that form the primary emphasis of this.

Historians now understand southern Baptists as part of the mainstream rather than the exotic fringes of American religious and cultural history. Evangelical Protestantism ordered the lives of millions of common folk in the South long after its central role in other parts of the country had been diminished. The southern evangelical emphasis on direct, immediate, and vibrantly emotional contact with God has given the South its distinctive religious coloration. This emphasis on experience remains firmly in the center rather than on the fringes of religious expression in the region.

Historians also have explored thoroughly the argument that southern churches languished in "cultural captivity." White southern churches rarely sought to overturn the southern social and racial hierarchy but rather reinforced and even defined it. In this sense they remained in bondage to southern culture, at least according to traditional definitions of this term. The cultural captivity thesis highlights the moral failings of white southern religion, as it was originally designed to do. But the argument fails to place southern religious history in a bicultural context. Based on studies of white churches and denominational organizations, the model ignores the presence and agency of black churches. It could just as easily be said, moreover, that southern culture fell captive to southern religion. But which "southern religion" and which "southern culture"? Would it be the southern religion of Thomas Dixon Sr., or his son, the famous novelist Thomas Dixon Jr., or Dixon's fundamentalist brother, Amzi Clarence Dixon? Would it be the southern religion of Martin Luther King Jr.'s father, or of Ned Cobb, the black cotton farmer and activist in the Sharecropper's Union in Alabama? By singularizing the terms southern religion and southern culture, the argument overlooks the multilayered nature of religious and cultural interactions.

Beyond the cultural captivity thesis, there remain deeper questions about the relationship of southern Baptists and southern cultures. Anthropologists have explained how religion provides mythological underpinnings for particular cultures, while it also allows dissident groups a chance to formulate alternative visions for a new order. When this idea is applied to southern religion, it is possible to replace the "captivity" metaphor altogether and use instead anthropological notions of religion and culture as inextricably intertwined. Southern culture has been identified closely with decentralized, localistic, traditionalist patterns of life and with highly persistent cultures. Well into the twentieth century, southern folk remained intensely defensive of local norms and reluctant to break from entrenched practices. They found in both their white and black Baptist churches a powerful theological and ecclesiastical tradition—congregational independence—that taught that God had sanctioned local men and women to run their own spiritual affairs and implied that they were meant to control their own destinies. The fierce localism of southern Baptist churches, the tenacity of rural religious practices, and the conflict between these practices and the centralizing desires of denominational reformers and Progressive Era activists suggest a fresh way to look at the relation of southern religion and southern culture. This same congregational control allowed black Baptists to nourish a unique religious culture that, though politically subdued during the early twentieth century and relentlessly criticized by both white and black Baptist denominationalists, was a wellspring from which flowed later movements for freedom....

The Civil War revolutionized southern religious life for both blacks and whites. Before the war, the white southern ministry reaffirmed the view that "pure religion" involved defining and enforcing the proper behavior of individuals in their divinely prescribed social duties, not questioning the roles themselves. Ministers led in the "sanctification of slavery," realizing that the defense of chattel slavery in a liberal democracy necessitated the divine stamp of approval for "our way of life." The axiom that politics should be left out of the pulpit effectively muffled religious dissent. White southern evangelicalism served conservative ends from the early nineteenth century forward. But this implicit prohibition against ministers engaging in "political-religion" loosened considerably during and after the war. Baptist ministers took an active part in secession discussions, some fervently supporting it, others fearing it as a rash and unwarranted move. The Alabaman Basil Manly Sr. exulted in his prominent role in secession discussions. The genteel Virginian John A. Broadus opposed secession but decided in 1861 that "it would be worse than idle to *speak* against it now" and that he should "resolve to do my duty as a citizen here." Southern political leaders understood the necessity of enlisting the spiritual authority held by Methodist and Baptist clerics for the war effort. A way thus opened for ministers to accept a greater sense of public responsibility. Chaplaincy in the Confederate army deeply informed the consciousness of a younger generation of evangelical ministers. Religious organizations such as the SBC flooded wartime camps with religious literature. After the war, elite ministers such as the Virginia Baptist John William Jones evangelized for the Lost Cause, the worship of Confederate heroes. They preserved the sense of the sacred in white southern history originally learned in the Confederate camps.

"Redemption" (meaning, in the religious sense, "washed in the blood") referred politically to the return of white Democrats to power in the 1870s. It also graphically symbolized the often bloody mixing of religion and politics in the postbellum South. During Reconstruction and into the 1880s, ministers preached a Lost Cause theology. The sacrifice of brave Confederate soldiers, they intoned, cleansed the South of its sin, while the cultural determination of whites after the war ensured the return of a righteous order. Once preached in this idiom—the language of the white evangelical South—this view hardened into an orthodoxy that pervaded southern historical interpretation for a century to come.

The Civil War revolutionized black religious life as well. African Americans interpreted the war as a conflict about slavery long before white political leaders North or South conceded as much. After the war, organizers of African American religious institutions used this biblical interpretation of current history—the war and Reconstruction—to galvanize support for the Republican Party. And the separate religious life that enslaved blacks developed before the Civil War, even while worshiping in white churches, took an institutional form after 1865, as African American believers withdraw from white congregations.

White and black Baptists profoundly influenced each other. Together, and separately, they created different but intertwined southern cultures that shaped Baptists in deep and lasting ways. Southerners of widely varying social groups, from plantation owners to yeoman farmers to enslaved blacks, accepted the evangelical Protestant mythology of mankind's unearned ability to achieve salvation. They rarely questioned the assuredness of salvation for the elect and damnation for the unconverted. They expected and demanded that believers exercise their faith by participating in a community of local Christians and by caring for those who were still "lost." By 1920 these beliefs had undergone challenges and some alteration, but the evangelical template still provided a pattern for the culture. The struggle against modernism marked southern religion as a distinctive element in the national culture. Fundamentalism originated as an intellectual movement in northern seminaries, but in the twentieth century it became identified with a group of southern evangelicals given to gloomy premillennial prophecies.

The congregationalism of Baptist church governance also continued to shape the lives of southern believers and the larger culture. To be a southern Baptist meant to worship in a local congregation that exercised ultimate authority in church matters. It meant voting on who would pastor the church, how the church would expend its funds, and how the church's worship service would be conducted. Local congregational control—termed "Baptist democracy" by denominational apologists—also ensured that southern vernacular styles could be exercised freely in congregational gatherings. The localism and traditionalism so entrenched in southern culture found safe haven within the walls of self-governing congregations, where the people of a community could practice "watchcare" on each other and suspiciously guard against sinful influences from the outside world. Denominational leaders found some success in implanting in their constituency Victorian bourgeois norms of private spiritualities and public behavior, but their "progress" in achieving this was slow. The resistance put up by congregants to the visions of the reformers—whether continuing to sing in southern oral dialect, refusing to cooperate with centrally organized denominational programs, or resisting modernizing trends in theology—demonstrated the tenacity of rural culture in southern Baptist life. This resistance also meant estrangement from an increasingly heterogeneous and urbanized America. But Southern religious forms survived the programmatic piety of denominational reformers and gradually penetrated American popular expressions later in the twentieth century.

Southern religion in the white sense has usually produced a profoundly conservative stance, while southern religion for blacks, though rarely assuming any revolutionary bent in the postwar South, has supported prophetic voices of change. The religious cultures of blacks and whites in the South provided the moral and spiritual force both for the Civil Rights movement and for the dogged resistance to it. Blacks transformed the hymn "Woke up this morning with my mind/Set on Jesus" into the civil rights anthem "Woke up this morning with my mind/Stayed on Freedom." Conservative southern whites adopted southern evangelical strictures and added to them the technology of modernity.

Into the 1940s, when white southern Baptists might be worshiping in a small church in Bakersfield, or black Baptists in scattered congregations in south Chicago, religious styles with rural roots endured and were adapted to new settings. Congregants lined out old hymns, listened to impassioned changed sermons, set aside mourners' benches for the benefit of the unsaved under conviction, and condemned the traditional vices of drinking, dancing, and gambling. Even while many Americans moved to secular ways of perception and action, southern Baptists (many of whom no longer lived in the South) deliberately and proudly remained outside of the national mold set during the era of modernization. They remained instead firmly inside the evangelical consensus of the nineteenth century. By staying where they were, they found themselves in the twentieth century marginalized from the dominant culture. Today, while still seeing themselves as outsiders, their styles have become part of the dominant national culture, and they have claimed a political inheritance denied their forebears. Southern Baptists, white and black, were two peoples divided by religious cultures with different historical roots that ultimately nurtured a tree that sprouted diverse and unique branches.

The Southern Rite of Human Sacrifice

DONALD G. MATHEWS

Human sacrifice to a vengeful deity conjures savage and exotic images that distance us from the practices they represent as being strangely inhuman. Just as savage but sadly less exotic are images of lynched African Americans in the Southern United States. The word, "lynched," rips from reluctant memories shame, guilt and anger at white atrocities. The stark reality behind the word is an historical presence that haunts heedless patriotic celebration and belies professions of national innocence; its condensation of white peoples' fury and black peoples' anguish is as intensely malevolent as human sacrifice.... Since the early eighties, scores of scholars have turned their attention to specific, dramatic incidents of violence, or to patterns within geographical areas or in relation to associated issues such as gender. The achievements have been impressive; but few have noticed what a few African Americans such as Gwendolyn Brooks understood when she observed that "the loveliest lynchee was our Lord." Few have wondered why it made sense to imagine a lynched black man as Christ upon the Cross, that is, to imagine lynching as a human sacrifice. Yet it is just this compound of sacrifice, crucifixion, and death and its association with the predominate religion of the lynching-South that begs discussion.

The causes of lynching are complex; there is no one explanation; but in the list of things still to study, it is important to add "studying religion and lynching."... The silence about the meaning of religion in discussions of lynching is strange because of the common knowledge that crucifixion, an act of violence, is at the very core of the Christian paradigm that was so essential a part of Southern culture. African Americans understood this; they understood that Christ, too, had been lynched.

Silence on the religious context is surprising because of the furtive presence of the sacred in studies of Southern violence....

Suzanne Marshall ... believes that [religion and violence] "were intertwined in the Black Patch [tobacco-growing] culture" of western Kentucky and north central Tennessee. This conclusion was suggested by encountering a religion that had scourged the area since the Great Revival with a wrathful, punitive divine Patriarch, draconian in His ways with men, women, children and nature, Whose punishments modeled the harsh penalties His devotees "meted to violators of community standards." The fusion of violence and religion flowed from family as well as church; violence seemed an appropriate way for patriarchs to rear children and train wives, and it was not always easy to distinguish divine from human wrath. Marshall does not argue that religion alone caused violence, nor does she explain how religion fused with other variables; but she does attempt to factor it into a cultural context that shaped a pervasive understanding of sanction, morality, and justice in an agricultural region under strain....

Segregation and Religion

The overlay of religion and lynching in the New South is a compelling problem because both were waxing in influence throughout the region at the same time and because it seems natural to believe that a simultaneous increase in religion and illegal collective violence throughout the same region is at least a paradox if not a contradiction. Southerners may have been sloughing off the rule of church discipline by the Great War but they had been joining the church in greater numbers since the 1880s.… During the 1890s, denominational bodies could report that new educational and missionary facilities were producing more members than ever before although percentages of church members in the general population did not surpass 50%. Statistics, however, under-report the percentages and numbers of people who could be said to have come under the influence of religion.… Moreover, an increase in support for temperance legislation also suggests a trajectory of moral influence mixed of course with political calculation and class imperialism. In addition, religion suffused the educational facilities of the New South.…

Religion may be understood as the complex symbolic representation of the social order through which we learn transcendence. The concept of god may be birthed from our social consciousness—the experience of which transcends self to make demands upon us through a sacred sense of the other. Historians, at least, should consider this broader and socially rooted insight of the classic sociologist Emile Durkheim who argued, a disciple observes, "that religious feeling is the individual's awareness of the group." Penalties—such as lynching—exacted of persons who were certified as having violated community in some way could be said to have been expiation rendered a power superior to individuals. The rite, "reverent manner" and "grave satisfaction" reported at Leo Frank's lynching were not, therefore, strange; they flowed naturally from the situations and culture in which they were observed.…

Lillian Smith certainly remembered segregation as sacred. In *Killers of the Dream*, she mused in a compelling, reflective and unforgiving manner about the ways in which "sin and sex and segregation" had suffused the lives of Southerners. She could not separate the three motifs. Although as an adult she believed that Christian love impugned segregation, as a child she had been taught together with other white children "to love God, to love our white skin and to believe in the sanctity of both." She had learned sin and guilt within the incubation of a "warm, moist evangelism and racial segregation" sanctified by a religion "too narcissistic to be concerned with anything but a man's body and a man's soul." The body was the "essence of morality" based as the latter was on the "mysterious matter of entrances and exits" with sin hovering "over all doors." Critics, favorable or not, commented on her weaving of Freudian insights into the fabric of her interpretation, but her primary focus was segregation. It was part of the mental process of pushing "everything dark, dangerous, and evil" to "the rim of one's life" where danger lurked. Evil was thought to have been purged from the sin-distressed self so that [white] Southerners had become fascinated with other people's evil rather than their own and had somehow been compelled to find personal salvation in the "death of Christ" without carrying the cross.…

Religion as Punishment

In a society where distinctions and dichotomies were so important, the clergy insisted upon polarity, too. Ultimately, perhaps, the dread polarity between God's Wrath and human sin was the most appropriate way of putting the matter; for "belief in someone's right to punish you," wrote Lillian Smith "is the fate of all children in Judaic-Christian culture." If the polarity were softened into Christian-and-world, or salvation-and-sin, or love-and-hate, binary opposition nonetheless persisted as it did in segregation. The word that reflected one side of the dichotomy has traditionally been "otherworldliness;" but it was an otherworldliness plunged deep into this world.... Wilbur J. Cash captured the meaning of this "otherworldly" religion that so affected this world as "primitive frenzy and the blood sacrifice."...

Citing a "primitive frenzy and the blood sacrifice" conveys the image of a savage South, a "savage ideal" that oversimplifies the region so cruelly that we are bereft of the generous ambiguity of a complexity that includes educated if tedious clergymen, tortured if ineffectual writers, prophetic if isolated dissenters, and quietly heroic women. But the phrase lingers because it is true; if "primitive frenzy" is translated as the result of repressed sexuality, challenged patriarchy, and reasoned violence fused in the act of murder, we may be able to understand it in less emotionally freighted ways. But the frenzy remains. The meaning of "blood sacrifice" is much more complex; and yet it is at the core of southern white fundamental Protestantism. Blood sacrifice is the connection between the purpose of white supremacists, the purity signified in segregation, the magnificence of God's wrath, and the permission granted the culture through the wrath of "justified" Christians to sacrifice black men on the cross of white solidarity.

To write that Christianity permitted lynching within a segregated society is not merely to make a homiletic point. Nor is it on the other hand a preface to linking specific acts of violence with specific people in a specific place who did hideous things because God told them to do so. To be sure, some people did believe they were absolutely justified, which amounts to the same thing; but that is not the point. The point is that because historians know that religious mood, ritual action, and moral outrage at black men were associated with illegal community acts of violence, students may want to go beyond mentioning such things to ask how we might understand this nexus.... At issue is neither the integrity of Christianity nor the ignorance and credulity of simple folk who believe myths that "sophisticated" modernists have rejected. At issue is the cultural reality behind what we have known existed but never had the temerity to confront; and the place to begin is with Lillian Smith's understanding of Christianity as punishment, and W. J. Cash's perception of the "blood sacrifice." It is important to ask: "How could Cash's words have come so easily; could he have meant that whites literally sacrificed blacks?" "Where could he possibly have conceived the fantastic metaphor that birthed such a preposterous idea?" The question is not rhetorical; there is a specific answer: "In church."...

Sacrificing Christ/Sacrificing Black Men

Conceiving of God as Supreme Hangman and the Christ as Divine Substitute Who paid the penalty for human sin in blood sacrifice did not make white Christians lynch black people. The formula did however reflect a state of mind; it reflected the ways in which views of moral accountability and penalty could allow—when fused with whites' racial antipathy, patriarchal prerogative, sexual apprehension, and economic tenuousness—public violence against a black man associated with a crime of rich symbolic significance. In such an event we are confronted with a myth as powerful as that of Christian atonement for it is a myth also of a specific kind of fall, a resulting collective disorder, and a punishment appropriate to the crime. The offense was defined by the myth of the "black beast rapist" intent on ravishing innocent white women; the myth inherent in the image became one of the most pervasive white Southern parables of sin, guilt, punishment and salvation. Both myths coincided in the shared recognition that punishment changes things in the community far beyond the mere effect of the act itself upon the "criminal". There is a shared sense that the one upon whom the myth is centered—the Christ or the "rapist"—must die to relieve the discord (sin, anguish, conflict) that is so dangerous to community.... This violent transference is justified by appeal in both cases to the justice of God. With regard to Christian atonement, the sacrificial reading of Christ's death lays responsibility for the victim's death upon Divine Justice. Killing the black victim is also understood to be the "will of God," that is, just. In both cases punishment is necessary to sustain sacred order, and in the case of the black victim, punishment may be a "sublimation of people's self-assertive instincts and hostilities."... White Southerners did not think of their executions of black men as similar to Christ's sacrifice although black Southerners did so.... What most whites did not understand was that, as Gwendolyn Brooks wrote, "the loveliest lynchee was our Lord."...

Religion permeated communal lynching because the act occurred within the context of a sacred order designed to sustain holiness. Holiness demands purity and purity was sustained in the segregated South by avoidance, margins, distances, aloofness, strict classification and racial contempt. To be sure, economic benefits flowed from whites' attempts to control black people but these were hidden even from white people themselves by fabricating sexualized myths of otherness about African Americans. Essential to these myths by the late 1880s was the image of the white woman whose innocence justified whatever violence white men might find "necessary" for her protection against the "black-beast-rapist." When myth brought violence, the deadly rituals that stripped the black victim of his sexuality were grisly evidence of a transfer to the black body of all the violence, guilt, and shame of the white community; the transfer re-enacted ancient scapegoating rituals. That the formal religion of Southerners should have been symbolized by "sacrifice" is not surprising. The cross had come to symbolize a salvation effected by Christ's paying just satisfaction for the sins of humanity: focus was on the justice of punishment. Even God had had to pay the price for human sin! His Justice required it. That African Americans could see lynching as a sacrificial act in which they identified with the victim meant that existentially at least they understood an alternative view to the orthodox (white) emphasis on penal sacrifice. A few whites could begin to see that Christ, too, had been lynched and to challenge both theology (implicitly) and white conceptions of justice (explicitly). A few white women could try to subvert the myth of immaculate protection because they understood its power to dominate themselves as well as black people. Because the myth of God's just vengeance permitted whites' obsession with punishment to rule their relations with blacks there was no restriction within the myth to the racism that clouded their vision. E. T. Wellford, however, had sensed that atonement demanded empathy with sacrificial victims so that there might be no more "victims"; but his insight remained hidden from most Southern whites. They could not see, as black Christians did, that in a sacrifice celebrated in such dramatic and public fashion, the Christ had become black.

The Churches, "Redemption," and Jim Crow

MARK A. NOLL

In broader historical perspective, the Civil War was as important for religion as for national politics. The evangelical Protestantism that had been such a dominant national force before the war certainly survived with considerable strength thereafter. But the era when evangelical priorities also dictated national priorities was over. When the Civil War showed evangelical Protestantism to be a force that could deepen social convictions and regional loyalties but could not harmonize social and regional antagonisms, the role of evangelical Protestantism in national politics, though still significant, moved from active to passive. A wide range of consequences followed.

Foundations for the Democratic Republic

To grasp the religious-political tectonics at work throughout American history, a rough schematization in terms of republican political theory is useful. From even before the United States came into existence, advocates of republicanism made almost as much of their fears as of their hopes. The republican hope was that a regime of checks and balances, of dispersed powers, of limited but responsible government, could avoid the tyranny that bedeviled Europe. The fear was that the populace would not maintain the moral character—in eighteenth-century terms, the virtue—without which even a republic was doomed to demagoguery and systemic injustice.

From the founding of the United States, national leaders had looked to religion as one of the most important guarantors of that moral character....

But religion was not the only support that national leaders looked to for the success of republican government. A comparable security for the republic was sought in the democratic dispersal of authority to industrious citizens. As first articulated by Thomas Jefferson, and then in a more democratic form by Andrew Jackson, the expectation was that a healthy nation would result from leaving self-sufficient, white working men alone to freely cultivate opportunities for free labor and free trade. The ideal of the agrarian yeoman, and then of the free white citizen, seemed almost as important as the inner discipline of religion for the health of the republic.

The Founders were not disappointed. For the first generations of national history, religious voluntarism along with free labor and free trade did produce a flourishing democracy of remarkable strength.

Slavery and sectional controversy, however, created problems that could not be solved by voluntary religion, free markets, or free white men.... Among the many revolutionary aspects of the Civil War was the extent to which the federal government (and the Confederate government as well) expanded its power to accomplish large national tasks.

That broad exercise of central government authority did not, however, last long. With the retreat from Reconstruction by the late 1870s, market forces—largely untrammeled by religious concerns—came to dominate the American polity. To be sure, between the end of Reconstruction and the beginning of the New Deal, many proposals were advanced that would have authorized government to address national problems with national solutions. Progressives especially led the appeal for a national income tax, for federal restraints on business monopolies, for national legislation to regulate the labor of women and children, and for many other reforms to be administered from the center. World War I strengthened the appeal for a more active central government.

To these pragmatic and utilitarian appeals for a more active federal government, a moral force was added by a number of religious reformers who petitioned the national government to find solutions for national problems. These included the National Association to Amend the Constitution (in order to add God, Jesus, and the Bible to the Preamble), the National Reform Association, the Woman's Christian Temperance Union, and the Anti-Saloon League.

The Eighteenth, or Prohibition, Amendment of 1919 represented the most visible success of these appeals. To its advocates, the Eighteenth Amendment brought the right kind of coercive authority to the nation's most destructive problem. It thus represented a continuation of the expanded federal power intimated in the Thirteenth, Fourteenth, and Fifteenth amendments. But compared with either the Civil War era or the period after the Great Depression, the years from roughly 1876 to 1932 witnessed a relatively ineffective national government and a diffused rather than concentrated religious influence on national affairs. The failure of Prohibition to resolve the practical and moral problems of alcohol abuse testified to the relative superficiality of hopes for its success. That failure also testified to the relative superficiality of the reformist religion supporting the Eighteenth Amendment, and the relative weakness of the government that attempted to enforce it.

The federal government moved back decisively into the center of political life only with the New Deal. To address an economic crisis of unprecedented depth and duration, the federal government exerted unprecedented energies to meet the national emergency. By contrast to the period of the Civil War, once the immediate economic crises were met through the expansion of the federal government in the New Deal, central authority did not retreat. Rather the unfolding of World War II hard on the heels of the Depression and the New Deal, permanently directed national expectations toward national solutions for national problems.

Not until after World War II did religion once again attain the national prominence it had exercised in the decades before the Civil War. The vehicles for that prominence were civil rights reforms and conservative movements quickened to life at least partly in reaction to those reforms. Thus, once religion did again begin to assert national influence, it was a fractured presence driving public life in contradictory directions, even though the two strongest national religious forces—as expressed, first, in the civil rights movement and then in the New Religious Right—were both descended from the evangelical religion that had been such a dominant force in the antebellum period....

The Political Weakening of Evangelical Religion

The exigencies of warfare and Reconstruction explain why the federal government became the nation's dominant political force from 1860 to 1876. But from a religious standpoint, there is more to be said. Evangelical Protestantism lost out in national political influence because, while it had the strength to animate the division over slavery, it did not display the political wisdom required to resolve the issue of slavery or the political strength to unify the halves of the nation divided by war over slavery....

Only because religious belief and practice had become such powerful civilizing forces before the conflict, only because they had done so much to create the nation that went to war, did that conflict result in such a great alteration in the influence of religious belief and practice on the nation. In the wake of the conflict, two great problems confronted the churches: one was the enduring reality of racism, which displayed its continuing force almost as virulently through the mob and the rope as it had in the chain and the lash. The other was the expansion of consumer capitalism, where unprecedented opportunities to create wealth were matched by large-scale alienation and new depths of poverty in both urban and rural America. For religion to have addressed these two problems constructively, America's believers needed the kind of intellectual and institutional vigor that evangelical Protestants had brought to bear on so many tasks in the generations between the Revolution and the Civil War.

Instead, the Civil War was won and slavery was abolished not by religious agency, but by an unprecedented expansion of central government authority and by a hitherto unimaginable degree of industrial mobilization. If the war freed the slaves and gave African Americans a constitutional claim to citizenship, it did not provide the moral energy required for rooting equal rights in the subsoil of American society or for planting equal opportunity throughout the land. If the war showed what could be accomplished through massive industrial mobilization, it did not offer clear moral guidance as to how that mobilization could be put to use for the good of all citizens.

To be sure, the evangelical Protestant traditions that had done so much to shape society before the war were not rendered powerless in its wake. Yet they were now much more deeply divided than before. North vs. South and black vs. white represented only two of such divisions. The nation's evangelical phalanx was now also riven between populist, lay-driven energies of the sort displayed by Dwight L. Moody, the era's leading urban evangelist, and the academic, formal energies of the sort found at the nation's first-rank colleges, which had begun to absorb evolutionary and higher critical conceptions of religion from Europe's elite intellectuals. The beliefs and practices that were so prominent nationally in the antebellum period did remain important after the war for millions of individuals, within networks dominated by the churches, and in many local regions. But because those beliefs and practices had not been able to resolve the issue of slavery, which had torn the nation apart, and because they were divided in meeting the practical and intellectual challenges that burgeoned after the war, they gave way in national influence to the expansion of federal power and the exercise of market forces that dominated the political landscape for the next two generations.

The Rise and Rapid Fall of Central Government Authority

With the relative decline of evangelical Protestantism as a *national* public force, the central government for a brief period became the dominant influence in the nation's public life. During the war itself, the unprecedented demands of conflict pushed the northern Republican Party reluctantly, and Confederates of all stripes even more reluctantly, to accept an ever-expanding role for the national state. After the end of the conflict, a muddle ensued until congressional Republicans seized control of Reconstruction from President Andrew Johnson, whose sympathies lay with white southern leaders who desired a speedy return to the status quo antebellum. Those sympathies were expressed in traditional small-r republican warnings against the threat of unchecked national power. But under congressional Reconstruction, the national government put troops on the ground in the South, coordinated the efforts of northern and southern voluntary agencies (many of them evangelical) who provided education and economic assistance to freed slaves, and taxed the whole country to pay for this exercise of national authority.

So long as central government retained the capacity to act nationally, it was conceivable that the abolition of slavery accomplished by the Thirteenth Amendment (1865) would go on to address the even more difficult task of guaranteeing civil rights for citizens of all races. The Fourteenth Amendment (1868) announced such a guarantee as applicable to all persons born in the United States, including former slaves. It boldly proclaimed that no state was "to make or enforce any law which shall abridge the privileges or immunities of citizens"; and it decreed that no state was to "deprive any person of life, liberty, or property, without due process of law; nor deny to any person within its jurisdiction the equal projection of the laws."

Shortly thereafter, the Fifteenth Amendment of 1870 went even further to guarantee the right to vote for all male citizens regardless of "race, color, or previous condition of servitude." Earlier, the Fourteenth Amendment had even spelled out in considerable detail the extensive penalties that would fall on states "when the right to vote at any election for the choice of Electors for President and Vice-President of the United States, Representatives in Congress, the executive and judicial officers of a State, or the members of the legislature thereof, is denied to any of the male inhabitants of such State ... or in any way abridged, except for participation in rebellion, or other crime."

For the brief span of years during which these amendments were approved, it seemed that a vigorous national government might therefore accomplish what antebellum exertions from the informal establishment of evangelical voluntarists had not been able to accomplish. The evangelical denominations and voluntary associations had made some efforts to translate the Bible's message of universal dignity for all humanity into the functioning practices of the land, but now the government itself seemed to secure a variation of that promise in the Constitution. Especially as African-American men began to exercise the franchise and when a few African Americans were voted into statewide and national office, it seemed as if the determined actions of central government against racism might begin to match the effectiveness of central government action against slavery.

But national willingness to support an active national government failed. Already the presidential election of 1868 was a harbinger, when the Democratic candidate Horatio Seymour of New York won more than 47% of the popular vote against the war's lionized military hero, Ulysses S. Grant, and at a time when military occupation gave Republicans a virtual lock on several states in the former Confederacy. Seymour's pledge to remove the federal presence from the former Confederacy as rapidly as practicable met with almost as much approval in the North as in the South....

Simultaneously, the process that white southerners called "redemption," whereby white supremacists regained control of state governments in the former Confederacy, was also well under way. Here the story involved another reassertion of republican fears that accompanied decisive maneuvers by the white population and the Democratic Party, both of which had been marginalized by black emancipation and federal Reconstruction. The process also involved the brutal application of naked terror. The graphic example of Mississippi leading up to the congressional elections of 1874 and then in the election seasons of 1875 and 1876 became an inspiring template for other aggrieved white Democrats throughout the South. These critical elections were accompanied by several pitched battles between Democratic militias and Republican forces loyal to Mississippi's elected government; many isolated bushwackings, murders, and executions; and a great tide of threat, beating, intimidation, and economic coercion. Against this violence, President Grant at first offered tentative assistance to the Republican-led Mississippi government. Then when the GOP's defense of

Reconstruction became less politically advantageous than establishing its reputation for "reform," the federal assistance dried up.

Meanwhile, a whirlwind of political rhetoric constantly reiterated the republican themes of corruption, unchecked central authority, and despotism....

Southern "redemption" represented a counterrevolution. It involved the violent transfer of power from liberated slaves and their Republican allies to an all-white Democratic Party. Significantly for the ideological conventions that dominated national politics into the mid-twentieth century, "redemption" also forged a strong bond between southern local control of racial matters and a rhetoric that pictured the exertion of national government authority as tyrannical, corrupt, and ungodly. The success of "redemption" fixed for the whole nation the pairing of local autonomy and racial exclusion as triumphant over the pairing that Nicholas Lemann succinctly labeled "black political empowerment and federal authority."

In sum, the door that the Civil War had opened to full political participation by all citizens, black as well as white, was rapidly closing.

The election of 1876 and its aftermath sealed the retreat from active Reconstruction. In that disputed election, the Republican Rutherford B. Hayes of Ohio gained the White House, despite receiving 3% fewer popular votes than his Democratic opponent, Samuel J. Tilden of New York. Tilden had campaigned aggressively for a pull-back of federal authority in all areas of national life....

Race and Religion, South and North

The national unwillingness to maintain support for an active central government opened the way, once again, for race and religion to act together with powerful political effects, but this time negatively, as promoters of social passivity, instead of positively, as promoters of social activism. The reasons for the failure of Reconstruction, and with it the failure to move beyond the elimination of slavery to the guarantee of civil rights for all Americans, are well known. Full-scale support for Reconstruction from an active central government appeared to violate deeply ingrained republican instincts about the dangers of large government. More specifically, southern white racism proved stronger than the federal defense of civil rights. But it was not just the South. The will of integrationists from all sections of the country was undermined, either by new causes that drew attention away from race, by weariness in pursuing the very difficult goals of legal and social equality, by visions of spirituality that downplayed worldly involvements, or by violence.

IN THE SOUTH

The role of vigilante violence in winning the white South a victory in peace that its armies could not gain in war has been the subject of a cascade of scholarship on lynching and the other physical means used to disenfranchise blacks and restore control of southern society to racist governments. In that literature, a prominent theme is the use of mob violence to defend the virtue of white women and the sanctity of the white Christian home against the depredations of black sexual assault. These violent measures, adopted as they were to defend white sexual purity, may reflect the most irrational moment in all of American history, since the ubiquity of lighter-skinned African Americans testified continually and unmistakably to the many generations of sexually predatory acts by white males upon black women....

Along with the willingness to use extralegal violence, a widespread willingness to exploit the resources of traditional evangelical religion also drove opposition to Reconstruction and played an important part in bringing central government action to a halt. On the religious factors in what was called at the time the "redemption" of the South, a number of authors have made outstanding recent contributions. Together, these historians have demonstrated that religion, in the North as well as the South, was critical in the process that brought Reconstruction to a close, restored white racist regimes to power, and turned the attention of the North away from defending citizens' rights for all.

Religiously inspired actions were usually passive, as pastors and church leaders stood by silently while the Ku Klux Klan, the Knights of the White Camellia, and other organized mobs menaced, assaulted, or murdered African Americans who attempted to take up the opportunities guaranteed by the Thirteenth, Fourteenth, and Fifteenth amendments, and the whites who, however cautiously, supported their efforts. Occasionally church leaders could be more active, as when John Ezell, a Baptist minister in Spartanburg County, South Carolina, joined the local Klan in mob actions against white and black Republicans, only to repent before a court with an admission that he "did not believe he was safe outside of the klan." During the early 1870s, the wife of Mississippi's Republican governor reported to relatives in the North that the state's ministers used their Sunday sermons to encourage disloyalty to the Union.

In later decades, influential religious leaders either simply accepted "redemption" or provided it active support. A particularly telling incident was the response of revivalist Sam Jones to the 1899 lynching and mutilation of Sam Hose, which took place in Georgia during the nadir of that state's lynching frenzy. At the time Jones was the South's most famous itinerant preacher, who also enjoyed a national reputation for his salty, straightforward preaching of homespun Christian morality. Hose was a farm laborer accused of murdering his employer and raping the employer's wife in an incident that probably involved violent provocation from the employer. Shortly afterwards, Jones publicly protested against the lynching as a breach of regular judicial procedure. But then when white opponents defended the act as a Christian defense of the home and of sexual purity, Jones shifted his stance and himself became a defender of what had happened. In this incident, the independent-mindedness for which Jones was famous as a preacher was of no avail in standing against the religious, as well as sociopolitical, conventions of his day. Whether actively or passively, white southern religion all but unanimously supported the imposition of white supremacist rule and for a very long time offered scant resistance to its continuation.

IN THE NORTH

From the North, the willingness of well-known public religious figures like the evangelist Dwight L. Moody, the preacher Henry Ward Beecher, the novelist Harriet Beecher Stowe, or the temperance advocate Frances Willard to sacrifice black civil rights to other religious goals made their own important contribution to the "redemption" of the South. Moody was a close friend of General O. O. Howard, the head of the Freedman's Bureau after whom Howard University in Washington, D.C., was named, and he had been inclined during his years in Chicago to act with considerable fairness toward African Americans. But when, in 1876, he conducted a preaching campaign in Augusta, Georgia, and local white leaders insisted upon segregating the audience, Moody reluctantly gave in to their wishes. Until the mid-1890s, and despite a willingness to speak before black audiences, Moody maintained a policy of segregation for his meetings. This general pattern was widespread....

AMONG EVANGELICALS

To the extent that D. L. Moody's type of evangelical religion represented widespread beliefs, it also contributed to racial difficulties. More in reflecting than in leading the white evangelical spirit of his age, Moody, as if in conscious reaction to the political overcommitments of evangelicals during and after the Civil War, guided his audiences away from external and social duties toward a consideration of inner and personal states of being. Along with large segments of the Protestant world, Moody's heightened stress on personal piety seemed to entail a decrease of interest in social conditions....

... The end result from shifting theological emphases toward the turn of the century was that the more conservative and pietistic elements of American Protestantism were neutering the social impact of Christian faith even as many evangelicals continued to find manifold resources in traditional Christianity for private devotion and domestic guidance.

AMONG PROGRESSIVES

The more progressive segments of the Protestant world that did retain an interest in social justice did not always include racial matters in these concerns. Notable social reformers who otherwise exerted unusual efforts at embodying biblical values in their reforms regularly turned aside from racial problems....

Walter Rauschenbush, the movement's most profound theologian, was representative. He saw much in American society that needed the rebuke of Christian reform, but he felt no particular urgency in challenging the era's conventions about race. For Rauschenbush, the sad plight of African Americans would be rectified by the same sort of economic improvements and Christianizing impulses that he felt were improving the circumstances of at least some immigrant communities. From all sides of the well-established American Protestant world, in other words, came silence, complicity, or active assistance to the "redemption" of the South....

The important point to be made about Reconstruction repeats what had been true as well for the Civil War. Just as the depth and intensity of antagonism in that war had been a product, in substantial part, of religious conviction, so too did religion figure crucially, and in many ways, to propel the national retreat from federally sponsored Reconstruction. The "redemption" of the South was, as the name suggests, a spiritual turning point, as well as a political turning point....

Domains of Continuing Religious Strength

It is important to be clear about the fate of religion in the late-nineteenth-century United States. When the evangelical Protestant phalanx receded as a dominant force in national politics after the Civil War, it did not mean that religion as a whole went into decline. To the contrary, religious energies may actually have been increasing during this period, but in diverse forms pushing in uncoordinated directions. Roman Catholics were growing stronger in many urban areas of the East, and in some of the western states, though this organization was still a few years removed from when Catholics would venture boldly into the national political arena. Catholics were joined—though in smaller numbers and over less territory—by other religious bodies that also were advancing from strength to strength. These bodies included Lutherans in the upper Midwest, Mormons in Utah, Hispanic Catholics in the Southwest, and what could be called the "Methodist belt" that stretched from Delaware to Kansas.

The strongest regional concentration of a specific religious tradition was, however, the former Confederate South, as recorded by the 1890 census. The Civil War that broke the national power of evangelical Protestant movements of British origin enabled those same movements to exert a new kind of hegemony throughout the southern region of the country. With the exception of Louisiana and its Catholic communities, the religious affiliations of the other ten states recorded extraordinary majorities for the Methodists and Baptists, who might have fought each other like cats and dogs, but only as an expression of what Freud called "the narcissism of small differences." Thus, in 1890 Methodists and Baptists made up over 90% of the churched population in Georgia and Mississippi; over 80% in Alabama, Arkansas, North Carolina, South Carolina, and Virginia; and at or over 70% in Florida, Tennessee, and Texas. The concentration of Baptists was especially important for ideology, since this was the American religious tradition with the strongest fears about outside influence from top-down national elites and the strongest commitment to the Christian faith understood as a personal, rather than social, force. These religious convictions merged easily with political fears of an intrusive national government and political commitment to the prerogatives of local government.

The religious transformation brought on by the Civil War actually solidified the place of the more or less sectarian evangelical bodies in the former Confederate states, even as it defused evangelical influence in the nation as a whole. The effect of these developments on political life was considerable, especially in the South where the white churches played such an important role in overthrowing Reconstruction. For the longer term, however, it was important that a very different story was also under way, since the postbellum configuration of southern religion also provided enough space for independent African-American churches to develop, and they would later play a similarly important part in overthrowing Jim Crow....

LONG-TERM EFFECTS

The religious-racial-political effects of the Civil War were extremely far-reaching. It was especially important that central government authority succeeded in reuniting the country and in making slavery illegal but failed to dislodge systemic racial discrimination. Yet it is also necessary to be realistic about what was actually possible at the time, especially from the perspective of the early twenty-first century when living memory is fading rapidly about how strongly the nineteenth-century racist assumptions prevailed in all segments of white society, religious and nonreligious, highly educated and illiterate, northern as well as southern. Only a massive federal presence maintained vigilantly for thirty, forty, or even fifty years might have rooted black political participation and black legal equality deeply enough to withstand the tempests of reaction and swelling undercurrents of indifference. In the event, the tempests, which were very strong in the South and also in a few areas elsewhere, and the undercurrents, which were strong in every region of the country, won out over central government action. Thereafter, central government inaction facilitated the process by which racial discrimination and racial prejudice, even in the absence of slavery, worsened from the 1870s for more than the next half-century.

The failure of the central government to move effectively against racial discrimination was not exactly *caused* by the failures of evangelical religion during and after the Civil War. But the acceptance by evangelicals, who had done so much to shape the nation in so many other ways, of a racist regime after the war was everywhere a contextual factor in the weakening of central government action during Reconstruction and its caving in to the "redemption" of a white racist South. This same acceptance was also an important factor in the retreat of the main white denominations from advocacy on behalf of African Americans. What was true for white evangelicals about sanctioning a racist America was for the most part just as true for other Protestants and Roman Catholics.

Nonetheless and critically, after the social hegemony of white evangelical Protestants gave way, it helped create enough free space for a distinctly African-American form of experiential, quasi-evangelical, universal, and reforming Christianity to get up from its bed and start to walk. That miracle, however underestimated at the time, would one day bring about a fundamental alteration in the shape of American political life.

FURTHER READING

Kenneth K. Bailey, *Southern White Protestantism in the Twentieth Century* (1964).

Edith L. Blumhofer, *Restoring the Faith: The Assemblies of God, Pentecostalism and American Culture* (1993).

John B. Boles, *The Great Revival, 1787–1805: The Origins of the Southern Evangelical Mind* (1972).

Paul Conkin, *American Originals: Homemade Varieties of Christianity* (1997).

Mark Cowett, *Birmingham's Rabbi: Morris Newfield and Alabama, 1895–1940* (1986).

Leonard Dinnerstein and Mary Dale Palsson, eds., *Jews in the South* (1973).

John Lee Eighmy, *Churches in Cultural Captivity: A History of the Social Attitudes of Southern Baptists* (1972).

Eli N. Evans, *The Provincials: A Personal History of Jews in the South* (1973).

Wilson Fallin, *The African American Church in Birmingham, Alabama, 1815–1963* (1997).

J. Wayne Flynt, *Alabama Baptists: Southern Baptists in the Heart of Dixie* (1998).

———, "Baptists and Reform," *Baptist History and Heritage* 7 (1972), 211–222.

Mary E. Frederickson, "'Each One Is Dependent on the Other': Southern Churchwomen, Racial Reform, and the Process of Transformation, 1880–1940," in Nancy Hewitt and Suzanne Lebsock, eds., *Visible Women: New Essays on American Activism* (1993).

Jean E. Friedman, *The Enclosed Garden: Women and Community in the Evangelical South, 1830–1900* (1985).

Willard B. Gatewood Jr., *Preachers, Pedagogues and Politicians: The Evolution Controversy in North Carolina, 1920–1927* (1966).

John M. Giggie, *After Redemption: Jim Crow and the Transformation of African American Religion in the Delta, 1875–1915* (2008).

David Edwin Harrell Jr., *All Things Are Possible: The Healing and Charismatic Revivals in Modern America* (1975).

———, *White Sects and Black Men in the Recent South* (1971).

———, ed. *Varieties of Southern Evangelicalism* (1981).

Paul Harvey, *Freedom's Coming: Religious Culture and the Shaping of the South from the Civil War through the Civil Rights Era* (2007).

———, *Redeeming the South: Religious Cultures and Racial Identities among Southern Baptists, 1865–1925* (1997).

Merrill M. Hawkins Jr., *Will Campbell: Radical Prophet of the South* (1998).

Evelyn Higginbotham, *Righteous Discontent: The Women's Movement in the Black Baptist Church, 1880–1920* (1993).

Samuel S. Hill Jr., *The South and the North in American Religion* (1980).

———, *Southern Churches in Crisis* (1966).

E. Brooks Holifield, *The Gentlemen Theologians: American Theology in Southern Culture, 1795–1860* (1978).

Charles A. Israel, *Before Scopes: Evangelicalism, Education, and Evolution in Tennessee, 1870–1925* (2004).

Anne C. Loveland, *Lillian Smith: A Southerner Confronting the South* (1986).

Bobbie Malone, *Rabbi Max Heller: Reformer, Zionist, Southerner, 1860–1929* (1998).

Robert F. Martin, "A Prophet's Pilgrimage: The Religious Radicalism of Howard Anderson Kester, 1921–1941," *Journal of Southern History* 48 (1982), 511–530.

Sally McMillen, *To Raise Up the South: Sunday Schools in Black and White Churches, 1865–1915* (2001).

William E. Montgomery, *Under Their Own Vine and Fig Tree: The African-American Church in the South, 1865–1900* (1993).

Mark A. Noll, *God and Race in American Politics* (2008).

Ted Ownby, *Subduing Satan: Religion, Recreation, and Manhood in the Rural South* (1990).

Barbara Diane Savage, *Your Spirits Walk Beside Us: The Politics of Black Religion* (2008).

Beth Barton Schweiger and Donald G. Mathews, eds., *Religion in the American South: Protestants and Others in History and Culture* (2004).

Beth Schweiger, *The Gospel Working Up: Progress and the Pulpit in Nineteenth-Century Virginia* (2000).

James Sellers, *The South and Christian Ethics* (1962).

Milton C. Sernett, *African American Religious History: A Documentary Witness* (1999).

Shelton Smith, *In His Image, But...: Racism in Southern Religion, 1780–1910* (1972).

Daniel Stowell, *Rebuilding Zion: The Religious Reconstruction of the South, 1863–1877* (1998).

Vinson Synan, *The Holiness-Pentacostal Tradition* (1971).

Noreen Dunn Tatum, *A Crown of Service: A Story of Woman's Work in the Methodist Episcopal Church South, from 1878 to 1940* (1960).

James J. Thompson Jr., *Tried as by Fire: Southern Baptists and the Religious Controversies of the 1920s* (1982).

Clarence E. Walker, *A Rock in a Weary Land: The African Methodist Episcopal Church during the Civil War and Reconstruction* (1982).

James M. Washington, *Frustrated Fellowship: The Black Baptist Quest for Social Power* (1986).

Edward L. Wheeler, *Uplifting the Race: The Black Minister in the New South, 1865–1902* (1986).

Charles Reagan Wilson, ed., *Religion in the South* (1985).

CHAPTER 8

Southern Memory and History

*It is an axiom that southerners have always valued their history. This interest manifests itself in the often asked family question, "Who are your people?" Virginia Foster Durr, from Birmingham, Alabama, calls this being "placed." Personal connections and family stories bring forth an individual's memory, but when people within a region or a nation hold a particular view of the past—whether accurate or not—this becomes collective memory. One way to see it is that history is the past, and memory is what people remember about the past even if they were not yet alive to record it. Collective memory can become a uniting premise of shared identities and values; it may incorporate themes around which people will rally. It can also become a powerful tool in the hands of politicians, entrepreneurs, and promoters who seek to "own" the past—or their version of it. Historian David Blight calls this the "*politics *of memory," and the way collective memory is used as a political or social force becomes a subject of interest to historians. Wielded by powerful groups, collective memory can be used to define what is acceptable, what should be remembered or forgotten, and who may be allowed access to economic or political power. Seemingly benign memories of the past can and do often shape societal norms related to power, class, gender, and race. It is the historian's task to decipher the ways in which collective memories have been appropriated to gain power or to maintain identity.*

Themes that speak to southern memory and history are found in books, pageants, reenactments, parades, entertainment parks, museums, or even sorority rush at Ole Miss. It was C. Vann Woodward who pointed to southern history as the South's most distinctive feature, and there seems to be no lack of interest in its most pivotal event—the Civil War. The four-year bloody conflict may represent a tiny percentage of the South's overall past, but the war looms as the *defining moment in the collective memory of the nation and the South. Historian David Goldfield writes that "The Civil War is like a ghost that has not yet made its peace and roams the land seeking solace, retribution, or vindication." The war, with its tragic consequences—600,000 dead and loss of property totaling tens of millions of dollars—left the nation united in principle and divided in reality. Most white southerners sank into an angry depressive state; their losses were enormous, their hopes for a separate nation dashed, their livelihoods threatened. Yet, almost as soon as the smoke had cleared they sought remedy for the pain by creating a memory that transformed defeat into a valorous cause. As the years unfolded they perfected this ideology, claiming that Confederates fought over states' rights, not slavery, and that Confederate soldiers, representing a noble cause, fought valiantly on the battlefields. Although some whites admitted to slavery's inhumanity, most defended it as a benevolent institution. They romanticized their Old South "civilization" and vilified Reconstruction as Union occupation—more horrific for white southerners than war itself. They remembered fondly faithful slaves and damned as ungrateful those servants who ran to freedom or were elected to Reconstruction governments. White southern women posed as heroines who maintained the home front, while members of the Ku Klux Klan became heroes who returned state government to white politicians. Labeling these notions the "Lost Cause," white southerners spread this version of the past through speeches, newspaper editorials, books, articles, organizations, veterans' reunions, catechisms for children, monument building, and cultural arts. Historian Karen Cox noted the lasting influence of the United Daughters of the Confederacy as they indoctrinated children in Lost Cause ideology through school textbooks and library holdings. Symbols abounded—the Confederate battle flag took on a new meaning in the postwar era—and Dixie became a mantra for spreading Lost Cause enthusiasm. Nowhere in this version of collective memory was there an appreciation of the hardships borne by slaves, the anticipation of freedom, or the realization of equal rights for freedpeople.*

Countering Lost Cause memory was a vibrant oppositional point of view expressed by ex-slaves. Their version of the past, as they encountered emancipation, consisted of recollections of a brutal system of bondage, a longing for freedom, and a joyful day of jubilee when they finally grasped their liberation. Lacking the means to build monuments or fill libraries with histories of African American experiences, freedpeople expressed themselves through celebrations of freedom that erupted all over the South. President Abraham Lincoln's Emancipation Proclamation, now a well-established document in emancipation memory, symbolized for African Americans the moment of national redemption. Denied freedom for 246 years, the Civil War became for slaves a defining moment as they recognized what it meant to belong to a nation that valued freedom enough to fight a long and bloody civil war. African Americans called it their Freedom War. In the wake of the Civil War, three constitutional amendments granted them emancipation, citizenship rights, and male voting rights. Unlike the frenzy of monument building that represented Lost Cause enthusiasm, African Americans created few monuments to their liberation. Rather, their collective memories are rooted in sermons, speeches, parades, floats, dramatizations, oral histories, newspapers, journals, university curricula, and the Association for the Study of African American Life and History (ASALH). Southern blacks organized around churches and schools, and they kept the memory of their past alive through emancipation celebrations such as Juneteenth (June 19, 1865), which commemorated the day the slaves of Texas—the last in the Confederacy—learned of their freedom.

Today, Lost Cause celebrations, such as those reported by Katharine Du Pre Lumpkin, are a faded memory. Juneteenth, however, celebrated annually in Washington, D.C., is well on its way to becoming the nation's emancipation celebration. Historically speaking, although the northern states accepted the white southern revisionist view of the past leading toward reunion at the turn of the twentieth century, one could argue that today the counter-emancipation memory of freedom has triumphed in national historical consciousness.

Historical collective memory and history have been closely intertwined. What role has collective memory played in U.S. or state legislative processes, in economic decisions, in cultural expressions? What role did gender play in the creation of a Lost Cause ideology? How have minorities in the United States kept collective memories alive? Why does it matter?

DOCUMENTS

In Document 1 Juneteenth, as it was celebrated in San Antonio, included marchers, buggies, bands, and observers who appropriated public space for the memorialization of freedom. In contrast to the impermanent Juneteenth parade, which lasted a day at best, stands the imposing statue of Robert E. Lee in Richmond, Virginia, still visible today. In Document 2, Jubal Early defends his own military actions. He makes the case for a state's right to "defend against the domination of a fanatical faction at the North" and argues that the conflict was not a defense of slavery but the "mere occasion of the development of the antagonism between the two sections." With this defense, he illustrates the enduring notions of the Lost Cause. In Document 4, Cornelia Branch Stone, author of the U.D.C. Catechism for Children, outlines the "correct" answers to questions regarding the Old South, the Civil War, and the South in 1912. The term *catechism* is defined as a summary of religious doctrines in the form of questions and answers. In the years of monument building, sustained largely by the United Daughters of the Confederacy (UDC), the Confederate Monument at Arlington National Cemetery, dedicated on June 4, 1914 (Document 5), represented "an extraordinary achievement for peace and reconciliation" between the North and South, vindicating the actions of the "generation of the sixties." The UDC claimed this monument as a Lost Cause victory because of the hundreds of statues to Confederates erected across the South, this was the only "national" memorial. Note the depiction of a faithful slave holding the soldier's child on his departure for the battlefield. Document 6, accompanies the article "The National Mammy Monument Controversy of the 1920s" as a satiric commentary to the very real designs to raise a monument to "Mammy" in the nation's capital. Katharine Du Pre Lumpkin, civil rights supporter and author of *The Making of a Southerner*, recalls with irony and sadness in Document 6 how the Lost Cause was sustained by her parents' instructions.

1. Southerners Remember the Past, 1890

"Juneteenth Celebration in San Antonio, 1890." (Daughters of the Republic of Texas Library)

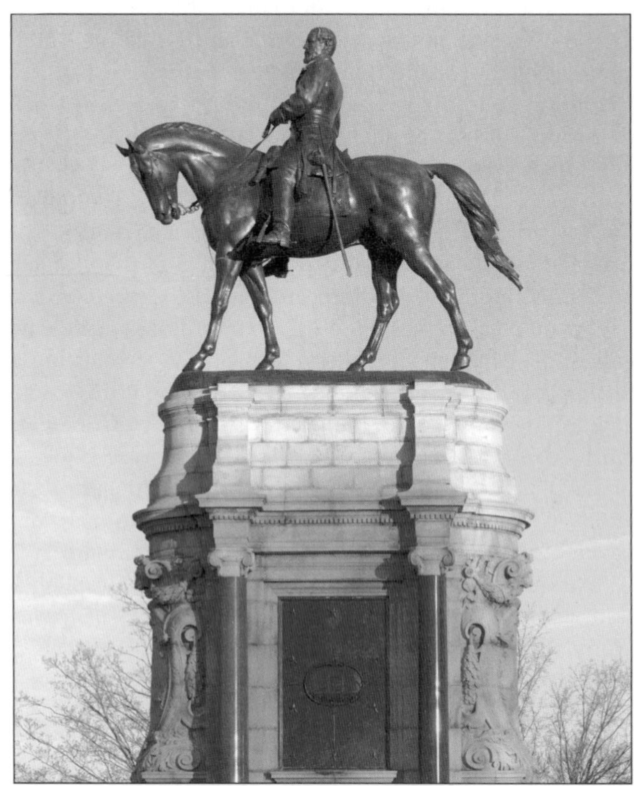

Robert E. Lee Monument, Richmond, Virginia, 1890. (Lee Sandstead)

2. Confederate General Jubal Early Memorializes the "Lost Cause," 1894

When the question of practical secession from the United States arose, as a citizen of the State of Virginia, and a member of the Convention called by the authority of the Legislature of that State, I opposed secession with all the ability I possessed, with the hope that the horrors of civil war might be averted and that a returning sense of justice on the part of the masses of the Northern States would induce them to respect the rights of the people of the South.

While some Northern politicians and editors were openly and sedulously justifying and encouraging secession, I was laboring honestly and earnestly to preserve the Union.

As a member of the Virginia Convention, I voted against the ordinance of secession on its passage by that body, with the hope that even then, the collision of arms might be avoided and some satisfactory adjustment arrived at. The adoption of that ordinance wrung from me bitter tears of grief; but I at once recognized my duty to abide the decision of my native State, and to defend her soil against invasion. Any scruples which I may have entertained as to the right of secession were soon dispelled by the unconstitutional measures of the authorities at Washington and the frenzied clamor of the people of the North for war upon their former brethren of the South. I recognized the right of resistance and revolution as exercised by our fathers in 1776 and without cavil as to the name by which it was called, I entered the military service of my State, willingly, cheerfully, and zealously....

During the war, slavery was used as a catch-word to arouse the passions of a fanatical mob, and to some extent the prejudices of the civilized world were excited against us; but the war was not made on our part for slavery. High dignitaries in both church and state in Old England, and puritans in New England, had participated in the profits of a trade by which the ignorant and barbarous natives of Africa were brought from that country and sold into slavery in the American Colonies. The generation in the Southern States which defended their country in the late war, found amongst them, in a civilized and Christianized condition, 4,000,000 of the descendants of those degraded Africans. The Creator of the Universe had stamped them, indelibly, with a different color and an inferior physical and mental organization. He had not done this from mere caprice or whim, but for wise purposes. An amalgamation of the races was in contravention of His designs or He would not have made them so different. This immense number of people could not have been transported back to the wilds from which their ancestors were taken, or if they could have been, it would have resulted in their relapse into barbarism. Reason, common sense, true humanity to the black, as well as the safety of the white race, required that the inferior race should be kept in a state of subordination. The conditions of domestic slavery, as it existed in the South, had not only resulted in a great improvement in the moral and physical condition of the negro race, but had

Lieutenant General Jubal Anderson Early, C.S.A., *Autobiographical Sketch and Narrative of the War Between the States* (Philadelphia: J. B. Lippincott, 1912), vii.

furnished a class of laborers as happy and contented as any in the world if not more so. Their labor had not only developed the immense resources of the immediate country in which they were located, but was the main source of the great prosperity of the United States, and furnished the means for the employment of millions of the working classes in other countries. Nevertheless, the struggle made by the people of the South was not for the institution of slavery but for the inestimable right of self-government, against the domination of a fanatical faction at the North; and slavery was the mere occasion of the development of the antagonism between the two sections. That right of self-government has been lost, and slavery violently abolished....

Each generation of men owes the debt to posterity to hand down to it a correct history of the more important events that have transpired in its day. The history of every people is the common inheritance of mankind, because of the lessons it teaches.

For the purposes of history, the people of the late Confederate States were a separate people from the people of the North during the four years of conflict which they maintained against them.

No people loving the truth of history can have any object or motive in suppressing or mutilating any fact which may be material to its proper elucidation.

3. Katharine Du Pre Lumpkin Recounts her Childhood with the Lost Cause, 1946

Confederate reunions ... came infrequently. At least it was so for us children. We must wait until it was the turn of our town again to welcome the old men. Moreover, reunions could not do everything. They could be counted upon to arouse our Southern patriotism to a fervid pitch and spur us on to fresh endeavors. When all was said and done, however, something continuing and substantial should be going on if we children were indeed to fulfill the part our people had set their hearts upon.

My father put it this way. He would say of his own children with tender solemnity, "Their mother teaches them their prayers. I teach them to love the Lost Cause." And surely his chosen family function in his eyes ranked but a little lower than the angels. He would say: "Men of the South, let your children hear the old stories of the South; let them hear them by the fireside, in the schoolroom, everywhere, and they will preserve inviolate the sacred honor of the South."

Many other men like Father—men of his station and kind, men who like him still lived in the days of their lost plantations—also said such words, said them continually. For my home, I know it did not rest at words. I know that Father not alone preached these things. In very fact he lived them, at the same time impregnating our lives with some of his sense of strong mission....

My father devised one special means for teaching us....

Our "Saturday Night Debating Club" was … a training ground, although to us it seemed much more an absorbing family game. It was serious business, but never solemnly serious, nor would any of us have been left out of it for anything. Even I was allowed a small part in keeping with my tender years. On most weekdays Father must be away from home attending to the task of making a living. Each Saturday night he would announce the topic for the next meeting, but being away, he left much of our advice in preparation to Mother. She was entirely qualified to give it, although of course when Father was there we naturally turned to him. Indeed, Mother turned to us, saying, "Ask your father. He knows about that better than I do." Occasionally the subject for debate would be an old-fashioned query—"Is the pen mightier than the sword?" Usually, and these were our favorites, we argued topics of Southern problems and Southern history. I say "we." The most I ever contributed were a few lines which Mother had taught me. After that I was audience.

We would hurry through Saturday-night supper and dishes. A table would be placed in the parlor, Father seating himself behind it, presiding. On either side were chairs for the debaters. Mother and I comprised the audience, although at the proper time she would retire with Father to assist in judging. All being assembled, Father would rap firmly for order, formally announce the subject, introduce the first speaker on the affirmative, and the game was on.

And what a game! What eloquence from the speakers! What enthusiasm from the "audience"! What strict impartiality from the chairman! And how the plaster walls of our parlor rang with tales of the South's sufferings, exhortations to uphold her honor, recitals of her humanitarian slave regime, denunciation of those who dared to doubt the black man's inferiority, and, ever and always, persuasive logic for her position of "States Rights," and how we must at all times stand solidly together if we would preserve all that the South "stood for."…

There was the glamorous, distant past of our heritage. Besides this, there was the living, pulsing present. Hence, it was by no means our business merely to preserve memories. We must keep inviolate a way of life. Let some changes come if they must; our fathers had seen them come to pass: they might grieve, yet could be reconciled. It was inconceivable, however, that any change could be allowed that altered the very present fact of the relation of superior white to inferior Negro. This we came to understand remained for us as it had been for our fathers, the very cornerstone of the South.

It too was sanctified by the Lost Cause. Indeed, more than any other fact of our present, it told us our cause had not been lost, not in its entirety. It had been threatened by our Southern disaster (we would never concede the word "defeat"). No lesson of our history was taught us earlier, and none with greater urgency than the either-or terms in which this was couched: "Either white supremacy or black domination." We learned how Restoration—or the Redemption, as men still said in their more eloquent moments—had meant this as much as anything to our heritage. "The resounding defeat of the forces of darkness. The firm re-establishment of our sacred Southern principles." To be sure, we learned all this long after we had begun to behave according to the practical dictates of the "sacred principle" of white supremacy.

4. United Daughters of the Confederacy Prepare a Catechism for Children, 1912

What causes led to the war between the States, from 1861 to 1865?

The disregard, on the part of the States of the North, for the rights of the Southern or slave-holding States.

How was this shown?

By the passage of laws in the Northern States annulling the rights of the people of the South—rights that were given to them by the Constitution of the United States.

What were these rights?

The right to regulate their own affairs and to hold slaves as property.

Were the Southern States alone responsible for the existence of slavery?

No; slavery was introduced into the country in colonial times by the political authorities of Great Britain, Spain, France and the Dutch merchants, and in 1776—at the time of the Declaration of Independence—slavery existed in all of the thirteen colonies.

How many of the colonies held slaves when the federal constitution was adopted, in 1787?

All except one.

Did slavery exist among other civilized nations?

Yes, in most all; and our mother country, England, did not emancipate her slaves until 1843, when Parliament paid $200,000,000 to the owners.

After the first introduction of slavery into the colonies, how was the African slave trade kept up?

By enterprising shipowners of New England, who imported the slaves from Africa and secretly sold their cargoes along the coast, after the States of the North had abolished slavery.

Why did not slavery continue to exist in the States of New England?

Because they found it unprofitable, and they sold their slaves to the States of the South.

What great leader in the Northern army owned slaves?

Gen. U.S. Grant, who continued to live on their hire and service until the close of the war, and after the emancipation proclamation had been published, while he was leading armies to free the slaves of the South.

When the Northern States had sold their slaves to the South, what did they then do?

They organized a party to oppose slavery, called the "Abolition Party," which advocated all means to abolish slavery, with no intention of paying the people of the South for their property.

When did the South become alarmed?

At the election of Abraham Lincoln by this party, which was pledged to take away the slaves and offer no terms of payment to the owners.

Reprinted courtesy of the Rosenberg Library, Galveston, Texas.

Did the people of the South believe that slavery was right?

No, not as a principle; and the colonies of Virginia and Georgia had strongly opposed its first introduction, but after the Constitution of the United States had recognized the slaves as property, and the wealth of the South was largely invested in negroes, they did not feel it was just to submit to wholesale robbery.

How were the slaves treated?

With great kindness and care in nearly all cases, a cruel master being rare, and lost the respect of his neighbors if he treated his slaves badly. Self-interest would have prompted good treatment if a higher feeling of humanity had not.

What was the feeling of the slaves toward their masters?

They were faithful and devoted and were always ready and willing to serve them.

How did they behave during the war?

They nobly protected and cared for the wives of soldiers in the field, and widows without protectors; though often prompted by the enemies of the South to burn and plunder the homes of their masters, they were always true and loyal.

What were the principles of the Southern people?

They believed that each State should regulate her own affairs, according to its best interests, with no meddling with the management of other States, and that each State should loyally support the Constitution of the United States.

Who was most prominent in defining "State Rights?"

John C. Calhoun, of South Carolina.

What steps did the Southern people take after the election of Mr. Lincoln?

They seceded from the Union, and at once took possession of the forts, arms and ammunition within their borders.

Did the forts surrender without resistance?

In nearly all cases.

In what order did the States secede?

South Carolina, December 20, 1860.

Mississippi, January 9, 1861.

Florida, January 10, 1861.

Alabama January 11, 1861.

Georgia, January 19, 1861.

Louisiana, January 26, 1861.

Texas, February 1, 1861.

Virginia, April 17, 1861.

Arkansas, May 6, 1861.

North Carolina, May 20, 1861.

Tennessee, June 24, 1861.

Missouri, October 31, 1861.

Kentucky, November 20, 1861.

What other State attempted to secede?

Maryland.

How was this prevented?

The Maryland Legislature was closed by the United States marshal and the secession members were sent to prison on September 18, 1861.

What had happened before this in Baltimore?

Federal troops in passing through that city to invade the South, were attacked on April 19, 1861, by the citizens of Baltimore, and a fight ensued in the streets, and the first blood of the war was there shed.

Did Maryland take any part in the cause of the South?

Yes, most valiant part, by furnishing many regiments of men and other aid for carrying on the war, and those who gave this aid endured persecution and imprisonment by the Federal authorities, as well as from those at home who opposed secession. Maryland was only kept in the Union by force.

What honor did General Lee confer on Maryland officers?

In the last retreat of the world-famed fighting army of northern Virginia he appointed Col. H. Kyd Douglas and Col. Clement Sullivane, two staff officers, one twenty-four years of age, the other twenty-six, to command the rear guard of the two divisions of the little army on its way to Appomattox.

What was the first step taken by the seceded States?

They proceeded to organize a government, by uniting themselves under the name of the Confederate States of America, and adopted a Constitution for their guidance.

Whom did they elect as their President?

Jefferson Davis, of Mississippi, senator from that State in the Congress of the United States, when Mississippi seceded, and already distinguished as a soldier and statesman, having gallantly served in the Mexican war, and as secretary of war under President Pierce, and member of both houses of Congress.

Did he resign his seat in the Senate as soon as his State seceded?

No. His State seceded on January 9th, and he remained in the Senate until January 21st, pleading for some pledge from the North that would secure the interests of the people of the South.

Does it appear from this that he led his people to secession?

No; like General Lee, he was led by the people of his State, obeying their call, and believing that his first duty was to his State....

What purposes have the Daughters of the Confederacy?

To preserve the true history of the Confederacy and keep in sacred memory the brave deeds of the men of the South, their devotion to their country and to the cause of right, with no bitterness toward the government of the United States, under which we now live.

What other purpose have the Daughters of the Confederacy?

To teach their children from generation to generation that there was no stain upon the action of their forefathers in the war between the States, and the women of the South who nobly sustained them in that struggle, and will ever feel that their deathless deeds of valor are a precious heritage to be treasured for all time to come.

For what was the army of the South particularly noted?

For its great commanders—great as soldiers and great as men of stainless character—and for the loyalty of the men in the ranks, who were dauntless in courage, "the bravest of the brave," ever ready to rush into the "jaws of death" at the command of their great leaders.

5. The U.D.C. Raises a Monument to the Confederacy, Depicting a Soldier and Mammy in Arlington Cemetery, 1914

Detail of frieze showing "black mammy," Confederate Monument at Arlington National Cemetery. Karen L. Cox, "The Confederate Monument at Arlington: A Token of Reconciliation," in Cynthia Mills and Pamela H. Simpson, eds., *Monuments to the Lost Cause: Women, Art, and the Landscapes of Southern Memory* (Knoxville: University of Tennessee Press, 2003), 159. (Public Domain)

6. The *Baltimore Afro-American* Mocks the Idea of a Mammy Monument, 1923

"Another Suggestion for the 'Mammy' Monument," *Baltimore Afro-American*, March 30, 1923. Micki McElya, "Commemorating the Color Line: The National Mammy Monument Controversy of the 1920s," in Cynthia Mills and Pamela H. Simpson, eds., *Monuments to the Lost Cause: Women, Art, and the Landscapes of Southern Memory* (Knoxville: University of Tennessee Press, 2003), 214. (Public Domain)

ESSAYS

In the first essay David R. Goldfield discusses Civil War collective memory mainly from the perspective of southern whites who were struggling with defeat, learning to cope with emancipation, and elevating their surrender into a "heroic Lost Cause." In his essay, Goldfield argues that the healing process for whites required shaping the historical narrative: reinventing the Old South for continuity sake but creating a New South Creed to encourage economic development and political power. In the second essay W. Fitzhugh Brundage argues that an emancipationist memory encountered pervasive racism. Nonetheless,

African Americans fashioned a redemptive past that spoke to their advancements in freedom, pride in their sustainability, reminders of their citizenship, especially in service toward their country, and rejoinders to whites that Africans were "the inventors of civilization." Rather than erecting expensive monuments in the expression of their collective memories, they marshaled a public robust ceremonial life that challenged Lost Cause sensibilities. Southern whites, argues Micki McElya in the third essay, grew concerned over African Americans' strength and their growing radicalism in the wake of World War I. By hoping to create a national Mammy monument, the United Daughters of the Confederacy planned to mold concepts of a permanent ideal faithful servant and thereby shape public memory to their own romanticized view of slavery and race relations—a "history of their own invention."

The Past Is

DAVID R. GOLDFIELD

One of the most frequent comments from newcomers and visitors alike is that the South is still fighting the Civil War. The immanence of the war is a given for a southerner, at least for white southerners. Southerners tend to live in multiple time zones. Past, present, and future are conflated, and the past is the most important of all. We are comfortable with this; it has become second nature. The title character of Mississippi writer Barry Hannah's novel *Ray* (1984) admits, "I live in so many centuries. Everybody is still alive."

Some years ago I stood at the base of the massive equestrian statue of Robert E. Lee on Richmond's Monument Avenue. It was a bright Sunday summer morning, early but already suggesting the blazing heat to come. As I tried to position myself to take a photograph, I saw a well-dressed elderly gentleman shuffling toward me. He smiled, pointed up at the statue, and commented matter-of-factly before he ambled away, "Quite a man, isn't he." *Isn't* he? I should not have been surprised at the use of present tense in reference to a long-dead general, albeit a very special general. "There is no such thing really as was because the past is," William Faulkner wrote. And so it is in the South. Southerners may live in the past, as some charge, but it is incontrovertible that the past lives in southerners. Ben Robertson, a South Carolina journalist in the 1930s and '40s, put it this way: "All about me, on every side, was age, and history was continuous.... I was Southern, I was old."

In the South history is not learned; it is remembered, it is handed down like a family heirloom through generations. Much of this remembered past is no longer in history books, but it is valued all the more as a precious lifeline, ever more fragile, connecting southerners to the South and each other. The memories

---

David Goldfield, *Still Fighting the Civil War: The American South and Southern History* (Baton Rouge: Louisiana State University Press, 2002), pp. 14–28. Reprinted by permission of Louisiana State University Press.

invariably begin with the Civil War. And how white southerners remembered the Civil War and its aftermath defined and distinguished the South for the next century.

It is tempting to read history backward and see North and South as distinctive regions since time began. From the first European settlements, it is true, North and South were never identical, any more than two children from the same family are exactly alike. Plantation slavery distinguished the South early in our nation's history, and that difference grew through the first half of the nineteenth century. But, as historian Stephen Nissenbaum wrote, the sectionalism derived from slavery was "not an outgrowth of fundamentally different social systems, but instead was integral to republican ideology and the conception of the federal system itself." Put another way, the rhetoric of sectional antagonism often boiled down to which section espoused and practiced the Revolutionary ideals best. What galled southerners was not their difference from the North but that northerners refused to accept them as equal moral, political, and economic partners in the American enterprise.

When northerners and southerners defended their respective stands on sectional issues, they both appealed to the same time-honored nationalist and war democratic sentiments. Southern secessionists believed they were the true keepers of the ideals that had inspired the American Revolution. They were merely re-creating a more perfect Union. It was not they, but the Republicans, who had sundered the old Union by subverting the Constitution's guarantee of liberty. Abraham Lincoln similarly appealed to nationalist themes, telling northerners that the United States was "the last best hope on earth."

Even when the Republicans won the election of 1860, secession was by no means inevitable. The debates over secession highlighted the divisions in southern society, between the states and within the states. Save for South Carolina, long in the forefront of radical sentiment in the region, dissent surfaced in all the southern states. Some states, such as Virginia, North Carolina, Tennessee, and Arkansas, seceded reluctantly only after the war began and President Lincoln asked them for troops. Kentuckians never could make up their minds one way or the other and remained tenuously in the Union for the duration of the war. Western Virginians could not abide their state's secession decision and pulled a secession of their own, declaring the separate state of West Virginia in 1863. In the meantime, residents of northern Alabama, eastern Tennessee, western North Carolina, and parts of Texas took up sporadic armed resistance to Confederate authority. The Heroes of America, a pro-Union group in North Carolina, may have had as many as ten thousand members by 1863. It was possible during that year of fierce fighting to visit southern mountain towns, Delta plantations, and Texas ranches and see the Stars and Stripes flying proudly.

Even loyal Confederates found it difficult to transfer that loyalty to a new central government. Most southerners had rarely ventured beyond their counties; family and friends were their primary frames of reference. They identified with their localities, perhaps their state, but rarely with an entity called "the South." States' rights had been a great rallying cry for secession, and now southerners were called upon to sacrifice their local interests, wealth, and young men for a much broader cause. That was difficult; some governors balked at troop quotas, others withheld supplies, and many Confederates bickered with the government in Richmond. "Died of States' Rights" might arguably serve as the epitaph for the defeated Confederacy, at least according to one historian. The South was not a united country as it fought for independence.

After the war, this changed. Robert Penn Warren's simple dictum, "The South was created at Appomattox," holds. The war and defeat took a terrible toll on the South. From the outset, both sides depicted the conflict as a holy war. Julia Ward Howe's "Battle Hymn of the Republic" summarized the northern view that God would strike the South with "His terrible swift sword." Southerners, equally religious, claimed God's favor as well. Obviously, God could "choose" only one side in this conflict. From the white southerners' perspective, their defeat was more than a lost war; they had evidently fallen out of favor with God.

In addition to the terrible loneliness and abandonment such an event implied for a religious people, the physical destruction of the region testified to man's and God's wrath. The scorched-earth policies of General William T. Sherman and his comrades-in-arms not only eroded the southern will to fight but made recovery that much more difficult. There was no Marshall Plan to rescue the South. Union armies had destroyed two-thirds of the South's assessed wealth, two-fifths of the livestock, and one-quarter of the white men between the ages of twenty and forty. The invasion ruined half the South's farm machinery, destroyed many of its railroads, and shattered its industry. Northern wealth rose by 50 percent between 1860 and 1870; southern wealth declined by 60 percent. In 1860 the southern states possessed slightly less than one-third of the nation's wealth; by 1870 that share had declined to 12 percent.

When the young Confederate soldiers—many were boys, really—hobbled home, some broken, a few relieved, many with a sense of ruined dreams and lives askew, they came to a familiar place, a homestead, a town; but the time was unfamiliar. A civilization had vanished; an order was undone, the future a blank of uncertainty. Though Union armies had foretold the war's outcome with victories at Gettysburg and Vicksburg in July 1863, the end nearly two years later still came as a blow, for hope is a hardy perennial, and faith is still stronger. Stories filled the Bible of the weak inheriting victory and more. One more miracle, Dear Lord, please.

The soldiers came home to women and children who also had suffered the shock of war and deprivation. The women had waved gaily at departing sons, brothers, husbands, and fathers; had knitted uniforms, tilled the soil, tended the wounded, and buried the dead; and had come to rail against the Confederate government for keeping their husbands, hoarding their food, and leaving them vulnerable to friend and foe alike. The chivalry that promised protection and shelter proved a thin reed in war; their men could guarantee neither. God had rendered His judgment, these women believed, and had pronounced the South guilty. "The demoralization is complete," a Georgia girl lamented. But neither the meaning nor source of that guilt was altogether clear. Such riddles would await future decoding; in the meantime, food, livelihood, and life itself offered more than enough challenges.

It was easier to heal the body than to cure the mind. The holy war was lost, as was the civilization that drove it. White southerners confronted change, but change to what they knew not. Their worst fears and imaginations played wildly: Would the Negro work? Would the ex-slave seek vengeance? Would the Union soldiers maintain their subjects in permanent penury and fear? Would they persist in dependence as virtual slaves to their new black and federal masters?

For southern blacks, as for southern whites, time began in 1865. But to African Americans, the surrender at Appomattox marked the time of liberation, not capitulation. They greeted peace with celebration and began to craft a new lore from the wreckage of the old system....

As the freed slaves celebrated the Union victory, Confederates tried to live with defeat, but acceptance did not come easily. White southerners did not wait for answers; they fought back. *Reconstruction* is a misnomer; *Restoration* is a more accurate term to describe the events from the surrender at Appomattox in 1865 to the removal of the last federal troops from the South in 1877. Except for a brief three-year period, from 1867 to 1870, ex-Confederates reclaimed their region, their governments, and their dominion over their families and former slaves. It was a stunning reversal of fortune for the erstwhile Confederacy, so recently downtrodden, defeated, and demoralized. How could they have mustered the strength and will to restore so much of what the war had swept away?

Part of the answer is that the North allowed the ex-Confederates considerable leeway in governing themselves and in allowing them to govern others. But more significant, perhaps, was the mental alchemy white southerners performed on the war itself. They spun the straw of defeat into a golden mantle of victory. Not that they refused to accept the verdict of the war—the end of slavery and of southern independence—but they rejected the idea of defeat and the guilt such a result implied.

A rationale was born. White southerners elevated defeat into a heroic Lost Cause, their fallen comrades and faltering leaders into saintly figures, their crumbled society into the best place on earth, and their struggle to regain control over their lives and region into a victorious redemption. Memory offered salvation; they could not allow the past to slip into the past. They had to keep foremost the old proverb that the struggle of man against power is the struggle of memory against forgetting. And they remembered.

Transforming defeat into a heroic cause, made more noble by loss than by victory, resolved some of the humiliation white southerners experienced in the years after the war. But such an artifice could not persist in a vacuum. It required context. That context was the Old South. For if the war was heroic then so was the cause for which white southerners cast down their lives and fortunes. Recasting the war, they reformulated the Old South.

The invention of the Old South gave white southerners a tradition, a sense of continuity in a destabilized postwar world. Returning from war,

Confederate veterans entered a different world, a strange place with everything reversed, as if they were suddenly living in a mirror. From the simplicity of war to the complexity of life, soldiers groped for meaning and routine. They found solace in the collective experience of war and the view of that war as it evolved into the Lost Cause. They needed a sterling vision of the Old South, a heroic war, and eventually a glorious Redemption to extract them from the mirror, to set things right—maybe not exactly like before, but tolerable, and maybe someday better. Now they could hope. By creating a history from the story of the Old South, the Civil War, and Reconstruction, they erected legend to live by and for. Their history, like all good traditions, scrambled time, so that the war and Reconstruction became one event, an immediate and constant part of daily living, a reminder to do well and think right and remember that the legacy is watching.

White southerners often publicly professed good riddance to slavery in the postwar years, but they protested its shortcomings a bit too much. They cited the institution's burdens on masters and how it hampered the southern economy and limited opportunities for poorer whites. To hear them, one would think the Emancipation Proclamation liberated southern whites as much as black slaves. They rarely pronounced slavery a moral evil, however, for to do so would be to call the Cause into question. Instead, they created a memory of the Old South as a time of happy slaves, gracious masters, and beautiful chaste women. The creation of an Edenic Old South heightened the tragedy of its destruction. Like the fall of ancient Greece, the demise of southern civilization dissolved the beauty, grace, learning, and civility that flourished under enlightened men. "In simple truth and beyond question," Virginia novelist George W. Bagby intoned in 1884, "there was in our Virginia country life a beauty, a simplicity, a purity and uprightness, a cordial and lavish hospitality, warmth and grace which shined in the lens of memory with a charm that passes all language at my command."...

The Civil War and Reconstruction had accumulated new legends to justify contemporary needs. New "traditions" appeared throughout the twentieth century. Among the most popular novels of the early 1900s were Thomas Dixon's *The Clansman* and *The Leopard's Spots*. Both idealized the Old South and chronicled a Reconstruction that occurred only in vivid imaginations; such fictions were shared by most white southerners (and by most white Americans) as fact. The refurbished history of the Old South, coupled with white perspectives on the Civil War and Reconstruction, forged a new national identity in the South, what D. W. Griffith would refer to in the title of his 1915 film adaptation of Dixon's work as *The Birth of a Nation*....

The forward-looking publicity agents for a New South of great cities, industries, and commerce also paid homage to a sanitized Old South. This was not merely lip service to calm the doubts of those who feared the impact Yankee-style economic development on their traditional way of life. New South boosters avidly made the connection between their programs and their foundation in the Old South. The New South Creed of progress embraced an Old South Creed of tradition. Henry Grady, the cherubic Atlanta journalist who beat the drums of his city and region incessantly, offered no apologies for slavery and the civilization it supported. "The Northern man," he offered, "dealing with casual servants can hardly comprehend the friendliness that existed between the master and the slave." And, Grady continued, the warm relations between black and white had survived the war and distinguished the South's pursuit of progress. "It is the answer to abuse and slander," Grady professed. "It is the hope of our future."...

White southerners communicated these "traditions"—of the Old South, the Civil War, and Reconstruction—in various venues. Confederate president Jefferson Davis had given the charge to his and future generations to "keep the memories of our heroes green." And they did. Veterans shared their stories at family gatherings and church picnics. Just after the war, women's memorial associations maintained the graves and the memories of the young men who perished fighting for their country. Public spectacles, commemorations, monuments, and the naming of streets, schools, and public buildings after martyrs and leaders offered visual representations of white southern history. Political contests, that most public of engagements in the South, offered opportunities to articulate the past and connect candidates' current endeavors to a storied and gloried history. Popular songs and hymns celebrated saints and martyrs to the Cause.

As subsequent generations of white southerners emerged, more removed from the actual events than their predecessors, the written word in textbooks, novels, memoirs, and monographs added to oral and visual traditions. The Southern Historical Society, founded in 1869, published scholarly papers defending the Confederacy. By the early 1900s the professional historical writings of William A. Dunning and U. B. Phillips told about an Old South of benevolent slavery, a Civil War fought for states' rights, and a Reconstruction that began in tragedy and ended in triumph with Redemption. Little differentiated the professional from the popular perspective. When Margaret Mitchell conducted research for *Gone With the Wind*, she diligently devoured half a century's worth of scholarly work in southern history, much of which found its way into her novel. Both her story and her sources were fiction. Only beginning in the 1930s and 1940s, with the pioneering work of historians C. Vann Woodward and John Hope Franklin, did southern historians challenge the traditional view of southern history, and not in earnest until the 1950s. But even then, the stories from the earlier era enveloped young white southerners, for whom the war and Redemption seemed more immediate than ever, preservation more important than before.

White southerners growing up in the early twentieth century noted how vivid the war and Redemption seemed to them in the stories created and recreated by their elders, in the books they read, the tableaux they viewed. The war and Redemption were as immanent as today and as impending as tomorrow. Novelist Mary Johnston, of the first postwar generation, recalled that her parents raised her "in a veritable battle cloud, an atmosphere of war stories, of continual reference to the men and to the deeds of gigantic struggle."

Subsequent generations also heard and learned the heartfelt soliloquies; it was not enough to remember the past; it was necessary to *live* the past. The semblance of being there, of experiencing the pain and the glory, the martyrdom and the resurrection, made their preservation all the more precious. The sustenance of that Cause and that Redemption functioned both as a tribute to ancestors and a living memorial to the present, a gift that never stopped giving. Novelist Caroline Gordon grew up in Kentucky in the early 1900s, and as soon as she could carry a tune, she sang songs of praise for Confederate heroes interspersed by her grandmother's vivid commentary on battlefield exploits. As Gordon observed in the 1930s, "I do not think that my childhood experiences were very different from those of any southerner who is over thirty years old."

Years later, when war and Reconstruction generations could no longer reach out to their children and grandchildren, the legacy of storytelling, the textbooks replete with the legends of the Cause and Redemption, and the physical and social world they inherited still surrounded their progeny. As if performing the Passion Play, white southerners repeated the exploits of the war over and over again: not the defeats, desertions, and dissent, but the heroism against great odds, the sacrifices when no more could be offered, and the lives lost for a cause greater than man. Southerners growing up in the first half of the twentieth century found dating the war difficult because their elders often discussed the conflict as if it had happened yesterday or was still in progress. Writer Willie Morris recalled frightening his maiden aunts in the 1940s with fabricated radio reports that the Yankees were coming. Margaret Mitchell confessed, "I heard so much about the fighting and hard times after the war that I firmly believed Mother and Father had been through it all instead of being born long afterward. In fact I was about ten years old before I learned the war hadn't ended shortly after I was born."

Not only was the timing of the war uncertain to children coming of age enveloped in a "past" that was not quite past, but so was the outcome. James Eleazar, growing up in South Carolina in the early 1900s, did not learn that the South had lost the war until he was twelve years old: "And it was one of the saddest awakenings I ever had. For hours on end I had listened to Grandpa tell of whipping the lard out of the Yankees on a dozen battlefields." But the loss, Eleazar would learn, was only a temporary setback. So pervasive was the tendency to idealize the war and repeat its events like a rosary that even Yankees who settled in the region adopted the stories as their own. Shirley Abbott wrote that her father recounted the heroic deeds of the war incessantly even though he hailed from Indiana and his ancestors had fought proudly in the Union Army.

The histories made a lasting impression. George Wallace remembered his time as a fifteen-year-old page in the Alabama legislature, stealing out of the State House in Montgomery one sultry morning and standing on the star where Jefferson Davis was sworn in as president of the Confederacy, and how he would one day stand on that sacred spot, and how he would shield it from the bootheels of President John F. Kennedy's men when they came calling on him a century after Gettysburg.

The Confederate monument erected in Yazoo City, Mississippi, in 1909 by the United Daughters of the Confederacy (UDC) bears the inscription, "As at Thermopylae, the greater glory was to the vanquished." In the southern alchemy that turned failure to glory, here lay the soul of the New South. For southerners, like the ancient Spartans whom Xerxes' army had cut to ribbons, the outcome paled before the Cause. The civilization destroyed by the Union forces may have vanished, but its principles were immortal. The monuments that grew up, first of the leaders, then of the common soldiers, in every courthouse square in the South, reflected this noble lineage. They also indicated that the embodiment of these principles lay with the white South and, more particularly, with the white male South, embronzed in steadfast glory, gazing northward.

The recasting of the Civil War began before the ink dried on the surrender document. William Pittman Lumpkin enlisted in the Confederate army at the age of fifteen in 1864. Less than a year later, as he walked back to his Georgia home, he had reinvented himself as *William Wallace* Lumpkin, after the thirteenth-century Scottish patriot later immortalized in the film *Braveheart*. Like the first William Wallace, Lumpkin would not readily submit to rule by superior force, and that example girded his postwar life and the lives of countless other southern white men.

Honor was to remember and follow the example of those who sacrificed; dishonor to forget and walk the path of the enemy. Orthodoxy mattered, both in civil and religious terms: the public symbols of sacrifice were etched into the southern landscape in the numerous statues, monuments, and consecrated grounds; on the lips of political leaders who reminded their neighbors of that sacrifice and how close they came to suffering the ultimate defeat of Yankee and black rule; in the books and articles they read, primers for remembrance, Aesops' fables for the masses, with the moral always evident and always the same.

Black Memory in the Era of Jim Crow

W. FITZHUGH BRUNDAGE

On January 1, 1864, 15,000 blacks packed the streets of Norfolk, Virginia, to observe the first anniversary of the Emancipation Proclamation. The highpoint of the celebration was a huge parade that, even at a time when the outcome of the Civil War remained in doubt, attested to the resolve of blacks to embrace freedom and citizenship. The splendid marching of four regiments of black troops, the gusto of the brass bands, the obvious pride of the volunteer black

From Winfred B. Moore Jr., et al., eds., *Warm Ashes: Issues in Southern History at the Dawn of the Twenty-First Century* (Columbia: The University of South Carolina Press, 2003), pp. 341–353. Reprinted by permission.

fire companies, and the respect accorded the procession of black clergy-men were all facets of a cathartic, communal celebration of freedom.

Seventy-two years after the Emancipation celebration in Norfolk, tens of thousands of blacks flocked to Dallas to commemorate both the Lone Star State's centennial and the seventy-first anniversary of Juneteenth (the date in 1865 when General Gordon Granger arrived in Galveston and informed Texans that the United States government intended to enforce the Emancipation Proclamation throughout the region). Excited crowds followed a gigantic parade to the centennial fair grounds where they thronged the Hall of Negro Life. The festivities were intended to underscore, for generations of blacks born long after slavery, the continuity between their present circumstances and their race's past. Certainly, the Juneteenth ceremonies in Fort Worth, Texas, three years later did so. Beyond reminding the gathered crowd about past traumas and accomplishments, the presence of fifty-five former slaves as guests of honor at the local Prince Hall Masonic Mosque made the reality of bondage a living history, if only temporarily and symbolically.

The celebrations in Norfolk, Dallas, Fort Worth, and elsewhere attested to the dedication of blacks to acknowledge and ennoble what James Weldon Johnson called their gloomy past. These events are reminders of the existence of a powerful alternative to white historical memory in the New South. Scholars have done much to expose the labors of whites elites and others to define the meaning of the Civil War and the past in the postbellum South. But historians have devoted virtually no attention to the simultaneous expressions of black historical self-representation and dissent. Isn't it curious that we know more about Election Day and Pinkster Day parades in the antebellum North than we do about the complex tradition of ceremonial citizenship enacted in Norfolk, Dallas, and across the hinterland of the South?

Any attempt to reconstruct black historical memory should begin with these festivals of memory. Despite the oppressive conditions that Southern blacks faced, the public sphere remained sufficiently porous and open to voluntary, collective action that they could not be entirely excluded from it. They made creative use of the resources at their command and defiantly gave public expression to their collective memory, thereby offering a counter-memory to that of Southern whites. Diverse public ceremonies, which became the preeminent forum in which African Americans displayed their recalled past, enabled vast numbers of blacks to learn, invent, and practice a common language of memory. By providing blacks with highly visible platforms for the expression of black collective memory, celebrations ensured that their sense of the past was something more than a rhetorical discourse accessible principally to literate, elite African Americans. Instead, black memory existed as recurring events that could be joined in and appreciated collectively Such celebrations had a unique capacity to celebrate the recalled past before an audience that incorporated the breadth of the black community, from the college-trained preacher to the illiterate day laborer and the impressionable school child.

The conventions of nineteenth-century public life encouraged blacks to develop such spectacles of memory. Public festivals of all kinds proliferated in the Gilded Age until the collective display of patriotism and community spirit became a competitive process with a dizzying array of groups vying to exhibit their civic enthusiasm. Blacks understood the importance of interrupting their individual, day-to-day routines in order to enter into public space and perform coordinated roles in pageants of representation. By insinuating celebrations of black history into the region's civic life, Southern blacks strove to break down their historical exclusion from a ceremonial citizenship. And by providing blacks with an opportunity to stage complex self-portraits of their communities commemorative celebrations represented a bold act of both communal self-definition and cultural resistance.

Within a decade of Appomattox, African Americans had adopted at least a half dozen major holidays and countless lesser occasions during which they staged elaborate processions and ceremonies. New Year's Day, previously the most bitter day of the year because of its associations with slave auctions, now provided an occasion to commemorate with acclamations of the wildest joy and expressions of ecstasy, Lincoln's 1863 Emancipation Proclamation and the abolition of slavery. Southern blacks joined in the February commemoration of Washington's birthday, using it to highlight the cruel irony that their ancestors had fought beside Washington to found a nation that subsequently had rejected them. To the extent that Lincoln's birthday was celebrated in the South, it was by African Americans, who understandably were eager to link their history with that of their martyred liberator. They added February 18, Frederick Douglass's purported birthday, to their calendar of holidays after the beloved abolitionist's death in 1895.) In 1865 the eager participation of blacks in Charleston, South Carolina, and elsewhere helped to establish Memorial Day in late May as the fitting commemoration of military valor and sacrifice. They also gave new meaning to Independence Day. Only at the end of the nineteenth century, when the patriotic fervor aroused by the Spanish-American War swept the region, did most white Southerners resume celebrating the nation's founding. Blacks understood that if the Declaration of Independence was to be a resounding appeal to liberty and equality, the Fourth of July, its anniversary, was the appropriate occasion to present their unfulfilled claims to freedom.

The black commemorative calendar also included a panoply of celebrations of hallowed religious events. Perhaps the most widely observed denominational holiday was the birthday of Richard Allen, the founder of the African Methodist Episcopal (AME) Church. Initially adopted by the AME Church in 1876 as a way to arouse black interest in the nation's centennial, Allen Day became, by the late 1880s, an enduring region-wide celebration. Admittedly an affair exclusive to black Methodists, it and other religious anniversaries were conceived of as celebrations of collective black achievement and as important milestones in the day-to-day lives of black communities. Thus, even members of competing churches and organizations were encouraged to take pride in ceremonies honoring their rivals' history and accomplishments.

Blacks like wise set aside dates to commemorate anniversaries associated with the benevolent organizations that multiplied across the South. Although the principal objectives of these societies were benevolent and social, they also invariably cultivated an awareness of their own histories through meetings, parades, fairs, and anniversary celebrations. The nineteenth anniversary of the founding of the Covington, Virginia, chapter of the Order of Good Samaritans in July 1896 typified the public ceremonies that such groups staged. The men and women of the order, dressed in elaborate regalia, gathered at their hall and then, following behind a local cornet band, marched through the main streets of the small western Virginia mining town. Eventually the paraders reached the Covington Baptist Church, where officers of the order recounted the Good Samaritan's history and ministers blessed the occasion. Then the celebrants enjoyed a ceremonial feast and an evening of fellowship. Similar extravaganzas were commonplace in the region's larger cities, where month after month, year after year, the rhythms of everyday life were interrupted by spectacular parades of flamboyantly garbed black marchers honoring their respective benevolent and fraternal societies.

Seemingly, no black community was too small to nourish a commemorative tradition. In Purcellville and Hamilton, two neighboring rural villages in northern Virginia, for instance, blacks organized the Loudoun County Emancipation Association, which in turn planned and hosted an annual celebration every September 22. The fact that the association had its own printed letter head stationery was only one indication of its ambitions. Although both poor and obscure, the association nonetheless enlisted prominent figures, including W. Calvin Chase, the editor of the Washington *Bee,* to deliver the annual orations. So audacious were the association's directors that in 1922 they displayed no insecurity when they wrote, in labored and ungrammatical prose, to Mary Church Terrell, one of the most respected black clubwomen of the era, requesting her to deliver an address at the upcoming Emancipation Day celebrations. Although Terrell eventually begged off and the association had to make alternative plans, the organization's request itself revealed the initiative of even the most humble black organizations. The size and spectacle of black ceremonies testified to the significance that blacks attached to them. In Norfolk, Virginia, for instance, Emancipation Day on each January 1 routinely attracted tens of thousands of onlookers eager to watch parades that stretched for miles through the principal streets of the city. In Beaufort, South Carolina, Memorial Day evolved into a similar region-wide celebration that enticed visitors and black military units from the Carolinas and Georgia. In Vicksburg, Mississippi, Fourth of July festivities included grand parades of several hundred marchers and brass bands through the main thoroughfares of the city before celebrants gathered at the city's imposing courthouse and to listen to long slates of speakers. Similarly, the combination of pageantry and festive atmosphere in Charleston, South Carolina, each Independence Day attracted black excursionists from as far away as Columbia, Savannah, and Augusta.

The festivities staged by blacks were boisterous affairs that often challenged the racialized segregation of public spaces, including spaces that were especially hallowed to whites. Blacks in Richmond, for instance, pointedly included the grounds of the Virginia capitol in their July Fourth celebrations That the former capitol of the Confederacy would be the site for large crowds of blacks to celebrate the founding of the republic by parading, carousing, and selling lemonade, watermelons, and other holiday foods was abhorrent to white sensibilities. Even after conservative whites regained control of the state's government in the 1870s, black paraders continued to conduct imposing ceremonies that tweaked white sensibilities. After 1890, black militia units incorporated the imposing Robert E.

Lee statue on Monument Avenue into their ceremonial musters. By parading at the foot of the monument, they associated themselves with the memory of the city's most renowned military figure. As black men in uniform, they simultaneously reminded Richmond's whites of Lee's defeat at the hands of an army that included former slaves.

If blacks demonstrated the primacy of their racial identity by marching collectively, they made manifest their multiple affiliations by choosing to march as members of distinct social organizations. The organization evidenced much about the accelerating social and class differentiation among blacks during the late nineteenth century. As black communities separated themselves out into discrete groups on the basis of religion, class, occupation, education, and ancestry, they staged celebrations that reflected and acknowledged these same divisions. Driven by the vigorous competition for public prestige among black organizations, they understandably grasped opportunities, such as public ceremonies and parades, to establish their claims for public recognition and influence. Thus, the order of the procession revealed not just the organizational infrastructure of the black community but also what social attributes blacks valued and wanted to display before the larger world.

Unmistakable conventions emerged for ordering parades. The social and political symbolism of black military service suffused black commemorative celebrations. The privilege and prestige of occupying the front ranks of processions often went black veterans of the Civil War, and. later of the Spanish American and First World Wars. Joining the veterans at the front of many black parades were black militia. Parading black veterans were a reminder of the blacks who, by fighting at Port Hudson, Milliken's Bend, Ft. Wagner, San Juan Hill, and in the trenches in Europe, had proved that battlefield heroics knew no color line. Lines of Civil War veterans, in particular, connected the agency of ordinary men with great deeds, including the destruction of slavery and the eventual achievement of political rights.

The prestige attached to black men in uniform went beyond respect conferred upon them for their willingness to take up arms in times of crisis. The representation of blacks as soldiers took on particular significance at a time of flowering nationalism and shifting attitudes toward the commemoration of military valor. After the Civil War, whites in North and South alike engaged in a frenzy of monument building to celebrate the common (white) soldier. As historian Kirk Savage has observed, "this proliferation of soldier monuments militarized the landscape of civic patriotism." Black soldiers, however, were virtually invisible in the commemoration of war and soldiering. Because blacks were excluded from monumental representations of military valor, displays of military prowess by black militia during commemorative pageants were charged with symbolic significance. Black militia, consequently, seized. any pretext to muster and parade. These drills, especially on July Fourth, were intended to demonstrate black military competence and to rebut white criticism that black soldiers were little more than overdressed and undertrained poseurs. Well-dressed and well-ordered black troops came to symbolize the ideal of black masculine leadership. News accounts regularly praised the young men's "excellent marching," "neat appearance and splendid soldiery," and "very soldier-like appearance." A company's stylish and correct showing on the parade ground reflected equally on the troops and on their community. As the Savannah *Tribune* observed in 1897, the local black militia had "for over twenty years" borne the burden of representing their people."

In black communities without militia companies, black fire companies often occupied the front ranks of civic festivities. Volunteer fire companies offered another avenue for displays of public service while also contributing pomp and spectacle to civic ceremonies. Perpetuating a tradition that extended back to the earliest years of the republic, black firemen, like their white counterparts, used holidays, especially Independence Day, as a pretext for tournaments during which rival companies vied to see which was fastest in getting to and putting out mock fires. Sometimes the displays of firefighting skills were intended as pure farce. But more often the fire companies strove to demonstrate that black communities possessed courageous men dedicated to selfless public service. Like the militia, the fire companies helped to give meaning to commemorative celebrations by linking them with voluntarism, private association, and civic obligation.

Following behind the militia units, veterans, and fire companies, were labor organizations and trade groups. The 1888 Emancipation Day cavalcade in Washington D.C., for instance, included two floats of whitewashers and plasters who advertised their trades "with yells which would do credit to Comanche Indians." During Emancipation Day in Jacksonville in 1892, the longshoremen's association, the printer's union, the carpenter's union, and a "Trade display" float joined the procession through the city's streets. A quarter century later, approximately one thousand longshoremen paraded the streets of Savannah in honor of Emancipation Day. These street dramas linked outward displays of occupational pride with both the honored past and contemporary concerns. They announced the workers' determination to be part of the body politic, appearing for all to see on important civic occasions, marching in orderly formation under their various banners. A few even perpetuated ancient traditions associated with European celebrations by performing defacto craft pageants in mock workshops. An enterprising black butcher in Jacksonville, for example, used the July Fourth parade in 1887 as an opportunity to sell literally "his fine fresh meats" from the back of his "well arranged float." When black workers affiliated their collective identity with the commemoration of American independence and emancipation, they linked the blessings of democracy and freedom with their own economic opportunities. And to insist upon the variety and dignity of their labor at a time of systematic discrimination against black tradesmen and workers was to liberate blacks of the stigma of being mere hewers of wood and drawers of water. However much these demonstrations of craft pride and organization by blacks borrowed from older labor iconography, they achieved particular symbolic power because they were staged by former slaves and their descendants whose labor previously had been denied either social status or recompense.

At century's end, the parade lines were joined by business floats that advertised the wares and skills of black entrepreneurs. To some extent, the business floats reflected the commercialism that crept into all manner of public commemoration during the late nineteenth century. In an age when monument companies pandered to white veterans' groups and women's organizations by adopting the latest marketing and advertising techniques, black businessmen could hardly have been expected to forgo similar tactics. Funeral home operators in Charleston, for example, used the 1917 Emancipation Day parade to introduce automobile hearses to the public. The increasing prominence of business floats after the turn of the century also testified to the efforts of black business organizations such as the National Negro Business League to stimulate local black enterprise, inform the public of advances made by black businesses, and inspire community pride. Although black business organizations sometimes were ridiculed for their tub-thumping bluster, their advertising campaigns meshed well with the traditions of communal uplift that were central to black celebrations. Moreover, each business float offered further symbolic confirmation of the black progress that the ceremonies were intended to demonstrate and celebrate.

Just as the processions provided an opportunity for black communities to engage in ceremonial collective representation, commemorative festivities provided black orators with a platform from which to transform the discordant and tragic reality of the black past into something grand and ennobling. At a time when famous speeches were still printed, bound, and sold in editions, numbering in the tens of thousands, and in a region where the more ordinary productions of high culture were seldom found and little encouraged, oratory enjoyed continuing prestige and therefore figured prominently in black commemorative celebrations. With eloquent learnedness, stately gestures, studied solemnity, and expertly moderated delivery, black orators shaped the meaning of black celebrations. During orations that commonly lasted two, three, or even four hours, they turned the parade grounds and parks into open-air schools where they informed and inspired as well as entertained.

Black commemorative orators turned the era's civilizationist ideology on its head by insisting that blacks not only had contributed to humankind's progress but were, indeed, the inventors of civilization. This claim demanded a profound revision of ideas about the history of Africa's peoples. Africa, for whites, was a metaphor for barbarism, and Africa's purported lack of civilization was a stigma borne by black people everywhere. Rejecting this dominant vision of African history, black orators responded that Africa had been the cradle of much that the world had come to define and salute as Western. Black celebrations disseminated the distinctive translation of the civilizationist ideology deep into the Southern hinterland so that black lumbermen in East Texas; mill workers in Birmingham, Alabama; and self-sufficient farmers in Glynn County, Georgia, who almost certainly never read the learned writings of Alexander Crummell and other black intellectuals, encountered interpretations of the black past that meshed seamlessly with the more erudite renderings of distant black intellectuals. At the very least, audiences heard a narrative of ancient black accomplishments that contrasted sharply with white accounts of African savagery.

Black orators differed no less sharply with whites over the meaning of the Civil War. Southern whites, of course, strenuously defended secession and were acutely sensitive to any suggestion that the defense of slavery had motivated their failed rebellion. The black counter-narrative was equally unambiguous. Over and over again, black orators insisted that the Civil War had been God's punishment for slavery and that the plight of African Americans had been the catalyst for the nation's Armageddon. Rather than a tactical sleight of hand dictated by wartime exigencies (as many white Southerners claimed), the Emancipation Proclamation was a redemptive act through which God wrought national regeneration. By so explaining the mystery of slavery and the jubilee of freedom, black orators insisted that the divine providence of history had worked (and might work again in the future) to elevate the African peoples. Emancipation anticipated some profound, imminent and millennial transformation in the status of black people. At the very least, it held out to blacks the promise of social justice and suggested that the ascendancy of the white race was only temporary.

That the United States was a nation with a millennial destiny and that blacks had an important role to play in that future was apparent to most commemorative orators. The future of civilization in general and the black race in particular would be played out on this continent where black orators already discerned ample evidence of their race's rapid ascent of the ladder of civilization. They viewed the history of Southern blacks paradigmatically, as a parable of racial elevation. Whereas most whites presumed that centuries would be required to elevate blacks above abject barbarism, black orators dwelled on the exceptional, indeed unparalleled strides that blacks had made since slavery.

Although blacks had to watch as the promise of Reconstruction receded, they refused to join in the increasingly shrill denunciation of the postbellum experiment. At the same time that whites, ranging from the playwright Thomas Dixon and filmmaker D. W. Griffith to the historian William Dunning, compiled the dark record of Reconstruction, black commemorative orators recalled with reverence the courage and integrity with which blacks had conducted themselves then. The defense of the legitimacy of Reconstruction in commemorative orations was an important political exercise because blacks had few other venues to challenge the ascendant interpretation of the postwar period. The audience who listened to J. C. Lindsay of Savannah in 1917 lament that the old wail is still heard that the period that followed emancipation was filled with mistakes did not need to wait for W. E. B. DuBois's revisionist account of Reconstruction in order to discover a correction to the virulently critical white commentaries on the postbellum years. Lindsay, like many orators, conceded that black suffrage may have been improperly used and the right abused, but he insisted that even then it served to check political outrages and political impositions. By defending the legitimacy of Reconstruction black orators dismissed white claims that the black fortunes had been raised by the redemption of the region and return of white rule.

Reflecting their refusal to promote the appearance of a passive, deferential black populace, orators gave voice to enduring political aspirations. Rev. W. H. Styles, for instance, strongly condemned lynching as barbaric in his address during the anniversary of the ratification of the 15th Amendment in Blackshear, Georgia. He stressed that the political rights guaranteed by the Constitution provided the only protection against white violence. Rev. J. J. Durham warned his Savannah audience in 1900 that any attempts to deal with the Negro as something less than a citizen would cost this country more blood and treasure than it took to establish its independence. Through speeches and resolutions, orators and celebrants made strenuous demands for black political rights, denounced racism, and defended black aspirations on the grounds that they have surpassed all reasonable tests of education, culture, morality, and patriotism they had faced. And when the gathered audiences at celebrations adopted resolutions of protest, they gave voice to concerns and opinions that were otherwise too seldom acknowledged in Southern public life.

By fusing protests, jeremiads, and memorials, black commemorative orations occupied a crucial role in black collective memory in the postbellum South. If black orators at times seemed to parrot the dominant strains of the American faith in a progressive unfolding historical drama, they did so in order to promote an African American collective identity, not because they necessarily identified with white values. This strategy of reversal—of appropriating purportedly American ideals and turning their back on their professors—was fundamental to expressions of black public memory after the Civil War.

Such inversions of white presumptions about the past understandably had especially strong purchase at a time when blacks struggled to establish that the large and central themes of the black experience were only traceable in history's processes. Commemorative addresses did so by serving as an oral archive of both black strivings and African American claims for justice. They historicized the black past for the broad expanse of Southern blacks who otherwise had few occasions to recall and ponder their shared history by situating the particular and individual lived experience of black audiences in larger historical events, revealing to them the political and cultural forces that influenced their lives. Speaking for a generation in transition from the folk memory to a broader historical consciousness, orators contributed mightily to turning the atomized memories of individuals into a collective past, one that could sustain black civic culture throughout the era of Jim Crow.

Taken together, the commemorative processions, orations, and festivities posed an unmistakable challenge to white understandings of the past. Indeed, the contest over the meaning of Southern history was not just between the North and the South, but also between white and black Southerners. White southerners, after all, had argued with their Northern counterparts for decades. But they had no previous experience with a challenge to their interpretative authority over the past from within the South. When white Southerners systematically set about codifying their heroic narrative and filling the civic landscape with monuments to it, they were conscious not only of a challenge from Northern counter-narratives, but also from Southern blacks. The resentment that Southern whites vented every Fourth of July, the mocking derision that they showered on black commemorative spectacles, and the frequency of legal and extralegal harassment directed against black revelers leave little doubt that whites understood that the rituals of black memory represented a form of cultural resistance. For all of the efforts of Southern whites to enshrine their historical understanding of slavery, the Civil War, and black failings, black commemorative celebrations made manifest a forceful and enduring black counter-narrative.

Of course, poverty and oppression sharply circumscribed the expression of this black counter-memory. As Southern whites strengthened their grip over the public realm in the late nineteenth century, some expressions of black memory eventually were marginalized or altogether suppressed. This competition between white and black Southerners over the meaning of the past was never equal: whereas white Southerners created a landscape dense with totemic relics, Southern blacks could never fix their memory in public spaces in the same manner or to the same extent. Not only did whites enjoy an advantage in establishing the materiality of their memory, but they also possessed the power to silence parts of the past; for instance, they reverently erected monuments to faithful slaves but raised no statues of black Civil War soldiers. Over the course of the late nineteenth century, Southern whites, with the complicity of white Northerners, secured the cultural resources necessary to make their memories authoritative while rendering those of blacks illegitimate or imperceptible to whites.

Yet even as whites used history as a tool with which to erase blacks from annals of civilization, blacks fashioned an alternative past that gave meaning to their sufferings and could sustain their ambitions. Charles Carroll, the orator at the 1896 Juneteenth celebrations in Waco, Texas, brilliantly expressed the desperate need blacks had to fashion a useable historical memory. We must not sink in despair, he entreated his audience. We must not give up the high hope of our race, for who could determine our existence today had our forefathers ignored the hope of this generation. He refused to believe that the sacrifice of brave Negro heroes during the Civil War, Frederick Douglass, and other redeeming fathers had not eased the way for their successors. Yes, blacks had been defrauded of the full meaning of citizenship by every means human ingenuity can devise. But, Carroll concluded, "as this race unfolds the canvas of time and recollection which represents it from bondage to freedom, it whispers consolation to generations unborn." To find consolation in the black experience in America was an act of extraordinary social imagination. We might well wonder how Southern African Americans would have survived the disappointments and hardships of this age had they not done so.

The National Mammy Monument Controversy of the 1920s

MICKI McELYA

In February 1923 Neval H. Thomas, a board member of the National Association for the Advancement of Colored People (NAACP), sent an open letter to the U.S. Senate, the United Daughters of the Confederacy, and two mainstream newspapers, the *New York World* and the *Washington Evening Star.* In this letter, which was reprinted in a number of black newspapers, Thomas decried a bill before the Senate to allot land in the nation's capital for a

Micki McElya, "Commemorating the Color Line: The National Mammy Monument Controversy of the 1920s" in Cynthia Mills and Pamela H. Simpson, eds., *Monuments to the Lost Cause: Women, Art, and the Landscapes of Southern Memory* (Knoxville, TN: The University of Knoxville Press, 2003) pp. 203–216. Reprinted by permission.

monument to the "faithful colored mammies of the South." Urging the senators to deny the land grant, he argued, "Democracy is the monument that the noble 'black mammy' wants erected to her, and not this marble shaft which can only be a symbol of servitude to teach white and black alike that the menial callings are the Negro's place in the scheme of things."

Thomas's letter and other early challenges to the UDC's proposal failed initially, as the Senate on February 28, 1923, approved Bill S4119 to grant the southern women a place in Washington, D.C., for their memorial. But a flood of protests followed, and the bill never reached the floor of the House of Representatives for a vote. While struggles continue to this day to realize the democracy Thomas sought, the national mammy monument drive came to its end in 1924 when it was left to languish in a House committee.

This brief episode in the history of the production of public memory has much to tell us about the formation of racial identities and categories, efforts to expand the parameters of American citizenship, and southern regionalism in the early twentieth century—the "scheme of things" in Thomas's words. From the Daughters who conceived of the monument to the various African American organizations and journalists who opposed it, those enmeshed in the controversy used the image of the mammy to articulate contrasting visions of what this scheme of things ought to be and where they should fall within it. The complex debate that ensued may be best understood by first considering the motivations of the United Daughters of the Confederacy, whose members shared a particular vision of segregation and racial fantasy embodied in the figure of the mammy. Any analysis of the battle over the monument also must explore the Daughters' choice of a medium—public sculpture—to promote their views.

Confronted with growing black radicalism after World War I and the continuing exodus of African Americans from the South, the monument's supporters nationwide longed for a black mammy. They wanted to render in stone and bronze a permanent marker of appropriate, safe, and appealing blackness. Significantly, the figure they chose for veneration held particular gender, class, sexual, and regional connotations. In popular representation, the mammy had been the most loyal, because she was content with her servitude and sanctioned white supremacy. For monument advocates, she embodied the best potential for interracial relations. Their support of the campaign and its initial success did not just indicate whites' belief in their own racial superiority but also affirmed whites' wish for African Americans to believe in that superiority too. In their view, mammy did not just serve, but was happy to do so, and held genuine affection—even unconditional maternal love—for her white masters and charges.

The desire to fix for all time the contours of such a devoted servant suggests the fear of another kind of blackness—presumed to be unruly, dangerous, and destabilizing—that was visible in America in the postwar period. In his compelling study of race and monuments in the nineteenth century, art historian Kirk Savage describes twin catalysts of commemorative movements: the hope of molding a particular historical narrative into concrete form and the participants' wish to claim a broad consensus for their view. Noting that public sculpture drives have often been controversial, Savage argues, "to commemorate is to seek historical closure" and to secure the past "against the vicissitudes of the present." Indeed, the United Daughters of the Confederacy and their supporters sought to locate black people and national race relations within a history of their own invention. Yet their monument drive was more than an attempt to herald a cause long lost and to portray slavery as a benign institution. The campaign reveals much more—the articulation of a new cause for an uncertain future.

Women's "Visible" Work

Founded in 1894, the United Daughters of the Confederacy initially acted as an umbrella organization for local Ladies' Memorial Associations and other Confederate women's groups. By the early 1900s, it was an exceedingly popular organization among white, bourgeois, and elite southern women. Its membership steadily increased in the early twentieth century, growing from about 17,000 members in 1900 to 68,000 by 1920. White women established chapters throughout the South and in areas as far flung as New York City; Helena, Montana; and Paris, France.

While commemorative activities and public spectacles of mourning for the Confederate dead remained central to the UDC in the early twentieth century, the group pursued a broader social and political agenda than the earlier Ladies' Memorial Associations. Of primary importance was the "preservation" of a glorious memory of the Confederacy as well as women's roles as keepers and disseminators of this "truth." Rather than simply maintaining an extant collective understanding of the historical past, however, the Daughters worked persistently to reinvent the Old South and Confederate traditions. Like other turn-of-the-century women's groups, UDC members saw themselves as particularly suited to reform and patriotic education. To this end, they not only raised monuments and orchestrated Confederate Memorial Day events throughout the South but also campaigned to remove from southern schools certain textbooks deemed hostile to the Confederacy, founded and staffed memorial homes to care for aged Confederate men and women, organized a children's auxiliary called the Children of the Confederacy, and sponsored historical research.

Public memorialization remained a crucial means for the dissemination of this history and Confederate pride. Writing of the UDC's extensive commemorative activities in an organizational history published in the early 1930s, Rassie Hoskins White asserted the special importance of public monuments in the group's social and political agenda. The Daughters devoted so much time, labor, and money to statues, White explained, because "they knew monuments would speak more quickly, impressively, and lastingly to the eye than the written or printed word—attract more attention." She wrote, "The [UDC] chapters, State Divisions, and the general organization have done remarkable work in other lines, unseen work, but it is this *visible* work—great monuments and memorials—that has brought the organization publicity and acclaim for these thirty-five years of work, for they have spoken and will speak to a world indifferent to that vast amount of work which is invisible." While the monuments commemorated martial honor and a patriarchal system, she argued that they also denoted the power and prowess of the women whose fund-raising, political savvy, and time had enabled their existence. White's insistent emphasis on making "visible" the Daughters' "work" points to this contradiction in UDC members' struggles to define public authority for white women by celebrating Old South hierarchies....

If African American contemporaries were excluded from the Daughters' circle of southern virtue in the twentieth century, their enslaved ancestors held a central place in the mythology upon which this "tradition" rested, embodied particularly in the figure of the "faithful slave." Histories and anecdotes written by UDC members abound with stories of slaves who resisted the opportunities for freedom during the Civil War to protect and serve white women and children on the home front or who risked their lives to serve their masters in battle. These romantic fictions were intended to demonstrate that an affection and mutual understanding stood at the heart of slavery. They masked the coercion and brutalities of forced labor.

Spearheaded by the Jefferson Davis Chapter No. 1650 of Washington, D.C., the 1922–23 mammy commemoration drive grew out of nearly twenty years of discussion within the UDC about erecting a monument to the "faithful slaves" of the South. This debate had intensified between 1904 and 1905 in a series of exchanges printed in the *Confederate Veteran*, the national magazine of various Confederate patriot groups including the United Confederate Veterans (UCV) and the Daughters. In September 1904, Mrs. G. Gilliland Aston of Asheville, North Carolina, publicly appealed for a monument to "faithful slaves," a call endorsed by Mrs. Fred A. Olds, president of the North Carolina Division.

In an open letter to the UDC, UCV and "all the women of the South," Aston argued that the Confederate Veterans' recent campaign to erect a monument to southern women should be redirected to fund a memorial to "faithful slaves." Aston juxtaposed the expectations placed on white southern women during the war with what she saw as the profoundly questionable support of enslaved people. White women, she said, had felt they were enduring the struggle "for the sacred ties of kindred and country. How different with the faithful slaves! They did it for love of masters, mistresses and their children. How nobly did they perform their tasks! Their devotion to their owners, their faithfulness in performing their labors and caring for us during these terribly disastrous years, and their kindness at the surrender, while we were powerless and helpless, have never been surpassed or equaled."

At the same time, Aston's letter reveals a certain ambivalence about the nature of these cross-race relationships, usually described by the UDC as benevolent and noncoercive. While white women on the home front could be assumed to support the Confederacy, the letter implies, the actions of the enslaved were "different" because they worked against their own interests in astounding ways. Slaves who remained loyal when they had the opportunity to free themselves or to attack those who held them in bondage must have made their choice, Aston contended, out of genuine love for their masters. This, she declared, was a loyalty worthy of commemoration....

Ready for Mammy

By the 1920s the UDC was ready to commemorate "faithful slaves," and some people beyond the South also were ready for such a monument. The years surrounding the First World War were marked by increasingly visible black challenges to American racism and imperialism. Having rallied for what Woodrow Wilson described as a war to make the world "safe for democracy," many in the United States found this "democracy" still terribly wanting after the war. Black soldiers who served in the segregated U.S. military faced a grim reality: they were expected to fight for a country that refused to recognize them as citizens. Black Americans also witnessed the global, anticolonial struggles of other peoples of African descent.

The NAACP put its money and legal expertise behind antilynching legislation movements and in 1919 took a decidedly more militant stance in its public voice, *The Crisis*. Editor W. E. B. Du Bois, who had advised putting aside racial politics in favor of national unity during the war, now wrote: "We return. We return from fighting. We return fighting. Make way for Democracy!" In that same year Du Bois hosted his first Pan-African Congress in Paris. With a distinctly different global vision and constituency, Marcus Garvey had shifted the base of his United Negro Improvement Association in 1916 to New York's Harlem, where its membership grew steadily during and after the war as black migrations from the South to northern and western urban centers escalated generally. This Great Migration and the twenty-five race riots that exploded in cities across the United States in 1919 were in the minds of many Americans in the 1920s. Confined to no single region, riots erupted in the North, South, and West; in Omaha, Nebraska; Chicago; New York; and Knoxville, Tennessee. NAACP Secretary James Weldon Johnson referred to the period between June and the end of 1919 as the "Red Summer"—a reference to the terror and bloodshed of that time.

It was within this postwar American landscape of racial turmoil that leaders of the United Daughters of the Confederacy sought to construct their vision for future race relations—a "solution" of sorts, modeled on southern segregation and embodied in the mammy. Their decision to focus on this particular figure, rather than the more elusive and often gender-neutral "faithful slave," is telling. The broad national popularity of mammy imagery and its connotations of maternal tenderness and domestic labor were central to the Daughters' notion of affectionate segregation.

Mammy had always been, and remains, the product of a white racial imagination. Invented by southern proslavery writers in the late antebellum period, the figure was defined as a beloved cook, caretaker, and grandmotherly slave woman in response to abolitionists' charges that slavery was wracked with sexual depravity, including the rape and concubinage of black women by white men. Through the concept of the mammy, these theorists of slavery sought to legitimize relations between white men and black women as maternal and nurturing, not sexual. Their elaborate construction of mammy included not only physical attributes that stressed her old age or wide girth but also her character. She loved her white "family" and would protect it fiercely, but she was simultaneously a bit cantankerous and a disciplinarian of white children. Endearing in her gruff demeanor and unrefined features, mammy always was the antithesis of desirable white femininity.

Images of mammy saturated early-twentieth-century American culture, promoting these notions of asexuality, big-hearted kindness, and Old South gloriana. This period saw the escalating production and consumption of racist imagery in everything from popular music and material goods to new forms of consumer advertising. The most prevalent representation of mammy was undoubtedly Aunt Jemima, who smiled from boxes of pancake mix in kitchens throughout the country while domestic worker Nancy Green toured the nation appearing at industry-sponsored pancake feeds as the embodiment of the still-popular trademark. In modern consumer capitalism, the mammy's southern origin was one of her key characteristics—she was (and is) an American icon, but always a southern figure....

It was within these interconnected contexts—increasingly visible black geographic movements and radicalism, and the wide, national popularity of mammy imagery—that the U.S. Senate concurred with the UDC that the "faithful mammies of the South" should be honored with a public monument in the nation's capital. Sen. John Sharp Williams of Mississippi had introduced his bill to set aside land for such a statue earlier that winter, the last piece of legislation of his thirty-year congressional career....

The Limits of Citizenship

[A]dvocates hoped that a mammy statue would offer a lesson about appropriate black conduct and expectations. One supporter said: "If the negroes of the present generation and generations to follow, measure up [to mammy] in citizenship, character, intellect, dependability, industry and godly living, they, as well as the white people of this country, will have a right to feel that they are doing mighty well." Note particularly in this passage the implication that black citizenship ought to be equivalent to the domestic labors of slavery. It was the monument's potential to solidify this intent, literally, within the national civic culture that so alarmed Neval Thomas as he wrote of its ability to "teach white and black alike that the menial callings are the Negro's place in the scheme of things."

This racialization of the domestic sphere had terrific potential for white women's reshaping of their own citizenship. In commemorating mammy, the UDC retained the maternal, feminine construction of domesticity through which "progressive" women's organizations had long articulated a gendered notion of political power in the United States while at the same time distancing white womanhood from private labor and the responsibilities of daily household upkeep. The UDC's construction of loving, servile blackness "emancipated" feminine whiteness from the domestic impediments to public activity. In this manner, the Daughters campaigned to recast the gendered dichotomy of public and private space—with public life traditionally reserved for men, and women confined to the domestic sphere—into a bifurcated, racial division. For them, black people's labors could enable a new white public, composed of both men and women unified through racial homogeneity. The UDC hoped that mammy's mythic traits of loyalty and contentment with slavery might be a model for African Americans living in future eras of segregation, disfranchisement, and white privilege....

Monumental Violence

The black press's challenge to this vision was swift as it opposed the monument bill and presented very different understandings of the enslaved, black mother's place in modern African American citizenship. In response to the Daughters' romanticization of slavery and their vision of "affectionate" segregation, black journalists focused on the abuses and sexual exploitation of slavery as well as the brutalities and disfranchisement of contemporary southern apartheid and the informal segregation prevalent across the nation. Assessing the controversy, one black newspaper, the *St. Louis Argus*, reported, "No subject has brought forth a more unanimous protest, except lynching, since the Civil War, than has the proposed Black Mammy statue."...

The black press wrote persistently of the injuries heaped upon the mammies of the past whom the Daughters professed to so love and honor. These newspapers often referred to mammies as tragic figures, unable to care for their own children or support their own black families as they were forced into mothering white children and as their labors were co-opted into the white family economy. Mary Church Terrell, one of the founders of the National Association of Colored Women, wrote in a widely printed editorial, for example, "The black mammy was often faithful in the service of her mistress's children while her heart bled over her own babies, who were thus deprived of their mother's ministrations and tender care, which the white children received."...

Woven through these images of violence and tragedy were strands of the sexual exploitation of African American women, under slavery as well as in the early twentieth century. Focusing on predatory white men, these discussions linked the mammy figure as an embodiment of the history of slavery with the position of modern-day African American women in a brutally segregated society. By drawing attention to the rape, exploitation, and endangerment of domestic workers, both enslaved and free, black journalists made it clear that the mammy figure was invented to conceal white desire and sexual violence....

By focusing on white men's sexual terrorism of black women, papers like the *Defender* disputed the assertions of black deviance and sexual transgression that underlay the brutal enforcement of southern segregation through lynching and assault. An expansive form of social control in the South, actual violence and the constant threat of lynching enabled white, patriarchal domination, the denial of African American citizenship, and the continued coercion of black labor. The black press sought to dismantle this system by turning the charges of rape against those who employed such accusations to fuel lynch mobs.

Journalists for the black press ripped away the veneer of maternal warmth and childlike innocence the UDC affixed to segregation and black exclusion in their drive to commemorate mammies. Exposing the white terrorism that enforced the color line, they also named as a form of violence the processes of denial, concealment, and domination that produced the mammy stereotype.

Monumental Vigilance

As the monument controversy roiled, supporters and detractors of the statue agreed on one thing: The stakes were incredibly high. Both sides believed that national monuments could deeply influence American civic life. Commemoration was not a mere reflection of larger tensions over citizenship, race, and gender but stood at the heart of them with the potential to shape a new citizenry as well as new levels of oppression or freedom. Thus, much of the public discussion was about monumentality itself, reflected in the common use of monumental language and imagery to frame protests to the commemoration drive.... The protest [cartoon] ... [makes] starkly clear the importance of the conflict over "representation," both visual and political [See Document 6]. In critics' view, a public sculpture based on mammy imagery would give concrete form to dangerous ideas and imbue them with a kind of "official truth."

This facet of the conflict was clearly expressed in a fascinating editorial decision made by a prominent, Washington, D.C.-based black newspaper, the *Washington Tribune*, a month before the mammy monument bill passed the Senate. In January 1923 the paper, which would become a leading voice in organizing objection to the commemoration, began reprinting the text of *Emancipation and the Freed in American Sculpture: A Study in Interpretation*, written by the newspaper's president, F. Morris Murray. The timing of this reprint is too suggestive to be simple coincidence. In his introduction to the study, Murray argued for a keen critical vision in the face of public commemoration: "When we look at a work of art, especially when 'we' [black people] look at one in which Black Folk appear—or do not appear when they should—we should ask: what does it mean? What does it suggest? What impression is it likely to make on those who view it? What will be the effect on present-day problems, of its obvious and also of its insidious teachings? In short, we should endeavor to 'interpret' it; and should try to interpret it from our own particular viewpoint." ... Murray asserted the political and social power of monuments and counseled vigilance in reading their potential effects.

A month later, a front-page headline urged *Tribune* readers to "Voice Protest Against 'Mammy' Statue." By framing its coverage of the monument campaign with this analytical study of artistic representation, the *Tribune* sought to provide readers with the conceptual tools for understanding the grave consequences of such a commemoration and for formulating a protest.

It was this fierce and varied protest that would ultimately spell the end of the mammy monument drive. The land grant proposal had never been as popular in the House. Drawing upon political and social relationships they had cultivated with southern lawmakers and journalists in Washington, the Daughters had won the Senate's backing in 1923. But the public controversy that followed Senate approval bolstered the representatives' lack of interest or active objections to the scheme, and the resolution was never allowed out of committee in the House. Quiet congressional inaction spared the city of Washington and the nation from witnessing construction of a memorial to the "faithful colored mammies of the South." The iconography of the mammy and the wider debate around it, however, would long remain powerfully present within American political culture.

FURTHER READING

Rod Andrew Jr., "Soldiers, Christians, and Patriots: The Lost Cause and Southern Military Schools, 1865–1915," *Journal of Southern History*, 64 (November 1998), 677–710.

Fred Arthur Bailey, "Mildred Lewis Rutherford and the Patrician Cult of the Old South," *Georgia Historical Quarterly* 77 (Fall 1994), 509–535.

———, "Textbooks of the 'Lost Cause': Censorship and the Creation of Southern State Histories," *Georgia Historical Quarterly* 75 (Fall 1991), 507–533.

David Blight, *Race and Reunion: The Civil War in American Memory* (2001).

Robert E. Bonner, *Colors and Blood: Flag Passions of the Confederate South* (2002).

W. Fitzhugh Brundage, *The Southern Past: A Clash of Race and Memory* (2008).

Gregg Cantrell and Elizabeth Hayes Turner, eds., *Lone Star Pasts: Memory and History in Texas* (2005).

Kathleen Ann Clark, *Defining Moments: African American Commemoration and Political Culture in the South, 1863–1913* (2005).

Thomas Lawrence Connelly, *The Marble Man: Robert E. Lee and His Image in American Society* (1977).

Thomas L. Connelly and Barbara L. Bellows, *God and General Longstreet: The Lost Cause and the Southern Mind* (1982).

John M. Coski, *The Confederate Battle Flag: America's Most Embattled Emblem* (2005).

Karen Cox, *Dixie's Daughters: The United Daughters of the Confederacy and the Preservation of Confederate Culture* (2003).

Gaines Foster, *Ghosts of the Confederacy: Defeat, the Lost Cause, and the Emergence of the New South* (1987).

David Goldfield, *Still Fighting the Civil War: The American South and Southern History* (2002).

Caroline E. Janney, *Burying the Dead but Not the Past: Ladies' Memorial Associations and the Lost Cause* (2007).

Joan Marie Johnson, " 'Drill into us … the Rebel Tradition': The Contest over Southern Identity in Black and White Women's Clubs, South Carolina, 1898–1930," *Journal of Southern History*, 66 (August 2000), 525–562.

Micki McElya, *Clinging to Mammy: The Faithful Slave in Twentieth-Century America* (2007).

Cynthia Mills and Pamela H. Simpson, eds., *Monuments to the Lost Cause: Women, Art, and the Landscapes of Southern Memory* (2003).

W. Scott Poole, *Never Surrender: Confederate Memory and Conservatism in the South Carolina Upcountry* (2004).

Michael K. Prince, *Rally 'round the Flag, Boys: South Carolina and the Confederate Flag* (2004).

Nina Silber, *The Romance of Reunion: Northerners and the South, 1865–1900* (1993).

Charles Reagan Wilson, *Baptized in Blood: The Religion of the Lost Cause, 1865–1920* (1980).

CHAPTER 9

The Progressive South in the Age of Jim Crow

Historians of the South have long grappled with the complexities of southern progressivism. As the nation experienced reform at the city, state, and national levels, so too did the South. The Progressive movement in the South, however, occurred in the context of disfranchisement, racial violence, segregation, woman suffrage, the Lost Cause, and the rise of a one-party South. Nonetheless, historians have shown that for at least three decades between 1895 and 1925, a vigorous spirit of reform took root in the South. These included the insistence that government take a larger role in promoting the welfare of its citizens by setting a minimum working age for children in factories; improving public schools; regulating the railroads; ending the convict lease system; eradicating diseases such as hookworm and pellagra; maintaining better oversight and inspection of foods sold in the marketplace; ensuring safe, clean water and public spaces; building better roads and promoting scientific agriculture for farmers; establishing well-baby clinics, antituberculosis hospitals, and parks and playgrounds for children; protecting families through prohibition; and extending rights to women (raising the age of consent, passing married women's property rights, and granting suffrage).

At the same time, progressives paradoxically believed that restricting the right to vote to those who were literate or who could pay a poll tax was a move toward improving the electorate. They believed that segregation ordinances would create harmony between the races, and that the sterilization of mentally deficient individuals (eugenics) would improve humankind. These laws, also a part of the Progressive movement, represented a desire to direct southern society in an orderly, efficient, and moral manner. Unlike Populists, the progressives did not offer any radical economic programs; rather, they actively pursued economic development as another method of improving southern society.

The champions of progressive reform came primarily from a new middle class emerging in cities and towns and comprised both men and women, whites and blacks. The movement may be traced to various sources: religion, higher education, urbanization, and a national momentum for change, to name just a few. Considering the South's inherent conservatism, historians have pondered the impact that southern progressivism may have had on society.

Did the promise of progressivism merely result in an improved version of the status quo? Or were the changes more fundamental, and did they establish a foundation for future advances in race relations, gender equality, labor, and education?

DOCUMENTS

The documents reflect both the diversity of southern progressivism and its relationship to regional culture. Documents 1 and 2 should be read together, as they present the opposing views of the two leading spokesmen for African Americans in the progressive South—Booker T. Washington and W. E. B. Du Bois. In 1895, as white supremacy movements gained momentum, Booker T. Washington accepted an invitation to speak at the Atlanta Exposition before a white audience. The text of his speech sheds light on black fears and reveals one leader's strategy for improving race relations. His speech was labeled "The Atlanta Compromise." W. E. B. Du Bois, Harvard-trained sociologist and cofounder of the NAACP in 1909, challenged Washington's compromise with white southerners and renounced his accommodationist policies. Document 3, a memoir from Charleston, South Carolina, describes the evening that Mary Church Terrell, first president of the National Association of Colored Women, came to enlist African American women in civic reform. The Progressive era vitalized women across the South, and for African American women a national figure such as Terrell encouraged their full participation in community activism. Charles W. Dabney was a leading southern educator and president of the University of Tennessee at the time he wrote "The Public School Problem in the South" (1901), reproduced here as Document 4. The essay candidly discusses the "disgrace" of public education in the South and its impact on politics and the regional economy. Dabney's views on disfranchisement and "industrial education" for blacks were typical of southern progressives. Edgar Gardner Murphy, an Episcopal priest in Montgomery, Alabama, joined many of his colleagues in the movement by participating in a wide variety of reform efforts. These included race relations, education, and, as can be seen in Document 5, child labor. Georgia's Governor Hoke Smith discussed an array of progressive measures in his 1907 inaugural address. His speech, seen here in Document 6, makes clear how black disfranchisement, paradoxically, fit well with white progressives' views of reform. The Southern Sociological Congress was dedicated in 1912 to coordinating social reform efforts and provided a major organizational response for the Progressive movement. In its 1914 meeting members drafted a plan "The Solid South for a Better Nation," presented here as Document 7. In 1914 President Woodrow Wilson refused to endorse the Susan B. Anthony Amendment for woman suffrage. His refusal encouraged southern antisuffragists, who raised their cry of alarm, as seen in Document 8, by bringing in issues of race and memories of "black rule" during Reconstruction. The logical result of extending the franchise—in Texas, women could vote in the primaries in 1918—was for women to run for public office. Document 9 is a campaign broadside for Annie Webb Blanton, who ran for Texas state superintendent of public instruction in 1918 and won.

1. Booker T. Washington's Atlanta Exposition Address, 1895

Mr. President and Gentlemen of the Board of Directors and Citizens: One-third of the population of the South is of the Negro race. No enterprise seeking the material, civil, or moral welfare of this section can disregard this element of our population and reach the highest success. I but convey to you, Mr. President and Directors, the sentiment of the masses of my race when I say that in no way have the value and manhood of the American Negro been more fittingly and generously recognized than by the managers of this magnificent Exposition at every stage of its progress. It is a recognition that will do more to cement the friendship of the two races than any occurrence since the dawn of our freedom.

Not only this, but the opportunity here afforded will awaken among us a new era of industrial progress. Ignorant and inexperienced, it is not strange that in the first years of our new life we began at the top instead of at the bottom; that a seat in Congress or the state legislature was more sought than real estate or industrial skill; that the political convention or stump speaking had more attractions than starting a dairy farm or truck garden.

A ship lost at sea for many days suddenly sighted a friendly vessel. From the mast of the unfortunate vessel was seen a signal, "Water, water; we die of thirst!" The answer from the friendly vessel at once came back, "Cast down your bucket where you are." A second time the signal, "Water, water; send us water!" ran up from the distressed vessel and was answered, "Cast down your bucket where you are." And a third and fourth signal for water was answered, "Cast down your bucket where you are." The Captain of the distressed vessel, at last heeding the injunction, cast down his bucket, and it came up full of fresh, sparkling water from the mouth of the Amazon River. To those of my race who depend on bettering their condition in a foreign land or who underestimate the importance of cultivating friendly relations with the Southern white man, who is their next-door neighbor, I would say: "Cast down your bucket where you are"—cast it down in making friends in every manly way of the people of all races by whom we are surrounded.

Cast it down in agriculture, mechanics, in commerce, in domestic service, and in the professions. And in this connection it is well to bear in mind that whatever other sins the South may be called to bear, when it comes to business, pure and simple, it is in the South that the Negro is given a man's chance in the commercial world, and in nothing is this exposition more eloquent than in emphasizing this chance. Our greatest danger is that in the great leap from slavery to freedom we may overlook the fact that the masses of us are to live by the productions of our hands, and fail to keep in mind that we shall prosper in proportion as we learn to dignify and glorify comman labor and put brains and skill into the common occupations of life; shall prosper in proportion as we learn to draw the line between the superficial and the substantial, the ornamental

Booker T. Washington's Atlanta Exposition Address, 1895, from Booker T. Washington, *Up From Slavery*. pp. 127–131.

gewgaws of life and the useful. No race can prosper till it learns that there is as much dignity in tilling a field as in writing a poem. It is at the bottom of life we must begin, and not at the top. Nor should we permit our grievances to overshadow our opportunities.

To those of the white race who look to the incoming of those of foreign birth and strange tongue and habits for the prosperity of the South, were I permitted I would repeat what I say to my own race, "Cast down your bucket where you are." Cast it down among the 8 millions of Negroes whose habits you know, whose fidelity and love you have tested in days when to have proved treacherous meant the ruin of your firesides. Cast down your bucket among these people who have, without strikes and labor wars, tilled your fields, cleared your forests, builded your railroads and cities, and brought forth treasurers from the bowels of the earth, and helped make possible this magnificent representation of the progress of the South. Casting down your bucket among my people, helping and encouraging them as you are doing on these grounds, and to education of head, hand, and heart, you will find that they will buy your surplus land, make blossom the waste places in your fields, and run your factories. While doing this, you can be sure in the future, as in the past, that you and your families will be surrounded by the most patient, faithful, law-abiding, and unresentful people that the world has seen. As we have proved our loyalty to you in the past, in nursing your children, watching by the sickbed of your mothers and fathers, and often following them with tear-dimmed eyes to their graves, so in the future, in our humble way, we shall stand by you with a devotion that no foreigner can approach, ready to lay down our lives, if need be, in defense of yours, interlacing our industrial, commercial, civil, and religious life with yours in a way that shall make the interests of both races one. In all things that are purely social we can be as separate as the fingers, yet one as the hand in all things essential to mutual progress....

Nearly 16 millions of hands will aid you in pulling the load upward, or they will pull against you the load downward. We shall constitute one-third and more of the ignorance and crime of the South, or one-third its intelligence and progress; we shall contribute one-third to the business and industrial prosperity of the South, or we shall prove a veritable body of death, stagnating, depressing, retarding every effort to advance the body politic....

The wisest among my race understand that the agitation of questions of social equality is the extremest folly, and that progress in the enjoyment of all the privileges that will come to us must be the result of severe and constant struggle rather than of artificial forcing. No race that has anything to contribute to the markets of the world is long in any degree ostracized. It is important and right that all privileges of the law be ours, but it is vastly more important that we be prepared for the exercises of these privileges. The opportunity to earn a dollar in a factory just now is worth infinitely more than the opportunity to spend a dollar in an opera house.

In conclusion, may I repeat that nothing in thirty years has given us more hope and encouragement, and drawn us so near to you of the white race, as this opportunity offered by the exposition; and here bending, as it were, over the altar that represents the results of the struggles of your race and mine, both starting practically empty-handed three decades ago, I pledge that in your effort to work out the great and intricate problem which God has laid at the doors of the South, you shall have at all times the patient, sympathetic help of my race; only let this be constantly in mind, that, while from representations in these buildings of the product of field, of forest, of mine, of factory, letters, and art, much good will come, yet far above and beyond material benefits will be that higher good, that, let us pray God, will come, in a blotting out of sectional differences and racial animosities and suspicions, in a determination to administer absolute justice, in a willing obedience among all classes to the mandates of law. This, this, coupled with our material prosperity, will bring into our beloved South a new heaven and a new earth.

2. W. E. B. Du Bois Denounces Washington's Accommodationist Policies, 1903

Easily the most striking thing in the history of the American Negro since 1876 is the ascendancy of Mr. Booker T. Washington. It began at the time when war memories and ideals were rapidly passing; a day of astonishing commercial development was dawning; a sense of doubt and hesitation overtook the freedmen's sons,—then it was that his leading began. Mr. Washington came, with a simple definite programme, at the psychological moment when the nation was a little ashamed of having bestowed so much sentiment on Negroes, and was concentrating its energies on Dollars. His programme of industrial education, conciliation of the South, and submission and silence as to civil and political rights, was not wholly original; the Free Negroes from 1830 up to war-time had striven to build industrial schools, and the American Missionary Association had from the first taught various trades; and Price and others had sought a way of honorable alliance with the best of the Southerners. But Mr. Washington first indissolubly linked these things; he put enthusiasm, unlimited energy, and perfect faith into this programme, and changed it from a by-path into a veritable Way of Life. And the tale of the methods by which he did this is a fascinating study of human life.

It startled the nation to hear a Negro advocating such a programme after many decades of bitter complaint; it startled and won the applause of the South, it interested and won the admiration of the North; and after a confused murmur of protest, it silenced if it did not convert the Negroes themselves.

To gain the sympathy and coöperation of the various elements comprising the white South was Mr. Washington's first task; and this, at the time Tuskegee was founded, seemed, for a black man, well-nigh impossible. And yet ten years later it was done in the word spoken at Atlanta: "In all things purely social we can be as separate as the five fingers, and yet one as the hand in all things essential to mutual progress." This "Atlanta Compromise" is by all odds the most notable thing in Mr. Washington's career. The South interpreted it in different ways: the

Selected portions from Of Mr. Booker T. Washington and Others by W. E. B. DuBois.

radicals received it as a complete surrender of the demand for civil and political equality; the conservatives, as a generously conceived working basis for mutual understanding. So both approved it, and to-day its author is certainly the most distinguished Southerner since Jefferson Davis, and the one with the largest personal following....

So Mr. Washington's cult has gained unquestioning followers, his work has wonderfully prospered, his friends are legion, and his enemies are confounded. Today he stands as the one recognized spokesman of his ten million fellows, and one of the most notable figures in a nation of seventy millions. One hesitates, therefore, to criticise a life which, beginning with so little, has done so much. And yet the time is come when one may speak in all sincerity and utter courtesy of the mistakes and shortcomings of Mr. Washington's career, as well as of his triumphs, without being thought captious or envious, and without forgetting that it is easier to do ill than well in the world.

The criticism that has hitherto met Mr. Washington has not always been of this broad character. In the South especially has he had to walk warily to avoid the harshest judgments,—and naturally so, for he is dealing with the one subject of deepest sensitiveness to that section....

Among his own people, however, Mr. Washington has encountered the strongest and most lasting opposition, amounting at times to bitterness.... [T]here is among educated and thoughtful colored men in all parts of the land a feeling of deep regret, sorrow, and apprehension at the wide currency and ascendancy which some of Mr. Washington's theories have gained. These same men admire his sincerity of purpose, and are willing to forgive much to honest endeavor which is doing something worth the doing. They coöperate with Mr. Washington as far as they conscientiously can; and, indeed, it is no ordinary tribute to this man's tact and power that, steering as he must between so many diverse interests and opinions, he so largely retains the respect of all....

But Booker T. Washington arose as essentially the leader not of one race but of two,—a compromiser between the South, the North, and the Negro. Naturally the Negroes resented, at first bitterly, signs of compromise which surrendered their civil and political rights, even though this was to be exchanged for larger chances of economic development. The rich and dominating North, however, was not only weary of the race problem, but was investing largely in Southern enterprises, and welcomed any method of peaceful coöperation. Thus, by national opinion, the Negroes began to recognize Mr. Washington's leadership; and the voice of criticism was hushed.

Mr. Washington represents in Negro thought the old attitude of adjustment and submission; but adjustment at such a peculiar time as to make his programme unique. This is an age of unusual economic development, and Mr. Washington's programme naturally takes an economic cast, becoming a gospel of Work and Money to such an extent as apparently almost completely to overshadow the higher aims of life....

Mr. Washington distinctly asks that black people give up, at least for the present, three things,—

First, political power,

Second, insistence on civil rights,

Third, higher education of Negro youth,—and concentrate all their energies on industrial education, the accumulation of wealth, and the conciliation of the South. This policy has been courageously and insistently advocated for over fifteen years, and has been triumphant for perhaps ten years. As a result of this tender of the palm-branch, what has been the return? In these years there have occurred:

1. The disfranchisement of the Negro.
2. The legal creation of a distinct status of civil inferiority for the Negro.
3. The steady withdrawal of aid from institutions for the higher training of the Negro.

These movements are not, to be sure, direct results of Mr. Washington's teachings; but his propaganda has, without a shadow of doubt, helped their speedier accomplishment. The question then comes: Is it possible, and probable, that nine millions of men can make effective progress in economic lines if they are deprived of political rights, made a servile caste, and allowed only the most meagre chance for developing their exceptional men? If history and reason give any distinct answer to these questions, it is an emphatic *No.* And Mr. Washington thus faces the triple paradox of his career:

1. He is striving nobly to make Negro artisans business men and property-owners; but it is utterly impossible, under modern competitive methods, for workingmen and property-owners to defend their rights and exist without the right of suffrage.
2. He insists on thrift and self-respect, but at the same time counsels a silent submission to civic inferiority such as is bound to sap the manhood of any race in the long run.
3. He advocates common-school and industrial training, and depreciates institutions of higher learning; but neither the Negro common-schools, nor Tuskegee itself, could remain open a day were it not for teachers trained in Negro colleges, or trained by their graduates.

This triple paradox in Mr. Washington's position is the object of criticism by two classes of colored Americans. One class is spiritually descended from Toussaint the Savior, through Gabriel, Vesey, and Turner, and they represent the attitude of revolt and revenge; they hate the white South blindly and distrust the white race generally, and so far as they agree on definite action, think that the Negro's only hope lies in emigration beyond the borders of the United States. And yet, by the irony of fate, nothing has more effectually made this programme seem hopeless than the recent course of the United States toward weaker and darker peoples in the West Indies, Hawaii, and the Philippines,—for where in the world may we go and be safe from lying and brute force?

The other class of Negroes who cannot agree with Mr. Washington has hitherto said little aloud.... Such men feel in conscience bound to ask of this nation three things:

1. The right to vote.
2. Civic equality.
3. The education of youth according to ability.

They acknowledge Mr. Washington's invaluable service in counselling patience and courtesy in such demands; they do not ask that ignorant black men vote when ignorant whites are debarred, or that any reasonable restrictions in the suffrage should not be applied; they know that the low social level of the mass of the race is responsible for much discrimination against it, but they also know, and the nation knows, that relentless color-prejudice is more often a cause than a result of the Negro's degradation, they seek the abatement of this relic of barbarism, and not its systematic encouragement and pampering by all agencies of social power from the Associated Press to the Church of Christ. They advocate, with Mr. Washington, a broad system of Negro common schools supplemented by thorough industrial training; but they are surprised that a man of Mr. Washington's insight cannot see that no such educational system ever has rested or can rest on any other basis than that of the well-equipped college and university, and they insist that there is a demand for a few such institutions throughout the South to train the best of the Negro youth as teachers, professional men, and leaders.

... They do not expect that the free right to vote, to enjoy civic rights, and to be educated, will come in a moment; they do not expect to see the bias and prejudices of years disappear at the blast of a trumpet; but they are absolutely certain that the way for a people to gain their reasonable rights is not by voluntarily throwing them away and insisting that they do not want them; that the way for a people to gain respect is not by continually belittling and ridiculing themselves; that, on the contrary, Negroes must insist continually, in season and out of season, that voting is necessary to modern manhood, that color discrimination is barbarism, and that black boys need education as well as white boys.

3. Mary Church Terrell Speaks on the Role of Modern Woman, c. 1916

Mamie and I joined the City Federation [Charleston, S.C.] together. It was Mrs. Ida Green, wife of Reverend Nathaniel Green, Centenary's pastor, who organized the city. But it was Mrs. Mary Church Terrell who really brought the excitement to us. I'll never forget the night she spoke. It was at Mt. Zion A.M.E.

Church. And it seemed like everybody in Charleston got there early, then packed into the pews so tight until you had to put even the smallest purse on the floor, between your toes. In a short time, you could hardly turn your head to see who was behind you. And, with all the people, it was hot. Although you had a pasteboard fan in the hymnal rack in front of you, the people sat so close that you could only work it back and forth in front of you—side to side, you were liable to elbow your neighbor. That's to show you how the city turned out to hear this fine educator from Washington, D.C. We sat in the heat, dresses clinging to us, ladies' hats almost touching, fans just a-going—*flickflick-flickflick.* All of Charleston was waiting to hear what Mrs. Terrell would say about the role of the Modern Woman. Oh, my, when I saw her walk onto that podium in her pink evening dress and long white gloves, with her beautifully done hair, she *was* that Modern Woman. And when her voice went out over that huge crowd—no microphones back then—the fans stopped flicking. No one wanted to miss a word.

We have our own lives to lead, she told us. We are daughters, sisters, mothers, and wives. We must care for ourselves and rear our families, like all women. But we have more to do than other women. Those of us fortunate enough to have education must share it with the less fortunate of our race. We must go into our communities and improve them; we must go out into the nation and change it. Above all, we must organize ourselves as Negro women and work together. She told the story about a letter that a Southern white man sent to England, insulting us all, which was the cause of starting the Federation. "Let us turn in our numbers to face that white man and call him *liar,*" she said, and she had a wonderfully resonant voice. Every word could be heard clearly from the very front pew downstairs to the very last one in the gallery. When she raised her voice to say "LIAR," you could almost feel it on your skin.

She walked back and forth across the podium. In fact, she didn't walk, she *strode.* Regal, intelligent, powerful, reaching out from time to time with that long glove, she looked and sounded like the Modern Woman that she talked about. "And who were the Negro women who knew how to carry their burden in the heat of the day?" she asked looking right at this one and then right at that one in the audience. Harriet Tubman knew. Harriet wore a bandanna on her head and boots on her feet, a pistol on her hip and a rifle in her hand. Mrs. Terrell talked until we could almost see Harriet Tubman rescuing slaves right there and then, in front of our eyes. And then, what about Sojourner Truth, not armed with a rifle or a pistol but with the truth spoken:

> Ain't I a woman?
> That man over there says, a woman needs to be helped into carriages and lifted over ditches, and to be given the best place everywhere. Nobody ever helped me into a carriage. I rode in one mule wagon and enjoyed it. I got out in the muddy places and jumped over. Ain't I a woman?

She went on quoting and telling about the great women who'd done their work in the yesteryears. Well now, what about us, the women who were sitting in the Mt. Zion Church, the women coming after our great ancestresses? "WHO OF YOU KNOW HOW TO CARRY YOUR BURDEN IN THE HEAT OF THE DAY?" Mrs. Terrell demanded. And then she stopped talking altogether for a good little while, time enough for everybody there to ask herself, "Do I?" Then she told us a quiet "Good evening." The women hardly knew what to do when Mrs. Terrell got through speaking. We felt so stirred up, nobody wanted to wait till morning to pick up our burden again. Everywhere you might look, there was something to do.

4. Charles W. Dabney Proposes Change for the Public Schools in the South, 1901

The South waiting for education.—Everything in the South waits upon the general education of the people. Industrial development waits for more captains of industry, superintendents of factories, and skilled workmen. The natural resources of the Southern States are great and varied; capital in abundance is ready for investment in them; only men are wanted who can plan, organize, and direct. This is true of all our industries, even of our agriculture. A director of an Agricultural Experiment Station says: "We can do little more to improve the agricultural methods of the farmers until a new generation is educated, who can read our bulletins, apply scientific methods, and keep simple farm accounts."

The colleges for liberal, and institutions for scientific and technical education as well, wait for preparatory schools and high schools. With the same population there were during 1899 in all collegiate and graduate courses in liberal arts only 16,351 students in the Southern States against 30,741 in the North Central States, where they have public high schools. A system of public education is a pyramid; the primary schools are the foundation; the secondary schools and high schools, the normal schools, the technical schools, and the colleges carry up the structure step by step, and the university is the capstone. Our old system of education in the South, so far as we had any, was a Greek column; the university was a beautiful carved capitol of classic design, supported by a slender column of literary colleges and academies, which stood upon a narrow and unsubstantial base of private schools.

The effects of war and reconstruction.—Good government in town and State and intelligent action in national affairs are impossible without educated voters. Pettifogging politicians, selfish demagogues, and corrupt lobbyists will continue to control our legislative and county governments until a majority of the voters can read and think for themselves. The Republic must have an educated citizenship or go down. The question of educating all the people is more critically important to the South than it is to the remainder of the nation. We must educate all our people, blacks as well as whites, or the South will become a dependent province instead of a coordinate portion of the nation.... The only remedy for the political situation in the South is to be found in public education....

Charles W. Dabney, "The Public School Problem in the South," from Capon Springs Conference for Education in the South Proceedings, Raleigh, 1901.

In North Carolina only 30 per cent of the children are in daily attendance upon the schools; less than 60 per cent are enrolled in them, and the annual school term is less than seventy-one days. There are in North Carolina on the average 65 enrolled pupils to each school and 54 to each teacher. The schoolhouse which is supposed to shelter the children is valued at $179.60, and the teacher who has charge of them receives $23.36 a month for seventy and eight-tenths days, or about $77 for the term. The amount expended per year per pupil in attendance is but $1.34, which is only 51 cents per capita. In Tennessee less than half of the children between 5 and 18 years of age are in daily attendance; only 70 per cent are enrolled in the schools; the school term is only ninety-six days, and the enrolled pupils attend an average of only sixty-three days in the year. In Tennessee they are taught in a schoolhouse which cost $426, by teachers who receive an annual salary of $134. The total expense per pupil is $5.17 a year, which is only 87 cents per capita....

The laws designed to disfranchise illiterate whites and blacks are likely to have a beneficent influence upon the educational situation in the South. Such laws, if impartially drawn and fairly carried out, will do almost as much good in promoting the elementary education, of males at least, as compulsory laws. The uneducated people of the Southern States, both whites and blacks, esteem their ballot to a degree that is almost ridiculous. In States like North Carolina, where the educational qualification has been applied, the colored people are already showing an earnest desire to get the little education required to qualify as voters. But these laws, even at best, touch only one-half the population. The only perfect solution of the problem is a compulsory attendance law carefully designed to reach every healthy child. We must put all the children in school, but before we do this we must have the schools and the teachers....

We should consider the negro as a man to be educated for work, independence, and citizenship like other men. Everything I have said applies to him, therefore, just as it does to the white man. The negro is in the South to stay—he is a necessity for Southern industries—and the Southern people must educate and so elevate him or he will drag them down. The human race is an organism, all its members being bound together by natural affinities and ministering to each other by natural law. If history, philosophy, and revelation teach us anything it is the solidarity of all mankind, that "no man liveth to himself" and "no man dieth to himself," but that we are each "his brother's keeper."...

But we must use common sense in the education of the negro. We must recognize in all its relations that momentous fact that the negro is a child race, at least two thousand years behind the Anglo-Saxon in its development, and that like all other races it must work out its own salvation by practicing the industrial arts, and becoming independent and self-supporting. Nothing is more ridiculous than the programme of the good religious people from the North who insist upon teaching Latin, Greek, and philosophy to the negro boys who come to their schools. Many of our Southern States make a similar mistake in trying to enforce in the schools of the black districts courses of study laid down for whites.

5. Edgar Gardner Murphy Denounces Child Labor in Alabama, 1901

A Reply to the Committee

On Wednesday, October 30, the following communication appeared in the *Evening Transcript* of Boston, Massachusetts.

To the Editor of the *Transcript:* ...

As treasurer of a mill in that State [Alabama], erected by Northern capital, I am interested in the subject [of child labor]. From the starting of our mill, I have never been South without protesting to the agent, and overseer of spinning (the only department in which small help can be employed), against allowing children under twelve years of age to come into the mill, as I did not consider them intelligent enough to do good work. On a visit last June, annoyed that my instructions were not more carefully observed, before leaving I wrote the agent a letter of which the following is a copy:—

"Every time I visit this mill, I am impressed with the fact that it is a great mistake to employ small help in the spinning room. Not only is it wrong from a humanitarian standpoint but it entails an absolute loss to the mill.... I again express the wish that you prevent the overseer, as far as possible, from employing children under twelve years of age....

In defence of our officials, it is doubtless true that the trouble comes largely from the parents, who make every effort to get their children into the mill, and often because of refusal, take their families containing needed workers, to other mills, where no objection is made to the employment of children....

Now in regard to the attempted legislation of last winter: The labor organizations at the North imported from England [Irene Ashby] a very bright and skilful [*sic*] female labor agitator and sent her to Alabama. She held meetings at central points, and when the Legislature convened appeared at Montgomery with her following, and a bill against employing children was promptly introduced. The manufacturers and other business men of Alabama resented this outside interference, well knowing the source from which it came, and they were also aware that manufacturers at the North were being solicited for funds with which to incite labor troubles in the South.

As they recognized that this bill was only the entering wedge, they determined that action must come from within the State, and not outside. They also felt that the adjoining State of Georgia, having double the number of spindles, should act first. With these considerations in mind, the manufacturers selected among others our agent, a native Alabamian, to appear before the legislative committee, with the result that the bill was defeated. I think it may be said with truth, that the interference of Northern labor agitators is retarding much needed legislation in all the manufacturing States of the South.

Edgar Gardner Murphy, *Child Labor in Alabama: An Appeal to the People and Press of New England with a Resulting Correspondence,* as appeared in the *Evening Transcript* of Boston, Massachusetts, October 30, 1901.

As to our mill and the little town of 2300 people which has grown up around it, there is nothing within the mill or without, of which any citizen ... need be ashamed.... From the inception of this enterprise, the purpose has been to build up a model town that should be an object lesson to the South, and we are assured that its influences have been helpful. In addition to a school supported by public tax, the company has always carried on a school of its own, with an experienced and devoted teacher, who has been instructed to make special effort to get in the young children, and thus allure them from the mill. We have built and have in operation a beautiful library—the first erected for this special purpose in the State of Alabama, and we have a church building which would be an ornament in any village of New England, and is in itself an education to our people. We are now building a modern schoolhouse from plans by Boston architects which will accommodate all the children of our community. These are a few of the things we have done and are doing, in our effort to meet the responsibility we have assumed, in dealing with a class of people who have some most excellent traits, and who appeal to us strongly, because many of them have hitherto been deprived of needed comforts and largely of elementary advantages....

J. Howard Nichols,
Treasurer Alabama City Mill, Alabama

A Rejoinder from Alabama

On the afternoon of November 2d, Mr. Edgar Gardner Murphy, of Montgomery, Alabama, the chairman of the Alabama Child-labor Committee, received a copy of the above letter. Mr. Murphy at once wrote and forwarded the following rejoinder:—

To the Editor of the *Transcript*:...

I thank you for publishing Mr. Nichols's letter. The well-known citizens of Alabama with whom I have the honor to be associated, have welcomed the discussion of this subject, and they desire the frankest and fullest showing of the facts.

I note, however, with some amazement, that the Treasurer of the Alabama City Mill begins his argument by conceding the two fundamental principles for which we are contending—the social wrong and the economic error of child labor under twelve. He declares that from the starting of that mill he has repeatedly protested against the use of children under this age and that last June he wrote to his local agent that the employment of such help "is not only wrong from a humanitarian standpoint, but it entails an absolute loss to the mill." Now this is substantially, and in admirable form, the whole case of our committee.

Yet what must be our added amazement when, in the next paragraph but one, we read the further admission that, in order to continue this economic and social wrong and in order to defeat a simple and effective remedy for this wrong, the salaried representative of his own mill, during the preceding February, had appeared in this city before our Legislature, in aggressive and persistent antagonism to the protection of little children under twelve! This, in the teeth of protests which Mr. Nichols declares he has made since "the starting" of his mill. Who, then, is the responsible representative of the actual policy of the Alabama City Mill—its Treasurer or its representative before the Legislature? Or is the policy of the mill a policy which concedes the principle, only to deny the principle its fruit? If this be the true interpretation of the conditions, what are we to say to the explanations which are suggested; explanations offered "in defence of our [Mr. Nichols's] officials."

Mr. Nichols assures us that the officials have been put under grave pressure from the parents. Let us concede that this is true. Yet Mr. Nichols himself is not satisfied with this "defence," and he declares wisely and bravely that his officials must take their stand against the pressure of unscrupulous and idle parents. His agents must resist the threat of such parents to leave the Alabama City Mill for mills having a lower standard of employment. Does not Mr. Nichols see that our legislation was precisely directed toward ending this pressure, toward breaking up this ignoble competition, and toward the preservation of the standard of employment which he professes? There could be no pressure to withdraw the children and to enter them in other mills, if such labor were everywhere prohibited by statute. But we are grateful to Mr. Nichols for his declaration. And yet, is he ignorant of the need of legislation in the State at large? His very argument is a confession of knowledge. If the Alabama City Mill is fairly represented by the profession of Mr. Nichols, why should the paid and delegated agent of that mill labor here for weeks to thwart a simple legislative remedy for the abuses he deplores?

Is it sufficient for your correspondent to declare that this legislation met with local opposition simply because such reforms should come "from within the State and not from outside"? ... When the younger children are thrust into the labor market in competition with the adult, they contend that the adult wage is everywhere affected. But the agent of the Federation of Labor—earnest and devoted woman that she is—did her work, not in the spirit of interference, but in the spirit of helpfulness. She was not responsible for the beginning of the agitation. The demand for this legislative protection of our children was made by the Minister's Union of Montgomery and by the Woman's Christian Temperance Union of Alabama, before she was ever heard of in the South.

Nothing could be more baseless than the assumption that our local effort for reforms is due to outside forces. But if it were—what of it? There is at stake here to-day the welfare of our little children, the happiness and efficiency of our future operatives; the moral standard of our economic life; and this committee frankly proposes, in every honorable way, to secure all the aid, from every quarter of our common country, which we can possibly command. The criticism of such a policy is a little out of place from the representative of a mill here operated upon investments from Massachusetts....

Mr. Nichols also declares that our reform measure was defeated because it was believed to be "the entering wedge" of other troublesome labor legislation. We must not protect our little children under twelve, we must not do a compassionate and reasonable thing, because, forsooth, somebody might then demand an inconsiderate and unreasonable thing! Do the corporate interests in Alabama wish to predicate their liberties upon such an argument? ...

That mill, with its great influences, has led the fight in this State against the protection of our factory children. Will it continue to represent a policy of opposition and reaction? Or, will it represent a policy of coöperation and of progress? ...

Edgar Gardner Murphy
Montgomery, Ala., November 2, 1901.

6. Hoke Smith's Gubernatorial Address, Touches on Education 1907

A government fails to reach its highest sphere if it does not protect the right of property, and at the same time constantly broaden opportunities for mental, moral and financial growth to the less fortunate.

A government by the people furnishes the only hope for such a result. To make it sure, ballot boxes must be pure, and legislative halls must be free from the influences of predatory wealth....

Education

The chief object of government should be to prevent special privileges and to give to all equal rights and opportunities. To this the men and women of Georgia are entitled, and you are preparing legislation which insures it to them.

The relation of the state to the children goes much further. It is the duty of the state to see that the children are given an opportunity for all preparation which their probable life work requires.

Education from books alone is not always of much value. It should be accompanied with practical training, having in view the future of the child.

Negro Children

Let me refer to the negro children in this connection. Any plan for the negroes which fails to recognize the difference between the white and black races will fail. The honest student of history knows that the negro had full opportunity for generations to develop before the days of slavery; that the negro race was improved by slavery, and that the majority of the negroes in this state have ceased to improve since slavery. Few have been helped by learning from books. All have been helped who have been taught or made to work.

It is not the difference of environment; it is the difference of race, deep seated, inherited for generations and generations through hundreds of years.

The large majority of negroes are incapable of anything but manual labor and many taught from books spurn labor and live in idleness. Few negroes are willing to work beyond the procurement of the hardest necessities of life.

The negro child should be taught manual labor and how to live. The negro teacher should be selected less by book than by character examinations.

Hoke Smith's gubernatorial address: *Journal of the Senate of the State of Georgia, Executive Minutes of Georgia* (Atlanta: Department of Archives and History, 1907), pp. 3–14.

The negro school to be useful needs less books and more work. I favor a complete change in the examination of teachers for the negro schools, and for them a different plan of management; I would have the schools help the negro, not injure him....

White Children

The white children of Georgia are prepared for the highest development: but I do not mean by this that they will necessarily obtain it through literary and classical studies.

For them it is at this time most important to improve the manual training and agricultural schools, and the rural schools. With a view to progress, I ask you to consider the unorganized condition of the educational work of Georgia....

University and Branches

We must require the corporations in Georgia to pay their just taxes. We must equalize taxation among all the people of Georgia. Who will object to paying taxes when he realizes that the money is to be intelligently spent for the children of the state? Instead of a burden, it should be a great privilege to help in so noble a cause.

7. The Southern Sociological Congress Creates an Agenda for Reforming the South, 1914

The Social Program of the Congress

The Southern Sociological Congress stands:

For the abolition of convict lease and contract systems, and for the adoption of modern principles of prison reform.

For the extension and improvement of juvenile courts and juvenile reformatories.

For the proper care and treatment of defectives, the blind, the deaf, the insane, the epileptic, and the feeble-minded.

For the recognition of the relation of alcoholism to disease, to crime, to pauperism, and to vice, and for the adoption of appropriate preventive measures.

For the adoption of uniform laws of the highest standards concerning marriage and divorce.

For the adoption of the uniform law on vital statistics.

For the abolition of child labor by the enactment of the uniform child labor law.

For the enactment of school attendance laws, that the reproach of the greatest degree of illiteracy may be removed from our section.

For the suppression of prostitution.

This document can be found in James E. McCulloch, ed., *Battling for Social Betterment: Southern Sociological Congress, Memphis, Tennessee, May 6–10, 1914* (Nashville: Southern Sociological Congress, 1914), p. 9.

For the solving of the race question in a spirit of helpfulness to the negro and of equal justice to both races.

For the closest co-operation between the Church and all social agencies for the securing of these results.

8. Antisuffragists Raise the Race Issue, c. 1915

Men of the South: heed not the song of the suffrage siren! Seal your ears against her vocal wiles. For, no matter how sweetly she may proclaim the advantages of female franchise,—*Remember,* that *Woman Suffrage* means a reopening of the entire *Negro* Suffrage question; loss of State [*sic*] rights; and another period of reconstruction horrors, which will introduce a set of female carpetbaggers as bad as their male prototypes of the sixties. *Do Not Jeopardize* the present prosperity of your sovereign States, which was so dearly bought by the blood of your fathers and the tears of your mothers, by again raising an issue which has already been adjusted at so great a cost. Nothing can be gained by woman suffrage and much may be lost.

9. Annie Webb Blanton Runs for State Office, 1918

Concerning the Race for State Superintendent of Public Instruction

Why you SHOULD vote for Annie Webb Blanton for State Superintendent of Public Instruction.

1. She has actually taught in every grade of the public schools, rural and urban, and has first-hand practical knowledge of their needs.
2. For seventeen years she has been engaged in training teachers in the North Texas Normal College at Denton.
3. She is a graduate of the University of Texas, and has done graduate work in the University of Chicago.
4. She has the absolute confidence of the teachers of the State, as was evidenced when they elected her, by an overwhelming majority, president of the State Teachers Association, the only woman accorded that honor in the last 39 years.
5. She has wonderful natural endowment, is a born leader, a splendid public speaker, whom Mr. Doughty—her opponent—steadfastly, and perhaps intelligently, refuses to meet on the stump during this campaign, although she challenged him to do so.

This document can be found in the Romulus A. Nunn Papers, North Carolina Division of Archives and History, Raleigh, North Carolina.

This document can be found in the Annie Webb Blanton Vertical File, Center for American History, University of Texas at Austin.

6. She will remove the State Department of Education from connection with every form of machine politics, and put the great Public School system of Texas solidly in the "American" column. She has no hyphenated connections.

Why you SHOULD NOT vote for W. F. Doughty for State Superintendent of Public Instruction.

1. He was on the "Red" list of the breweries—that is, O. K.'d by them, which secret alliance was disclosed on pages 1547–1559, record of the Sulphur Springs brewery case.
2. The breweries were allied with the German-American Alliance, whose declared purpose was to control the public schools and Universities in the interest of German *kultur*.
3. If he was acceptable to the breweries, was he not acceptable to the German-American Alliance? (See U. S. Senate Subcommittee report, Sixty-fifth Congress, page 647).
4. He appeared on the platform with James E. Ferguson when Ferguson called the University of Texas professors a lot of "two-bit" thieves, endorsing by his silence this statement, which he knew to be slanderous, for he is himself a graduate of the University and had for years been befriended, helped, and taught by these same men, whom he suffered to be called "two-bit thieves," when he knew them to be honest and upright. The head of the educational interests of Texas should be a person with enough nerve to defend its educational institutions from slander.
5. Declaring that he has had the "privilege" of serving with the "honorable" James E. Ferguson, he refuses to make a public statement of his position on the Ferguson issue, in spite of the impeachment and conviction of the former governor [Ferguson].

ESSAYS

In the first essay, historian William A. Link finds more paradox than promise in the southern progressive movement. He takes the view that southern urban reformers and northern philanthropists wanted to help enact reforms in such areas as education, public health, prohibition, child labor, and woman suffrage, but they encountered traditionalists whose values were informed by "an intensely localistic, rural participatory democracy." Reformers discovered that by using revival techniques to counter rural resistance, they were able to win the cooperation of some southern individualists. Reformers, ironically, believed that disfranchisement and segregation would eventually benefit African Americans through such programs as "industrial education" and funds from northern philanthropists. One of the areas of most marked reform in the South came not so much through state action but through federal law. When the nation ratified the

Nineteenth Amendment, granting women the right to vote, many southern women rose to embrace this civic duty and, to the surprise of male politicians, challenged their way of doing politics. Lorraine Gates Schuyler argues that the woman suffrage amendment forced southern men to change "the look and feel of southern politics" with cleaned up campaigns, decent polling places, honest elections, and more inclusive platforms. Woman suffrage "undermined the hierarchies of gender and race" as a new generation of African Americans followed with their own demands to end disfranchisement measures.

The Paradox of Southern Progressivism

WILLIAM A. LINK

In 1946, a young scholar of southern history barely out of graduate school advanced a reinterpretation of the Progressive Era South. The stereotype of the region as so "unbelievably backward, economically, politically, and socially" as to be incapable of sustaining any liberal reform movement needed exploding, wrote Arthur S. Link. A common objective of "greater economic, political, and social justice" united southern social reformers as diverse as Grangers, Greenbackers, Alliancemen, and Populists; along with early twentieth-century progressives, they sought to restructure the political system, stabilize the social structure, and extend popular control over the economy through the extension of the role of government. Link's reformers were governors, congressmen, legislators, and newspaper editors, whose primary objectives included state regulation and restrictions on the power of party machines; southern progressivism's culmination came during the presidency of Woodrow Wilson.

Although an admiring portrait, Link's assessment acknowledged "serious deficiencies." Committed to political reform, progressives were concerned neither with such deeply rooted social problems as the increase in farm tenancy nor with, implicitly, meaningful economic change for the mass of southerners. Similarly, they ignored the plight of blacks; while they condemned lynching,  they opposed black political rights. "As far as progressive democracy went in the South," he concluded, "it was progressive democracy for the white man." Still, the reformers came out well; according to Link, they articulated the attitudes and political aspirations of most white southerners and led the fight against "conservatives and reactionaries."

Four and a half decades after the publication of this seminal article, scholars continue to debate the origins, motivations, and consequences of reform along the lines just described. By including the category of social alongside political reform, subsequent historians of the Progressive Era South filled in the details of southern progressivism which Link initially sketched out. Still, by focusing on the narrow issue of whether reformers' stated motivations were genuine, the scholarly debate remains limited. Some historians, generally optimistic about the causes and consequences of progressivism, have stressed that reformers were motivated by humanitarian impulses and wanted, as Hugh C. Bailey enthusiastically writes, to "restore the mythical equality of opportunity which supposedly existed in the society of the past." Most of these optimists, like Link, have qualified their praise, but they agree that the reformers, impelled by humanitarianism and their view of regional progress, acted in accord with their announced objectives. Other historians paint a more pessimistic portrait. In his classic *Origins of the New South, 1877–1913,* C. Vann Woodward characterized southern reform as a "paradoxical combination of white supremacy and progressivism" which had little relevance for the "political aspirations and deeper needs of the mass of the people"; despite the heralding of a new era of "washed, wormed, and weeviled Southerners," the condition of the rural masses probably worsened during the Progressive Era.

Recently historians have grown even more critical. David L. Carlton contends that South Carolina child-labor reformers actually sought to extend middle-class control over mill families; their main objective was class stabilization. James L. Leloudis II asserts that while women school reformers in North Carolina espoused a humanitarian rhetoric, their goal was the molding of children into a manageable labor force. Extending this argument to the role of northern philanthropists in southern black education, James D. Anderson argues that their primary motivation in promoting "industrial" education was to develop an "economically efficient and politically stable" southern social system. Taken together, these pessimist historians have turned the optimist orthodoxy about progressivism on its head. Whereas optimist historians take reformers at their word and portray them as well-intentioned, democratic, and responding to documented social problems, pessimists assert that a mask of liberal rhetoric hid darker purposes and intentions. As J. Morgan Kousser writes, reality "differed ... from the 'progressive' myth," for progressivism was for middle-class whites only.

This essay suggests another model for understanding southern progressivism. Most scholars have examined only one part of southern progressivism—the reformers themselves—while they have neglected the social contexts that reformers encountered. They have assumed, incorrectly, that reform was primarily a personal, political process which can best be comprehended in the setting of elections, legislatures, and governors. Whereas scholars' emphases have been political and biographical, reform had its most important impact outside of politics: on processes, institutions, and communities. Although the traditional approach makes most rural southerners passive participants in reform, they in fact played a dynamic role.

In order to understand the full consequences of reform, we need to know less about the problematic category of motivation and more about reform's social context. In particular, we need to comprehend how social policy functioned in pre-bureaucratic culture; why reformers came to see traditional social policy as inadequate; with what consequences they began to transform it in the early decades of the twentieth century; and, perhaps most important, how rural southerners responded to these policy changes.

Pre-bureaucratic Social Policy and the Emergence of Reform ...

In the rural South, centuries of isolation helped to form a restrictive definition of community. Localism fused with a rural republican ideology that articulated autonomy and self-reliance, stressed the dangers of concentrated power, and provided a political language for suspicion of outsiders. Southerners were the "historical partisans of personal liberty," explained one observer, and they were "naturally opposed to sumptuary laws of any kind."

Two disparate instances of social policy, public health and liquor licensing, supply examples of the decentralized but also democratic style of pre-bureaucratic governance. Into the early years of the twentieth century, poor sanitary conditions produced major outbreaks of cholera, yellow fever, and smallpox. Mosquitoes, one of many menaces, made nights in Texas "memorable," a nineteenth century visitor remembered; there was no escape from them "except to hang yourself or run away." A Republican governor in Reconstruction Mississippi found his room "full of the hungriest, blood thirstiest crew of mosquitoes that ever presented a bill to me." Going from room to room to escape, he finally slept in his boots to protect his ankles and feet.

Southern public health bureaucracies, despite efforts after Reconstruction to strengthen them, proved nearly powerless in practice....

Even after the discovery of microscopic origins of disease revolutionized public health in the late decades of the nineteenth century, southern state health officials received necessary funds and political support only after epidemic disease had begun its periodic sweep. Few late nineteenth- and early twentieth-century state health officers could do more than gather scattered, inaccurate statistics and make pronouncements about the general condition of health. Even if localities did request help, state health officials were effectively limited to advice. When physicians in a western North Carolina county requested that the state test local dairies, the state health officer replied with undisguised sarcasm that, with an annual budget of only $2,000, he could ill afford "to indulge in 'luxuries.' "

An even more serious problem was the lack of effective local health organization. Although most states provided for some form of local health organizations, in practice these were informal and almost completely powerless. In most states, local health officials performed few duties: periodically visiting the jail, fumigating the courthouse, and examining lunatics—for a minimal salary. They exercised supervisory powers over disease only in times of epidemic....

Local health officials also knew that little support would be forthcoming from state officials. Florida's health bureaucracy came into existence after a devastating outbreak of yellow fever in 1888, when the state legislature provided a State Board of Health with an assured revenue and with authority to restrict the inflow of yellow fever and smallpox from the Caribbean. Even so, the Board's actual power to aid local health officials—and to engage in any form of preventive public health—remained sharply curtailed....

Government's power over alcohol consumption provides another example of the limited scope of pre-bureaucratic southern social policy. The spread of the market economy during the nineteenth century spurred the commercialization of alcohol production, especially of corn whiskey; rising consumption, and excessive drinking, were commonplace in nineteenth-century southern life. In antebellum Mississippi, not only was it common to see "one who reeled as he walked," but only if Mississippians "lay and wallowed" were they regarded as drunk. Despite overdrinking, state and local governments before about 1905 avoided assuming a regulatory function over the distribution, sale, or consumption of alcohol. Although local option spread across the rural South in the post-Reconstruction period, illegal saloons, or "blind tigers," and bootleggers violated the law almost routinely, while federal internal revenue agents regularly collected taxes from dry counties in the South....

Lacking any tradition of state intervention, southern state and local administrators were uniformly unsuccessful in constructing an effective bureaucracy. Instead, local communities held the upper hand.... [S]outherners, white and black, were far from passive on the subject of governance. Because of the strength of community power, social policy in the nineteenth century remained decentralized and always required the approval of local communities.

Set in this social context, the emergence of southern progressivism takes on new significance. What reformers often portrayed as problems were actually social and political conditions long taken for granted. What reformers lamented as a decline in "community" was a contentious, intensely localistic, rural participatory democracy. Their prescription for social improvement and the means of enforcing it ran squarely into strong southern traditions of personal liberty and fear of and hostility toward outside intrusions.

If southern social reformers possessed a common characteristic, it was the belief that their region had undergone a serious crisis in the late decades of the nineteenth century and that it faced renewed crises in the near future. To many, the problems were primarily moral rather than political or social, and southern progressivism drew from a grass-roots swell of moral reformers. Beginning in the 1880s, evangelical churchmen began to mobilize against what they perceived as increasing secularization and moral decline in southern society. Post-Reconstruction churchmen witnessed rapid social change that seemed to erode social, racial, and gender order. Assertive children and adolescents, the rising incidence of divorce, and urban-centered evils like dancing, card-playing, theater, and, above all, prostitution, all indicated a moral order in decline.

The menace of alcohol, which embodied both individual and community corruption, became the central issue for moral reformers. To reformers, the connections between the saloon and moral decline were obvious, but they went a step further by linking corruption and moral decline to a passive social policy....

Near the turn of the twentieth century, reformers began to criticize and publicize what they considered evils in existing southern social and political institutions. The national popular press portrayed the South as a problem in need of solution.... The South retained a large, mobile, and ever-increasing rural population that would remain its majority well into the twentieth century. Social reformers in the North and Midwest addressed problems of rapid industrialization and the social and economic change that came with it. Not so with southern social critics. They believed that their social crisis came from underdevelopment and poverty, and their solutions were aimed at modernizing an entire people and an entire society. In the South, explained rural sociologist Eugene Cunningham Branson in 1902, isolation and poverty caused "social degeneracy and decay." To avoid stagnation and eventual social and political instability, reformers believed that the South's entrenched patterns of individual and community conduct needed to change. They favored not only expanding railroad and hard-surfaced transportation to the hinterlands, but also extending the values of the outside world: an outward-directed standard of conduct and adherence to a modernized, cohesive "community." In advocating these changes, reformers clashed with rural precepts of personal honor, individualism, and community control that were cardinal principles of the nineteenth-century South. Thus establishing a refashioned notion of community with reinvigorated institutions ultimately meant wrenching those institutions from their social context.

Social reformers inaugurated their assault on traditional social policy with evangelical-style crusades. The first such crusade began in 1901, when reformers established the Southern Education Board (SEB) to coordinate a regional public-school campaign. Other crusades followed: a long campaign, beginning about 1902, to institute prohibition, first by state legislation, then by state constitutional amendment, and finally by federal constitutional amendment; a campaign, organized in 1904, to limit or eliminate child labor in factories; a campaign, inaugurated in 1909, to eradicate hookworm disease; and a campaign, which began in the South in the same year, to grant women the right to vote.

These crusades were closely connected. Educational reform attracted a variety of reformers who saw the schools as vehicles of wider societal changes and who later applied the methods of the educational crusade to other reform campaigns. Edgar Gardner Murphy, executive secretary of the SEB, spearheaded the child-labor crusade; Madeline McDowell Breckinridge, a veteran of Kentucky school reform, became a leading regional and national suffragist; and Wickliffe Rose, a Tennessee university professor and educational reformer, later headed the hookworm crusade and the Rockefeller Foundation's International Health Board.

Studies of southern progressivism have said little about the organizational bases of these crusades and how they mobilized public opinion and translated a crusade into long-term social policies. As several historians have suggested recently, trends in American Protestantism strongly influenced progressive reform, and, in the South, this was nowhere more apparent than in the crusades' style, organization, and objectives. Reformers, themselves suffused with evangelical values, adopted the technique and approach of the religious revival. Like the revival, the reform crusades sought to move public opinion toward a dramatic conviction of social sin. In the case of the educational crusade, the objective was public support for schools and higher local taxes. In the case of the hookworm crusade, the reformers sought to alter public attitudes about public health so as to make parasitic infection impossible.

Careful advance preparations, including consultation with local leaders, assured success and public approval for the crusades. An example of thorough preparation modeled on evangelical methods comes from the Rockefeller Sanitary Commission, which was created in 1909 with a million-dollar endowment and led a five-year crusade to eradicate hookworm in the South. The commission's Administrative Secretary, Wickliffe Rose, endorsed a program of county dispensaries, traveling clinics that treated hookworm sufferers and preached the virtues of sanitation.

Rockefeller operatives laid a solid groundwork for each county crusade. They persuaded prominent citizens to endorse the dispensary and then organized a large delegation to meet with local officials to urge them to appropriate money for the dispensary. Success also depended on a massive publicity campaign, with printed placards and handbills announcing the dispensary and warning of the dangers of hookworms. "Parents who do not use this opportunity to rid their children of this dreaded-disease," read one placard in Alamance County, North Carolina, stood "squarely across their offspring's future, condemning them of times to an early death or a life of misery." These methods enabled the crusaders to reap a harvest of heavy turnout and public approbation.

Among the most sophisticated employers of these evangelical-style methods were the prohibitionists, who conducted their campaign under the auspices of the Anti-Saloon League (ASL). Organized nationally in 1895, the ASL began to penetrate the South after the turn of the century. The league organized state chapters which conducted local campaigns and lobbied state legislatures. Like hookworm campaigners, ASL prohibitionists emphasized advanced preparation and publicity. Relying on donations from local churches, the Virginia league—like all the ASL state chapters, an interdenominational coalition—had an operating budget of $16,000 by 1906, only five years after its founding. As did other southern prohibitionists, the Virginia reformers used these funds to develop a sophisticated system of publicity.

Examples abound of the staged preparation of early twentieth-century reform crusades....

The centerpiece of all these crusades, as for nineteenth-century revivalists, was a public event designed to reverse popular attitudes. Crusaders spread the word through familiar means: a courthouse meeting, often held under a tent, before throngs streaming in from adjoining rural areas. During the early years of the crusade, educational rallies coincided with the visits of outside speakers; during the later years, local school improvement leagues, led and run by women, orchestrated the rallies. The results were often dramatic. Wickliffe Rose described a typical scene at a hookworm dispensary held in Sampson County, North Carolina. "As we neared the place," he wrote, "we met a line of buggies and wagons with whole families coming away; ... a hundred or more people of both sexes and of all ages [were] waiting for attention."

By the time southern suffragists emerged after 1910, these crusading techniques were well established. Like the other reformers, suffragists employed public events to rally public opinion behind the cause. The suffrage crusaders often organized parades which became, in the setting of southern towns, a startling dramatization of feminine assertiveness. The early suffrage parades occurred more or less spontaneously. Elisabeth Perry Collins remembered that suffragists in Greenville, South Carolina, attempted to join a community parade but were greeted by jeers and taunts. Lila Meade Valentine similarly remembered that it was "considered indecent for women to speak in public" and "to march in processions with their brothers." Yet parades, and other public suffrage demonstrations, soon became commonplace across the South.

Like other crusaders, suffragists sent out visiting speakers, who usually made their addresses at county seats. In some localities, suffragists organized "suffrage schools," which invited speakers and distributed suffragist literature. "Suffrage speakers have been present at the State Fair, most of the County Fairs, Farmers' meetings, and many picnics and other public gatherings and have aided greatly in extending the suffrage 'gospel,'" reported a Virginia suffragist in 1915. The most successful of these meetings featured speeches by suffragists of noted oratorical ability and statewide reputation, such as Lila Meade Valentine of Virginia or Madeline McDowell Breckinridge of Kentucky....

The chief object of the reform revival became a kind of conversion experience through which collective public opinion radically recast its attitudes. The reformers' confidence in revival-based reform was not just based on its organizational style; they were convinced that reform would come suddenly. As in a revival, popular enthusiasm was carefully managed, staged, and manipulated....

By reaching out to public opinion in terms which rural southerners easily comprehended, the crusades reaped a full harvest. Their success provides additional evidence that the mass of southerners, far from passive objects of reform, performed an active role. Without the popular enthusiasm generated by the campaigns, it seems unlikely that political support for reform-oriented legislation would have materialized. And with what appeared to be a public consensus, reformers were able to convince legislators in state capitals to endorse sweeping new legislation that redefined governance and social policy in the South. Yet in redefining social policy, reformers clearly overstepped the mandate of the crusades. For if southern public opinion became aroused at the exposure of social conditions, it remained strongly committed to a pre-bureaucratic conception of governance.

A New Social Policy: Implementation and Resistance

Even as the reform crusades enjoyed early successes, a process had begun that would redefine the role of government in southern society. Early social reformers had criticized governance and endorsed a new degree of activism, but probably not all of them envisioned a full-blown bureaucratic, interventionist state. With the secular revival-crusades, reformers expressed common cultural attitudes and embraced traditional views of local autonomy and the solution of social problems. They believed that by altering public opinion, changed social conditions would follow.

In reality, the experience of implementing southern social reform would prove far more complex. At the root of social change, reformers came eventually to believe, lay the alteration of firmly rooted and popular folkways; democratically executed social policy would mean leaving the status quo unchanged. In taking the process of reform a step beyond the crusade model, then, reformers confronted a thorny dilemma. They discovered that implementing what they believed was a needed social change ran against local traditions and would necessitate the abandonment of community control. Operating within a restricted, disfranchised state made easier the rationalization of antidemocratic methods, as did cultural and attitudinal differences separating reformers and reformed. Yet continued problems in enforcing innovations in governance forced its practitioners to adapt and even to alter the new social policy.

The success of the reform crusades resulted in a host of new legislation. Southern state legislatures responded to the educational revival with new laws increasing state funds for schools and granting stronger powers to state school superintendents. Child-labor reformers persuaded most southern states to enact laws banning the employment of children in factories. Prohibitionists enjoyed a string of victories after 1905 in which statewide prohibition came into force by popular referendum or legislative enactment. Other reformers, operating in urban communities, obtained new laws or pressured municipal governments into enforcing existing ones to limit organized prostitution and ban business transactions on Sunday. In the wake of the hookworm campaign, state health departments experienced a dramatic growth in their coercive and regulatory powers. An offshoot of the general crusade for social betterment was the introduction of responsibility for social work and social welfare as part of state and local governments.

Increasingly, the agencies which these laws revitalized or created exercised centralized, bureaucratic governance. In some instances, as in the case of social efficiency modernizers, the transition from revival to bureaucracy was quick and almost unthinking. These reformers sought to change southern folkways by eliminating rural individualism and localism and substituting urbanized, dynamic values that would make social development along progressive lines possible. Social efficiency policy manifested itself primarily in a revamped approach to public schools and public health. With larger budgets and greater powers, educational and health bureaucracies expanded staff and exerted a supervisory role over local communities....

[I]n state health bureaucracies ... [m]ost of the new power went to the executive officers of the state boards of health, and from their offices grew new supervisory staffs. Their powers were probably the most coercive of any agency of the new social policy. With new authority to establish quarantine—powers that had before only theoretically existed—state health officials expanded their role in preventive health care. They acquired increased control over public sanitation and, beginning in urban areas, enforced new standards with new rigor. Health officials also began to examine and treat schoolchildren. They introduced new programs of child and maternal welfare, of disease prevention through inoculation and basic sanitation, and participated in energetic programs to combat venereal disease and tuberculosis.

Expansion of the state's welfare role constituted another category of the redefined social policy. The crusade to limit child labor was only one part of a broad effort to transform conceptions of the causes and solutions of poverty, social dislocation, and family disarray. The crusade for woman suffrage could also be lumped, not inappropriately, into this category. Suffragists frequently contended that extending the franchise to women would make government more nurturing and maternal toward its citizens. Suffragists assumed—incorrectly as it turned out—that the vote for women would create a constituency for new legislation to uproot vice, wife-beating, child labor, and bad working conditions for women and to establish an equal role for women within the family.

Another category of revised social policy involved the most ambitious effort to shape moral behavior in American history, state and national prohibition. In the South and elsewhere prohibitionists sought to redefine the relationship between government and the individual through a transformed social policy. Prohibitionists were the first to admit that there was never any time in which either statewide or later national prohibition was completely effective. Continued violations of prohibition, however, did not render it a failure, they argued. All civilized societies banned murder, but there would always be murder; larceny was illegal, yet it would always occur. Similarly, reformers reasoned, continued drinking was hardly an argument for prohibition's failure.

In a different category of social policy, race relations, most white social reformers welcomed disfranchisement and legally enforced racial segregation as necessary. Combined with a paternalism that dominated the thinking of social reformers, their belief in racial hierarchy exposed a dark, almost sinister side to southern progressives. But they also viewed political exclusion and *de jure* segregation as reforms that would stabilize white-black relations—which experienced a crisis of disturbing proportions during the 1890s—and, at least as they saw it, pave the way for black progress. To reformers, the disfranchised, one-party state provided opportunities for moderate, paternalistic racial policies. They believed that unlimited democracy and control by the mass of whites meant complete exclusion; the new administrative state, ironically, offered some benefits and services to blacks, those southerners most disinherited by progressive reform.

On the eve of World War I, then, a new approach to race relations was beginning to gain wider currency. Black education became a vehicle through which white reformers could seek black progress under the Jim Crow system. Programs, such as those which the General Education Board and the Rosenwald Fund sponsored, provided financial resources for the improvement of black schools under the vague rubric of "industrial education." Black educational reform also provided a model for future white southern reformers who accepted segregation while endorsing a program of black progress. By the 1920s, however, white race reformers discovered an erosion of white and black support for industrial education. In the pre-World War I period, white moderates defined the "Negro Problem" primarily in terms of black inadequacy; they believed that industrial education would transform black folkways with an infusion of Victorian standards of thrift and hard work. By the 1920s, moderates allied with the Commission on Interracial Cooperation (CIC), founded in 1919, espoused a different view: the primary problem was "discrimination" and "prejudice," not black inadequacy. Rejecting Victorian racial attitudes, CIC reformers—despite rampant racism and generally bleak prospects for blacks—sought improvements for blacks through the bureaucratic structures erected during the Progressive Era. Increasingly attracted to empirical definitions of racial problems, the CIC turned toward the new social scientists of the South for answers. Will Winton Alexander, the director of the CIC, thus established a close relationship with the Chapel Hill social scientist Howard W. Odum, who relied in turn on Alexander for advice, contacts with northern philanthropic foundations, and a supply of some of the earliest southern students of race relations.

Working closely with other practitioners of a new southern social policy, CIC reformers enjoyed access to the educational and health bureaucracies, and with them, they participated in state interracial groups and conferences. Black public education and public health assumed a greater priority during the 1920s. A new network of social scientists, typified by Odum and Wilson Gee of the University of Virginia, sponsored the incorporation of black welfare work into state social welfare systems. By the end of the 1920s, what Alexander called the "integration of the interracial movement with the official and volunteer social welfare agencies of many communities and states" had already occurred in Alabama, Georgia, the Carolinas, Louisiana, Virginia, and Tennessee. In the remaining states interracialists claimed "close and sympathetic relations" with social welfare agencies.

In attempting to alter some fundamental characteristics of southern life, reformers had traveled a long road during the first three decades of the twentieth century. From the educational revival in 1901 to the triumph of the woman suffrage movement in 1919, a series of regional crusades popularized new ways of identifying and attempting to solve social problems. These crusades enjoyed widespread support from public opinion—a major objective—yet they also betrayed a leadership style whose attitudes and intentions were far removed from those of most rural southerners. It should come as little surprise that reformers—who were infused with the cultural and social values of the new industrial order, who came from self-confident and assertive town classes, and who regarded the traditional village and rural culture with disdain—would favor a new form of interventionism.

That the attempt to implement these changes met frequent opposition supplies still more evidence that rural southerners were more active than passive regarding both reform and its implementation. Although reformers and rural communities converged in the crusades because of their familiarity with rural evangelical traditions, the attempt to introduce bureaucratic governance was another matter. Indeed the introduction of policy innovations began a long struggle between reformers and local communities. Still, the nature of this opposition must be placed in context, for the great majority of those who opposed reform possessed no unifying ideology or group consciousness. Although social distinctions and conflicts affected almost every aspect of southern life, few country folk reacted to social reform and accompanying policy changes exclusively or even primarily in terms of class. Rather, usually viewing the issue as a contest between their community and outsiders, they resisted reforms because they and their parents had always opposed interference in local matters. Significantly, in almost every instance of resistance to southern social reform, the resisters refused to link arms with one another for one very clear reason: they were as suspicious, perhaps even more suspicious, of other rural southerners as they were of outside centralizers.... Resistance was thus strongest wherever communities, especially rural communities, faced the deprivation of traditional autonomy....

This essay has argued that a clearer assessment of early twentieth-century reform requires a reexamination of its social context and consequences. Most historians of southern progressivism have neglected the social environment that reformers sought to change and the impact on it of their policy innovations. By focusing on reformers and their motivations, scholars have placed responsibility for major intergenerational social and political changes on their shoulders.

The real significance of Progressive Era social reform is to be found in the society which reformers confronted: a dispersed, rural population with strong traditions of individualism and localism. What the reformers sought amounted to revolutionary changes in governance and the administration of social policy, and they succeeded in introducing a new measure of interventionism in state and local government, designed to reorient fundamental qualities of southern culture. Popular antagonism to these changes, although not always fully or effectively articulated, frequently imperiled programs of modernization and administrative centralization. The implementation of the reformers' new social policy brought about not only centralized governance, but also localized community resistance. Historians of Progressive Era reform in the South must include both in their analyses.

"Now You Smell Perfume": Women Voters in the South

LORRAINE GATES SCHUYLER

WHAT WILL YOU BE? A Man or a Jelly Bean? This is the question that antisuffragists posed to southern men on the eve of ratification. For years, and at an even more fevered pitch in the last months before the Nineteenth Amendment was ratified, antisuffragists made apocalyptic predictions of the doomsday that would arrive in the South if women received the vote. According to these "antis" the entire southern social order would collapse in the wake of woman suffrage, as it threatened to bring "Negro Domination" and the ruin of the white southern family. While the antis' most dramatic claims failed to materialize, the sudden influx of women into public politics transformed the social drama of politics and challenged the supremacy of white males in ways that many antisuffragists had predicted with dread. As white and black women embraced their new status as voters, the Nineteenth Amendment blurred the lines of gender and race that were so central to the order of the Jim Crow South.

In the years immediately preceding the ratification of the Nineteenth Amendment, white southern men sat atop a political system exclusively within their control. The threats from Populists, Republicans, African Americans, and even poor whites had been answered with poll taxes, understanding clauses,

---

literacy tests, violence, and other legal and extralegal means of disfranchising disruptive voters. Voter participation rates in the South were appallingly low, even by low national standards, and on election days politically active southern white men gathered at the polls to share in the male political rituals of smoking, spitting, brawling, coarse joke-telling, drinking (despite laws to the contrary), and, not least, casting ballots, which symbolized their superiority to white women and children, all African Americans, and even other white men who lacked the means or education to share in southern political life.

Determined to protect this status quo, southern antisuffragists, both male and female, used theological, "scientific," and sociological arguments to condemn women's demands for the ballot. Ministers, leading male politicians, and female antisuffragists used biblical injunctions to remind southerners of the divine inspiration for woman's separate sphere. Moreover, they argued, women were mentally and physically unfit for the strenuousness of politics and public life. But more often, antis based their attacks on the threat that woman suffrage posed to the southern social order. Woman suffrage, they argued, would foster unhealthy competition between men and women, "discourage marriage," and "lessen women's attractive qualities of modesty, dependence, and delicacy." While antisuffragist men were often content to let the women antis take center stage in public debates over the issue, thereby furthering their contention that southern ladies did not really want the ballot, antisuffragist broadsides reveal surprisingly frank concerns about the effects of woman suffrage on southern manhood.

One broadside put it simply, "Block woman suffrage, that wrecker of the home." Another pamphlet warned that "more voting women than voting men will place the Government under petticoat rule." It was a cartoon published in Nashville, however, that really got to the heart of the matter. Titled "America When Femininized [*sic*]," it pictured a rooster left to care for a nest full of eggs as the hen departed the barn wearing a "Votes for Women" banner. This scene was supplemented by text that cautioned "Woman suffrage denatures both men and women; it masculinizes women and feminizes men." The broadside warned that the effects of woman suffrage, this "social revolution … will be to make 'sissies' of American men—a process already well under way." Another notice printed in Montgomery, Alabama, highlighted the same themes when it asked: "Shall America Collapse from Effeminacy? … The American man is losing hold. He is swiftly but surely surrendering to the domination of woman."

As these broadsides suggest, white southern men had a lot to be anxious about in 1920. In addition to the threat of woman suffrage, recurrent agricultural crises, labor unrest, a rising tide of African American activism, the Great Migration, and social changes symbolized by flappers and an increasingly independent youth culture all combined to make white southern men feel very uneasy as they entered the postwar decade. Historian Nancy MacLean has demonstrated that many white southerners believed that the hierarchical relations of power that provided the foundation for southern society were in danger of collapse, and hundreds of thousands turned to the Second Ku Klux Klan as a way to restore order. Nevertheless, many historians looking back on the 1920s have contended that antisuffragists' claims were mere "political hyperbole." To many white men who

America When Femininized

SUFFRAGIST—FEMINIST IDEAL FAMILY LIFE.

The More a Politician Allows Himself to be Henpecked The More Henpecking We Will Have in Politics.

A Vote for Federal Suffrage is a Vote for Organized Female Nagging Forever.

"American pep which was the result of a masculine dominated country will soon be a thing of the past. With the collapse of the male ascendancy in this country we can look forward to a nation of degeneration. The suppression of sex will ultimately have its harvest in decadence, a phenomenon already beginning. The effect of the social revolution on American character will be to make "sissies" of American men—a process already well under way."—Dr. William J. Hickson, Chicago University.

WOMAN SUFFRAGE denatures both men and women; it masculinizes women and femininizes men. The history of ancient civilization has proven that a weakening of the man power of nations has been but a pre-runner of decadence in civilization.

Will you stand for this? Prove that you will not by voting to **Reject** the Federal Woman Suffrage Amendment to the Constitution of the United States.

SOUTHERN WOMAN'S LEAGUE FOR REJECTION OF THE SUSAN B. ANTHONY AMENDMENT

WE SERVE THAT OUR STATES MAY LIVE, AND LIVING, PRESERVE THE UNION

Brandon-Nashville

Antisuffrage broadside (University of North Carolina Press)

watched southern women go to the polls for the first time in 1920, however, the dire predictions of antisuffragists must have seemed eerily prescient.

Despite determined opposition from the region's leading men, women in nearly every southern state cast their first ballots in November 1920. In August 1920, Tennessee's legislature provided a narrow margin in support of ratification, becoming the essential thirty-sixth state to ratify the Nineteenth Amendment and joining Arkansas, Kentucky, and Texas as the only southern states to vote in support of the federal amendment. By contrast, many other southern states not only refused to ratify the amendment but passed rejection proclamations. Alabama, Georgia, South Carolina, and Virginia sent such resolutions to Washington, announcing to the nation their antipathy for woman suffrage. Even after the Nineteenth Amendment was added to the Constitution, Mississippi and Georgia refused to make the necessary changes in their registration laws to permit women to vote in the 1920 presidential election. Indeed, as one historian has noted, "the all-male electorate of Mississippi rejected woman suffrage in a referendum the same day that women in most of the country voted for the first time." Up until the last moment, it seemed, southern white men fought to maintain the political sphere as their own domain.

Once that moment had passed, the presence of women voting, politicking, and lobbying in spaces formerly reserved for men marked a profound change on the southern political landscape. The appearance of women, both white and black, made the polls look different on election day and signaled that formal politics would no longer be the exclusive privilege of white men. As the *Richmond Times Dispatch* editorialized in 1923, "Somehow we couldn't visualize members of the fair sex in Virginia taking part in 'unfair' politics. The whole thing was incongruous." Figure 1 and Table 1, showing the increase in the popular vote in the first presidential election in which women voted, provide visual evidence of how widespread the disruption was for white men who had gone to such lengths to retain control of southern politics.

In Alabama, 79 percent more voters, more than 100,000 additional people, cast their ballots for president in 1920 than had done so in 1916. In North Carolina, nearly a quarter million additional voters crowded the polls on election

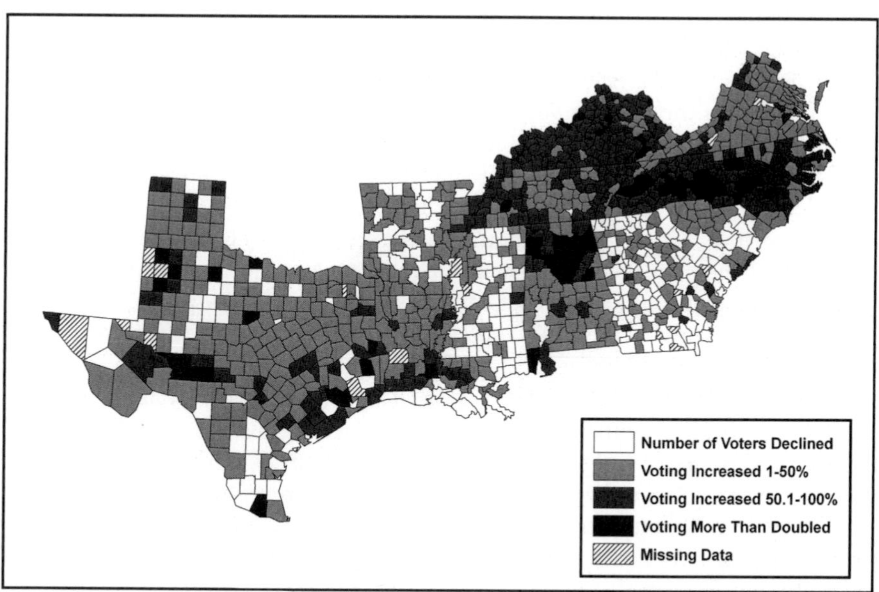

FIGURE 1 Change in Voter Turnout after Suffrage, 1920 Presidential Election (From Lorraine Gates Schuyler, *The Weight of Their Votes: Southern Women and Political Leverage in the 1920s* [Chapel Hill: The University of North Carolina Press, 2006], p. 18.)

TABLE 1 Trends in Voter Turnout before and after Suffrage, 1912–1920

	Change in Turnout 1912–1916	Change in Turnout 1916–1920	Change in No. of Voters 1916–1920
Alabama	11%	79%	103,516
Arkansas	36%	8%	13,517
Georgia	32%	−7%	−11,030
Kentucky	15%	77%	398,264
Louisiana	17%	36%	33,262
Mississippi	34%	−4%	−3,741
North Carolina	19%	86%	248,812
South Carolina	27%	4%	2,858
Tennessee	8%	57%	155,846
Texas	24%	30%	113,139
Virginia	11%	52%	78,975

SOURCE: The data utilized to create this table and table 2 were made available through the online database *U.S. Historical Election Returns* from the University of Virginia Geospatial and Statistical Data Center, http://fisher.lib.virginia.udu/collections/stats/elections/us.elections.

day in 1920, an increase of 86 percent. In Louisiana, more than 47,000 women registered to vote in the 1920 presidential election. Regionwide, the increase in voting was 56 percent in the states in which women were permitted to vote. The addition of more than one million new voters to the southern polls in November 1920 was not due exclusively to the entrance of women into the system, but in the absence of new women voters, Georgia and Mississippi suffered declines in the popular vote cast for president that year of 7 and 4 percent, respectively. While we cannot know precisely how many southern women voted in 1920, the presence of women at the polls was widespread and numerically strong enough to make southern white men take note.

Newspapers across the South took great notice of the first ballots cast by members of the "fair sex." On election day 1920, Virginia women went to the polls by the tens of thousands, and the state's largest newspaper noted that women "were early at the polls and stayed late" providing instructions to first-time voters and working diligently to get out the vote. On the day after the election, the editor of the *Richmond Times Dispatch* hailed the political involvement of the state's women: "Because of the lack of a strong minority party, Virginia campaigns have become rather cut and dried, but this year the women have given the color and zest needed for a complete revivification."...

Once the Nineteenth Amendment was ratified, politically active white women worked to make the polling places their own, and they transformed the polls into respectable spaces....

With the advent of woman suffrage, men not only had to acquiesce to the presence of women at the polls, but they also had to contend with the designs of women determined to make polling places more like parlors than saloons. In North Carolina, members of the Franklin League of Women Voters urged the sheriff to clean up the courthouse and construct a ladies restroom in advance of the election, and a Wake County woman voter complained that "much improvement was necessary" in the condition of her polling place. The Charleston, South Carolina, Democratic Executive Committee acted in 1924 to change its rules for the enrollment of primary voters so that "no enrollment books shall be opened or kept in a place conducting an illegal business." Apparently, local male party activists had previously enjoyed practicing their politics in shadier establishments....

The changes that followed in the wake of woman suffrage did more than render previously male spaces gender-neutral. Masculine political spaces became feminized. Indeed, in calling on Democratic men to move the location of voting and registration in Tennessee, one woman highlighted the contrast, as well as the cultural import of the change: "You know how many women won't go to the polls because only men are there and tobacco smoke or worse," she admonished, "think how you'd feel if obligated to go into a women's pink tea parlor to vote and could only vote for a woman." While most southern polling places were not moved to "pink tea parlors" in the aftermath of the Nineteenth Amendment, they increasingly resembled feminized domestic spaces. As one Georgia man said to the newly elected female legislator from his district, "You used to smell liquor at the polls, but now you smell perfume." The robust masculinity of polling places before 1920 was a reflection of women's distance from political power. The feminization of those same spaces after 1920 was a corollary to women's increasing political authority....

It was not just white women who made southern politics look different; newspapers and observers took particular note of the presence of African American women at the polls. Just two decades after Democratic leaders had ended the Republican threat and nearly eliminated the participation of African Americans in the South's political system through disfranchisement, African American women set about to take advantage of the federal amendment and exercise their rights as citizens. In South Carolina, one report on the number of women registering to vote was headlined, "960 Women Register in Union County, Some Are Negroes." In a front-page story about women voters, the *Chattanooga News* noted, "At several of the voting places some colored women were voting, and from the dispatch with which they marked and handed in their ballots they showed they were adept pupils."...

If the feminization of the polls threatened white southern manhood on a psychic level, many white men believed that the feminization of the polls threatened white supremacy more concretely. The disfranchisement of African Americans rested on violence, or at least the threat of violence. Yet it was assumed that white women could not be counted on to defend the polls with force, and the feminization of polling spaces made it increasingly unlikely that white men would exercise such violence in white women's presence. Moreover, some African Americans believed that white men would have more difficulty keeping black women from the polls than black men. As one observer put it, "Not even the 'cracker' can treat a woman with quite the same brutality with which he treats a man." Thus, while white men surely did not doff their hats to African American women, the Nineteenth Amendment provided some African American women with an opportunity to exercise their rights as citizens. The feminization of the polls even may have, as one historian argued, "cleared a narrow path for black men to return to electoral politics."

Just as antisuffragists had warned, the ratification of the Nineteenth Amendment fueled the demands of African Americans for full citizenship rights. Precise figures are not available, but accounts from around the region signaled the determination of African Americans to vote. In Louisiana, nearly 2,000 African American women registered to vote in less than two months, joined by more than 300 African American men who had not previously been registered. In Lexington, Kentucky, 3,067 "Negro Republican women" had registered by the end of the first week in October. "Thousands" of African American voters "stormed" the polls in Houston. Even in Edgefield, South Carolina, a white woman reported that nearly 10 percent of the new women registrants were African American. One southern black woman put it plainly, "We are going to exercise our rights under the law. We fear no evil; we will not be bluffed away from the polls. If bodily harm is resorted to, there are two sides to the question, and we may as well begin to prepare for a decision, a peaceful one, we fondly hope. Why should we be denied our votes?"...

Throughout the debates over woman suffrage, antisuffragists warned that a federal amendment would result in votes for both white and African American women. Though suffragists accurately countered with the argument that white women would out-vote black women, and that black women would be kept from the polls by the same methods that disfranchised their husbands, the Nineteenth Amendment did provide a very small number of African American women with an opportunity to participate in southern politics as citizens. With much fanfare, the Nineteenth Amendment brought new people to the polls—people who not only made politics look different but whose presence forced white men to acknowledge the symbolic equality of the ballot and the consequent diminution of their own manhood. As they stood alongside, or behind, women voters to cast their ballots and were forced to abandon the male rituals of election day, some southern white men must have thought that the antisuffragists' dire predictions had come true....

While the notions of gender equality implied by woman suffrage unsettled white men who stood atop the region's social hierarchy, African American men were much less threatened by the efforts of their wives and daughters to cast ballots. Instead, African American men generally viewed the Nineteenth Amendment as an opportunity to enhance their own political power and that of their race. Immediately after ratification, southern black men looked to the women of the race to seize their citizenship rights. The *Atlanta Independent*, for example, called on black women to "pay their taxes and register." As a result of the cumulative poll tax laws, many black and white men in Georgia could not afford to become enfranchised. Many black men consequently called on black women to register, noting that "it is much easier for our women to qualify and vote than the men," because new women voters as yet owed no back taxes at the polls. The *Savannah Tribune* issued a similar call to black women, insisting that registration "will never be easier than now!" "Now that our women are going up in such large numbers to be registered," the *Tribune* continued, "the men should be put upon their mettle to keep pace with them." *The Crisis* put it simply, "Every black man and woman ought to vote."...

African American women organized to take advantage of the Nineteenth Amendment in 1921, Ettrick, Virginia (From the Evie Spencer DeCosta Papers, 1984-26, Special Collections and Archives, Johnston Memorial Library, Virginia State University, Petersburg, Virginia.)

In contrast to white political women who routinely complained that the antisuffragism of husbands prevented white women from voting, African Americans, both male and female, focused on the hostile white registrars and the legal structure of disfranchisement that posed the greatest obstacles to black women's political participation. Indeed, an African American woman from Louisiana specifically denied that antisuffragist black men in her state "influenced their wives not to vote." Instead, she blamed the small number of African American women voters in her state on "unfair methods used by registrar[s]" and demanded that "national elections be controlled by U.S. Marshalls [*sic*] in the South." In the face of these "unfair methods," African American men actively demonstrated their support for women voters. In Columbia, South Carolina, the president of the local NAACP branch wrote to the national headquarters to describe the conditions that faced would be voters in his area and to express his determination to fight their disfranchisement "until hell freezes over." Women in South Carolina were exempt from the poll taxes that men had to pay, and as he lauded black women's efforts to enroll as voters, this local leader made clear his support for woman suffrage as a political strategy for his race. "We mean to stay in the fight," he explained, "until every woman who possesses the qualification is registered or fight the case through the Supreme Court." When black women in Birmingham organized a "women voters' club," the *Birmingham Reporter* applauded their efforts and urged the support "of the sober and thoughtful male members of the race." In contrast to the white southern men who effectively disfranchised their wives by refusing to pay the women's poll taxes, black men in the South were outraged by the "flagrant manner in which our women were discriminated against" and, in most cases, eagerly joined the women of their communities to fight for black women's right to vote....

While African American women and men struggled to obtain basic access to the polls and white men grappled with the challenge that woman suffrage posed to established patterns of private gender relations, some white women staged increasingly determined attacks on men's public authority as well. On the day of the primary election in the summer of 1922, Gertrude Weil went to her polling place near the Wayne County (N.C.) Courthouse. When she arrived she found the election judges and managers, all men, fraudulently marking "all the ballots in sight" for the candidate of their choice. Horrified, she proceeded to tear all the marked ballots into small pieces before the eyes of the "dumfounded" men. When one of the election officials finally recovered his senses, he challenged the woman voter to "bring a man in the court house to do her fighting." But, in an act that only furthered the poor official's humiliation, Weil turned, "paid no attention to him, but continued to look for marked ballots."

The story of Weil's "spunk" was widely reported in the state's newspapers, and reporters and editors lauded her for cleaning up politics, declaring that more such women were needed to protect North Carolina ballot boxes....

The presence of female poll watchers, election officials, and registrars was a sudden and ubiquitous example of the new public power of enfranchised white women. Female political leaders across the region demanded that white women be named to these posts, and in order to make their sisters comfortable at the polls, white female political leaders made themselves conspicuous. Moreover, in order to ensure that newly enfranchised women took advantage of their new voting rights, many white women worked as registrars. Though they frequently sought such posts in order to encourage other women to enroll as voters, official duties made these white women responsible for the registration of men as well as women. Some white southern men had resigned their posts in 1920 rather than register women voters." In the decade that followed, many white men found women registrars more than willing to sit in judgment of men's fitness for the franchise. And in those areas where black men dared attempt to register, white women registrars served as the guardians of white supremacy....

While southern white men struggled to adapt to the new political realities of woman suffrage, many white women demanded acceptance as equal partners in politics and access to all of the privileges attendant to citizenship. For some politically active white women, membership on Democratic Party committees ranked chief among those privileges....

In Alabama, the state's national committeewoman petitioned for greater female representation on the state Democratic Executive Committee. By a very narrow vote, male party leaders agreed to increase the number of voting members temporarily, allowing one woman from each congressional district to be added to the committee....

In North Carolina, male party leaders were described as "speechless" and "too dumbfounded to remember their manners" when white women made their first appearance at Democratic precinct meetings. In what the *News and*

Observer described in its front-page story as a "coup," the white women of Raleigh made a surprise appearance at city precinct meetings in 1920 to "demand recognition as Democrats" and their rightful representation at the state convention. When the men of the party recovered from the shock of this "invasion," they acknowledged the political authority of the women of their state and sent several of them as delegates to the state convention....

The spectacle of women running for office was perhaps the most dramatic change in the social drama of southern politics following the Nineteenth Amendment. As early as the November elections of 1920, southern women ran for and were elected to public office. Throughout the decade, newspapers reported on the elections of white southern women as aldermen, sheriffs, mayors, and state legislators. The widespread coverage of women's political campaigns testified to the spectacle....

For white women, the challenge was to compete aggressively against their male opponents without appearing to dismiss the cultural expectations about appropriate femininity. The spectacle of female candidates publicly promoting themselves and stumping for office upended southern gender hierarchies and made a mockery of southern notions of female deference. In a letter to the editor, an anonymous man from middle Georgia wrote in to comment on the "young lady" running for state legislature. While "everybody knows she is a nice girl and very able," he reported, "everybody" agrees the Georgia legislature "is no place for a woman." In Cabon Hill, Alabama, the editor of the local newspaper lambasted a female candidate for state legislature who had the temerity to question the policies of Alabama Power Company while touring the company's steam plant. As the editor described it, "Mrs. Maner in her zeal to further her political ambitions went so far as to completely overlook the fact that she should above all else conduct herself as a lady." For southerners in the 1920s, however, it was not altogether clear how one could successfully run for office and "conduct herself as a lady."

Just as white southern voters insisted that candidates conduct their competition for votes within the boundaries of the established social order, many southern newspapers downplayed the threat of female political authority by focusing attention on officeholders' "ladylike" qualities. A Kentucky newspaper story was headlined "Mrs. Flanery, Politician, Likes Housework." That article went on to describe the "rest" this state legislator found "among flowers and vegetables after [a] strenuous [legislative] session." South Carolina senator Mary Gordon Ellis was a determined politician; she had run for her senate seat as an act of revenge after the incumbent state senator sponsored legislation stripping her of her powers as county superintendent of education. Despite this obvious willingness to assert her authority, or perhaps because of it, a local reporter emphasized Ellis's domestic credentials in his article. "Senator Ellis can go into the kitchen and broil a steak to perfection," the reporter declared, "a meal good enough to put before a king." Miriam "Ma" Ferguson was the first woman to serve as governor in the South, but one newspaper article nevertheless described her as "a kindly, motherly woman ... a typical middle-class housewife." With great regularity, news reports about female politicians also made note of the woman's appearance. Emma Guy Cromwell, Kentucky's secretary of state, was described as a "slender little woman" with "dedicate features" and "delightfully feminine smiles." Less flatteringly, when Minnie

Fisher Cunningham opened her campaign for U.S. Senate in 1928, one Texas newspaper described her as "less mannish and political looking" than one would expect a "woman candidate for the Senate to be." To "prove that a woman politician is also a home keeper," southern observers praised women officeholders for their femininity, their cooking, their housekeeping, and their attention to maternal duties. Newspapers' stubborn insistence on the stability of the domestic order did little to reassure white southerners, though. Throughout the decade female officeholding remained rare and noteworthy as white men resisted this most powerful symbol of the increased authority of enfranchised women....

After 1920, white southern men were forced to adapt their campaigns, their public polling places, and their notions of southern ladyhood to accommodate new women voters. Woman suffrage transformed the look and feel of southern politics, and white men could no longer refer to the franchise as evidence of their superiority over white women or even African American women. For the first time in decades, a trickle of new African American voters demanded the right to vote. Moreover, the spectacle of white women representing themselves in public undermined one of the pillars of white southern manhood: white men as protectors of white women. In the words of one Alabama newspaper, women acquired "the status of male voters" when the Nineteenth Amendment was ratified. And just as antisuffragists had warned, the enfranchisement of women undermined the hierarchies of gender and race that ordered the Jim Crow South.

FURTHER READING

Raymond Arsenault, *The Wild Ass of the Ozarks: Jeff Davis and the Social Bases of Southern Politics* (1984).

Edward Ayers, *The Promise of the New South: Life after Reconstruction* (1992).

Hugh C. Bailey, *Edgar Gardner Murphy: Gentle Progressive* (1968).

———, *Liberalism in the New South: Southern Social Reformers and the Progressive Movement* (1969).

Patricia Bellis Bixel and Elizabeth Hayes Turner, *Galveston and the 1900 Storm: Catastrophe and Catalyst* (2000).

Paul D. Casdorph, *Republicans, Negroes, and Progressives in the South, 1912–1916* (1981).

Bruce Clayton, *The Savage Ideal: Intolerance and Intellectual Leadership in the South, 1890–1914* (1972).

Debbie Cottrell, *Pioneer Women Educator: The Progressive Spirit of Annie Webb Blanton* (1993).

Michael Denis, *Lessons in Progress: State Universities and Progressivism in the New South, 1880–1920* (2001).

John Dittmer, *Black Georgia in the Progressive Era, 1900–1920* (1977).

W. E. B. Du Bois, ed., *Efforts for Social Betterment among Negro Americans* (1909).

Elizabeth E. Etheridge, *The Butterfly Caste: A Social History of Pellagra in the South* (1972).

John Ettling, *The Germ of Laziness: Rockefeller Philanthropy and Public Health in the New South* (1981).

J. Wayne Flynt, *Dixie's Forgotten People: The South's Poor Whites* (1979).

———, *Poor but Proud: Alabama's Poor Whites* (1989).

Glenda Gilmore, *Gender and Jim Crow: Women and the Politics of White Supremacy in North Carolina, 1896–1920* (1996).

David F. Godshalk, *Veiled Visions: The 1906 Atlanta Race Riot and the Reshaping of American Race Relations* (2005).

Dewey W. Grantham, *Southern Progressivism: The Reconciliation of Progress and Tradition* (1983).

Elna C. Green, *Southern Strategies: Southern Women and the Women Suffrage Question* (1997).

Louis R. Harlan, *Separate and Unequal: Public School Campaigns and Racism in the Southern Seaboard States, 1901–1915* (1958).

———, *Booker T. Washington: The Making of a Black Leader* (1972).

———, *Booker T. Washington: The Wizard of Tuskegee, 1901–1915* (1983).

Carl V. Harris, *Political Power in Birmingham, 1871–1921* (1977).

Nancy Hewitt, *Southern Discomfort: Women's Activism in Tampa, Florida, 1880s–1920s* (2001).

William F. Holmes, *The White Chief: James Kimble Vardaman* (1970).

Joan Marie Johnson, *Southern Ladies, New Women: Race, Region, and Clubwomen in South Carolina, 1890–1930* (2004).

Jack Temple Kirby, *Darkness at the Dawning: Race and Reform in the Progressive South* (1972).

J. Morgan Kousser, "Progressivism—For Middle-Class Whites Only: North Carolina Education, 1880–1910," *Journal of Southern History* 46 (1980), 169–194.

———, *The Shaping of Southern Politics: Suffrage Restriction and the Establishment of the One-Party South, 1880–1910* (1974).

Edward J. Larson, *Sex, Race, and Science: Eugenics in the Deep South* (1995).

Elisabeth Lasch-Quinn, *Black Neighbors: Race and the Limits of Reform in the American Settlement House Movement, 1890–1945* (1993).

James L. Leloudis, *Schooling the New South* (1996).

————, "School Reform in the New South: The Woman's Association for the Betterment of Public School Houses in North Carolina, 1902–1919," *Journal of American History* 69 (March 1983), 886–909.

David Levering Lewis, *W. E. B. Du Bois: Biography of a Race* (1993).

Alex Lichtenstein, "Good Roads and Chain Gangs in the Progressive South: The Negro Convict Is a Slave," *Journal of Southern History* 59 (February 1993), 85–110.

Arthur S. Link, "The Progressive Movement in the South, 1870–1914," *North Carolina Historical Review* 23 (1946), 172–195.

William A. Link, *A Hard Country and a Lonely Place: Schooling, Society, and Reform in Rural Virginia, 1870–1920* (1986).

———, *The Paradox of Southern Progressivism, 1880–1920* (1993).

Judith N. McArthur, *Creating the New Woman: The Rise of Southern Women's Progressive Culture in Texas, 1893–1918* (1998).

Patrick McDowell, *The Social Gospel in the South: The Woman's Home Mission Movement in the Methodist Episcopal Church, South, 1886–1939* (1982).

August Meier, *Negro Thought in America, 1880–1915* (1963).

Rebecca S. Montgomery, *The Politics of Education in the New South: Women and Reform in Georgia, 1890–1930* (2006).

Thomas R. Pegram, "Temperance Politics and Regional Political Culture: The Anti-Saloon League in Maryland and the South, 1907–1915," *Journal of Southern History* 63 (February 1997), 57–90.

Bradley R. Rice, *Progressive Cities: The Commission Government Movement in America, 1901–1920* (1977).

Darlene R. Roth, *Matronage: Patterns in Women's Organizations, Atlanta, Georgia, 1890–1940* (1994).

Jacqueline A. Rouse, *Lugenia Burns Hope: Black Southern Reformer* (1989).

Dorothy Salem, *To Better Our World: Black Women in Organized Reform, 1890–1920* (1990).

Shelley Sallee, *The Whiteness of Child Labor Reform in the New South* (2004).

Anne Firor Scott, *Natural Allies: Women's Associations in American History* (1992).

————, *The Southern Lady: From Pedestal to Politics, 1830–1900* (1970).

Lorraine Gates Schuyler, *The Weight of Their Votes: Southern Women and Political Leverage in the 1920s* (2006).

Zamir Shamoon, *Dark Voices: W. E. B. Du Bois and American Thought, 1888–1903* (1995).

Stephanie Shaw, *What a Woman Ought to Be and to Do: Black Professional Women Workers during the Jim Crow Era* (1996).

Bryant Simon, *A Fabric of Defeat: The Politics of South Carolina Millhands, 1910–1948* (1998).

Anastatia Sims, *The Power of Femininity in the New South: Women's Organizations and Politics in North Carolina, 1880–1930* (1997).

Roslyn Terborg-Penn, *African American Women in the Struggle for the Vote, 1850–1920* (1998).

Mary Martha Thomas, ed., *Stepping Out of the Shadows: Alabama Women, 1819–1990* (1995).

George B. Tindall, *Emergence of the New South, 1913–1945* (1967).

Elizabeth Hayes Turner, *Women, Culture, and Community: Religion and Reform in Galveston, 1880–1920* (1997).

Marjorie Spruill Wheeler, *New Women of the New South: The Leaders of the Women Suffrage Movement in the Southern States* (1993).

LeeAnn Whites, "The De Graffenried Controversy: Class, Race, and Gender in the New South," *Journal of Southern History* 54 (1988), 449–478.

Cary Wintz, ed., *African American Political Thought, 1890–1930* (1996).

George C. Wright, *Life behind a Veil: Blacks in Louisville, Kentucky, 1865–1930* (1985).

Robert I. Zangrando, *The NAACP Crusade against Lynching 1909–1950* (1980).

CHAPTER 10

In Search of the Modern South

In a 1917 article, journalist and critic H. L. Mencken referred to the South as "the Sahara of the Bozart," ridiculing the South's lack of "beaux arts." By the 1940s, this had changed; millions of Americans read the novels of Thomas Wolfe, Zora Neale Hurston, Lillian Smith, and William Faulkner. Sociologist Howard W. Odum and his colleagues at the University of North Carolina had established national reputations for their social-scientific explorations of southern problems; a creative group at Vanderbilt University, the Nashville Agrarians, had offered a stunning, although nostalgic, critique of urban-industrial society.

In fact, the South was changing. The literary renaissance and the accompanying developments in critical thought and the social sciences demonstrated that southerners were capable of insightful self-analysis and creative genius. Cities, which had always brought fresh ideas to a region, were growing in the South, fostering better education and employment opportunities for residents away from their rural roots. By 1920, women had the right to vote and the social freedom to smoke, drink, cut their hair, and raise their hemlines. Southerners bought automobiles and began to see the region from a new perspective. Educators, influenced by the theories of Charles Darwin and others, sought more scientific methods for explaining their world. Black veterans, home from the front, questioned the place of segregation in a democracy.

While intellectuals and modernists waged a campaign of words over southern culture, some southerners, fearful of change and made nervous by gender and race expectations, revolted against modernism. In their opinion, secular values were undermining traditional evangelical beliefs. Through legislation and extra-legal violence, antimodernists attempted to recapture the "safety" of the traditional South. Fundamentalist Christianity, a northern religious innovation that made enormous headway in the South, flourished in some evangelical churches, adding a moralistic tone to antimodernist rhetoric. Such events as the rise of the Ku Klux Klan and the Scopes "Monkey" trial indicate the level of disturbance felt by traditionalists in the South.

Scholars today still ask why the cultural renaissance occurred in the 1920s. How did the growth of cities, increasing public opportunities for women, rising secularization, and new ideas from World War I shape the direction of the modern South? What were the consequences of antimodernist impulses for the South? How important has anti-evolutionist thinking been to the history of the South?

DOCUMENTS

H. L. Mencken, co-editor of the *American Mercury* in Baltimore, wrote one of the most scathing indictments of the South when he penned "The Sahara of the Bozart," featured here as Document 1. Mencken considered the South culturally barren, but he also noted the absurdity of Jim Crow laws. Mencken claimed that this article brought "a ferocious reaction in the South," but many rising southern writers who already had begun to criticize southern "civilization" were emboldened by his public denouncement. As if to emphasize Mencken's point, the Ku Klux Klan rose again in the South during the 1920s. Sinister in their white apparel, as shown in Document 2, members of the Klan used secrecy, intimidation, and violence against Catholics, Jews, blacks, labor union organizers, and whites who violated traditional moral codes. In Document 3, a sermon delivered in Raleigh, North Carolina, the Reverend Amzi Clarence Dixon attributes an array of global evils, including World War I and divorce, to Darwin's theory of evolution. Few causes stirred evangelical zeal more than state legislation to outlaw the teaching of evolution in public schools. In Document 4, attorney for the defense, Clarence Darrow, challenges the very premise posed by William Jennings Bryan and anti-evolutionists in the Scopes "Monkey Trial" in Dayton, Tennessee. Bryan, former Secretary of State, supported the biblical version of Earth's creation as presented in the book of Genesis, while Darrow spoke for modern science. The Scopes trial turned into a cause célèbre when it became the first trial to be broadcast for radio, when H. L. Mencken satirized the proceedings, and when a live chimpanzee was brought into the courtroom. William L. Poteat, Baptist president of Wake Forest College, in Document 5 concludes that fundamentalism and its insistence on the divorce between scientific evidence and the biblical story of creation "is compromising Christianity before the intelligence of the world." The Nashville Agrarians, in their manifesto entitled *I'll Take My Stand*, warned that modernization of the South would destroy some important regional values. In Document 6, Vanderbilt University English professor John Crowe Ransom, who wrote the introduction to *I'll Take My Stand*, criticizes the negative effects of the industrial society in contrast to the South's traditional agrarian folkways. The final document in this chapter, written by Richard Wright in *Black Boy*, reminds the reader that the South of the 1920s offered little hope for young black men whose words and actions were scrutinized by whites for signs of insubordination. His fearful encounter with a white northerner remains one of the best examples of the limits whites imposed on black citizens. Anything that suggested black achievement was off limits in conversation, including the boxing title earned by Jack Johnson!

1. H. L. Mencken Blasts the South as "The Sahara of the Bozart," 1917

Alas, for the South! Her books have grown fewer—
She never was much given to literature.

In the lamented J. Gordon Coogler, author of these elegiac lines, there was the insight of a true poet. He was the last bard of Dixie, at least in the legitimate line. Down there a poet is now almost as rare as an oboe-player, a dry-point etcher or a metaphysician. It is, indeed, amazing to contemplate so vast a vacuity. One thinks of the interstellar spaces, of the colossal reaches of the now mythical ether. Nearly the whole of Europe could be lost in that stupendous region of worn-out farms, shoddy cities and paralyzed cerebrums: one could throw in France, Germany and Italy, and still have room for the British Isles. And yet, for all its size and all its wealth and all the "progress" it babbles of, it is almost as sterile, artistically, intellectually, culturally, as the Sahara Desert. There are single acres in Europe that house more first-rate men than all the states south of the Potomac....

In all that gargantuan paradise of the fourth-rate [the South] there is not a single picture gallery worth going into, or a single orchestra capable of playing the nine symphonies of Beethoven, or a single opera-house, or a single theater devoted to decent plays, or a single public monument that is worth looking at, or a single workshop devoted to the making of beautiful things. Once you have counted James Branch Cabell (a lingering survivor of the *ancien regime:* a scarlet dragon-fly imbedded in opaque amber) you will not find a single Southern prose writer who can actually write. And once you have-but when you come to critics, musical composers, painters, sculptors, architects and the like, you will have to give it up, for there is not even a bad one between the Potomac mudflats and the Gulf. Nor a historian. Nor a philosopher. Nor a theologian. Nor a scientist. In all these fields the South is an awe inspiring blank....

Virginia has no art, no literature, no philosophy, no mind or aspiration of her own. Her education has sunk to the Baptist seminary level; not a single contribution to human knowledge has come out of her colleges in twenty-five years; she spends less than half upon her common schools, *per capita* than any Northern state spends. In brief, an intellectual Gobi or Lapland. Urbanity,

---

From *Prejudices: Second Series* by H. L. Mencken (New York: Alfred A. Knopf, 1920) Originally printed, in shorter form, in the New York *Evening Mail,* Nov. 13, 1917.

Document 1 from H. L. Mencken, *Prejudices: Second Series,* 1920. "This produced a ferocious reaction in the South, and I was belabored for months, and even years afterward in a very extravagant manner.... On the heels of the violent denunciations of the elder Southerners there soon came a favorable response from the more civilized youngsters, and there is reason to believe that my attack had something to do with that revival of Southern letters which followed in the middle 1920's."

politesse, chivalry? ... The mind of the state, as it is revealed to the nation, is pathetically naive and inconsequential. It no longer reacts with energy and elasticity to great problems. It has fallen to the bombastic trivialities of the camp-meeting and the stump. One could no more imagine a [Robert E.] Lee or a [George] Washington in the Virginia of today than one could imagine a [Aldous] Huxley in Nicaragua. I choose the Old Dominion, not because I disdain it, but precisely because I esteem it. It is, by long odds, the most civilized of the Southern states, now as always. It has sent a host of creditable sons northward; the stream kept running into our own time. Virginians, even the worst of them, show the effects of a great tradition. They hold themselves above other Southerners, and with sound pretension. If one turns to such a commonwealth as Georgia the picture becomes far darker. There the liberated lower orders of whites have borrowed the worst commercial bounderism of the Yankee and superimposed it upon a culture that, at bottom, is but little removed from savagery. Georgia is at once the home of the cotton-mill sweater, of the Methodist parson turned Savonarola and of the lynching bee.... There is a state with more than half the area of Italy and more population than either Denmark or Norway, and yet in thirty years it has not produced a single idea. Once upon a time a Georgian printed a couple of books that attracted notice, but immediately it turned out that he was little more than an amanuensis for the local blacks—that his works were really the products, not of white Georgia, but of black Georgia. Writing afterward *as* a white man, he swiftly subsided into the fifth rank. And he is not only the glory of the literature of Georgia; he is, almost literally, the whole of the literature of Georgia—nay, of the entire art of Georgia.[1]

Virginia is the best of the South today, and Georgia is perhaps the worst. The one is simply senile; the other is crass, gross, vulgar and obnoxious. Between lies a vast plain of mediocrity, stupidity, lethargy, almost of dead silence....

The South has simply been drained of all its best blood. The vast hemorrhage of the Civil War half exterminated and wholly paralyzed the old aristocracy, and so left the land to the harsh mercies of the poor white trash, now its masters....

The South has not only lost its old capacity for producing ideas; it has also taken on the worst intolerance of ignorance and stupidity....

Curious sidelights upon the ex-Confederate mind! Another comes from a stray copy of a Negro paper. It describes an ordinance passed by the city council of Douglas, Ga., forbidding any trousers presser, on penalty of forfeiting a $500 bond, to engage in "pressing for both white and colored." This in a town, says the Negro paper, where practically all of the white inhabitants have "their food prepared by colored hands," "their babies cared for by colored hands," and "the clothes which they wear right next to their skins washed in houses where Negroes live"—houses in which the said clothes "remain for as long as a week at a time." But if you marvel at the absurdity, keep it dark! A casual word, and

[1]The reference here, of course, was to Joel Chandler Harris.

the united press of the South will be upon your trail, denouncing you bitterly as a scoundrelly damnyankee, a Bolshevik Jew.

Obviously, it is impossible for intelligence to flourish in such an atmosphere. Free inquiry is blocked by the idiotic certainties of ignorant men. The arts, save in the lower reaches of the gospel hymn, the phonograph and the political harangue, are all held in suspicion....

That philistinism regards human life, not as an agreeable adventure, but as a mere trial of rectitude and efficiency. It is overwhelmingly utilitarian and moral. It is inconceivably hollow and obnoxious. What remains of the ancient tradition is simply a certain charming civility in private intercourse—often broken down, alas, by the hot rages of Puritanism, but still generally visible. The Southerner, at his worst, is never quite the surly cad that the Yankee is. His sensitiveness may betray him into occasional bad manners, but in the main he is a pleasant fellow—hospitable, polite, good-humored, even jovial.... But a bit absurd.... A bit pathetic.

2. The Ku Klux Klan Initiates New Members, 1915

A Ku Klux Klan Night Ceremony Inducting New Members in 1915. (© Bettmann/CORBIS)

3. The Reverend Amzi Clarence Dixon Preaches on the Evils of Evolution, 1922

Evolution with its "struggle for existence" and "survival of the fittest," which gives the strong and fit the scientific right to destroy the weak and unfit is responsible for the oppression and destruction of the weak and unfit by the strong and fit. It has fostered autocratic class distinctions and is no friend to those who stand for the protection of the weak against the oppression of the strong. The greatest war in history, which has drenched the world with blood and covered it with human bones, can be traced to this source. If the strong and fit have the scientific right to destroy the weak and unfit, that human progress may be promoted, then might is right, and Germany should not be criticized for acting upon this principle.

The "Superman"

Nietzsche, the neurotic German philosopher, hypnotized the German mind with his Pagan brute philosophy. "The weak and botched," said he, "shall perish; first principle of humanity. And they ought to be helped to perish. What is more harmful than any vice? Practical sympathy with the botched and weak Christianity." "If what I publish be true," he wrote to an invalid woman, "a feeble woman like you would have no right to exist."

"Christianity," he said, "is the greatest of all conceivable corruptions, the one immortal blemish of mankind." And he hated it because of its sympathy with the botched and weak. He glorified his ideal "blond beast" and gave to the world a "superman," one-third brute, one-third philosopher. Under the spell of his daring brutality, Germany adopted the motto, "Corsica has conquered Galilee." Nietzsche's philosophy of beastliness has its roots in the evolutionary assumption that the strong and fit, in the struggle for existence, have the scientific right to destroy the weak and unfit.

The Super-Nation

Under the spell of Nietzsche's "superman" there came into the heads of the German politicians and militarists the vision of a super nation, with the scientific right to destroy weaker nations and build its throne upon their ruins....

I tremble for the future of the world if the millions of China are to be moulded and dominated by a philosophy which gives to the strong and fit the scientific right to destroy the unfit. It is easy for the patriotism of any nation to make its people believe that they are the fittest nation in the world; only, if China with the conviction should become conscious of her strength, she could become, under masterful military leadership, the menace of the future. Any nation

---

"Dr. Dixon Claims Evolution Started in Unscientific Age," as appeared in *Raleigh News & Observer*, December 31, 1922, p. 5.

that teaches this pernicious delusion to its youth is now a menace to the peace of the world; and if all nations teach it, war will be the normal method of settling all disputes. Universal peace can never come until nations turn from this voice of the jungle to the song of the angels floating from the skies above the plain of Bethlehem: "Peace on earth among men of good will."

If the home is to be preserved as a sacred institution, the Bible which teaches that marriage came down from God and not up from the beast must be believed. The jungle theory as to the origin of marriage is today keeping busy the divorce courts of the civilized world. If government came down from God, so that "the powers that be are ordained of God," law will rule in righteousness and courts will mete out justice, but if the basis of government came from the jungle where brute force prevails the Bolshevist rule by bullet and bayonet is scientific and the scientific mind ought to accept it. This jungle origin of government is today a world-wide peril. If the Bible is a revelation from God through inspired men, its teaching is authoritative and its truths have in them an irresistible dynamic, but if the Bible is a mere record of human experience as men have struggled upward from their jungle origin, its teaching has no authority and its sayings are to be accepted or rejected by the inner consciousness of men, which is itself a product of the jungle.

If man came down from God, created in His image and has been wrecked by sin, then sin is an intrusion, an enemy that ought to be expelled; but, if man came up from the beast through the jungle, sin is "embryonic goodness," "righteousness in process of formation," even a search after good; of course such sin has no guilt and may be condoned, if not coddled. Such a delusion makes it easy to believe that sin has no existence and all things, even theft, falsehood and murder are good, because there is no evil in the world.

If the church came down from God in the sense that its members are "born from above," we have on this world a unique spiritual organism, of which Jesus Christ is the head, endued with an irresistible dynamic, "power from on high." But if the church came up from the beast through the jungle and is the expression of man's struggle out of beastliness into spirituality, we have simply one earth-born institution among many and cannot be optimistic regarding its destiny.

If Christ came down from heaven, as He says He did, "the only begotten Son of God" in the sense that He is the only one in the universe begotten of God in a virgin's womb, "God manifest in the flesh," "the Word made flesh and dwelling among men," we have in Him a unique personality; God, who is a Spirit, made concrete, thinkable, approachable and lovable; God, lowering Himself to our level, that He may lift us to His level. But if Christ is the expression of humanity's struggle up from the beast through the jungle, we have in Him simply a combination and culmination of jungle life in body, soul and spirit, detached from heaven, on the same plane with others, with little power to lift or transfigure.

The Beast-Jungle theory of evolution robs a man of his dignity, marriage of its sanctity, government of its authority, the church of her power and Christ of His glory.

4. Defense Attorney Clarence Darrow Interrogates Prosecutor William Jennings Bryan in the Scopes Trial, 1925

Examination of W. J. Bryan by Clarence Darrow, of counsel for the defense:

Q—You have given considerable study to the Bible, haven't you, Mr. Bryan?

A—Yes, sir, I have tried to....

Q—Do you claim that everything in the Bible, should be literally interpreted?

A—I believe everything in the Bible should be accepted as it is given there; some of the Bible is given illustratively. For instance: "Ye are the salt of the earth." I would not insist that man was actually salt, or that he had flesh of salt, but it is used in the sense of salt as saving God's people.

Q—But when you read that Jonah swallowed the whale—or that the whale swallowed Jonah—excuse me please—how do you literally interpret that?

A—When I read that a big fish swallowed Jonah—it does not say whale.

Q—Doesn't it? Are you sure?

A—That is my recollection of it. A big fish, and I believe it, and I believe in a God who can make a whale and can make a man and make both do what He pleases....

Q—You believe the story of the flood [Noah] to be a literal interpretation?

A—Yes, sir.

Q—When was that flood?

A—I would not attempt to fix the date. The date is fixed, as suggested this morning.

Q—About 4004 B.C.?

A—That has been the estimate of a man that is accepted today. I would not say it is accurate.

Q—That estimate is printed in the Bible?

A—Everybody knows, at least, I think most of the people know, that was the estimate given.

Q—But what do you think that the Bible, itself, says? Don't you know how it was arrived at?

A—I never made a calculation.

Q—A calculation from what?

A—I could not say.

Q—From the generations of man?

A—I would not want to say that.

Q—What do you think?

A—I do not think about things I don't think about.

Q—Do you think about things you do think about?

A—Well, sometimes....

Mr. Darrow—How long ago was the flood, Mr. Bryan? ...

The World's Most Famous Trial: Tennessee Evolution Case (Cincinnati: National Book Co.), 284–291.

The Witness—It is given here, as 2348 years B.C.

Q—Well, 2348 years B.C. You believe that all the living things that were not contained in the ark were destroyed.

A—I think the fish may have lived....

Q—Don't you know there are any number of civilizations that are traced back to more than 5,000 years?

A—I know we have people who trace things back according to the number of ciphers they have. But I am not satisfied they are accurate....

Mr. Darrow—You do know that there are thousands of people who profess to be Christians who believe the earth is much more ancient and that the human race is much more ancient?

A—I think there may be.

Q—And you never have investigated to find out how long man has been on the earth?

A—I have never found it necessary....

Q—Don't you know that the ancient civilizations of China are 6,000 or 7,000 years old, at the very least?

A—No; but they would not run back beyond the creation, according to the Bible, 6,000 years.

Q—You don't know how old they are, is that right?

A—I don't know how old they are, but probably you do. (Laughter in the courtyard.) I think you would give the preference to anybody who opposed the Bible, and I give the preference to the Bible.

5. Dr. William L. Poteat Criticizes Fundamentalism, 1925

We subject religious doctrine and the interpretation of the Bible to the test of the rational faculty, just as we apply that test to all other bodies of literature and doctrine. And however partial and dangerous it may be to rely upon one of our faculties and ignore the rest, many among us add to the habit of rationalism the offensive attitude of bigotry. The rationalism of science will set down as absurd what it is unable to explain or handle with its apparatus of the foot-rule, the clock, and the balance. So Salomon Reinach will declare that "religion is a collection of scruples which impede the free exercise of our faculties." The rationalism of orthodoxy will deny any fact which does not fit neatly into its system without deranging it, will go beyond what is written and seek to enforce with anathemas subscription to the decrees of an alien logic. So Mr. [William Jennings] Bryan will say that evolution is "a false, absurd, and ridiculous doctrine without support in the written Word of God and without support also in nature."

Fundamentalism. An interesting phenomenon in the religious thought of today springs out of this Western and modern tendency to rationalize the religious experience. Fundamentalism is an active movement which it is impossible to ignore, even if one wishes to do so. In so far as it succeeds it is likely to impose

---

on popular opinion the view that religion and science cannot dwell together in peace in the same mind. Such a practical result the propaganda does not seek, but it follows of necessity.The gentlemen who are promoting this movement appear to have learned nothing from history, illustrating a saying of the German author of the "Philosophy of History" that we learn from history that men never learn anything from history. They are loyal to a closed logical system and are repeating a blunder against which the past is full of warnings, and they are courting the disaster which has invariably followed the blunder,—the disaster of raising a perilous issue and later pulling it down. After a bitter resistance Christian theology in England came to see that the discovery of the method of creation did not dispense with the Divine agency in creation, and along with other human disciplines accepted and incorporated the great conception of evolution. That modus, as we have seen, was established some forty years ago. But only yesterday a few gentlemen, sincere, devout, and capable, old enough to remember it if they were even slightly in touch with the thought of that period, waked up to find, as they thought, the scientists secretly digging out the foundations of Christianity. Their excitement and alarm spread rapidly and widely. Trained for the most part in pre-laboratory days, they could not be expected to have the scientific habit or attitude. Invoking a man-made theory of inspiration most unfair to the precious documents of our faith, and committed to a bald literalism of interpretation, they take the rôle of defenders of the faith and in its name propose, by ecclesiastical and legislative enactment, by executive order, by organized propaganda, by inquisition and the refinements of modern torture, to crowd the eagle back into the shell and then, in Voltaire's famous phrase, crush the infamous thing. An organ of the movement announces that its purpose is "to drive out of all tax-supported schools every evolution teacher and every book teaching evolution. It is going to mean war to the knife, knife to the hilt." Once more the old slogan comes out of retirement—"religion or science," "Moses or Darwin." These earnest but misguided men are producing no effect whatsoever upon scientific opinion. Their solicitude comes in the wrong century. It might have been more effective in the nineteenth. In another direction, however, Fundamentalism is not without influence, and there lies the tragedy of it. It is compromising Christianity before the intelligence of the world. The young men and women who are trained in the laboratories of our colleges and universities, so far as they are affected at all, will find it difficult, under this interpretation, to keep their place in the Christian communion, or unpromising to enter. Without intending it, these ardent propagandists are, in reality, scattering thorns in the path of the young Greeks of our day who would see Jesus. We are witnessing another case of conservatism putting in jeopardy the cause which it seeks to save. The spectacle is amazing and disheartening.

Modernism in its newer phase is the reaction from Fundamentalism. As there are extreme Fundamentalists, so there are extreme Modernists. If the one says he believes everything in the Bible from cover to cover, including the covers,—everything read as it was written, interpreted with severest literalism, the other says he believes nothing in the Bible, interpreted with never so much freedom of figure and allegory: science has displaced religion as religion displaced magic. These two categories are neither exclusive nor exhaustive. Most intelligent

Christians decline both labels. In French and other legislative assemblies three groups of members are recognized,—the Right or conservatives, the Left or radicals, and the Center, the group holding intermediate or moderate views. The Center is most likely to be both clear and dependable. A great artist once said to me, "Perfection lies midway between perfection and barbarism."

6. John Crowe Ransom Takes a Stand for the Agrarian Way of Life, 1930

Nobody now proposes for the South, or for any other community in this country, an independent political destiny. That idea is thought to have been finished in 1865. But how far shall the South surrender its moral, social, and economic autonomy to the victorious principle of Union? That question remains open. The South is a minority section that has hitherto been jealous of its minority right to live its own kind of life. The South scarcely hopes to determine to other sections, but it does propose to determine itself, within the utmost limits of legal action. Of late, however, there is the melancholy fact that the South itself has wavered a little and shown signs of wanting to join up behind the common or American industrial ideal.... The younger Southerners, who are being converted frequently to the industrial gospel, must come back to the support of the Southern tradition. They must be persuaded to look very critically at the advantages of becoming a "new South" which will be only an undistinguished replica of the usual industrial community.

But there are many other minority communities opposed to industrialism, and wanting a much simpler economy to live by. The communities and private persons sharing the agrarian tastes are to be found widely within the Union. Proper living is a matter of the intelligence and the will, does not depend on the local climate or geography, and is capable of a definition which is general and not Southern at all. Southerners have a filial duty to discharge to their own section. But their cause is precarious and they must seek alliances with sympathetic communities everywhere. The members of the present group would be happy to be counted as members of a national agrarian movement.

Industrialism is the economic organization of the collective American society. It means the decision of society to invest its economic resources in the applied sciences. But the word science has acquired a certain sanctitude. It is out of order to quarrel with science in the abstract, or even with the applied sciences when their applications are made subject to criticism and intelligence. The capitalization of the applied sciences has now become extravagant and uncritical; it has enslaved our human energies to a degree now clearly felt to be burdensome. The apologists of industrialism do not like to meet this charge directly; so they often take refuge in saying that they are devoted simply to science! They are really devoted to the applied sciences and to practical production. Therefore it is necessary to employ a certain skepticism even at the expense of the Cult of Science, and to say, It is an Americanism, which looks innocent and disinterested, but really is not either.

The contribution that science can make to a labor is to render it easier by the help of a tool or a process, and to assure the laborer of his perfect economic security while he is engaged upon it. Then it can be performed with leisure and enjoyment. But the modern laborer has not exactly received this benefit under the industrial regime. His labor is hard, its tempo is fierce, and his employment is insecure. The first principle of a good labor is that it must be effective, but the second principle is that it must be enjoyed. Labor is one of the largest items in the human career; it is a modest demand to ask that it may partake of happiness.

The regular act of applied science is to introduce into labor a labor-saving device or a machine. Whether this is a benefit depends on how far it is advisable to save the labor. The philosophy of applied science is generally quite sure that the saving of labor is a pure gain, and that the more of it the better. This is to assume that labor is an evil, that only the end of labor or the material product is good. On this assumption labor becomes mercenary and servile, and it is no wonder if many forms of modern labor are accepted without resentment though they are evidently brutalizing. The act of labor as one of the happy functions of human life has been in effect abandoned, and is practiced solely for its rewards.

Even the apologists of industrialism have been obliged to admit that some economic evils follow in the wake of the machines. These are such as overproduction, unemployment, and a growing inequality in the distribution of wealth. But the remedies proposed by the apologists are always homeopathic. They expect the evils to disappear when we have bigger and better machines, and more of them. Their remedial programs, therefore, look forward to more industrialism....

Religion can hardly expect to flourish in an industrial society. Religion is our submission to the general intention of a nature that is fairly inscrutable; it is the sense of our rôle as creatures within it. But nature industrialized, transformed into cities and artificial habitations, manufactured into commodities, is no longer nature but a highly simplified picture of nature. We receive the illusion of having power over nature, and lose the sense of nature as something mysterious and contingent. The God of nature under these conditions is merely an amiable expression, a superfluity, and the philosophical understanding ordinarily carried in the religious experience is not there for us to have.

Nor do the arts have a proper life under industrialism, with the general decay of sensibility which attends it. Art depends, in general, like religion, on a right attitude to nature; and in particular on a free and disinterested observation of nature that occurs only in leisure. Neither the creation nor the understanding of works of art is possible in an industrial age except by some local and unlikely suspension of the industrial drive.

The amenities of life also suffer under the curse of a strictly-business or industrial civilization. They consist in such practices as manners, conversation, hospitality, sympathy, family life, romantic love—in the social exchanges which reveal and develop sensibility in human affairs. If religion and the arts are founded on right relations of man-to-nature, these are founded on right relations of man-to-man.

Apologists of industrialism are even inclined to admit that its actual processes may have upon its victims the spiritual effects just described. But they think that all can be made right by extraordinary educational effects, by all sorts of cultural institutions and endowments. They would cure the poverty of the contemporary spirit by hiring experts to instruct it in spite of itself in the historic culture. But salvation is hardly to be encountered on that road....

The tempo of the industrial life is fast, but that is not the worst of it; it is accelerating.... But a fresh labor-saving device introduced into an industry does not emancipate the laborers in that industry so much as it evicts them. Applied at the expense of agriculture, for example, the new processes have reduced the part of the population supporting itself upon the soil to a smaller and smaller fraction....

It is strange, of course, that a majority of men anywhere could ever as with one mind become enamored of industrialism: a system that has so little regard for individual wants. There is evidently a kind of thinking that rejoices in setting up a social objective which has no relation to the individual. Men are prepared to sacrifice their private dignity and happiness to an abstract social ideal, and without asking whether the social ideal produces the welfare of any individual men whatsoever. But this is absurd. The responsibility of men is for their own welfare and that of their neighbors; not for the hypothetical welfare of some fabulous creature called society.

Opposed to the industrial society is the agrarian, which does not stand in particular need of definition. An agrarian society is hardly one that has no use at all for industries, for professional vocations, for scholars and artists, and for the life of cities. Technically, perhaps, an agrarian society is one in which agriculture is the leading vocation, whether for wealth, for pleasure, or for prestige—a form of labor that is pursued with intelligence and leisure, and that becomes the model to which the other forms approach as well as they may. But an agrarian regime will be secured readily enough where the superfluous industries are not allowed to rise against it. The theory of agrarianism is that the culture of the soil is the best and most sensitive of vocations, and that therefore it should have the economic preference and enlist the maximum number of workers.

What anti-industrial measures might promise to stop the advances of industrialism, or even undo some of them, with the least harm to those concerned? What policy should be pursued by the educators who have a tradition at heart? These and many other questions are of the greatest importance, but they cannot be answered here.

For, in conclusion, this much is clear: If a community, or a section, or a race, or an age, is groaning under industrialism, and well aware that it is an evil dispensation, it must find the way to throw it off. To think that this cannot be done is pusillanimous. And if the whole community, section, race, or age thinks it cannot be done, then it has simply lost its political genius and doomed itself to impotence.

7. Richard Wright Describes Jim Crow Etiquette, 1945

One day I went to the optical counter of a department store to deliver a pair of eyeglasses. The counter was empty of customers and a tall, florid-faced white man looked at me curiously. He was unmistakably a Yankee, for his physical build differed sharply from that of the lanky Southerner.

"Will you please sign for this, sir?" I asked, presenting the account book and the eyeglasses.

He picked up the book and the glasses, but his eyes were still upon me.

"Say, boy, I'm from the North," he said quietly.

I held very still. Was this a trap? He had mentioned a tabooed subject and I wanted to wait until I knew what he meant. Among the topics that southern white men did not like to discuss with Negroes were the following: American white women; the Ku Klux Klan; France, and how Negro soldiers fared while there; French-women; Jack Johnson; the entire northern part of the United States; the Civil War; Abraham Lincoln; U.S. Grant; General Sherman; Catholics; the Pope; Jews; the Republican party; slavery; social equality; Communism; Socialism; the 13th, 14th, and 15th Amendments to the Constitution; or any topic calling for positive knowledge or manly self-assertion on the part of the Negro. The most accepted topics were sex and religion. I did not look at the man or answer. With one sentence he had lifted out of the silent dark the race question and I stood on the edge of a precipice.

"Don't be afraid of me," he went on. "I just want to ask you one question."

"Yes, sir," I said in a waiting, neutral tone.

"Tell me, boy, are you hungry?" he asked seriously.

I stared at him. He had spoken one word that touched the very soul of me, but I could not talk to him, could not let him know that I was starving myself to save money to go north. I did not trust him. But my face did not change its expression.

"Oh, no, sir," I said, managing a smile.

I was hungry and he knew it; but he was a white man and I felt that if I told him I was hungry I would have been revealing something shameful.

"Boy, I can see hunger in your face and eyes," he said.

"I get enough to eat," I lied.

"Then why do you keep so thin?" he asked me.

"Well, I suppose I'm just that way, naturally," I lied.

"You're just scared, boy," he said.

"Oh, no, sir," I lied again.

I could not look at him. I wanted to leave the counter, yet he was a white man and I had learned not to walk abruptly away from a white man when he was talking to me. I stood, my eyes looking away. He ran his hand into his pocket and pulled out a dollar bill.

"Here, take this dollar and buy yourself some food," he said.

"No, sir," I said.

"Don't be a fool," he said. "You're ashamed to take it. God, boy, don't let a thing like that stop you from taking a dollar and eating."

The more he talked the more it became impossible for me to take the dollar. I wanted it, but I could not look at it. I wanted to speak, but I could not move my tongue. I wanted him to leave me alone. He frightened me.

"Say something," he said.

All about us in the store were piles of goods; white men and women went from counter to counter. It was summer and from a high ceiling was suspended a huge electric fan that whirred. I stood waiting for the white man to give me the signal that would let me go.

"I don't understand it," he said through his teeth. "How far did you go in school?"

"Through the ninth grade, but it was really the eighth," I told him. "You see, our studies in the ninth grade were more or less a review of what we had in the eighth grade."

Silence. He had not asked me for this long explanation, but I had spoken at length to fill up the yawning, shameful gap that loomed between us; I had spoken to try to drag the unreal nature of the conversation back to safe and sound southern ground. Of course, the conversation was real; it dealt with my welfare, but it had brought to the surface of day all the dark fears I had known all my life. The Yankee white man did not know how dangerous his words were.

(There are some elusive, profound, recondite things that men find hard to say to other men; but with the Negro it is the little things of life that become hard to say, for these tiny items shape his destiny. A man will seek to express his relation to the stars; but when a man's consciousness has been riveted upon obtaining a loaf of bread, that loaf of bread is as important as the stars.)

Another white man walked up to the counter and I sighed with relief.

"Do you want the dollar?" the man asked.

"No, sir," I whispered.

"All right," he said. "Just forget it."

He signed the account book and took the eyeglasses. I stuffed the book into my bag and turned from the counter and walked down the aisle, feeling a physical tingling along my spine, knowing that the white man knew I was really hungry. I avoided him after that. Whenever I saw him I felt in a queer way that he was my enemy, for he knew how I felt and the safety of my life in the South depended upon how well I concealed from all whites what I felt.

ESSAYS

In the first essay, historian James C. Cobb asserts that the New South Creed, in which "a glorious past, a reassuring present, and a glittering future" pervaded southern thinking, came under attack in the 1920s. Historians, fiction writers, economists, and political scientists put southern society under the microscope and began to see its faults and failures. Cobb recognizes the role that the New

South Creed played in "retarding the growth of intellectual modernism in the region" in part as the result of a romantic mindset following the Civil War. Societal tensions emanating throughout the South brought an awareness of the need for change, socially and intellectually. Cobb argues that the post–World War I industrial spirit helped in the creation of a Southern Renaissance, an intellectual awakening. Nancy MacLean and Willard B. Gatewood Jr. argue that the same tensions led to a spirit of anti-modernism among southern whites. Whereas Cobb presents extraordinary intellectuals willing to break the bonds of traditional thinking, MacLean, in her history of the Ku Klux Klan, writes about the ordinary middle-class southerners, including pastors, who became klansmen to halt the process of modernization. Hannah Arendt's phrase the banality of evil becomes appropriate when looking at MacLean's depiction of Klan membership and ideology. In the final essay, Gatewood documents the effects of the Scopes trial on southern laws regarding the teaching of evolution in schools and the lingering adherence in the South to fundamentalist principles. The Scopes trial, rather than effecting change in state laws on the teaching of evolution, actually did the opposite. Tennessee still had a ban on teaching evolution in public schools as late as 1961.

The Southern Renaissance and the Revolt against the New South Creed

JAMES C. COBB

Daniel J. Singal has pointed to the pervasive influence of the New South Creed and its role in retarding the growth of intellectual modernism in the region. Because it was grounded so firmly and rigidly in a carefully constructed historical narrative, the weight of New South orthodoxy fell heavily on an emerging cadre of southern historians who faced especially strong pressure to fit their version of the region's past within the framework of the New South identity. To question the New South Creed's historical tenets "at any point," C. Vann Woodward explained, "was not only to make judgments about history, but to pass judgment on the legitimacy of the social order sustained by the assumptions questioned." Consequently, the early postbellum generation of southern historians were expected to occupy themselves with "vindicating, justifying, rationalizing, and often celebrating the present order," and as the outspoken John Spencer Basset pointed out in 1897, anyone who failed to do so faced "denunciation as a traitor and a mercenary defiler of his birthplace."...

Paul Gaston has argued that because myths such as the New South Creed "create mental sets which do not ordinarily yield to intellectual attacks ... they may be penetrated by rational analysis only as the consequence of dramatic, or even traumatic, alterations in the society whose essence they exist to portray." As a consequence, "the critique and dissipation of myths becomes possible only when tension between the mythic view and the reality it sustains snaps the

From *Away Down South: A History of Southern Identity* by James C. Cobb.

viability of their relationship." By the 1920s tensions between the New South's myths and its realities seemed to be approaching the snapping point.

Events such as the 1915 lynching near Atlanta of Leo Frank, a Jewish factory superintendent wrongly accused of murdering a female employee, as well as the resurgence of the Ku Klux Klan and the wave of post–World War I racial violence had helped to draw unprecedented attention to the South's enduring problems and deficiencies. In the wake of the war, a multitude of observers within the region and without began a critical reassessment of the New South version of the status quo below the Mason-Dixon line. Published in 1924, Frank Tannenbaum's *The Darker Phases of the South* only reaffirmed growing perceptions of southern benightedness.... Meanwhile, Oswald Garrison Villard repeatedly deplored the barbarity of lynching in the pages of *The Nation,* while W. E. B. DuBois assailed southern racial customs in a variety of publications. Focusing on Georgia, the supposed exemplar of New South progress, DuBois argued that "Georgia connotes to most men national supremacy in cotton and lynching, Southern supremacy in finance and industry, and the Ku Klux Klan."

DuBois was no tougher on Georgia than the Baltimore essayist, critic, and editor of the *American Mercury,* H. L. Mencken, who dismissed it as "at once the home of the cotton-mill sweater and of the most noisy and vapid sort of chamber of commerce, of the Methodist parson turned Savoranola and of the lynching bee." Meanwhile, the entire South, "for all the progress it babbles of," was "almost as sterile, artistically, intellectually, culturally as the Sahara Desert."...

In reality through his caricatured critiques of the contemporary scene, the acerbic Mencken seemed to be trying to goad white southerners into restoring the erudition and gentility that, so he believed, had characterized the South before the political and cultural ascent of the ignorant white masses in the late nineteenth and early twentieth centuries. Mencken's various attacks on southern cultural and intellectual backwardness won him a significant following among young southern journalists. Among them was North Carolina's Gerald W. Johnson, who saw the South as the "Congo," rather than the "Sahara" of the "Beaux Art" that Mencken described. In Mencken's *American Mercury,* Johnson assailed and spoofed the region in a variety of ways. In the aftermath of a successful tent revival, he found Raleigh, North Carolina, "so thoroughly sterilized morally that it is doubtful that liquor would have been sold to a justice of the Supreme Court, not to mention the parched drummers in the city's hotels." Johnson found both these frenzied religious rituals and the Ku Klux Klan flourishing in the South and the Midwest because "both sections are generally ill-provided with public amusements," and he worried that "impressionable children, caught in one of these orgies may never recover."...

Mencken had his black disciples as well, and in fact, he played a role in encouraging some of the key literary figures in the "Harlem Renaissance" that blossomed after World War I. Even as a nineteen-year-old, Richard Wright was both captivated by the way Mencken used words "as one would use a club" and stunned by the substance of what he wrote: "What amazed me was not what he said, but how on earth anybody had the courage to say it." By the time Wright discovered him, Mencken had already influenced many of the leading black intellectuals of the day.

In 1918 James Weldon Johnson praised Mencken as "the cleverest writer in America today."...

Generally, however, Mencken encouraged black writers to write with less anger and more detachment, from the perspective of one intrigued and amused rather than wounded by the white South's ignorance and insanity. He urged George Schuyler to craft a piece on "how the whites look to an intelligent Negro" and to do it "realistically and fearlessly." When Schuyler expressed a desire to write a spoof about the white man, an enthused Mencken responded, "Lay on.... I'd be delighted to see him dosed with the same kind of medicine that he has been giving Ethiop for so many years. Certainly he must be a ridiculous figure seen from without."

From 1929 to 1953, Mencken published fifty-four articles by or about blacks in the *American Mercury*. One of these, "I Investigate Lynchings" by Walter White, chronicled the racist insanity and ignorance that White encountered as he conducted his research into lynching. "Nothing contributes so much to the continued life of the investigator of lynchings and his tranquil possession of all his limbs as the obtuseness of the lynchers themselves," he explained. Published a year earlier, even White's book *Rope and Faggot: The Study of Judge Lynch* was often less scientific and objective than satiric in the Menckenian fashion. Quoting Mencken frequently, White also echoed his contention that the white South was a pathology-ridden, sick society lacking anything approaching real civilization....

Within five years after Mencken's essay appeared, contemporary observers were beginning to speak of the "renaissance" that was by then under way throughout southern thought and letters. The most notable explanation for the timing of this flurry of intellectual activity came from writer and critic Allen Tate, who argued that a post–World War I economic transformation in the South had ignited "a curious burst of intelligence that we get at the crossing of the ways, not unlike on an infinitesimal scale, the outburst of poetic genius at the end of the sixteenth century when commercial England had already begun to crush feudal England." Robert Penn Warren agreed that "after 1918, the modern industrial world, with its good and bad, hit the South" bringing a "cultural shock to a more or less closed and static society" comparable "to what happened on a bigger scale in the Italian Renaissance or Elizabethan England." As a result, Warren believed, "all sorts of ferments began" out of a "need to 'relive,' redefine life."

Some skeptics have challenged attempts to link the Southern Renaissance to economic and social modernization by arguing that the really significant changes in the South's economy and society did not even begin until the New Deal and World War II era when the Renaissance was already well under way, if not actually on the wane. As Reinhard Bendix has pointed out, however, in many modernizing societies "changes in the social and political order were apparent before the full consequences of the industrial revolution were understood." At the very least, Richard King contended, many of the key participants in the Southern Renaissance clearly shared "a pervasive, subjective sense that *something* fundamental had changed in and about the South."

Thomas Wolfe set his classic novel *Look Homeward, Angel* against the backdrop of Asheville's tumultuous emergence as a tourist mecca. His hometown's rapid growth brought prosperity to Wolfe's hard-charging, hard-bargaining mother but left Wolfe decrying the New South definition of "Progress" as "more Ford automobiles [and] more Rotary Clubs." He admonished his mother that "Greater Asheville" did not necessarily mean "100,000 by 1930" and insisted "we are not necessarily four times as civilized as our grandfathers because we go four times as fast in our automobiles" or "because our buildings are four times as tall." Ellen Glasgow seemed to agree, observing in 1928 the rising influence of "noise, numbers, size, quantity," and warning that "the modern South is in immediate peril less of revolution than of losing its individual soul in the national Babel."

Though he often focused on the depravity of southern poor whites, Erskine Caldwell also presented them as victims trapped between an outmoded agricultural system and the brutal, depersonalized industrial system that had begun to supplant it. In Caldwell's *Tobacco Road,* Jeeter Lester struggles to grow just one more cotton crop on worn-out land and refuses to go into the mills, which he condemns as "no place for a man to be." Caldwell envisioned his next novel as a sympathetic treatment of tenant farmers and mill workers "and all those living somewhere between those two occupations," and in *God's Little Acre,* the virile mill worker, Will Thompson, presents a stark contrast to the pathetic Jeeter. Although Thompson announces that he is as strong as "God Almighty himself," when he leads his fellow strikers in an abortive takeover of a mill about to be reopened with replacement workers, he is shot dead in front of the looms that were so much a part of his life. Will's death exposes the crushing indomitability and heartlessness of the New South's industrial system and the plight of those who had exchanged the poverty and frustration of the farm for the brutality and exploitation of the mill....

Elsewhere, writing in 1933 from what appeared to the casual observer a still sleepy Oxford, Mississippi, William Faulkner bemoaned the passing of the traditional, communal South that he pronounced "old since dead" at the hands of "a thing known whimsically as the New South." This, he was quite certain, was "not the South" but "a land of immigrants" intent on rebuilding Dixie in the image of "the towns and cities in Kansas and Iowa and Illinois" complete with filling station attendants and waitresses saying "Oh yeah?" and speaking with "hard r's" and once quiet intersections that now boasted "changing red-and-green lights and savage and peremptory bells."...

Bombarded with the New South's mythology of progress, but confronted everywhere with overwhelming contemporary evidence of their region's backwardness and decline, southern white intellectuals did in fact have much in common with their counterparts in other "developing" societies. Certainly, in the 1920s the South appeared to reach a point at which, as Dewey Grantham put it, "the earlier equilibrium between the forces of modernization and those of cultural tradition could no longer be sustained."...

As New South advocates sought to beat the North at its own game by emulating and even surpassing its economic achievement, [John Crowe] Ransom, [Donald] Davidson, and [Allen] Tate began to argue that the South's way of life was already superior to that of the North, and therefore, the effort to "northernize" the region would pull it down rather than lift it up. In 1930 Ransom, Davidson, and Tate joined forces with several of their current or former Vanderbilt colleagues ... to publish

I'll Take My Stand: The South and the Agrarian Tradition. Identifying themselves collectively as "Twelve Southerners," the authors contributed essays that varied widely in subject matter, emphasis, and quality. In general, however, they offered consistently vague tributes to the virtues of "agrarian" life and moderate to severe critiques of "industrialism."

In reality, most of the "Agrarians" who contributed to *I'll Take My Stand* were less intent on defending agrarianism or even deriding industrialism than on inciting their fellow white southerners to rise in revolt against what they saw as the ongoing New South effort to northernize their economy and society and thereby destroy their regional identity. Lifted from the lyrics of "Dixie," the title of the controversial volume came across as "fightin' words," but the cause at issue was not, as the subtitle suggested, preserving "the Agrarian tradition" so much as defending "a Southern way of life against what may be called the American or prevailing way."

In essence, the Agrarians sought in their erudite but diffuse treatises to discredit the dynamic, appealing, economically and politically pragmatic New South doctrine by emphasizing the threat that it posed to southern cultural identity. "How far," asked Davidson in his introduction, "shall the South surrender its moral, social, and economic autonomy?" as he urged young southerners to "look very critically at the advantages of becoming a 'new South' which will be only an undistinguished replica of the usual industrial community."...

The attempt by the "Twelve Southerners" to save the South from northernization by constructing an agrarian identity for their region was in no small sense a by-product of the modernization effort that they opposed so vehemently. Reinhard Bendix provided a useful comparative framework for understanding the historical setting from which the Agrarians emerged and, for that matter, the context in which the larger intellectual awakening of the Southern Renaissance began. Observing that in backward nations governments typically play a major role in instigating efforts to promote economic modernization, Bendix also cited the tendency of such nations to emphasize education in the hope of finding a shortcut to bridge the gap between themselves and more advanced societies....

New South proponents sought to build an "imagined community" organized around an identifiable and appealing economic and political agenda. On the other hand, despite their cultural objections to the New South program, the Agrarians offered no practical alternatives other than a romanticized historical vision of the country life that Depression-era southerners were then fleeing by the thousands. Still, as southern cultural supremacists they persisted in attacking those who occupied themselves with documenting and publicizing the South's defects and working tirelessly to help the region "catch up" with the rest of the nation. One of the principal targets of the Agrarians (within the South, at least) was University of North Carolina sociologist Howard W. Odum, who led his "regionalist" disciples at Chapel Hill in unloosing an avalanche of statistics and social research data pointing to the need to modernize the South's economy and institutions through a scientific, planned effort to promote both industrial development and agricultural revitalization.

Odum actually shared many of the Agrarians' concerns about the cultural consequences of wholesale industrialization. Still, his insistence on a realistic appraisal of southern problems led him to see their treatises as fanciful at best, even as it also set him squarely at odds with "the gross spirit of materialism" and the self-serving optimism that characterized the New South Creed. Established in 1922, Odum's *Journal of Social Forces* became the principal outlet for serious discussions of the South's deficiencies and failures and the inadequacies of southern leadership and institutions. Odum boldly proclaimed that the South needed "criticism and severe criticism," and H. L. Mencken, who had certainly done his share of criticizing, cited Odum as the embodiment of "the new spirit of the region" and the key figure in getting the new movement toward serious self-criticism that lay behind the Southern Renaissance "in motion."

The South was hardly lacking for critics in the 1920s, but one of the things that set Odum apart was the scholarly approach and sober tone of his writings, a tone that contrasted sharply with the caricature and superficial mockery favored by Mencken and his followers. As it evolved during the 1920s, Odum's approach also entailed not simply documenting the South's contemporary problems but searching for their roots in its past. Unlike Odum, many of the critical commentators on the South in the 1920s seemed too astonished by the ongoing panorama of ignorance and depravity that it presented to reflect seriously on the historical context from which this sorry state of affairs had evolved....

As Odum's colleague and protégé, Rupert B. Vance emphasized the importance of southern history even more strongly than Odum himself.... Vance saw the plantation retaining "many of the frontier traits" and passing them from the Old South to the New. (Odum had suggested almost the same thing when he noted "a sort of arrested frontier pattern of life" in the Southeast.) As Singal observed, "Almost everywhere he turned in surveying the modern South, Vance discovered that the basic patterns of the frontier still prevailed. The region continued to make its living by exploiting its natural resources heedlessly, applying little capital, skill or technology, with dramatically low levels of income and living standards the result."...

For Vance and Odum, the fusion of history and sociology was a means of offering a sound scholarly rationale for socioeconomic and political reform. This commitment to activist scholarship was enormously appealing to the young C. Vann Woodward, a native Arkansan who had graduated from Emory University with a degree in philosophy and earned an M.A. in political science from Columbia....

By the time he arrived in Chapel Hill, the twenty-five-year-old Woodward's activist credentials were well established. He had already visited the Soviet Union twice, and as an English instructor at Georgia Tech, he had participated actively in the defense of black Communist Angelo Herndon, who was convicted in Atlanta in 1932 of inciting insurrection. During his stint at Columbia, Woodward had also formed friendships with African American poets J. Saunders Redding and Langston Hughes and other participants in the Harlem Renaissance.

Despite his admiration for Odum and Vance, Woodward came to the University of North Carolina in 1934 to pursue a Ph.D. in history, rather than sociology. He was motivated primarily by his desire to secure the financial support (in the form of the Rockefeller Fellowship) necessary to complete his partially written biography of Populist leader Thomas E. Watson, which would also serve as Woodward's dissertation. For all his excitement about being on the same campus with Odum and especially Vance, however, when Woodward began his tutelage under the southern historians at Chapel Hill, he was soon and sorely disappointed. Owing to the stifling influence of the New South Creed on any impulse toward historical objectivity or candor, as the 1930s began, the formal study of southern history remained what Richard King called largely "an exercise in hagiography ... monumentalizing and devoted antiquarianism," and its "dominant mood" was "celebratory and/or defensive." Hence, Woodward quickly discerned that far from "making waves," the masters of southern history seemed "united not so much in their view of the past as in their dedication to the present order, the system founded on the ruins of Reconstruction called the New South."...

In reality, Woodward had come to Chapel Hill... to tell the dramatic personal story of a single Populist, Tom Watson, who had been at his best in the 1890s with his passionate articulation of the plight of the South's small farmers and tenants of both races, apparently only to sink thereafter into a relentless and sometimes blood-thirsty persecution of blacks, Roman Catholics, and Jews. Still, Woodward explained, Watson's life not only presented "a fascinating story in itself, but it plunged the historian into all the dark, neglected, and forbidden corners of Southern life shunned by the New South school."

As they appeared in *Tom Watson, Agrarian Rebel,* the Populists seemed more radical and better organized in the South than many had thought, and by emphasizing Watson's attempts to form a biracial political coalition, Woodward suggested that neither the Democratic party nor white unity and supremacy had always prevailed in post-Reconstruction politics. Anticipating one of the principal themes of his later study, *Origins of the New South,* Woodward also offered a distinctively unflattering portrait of the Redeemers, exposing their corruption and challenging their claims to descent from the old antebellum plantation order....

As he had begun his studies at Chapel Hill, Woodward had contrasted his own uninspiring impressions of the sorry state of southern historical scholarship ("no renaissance here, no rebirth of energy, no compelling new vision") with his excitement over the contemporary "explosion of creativity ... in fiction, in poetry, in drama." Nor could he help noting that the writers in these fields were "writing about the same South historians were writing about and making the whole world of letters at home and abroad ring with their praise." More than that, for the most part, the leading literary contributors to the Southern Renaissance were creating such a stir by holding the New South's vision of a glorious past up for inspection against the glaring light of contemporary injustice, poverty, and depravity.

Writing in 1938, Donald Davidson pointed out that every major literary or scholarly contribution of the last fifteen years had explored "the historian's question—what the South was?—and the related question—what the South is?" as part of an ongoing search for "Southern policies that will be well founded historically and at the same time applicable to the existing situation." Still largely in the grip of New South orthodoxy at that point, however, as a group, no segment of the white South's intellectual community seemed less inclined to make "the historian's question" part of a larger effort to understand the southern present than its historians themselves.

Mobilizing the Invisible Army

NANCY MACLEAN

If there were such a thing as a typical Klan meeting, the klonklave held by the Athens Klan on the night of September 15, 1925, would qualify. Exalted Cyclops *J.P. Mangum*,* a fifty-two-year-old policeman, called the meeting to order at 8:30 in the Klan's klavern (meeting hall). Presiding over the evening's events with *Mangum* was a full complement of twelve "terrors" (officers). In many regards, the meeting resembled one any other organization might hold: minutes read and approved, new members voted in, dues collected, plans laid for a recruitment campaign, an educational discussion, and even niceties: members received thanks from *Mangum* for having visited him when he was sick and from the board of stewards of a local church for having attended its recent revival meeting with a contribution.

Yet, mundane as the proceedings were, a few signs indicated that this club differed from others—notwithstanding the order's policy of not allowing discussions in meetings of "any subject, which, if published, would reflect discredit upon our great movement." Among the humdrum bills paid, for example, was one for labor and materials for a "fiery cross." Then there were the applications to join, some from previous members, that the Klansmen in attendance voted to reject. The chapter had recently reorganized due to a public scandal over the use of extralegal methods to combat vice, and it seems these men were viewed as possibly disloyal—"loose-mouth," "weak-kneed," or "traitors," in Klan parlance. Finally, one brief item in the minutes hinted at why absolute loyalty was so necessary. *L.S. Fleming*, the chapter Klokan (investigator), reported the case of a man who had been brought to the Klan's attention for failing to support his family. Not a few such delinquents found themselves kidnapped and flogged by crews of masked men in the 1920s.

Such blending of the ordinary and the extreme was common in the Klan of the 1920s; indeed, the blurring proved a source of strength....

The second Klan's founder, William Joseph Simmons, had not explicitly included such things among the Klan's goals when he established the order in 1915. The son of a poor Alabama country physician, Simmons was a man chronically on the make. Having tried his hand at farming, circuit-riding as a Southern

From *Behind the Mask of Chivalry* by Nancy MacLean.

*Names in italics have been changed.

Methodist Episcopal Church preacher, and lecturing in Southern history at Lanier University, by 1915 he had settled into a mildly lucrative position as the Atlanta-area organizer for the Woodmen of the World, a fraternal benefit society. Unsatisfied, Simmons dreamed of reviving the hooded order his father had served in as an officer after the Civil War.

For years, he thought about creating a new Ku Klux Klan. By October of 1915, he was ready to unveil the plans to a group of like-minded friends. Together, the group petitioned for a charter from the state. Then, on Thanksgiving night, they met atop Stone Mountain, an imposing several-hundred-foot-high granite butte just outside Atlanta. With a flag fluttering in the wind beside them, a Bible open to the twelfth chapter of Romans, and a flaming cross to light the night sky above, Simmons and his disciples proclaimed the new Knights of the Ku Klux Klan. Their passion for ceremony was not matched by a talent for organizing, however. Unclear about exactly what their message was, Simmons and his partners floundered over how to spread it. By early 1920, they had only enrolled a few thousand men.

That would soon change. In June of that year, Simmons signed a contract with Mary Elizabeth Tyler and Edward Young Clarke, partners in the Southern Publicity Association. Having organized support for the Red Cross, the Anti-Saloon League, the Salvation Army, and the War Work Council, the two had mastered the art of modern propaganda. Hiring a staff of seasoned organizers, they set to work to amass a following for the Klan and a small fortune for themselves. Within a few months, membership jumped to an estimated 100,000. A wife at age fourteen and a widowed mother at fifteen who went on to make a career as a businesswoman, Tyler had a knack for turning adversity to advantage. When in 1921 the *New York World* set out to destroy the Klan by documenting over one hundred and fifty separate cases of vigilante violence charged to it—an exposure so damning that it prompted a congressional investigation of the order—Tyler turned both into recruiting opportunities. In the four months after the *World's* exposé, the Klan chartered two hundred new chapters; overall membership leapt to some one million.

Seasoned promoters, Tyler and Clarke knew not only how to sell, but what would sell. To Simmons' initial blend of white supremacy, Christianity, and the male-bonding rituals of fraternalism, they added elements geared to tap the fears of many white contemporaries in the anxious years after the Great War. Declaiming against organized blacks, Catholics, and Jews, along with the insidious encroachments of Bolshevism, the order put itself forward as the country's most militant defender of "pure Americanism." It stood for patriotism, "old-time religion," and conventional morality, and pledged to fend off challenges from any quarter to the rights and privileges of men from the stock of the nation's founders. The message took. Although Tyler and Clarke had expected only Southerners to respond, men from all over the country did. "In all my years of experience in organization work," Clarke told Simmons, "I have never seen anything equal to the clamor throughout the nation for the Klan."...

Following a strategy devised by the Atlanta-based national office, Athens Klan promoters worked existing networks in the community to accumulate members. They looked to two areas in particular where it seemed their message might be well-received: fraternal orders and Protestant churches. The Klan presented itself to prospective members as the active embodiment of "the principles of the better class of lodges." Simmons, a member of fifteen other fraternal organizations himself, rallied men with odes to "the united powers of our regal manhood." To enhance the Klan's mystique, he designed a special alliterative lexicon for the movement. And he painstakingly worked out the details of elaborate rituals whereby members advanced in the order by obtaining "degrees" as they did in other fraternal orders. When he first came to Athens to advertise the new order in 1915, Simmons in fact emphasized "its unrivaled degree work." Many local Klansmen took the bait; they delighted in impressing their fellows with their mastery of Klan ritual.

In presenting their order thus, Klan organizers staked a bid for the loyalties of participants in the long tradition of fraternal association. The country had over six hundred secret societies by the mid-1920s; together, they enlisted over thirty million people. The Klan curried support from a number of these groups, especially those of common mind. It endorsed the *Fellowship Forum*, an anti-Catholic publication that claimed a readership of one million white, Protestant fraternalists. The Junior Order of United American Mechanics (JOUAM), an anti-Catholic, nativist fraternity whose better-known members included populist leader Tom Watson and President Warren Harding, was also known as "a close ally" of the Klan. Indeed, the Georgia JOUAM shared its weekly Atlanta-based publication, *The Searchlight*, with the Klan until the Klan formally took it over in October of 1923. The distinction between the two was moot in any case, since Klan leader J. O. Wood edited the newspaper.

Klan leaders cultivated their common ground with fraternal orders to reap a bumper crop of recruits....

The strategy worked. Even the meager records available for local fraternal orders reveal that a minimum of 120 Athens Klansmen, or twenty-nine percent, belonged to at least one. Among those that shared members with the Klan were the Woodmen of the World, the Elks, the Masons, the Odd Fellows, the Knights of Pythias, and the Shriners. Several Clarke County Klansmen also held office in these groups....

Nationwide, the Klan boasted that 500,000 Masons had joined by 1923. Along with members of other fraternal organizations, they often formed the backbone of local chapters.

Throughout the country, evangelical Protestants in particular flocked to the Klan, primarily Baptists, Methodists, and members of the Church of Christ, the Disciples of Christ, and the United Brethren. Men in more élite or liberal denominations, in contrast, such as Unitarians, Congregationalists, Lutherans, or Episcopalians, appeared less likely to join.... Even the patchy church records available showed that at least forty-three percent of Athens Klansmen belonged to a church—about the same proportion as that of all white county residents. Of these, thirty-seven percent were Baptists; thirty percent, Methodists; and smaller proportions scattered among other denominations.

Many Athens Klan laymen helped lead their churches. At least forty-six held positions such as deacon, elder, steward, committee member, usher, or Sunday School participant. Twelve Klansmen took part in the Men's Sunday School class at First Methodist Church alone. Some members advanced the cause in other ways. Klansman *L.T. Curry* served as Treasurer of the Businessmen's Evangelistic Club, while *N.O. Bowers* championed "personal evangelism" among young people through the Christian Endeavor Society. The wives and mothers of many local Klansmen, for their part, participated in the women's missionary societies of their churches.

Like laymen, many clergymen cooperated with the Klan. Of the thirty-nine national lecturers working for the Klan at one point, two-thirds were said to be Protestant ministers. Each Klan chapter, meanwhile, had its own kludd (chaplain). By 1924, the Klan boasted that it had enrolled 30,000 ministers. In that year, the Klan also claimed as members three-quarters of the 6,000 delegates to the Southeastern Baptist Convention. In Clarke County, most of the white Protestant churches had some connection to the Klan. Either their pastors belonged, or they allowed announcements of Klan meetings or robed visits of Klansmen during services, or they accepted Klan aid in evangelistic efforts....

Through such channels, the Klan built up its numbers. By 1923, its ranks included "three hundred of the finest men in Clarke County." Confident of their future, they began building a new klavern to hold their meetings. Members proudly announced that the hall would sport a forty-foot-tall electric cross. With its membership hovering around three hundred the next few years, the local chapter was a "baby Klan," as *The Searchlight* put it. The chapter drew in approximately one in ten of the native-born, Protestant white men eligible for membership—a considerable proportion, but small relative to some of its counterparts.

Statewide, the Klan also thrived in the first half of the decade. Since Atlanta hosted the Klan's national office, or Imperial Palace, Georgia always played a significant role in Klan affairs. The Atlanta Klan enrolled upwards of fifteen thousand members and boasted the largest fraternal hall in the city. By the mid-'twenties, chapters blanketed the state....

In the nation as a whole, Georgia ranked eighth among states in estimated membership. Among regions, the North Central and Southwestern states enrolled the most members, followed by the Southeast, the Midwest and Far West, and, finally, the North Atlantic states. By mid-decade, the total reached perhaps as high as five million, distributed through nearly four thousand local chapters. Yet the numbers barely suggest the reach of the Klan's tentacles. If its membership claims were true, the order enrolled as many members as the American Federation of Labor at the peak of its strength....

But their effect was enhanced by the kind of men the Klan was able to attract. The typical member, in Athens as elsewhere, was not the uprooted angry young man one might expect; he was middle-aged, married, and probably a father as well. Ninety-two percent of Athens Klan members were married men; more than two-thirds were fathers, with an average of between three and four children. While most local Klansmen were family men, not a few were civic leaders....

Just as the Klan recruited men from the mainstream, so it boosted members' morale with the kinds of family and community activities that clubs and churches also sponsored. Although excluded from the Klan itself, Klansmen's wives and sons could join parallel orders: the Women of the Ku Klux Klan, created in 1923, and the Junior Klan, created in 1924. Here, without distracting attention from the leading roles of their menfolk, family members might work for shared ends. Athens Klanswomen and men thus cooperated to reward a visiting minister with an automobile for his leadership of a successful revival at East Athens Baptist Church in 1926, winning themselves the gratitude of the church's chairmen and deacons. The following year, they collaborated on a fund-raiser whose end was "to place a Flag and Bible" in the city high school....

And yet Klansmen were not just Odd Fellows in robes and hoods. For all the ties that bound Klansmen to commonplace community networks and habits, the Klan was different. Leaders reminded members that their organization was "not a lodge," but "an army of Protestant Americans." As a "*mass movement*" to secure the alleged birthright of Anglo-Saxon Americans, it could achieve that goal only through "an aggressive application of the art of Klan craft." That required winning the confidence of the community by recruiting respected local men and making the Klan a "*civic asset*." In short, breaking into church and fraternal networks was part of a larger strategy to accrue power. And that power would be used toward ends some people in these networks might balk at.

Signs that the second Klan would be more than just another community organization were there from the beginning, not least in its name. The first call to reestablish the Klan came, not from William Joseph Simmons, but from Tom Watson. The foremost leader of Georgia's Populist movement in the 1890s, Watson had long since given up the struggle for interracial economic justice. Recently, he had turned his attention to Catholic and Jewish subversion. In August of 1915, he informed readers of his Georgia-based *Jeffersonian* magazine that "another Ku Klux Klan may have to be organized to restore Home Rule." Georgia's governor had just commuted the death sentence of Leo Frank, a Jewish factory supervisor convicted of the murder of Mary Phagan, a young white woman in his employ. The governor's mercy enraged those who believed Frank guilty, Watson among them. Four days after he issued his incitement, a body of men calling themselves the Knights of Mary Phagan kidnapped Frank from the state prison farm, took him to her home town, and hanged him from a tree.

Three months later, Simmons resurrected the Knights of the Ku Klux Klan in Atlanta, where Frank's alleged crime and his trial had taken place. The Frank case has often been cited as a catalyst for the creation of the second Klan, whose founding members, according to popular myth, included some of the Knights of Mary Phagan. In fact, no one has ever documented a direct connection between the two. The "truth" of the link lay less in personnel than in a common vigilante spirit. An appeal to that spirit would always be part of the Klan. Its promise of swift and secret vengeance, more than anything else, distinguished it from contemporary organizations with whom it shared ideas, rituals, and members.

Nothing in the early years helped more to make that promise come to life than D. W. Griffith's film extravaganza, *Birth of a Nation*, released in the same year as the second Klan's creation. In this racist epic of the Civil War, Reconstruction, and the restoration of white rule, Griffith harnessed all the emotive power of modern film-making technique to convince viewers that black men were beasts and white vigilantes were the saviors of American civilization. Given the right to vote and hold office, the film averred, African-American men dragged society into chaos; worse, they used such power to stalk white women. Griffith left no doubt about how this fate had been averted. In the final, climactic scene, the hooded and robed members of the Ku Klux Klan rode in to save his young white heroine from rape—by castrating and lynching her black would-be assailant. Their act ended sectional fratricide among white men and gave birth to a reunited America.

For the Klan, the film proved a boon. When it came to Atlanta for a three-week showing, record-breaking white crowds packed the theaters to cheer on the white-robed crusaders. Recognizing an opportunity, Simmons ran newspaper advertisements for the revived order next to those for the film. Thereafter, the Klan routinely exploited showings of *Birth of a Nation* to enlist new members, for it sent the message the Klan wanted delivered. "No one who has seen the film," commented journalist Walter Lippmann in 1922, "will ever hear the name [Ku Klux Klan] again without seeing those white horsemen." Not surprisingly, the NAACP sought—in vain—to have the film removed from circulation.

Black Americans in fact understood from the beginning that the second Klan was different, even from other racist organizations. In the view of many, it was an immediate threat. One month after the second Klan's founding ceremony, Georgia Republican leader Henry Lincoln Johnson begged the governor to make the order change its name, on the grounds that the Klan's re-establishment would encourage "mob outlawry." "My people (the colored people)," Johnson predicted, "will be the helpless, and often vicarious, victims." He was right. "Nobody knows," complained a Black Atlanta lodge officer to the NAACP in 1921, "the great destress" that this "great evil" had brought upon the black people of Georgia. The state's leading African-American newspaper, *The Atlanta Independent*, for its part, said of the second Klan that, like the first, its "aim and purpose is to terrorize helpless black men and women." "The epitome of race hatred and religious intolerance," it constituted "the most dangerous menace that ever threatened popular government."...

[T]he Klan steamrollered opposition and gained influence in Georgia. Broker of the votes of an estimated 100,000 of the state's 300,000 Democrats by 1923, the Klan held "the balance of power" in state politics, as even a reporter who sought to play down its domination had to admit. The order enrolled such well-placed officials as Governor Clifford Walker, Chief Justice of the State Supreme Court Richard B. Russell, Sr., State Attorney General George M. Napier, Atlanta Mayor Walter A. Sims, Solicitor General (district attorney) of Fulton County John M. Boykin, and Fulton Superior Court Judge Gus H. Howard, in addition to many less strategically placed men. Some evidence suggests that the roster also included Georgia's United States senators Tom Watson, Walter George, and William J. Harris; United States congressman and past president of the Anti-Saloon League W. D. Upshaw, and President of the Georgia State Senate Herbert Clay.

Similar patterns prevailed elsewhere. In 1923, for example, at least seventy-five congressional representatives were said to owe their seats to the Klan; at the annual conference of state governors the year before, only one was willing to discuss, let alone condemn, the Klan. The reason was not hard to find. The Klan held sway in the political life of many states; it dominated some outright, such as Indiana and Colorado; and it swept anti-Klan governors from office in a number of others, most spectacularly in Oregon and Kansas.

The ability to dispose of opponents so handily where it had the requisite numbers gives an indication of why Klan leaders put such a high premium on electoral politics. "It is of vital importance that our friends be placed in office," Georgia's Grand Dragon explained; "the life of our organization" might hinge upon the outcome of elections....

But it was back at home that the insulation mattered most. With it, the Klan could fend off measures that might have made its night-riding operations more difficult, such as a 1922 bill—aimed at the Klan—to prevent the wearing of masks on Georgia's public highways. The order went on to deliver one of the biggest electoral defeats in state history to the governor who proposed it, Thomas W. Hardwick. His successor, Clifford Walker, a Klansman himself, learned the lesson. As governor, he consulted Klan leaders before introducing new initiatives to the state assembly. On the local level, prosecution of Klan violence was hardly likely when municipal governments, police departments, and courts were rife with Klan members and sympathizers. "Everybody in the courthouse belonged to the Klan" in Atlanta, recalled a local city attorney; "virtually every judge, the prosecuting officers ... all the police and the mayor and the councilmen." If he exaggerated, it was not by much. With the cards thus stacked in its favor, the Klan could act with impunity.

Indeed, newspaper editors in the South, like politicians, tended to quaver in the face of Klan's power. Clearly, they did not view the order as an innocent analogue of other fraternal lodges. While local papers boosted these, most maintained an eerie silence regarding the Klan's activities. Few offered outright support, yet neither would they investigate or expose it. With the notable exceptions of the *Columbus Enquirer-Sun* and eventually the *Macon Telegraph*, no Georgia newspapers condemned the Klan until the second half of the decade, when its power had begun to wane. The Athens press was no exception.... "Nothing unpleasant must ever be printed" seemed to be the operating principle of most newspapers, observed one Athens educator and resident; another later recalled, "they put only nice things in the *Banner-Herald*."

Night-riding and inciting hatred were not nice; neither were they "newsworthy" if their targets were blacks or poor whites. The topic was just too ticklish to touch. Coverage of the Klan's activities, after all, might deter outside investors, agitate blacks, and stimulate discord among whites—to say nothing of losing subscriptions. Yet, uneasiness about the Klan's methods remained. The Athens press thus gave editorial support to two area judges who came out against the Klan in 1926 for its "lawlessness," its efforts "to intimidate men and ... dominate who shall run for office," and its habit of "trying men in secret." Throughout the South, in fact, the most commonly stated rationale for élite opposition to the Klan was, in the words of one Texas judge, that society could not abide "two systems of government for punishing crime," one "working at night with a bucket of tar and a sack of feathers."

After Scopes: Evolution in the South

WILLARD B. GATEWOOD JR.

Whether the so-called monkey trial at Dayton, Tennessee, in July 1925 was a decisive moment in the history of Christianity as William Jennings Bryan suggested or "an obscenity of the very first calibre" as Henry L. Mencken believed, it was the biggest and best newspaper story in the decade after World War I. On hand to witness the trial of John Thomas Scopes, the local football coach and high school teacher accused of violating Tennessee's new law against the teaching of Darwin's theory of evolution, was a larger contingent of newsmen than covered the naval limitation conference in Washington four years earlier. The principal attraction in the sleepy town in the Tennessee hills—"forty miles from the nearest city and a million miles away from anything urban, sophisticated and exciting"—was not young Scopes, but rather two nationally known verbal pugilists, William Jennings Bryan, whom the World's Christian Fundamentals Association dispatched to assist the prosecution, and Clarence Darrow, who headed the legal team sent by the American Civil Liberties Union to defend Scopes.

The Scopes trial quickly took its place alongside the Ku Klux Klan as a standard ingredient in the version of a Benighted South that emerged in the 1920s. That the South was the scene of a succession of well publicized battles over Darwin's theory and the only region of the country that kept monkey laws on the statute books for over forty years lent credence to the view that militant opposition to biological evolution was as southern as racism and states' rights. In one form or another the idea that campaigns against Darwin were rustic capers by ignorant religious zealots of the southern hinterlands has persisted since the 1920s. Such a view, while not without elements of truth, tends to distort the role of the South in the controversies over evolution that have periodically erupted in the twentieth century and to obscure the scope and meaning of these struggles.

To interpret the disturbances over Darwin as rural in origin, much less as mere regional phenomena, is to fly in the face of considerable evidence to the contrary. The antievolution campaigns, whether in the form of laws banning the theory from public schools in the 1920s or of acquiring "equal time" for creation science more than a half century later, were not isolated local efforts by a handful of untutored clerical zealots hostile to science per se. Rather they represented the most publicized aspect of a larger, more complex movement known as fundamentalism, a version of evangelical Protestantism that emerged in the late nineteenth century. Northern and urban in origin, fundamentalism was a

---

supernatural, biblically-based faith, often with a premillenialist orientation and always militantly opposed to liberal theology and the cultural changes it accommodated. Constituting a formidable coalition by the end of World War I, fundamentalists embarked upon a nationwide offensive in the 1920s that for a time filled the air with the sounds of ferocious combat and that polarized American Protestantism into warring camps....

The fundamentalist theology that came to maturity in the era of World War I was in many respects similar to what Victor I. Masters, a prominent southern Baptist, described in 1915 as "the Anglo-Saxon evangelical faith" of the South. Essential in both was a belief in a divinely inspired, errorless Bible as the source of all that was "decent and right in our civilization." For fundamentalists, their battle for the Bible was a battle for civilization. In the South, where the "Anglo-Saxon evangelical faith" was linked with cultural conservatism, the battle for the Bible easily became a battle for the southern way of life....

The strong antimodernist impulse, evident throughout southern Protestantism, early identified Darwin's theory as a threat to the integrity of the errorless Scriptures. Among the victims of the bias against evolution in the late nineteenth century was James Woodrow, an uncle of Woodrow Wilson, who in 1886 was dismissed from the Southern Presbyterian Seminary in South Carolina for insisting that evolution was compatible with the book of Genesis. Concern about the dangers of the "new theology" that accompanied the emergence of fundamentalism not only caused southerners to be on guard against its appearance in their midst but also prompted greater attention to what was viewed as a critical component of that theology, namely evolution....

In a region so proud of its reputation as "the stronghold of orthodox Christianity in this country" and traditionally hostile to Darwin, the antievolutionist rhetoric proved extraordinarily effective in galvanizing public opinion in favor of statutes to outlaw evolution. The crusade against evolution in the South, as Wilbur J. Cash observed, was not the work of a "small, highly organized pressure group," but rather "an authentic folk movement."... Ultimately five states—Oklahoma, Florida, Tennessee, Mississippi and Arkansas—enacted antievolution measures. More remarkable, perhaps, in view of the regional obsession with Darwin, was the failure of similar legislation elsewhere in the South....

Individuals active in the antievolution crusade of the 1920s who continued to oppose Darwin's theory throughout the quarter of a century afterward kept the issue alive and prepared the soil in which creation science would flourish in the 1970s.... [One who was] significant was the flamboyant, controversial J. Frank Norris of Texas, editor of *The Fundamentalist* and "the epitome of the independent fundamental Baptist" who exerted a powerful influence in fundamentalist circles for almost three decades after the Scopes trial. A whole generation of preachers and evangelists were "inspired by his example" and "hundreds of churches" organized through his influence. By his own admission one of his most notable achievements was his war on evolution that resulted in the purging of the Baylor University faculty of "seven evolution professors." The ever broadening base of southern fundamentalism and the virile legacies bequeathed by ... Norris and others insured the survival of antievolution sentiment in the South....

By 1931 five southern states required Bible reading and six others permitted it. Except for Louisiana, where a large Catholic population precluded a Protestant consensus, Bible reading became virtually a universal practice in public schools throughout the South. While the pattern in regard to the teaching of biological evolution was probably less uniform, there is substantial evidence to indicate that Darwin's theory was a topic that teachers in the region either chose to ignore altogether or to approach with great caution.

After the enactment of the Arkansas antievolution measure in 1929, which marked the end of legislative activity for almost fifty years, a common observation, especially by apologists for the South, was that the existence of monkey laws in three states posed no threat and were in fact meaningless....

The mere existence of antievolution laws not only acted as a deterrent to free discussions of evolution, but they also made available to disgruntled citizens legal instruments for disciplining teachers and administrators they found objectionable on other grounds. In 1929, for example, a high school principal in Fentress County, Tennessee, who incurred the enmity of two citizens because he suspended their children from school for a fireworks prank, was brought to trial and accused, among other things, of teaching evolution. Although the evolution charge was obviously added in an attempt to arouse community opinion against the principal, he was ultimately cleared of all charges....

In 1971 ... popular hostility to Darwin's theory may have subsided but had scarcely disappeared in North Carolina. In that year Gaston County school officials summarily dismissed George Ivey Moore, a student teacher in a junior high school, "for having responded to students' questions with answers approving the Darwinism theory, indicating personal agnosticism and questioning the literal interpretation of the Bible." Moore filed suit in federal court and won. The judge ruled that Gaston County school authorities had violated the establishment clause of the First Amendment by officially approving, in effect, "local orthodoxy" in regards to Darwin's theory of evolution. As the judge noted, the very word "evolution" still "struck a nerve" in Gaston County.

In view of the lucrative market in school textbooks it is hardly surprising that publishers were careful to avoid striking the same nerve. As a result, during the decades following the Scopes trial high school biology textbooks underwent significant revision in deference to antievolution opinion in the United States....

Throughout the fifty years after the Scopes trial various individuals and organizations, including scientific and academic groups, attempted in vain to secure the repeal of the monkey laws in Tennessee and Arkansas....

A bill to repeal the Tennessee antievolution law in 1929 met with no more success than those in Arkansas. Later efforts to repeal the Tennessee measure in 1931, 1935, 1939, 1951, and 1961 also failed but not before sparking legislative debates remarkably similar in content and tone to those during the 1920s. Legislators favoring repeal spoke as advocates of liberty and enlightenment who deeply resented the injury to "the good name of the state" prompted by the antics of what they called "a few narrow, prejudiced religious fanatics." Those who opposed repeal included some who preferred to leave the monkey law "quietly and peacefully sleeping" rather than remind the world of its existence.

But the majority of the opponents still believed that Darwin's theory was incompatible with their religious faith and a serious threat to morality, ethics, and decency. "If this act is repealed," a Tennessee legislator declared in 1931, "we may as well close our Bibles, turn our backs on Christian people and let this state go to hell." Thirty years later Tennessee legislators, among many others throughout the South, voiced identical sentiments.

In the half century after the Scopes trial the South underwent dramatic social and economic changes; industrialization, urbanization, a steady climb out of education deprivation, a Second Reconstruction that destroyed the legal foundations of racial segregation and prompted references to a "post-racial south," and increased per capita wealth substantially reduced some of the statistical disparities that traditionally distinguished the region from the rest of the nation. Much of the progress in education that commentators in the 1920s considered essential to overcome public hostility to evolution in the South had been achieved by a half century later, but somehow more and better public schools failed to eradicate opposition to Darwin's theory. Notwithstanding the preference of chambers of commerce and other regional boosters for the label "sunbelt," the South remained the Bible Belt. A sociologist writing in 1972 concluded that there was no substantial decrease in "Southern religious peculiarity in the recent past and no prospects for the decrease in the near future." In 1925 Henry L. Mencken observed while returning to Baltimore from Dayton that one could throw a brick out of the train window anywhere in route and hit a fundamentalist on the head. Allowing for Mencken's imprecise use of "fundamentalist" as a pejorative term for a broad spectrum of southern churchmen, his observation possessed considerable validity—and still did a half century later. The typical nonsouthern image of southern Baptists as late as 1967, according to a denominational paper, was that of "fundamentalists and hillbillies," devoted to "ideas and practices of day-before-yesterday," but who somehow appeared "too well dressed." Southern fundamentalists in the 1960s and 1970s were, in fact, different from those of Mencken's era: their ranks exhibited greater affluence and respectability, higher levels of education and sophistication, a broader institutional base, and an increasing political consciousness. The fundamentalism bequeathed by the generation at the turn of the century that was primarily northern and urban in origin lost something and gained something in its sojourn in the South. Hence, the fundamentalism that the South fed back to the nation after World War II, while deeply indebted to those who had formulated the doctrinal statements known as "the fundamentals," was not quite the same. From the ranks of this southern-type fundamentalism emerged the likes of Billy Graham, Jerry Falwell, Oral Roberts, and others who presided over expensive, nationwide religious empires and whose collective influence resulted, to an extraordinary degree, in what David Edwin Harrell, Jr., has termed "the southernization of American evangelicalism." Their message and style revealed the unmistakable influence of those who battled modernism and evolution in the generation of the Scopes trial. The idea of the South as "the nursery, the training ground, the granary, the source of supplies" for evangelizing America and the world was thoroughly familiar for them. Although Graham and most others associated with the post–World War II religious revival in the United States largely ignored Darwin's theory, they contributed significantly to a cultural milieu that nourished antievolutionism....

Although the South was the scene of noisy struggles over Darwin's theory and the only section of the country to invoke the coercive power of the state to ban it from the classroom, the region was never monolithic in its hostility to evolution. Those in the South intent upon enacting monkey laws encountered strong opposition from some conservative churchmen, including Southern Baptists, as well as from academic, scientific, and diverse other groups. Among Southern Baptists there were always leaders who boldly and eloquently opposed antievolution statutes as inconsistent with the denomination's historic commitment to religious liberty and to the principle of church-state separation. But the popularity of the antievolution position in the South meant that those who spoke against such laws, especially elected officials, did so at considerably greater risk than those elsewhere. In the South one was almost certain to be condemned and ostracized as a cultural scalawag who had sold out to alien forces bent on obliterating the southern way of life. Most opponents of antievolution legislation in the region recognized, as did Wilbur J. Cash, that such measures were usually "the focal point of attack for a program, explicit or implicit, that went far beyond evolution laws."...

Yet the fact remained that the South's response to evolution has been more intense, noisier, and more productive of coercive legislation than that of the rest of the country. Explanations of the region's exceptionalism on this particular issue have usually included references to two of the three R's of southern distinctiveness in general, ruralism and religion, and on rare occasions to the third R, race. Undoubtedly the South's rural character, low church, Bible centered, individualistic Protestantism, relatively low level of literacy and traditional educational deficiencies, as well as the existence in the region of a populist bias against established authority and elitism, have influenced its reaction to the theory of evolution. Perhaps more important, however, has been the peculiar relationship between regional faith and culture, a relationship in which consensual attitudes have been equated with a divinely ordained order of things. Whatever else antievolution and scientific creationist laws may have symbolized, as Clarence Cason observed in 1935, southerners perceived them as devices "to conserve their customs" and protect "the church about which their social patterns, their essential culture, foregathered to an important extent."

FURTHER READING

Kathleen M. Blee, *Women of the Klan: Racism and Gender in the 1920s* (1991).

Joseph Blotner, *Faulkner: A Biography,* 2 vols. (1974).

John M. Bradbury, *Renaissance in the South: A Critical History of the Literature, 1920–1960* (1963).

Wayne D. Brazil, "Social Forces and Sectional Self-Scrutiny," in Merle Black and John Shelton Reed, eds., *Perspectives on the American South: An Annual Review of Society, Politics and Culture*, vol. 2 (1984), 73–104.

Cleanth Brooks, *William Faulkner: The Yoknapatawpha Country* (1963).

Walter Buenger, *The Path to a Modern South: Northeast Texas between Reconstruction and the Great Depression* (2001).

Wilbur J. Cash, *The Mind of the South* (1941).

David Chalmers, *Hooded Americanism: The History of the Ku Klux Klan* (1981).

Paul K. Conkin, *The Southern Agrarians* (1988).

David Herbert Donald, *Look Homeward: A Life of Thomas Wolfe* (1987).

Don H. Doyle, *Faulkner's Country: The Historical Roots of Yoknapatawpha* (2001).

Paul D. Escott, ed., *W. J. Cash and the Minds of the South* (1992).

Ray Ginger, *Six Days or Forever: Tennessee* v. *John Thomas Scopes* (1974).

E. Stanley Godbold Jr. *Ellen Glasgow and the Woman Within* (1972).

James M. Gregory, *The Southern Diaspora: How the Great Migrations of Black and White Southerners Transformed America* (2007).

Jacquelyn Dowd Hall, *Revolt Against Chivalry: Jessie Daniel Ames and the Woman's Campaign Against Lynching* (1974).

William C. Harvard and Walter Sullivan, eds., *A Band of Prophets: The Vanderbilt Agrarians after Fifty Years* (1982).

Georgina Hickey, *Hope and Danger in the New South City: Working-Class Women and Urban Development in Atlanta, 1890–1940* (2003).

Thomas S. Hines, *William Faulkner and the Tangible Past: The Architecture of Yoknapatawpha* (1996).

Fred C. Hobson Jr. *Serpent in Eden: H. L. Mencken and the South, 1920–1935* (1974).

———, *Tell About the South: The Southern Rage to Explain* (1983).

Hugh C. Holman, *Three Modes of Southern Fiction: Ellen Glasgow, William Faulkner, Thomas Wolfe* (1966).

Anne Goodwyn Jones, *Tomorrow Is Another Day: The Woman Writer in the South, 1859–1936* (1981).

Richard H. King, *A Southern Renaissance: The Cultural Awakening of the American South 1930–1955* (1980).

Jack Temple Kirby, *Rural Worlds Lost: the American South, 1920–1960* (1987).

Michael Kreyling, *Inventing Southern Literature* (1998).

Lawrence Levine, *Defender of the Faith: William Jennings Bryan; The Last Decade, 1915–1925* (1965).

Nancy MacLean, *Behind the Mask of Chivalry: The Making of the Ku Klux Klan* (1994).

David Minter, *William Faulkner: The Writing of a Life* (1980).

Jack Nelson, *Terror in the Night: The Klan's Campaign Against the Jews* (1993).

Michael O'Brien, *The Idea of the American South, 1920–1941* (1979).

Ted Ownby, *American Dreams in Mississippi: Consumers, Poverty, and Culture, 1830–1999* (1999).

William Alexander Percy, *Lanterns on the Levee: Recollections of a Planter's Son* (1941).

Darden Asbury Pyron, *Southern Daughter: The Life of Margaret Mitchell* (1991).

Elizabeth Robeson, "The Ambiguity of Julia Peterkin," *Journal of Southern History* 61 (1995), 761–786.

Louis D. Rubin Jr., ed., *The American South: Portrait of a Culture* (1980).

———, *The Wary Fugitives: Four Poets and the South* (1978).

———, *Writers of the Modern South: The Faraway Country* (1963).

Louis D. Rubin Jr. and Robert D. Jacobs, eds. *Southern Renascence: The Literature of the Modern South* (1959).

Milton C. Sernett, *Bound for the Promised Land: African American Religion and the Great Migration* (1997).

Patsy Sims, *The Klan* (1996).

Daniel J. Singal, *The War Within: From Victorian to Modernist Thought in the South, 1919–1945* (1982).

———, *William Faulkner: The Making of a Modernist* (1997).

John David Smith, ed., *Disfranchisement Proposals and the Ku Klux Klan* (1993).

Morton Sosna, *In Search of the Silent South: Southern Liberals and the Race Issue* (1997).

Walter Sullivan, *A Requiem for the Renascence: The State of Fiction in the Modern South* (1976).

George B. Tindall, "The Significance of Howard W. Odum to Southern History: A Preliminary Estimate," *Journal of Southern History* 24 (1958), 285–307.

Twelve Southerners, *I'll Take My Stand: The South and the Agrarian Tradition* (1930).

Pam Tyler, *Silk Stockings and Ballot Boxes: Women and Politics in New Orleans, 1920–1963* (1996).

Susan Millar Williams, *Devil and Good Woman, Too: The Lives of Julia Peterkin* (1997).

Joel Williamson, *William Faulkner and Southern History* (1993).

CHAPTER 11

Turning Points? The New Deal to Post–World War II

When the Great Depression struck, the South was already reeling from agricultural and industrial miseries. By 1932, the meager financial resources of states and localities had disappeared under the avalanche of unemployment and low crop prices. A few years later, the southern economy was scarcely better, but posters bearing the likeness of President Franklin D. Roosevelt seemed to be tacked to every tobacco barn, county courthouse bulletin board, and filling station in the South. The New Deal gave southerners some work and much hope.

The Roosevelt administration did not intend to change the region's society and traditions. Southern politicians held important committee posts in the U.S. Congress and Senate and were wary of massive federal expenditures that could short-circuit their control over some whites and most blacks. But with $4 billion of federal money poured into programs, accompanied by the upheaval in farm prices and the dislocation of farm workers, change was bound to happen. What did it mean to long-time farming families and to rural traditions to leave the land? What did it mean to farmers to receive a paycheck from the federal government instead of from the plantation or local store owner? Scholars are sorting out the extent of these changes and especially their legacy for the modern South.

More important, many historians have argued, was the impact of World War II on the South. The migration from farms to cities and factories, sparked by federal defense factory jobs, increased employment opportunities. The war heightened the aspirations of women, who found that they could be fully employed if they so desired, and of blacks, who hoped for racial progress in the courts, on the battlefields, at polling places, and in their towns. The South was on the move: Millions left their communities to work in distant cities or fight in remote places. What impact these changes had on the South and on its future is a question debated by historians today. Some believe that World War II brought greater change to the South than had the Civil War. As with the New Deal, it is not yet clear whether the war was a watershed or the continuation of earlier trends in southern society.

DOCUMENTS

Staying alive during the difficult years of the Great Depression depended on the resourcefulness of all family members, but what happened when women, often working for lower wages than men or laboring in the home, ended up alone or as sole caretakers of the family? Letters to Florida officials and to Eleanor Roosevelt demonstrate, as seen in Document 1, that desperation often haunted these women and their families. The grim conditions on the farms and in the mines and factories played a role in thrusting the author of Document 2, Louisiana governor and senator Huey P. Long, into the national spotlight. The "Kingfish," as he was known, was a dyed-in-the-cotton demagogue in a region already famous for the genre, but his deeds matched his rhetoric more closely than others. This selection demonstrates why he generated such loathing and love in the South and elsewhere. The Farm Security Administration sent photographers, including Dorothea Lange, into the South during the late 1930s to capture the impact of the New Deal and to record what remained to be accomplished. Lange hoped that these photographs would help the nation understand the continuing needs in the South. The Great Depression muted the brash boosterism of the 1920s, and the federal government laid out the truth about the region's poverty. The two photographs in Document 3, tell different stories. The first, "People Living in Miserable Poverty, Elm Grove, Oklahoma County, Oklahoma," speaks of displacement, perhaps due to the dust storms that ravaged parts of the upper South making refugees out of parents and children as seen here in Oklahoma. The other, "Plantation Owner. Mississippi Delta, near Clarksdale, Mississippi," suggests a static hierarchical social order. The plantation owner's position in the photograph, his shiny automobile, the field workers in the background all conjure up an image of a racially exploitative environment exacerbated by the Great Depression. Document 4, an excerpt from *Report on Economic Conditions of the South* details how far the South lagged behind the rest of the country in economic, educational, and social development. Document 5, a portion of Virginia Foster Durr's autobiography, *Outside the Magic Circle*, gives a behind-the-scenes description of the first meeting of the Southern Conference for Human Welfare (SCHW) and her own campaign to end the poll tax. Virginia Foster Durr and her husband Clifford Durr, a lawyer for the Reconstruction Finance Corporation under FDR, were activists for civil rights. Virginia belonged to the SCHW, an interracial group founded in Birmingham in 1938. It was created in response to the needs put forth in the National Emergency Council's *Report on Economic Conditions of the South*, which was drafted by Clifford Durr and others. Document 6 is an excerpt from *Mothers of the South*, the result of research into the lives of southern tenant farm women conducted by sociologist Margaret J. Hagood. For girls, poverty, lack of education, and male privilege left lasting scars. W. T. Couch, director of the University of North Carolina Press, commissioned a book written by African Americans designed to explicate their aspirations during and after the war. The resulting manuscript, edited by Howard University history professor Rayford W. Logan with writings by veteran black educator Gordon B. Hancock, are excerpted here as Document 7. They reflect a less patient generation of blacks, who sought national solutions to regional racial problems.

1. Florida Women Desperate for Help Turn to the Government in Letters from the Depression, 1931, 1933, 1934

Mrs. Annie Esser Bartenfels (Miami) to [Governor Doyle E.] Carlton, 21 April 1931

1930 census: This may be Anna Bartonsfield, a 40-year-old German immigrant. She lives as a "lodger" and works as a cleaner at the city hospital. She is listed as single.

Pardon the liberty I take in writing you in regard to my personal affair concerning the Bank of Bay Biscayne (a State Bank), which closed its doors June 11, 1930.

This was a terrible blow to me for today I am penniless after such hard struggle for my living.

I have no home, nowhere to go! I am not able to take out insurance that would carry me through illness or death on account of all my money being tied up in the closed bank.

I am a widow. I have worked steady and faithful for a period of twenty years by long hours, small salary and hard work. I saved all I could without spending anything on myself, for the reason I wanted to protect myself in my age. Now my strength is gone and my health is poor—I have no one to depend on.

All that I saved I deposited in this State Bank. I had both a savings and checking account. My Pass Book No. is 8101. The very last amount of $100.00 I deposited on June 3rd, 1930—it was a holiday, the front door was closed, but was advised to go to the side door to enter the bank. My deposit and my statement were marked the "4th of June."

My suffering and distress is very heavy and urgent. I have to depend on domestic work so long as it will last, to support myself and avoid starvation.

Under the circumstances as explained above, I ask you kindly for a widow's right as a citizen. Please will you kindly aid me in this earnest matter to get my hard earned money back in full as I need it so much for my living? I shall appreciate your kindness very much.

Please reply to this matter strictly private as I do not want any publicity.

From Elna C. Green, ed., *Looking for the New Deal: Florida Women's Letter's During the Great Depression* (Columbia: University of South Carolina Press, 2007), pp. 30, 38, 50, 53. Reprinted by permission.

Miss Lola Nowling (DeFuniak Springs) to [Governor David] Sholtz, 28 January 1933

1930 census: She is the 11-year-old daughter of Miles, who is a laborer in the turpentine industry.

I am writing you this letter. Not because I won't to but because I need to. I won't to tell you my daddy died last April and left me and my mother and one boy[.] He is eight years old. I am 14 years of age. My daddy left mother a car and three heads of cows. she has sold them to make a living for us. My mother is in bad health can't work and only weighs (91) lbs. She hasn't any relatives but one that helps her and they don't much because they are not able hardly. Me and my brother gets ($2.00) a month each from the country [county]. and we are living on that now part of the time. We don't have much to eat. but we are in a bad shape now. and I want to ask you is they any chance for mother to get a widows pension if you can do anything for her. I surely would be glad and thank you so much. She gave you her vote and mother said if she ever lived till you get this. Please give me a quick reply[.] if you don't believe what I have said come and see.

Mrs. E. C. Scott (Lee) to [Governor David] Sholtz, 28 November 1933

Am writing you to know if you could issue me any State Peddling licenses. With[out] any funds.

As I'm a widow have three children ages 1-5-8 yrs whom are wholy depending on me for a living, and a mother[,] one sister[,] one brother who is partily depending on me. Mother unable to work, and very feeble. brother too small to work. and sister is sickly.

I have taught school 1 yr. but under the new laws of Fla. I cant teach any more as I have no college training.

My husband supported us all while he was with us. But he got injured in an auto wreck and passed away five days later. and Funeral, hospital, and operation expenses taken the $1000 insurance he carried.

My children and I had to come to live with my mother on a farm but the farm is not large enough to support us all without some other help.

I've tried to get along without asking this favor of you. But seems like everything goes wrong.

So winter is knocking at our door and we have no winter clothing.

My sister is working on the Relief Force but that only keeps us in groceries. Mother underwent an opration in St. Vincent's Hospital July 8 in Jacksonville, Fla. and we owe over $250.00 to the Dr's. that did the opration. besides our grocery bill and medicine bill.

I tried to get work on the relief but they said I could not work because I lived in the house with my mother and my sister working. My mother's house and farming fence needs to be repaired very badly. and if some one don't get some way of helping my sister work will go down soon.

Hoping you can grant me this favor which will not only be appreciated by myself but by all. And will thank you for your kindness. Many times over.

Mrs. Virginia Clements (Jacksonville) to ER [Eleanor Roosevelt], 7 January 1934

Pardon me for troubling you. I guess you remember me writeing you once before this. I was in trouble about looseing my little home. I had a loan on it and asked you to help me out, so I guess I have lost it.

I hate to be so persistent and ask for your help again when I was refused. Just two old people 72 yrs old and no way to help ourselves. Mr. Clements has been paralized since last May cant talk or walk. I cant begin to tell you the worry and trouble I have had; just how I have stood up under it I cant tell.

I left Macon[.] a friend paid our way to Jacksonville, Fla thinking it would help Mr. Clements. The Government is helping so many things cant you get some help for me? $10.00 or $15.00 per week would be wonderful to help me pay rent and get a little something to eat, or any thing that you are willing to give me would certainly be appreciated. I owe a big Dr's bill nothing to pay with. If you could know what I have gone through with I believe you would help me. If you would help me every week or once a month. If you send anything dont make it public. I am poor but proud. I have seen better days.

Hope this wont fall on deaf ears.

2. Huey P. Long Wants to Make "Every Man a King," 1933

The increasing fury with which I have been, and am to be, assailed by reason of the fight and growth of support for limiting the size of fortunes can only be explained by the madness which human nature attaches to the holders of accumulated wealth.

What I have proposed is:—

The Long Plan

1. A capital levy tax on the property owned by any one person of 1% of all over $1,000,000; 2% of all over $2,000,000 etc., until, when it reaches fortunes of over $100,000,000, the government takes all above that figure; which means a limit on the size of any one man's fortune to something like $50,000,000—the balance to go to the government to spread out in its work among all the people.
2. An inheritance tax which does not allow any one person to receive more than $5,000,000 in a lifetime without working for it, all over that amount to go to the government to be spread among the people for its work.

Huey P. Long, "The Maddened Fortune Holders and Their Infuriated Public Press," in *Every Man a King: The Autobiography of Huey P. Long* (New Orleans: National Book Co., 1933), pp. 338–340.

3. An income tax which does not allow any one man to make more than $1,000,000 in one year, exclusive of taxes, the balance to go to the United States for general work among the people.

The foregoing program means all taxes paid by the fortune holders at the top and none by the people at the bottom; the spreading of wealth among all the people and the breaking up of a system of Lords and Slaves in our economic life. It allows the millionaires to have, however, more than they can use for any luxury they can enjoy on earth. But, with such limits, all else can survive.

That the public press should regard my plan and effort as a calamity and me as a menace is no more than should be expected, gauged in the light of past events. According to Ridpath, the eminent historian:

> The ruling classes always possess the means of information and the processes by which it is distributed. The newspaper of modern times belongs to the upper man. The under man has no voice; or if, having a voice, he cries out, his cry is lost like a shout in the desert. Capital, in the places of power, seizes upon the organs of public utterance, and howls the humble down the wind. Lying and misrepresentation are the natural weapons of those who maintain an existing vice and gather the usufruct of crime.
>
> —Ridpath's History of the World, Page 410.

In 1932, the vote for my resolution showed possibly a half dozen other Senators back of it. It grew in the last Congress to nearly twenty Senators. Such growth through one other year will mean the success of a venture, the completion of everything I have undertaken,—the time when I can and will retire from the stress and fury of my public life, maybe as my forties begin,—a contemplation so serene as to appear impossible.

That day will reflect credit on the States whose Senators took the early lead to spread the wealth of the land among all the people.

Then no tear dimmed eyes of a small child will be lifted into the saddened face of a father or mother unable to give it the necessities required by its soul and body for life; then the powerful will be rebuked in the sight of man for holding that which they cannot consume, but which is craved to sustain humanity; the food of the land will feed, the raiment clothe, and the houses shelter all the people; the powerful will be elated by the well being of all, rather than through their greed.

Then, those of us who have pursued that phantom of Jefferson, Jackson, Webster, Theodore Roosevelt and Bryan may hear wafted from their lips in Valhalla:

EVERY MAN A KING

3. Dorothea Lange Photographs the Depression, 1936

"People living in miserable poverty, Elm Grove, Oklahoma County, Oklahoma," 1936. (Dorothea Lange/Library of Congress)

"Plantation Owner. Mississippi Delta, near Clarksdale, Mississippi," 1936. (Dorothea Lange/Library of Congress)

4. The President's Council Reports on Southern Economic Conditions, 1938

The President's Letter

To the Members of the Conference on Economic Conditions in the South: My intimate interest in all that concerns the South is, I believe, known to all of you; but this interest is far more than a sentimental attachment born of a considerable residence in your section and of close personal friendship for so many of your people. It proceeds even more from my feeling of responsibility toward the whole Nation. It is my conviction that the South presents right now the Nation's No. 1 economic problem—the Nation's problem, not merely the South's. For we have an economic unbalance in the Nation as a whole, due to this very condition of the South.

It is an unbalance that can and must be righted, for the sake of the South and of the Nation....

FRANKLIN D. ROOSEVELT.

THE WHITE HOUSE
Washington, D.C., July 5, 1938.

Report to the President

POPULATION

The population of the South is growing more rapidly by natural increase than that of any other region. Its excess of births over deaths is 10 per thousand, as compared with the national average of 7 per thousand; and already it has the most thickly populated rural area in the United States. Of the 108,600,000 native-born persons in the country in 1930, 28,700,000 were born in the Southeast, all but 4,600,000 in rural districts.

These rural districts have exported one-fourth of their natural increase in sons and daughters. They have supplied their own growth, much of the growth of southern cities, and still have sent great numbers into other sections. Of these southerners born in rural areas, only 17,500,000 live in the locality where they were born, and 3,800,000 have left the South entirely....

PRIVATE AND PUBLIC INCOME

Ever since the War between the States the South has been the poorest section of the Nation. The richest State in the South ranks lower in per capita income than the poorest State outside the region. In 1937 the average income in the South was $314; in the rest of the country it was $604, or nearly twice as much.

Even in "prosperous" 1929 southern farm people received an average gross income of only $186 a year as compared with $528 for farmers elsewhere. Out of that $186 southern farmers had to pay all their operating expenses—tools, fertilizer, seed, taxes, and interest on debt—so that only a fraction of that sum was

Report on Economic Conditions in the South. Prepared for the President by the National Emergency Council., 1938.

left for the purchase of food, clothes, and the decencies of life. It is hardly surprising, therefore, that such ordinary items as automobiles, radios, and books are relatively rare in many southern country areas.

For more than half of the South's farm families—the 53 percent who are tenants without land of their own—incomes are far lower. Many thousands of them are living in poverty comparable to that of the poorest peasants in Europe. A recent study of southern cotton plantations indicated that the average tenant family received an income of only $73 per person for a year's work. Earnings of share croppers ranged from $38 to $87 per person, and an income of $38 annually means only a little more than 10 cents a day.

The South's industrial wages, like its farm income, are the lowest in the United States. In 1937 common labor in 20 important industries got 16 cents an hour less than laborers in other sections received for the same kind of work. Moreover, less than 10 percent of the textile workers are paid more than 52.5 cents an hour, while in the rest of the Nation 25 percent rise above this level. A recent survey of the South disclosed that the average annual wage in industry was only $865 while in the remaining States it averaged $1,219....

Since the South's people live so close to the poverty line, its many local political subdivisions have had great difficulty in providing the schools and other public services necessary in any civilized community. In 1935 the assessed value of taxable property in the South averaged only $463 per person, while in the nine Northeastern States it amounted to $1,370. In other words, the Northeastern States had three times as much property per person to support their schools and other institutions.

Consequently, the South is not able to bring its schools and many other public services up to national standards, even though it tax the available wealth as heavily as any other section. In 1936 the State and local governments of the South collected only $28.88 per person while the States and local governments of the Nation as a whole collected $51.54 per person.

Although the South had 28 percent of the country's population, its Federal income-tax collections in 1934 were less than 12 percent of the national total. These collections averaged only $1.28 per capita throughout the South, ranging from 24 cents in Mississippi to $3.53 in Florida.

So much of the profit from southern industries goes to outside financiers, in the form of dividends and interest, that State income taxes would produce a meager yield in comparison with similar levies elsewhere. State taxation does not reach dividends which flow to corporation stockholders and management in other States; and, as a result, these people do not pay their share of the cost of southern schools and other institutions.

Under these circumstances the South has piled its tax burden on the backs of those least able to pay, in the form of sales taxes. (The poll tax keeps the poorer citizens from voting in eight southern States; thus they have no effective means of protesting against sales taxes.) In every southern State but one, 59 percent of the revenue is raised by sales taxes. In the northeast, on the other hand, not a single State gets more than 44 percent of its income from this source, and most of them get far less....

WOMEN AND CHILDREN

Child labor is more common in the South than in any other section of the Nation, and several Southern States are among those which have the largest proportion of their women in gainful work. Moreover, women and children work under fewer legal safeguards than women and children elsewhere in the Nation.

Low industrial wages for men in the South frequently force upon their children as well as their wives a large part of the burden of family support. In agriculture, because of poor land and equipment, entire families must work in order to make their living.

The 1930 census, latest source of comprehensive information on child labor, showed that about three-fourths of all gainfully employed children from 10 to 15 years old worked in the Southern states, although these States contained less than one-third of the country's children between those ages....

In a region where workers generally are exploited, women are subjected to an even more intense form of exploitation. Many women work more than 50 hours a week in cotton and other textile mills, and in the shoe, bag, paper box, drug, and similar factories in certain Southern States.

The South has two of the four states in the entire Nation that have enacted no laws whatever to fix maximum hours for women workers. Only one of the Southern States has established an 8-hour day for women in any industry. Only four of the Southern States have applied a week as short as 48 hours for women in any industry.

Reports for a number of industries, including cotton manufacturing, have shown wage earners receiving wages well below those estimated by the Works Progress Administration as the lowest which would maintain a worker's family.

Women's wages ordinarily amount to less than men's. However, only two of the Southern States have enacted a law providing a minimum wage for women, though several others are attempting to pass such legislation. Recent pay-roll figures show women textile workers in an important southern textile State receiving average wages 10 percent below the average outside the South. Other figures show that a week's wage of less than $10 was received by more than half the women in one State's cotton mills, and by a large part of the women in the seamless hosiery plants of three States and in the men's work-clothes factories of two States.

Many women, even though employed full time, must receive public aid because their wages are insufficient to care for themselves and their children. The community thus carries part of the burden of these low wages and, in effect, subsidizes the employer.

One condition tending to lower women's wages is the system by which factories "farm out" work to be done in homes. Women have been found at extremely low pay doing such work as making artificial flowers, sewing buttons on cards, clocking hosiery, embroidering children's clothing, stuffing and stitching baseballs. Although this is a relatively recent tendency in the South, there are indications that such work is increasing. Usually the pay is far below that paid in the factory. A study of industrial home work on infants' wear disclosed that the women worked much longer hours than in the factory, though half of them received less than $2.73 for their week's work.

A low wage scale means low living standards, insufficient food for many, a great amount of illness, and, in general, unhealthful and undesirable conditions of life....

5. Virginia Foster Durr Describes the Southern Conference for Human Welfare and the Campaign to End the Poll Tax, 1938

About 1936 Cliff [Clifford Durr] joined the Southern Policy Committee, a group of young Southerners in the New Deal who met for dinner together once to twice a month to discuss the South. It was all white and all high-echelon people in the Senate and the House and New Deal agencies: Cliff, Lister Hill, Senator John Sparkman, Clark Foreman, Tex Goldschmidt, Abe Fortas, and some others.

At one of these meetings of the Southern Policy Committee, Clark Foreman and a very bright fellow named Jerome Frank, who had been general counsel of the Agricultural Adjustment Administration, had the idea that a pamphlet should be written on the South. In 1938 they sold the idea to the president, and he asked Lowell Mellett of the National Emergency Council to direct the Project.

The result was the *Report on Economic Conditions of the South*, referred to as *The South: Economic Problem Number One*, written mostly in my living room. Arthur Raper, a noted sociologist from North Carolina; Jack Fisher, who later became editor of the *Atlantic;* Tex Goldschmidt; and Cliff all worked on the pamphlet. I wasn't included in the group—no women were—but I was always bringing in coffee and food and hearing the fights among them. Sometimes they worked at Lowell Mellett's house, right down the road from us. The report had articles on agriculture and industry. Cliff wrote an article for it on credit and he wrote the letter that the president signed that introduced the pamphlet. The pamphlet was written as a manifesto of what had to be done in the South and is really very good....

In the end, the New Dealers, the Southern Policy Committee, the labor people, and the black people all got together in Birmingham in November 1938, for the first meeting of the Southern Conference for Human Welfare.

A variety of groups came together at the conference in Birmingham. I attended as a delegate from the Women's Division of the Democratic National Committee. Miss Lucy [Randolph Mason] and Joe Gelders represented labor. Cliff and Clark Foreman and Tex Goldschmidt represented a group of young Southerners in the New Deal. Jane and Dolly Speed, who now ran a Communist bookstore in Birmingham, and Rob Hall, the Communist secretary for Alabama, were there. Bill Mitch and others represented the mine workers and the steel workers. I understand that Mrs. Rossevelt was the one who insisted that blacks

---

From *Outside The Magic Circle: The Autobiography of Virginia Durr* edited by Hollinger F. Barnard. (UAP 1985) excerpts from Chapter 7, "The Southern Conference for Human Welfare," pp. 116-134. Reprinted by permission.

be included, and Mary McLeod Bethune was her emissary. Frank Graham [UNC president] and many other University of North Carolina people were there. Myles Horton was there with the people from the Highlander Folk School, a settlement house in rural Tennessee that had become involved in the union movement....

The conference opened on a Sunday night in the city auditorium in downtown Birmingham. Oh, it was a love feast. There must have been 1,500 or more people there from all over the South, black and white, labor union people and New Dealers. Southern meetings always include a lot of preaching and praying and hymn singing, and this meeting was no exception. The whole meeting was just full of love and hope. It was thrilling. Frank Graham was elected temporary chairman and he made a beautiful speech. He set the tone for the meeting, and we all went away from there that night just full of love and gratitude. The whole South was coming together to make a new day.

We were to meet the next morning to elect a permanent chairman and then break up into workshops, but when we got there we found the auditorium surrounded by black marias. Every police van in the city and county was there. Policemen were everywhere, inside and out. And there was Bull Connor [Public Safety Commissioner] saying anybody who broke the segregation law of Alabama would be arrested and taken to jail. No ifs, ands, or buts about it.

The city auditorium had a central aisle, and Connor said the blacks had to sit on one side and the whites on the other. Then a great debate began about whether blacks and whites could sit and stand on the stage together.

That same day Mrs. Roosevelt arrived. She was ushered in with great applause. Everybody clapped and clapped and clapped and clapped. She got a little folding chair and put it right in the middle of the aisle. She said she refused to be segregated. She carried the little folding chair with her wherever she went. The workshops were held in various churches and other buildings, and of course they had to be segregated too. Policemen followed us everywhere to make sure the segregation laws were observed, but they didn't dare arrest Mrs. Roosevelt.

The South's etiquette of race was challenged in another episode during the conference. Louise Charlton, who had been one of the organizers, was presiding until Dr. Graham was officially elected president. At one point she called on Mary McLeod Bethune. She said, "Mary, do you wish to come to the platform?" Mrs. Bethune rose. She looked like an African queen, a large woman and homely but with an air of grandeur. She always carried a stick engraved with her name on it that President Roosevelt had given her. She was very proud of that stick. Mrs. Bethune got up with the stick and she said, "My name is Mrs. Bethune." So Louise had to say, "Mrs. Bethune, will you come to the platform?" That sounds like a small thing now, but that was a big dividing line. A Negro woman in Birmingham, Alabama, was called Mrs. at a public meeting....

This is the way I felt in 1938 at the Southern Conference meeting in Birmingham; it was silly to argue ideology when there were so many hard jobs to be done. I was concentrating on the poll tax and on getting women to vote.

As time went on, I felt more strongly about women's rights. I had a good husband, so I don't personally have passionate feelings about women's rights. But I had passionate feelings about the way Southern girls were treated and the position I was in as a young girl. It was supposed to be bad for you to be smart and to go to college, because men liked dumb women. My aunt, I remember, would say, "Don't discuss books with boys. That always scares them off."...

The whole group of 1,500 or more people, when they finally met, wanted to get rid of the poll tax. That was the first resolution. There were resolutions on credit and on agriculture and this, that, and the other, but the main concern was the right to vote—to get rid of the poll tax and to get rid of the registration laws. We formed a subcommittee of the Southern Conference for Human Welfare on the poll tax. It was named the Civil Rights Committee, but we worked on getting rid of the poll tax mostly. Maury Maverick, a congressman from Texas, was president of the subcommittee....

Soon after the Birmingham meeting of the Southern Conference for Human Welfare, Joe Gelders came to Washington to get someone to introduce a bill in Congress to abolish the poll tax. Joe was executive secretary of the poll tax committee and I was vice-president. Lee Geyer, a congressman from California, agreed to introduce the bill, and he agreed to let us use his office as a place to work.... He thought to deny people the right to vote was a sin and a shame and an outrage. Unfortunately, he had the beginnings of cancer of the throat, so he had difficulty speaking. But he did introduce the bill in late 1939.

The bill was sent to the Judiciary Committee. The head of the Judiciary Committee at that time was Congressman Hatton Sumners from Texas. He was an old gentleman who'd been in the House forever and a day. He was the epitome of the Southern conservative. I believe he even wore a frock coat. He looked like a relic of the past. And he did everything he could to keep the bill from ever coming to a hearing. He used every device and maneuver.

Maury Maverick, the president of the poll tax committee, was still in the Congress at that time. Maury was young and lively and very bright. He was full on vim and vigor and he wasn't scared of anybody, so he got old Hatton Sumners to hold the hearings. Maury testified and so did Clark Foreman and Miss Lucy. We were treated in a very hostile way by the committee, particularly by Hatton Sumners, who was just burning with rage and indignation at the idea of this bunch of upstarts.

The evidence was all there—the fact that not more than 12 percent of the voting population in Virginia voted and 13 percent in Mississippi. The facts were incontrovertible. That is, since the disenfranchising provisions of the 1800s and early 1900s, starting with Mississippi, the number who voted in the South, both blacks and whites, had gone down, down, down. The South in 1939 had an extremely small vote. It was argued that Southerners weren't interested in voting. They just didn't care about it.

Hatton Sumners never printed the hearings. He was a man of so much prestige and power in the House that he wouldn't budge. The Southerners controlled most of the big committees. They had been in office forever and a day because of the small electorate in the South. Many were seventy or eighty and they had been in Congress thirty or forty years. They just ran the show....

We began to lobby on the Hill in an effort to get support for the poll tax bill. I was about thirty-six—a good deal younger and better looking than I am now, and I was subjected for the first time to passes from senators and congressmen. To be a senator or congressman you had to have a rather large ego, because it takes an awful lot of work and strength and vitality and vigor. Well, frequently they'd chase you around the desk, literally. You'd see this large mountain of a man rise up and come toward you, and you'd back toward the door. So many of them were men of strong sexual urges, I would say. But you really couldn't take it personally. You didn't feel that you were being particularly distinguished for unusual charms or beauty; it was just that you were female and fair game....

The poll tax committee was, at that time, part of a Roosevelt coalition. I was in it for the women, but the blacks had stronger feelings. They always said that even when we got the poll tax abolished, they still had registration restrictions to get around. So while they favored abolishing the poll tax, they always realized that they would have to do away with the registration provisions and the property and literacy provisions. In some of the states, if a man was illiterate, he couldn't vote unless he owned three hundred dollars worth of property. The NAACP and the black Elks and all the black organizations supported us.

Abolition of the poll tax would bring more working-class white voters into the Roosevelt coalition, too. The disenfranchising provisions had been aimed at poor whites as well as blacks. The poor whites have continually cut their own throats. They voted for the voting restrictions because they thought it would keep the blacks from voting, but at the same time, it kept *them* from voting, too....

Because of the disenfranchisement provisions, the South was ruled by an oligarchy. The planters in the black belt were in alliance with the corporate interests in Birmingham—we called them the "Big Mules." We thought the first step in breaking this oligarchy was to abolish the poll tax, but progress was slow. A bill would be signed out of committee and pass in the House. Then it would be filibustered to death in the Senate. Almost everyone from the South would filibuster, of course. The only support we got from the South was from Claude Pepper of Florida, who introduced the bill to abolish the poll tax several times. Florida had already abolished the poll tax by state action in 1937. Frank Graham helped, of course. He was in the Senate for a while. But I can't remember getting support from any other North Carolina politician. From 1940 until the poll tax committee folded in 1948, we would get a bill to abolish the poll tax introduced, but it never was approved by the whole Congress.

Poll taxes were finally abolished through the Twenty-fourth Amendment ratified in 1964.

6. Margaret J. Hagood Recounts the Life of a Tenant Child, 1939

The story of the tenant child begins more than a quarter of a century ago. On Monday ten-year-old Mollie [Goodwin] woke up when her mother lifted the stove lid and began making the fire. She slipped from underneath the cover easily, so as not to disturb her little brother, and took down her last year's red dress, which had been fleecy and warm, but now was slick and thin. Their bed was in the log kitchen of the Goodwin's two-room cabin, which would be warm enough in a half hour for the sickly knee-baby, who slept with Mollie, to face the December morning.

Mollie's father came from the main room of the cabin to lace up his shoes in front of the kitchen stove. He never made the fire unless his wife was sick in bed, but he got up at the same time she did to go out to the smokehouse and measure out the day's allowance of meat. Ben Goodwin was a saving man who could not abide waste. He made his share of the proceeds from the small, cotton tenant farm buy the annual fall clothing supply for his family of seven and run them through the winter and spring until midsummer or later. Even then, he kept his account at the country store the lowest of any family's in the neighborhood, doing all the buying himself and measuring out the rations every morning.

Mollie's plump arms stretched tight the seams of her outgrown dress, and as she leaned over to pick up fresh wood for the fire, she felt her dress split at the shoulder. She wondered what she would do the washing in if she couldn't get into the old dress next Monday or the one after that. Her father's rule was that her two new dresses of the same cotton fleece lined material, one red and one blue, must never be worn except for school or Sunday School. She had no sisters to hand down clothes to her, for the other four children were boys. Some girls she knew wore overalls for working, but her father would not allow that either. A wicked thought came to her mind—maybe if she had nothing to wear to wash in next Monday, she wouldn't have to wash and instead could go to school with her brothers. She could iron on Tuesday inside the house in her underwear—then a vision of her mother bending over the wash tubs, moaning with the pain in her back, made her put aside the daydream of a washless Monday.

After breakfast Mollie's older brother cut wood and started a fire under the wash pot while she and the brother next younger drew and carried water from the well. Then the boys left for the mile walk to the one-teacher school and Mollie started back for the house to get up the clothes. She lingered on the way, debating whether her father's overalls, stiff with a week's accumulation of winter mud and stable stains, were harder to wash than the baby's soiled diapers. They *were* harder, but the odor from the diapers made you feel you couldn't go on. It was a sensory symbol of babies, of her sick mother, of crying, little

---

From *Mothers of the South: Portraiture of the White Tenant Farm Woman* by Margaret Hagood.

brothers, and now was vaguely mixed with her distaste for what two girl friends had told her at recess last week about how babies come. Mollie tried not to think about this and hoped she never had any babies.

The school bell's ringing interrupted her musing and reminded Mollie of how much she wanted to be there. Her dress was as new as any in school and its color still bright. The teacher had smiled approvingly at Mollie last week when the visiting preacher pinched her dimpled cheek and said, "Miss Grace, you have a fine looking bunch of little girls." Mollie thought now of having, when she was grown, a dress like Miss Grace's Sunday one. The bell stopped ringing and Mollie resolved to stop thinking and to work very hard and fast. Once before she had finished all the washing in time to go back with the boys after dinner. And so she scrubbed with all her force against the washboard and paid no attention to the pain from her knuckles scraped raw.

By dinner time all the clothes were on the line and the first ones out already frozen stiff. Mollie, numbed by cold and fatigue, ate peas, fat pork, and cornbread without joining in the family talk. When she got up from the table, her back ached—she wondered how many years of washing it would take to make it as bent over as her mother's. She changed to her new dress in time to set off for the afternoon session of school. She pulled herself together to respond to the teacher's beaming look of approval for having come to school that afternoon, and then relaxed into a lethargy from weariness and missed words she knew in the Third Reader and was spelled down quickly....

Mollie liked summer time best after the cotton had been chopped, hoed, and laid by. Once or twice a week she was allowed to go spend the afternoon with Mrs. Bynum, the nearest neighbor, who had no daughters. They sat on the front porch and rocked and talked. This was a treat for the little girl because her own mother always had to lie down when she could stop working, and pain limited her words to necessary instructions. One summer Mrs. Bynum bought some flowered dimity and made Mollie a visiting dress. They used to hitch up her horse to the buggy and drive four miles to visit a sister who had twelve children, most of them girls. The older girls let Molly try on hats and brooches and Mollie loved these afternoons. On the trip Mrs. Bynum taught Mollie to drive the horse. In her own family's wagon there were always boys who claimed this privilege.

One stormy winter night three months before Mollie was twelve, she was put to bed early. Her father moved the trundle bed from the main room and all the children went to sleep in the kitchen—all but Mollie. She had a terrible feeling of impending disaster to her mother and herself. When she had asked her mother about babies not long before, her mother had told her she was going to have another and that something would happen to Mollie soon, too. From the front room Mollie heard groans and knew her mother was suffering. Her own body began to ache. Her mother's sounds grew louder and each time an anguished scream reached Mollie's ears, a shooting pain went through her. Hardly daring, Mollie reached down under the cover and felt that her legs were wet. All the boys were asleep and so she drew back the cover and in the moonlight saw black stains which had come from her body. Suddenly she thought she was having a baby. She tried to scream like her mother, but the terror of the realization paralyzed her. Fright overwhelmed her until she was no longer conscious of pain. She remained motionless for a long time, knowing and feeling nothing but a horrible fear of disgrace and dread. Then she became aware that the moaning in the next room had stopped and that someone had unlatched the kitchen door. Trembling, she eased out of bed and crept into her mother's room. There was a new baby lying on one side, but she slipped into the other side of the bed and nestled against her mother. The relaxing warmth and comfort of another's body released the inner tensions and Mollie melted into tears and weak, low sobs. Her mother stroked her but said nothing. She lay there for some minutes until the Negro "granny" said she must leave her mother and led her back to bed. Early in the morning she hid the soiled bedclothes in a corner until she could wash them secretly in the creek and found some cloths in her mother's drawer which she asked for without giving any reason. Not for two years, when a girl friend told her, did she have any instruction about how to fix and wear sanitary pads.

7. Gordon P. Hancock Gives His Perspective on "What the Negro Wants," 1944

Gordon B. Hancock on a Southern Solution to Race Relations

THE DURHAM CONFERENCE

What is probably the most constructive departure in race relations since the emancipation of the Negro was made in the historic conference held at Durham, North Carolina, October 20, 1942. Sixty of the most influential Negroes of the South representing all shades of thought and occupational affiliation met of their own free will and accord—and at their own expense—and drew up a statement now known as the Durham Manifesto, which has had a far reaching effect on the thought and thinking of this country. Six thousand copies of the printed statement have been sent upon request to every state of the Union where interested persons are seeking more intimate knowledge of a document that has had such dramatic reception throughout the country. The conferees not only brought forth the statement, but assumed the financial responsibility for its publication. This forthright statement by a group of Southern Negroes caught the imagination of the country and the first edition of seven thousand copies is nearing exhaustion. A prominent churchwoman recently requested sufficient copies to supply the missionary circles of her entire state where it is to be used for study groups. In the *Statement of Purpose* we read:

> The inception of this conference hinges about the tragedy that took place at the close of World War I, when returning Negro soldiers were

met not with expressions and evidences of the democracy for which they had fought and for which thousands of their fellow race men had died. Instead, there was a sweeping surge of bitterness and rebuff that in retrospect constitutes one of the ugliest scars on the fair face of our nation. Interracial matters were left adrift and tragic was our experience and distressing was our disillusionment. Today the nations are again locked in mortal combat and the situation is desperate and dangerous, with the scales of fortune so delicately poised that we dare not predict what a day may bring forth; but this we know, that the Negro is again taking the field in defense of his country. Quite significant also is the fact that whereas the pronounced anti-Negro movement followed the last war, it is getting under way before the issues of the current war have been decided. In an hour of national peril, efforts are being made to defeat the Negro first and the Axis powers later. Already dire threats to throw again the Negro question into the politics of the South is becoming more and more dangerous. This is a direct challenge to the Negroes of the South who have most to gain if this threat is throttled and most to lose if it is fulfilled.

The purpose then of this conference is to try to do something about this developing situation. We are proposing to set forth in certain "Articles of Cooperation" just what the Negro wants and is expecting of the postwar South and nation. Instead of letting the demagogues guess what we want, we are proposing to make our wants and aspirations a matter of record, so clear that he who runs away may read. We are hoping in this way to challenge the constructive cooperation of that element of the white South who express themselves as desirous of a New Deal for the Negroes of the South.

In our "Articles of Cooperation" we are seeking for a common denominator of constructive action for the Negroes and this element of whites who are doing many of the things that we want done, and cannot do ourselves. In other words, we are proposing to draft a "New Charter of Race Relations" in the South. The old charter is paternalistic and traditional; we want a new charter that is fraternal and scientific, for the old charter is not compatible with the manhood and security of the Negro, neither is it compatible with the dignity and self-respect of the South. It ever leaves the South morally on the defensive! The Negro has paid the full price of citizenship in the South and nation, and the Negro wants to enjoy the full exercise of this citizenship, no more and no less.

The Durham Manifesto broke down the whole area of race relations into seven categories relating to political and civil rights, industry and labor, service occupations, education, agriculture, military service, social welfare and health. The statement was widely and favorably received throughout the nation, with white and Negro press not only lavish in their praise of the document but generous in the space allotted to its publicity.

ESSAYS

Cambridge University Professor Anthony J. Badger in the first essay asks the question, "How did the New Deal transform the South?" The essay would lead one to conclude that not much of significance changed. After ten years the South was still mainly a single-crop rural region with few labor laws, a tightly segregated racial environment, and a section dominated by planters, industrialists, and elites. "What brought dramatic change to the South ... was the war," writes Badger since the New Deal only "shored up the traditional structures of southern society." Historian Patricia Sullivan, in the second essay, argues that the New Deal provided many openings for racial justice and was supported by masses of impoverished southerners. By examining the lives of many of the energetic idealistic young New Dealers, Sullivan suggests that FDR was more race conscious than Badger would allow. Yet, when FDR tried to purge conservative southern congressmen, voters in the South opposed him. Nonetheless, when the Southern Conference for Human Welfare convened with 1,200 people of both races in Birmingham, Alabama, the idealists for change in the South "had shaken the foundations of the 'Solid South.'" Professor James C. Cobb takes the long view of the impact of the New Deal and World War II on the South. He sees evidence of the "changes in southern agriculture, the outmigration of blacks, and the move to industrialize" beginning before World War I. But New Deal programs and massive federal expenditures on defense pushed the South down the road to moderate prosperity. Cobb's depiction of the South's turning point includes economic, cultural, literary, racial, and political changes, although he also points to the limitations of change brought on by World War II.

How Did the New Deal Change the South?

ANTHONY J. BADGER

At first sight the New Deal could not fail to have a profound impact on the South.... The Tennessee Valley Authority rejuvenated an entire river basin. What the *Progressive Farmer* called the power revolution brought electrification for the first time to the countryside. The New Deal introduced unemployment compensation and old-age insurance. It provided undreamt of levels of welfare assistance to the poor. In the cities federal public works programs left a lasting physical imprint on the community by building the capital facilities which in the North had been constructed by private investors.

Most communities in the South still bear the traces of the New Deal in a school, a housing project, a library, a park, or a historic building restored—all provided by the federal government in the 1930s. In Memphis the Works Progress Administration constructed a $25,000 building that was modernistic in design,

From Anthony J. Badger, *New Deal/New South: An Anthony J. Badger Reader* (Fayetteville: The University of Arkansas Press, 2007), pp. 32–44. Reprinted by permission of the author.

with curtained windows, shower baths, spacious runways, individual rooms, and offering a daily change of bedding. This was the municipal dogpound.

Yet the New Deal left the basic economic, social, racial, and political structure of the region largely untouched. In 1930 the South was a poor, rural, one-crop society in which too many people chased too little farm income. In 1940 the South was still a poor, rural, one-crop society in which too many people chased too little farm income. In 1930 the South was a bastion of the open shop. In 1940 it was still an anti-union stronghold. In 1930 the South was rigidly segregated and blacks were economically and politically powerless. In 1940 blacks were still economically dependent, politically impotent, and rigidly segregated. In 1930 southern politics were dominated by a conservative alliance of county seat elites, planters, and industrialists, largely immune to popular pressure because of their economic dominance and the restricted nature of the electorate. In 1940 those same political leaders still controlled the South. As V. O. Key Jr., noted, the have-nots continued to lose out in the region's disorganized politics.

The New Deal rescued cotton and tobacco farmers. Josiah Bailey wrote in December 1933, "Eastern North Carolina, a very large section devoted to agriculture has been prostrated for five years. This year the people are really prosperous ... with one accord they give the credit to the President." A Mississippi banker told Turner Cartledge in 1935 about his county's cotton farmers. "I can show you papers in our current portfolio that had been cancelled us uncollectable years ago. People come in here and ask to pay back interest on notes we literally have to fish out of the waste basket." The Agricultural Adjustment Administration established the mechanisms of production control, price support loans, and ample credit that would enable those farmers who stayed on the land to work in a relatively risk-free environment and to enjoy prosperity when it returned during World War II. The AAA also established the political processes whereby organized commodity groups could guarantee favorable government response in the future.

But New Deal planners had more ambitious plans to modernize southern agriculture. Recognizing that high-cost American cotton could not compete on the glutted world market, they wanted to subsidize the gradual switch of southern agriculture from high-cost cotton production to a more diversified farming. Recognizing that there were too many farmers in the South working on submarginal land in too small units they wanted to resettle those farmers on better land in new communities with model housing, ready credit, supervision, and cooperative services. Both goals failed. The Farm Bureau, the pressure group that had been rescued by the New Deal, resisted any efforts to subsidize cotton agriculture other than by rigging a fair price in the marketplace. The Resettlement communities aroused bitter congressional opposition and catered to a very small number of farmers. In any case farmers were reluctant to move; they resented the obstacles placed in the way of acquiring their own farms; the individual units were too small to be viable; and the turnover of clients was high. Economic forces during the war and after would ultimately achieve the diversification and reorganization of southern agriculture, not government planners.

What of the rural poor, the tenants, and the sharecroppers? David Conrad described them as the forgotten farmers of the New Deal.... The story is now familiar enough: initial indifference to the tenants' plight on the part of the Cotton Section and the landlord-dominated local committees of the AAA; the discrimination against tenants in the allocation of rental and benefit payments; the lack of any guarantees that tenants received the payments due to them; the eviction of tenants in defiance of the Cotton Contract, particularly in the western part of the region; the remarkable, but ultimately doomed, desperation militancy of the biracial, socialist-led Southern Tenant Farmers' Union; and the belated and ineffective assault on rural poverty by the Farm Security Administration....

In the North in the 1930s the combination of worker militancy and the federal government protection of trade union rights under the Wagner Act produced the great breakthrough in union organization as labor organized mass production workers and moved from the fringes of the economy to the centrally important industries. In the South that combination of rank-and-file protest and government assistance failed to shake the power of anti-union employers. There was no breakthrough in labor organization.

The worker militancy was certainly there. Southern workers in the 1930s were not conservative, individualistic rural migrants hostile to collective action. Weary of paternalism, angry at wage cuts and stretch outs, hopeful of help from Roosevelt, they demonstrated unaccustomed determination in flocking to the union banner. In the depths of the Depression miners waged a futile battle against wage cuts and evictions in Harlan County, Kentucky. Inspired by Section 7a of the NRA, 20,000 Alabama coal miners joined the UMW in 1933–34. In a massive explosion of frustration, Piedmont textile workers joined the moribund United Textile Workers, at the same time forcing their leaders into a disastrous and premature strike in September 1934. Rubber workers in Gadsden, Alabama, made repeated efforts to organize in the face of violent repression. Steel workers in Birmingham unionized the Tennessee Coal and Iron subsidiary of U.S. Steel in 1937.

But determined protest was not enough. Nor could the new federal protections always help. In the case of steel economic circumstances—the prospect of rapidly filling order books—might persuade a national corporation like U.S. Steel to sign a union contract to ensure continuous production and order its southern subsidiaries to do likewise. Even in Birmingham, however, other employers saw no need to do likewise. The final employer to sign a union contract did not do so until 1974. In textiles employers had absolutely no incentive to concede to union demands. In 1934 at the time of the great textile strike the industry was already producing in excess of demand. In 1937–38 when the Textile Workers Organizing Committee launched its campaign, recession had once again gripped the industry.

Where employers were determined to resist they could utilize local community sentiment to defeat the unions. Rubber is the classic example. When the URW attempted to organize Goodyear in Akron, Ohio, Goodyear found that they could not sustain a vigilante strikebreaking organization in the face of local community hostility. In Gadsden, Alabama, on the contrary, the local press denounced outside agitators, and local law enforcement officers co-operated in beating up and kidnapping union organizers and breaking up picket lines. (Employers also used more mundane tactics: they held a strip-tease show in the local YMCA to attract workers away from a union meeting.) In the South labor was too politically powerless to impose its will on local sheriffs, on state legislatures, which passed a host of anti-labor laws after 1937, and on state governors who would usually be prepared to call out the National Guard to help break strikes. (Bibb Graves of Alabama and Olin Johnston of South Carolina were two exceptions to the general rule in the 1930s: they both turned down at least once employer requests to call out the Guard.)

The workers' political impotence was starkly illustrated in Birmingham, Alabama. The poll tax disenfranchised so many in Birmingham that 20,000 votes in a voting-age population of half a million in Jefferson County were enough to win local elections. There were 57,000 potential union members, half of them black. At most only 5,000 CIO members could vote. Political weakness like this meant that unions were unable to offset traditional anti-union tactics by the employers. As a result neither rank-and-file militancy nor federal protection was enough to break down the long-standing pattern of worker dependency in industrial relations.

Before the New Deal, welfare provision in the South was firmly ensconced in the old Poor Law traditions. No state made any provision for relief for the able-bodied unemployed. Nor did most counties. Birmingham had abolished its welfare department in 1924. Until 1933 most southern efforts to alleviate the plight of the unemployed were confined to coordinating private charity efforts.... But it was Harry Hopkins's Federal Emergency Relief Administration that revolutionized relief provision in the South. Ninety percent of relief spending under the FERA in the South was provided by federal money, compared to 62 percent in the rest of the country. To qualify for such aid, states had dramatically to professionalize their welfare organizations. As Michael Holmes noted, "Many counties in Georgia that had never seen a social worker now had one permanently stationed within their borders." Later, to qualify for federal matching funds for categorical assistance to the old, the blind, and dependent children, southern states had to maintain that revolution in professionalism. Southern cities established departments of public welfare for the first time. Southern states were forced to develop unemployment compensation programs. Old-age insurance for southerners became a federal responsibility.

But this welfare revolution was plagued by two persistent problems: local administration and joint federal state responsibility. It was difficult to find qualified staff to run relief programs in the South. Those in South Carolina were described as "conscientious, hard working, sincere and incompetent." Hostility to women appointments and to nonpartisan appointments was widespread. So too was traditional local hostility to the whole idea of relief. State legislatures were reluctant to make appropriations. Governor Eugene Talmadge of Georgia simply believed that castor oil was all the unemployed needed. Everywhere FERA and WPA operations were curtailed at harvest time to ensure the availability of as large a force as possible for cotton picking. Later in the 1930s assistance for the unemployed who were not given WPA jobs was patchy. At least five South Carolina counties, for example, made no relief provision for them at all.

The federal state operation of Social Security not only meant that states varied considerably in the generosity of the benefits they offered and the conditions they imposed on recipients, but also that many southern states could scarcely afford to participate in the system at all. The principle of matching funds meant that the poor southern states received less per capita from New Deal spending than any other region. It was not only Huey Long who called for a purely federal system of social security to offset southern poverty and southern discrimination against blacks. William Colmer, later one of the most reactionary, and states rights Mississippi congressmen, also called for a federal social security system because his state was simply too poor to take advantage of matching funds. Mississippi was the last state in the union to enter the Aid to Dependent Children Program. The ramshackle nature of the New Deal's welfare state was compounded by the exclusion of farm laborers from Social Security. Lee Alston and Joseph Ferrie have argued that southern landlords opposed the inclusion of farm laborers and lobbied to keep benefit payments low in the South because they did not want to see government welfare undermine their own paternalist in-kind benefits. They feared government benefits would loosen the control over their tenants which in-kind benefits enabled them to maintain. Thus the

impact of the New Deal's welfare revolution on the South was severely restricted by local poverty and entrenched conservative hostility.

As is well known, the New Deal, conscious of the need to maintain southern congressional support, did little for southern black civil rights. Roosevelt did not wholeheartedly commit himself to the fight for anti-lynching legislation or to abolish the poll tax. New Deal programs in the South routinely discriminated against blacks and perpetuated segregation. At best, as in the tenant purchase schemes and in the rehabilitation grants of the FSA, blacks received assistance in proportion to their share of the population, not in proportion to their need. Blacks, so many of whom were sharecroppers and farm laborers, disproportionately suffered from the failure of the New Deal rural poverty programs. Southern employers routinely solved the problem of higher costs resulting from the NRA and minimum-wage legislation by discharging black workers.

Southern blacks were, nevertheless, grateful to Roosevelt because what aid they did receive from the New Deal was vastly greater than any assistance they had received in the past or were likely to receive from white state and local governments. Discriminated against they may have been, but southern blacks were not excluded as they had so often been before. In New Orleans, for example, at the outset of the Depression, the city council had restricted employment on public works projects entirely to poll tax payers—that is, whites—and even tried to make the same stipulation for employment on the municipal dock wharves. New Deal officials fairly quickly stamped out any similar efforts to exclude blacks from FERA and CCC programs in 1933 and 1934. Similarly FERA and WPA spending both on school building and on emergency teachers virtually rescued black education in the South, which had been the first target of economy-minded school boards and state legislatures.

Southerners such as Will Alexander, Aubrey Williams, Clark Foreman, Brooks Hays, Frank Graham, C. B. "Beanie" Baldwin, and Clifford Durr were all radicalized by their service in Washington in New Deal agencies. They began to look critically at traditional patterns of race relations in the South and began to envisage the end of segregation. But, as Morton Sosna and John Kneebone have shown, southern liberals who remained in the South, notably the much-celebrated liberal newspapermen, clung tenaciously to the doctrines of paternalism and gradualism and to the hostility to federal intervention....

New Dealers hoped they could avoid the devisive racial issue by concentrating on the economic needs of the South. New Deal relief agencies first uncovered the full, hitherto unsuspected, dimensions of rural poverty. Social scientists at Chapel Hill and southerners in federal agencies in Washington pulled this data together to proclaim the South in 1938 as the nation's number-one economic problem. Capitalizing on this diagnosis New Dealers formed the Southern Conference for Human Welfare to lobby for a dramatically new way of modernizing the South. The key was the creation of mass purchasing power through federal intervention. Minimum-wage legislation, welfare legislation, the extension of social security, and a farm tenancy program were to be the economic core of this strategy. But to attain this goal there would have to be a political transformation. Economic democracy would require the protection of the civil liberties of trade union organizers and the abolition of the poll tax. But whereas the New Dealers saw Washington as the region's salvation, conservative leaders saw "Washington as the South's No 1 economic problem." Conservatives preferred the traditional model for securing economic growth in the South: the attraction of low-wage industry by the promise of a sympathetic context of cheap government and a cheap docile labor force. There was never much doubt that southern conservatives would win this argument, Ironically, they were forced to be more active in the search for low-wage industry because existing industries in the South had had to raise wages in response to federal legislation. Consequently, starting with Mississippi, southern states began actively seeking outside investment by promising attractive tax concessions and subsidies. James C. Cobb in *The Selling of the South* shows that this conservative modernization strategy was the policy followed by southern governments right through the 1940s and 1950s. The strategy had an additional advantage. The sort of businessmen likely to be attracted to the South were perfectly happy with the existing pattern of traditional race relations in the region.

The triumph of the conservative modernization strategy and the failure of the Southern Conference for Human Welfare highlighted the persistence of political conservatism in the South....

Above all, most southern congressmen became increasingly alarmed by the nonemergency direction of the New Deal. Vast spending, large welfare programs, and support for organized labor might have been tolerable in an economic emergency, but once a semblance of agricultural recovery had been secured by 1937 congressmen began to resent the increasingly northern, urban orientation of the New Deal. Closer to home, local county seat elites in the South feared the threat the New Deal posed to existing patterns of dependence in the region. The traditional power of landlords and employers was threatened by labor organizers, rural poverty programs, and minimum-wage legislation....

The fundamental problem was that the New Deal had scarcely touched the basic political structure of the South. Most potential beneficiaries and supporters of the New Deal were effectively disenfranchised. When Lister Hill was elected to the Senate in 1938 less than 10 percent of Alabama's voting-age population voted. Hill summed up his dilemma to Virginia Durr, who advocated the abolition of the poll tax as a solution to the problems of southern liberals: "If you will guarantee that this thing will pass, I'll vote for it, because the kind of people that will be voting after the poll tax is off, they'll be the kind of people that will be voting for me. But unless you guarantee it's going to pass the House and the Senate, I can't do it." Here was the classic statement of the attitude that would plague southern liberals in the postwar world as well. They lamented that they operated in a conservative political structure. But they would not lift a finger to change that structure. They willed the end but not the means. Change could only be imposed by federal authority, but supporting such change might imperil their political careers. Instead, they counseled caution and moderation in order to preserve their influence. This influence, which they so assiduously protected, was of no avail when the racial crises of the 1950s and 1960s finally came. Moderates like Lister Hill and John Sparkman were completely unable to influence events or to dictate the timetable of change....

What brought dramatic change to the South, however, was not the New Deal but the war. World War II was the juggernaut that ran over southern society. Jobs in defense industries at last enabled a surplus rural population to leave the land. Soaring farm prices gave southern farmers the means to mechanize: a potential labor shortage gave them the incentive to do so. Southern agriculture was about to be modernized.

The wartime and postwar boom enabled blacks to move into southern cities where they would have a degree of economic independence and living space—essential pre-conditions of the civil rights movements of the 1950s and 1960s. World War II permanently heightened black expectations.

Federal spending in the South on defense, and later on space, in both the war and the cold war was the catalyst that enabled the southern economy to take off into self-sustaining economic growth. Low wages and rural poverty persisted, but the South was to become also a region of high-tech industry and diversified agriculture that would attract in-migration from affluent whites and, eventually, from returning blacks.

New Dealers dreamt ambitious dreams of a modernized South in which small farmers prospered, low-wage industry was eliminated, workers were unionized, and the federal government guaranteed adequate wages and welfare. It was to be a democratized South in which the have-nots would at last have political power.

For the more ambitious among the reformers, the advent of economic democracy in the region would also herald the breaking down of traditional patterns of race relations. Such dreams were unrealized. In the economic emergency of 1933 the federal government lacked the bureaucratic and administrative capacity to impose radical change on the South. New Dealers had to work with, not against, southern congressmen, the economic interests that were to be regulated, and local state government agencies. Inevitably these institutions were buttressed. By the time New Dealers had developed plans to transform the South, these conservative forces which the New Deal had rescued would be in a position to stifle New Deal aspirations. The unanticipated consequences of the New Deal were the strengthening of the position of large planters, the triumph of conservative strategies of securing economic growth, and the hardening of resistance to changes in race relations. The New Deal shored up the traditional structures of southern society. Consequently, when economic modernization came to the South in the aftermath of World War II, the destiny of the South was not in the hands of New Deal–style reformers but of the familiar local elites who

were determined that economic growth should not undermine traditional patterns of dependency and deference and of white supremacy. It would take two forces that New Dealers had not envisaged to break that control: coercive intervention in race relations by the federal judiciary on the one hand, and a massive popular protest from below by the civil rights movement on the other. It was World War II and these later unexpected phenomena, not the ambitious federal plans of the New Dealers, that eventually transformed the South.

Challenge to the Solid South, 1933–1938

PATRICIA SULLIVAN

"The New Deal was so abruptly different it was startling," recalled a reporter who had been covering national politics since the presidency of Calvin Coolidge. "Suddenly Washington was alive." The feverish activity of the first one hundred days transformed the nation's capital. New agencies sprang up, and old departments were made over; the rash of New Deal programs gave Washington a grip on every phase of the nation's economic life.

If the legislative whirlwind that produced the early New Deal was embedded with contradictions and crosscurrents, there was no question that a fundamental reordering of government was under way. Process prevailed over form. Franklin Roosevelt's endorsement of government as a tool to advance economic security and human betterment promised to stretch the parameters of government and politics. This national experiment implicitly challenged the static and insular political culture that had prevailed in the South since the turn of the century.

The urgency of the depression combined with the innovative and confident milieu of New Deal Washington to create "a freedom of experimentation that

From *Days of Hope: Race and Democracy in the New Deal Era* by Patricia Sullivan.

was unexampled." Roosevelt orchestrated a new concept of government through the constellation of policymakers he convened. Among the boldest strategists were Relief Administrator Harry Hopkins and the cabinet secretaries Harold Ickes, Henry Wallace, and Frances Perkins....

[T]he Roosevelt administration enlisted the talents and enterprising spirit of the legion of young lawyers, social workers, and economists who flocked to Washington to "help right the wrongs that had befallen the country."

Clark Foreman, who never anticipated a career in government or politics, was, in many ways, typical of this group. He also represented a very different kind of southerner on the national scene, one who offered a stark contrast to those southern statesmen who had risen through the ranks of the Democratic Party to powerful positions on Capitol Hill.

In addition to Foreman were Will Alexander, C. B. "Beanie" Baldwin, Clifford Durr, Aubrey Williams, Mary McLeod Bethune, Arthur "Tex" Goldschmidt, Oscar Chapman, and others. Brilliant, young black professionals, such as Robert C. Weaver and William Hastie, were also drawn to the potential for social engineering inherent in the New Deal. As policymakers, lobbyists, and activists, these individuals endorsed and helped to create new forms of political participation and alliances that gave voice to constituencies long disfranchised by law and custom in the South. They also played a pivotal role in drawing national attention to the poverty that pervaded southern life and that thwarted the recovery effort.

As Anthony Badger's history of the New Deal demonstrates, the depression created constraints as well as opportunities. The experimental and "refreshingly self-critical" spirit that animated the New Deal was contained by persistent political realities that "sharply limited the room of ... policymakers to maneuver." The predominantly conservative southern bloc in Congress, coupled with the traditional emphasis on localism and volunteerism in the region, stood as the greatest obstacle to the New Deal aspirations toward a new, more equitable social order. As has been amply documented, the National Industrial Recovery Act (NIRA) and the Agricultural Adjustment Act, the cornerstones of the early New Deal, were easily tailored by local southern elites and their powerful representatives in Congress to fit the prevailing economic and political arrangements in the region.

But the persistence of old forms and old allegiances masked subtle shifts in the expectations and political consciousness of people who responded directly to the emergence of the federal government as a dominant force in the economic life of the nation. The unfair and racially inequitable administration of federal programs in the South became a focus of protest, an occasion for organized action....

The creation of a position to ensure the participation of black Americans in the recovery effort was emblematic of the new departure heralded by the New Deal. Commenting on Clark Foreman's appointment as "Special Adviser on the Economic Status of Negroes," the *New Republic* called it "an experiment ... worth watching." The editorial observed that wage differentials based on race were the major contributing factor in "the appalling plight of the Negro, particularly in the South." Yet, the editorial explained, enforcement of an equal wage often led to the replacement of black workers by whites. "Of course," it was assumed that no government official could "compel employers to end this discrimination." Foreman could be most useful, the *New Republic* predicted, by helping to "create conditions under which the Negroes [could] organize and fight for their own rights."...

Among FDR's major appointments, [Harold] Ickes was exceptional in his willingness to act unequivocally in behalf of racial fairness and inclusion, providing Foreman and Weaver with an important wedge for stretching the limits of an often inflexible bureaucratic structure. Foreman's success in cracking the Civilian Conservation Corps (CCC) policy of barring blacks from supervisory positions offers a useful example. The CCC, which provided employment for young men under army supervision, maintained segregated camps. All of the officers and supervisory personnel, however, were white. Foreman's appeals to the army to hire black supervisors for the black camps were rebuffed. Since the Interior Department had authority over the camps located in the national parks, Foreman obtained an order from Ickes requiring that a black person be hired to fill the next supervisory position available in a black camp on park land.

When an opening for an archaeologist occurred for a project restoring the Civil War battlefields in Gettysburg, Foreman and Weaver located Dr. Louis King of West Virginia to fill the position. A delegation from the National Park Service protested the appointment and warned that there was no place for King to eat and that white people in Gettysburg were not used to associating with black people. King's very presence could easily provoke violence and bloodshed. Their grim warnings made Foreman fearful for King's safety, but he did not retreat. King took the job and got along very well. His appointment was an incremental change, which failed to secure any fundamental reform in hiring policies. But beyond the singular victory, Foreman later recalled that the experience afforded a useful lesson. "I became convinced that fear was the tool of reaction and that a person who wanted to fight for decent conditions for all human beings had to make up his mind that he would not be frightened away from a position he knew to be correct."

The $3.3 billion Public Works Administration (PWA), administered by Ickes, provided an unprecedented opportunity to develop a mechanism for defining and enforcing a no-discrimination policy on federally funded work projects. Ickes's initial order that a no-discrimination clause be included in all PWA contracts met with cautious enthusiasm from black spokesmen. A black newspaperman warned that a previous federal no-discrimination order, enacted by Secretary of the Treasury Ogden Mills in 1932, had been easily ignored, since no criteria existed to measure discrimination. Ickes referred the matter to the Office of Negro Affairs. In preparation for the establishment of the Housing Division of the PWA, he advised Foreman and Weaver to devise an affirmative policy to ensure the full participation of black labor in federally funded projects.

Weaver was primarily responsible for developing the new policy. Working closely with William Hastie [Howard University Law Professor], he devised a procedure whereby PWA contract recipients were required to employ a minimum percentage of black skilled labor, based on the percentage of skilled black laborers in the local population according to the 1930 occupational census. Meeting this minimum requirement would serve as prima facie evidence that contract recipients were complying with the no-discrimination policy. Implementation of the new policy was complicated by the exclusion of blacks from the building trade unions and from the licensing procedures for plumbers and electricians in northern and southern cities. In these cases, the Department of Labor was able to negotiate agreements with local union officials. By 1936, the policy had been implemented in twenty-nine cities, including Birmingham, Atlanta, Columbia, and Memphis. The Housing Program, under Weaver's supervision, proved to be the most racially inclusive New Deal initiative, securing black participation in all phases of the slum-clearance and low-rent housing programs.

The PWA's quota system was not devised to open new job opportunities for black workers. Developed in a time of depression and unemployment, it served as a holding action, ensuring that black workers retained past occupational advantages. New Deal policy efforts in behalf of racial and economic reform were piecemeal and limited. Although opponents had blocked official racial wage differentials, regional wage differentials and local subterfuge maintained racial-based wages. In the short term, progressives in the Roosevelt administration had to accommodate conservative southerners, whose support was deemed essential to the president's overall program. Foreman later reflected, "Almost all of the work I was doing seemed to be patchwork, getting a man here, protesting there, but not solving anything fundamental."

Nevertheless, the process surrounding the New Deal offered a unique opportunity to test strategies, establish new precedents, and stretch the boundaries of participation. As they engaged the social forces released by the depression and the New Deal, Foreman, Weaver, and other young progressives were participating in a broader movement. "More important than the factual representation of New Deal programs," Weaver advised the annual convention of the NAACP in 1937, "is the interpretive analysis of results and the evolution of techniques for the future.... Unless a group like ours is constantly developing, consciously or unconsciously, such techniques, it will not only fail to advance, but must rapidly lose ground."

The political struggle unleashed by the implementation of the New Deal farm program fed the process that Weaver described. The success of southern planters in tailoring the Agricultural Adjustment Act to their interests sparked a reaction that drew national attention to the problem of chronic rural poverty in the South. When the Arkansas-based STFU entered the debate over the New Deal farm program, it created an opportunity for liberal and progressive New Dealers to publicly explore the economic and political underpinnings of the South's impoverishment. The plight of the rural poor, black and white, stood as compelling testimony to the inadequacy of "recovery" measures and documented the need for far-reaching, federally sponsored reforms. It was an issue that informed the debate surrounding the 1936 presidential campaign and the shifting political alignments that led Franklin Roosevelt to identify the South as "the nation's number one economic problem."

Henry Wallace's Department of Agriculture, probably more than any other New Deal agency, reflected the eclectic mixture of policymakers that composed the Roosevelt administration. Veterans of the decade-long struggle to secure federal price-support policies for agricultural products rubbed shoulders with energetic young reformers whom the director of the Agricultural Adjustment Administration (AAA), George Peek, cryptically described as "an entirely new species." Lodged primarily in the general counsel's office under Jerome Frank, the young reformers were among the most brilliant legal minds of the New Deal, including Alger Hiss, Thurman Arnold, Telford Taylor, Lee Pressman, and John Abt, along with Gardiner Jackson, who worked in the consumer counsel's office. These young urban lawyers arrived in Washington imbued with the confidence and hope of the early New Deal days but with little first-hand knowledge about agriculture. "The spirit was rather as though we were going to fight for the country," Hiss recalled. "We were like a militia in mufti and we had enlisted for the duration."

Conflicting interpretations of the authority and objectives of the farm program quickly divided the representatives of large agricultural interests and the lawyers in the general counsel's office, who were concerned about the full implications of the farm program for all who made their living from the land. Tensions were briefly obscured by the economic emergency and institutional political factors that guided the implementation of the Agricultural Adjustment Act, the centerpiece of the recovery effort. Described as "the greatest single experiment in economic planning under capitalist conditions ... in a time of peace," the act provided for a voluntary program of acreage reduction, supported by government payments, to decrease production and raise prices. Southern planters, working through established networks of the Extension Service and the American Farm Bureau, easily controlled the implementation of the act in the region. John P. Davis, sent to the South by the NAACP in 1934 to interview black tenant farmers, and Socialist Party leader Norman Thomas were among those who reported on the devastating consequences. By pouring millions of dollars into southern agriculture without addressing the evils of the plantation system, critics charged, the federal government shored up the old system and aggravated the desperate plight of tenant farmers and sharecroppers, who composed more than 45 percent of the South's farming population.

AAA policy required landowners to pay a portion of the government payment for crop reduction to their tenants, but there was no adequate enforcement mechanism. Widespread cheating by landowners precipitated the organization of the STFU in Tyronza, Arkansas, in July 1934. An organizer of the interracial union recalled: "The sharecroppers wanted their share of the government money. It was that simple. That's why they organized." The STFU, which enjoyed the support of the young liberals in the AAA, mounted a vigorous critique of New Deal farm policy, charging that it intensified the displacement of tenant farmers and denied them any representation in the local administrative structure of the AAA. When Hiram Norcross, chairman of the local AAA committee, evicted twenty-seven STFU members from his plantation, the union sued Norcross in court. The plaintiffs argued that the widely disputed section seven of the cotton contract required that landlords participating in the AAA program keep the same tenants, not simply the same number of tenants.

Emboldened by the STFU's action, AAA General Counsel Jerome Frank issued an interpretation of the cotton contract. He endorsed the STFU's position, arguing that it was essential to protect the rights of sharecroppers and tenants. Frank's ruling challenged the autonomy of southern landowners and contested the political clout of cotton growers, political power that was lodged securely with the Democratic leadership in the Senate, including Majority Leader Joseph Robinson of Arkansas. Henry Wallace conceded that Frank and his associates had acted on the highest of motives but that their interpretation of section seven was indefensible in view of the political realities and the larger agricultural picture. The ruling would result in the collapse of the entire cotton program. Thus, in the well-known "purge" of 1935, Wallace dismissed Frank and several of his top assistants.

Assistant Secretary of Agriculture Rexford Tugwell persuaded C. B. "Beanie" Baldwin, his young protégé from Virginia, not to resign from Secretary Wallace's staff in the wake of Frank's expulsion, advising him that "the fight was only beginning" and that he should save himself for another day. The failure of Frank's blunt strike on behalf of the rural poor did not slow the political momentum gathering behind the cause of tenant farmers and sharecroppers. Early in 1935, Will Alexander, Edwin Embree, and Charles Johnson published the findings of a year-long study of cotton tenancy. Funded by the Rockefeller Foundation and the Rosenwald Fund, the study documented how the government, under the AAA, had assumed "many of the risks of the landowners and thrown them on the tenants." The STFU continued to organize and protest, growing to thirty thousand members in six states by 1937, one-third of whom were black. Their efforts met with evictions and a widely publicized reign of terror. "There can be no doubt of the reversion to slave law, mob violence and fascist methods in Arkansas," editorialized the *New York Post*. Growing pressure from national organizations and liberal groups, along with the populist challenge of Huey Long, convinced Roosevelt of the need to establish a separate organization to redress the plight of the rural poor. In April 1935, he authorized Tugwell's plan for such an agency. Tugwell organized the Resettlement Administration, with Will Alexander as deputy administrator and C. B. Baldwin as assistant administrator.

The STFU, in conjunction with its sympathetic supporters in the Roosevelt administration, succeeded in broadening the debate over federal farm policy and compelling the government to address the issues of rural poverty and displacement. The process focused national attention on the South and put a human face on the economic misery that plagued the region. Tugwell's Resettlement Administration undertook an ambitious campaign of public information, which "harnessed the creative abilities of writers, journalists, and scholars to the purpose of educating the country about impoverished land and people." The Photographic Section of the Resettlement Administration (which continued under its successor organization, the Farm Security Administration) employed the nation's most creative young photographers; whose visual rendering of rural poverty was unsurpassed. Late in 1936, at Tugwell's urging, Secretary of Agriculture Henry Wallace traveled through the Deep South with Will

Alexander and C. B. Baldwin to examine conditions firsthand. Wallace, who carried Arthur Raper's newly published *Preface to Peasantry* with him, was visibly shocked by what he found. He became increasingly attentive to the South and its peculiar relationship to the politics of the New Deal. As a region, it was most desperately in need of federally sponsored economic reforms to break the cycle of poverty that drained the region's human and natural resources. Yet the South's elected representatives became the leading opponents to the more reformist course of the Roosevelt administration, heralded by the 1936 election.

The "discovery" of rural poverty in the South was played out against growing polarization in Washington over the course of the New Deal. In a series of decisions during 1935 and 1936, the Supreme Court struck at the heart of the New Deal when it overturned the National Industrial Recovery Act, the Agricultural Adjustment Act, the Railroad Retirement Act, and a New York State minimum-wage law. These rulings severely restricted "the government's right to regulate the economy under the commerce clause, to tax and spend for the general welfare, and to interfere with the freedom of contract." Roosevelt blasted the Court for creating a constitutional "no-man's land" where neither federal nor state government could function. The judicial revolt reinforced increasingly vocal attacks by conservatives, wed to a strict laissez-faire ideology, compelling Roosevelt to take the offensive. During the summer and fall of 1935, the president embarked on the legislative battle of the second hundred days. Under intense lobbying from the White House, Congress passed the Wagner Act, the Social Security Act, a holding company bill curbing the power of giant utilities, and a new tax law that increased rates for higher incomes and corporations. Countering the Supreme Court's assault on the New Deal, Roosevelt told a group of young Democrats, "My friends, the period of social pioneering is just beginning."

"We will win easily next year," Roosevelt told his cabinet late in 1935, "but we are going to make it a crusade." Roosevelt had presided over a dramatic upsurge in the economy and a multibillion-dollar program of jobs, credit, and relief that touched the lives of a broad cross section of the citizenry. Allowing for its deficiencies and inequities, the New Deal marked a decisive break with the past. New Deal legislation fundamentally altered the relationship between the government and the individual citizen and invested the newly revived labor movement with strength and confidence. Roosevelt made the 1936 election a referendum on the role of government in a modern society. Campaigning against those "economic royalists" who had come to see government "as a mere appendage of their own affairs," Roosevelt pledged an activist federal government, committed to the "establishment of a democracy of opportunity, for all the people." He proclaimed, "Freedom is no half and half affair."...

Secure in his electoral mandate, Roosevelt pressed ahead in his effort to redefine and sharpen the tools for sustaining an expansion of New Deal reform. Woven through his inaugural address was a litany describing the poverty and despair that continued to proscribe the opportunities of millions of citizens. He ended with the immortal refrain, "I see one-third of a nation ill-housed, ill-clad, ill-nourished." He reminded the nation of the vision guiding the collective experiment that had begun four years earlier, in the darkest days of the depression, "a vision—to speed the time when there would be for all the people that security and peace essential to the pursuit of happiness."...

As Roosevelt pushed to expand the New Deal during 1937, southern Democrats steadily joined the ranks of the opposition. The Fair Labor Standards Act, which, along with a revived labor movement, promised to further erode regional wage differentials, met strong opposition from key southern congressmen, including Finance Committee Chairman Byron "Pat" Robinson of Mississippi. In the wake of the fall recession in 1937, a number of Republican and Democratic senators ... met in November at the instigation of Senator Josiah Bailey of North Carolina. Their "Conservative Manifesto" claimed that a restoration of business confidence was essential to economic recovery. Toward this end, they recommended the reduction of taxes, the primacy of a balanced budget, a restoration of states' rights, and the strict observation of private property rights and the rights of capital. Facing an increasingly recalcitrant southern bloc, Roosevelt prepared to take the battle for the New Deal directly to the southern people.

The South, more than any other region, offered a striking dichotomy between mass popular support for New Deal initiatives and a stiffening opposition among its elected representatives in Congress. Indeed, the South was the one region where, according to a Gallup poll, a majority of the people backed the Court-packing plan. Lyndon Johnson's vigorous support of the president's plan won him a Texas congressional seat in 1937. Even though there were a notable number of young, southern supporters of the New Deal in the House and the Senate, supporters like Lyndon Johnson and Claude Pepper, seasoned representatives of the South's landowners and industrialists had emerged as key opponents.

In February 1938, Lucy Randolph Mason, the southern director of public relations for the Congress of Industrial Organizations (CIO), reported to Eleanor Roosevelt on the precarious political situation in the region. She warned of a growing opposition to the Roosevelt administration "among the power holding group," regardless of the "lip service" they might be giving it. If a vote was taken among this group, she was confident the president would lose. "The only hope for progressive democracy in the South," she observed, "lies in the lower economic groups, particularly the wage earner." They adored Roosevelt. Yet most of these people did not vote. Mason advised that the poll tax be abolished and that a deliberate campaign be waged to enfranchise the great majority of nonvoting southerners, "a hope more likely filled if the mass production industries" could be organized to give the unions "real strength." Robert Weaver recalled that for people in Washington who were concerned with the situation in the South, one fact had become increasingly evident: "If you were going to make real basic changes, you had to do something about the electorate."...

[F]or the president to mobilize support for the New Deal in the South, it was essential that the people of the South understand what the New Deal meant to them ... Roosevelt and Foreman agreed that a pamphlet on this subject could be useful during the summer primaries by illustrating how the South had benefited from the New Deal and by describing the serious economic problems that remained. Roosevelt authorized Foreman to implement the project under the aegis of Lowell Mellett, executive director of the National Emergency Council (NEC).

Early in the summer of 1938 Foreman convened a small group of southerners working in the Roosevelt administration to draft the report anonymously. The report was then reviewed and endorsed by an advisory committee of prominent southerners. Many people throughout the government provided assistance, but the core group consisted of Clifford Durr of Alabama, who was a lawyer for the Reconstruction Finance Corporation, John Fisher of Oklahoma, who worked for the Farm Security Administration, and Arthur "Tex" Goldschmidt of Texas, who had been instrumental in establishing the Works Progress Administration (WPA) and was then working for the Consumer's Counsel of the Bituminous Coal Administration and serving as vice-president of the Federal Workers Union. Foreman consulted frequently with southern representatives during the preparation of the draft. On the recommendation of Senator Lister Hill of Alabama, the group limited their discussion of the fifteen subjects covered in the report to four pages each so that individual sections could be easily reproduced and widely distributed as pamphlets and campaign literature. The topics ranged from "Soil," "Water," and "Ownership and Use of Land" to "Health," "Education," and "Women and Children." The concise style and the simple straightforward language were aimed to ensure a wide audience....

Clark Foreman edited the final copy, and on 25 July ... transmitted the *Report on the Economic Conditions of the South* to the president.

The president announced the publication of the NEC report during a speech in Barnesville, Georgia, where he shared the platform with Senator Walter George, former Governor Eugene Talmadge, and U.S. Attorney Lawrence Camp. Explaining how sectional imbalance drained the potential for southern development, Roosevelt declared that the South was "the nation's number one economic problem." Discriminatory freight rates, depressed wages, and purchasing power that fell well below the national average not only were problems for the region but contributed to an economic imbalance in the nation as a whole and required national solutions. The Rural Electrification Administration (REA), which the president dedicated that day, was a "symbol of the progress" being made. The REA aimed to bring electricity "to every village, every home and every farm in every part of the United States" and promised to be especially beneficial to the South.

The support of Congress was essential if New Deal initiatives like the REA were to continue. It was for this reason, Roosevelt explained, that he felt compelled to intervene in the 1938 primary elections on behalf of liberal candidates who shared his commitment to a broad program of economic and social reform. He closed his speech by endorsing U.S. Attorney Lawrence Camp over incumbent Walter George for the U.S. Senate. The president traveled on to Greenville, South Carolina, where he endorsed Governor Olin Johnston in a bid for "Cotton" Ed Smith's seat in the U.S. Senate.

Roosevelt also endorsed William Dodd Jr.'s challenge to Congressman Howard Worth Smith of Virginia, the powerful chairman of the House Rules Committee.

Walter George called the president's Barnesville speech "a second march through Georgia." He reminded his fellow Georgians, "We answered this question before when federal bayonets stood guard over the ballot box ... honest men cast honest ballots for the Redemption of this State." Generally, the southern press, southern public figures, and many southern liberals outside of the New Deal shared George's sentiments and resented the president's interference in state political contests. Commenting on the reaction to Roosevelt's challenge to George, *New York Herald Tribune* columnist Mark Sullivan observed that just below the surface was the issue of states' rights, namely the right to control elections. The principal use the South had for this right, Sullivan explained, was to exclude blacks from voting in Democratic Party primaries. Half of Senator "Cotton" Ed Smith's final speech before the primary election was a strident defense of white supremacy....

In the South, the poll tax and other restrictions kept most blacks and a majority of low-income whites from voting. This was the constituency of the New Deal, and the great majority of them did not participate in the 1938 primary elections. In Georgia, for example, Tom Stokes observed that four-fifths of the fifty-three thousand WPA workers in the state were black. They were legally excluded from voting in the Democratic primary. In addition, voter registration was low among white WPA workers in the state. Thus, Roosevelt's attempt to purge conservative southern Democrats seemed destined to fail in the short term, and it did. But it marked the opening battle in a growing movement to open up the political process in the South.

The significance of the NEC report reached beyond the 1938 primary season. It turned a national spotlight on the South and on the economic and political significance of the region....

The NEC report became "a kind of Bible" for southern New Dealers, anti-poll-tax activist Virginia Durr recalled. Jonathan Daniels, then the editor of the *Raleigh News and Observer*, ... advised that the president pay little mind to those southerners who resented his description of the South as the nation's number-one economic problem. These critics, he confided, were the "same old Daughters of the Confederacy—though some in pants—who in all the long years" had been "a more destructive crop than cotton." He added: "They are not talking for the thoughtful men and women in every class in the South.... We know we are in a hell of a fix even when we sit in the shade and we are grateful for his help out of the hole."...

Clark Foreman and other members of the SPC joined with labor representatives Joseph Gelders and Lucy Randolph Mason in organizing a southern-wide conference in response to FDR's challenge. Over Thanksgiving weekend in 1938 more than twelve hundred people—"representing all classes and conditions," black and white, from each of the southern states—met in Birmingham to consider the subject matter of the NEC report and to establish a permanent organization that would work toward some solution of the problems it described. The result was the Southern Conference for Human Welfare (SCHW). According to Frank Graham, president of the newly formed SCHW, the organization had grown from a combination of influences and forces.... But the SCHW ... provided a forum for all people of the South, "regardless of party, religion or race," to prepare for political action. Arthur Raper, a founding member of the SCHW, believed that the time was ripe for such an organization. The depression and the New Deal had shaken the foundations of the "Solid South." He noted: "A lot of folks were standing up on their feet and talking and expecting things that they had never expected before.... Here was a ferment, a very basic, vital ferment, and people needed to respond to it in some way."

The Impact of World War II on the American South

JAMES C. COBB

While it was difficult at the end of the 1940s to look back much beyond the War itself, the perspective of the 1990s both affords us the luxury of the longer view and requires that we take it. When we do, we can see that, to some extent, the changes in southern agriculture, the outmigration of blacks, and the move to industrialize were actually rooted in conditions and trends visible as early as or even before World War I. In fact, the years from the boll weevil invasion of the early twentieth century through the beginnings of the Great Migration of blacks to the North and the descent into the Great Depression might be seen as the harbingers of a great turning period, a protracted drama for which the New Deal and World War II constituted the final acts.

Most scholars have argued that of the two acts, World War II clearly deserves top billing, but it is virtually impossible to assess the impact of the New Deal and World War II separately. Both the New Deal and the war contributed heavily to the modernization of southern agriculture and the South's subsequent efforts to industrialize. While the New Deal's acreage-reduction programs rendered much of the old farm labor force marginal, if not superfluous, however, the war offered alternative employment opportunities and threatened to create a labor scarcity sufficient to boost farm wages above levels that southern landlords were willing to pay. Meanwhile, although the war seemed ultimately to undermine southern liberalism and strengthen anti-New Deal conservatism, the conflict did not cancel the Roosevelt administration's stated commitment to improving economic conditions in the South and arguably even facilitated it by removing the restrictions on spending that had hampered New Deal recovery efforts.

The $52 billion paid out on just the ten largest government defense contracts between 1940 and 1944 was roughly equivalent to total government expenditures between 1932 and 1939. Not surprisingly, southern manufacturing employment grew by 50 percent during the war, and annual wages climbed by

---

James C. Cobb, "World War II and the Mind of the Modern South," from *Remaking Dixie: The Impact of WWII on the American South* edited by Neil R. McMillen (Jackson, MS: University Press of Mississippi). Copyright © 1997. Reprinted by permission of the publisher.

40 percent between 1939 and 1942 alone as war-induced competition for labor quickly rendered the New Deal's Fair Labor Standards minimums obsolete in some southern industries. For all the undue influence still wielded by reactionary southern politicians, the Roosevelt administration also seized numerous wartime opportunities to exempt the South from its official "hold the line" policy on wages while affording significant support to organized labor as well. Although the South remained a decidedly low-wage region, it emerged from the conflict with an expanded industrial labor force and a markedly more affluent consumer pool which became a crucial part of the region's postwar attraction for market-oriented industries. If it is correct to credit the war with finishing what the New Deal started, it seems reasonable as well to think of World War II functioning, at least in part, as a sort of unarticulated Third New Deal, one freed from some of the most severe economic constraints that hampered the first two.

Wartime spending created many new job opportunities for southerners, although not all enjoyed equal access to them. On any construction site, as one black southerner who spoke from experience explained, "If a white man and a black man both walk up for an opening and it ain't no shovel in that job, they'd give the job to a white man." This generalization applied to black veterans as well. Promiseland, South Carolina, veteran Isaac Moragne angrily rejected a Veterans Administration staffer's recommendation that he apply for a common laborer's position, explaining later, "I was a staff sergeant in the Army, ... traveled all over England ... sat fourteen days in the English Channel ... I wasn't going to push a wheel barrow."...

During the war, men and women left the South's farms for its factories in almost equal numbers, and in many cases, employers preferred to hire the women. This was especially true when the choice lay between a white woman and a black man. In some instances, defense employers simply drew on the existing textile labor pool where white women were heavily represented and blacks hardly at all. Although many of these white women withdrew or were pushed out of the industrial workforce when the war ended, postwar economic expansion soon afforded them new opportunities to return to the factories while the concomitant shrinkage of the South's agricultural sector often made such a move a matter of absolute necessity. In Mississippi, the number of women employed in manufacturing increased by nearly 60 percent between 1940 and 1950, a rate  nearly twice as high as that for their male counterparts. At the same time, continuing discrimination forced blacks of both sexes to pursue wartime opportunities in the North.

In both the short and long terms, the war's impact on worker mobility was crucial in a number of ways. At the national level, while 12 million Americans were being shipped overseas, another 15 million moved to cities elsewhere in the nation, with half of these moving to different states. Meanwhile, between 1940 and 1945, three times as many people left the South each year as had departed during the preceding decade. A total of 1.6 million civilians moved out of the  South during the war, and almost as importantly, three times that many moved elsewhere within the region. Prior to the war, southern workers had been far less mobile, sticking close to home either because they could not afford to move, had no incentive to move, or simply could not bring themselves to move. This labor market inflexibility was far less pronounced in the postwar South as outmigration, inmigration, and intraregional migration continually responded to and shaped economic, racial, political, and cultural trends.

Among the cultural trends most affected by this newfound mobility and other war-induced changes was the evolution of southern music.... Country music went both national and international thanks not only to the proliferation of country radio programming in response to the outmigration of southern whites but to the Armed Forces Radio Network, which carried what had once been seen as strictly regional "hillbilly" music all over the world....

During the war and after, younger and more urbane black audiences readily demonstrated their preference for the amplified dance-oriented stylings that became known as "rhythm and blues." Researchers who studied black life during the war had discovered a marked trend toward secularization as rural blacks acquired radios, automobiles, and telephones and generally transcended the barriers that had once insulated them from mass-society influences. Disgusted by the changes she observed, lifelong Mississippi Delta churchgoer Matilda Mae Jones complained, "Songs they sing in church now feel like fire burning.... all fast and jumpy and leapy like.... that's just the way these swing church songs are now." Jones's complaint foreshadowed a trend that would see performers like Clarksdale-born gospel singer Sam Cooke, who began his career singing songs such as "Jesus Gave Me Water," go on to fame as a rhythm and blues superstar with hits like "Chain Gang" and "Everybody Loves to Cha Cha Cha." Cooke's career paralleled those of countless others, such as James Brown and Otis Redding and Ray Charles, who, in succeeding years, not so much left gospel music as took it with them when they entered the secular, sensual world of rhythm and blues....

Writing in 1935, Greenville writer David L. Cohn described the Mississippi Delta as a land of "complete detachment," explaining that "change shatters itself on the breast of this society as Pacific breakers upon a South Sea reef." "Disturbing ideas" might "crawl like flies around the screen of the Delta," wrote Cohn, but "they rarely penetrate." In the wake of World War II, Cohn painted a decidedly different portrait, however, noting that "many changes have occurred in the life of the Mississippi Delta as elsewhere. We had scarcely emerged from a shattering economic depression before we were plunged into man's most catastrophic war. The foundations of our faith are severely shaken. We no longer believe, as we once did, in the inevitability of progress. Our compass is aberrant, our course erratic. We are more than a little fearful that we shall not make our landfall."...

The contradictions raised by World War II and subsequently magnified by the tensions of the Cold War focused national and international attention on the South's deficiencies. World War II brought more than twice as many Yankee soldiers to the South as the Civil War and their wartime experiences often

yielded specific and personal testimony to the South's backwardness.... The result was the creation of what [Morton] Sosna called "a bull market ... for regional exposure, explanation, and analysis."

Certainly, the war years inspired and nurtured a host of writers of both fiction and nonfiction who wrote with the clear purpose of focusing attention on the South's problems and stressing the urgency of finding solutions. Serving as a Naval officer in India, young historian C. Vann Woodward was struck by his visit with the leader of India's untouchables who "plied me with questions about the black 'untouchables' of America and how their plight compared with that of his own people." Already the author of a revisionist biography of Populist Tom Watson, Woodward returned from the war to write a sweeping reinterpretation of the Redeemer Era South and then to pen *The Strange Career of Jim Crow*, an enormously influential volume that struck at both the legal and emotional underpinnings of segregation.

Meanwhile, Woodward contemporary John Hope Franklin, who had just received his Ph.D. from Harvard, offered his services as a historian to the War Department. Because he was black, he was rebuffed without receiving serious consideration. Then, responding to Naval recruiters' appeals for clerical personnel, Franklin was again rejected solely on the basis of his race. Finally, ordered to report for a draft physical, Franklin was subjected to further indignities, leading him to conclude that "the United States did not need me and did not deserve me." Consequently, he spent the rest of the war outwitting the draft board and "feeling nothing but shame for my country—not merely for what it did to me, but for what it did to the millions of black men and women who served in the armed forces under conditions of segregation and discrimination." Franklin went on to revise the traditional historical view of Reconstruction and of the role of blacks in southern history and to serve (as did Woodward, in a lesser capacity) as an adviser to the NAACP Legal Defense Team representing the plaintiffs in the *Brown* v. *Board of Education* case.

Franklin's wartime experience reflected the ambivalence and frustration with which many black intellectuals approached the conflict. Determined to link the fighting abroad to the struggle for racial justice at home, poet Langston Hughes exulted in "Jim Crow's Last Stand" that "Pearl Harbor put Jim Crow on the run/That Crow can't fight for Democracy/And be the same old Crow he used to be." Hughes also urged black soldiers to get those "so bad, evil and most mad, GO AND GET THE ENEMY BLUES." As segregation continued to flourish throughout the war effort, however, a disappointed Hughes also mocked, "Jim Crow Army and Navy, Too/Is Jim Crow freedom the *best* I can expect from you?"

By the time the war began, Richard Wright's angry fiction had already established him as the nation's preeminent black writer. As an increasingly disenchanted member of the Communist Party, however, Wright found himself zigging and zagging in response to a party line that was zigging and zagging as well. In the wake of the Nazi-Soviet Pact, he insisted that the conflict was "Not My People's War," pointing out that "the Negro's experience with past wars, his attitude towards the present one, his attitude of chronic distrust, constitute the most incisive and graphic refutation of every idealistic statement made by the war leaders as to the alleged democratic goal and aim of this war." After Hitler's invasion of Russia, however, the party suddenly had no more use for

Comrade Wright's pacifism, and slightly more than a week after Pearl Harbor, a frustrated Wright pledged his "loyalty and allegiance" to the American cause, promising that "I shall through my writing seek to rally the Negro people to stand shoulder to shoulder with the administration in a solid national front to wage war until victory is won."

Meanwhile, irreverent novelist and folklorist Zora Neale Hurston had drawn consistent criticism from Richard Wright and other black intellectuals for her failure to use her writings as a weapon in the struggle against racism and Jim Crow. Yet for all her apparent reluctance to devote her energies to solving the race problem, in the original manuscript for her autobiographical *Dust Tracks on a Road*, she pointed out that "President Roosevelt could extend his four freedoms to some people right here in America.... I am not bitter, but I see what I see.... I will fight for my country, but I will not lie for her." Like several others, this passage was subsequently excised after Hurston's white editor deemed it "irrelevant." After the war, however, writing in *Negro Digest*, Hurston cited Roosevelt's reference to the United States as "the arsenal of democracy" and wondered if she had heard him correctly. Perhaps he meant "arse-and-all" of democracy, she thought, since the United States was supporting the French in their effort to resubjugate the Indo-Chinese, suggesting that "the ass-and-all of democracy has shouldered the load of subjugating the dark world completely." Hurston also announced that she was "crazy for this democracy" and would "pitch headlong into the thing" if it were not for the numerous Jim Crow laws that confronted her at every turn.

World War II also stiffened white crusader Lillian Smith's resolve to fight against segregation. She insisted in 1943 that fighting for freedom while acquiescing to Jim Crow amounted to "trying to buy a new world with Confederate bills." Condemned by Georgia governor Eugene Talmadge as "a literary corn cob," Smith's 1944 novel *Strange Fruit* was a searing story of miscegenation and murder that concluded with the lynching of an innocent young black man. It lay bare the pain and suffering caused by white racism and the hypocrisy and sexual repression that festered just beneath the surface of the southern way of life.

The uncompromising Smith was hardly more contemptuous of those who defended Jim Crow than those who urged moderation in the fight against it. Yet, with external pressures mounting as the Supreme Court struck down the white primary in 1944, many white southerners who had once seemed most dedicated to racial justice found themselves urging the proponents of desegregation to slow down. Ardent and courageous spokesmen like Hodding Carter and Ralph McGill insisted that ending segregation would take time, and when they bristled at northern critics—members of the "hit-and-run school of southern writing," as Carter called them—they sounded a great deal like Faulkner's Gavin Stevens in *Intruder in the Dust* and Faulkner himself a few years thereafter. As Numan V. Bartley observed, in the wake of the war "the very word 'liberal' gradually disappeared from the southern political lexicon, except as a term of opprobrium." Meanwhile, although the contradictions raised by Jim Crow were inconsistent with the United States's rise to free-world leadership, the anti-Communist hysteria of the early Cold War years made even northern liberals initially reluctant to encourage antisegregation litigation and protests....

Even before World War II, some southern intellectuals were beginning to behave according to a pattern that now seems fairly typical of emerging or developing nations around the world, agonizing about their region's backwardness but also expressing their fears about the loss of cultural identity and virtue that might accompany the accelerating effort to modernize their society. No writer struggled more painfully or brilliantly with the persistence of the South's deficiencies or the decay of its virtues than William Faulkner. In the wake of World War II, Faulkner's fictional Jefferson was already experiencing what Walker Percy later called "Los Angelization," its "old big decaying wooden houses" giving way to antiseptic one-story models crammed into subdivisions "with their neat plots of clipped grass and tedious flowerbeds" and its housewives "in sandals and pants and painted toe nails," puffing "lipstick-stained cigarettes over shopping bags in the chain groceries and drugstores." Meanwhile, mechanization of agriculture brought a dramatic change in the rhythm of southern rural life as machines came between men and women and the land and further separated them from the product of their labors. "I'd druther have a mule fartin' in my face all day long walkin' de turnrow than dem durned tractors," a Delta farmhand told David Cohn. "There ain't nothing about a tractor that makes a man want to sing," complained another worker. "The thing keeps so much noise and you so far away from the other folks."...

On another front, the war's acceleration of black migration from states where blacks could not vote to states where they could played a key role in spurring the Democratic Party's advocacy of civil rights, but in doing so, it also fed the nationwide white blacklash that all but derailed the civil rights movement. Similarly, if the war-inspired Civil Rights revolution allowed southern blacks to claim the political rights and influence so long denied them, it also triggered the massive exodus of racially conservative southern whites from the Democratic Party, the cumulative result being a South that quickly amassed the nation's largest concentration of black officeholders while becoming its most predictably Republican region in presidential elections and a growing number of lesser contests as well.

While [W. J.] Cash would have found officeholding by Republicans or blacks almost equally startling, he would probably have been even more amazed to see that the changes set in motion or intensified by the war had rendered his version of the southern mind essentially obsolete, replacing it with a more heterogeneous and less exclusionary model, one open to anyone who saw themselves as southerners regardless of race or gender or even regional or national origin. Not only were blacks just as likely as whites to identify themselves as southerners by the 1990s, but in many cases, they actually seemed more confident of what that meant. Enduring taunts and threats and all manner of abuse from those who sought to preserve Cash's South, Charlayne Hunter-Gault had broken the color barrier at the University of Georgia in 1961. In 1988 she returned to Athens to deliver the commencement address, embracing the South as "my place" and paying tribute to southerners of both races whose "tumultuous" but shared history had melded them into the nation's only "definable people." Numerous such examples along with contemporary polls identifying Robert E. Lee and Martin

Luther King as the South's most revered historical figures seem to point to a southern mind dramatically different though hardly less paradoxical or contradictory than the one that tormented Cash.

Confirming the anxiety Cash had felt in 1940, Morton Sosna concluded that the South had emerged from World War II as "an arena where the forces of good and evil, progress and reaction, rapid change and seemingly timeless continuity were about to engage in a battle of near mythological proportions." As Sosna indicated, for the South, the end of the war meant not peace but another quarter century of struggle. More than any single preceding event, World War II helped to shape not only the contours of this struggle but its outcome, an outcome that finally allowed us to contemplate a South whose virtues, if they did not tower over its faults, were at least no longer totally obscured by them. All of this seems to have come out far better than Cash dared to hope. Yet, before we credit World War II with unloosing forces that destroyed Cash's South, we should first take note of the racism, violence, anti-intellectualism, and social indifference that now permeate American society at large and ask how the postwar historical context so clearly conducive to mitigating these characteristic vices of the southern mind in 1940 could have also set the stage for their ominous emergence as defining features of the national mind in 1996.

FURTHER READING

Anthony J. Badger, *Prosperity Road: The New Deal, Tobacco, and North Carolina* (1980).

Roger Biles, *Memphis in the Great Depression* (1986).

———, *The South and the New Deal* (1994).

Julia Blackwelder, *Women of the Depression: Caste and Culture in San Antonio, 1929–1939* (1984).

George T. Blakey, *Hard Times and New Deal in Kentucky, 1929–1939* (1986).

Jennifer Brooks, *Defining the Peace: World War II Veterans, Race, and the Remaking of Southern Political Tradition* (2004).

James A. Burran, "Urban Racial Violence in the South During World War II: A Comparative Overview," in Walter J. Fraser Jr. and Winfred B. Moore Jr., eds., *From the Old South to the New: Essays on the Transitional South* (1981), 167–177.

Dominic J. Capeci Jr., "The Lynching of Cleo Wright: Federal Protection of Constitutional Rights During World War II," *Journal of American History* 72 (1986), 859–887.

Robert A. Caro, *The Years of Lyndon Johnson: The Path to Power* (1983).

Dan T. Carter, *Scottsboro: A Tragedy of the American South* (1969).

Charles D. Chamberlain, *Victory at Home: Manpower and Race in the American South during World War II* (2003).

James C. Cobb, *The Most Southern Place on Earth: The Mississippi Delta and the Roots of Regional Identity* (1992).

———, *The Selling of the South: The Southern Crusade for Industrial Development, 1936–1980* (1982).

James C. Cobb and Michael V. Namorato, eds., *The New Deal and the South* (1984).

Pete Daniel, *Breaking the Land: The Transformation of Cotton, Tobacco, and Rice Cultures since 1880* (1985).

———, *Standing at the Crossroads: Southern Life since 1900* (1986).

Keith Dix, *What's a Coal Miner to Do?: The Mechanization of Coal Mining* (1988).

Alan Draper, "The New Southern Labor History Revisited: The Success of the Mine, Mill and Smelter Workers Union in Birmingham, 1934–1938," *Journal of Southern History* 62 (February 1996), 87–108.

Anthony P. Dunbar, *Against the Grain: Southern Radicals and Prophets, 1929–1959* (1981).

Charles W. Eagles, *Jonathan Daniels and Race Relations: The Evolution of a Southern Liberal* (1982).

John Egerton, *Speak Now Against the Day: The Generation Before the Civil Rights Movement in the South* (1994).

Gilbert C. Fite, *Cotton Fields No More: Southern Agriculture, 1865–1980* (1984).

J. Wayne Flynt, *Dixie's Forgotten People: The South's Poor Whites* (1979).

Kari Frederickson, *The Dixiecrat Revolt and the End of the Solid South, 1932–1968* (2001).

Frank Freidel, *FDR and the South* (1965).

Glenda Elizabeth Gilmore, *Defying Dixie: The Radical Roots of Civil Rights, 1919–1950* (2008).

John Temple Graves, *The Fighting South* (1943).

Barbara Griffith, *The Crisis of American Labor: Operation Dixie and the Defeat of the CIO* (1988).

Donald H. Grubbs, *Cry from the Cotton: The Southern Tenant Farmers' Union and the New Deal* (1971).

Margaret Jarman Hagood, *Mothers of the South: Portraiture of the White Tenant Farm Woman* (1939).

William Ivy Hair, *The Kingfish and His Realm: The Life and Times of Huey P. Long* (1991).

Ronald L. Heinemann, *Depression and New Deal in Virginia: The Enduring Dominion* (1983).

John W. Hevener, *Which Side Are You On? The Harlan County Coal Miners, 1931–1939* (1978).

James A. Hodges, *New Deal Labor Policy and the Southern Cotton Textile Industry, 1933–1941* (1986).

Donald Holley, *Uncle Sam's Farmers: The New Deal Communities in the Lower Mississippi Valley* (1975).

Preston J. Hubbard, *Origins of the TVA: The Muscle Shoals Controversy, 1920–1932* (1961).

———, ed., *Huey at 100: Centennial Essays on Huey P. Long* (1995).

Glen Jeansonne, *Messiah of the Masses: Huey P. Long and the Great Depression* (1993).

James H. Jones, *Bad Blood: The Tuskegee Syphilis Experiment* (1992).

Robin D. G. Kelley, *Hammer and Hoe: Alabama Communists During the Great Depression* (1990).

Jack Temple Kirby, *Rural Worlds Lost: The American South, 1920–1960* (1987).

Thomas A. Krueger, *And Promises to Keep: The Southern Conference for Human Welfare, 1938–1948* (1967).

Michael J. McDonald and John Muldowny, *TVA and the Dispossessed: The Resettlement of Population in the Norris Dam Area* (1982).

Paul Mertz, *New Deal Policy and Southern Rural Poverty* (1978).

H. L. Mitchell, *Mean Things Happening in This Land: The Life and Times of H. L. Mitchell, Co-Founder of the Southern Tenant Farmers Union* (1979).

Chester M. Morgan, *Redneck Liberal: Theodore G. Bilbo and the New Deal* (1985).

Robert J. Norrell, "Caste in Steel: Jim Crow Careers in Birmingham, Alabama," *Journal of American History* 73 (December 1986), 669–694.

Nell Painter, *The Narative of Hosea Hudson: His Life as a Negro Communist in the South* (1979).

Merl E. Reed, *Seedtime for the Modern Civil Rights Movement: The President's Committee on Fair Employment Practice, 1941–1946* (1991).

John A. Salmond, *A Southern Rebel: The Life and Times of Aubrey Willis Williams, 1890–1965* (1983).

Rebecca Sharpless, *Fertile Ground, Narrow Choices: Women on Texas Cotton Farms, 1900–1940* (1999).

Harvard Sitkoff, *A New Deal for Blacks: The Emergence of Civil Rights as a National Issue*, vol. 1: *The Depression Decade* (1978).

John R. Skates, "World War II as a Watershed in Mississippi History," *Journal of Mississippi History* 37 (1975), 131–142.

Douglas L. Smith, *The New Deal in the Urban South* (1988).

Morton D. Sosna, *In Search of the Silent South: Southern Liberals and the Race Issue* (1977).

Patricia Sullivan, *Days of Hope: Race and Democracy in the New Deal Era* (1996).

Martha Swain, *Ellen Woodward: New Deal Advocate for Women* (1995).

Tom Terrill and Jerrold Hirsch, eds., *Such As Us: Southern Voices of the Thirties* (1979).

Melissa Walker, *All We Knew Was to Farm: Rural Women in the Upcountry South, 1919–1941* (2000).

Nancy J. Weiss, *Farewell to the Party of Lincoln: Black Politics in the Age of FDR* (1983).

T. Harry Williams, *Huey Long* (1969).

Nan Elizabeth Woodruff, *As Rare as Rain: Federal Relief in the Great Southern Drought of 1930–1931* (1985).

CHAPTER 12

Race Relations and Freedom Struggles

Historians of the South have labeled the civil rights movement the Second Reconstruction. It attempted to accomplish what the first Reconstruction movement failed to do, that is, to give enduring civil rights to African Americans. In terms of its importance to the history of the South, the civil rights movement ranks with the Civil War and World War II. There is no doubt that the war's theme of greater diplomacy challenged white supremacists, who reacted with intimidation and violence, especially after the U.S. Supreme Court's Brown *decision in 1954. Black southerners acted, too: They pressed to desegregate schools, reinstate voting rights, and end segregation in public accommodations through boycotts, sit-ins, freedom rides, and protest marches.*

Freedom struggles begin with those who envision justice and courageously act to secure it. The movement to gain freedom and democracy stemmed in part from black churches, which had fostered solidarity and had brought forth pastors such as Martin Luther King Jr., Fred Shuttlesworth, and Andrew Young and lay leaders such as Ella Baker and Fannie Lou Hamer. Black colleges and universities became proving grounds for civil rights activists, men and women, faculty and students alike. The NAACP, the Southern Christian Leadership Conference (SCLC), Congress of Racial Equality (CORE), and the Student Non-Violent Coordinating Committee (SNCC) were among the many organizations founded to ensure that the movement for civil rights would not lose momentum. These groups and individuals in communities across the South took the freedom struggle to the courts, to the streets, and to the jury of public opinion; thousands of volunteers learned to practice nonviolent direct action, which often led to abuse from white supremacists, arrest, and even death. Thousands of citizens in towns and cities found their own ways to protest.

Segregation finally began to fall across the South with the 1964 Civil Rights Act, and, after a series of bloody demonstrations in Mississippi and Alabama, Congress in 1965 enacted the Voting Rights Act. In 1964 the nation ratified the Twenty-fourth Amendment to the Constitution, ending poll taxes. The integration of schools through busing and the desegregation of neighborhoods followed as the U.S. Supreme Court further defined the term civil rights. *Liberation movements for one group often inspire others to take action. It is well known that the movement for civil rights led to a renewed national movement for women's rights as many women volunteers for civil rights found themselves discriminated against even by their own colleagues.*

The historiography of the movement has changed since scholars began writing its history. Until the early 1980s, most authors concentrated on national figures and the major sites of the movement. More recently, studies at the state and community levels have examined the movement from the viewpoint of local people, demonstrated the existence of factions within the movement, and showed the diversity of actors—black and white, male and female, young and old. Still, questions remain. What role did the federal government play in promoting civil rights? What was the nature of white resistance, and where has white supremacy found expression today? What was the relationship between local activists and protest movements and regional and national civil rights organizations? What has been the legacy of the movement for women's rights? What has the civil rights movement brought to the nation?

DOCUMENTS

Document 1 is a personal recollection written by historian Melton A. McLaurin, who grew up in Wade, a small town in North Carolina. There he learned (and repudiated) the meaning of white supremacy. In this selection, he illustrates how profoundly whites believed in the inferiority of blacks and how in one afternoon he came to the full realization of its importance in his own life. By the mid-1950s segregation was beginning to be fully challenged. Since the 1930s, the U.S. Supreme Court had been eroding the *Plessy v. Ferguson* (1896) ruling, which held that separate but equal accommodations were constitutional. In May 1954, the Court decisively overturned that precedent in *Brown v. Board of Education of Topeka*, declaring that segregation was inherently unequal. A portion of Chief Justice Earl Warren's opinion appears in Document 2. This decision and subsequent protests by southern blacks provoked strong reaction in the South, fueled in part by opportunistic politicians. As white supremacy increasingly became the litmus test for officeholding and as the courts continued to rule in favor of black plaintiffs, a period of massive resistance emerged in the South. Document 3, popularly known as the Southern Manifesto, marks an important stage in this resistance. Signed by almost all southern senators and congressmen, it aims to demonstrate white southern solidarity and thereby forestall federal efforts to implement the *Brown* decision. The Supreme Court unwittingly aided segregationists when it decided in *Brown II* that schools should desegregate "with all deliberate speed." Many whites responded with "Never." In 1957, Virgil Blossom, the superintendent of Little Rock Schools, prepared a plan for the gradual desegregation of Central High School in 1957. The "Blossom Plan" was adopted and nine black students transferred to Central High, becoming the first in the state to attempt to integrate a white high school. The plan was sabotaged by white extremists intent on stopping all integration in Arkansas. Governor Orval Faubus supported the segregationists and brought in the

Arkansas National Guard on September 4, 1957, to bar the entrance to Central High School. This resulted in national embarrassment in the midst of the cold war and a meeting with President Dwight Eisenhower, who nationalized the Arkansas guardsmen and sent in the 101st Airborne Division to protect the African American students as they entered the school. The photograph of the nine students and Mrs. Daisy Bates, president of the Arkansas NAACP, seen in Document 4, shows them in happy anticipation before entering Central High. In the months following their entrance, the nine students endured a year of almost unrelenting bullying by some white students, despite the presence of national guardsmen. Melba Pattillo Beals recounts her experiences of abuse, real danger, and rescue in Document 5. In 1963 the civil rights movement came to Birmingham, where many members of the SCLC led boycotts and marches to protest the city's segregated stores and facilities. Martin Luther King Jr. stirred the ire of the state's most prominent clergy, who wrote a letter to the *Birmingham News* asking him to stop the demonstrations (Document 6). King replied with his "Letter from Birmingham Jail" (Document 7), which has since become one of the classic pieces of civil disobedience literature. King began the letter while imprisoned for violating a court injunction; he used religious principles, a stubby pencil, and the margins of a newspaper to discuss the reason why blacks could no longer wait for civil rights. With logic he explained how nonviolent direct action was necessary to "create such a crisis and establish such creative tension that a community that has constantly refused to negotiate is forced to confront the issue." In that same year, Anne Moody and cohorts from Tougaloo College confronted segregation head-on. In her classic account, *Coming of Age in Mississippi,* Moody describes the student sit-in movement in Jackson, Mississippi (Document 8). The photograph that follows (Document 9) shows John Salter, Joan Trumpauer, and Anne Moody at the Woolworth's lunch counter and illustrates the mob mentality. Congress finally acted in 1964 and 1965 by passing the Civil Rights Act and the Voting Rights Act. These laws forbade discrimination, mandated equal access to public facilities, and assured voting rights for African Americans. Document 10 provides evidence of a sizable increase in black voter registration in the South after 1965.

1. Melton A. McLaurin Recalls His "Separate Past" in Wade, North Carolina, 1953

In the South of my youth "good breeding" was still extremely important. Adults who abused blacks "for no good reason" were held in contempt by my family, and as late as the 1950s the older generation talked disparagingly about whites who "treated their colored people mean," as if whites still owned blacks and were compelled by some social code to handle their laborers gently. *Nigger* was a word poor whites used, a term they hurled at blacks (whom the adults in my

Separate Pasts: Growing Up White in the Segregated South by Melton A. McLaurin. Athens, G.A.: University of Georgia Press.

family always referred to as "colored people") the way my childhood friends from less affluent families hurled pieces of granite from the railway track beds at hapless black children their age or younger. Despite linguistic niceties, however, all whites knew that blacks were, really, servants. It was their destiny to work at menial tasks, supervised, of course, by benevolent whites. All this was according to God's plan and was perfectly obvious to all but dimwitted Yankees and Communists. As a young child I could sit in church with the other white children of the village and sing "Jesus loves the little children … Red and yellow, black and white" and never wonder why no black children were in our group. Until I began to work at the store the thought that they should have been in church with us never occurred to me. It also probably never occurred to the adult church members, including the minister.

Race, then, was something I rarely thought about and never pondered—that is, until a single incident, a commonplace occurrence involving Bobo, made me aware of the tremendous impact a segregated society had upon my life. Unlike schoolmates like my best friend, Howard Lee Baker[,] … Bobo was never an important part of my life. Bobo was merely there, a child whom I saw frequently and played with on occasion, but who was of no real consequence to me. Because of his relative unimportance, because I had known him all my life, because he had been a part of my childhood environment in the same way as the trees and the school playgrounds and the dusty streets, because, like them, he had always been there, Bobo changed that comfortable, secure racist world for me. He did so unintentionally, yet irrevocably, in the fall of my thirteenth year….

There was certainly nothing extraordinary about physical contact with Bobo. As a child I played football and basketball with him, wrestled with him, and competed against him in other games that were actually boyhood tests of physical strength….

The realization occurred in a comfortable, familiar setting on the playground. It was one of those uncommon common incidents of ordinary life which, because of some inexplicable turn of events or perhaps because of their timing, unmask some aspect of our life that we have always accepted as a given, place it in another perspective, and cause it to assume an entirely different face. Often such perceptions are not a result of either education or training but are instead mere happenstances, accidents of understanding, and are as unwelcome as they are unintended.

A basketball court was as appropriate as any place to gain some understanding of the larger implications of segregation and racism. In Wade basketball was the premier sport, played continually by boys, black and white, from September through May….

Pickup games between integrated teams were nothing unusual; in fact, they were the norm when blacks and whites played on the same court…. Although race was not completely ignored on the courts, it rarely influenced the conduct of a game. In all the years I played in such integrated contests, I never saw a fight provoked for racial reasons, though disputes over fouls, out of bounds plays, and other technicalities occurred with monotonous regularity during practically every game. The lack of racial tensions on the court probably stemmed from the fact that the society accepted, and in many ways encouraged, the practice of integrated play. Young southern males had traditionally engaged in integrated informal sports events, especially such outdoor sports as hunting and fishing. Integrated pickup basketball games, as opposed to organized play, were merely an extension of this practice. It was only contact with females of the opposite race that was proscribed, and that only after puberty....

One fall Saturday afternoon six of us were matched in a hotly contested game, neither of the equally untalented threesomes able to gain much of an advantage. Howard Lee and I, the only whites in the game, were joined by an awkward young black named Curtis, whose reasonably accurate jump shot was negated by his general lack of coordination. Bobo played on the other team, opposite me as usual....

We were using Howard Lee's ball, which presented a challenge because it leaked air and had to be reinflated every thirty minutes or so. Since there was an air compressor at the store, I was charged with keeping the ball inflated. Although we played on a black playground, the white kids controlled the situation because we controlled the ball. None of the black players had a ball, so without us there was no game....

We played into the afternoon, our play interrupted by frequent trips to the air compressor. When enough air leaked from the ball to cause it to lose its bounce and begin to interfere with the game, I would take it to the air compressor to pump it up.... When we reached the air compressor I pulled from my pocket the needle required to inflate the ball and without thinking handed it to Bobo.

The procedure followed for inserting a needle into a basketball had long been sanctioned by the rituals of kids playing on dirt and asphalt courts. First, someone wet the needle by sticking it into his mouth or spitting on it. Thus lubricated, the instrument was popped neatly into the small rubber valve through which the ball was inflated. This time chance dictated that playground procedure would fail; we couldn't insert the needle into the valve. Bobo stuck the needle in his mouth, applied the usual lavish amount of saliva, and handed it to Howard Lee, who held the ball. Howard struggled to push the needle into the valve, with no luck. Irritated by what struck me as their incompetence and anxious to return to the game I decided to inflate the ball myself. I took the ball from Howard, pulled the needle from the valve, and placed it in my mouth, convinced that my spit would somehow get the needle into the ball and us back onto the court. A split second after placing the needle in my mouth, I was jolted by one of the most shattering emotional experiences of my young life. Instantaneously an awareness of the shared racial prejudices of generations of white society coursed through every nerve of my body. Bolts of prejudice, waves of prejudice that I could literally feel sent my head reeling and buckled my knees.

The realization that the needle I still held in my mouth had come directly from Bobo's mouth, that it carried on it Bobo's saliva, transformed my prejudices into a physically painful experience. I often had drunk from the same cup as black children, dined on food prepared by blacks. It never occurred to me that such actions would violate my racial purity. The needle in my mouth, however, had been purposely drenched with Negro spit, and that substance threatened to defile my entire being. It threatened me with germs which, everyone said, were common among blacks. These black germs would ravage my body with unspeakable diseases, diseases from the tropics, Congo illnesses that would rot my limbs, contort my body with pain.... Those awful African diseases, I now imagined, would claim me as a victim.

The tainted substance on the needle also threatened, in a less specific but equally disturbing manner, my white consciousness, my concept of what being white meant. Bobo's spit threatened to plunge me into a world of voodoo chants and tribal drums. Suddenly the *Saturday Evening Post* cartoon world of black savages dancing about boiling cauldrons filled with white hunters and missionaries seemed strangely real. I felt deprived of the ability to reason, to control the situation. All threats to mind and body, however, failed to compare to the ultimate danger posed by the saliva on the needle. It placed in jeopardy my racial purity, my existence as a superior being, the true soul of all southern whites....

The urge to gag, to lean over and vomit out any of the black saliva that might remain to spread its contamination throughout my body, was almost unbearable. Yet I could neither gag nor vomit, nor could I wipe my mouth with the back of my hand. Ironically, the same prejudices that filled me with loathing and disgust also demanded that I conceal my feelings. The emotional turmoil exploding inside me had to be contained, choked off. Not for a second could I allow Bobo to suspect that I was in the least upset, or to comprehend the anguish his simple act of moistening the needle with his saliva had caused me.... More than the poison of Bobo's saliva I feared the slightest indication of loss of self-control, the merest hint that this black child I knew so well had the power to cut me to the emotional quick, to reach the innermost regions of my being and challenge the sureties of my white world. He could never be allowed to cause me to deviate in the least from the prescribed pattern of white behavior....

Yet my vindication of white supremacy was incomplete. While I had asserted my superiority and my right to that status because of my skin color, I still felt defiled. The thought that some residual contamination, some lingering trace of the essence of Bobo's blackness remained with me became an obsession. I could feel his germs crawling through my body, spreading their black pestilence from head to toe. I had to cleanse myself—to purify my body of Bobo's contaminants and to rid my person of any remaining trace of his negritude. Only then could I fully reclaim my racial purity and restore my shaken sense of superiority. And I had to do so quickly, without the knowledge of others, before I could return to the game....

From the side of the building protruded a faucet, used by thirsty ball players who had no money for Cokes. Bending over, I turned the tap and watched the clear, clean water burst from the spigot and spatter into the sand. I cupped my hands beneath the flow, watched them fill with the crystal liquid, then splashed it to my face, felt it begin to cleanse me of Bobo's black stain.

Bending farther, I placed my mouth against the grooved lip of the faucet.... I let the cleansing stream trickle through my mouth, removing any remaining Negro contaminant. I splashed more water over my face and head, then washed my hands and forearms. Finally, I swallowed a large gulp of water, felt it slide down my throat, and in my mind's eye saw it wash away the last traces of Bobo's blackness. My rite of purification was completed. With this baptism of plain tap water I was reborn, my white selfhood restored. I stood straight, shook the water from my face and hands, and walked back to rejoin the game....

What I remember is an awareness that things had changed. I knew that Bobo was black, that he would always be black, and that his blackness set him apart from me in ways that I had never understood. I realized, too, that his blackness threatened me, that in a way I did not comprehend it challenged my most securely held concepts about who I was and what I might become.... I also knew that there was something very wrong, even sinister, about this power Bobo held over me, this ability to confound my world simply because he was black. None of it made much sense at the time. But the knowledge, the understanding that segregation was so powerful a force, that it could provoke such violent emotional responses within me, for the first time raised questions in my mind about the institution, serious questions that adults didn't want asked and, as I would later discover, that they never answered.

2. *Brown* v. *Board of Education of Topeka, Kansas,* 1954

Mr. Chief Justice Warren delivered the opinion of the Court....

Today, education is perhaps the most important function of state and local governments. Compulsory school attendance laws and the great expenditures for education both demonstrate our recognition of the importance of education to our democratic society. It is required in the performance of our most basic public responsibilities, even service in the armed forces. It is the very foundation of good citizenship. Today it is a principal instrument in awakening the child to cultural values, in preparing him for later professional training, and in helping him to adjust normally to his environment. In these days, it is doubtful that any child may reasonably be expected to succeed in life if he is denied the opportunity of an education. Such an opportunity, where the state has undertaken to provide it, is a right which must be made available to all on equal terms.

We come then to the question presented: Does segregation of children in public schools solely on the basis of race, even though the physical facilities and other "tangible" factors may be equal, deprive the children of the minority group of equal educational opportunities? We believe that it does.

In *Sweatt* v. *Painter* ..., in finding that a segregated law school for Negroes could not provide them equal educational opportunities, this Court relied in large part on "those qualities which are incapable of objective measurement but which make for greatness in a law school." In *McLaurin* v. *Oklahoma State*

This document can be found in *Brown* v. *Board of Education*: 349 U.S. 483 (May 17, 1954).

Regents, ... the Court, in requiring that a Negro admitted to a white graduate school be treated like all other students, again resorted to intangible considerations: "... his ability to study, to engage in discussions and exchange views with other students, and, in general, to learn his profession." Such considerations apply with added force to children in grade and high schools. To separate them from others of similar age and qualifications solely because of their race generates a feeling of inferiority as to their status in the community that may affect their hearts and minds in a way unlikely ever to be undone. The effect of this separation on their educational opportunities was well stated by a finding in the Kansas case by a court which nevertheless felt compelled to rule against the Negro plaintiffs:

> Segregation of white and colored children in public schools has a detrimental effect upon the colored children. The impact is greater when it has the sanction of the law; for the policy of separating the races is usually interpreted as denoting the inferiority of the negro group. A sense of inferiority affects the motivation of a child to learn. Segregation with the sanction of law, therefore, has a tendency to [retard] the educational and mental development of Negro children and to deprive them of some of the benefits they would receive in a racial[ly] integrated school system.

Whatever may have been the extent of psychological knowledge at the time of *Plessy* v. *Ferguson*, this finding is amply supported by modern authority. Any language in *Plessy* v. *Ferguson* contrary to this finding is rejected.

We conclude that in the field of public education the doctrine of "separate but equal" has no place. Separate educational facilities are inherently unequal. Therefore, we hold that the plaintiffs and others similarly situated for whom the actions have been brought are, by reason of the segregation complained of, deprived of the equal protection of the laws guaranteed by the Fourteenth Amendment.

3. White Southerners Refute *Brown* v. *Board of Education* and Write Their Own Southern Manifesto, 1956

The unwarranted decision of the Supreme Court in the public school cases is now bearing the fruit always produced when men substitute naked power for established law.

The Founding Fathers gave us a Constitution of checks and balances because they realized the inescapable lesson of history that no man or group of men can be safely entrusted with unlimited power. They framed this Constitution with its provisions for change by amendment in order to secure the fundamentals of government against the dangers of temporary popular passion or the personal predilections of public officeholders.

This document can be found in *Southern School News*, April, 1956.

We regard the decision of the Supreme Court in the school cases as a clear abuse of judicial power. It climaxes a trend in the Federal Judiciary undertaking to legislate, in derogation of the authority of Congress, and to encroach upon the reserved rights of the States and the people.

The original Constitution does not mention education. Neither does the 14th amendment nor any other amendment. The debates preceding the submission of the 14th amendment clearly show that there was no intent that it should affect the system of education maintained by the States.

The very Congress which proposed the amendment subsequently provided for segregated schools in the District of Columbia.

When the amendment was adopted in 1868, there were 37 States of the Union. Every one of the 26 States that had any substantial racial differences among its people, either approved the operation of segregated schools already in existence or subsequently established such schools by action of the same law-making body which considered the 14th amendment.

As admitted by the Supreme Court in the public school case (*Brown* v. *Board of Education*), the doctrine of separate but equal schools "apparently originated in *Roberts* v. *City of Boston* (1849), upholding school segregation against attack as being violative of a State constitutional guarantee of equality." This constitutional doctrine began in the North, not in the South, and it was followed not only in Massachusetts, but in Connecticut, New York, Illinois, Indiana, Michigan, Minnesota, New Jersey, Ohio, Pennsylvania and other northern States until they, exercising their rights as States through the constitutional processes of local self-government, changed their school systems.

In the case of *Plessy* v. *Ferguson* in 1896 the Supreme Court expressly declared that under the 14th amendment no person was denied any of his rights if the States provided separate but equal public facilities. This decision has been followed in many other cases. It is notable that the Supreme Court, speaking through Chief Justice Taft, a former President of the United States, unanimously declared in 1927 in *Lum* v. *Rice* that the "separate but equal" principle is "within the discretion of the State in regulating its public schools and does not conflict with the 14th amendment."...

This unwarranted exercise of power by the Court, contrary to the Constitution, is creating chaos and confusion in the States principally affected. It is destroying the amicable relations between the white and Negro races that have been created through 90 years of patient effort by the good people of both races. It has planted hatred and suspicion where there has been heretofore friendship and understanding.

Without regard to the consent of the governed, outside agitators are threatening immediate and revolutionary changes in our public-school systems. If done, this is certain to destroy the system of public education in some of the States.

With the gravest concern for the explosive and dangerous condition created by this decision and inflamed by outside meddlers:

We reaffirm our reliance on the Constitution as the fundamental law of the land.

We decry the Supreme Court's encroachment on rights reserved to the States and to the people, contrary to established law, and to the Constitution.

We commend the motives of those States which have declared the intention to resist forced integration by any lawful means.

We appeal to the States and people who are not directly affected by these decisions to consider the constitutional principles involved against the time when they too, on issues vital to them, may be the victims of judicial encroachment....

In this trying period, as we all seek to right this wrong, we appeal to our people not to be provoked by the agitators and troublemakers invading our States and to scrupulously refrain from disorder and lawless acts.

4. The Little Rock Nine and Daisy Bates Pose in Mrs. Bates's Living Room, c. 1957

Little Rock Nine and Daisy Bates posed in living room (Library of Congress). Seated, left to right: Thelma Mothershed, Minnijean Brown, Elizabeth Eckford and Gloria Ray. Standing, left to right: Ernest Green, Melba Pattillo, Terrance Roberts, Carlotta Walls, Daisy Bates and Jefferson Thomas. (Everett Collection Inc.)

5. Melba Pattillo Beals Reflects on 'Integration' at Central High, 1958

February 18, 1958.

A red-haired, freckle-faced girl, the one who taunts me in homeroom, keeps trailing me in the hallway between classes. Today she spit on me, then slapped me. Later in the day as I came around a corner, she tripped me so that I fell down a flight of stairs. I picked myself up to face a group of boys who then chased me up the stairs. When I told a school official about it, he said she was from a good family and would never do such a thing and I needed a teacher to witness these incidents if he were going to take any action. He asked me what did I expect when I came to a place where I knew I wasn't welcome. He warned me to keep Minnijean's expulsion in mind.

February 19

Andy again. He's really beginning to frighten me. As I emerged from the cafeteria today, he walked right up, face to face, stepping on my toes so I couldn't move for a long moment. He shoved me backward and then held a wrench up to my face. He waved it around and shouted all sorts of threats that he could do a lot of awful things to my face with it. My knees were shaking and I didn't know what to do. I said, "Thank you." His eyes grew huge. Quicker than the speed of light, I jumped away from him and ran. "Just think all night about what I'm gonna do to you tomorrow," he shouted after me.

February 20

I got hit across the back with a tennis racquet. I managed to smile and say, "Thank you." Andy said, "What did you say, nigger?" I repeated, "Thank you very much." I spit up blood in the rest room. I felt as though someone had stuck a hot poker through my back, into my insides. I saw him several times during the afternoon, but I never let him see me cry, and I didn't report it to anybody.

I think only the warrior exists in me now. Melba went away to hide. She was too frightened to stay here....

By the beginning of March, I had sunk into the state of mind you get into when you know you have to take castor oil and there's no way out. I just did what had to be done, without discussing it or thinking about it. I would get up, polish my saddle shoes, bathe, get dressed, dump my bowl of oatmeal into the toilet so Grandma India would think I'd eaten it—but my nervous stomach wouldn't have to eject it—and go to the war inside that school. I listened to shouts, to ugly names, while I smiled and said "Thank you." I waited for a ride, came home, did homework, got to bed, and started over again the next day. I felt kind of numb, as though nothing mattered anymore.

I thought my routine must be like a soldier's fighting in wartime. Only I was lucky enough to have weekends in another world. One day I was doing just that, thinking about my other world and about the headline I had seen that read, "IT'S LOVELY, SAYS MINNIJEAN OF HER NEW YORK SCHOOL." What would it be like to have just one lovely day of school amid pleasant people who smiled when you looked them in the eye?

As I stood alone, outside the Sixteenth Street entrance of Central High, I was shivering against the cold, waiting for my ride home that Friday afternoon. I was immersed in fantasies about my quiet, safe weekend. My body was there, but my mind was somewhere else.

My 101st guard Danny had said, "When you let yourself lose your focus, you make big mistakes." I suddenly realized that I had done just that, made a foolish mistake. The Sixteenth Street entrance was one of the most dangerous areas of Central High's grounds. It was a place I would never have chosen to wait alone, had I been conscious of my action. It was an isolated spot with no teachers, principals, or guards keeping watch, but I was too weary to walk the two blocks to the other side where it was safer and where my driver expected to pick me up. I decided I'd be wiser to stand still and hope that the car-pool driver would figure out I wasn't waiting in the appropriate place and would come around to this side of the building looking for me. So I said a little prayer and allowed myself to lapse deep into my thoughts once more.

Suddenly there was a voice in the distance, calling my name, jolting me from my thoughts. "It's nigger Melba." It was Andy's voice shouting at me. My heart started beating fast. Where the heck was he? I looked to see how far off he was. He was more than a block away, coming up from the playing field with a group of his friends. They were walking fast, almost galloping. Even if I started running, I couldn't out-distance all of them. I looked around frantically, searching for help.

"Hey, Melba, you gotta get out of here." The second voice was much closer. I wasn't alone. There was a sleek, muscular boy, about six feet tall, wearing a varsity jacket and a cap, with a bushy shock of blond curls peeking from beneath it. He was leaning against the passenger side of a 1949 Chevy parked at the curb, only a few feet to my left. Was he one of Andy's friends, who'd come to corner me and hold me there? His face looked familiar to me. He resembled one of those big tough boys who got their kicks taunting me. But why wasn't he coming toward me, shouting ugly words at me like the others?

My mouth went dry. My feet seemed bolted to the ground. My knees were shaking so badly that I doubted whether I could run. Where would I go? Andy and his friends were dancing about each other in a circle, huddling to decide how they would have their fun with me. One boy started to run back in the direction from which they had come. Another boy joined them. What were they going back to get, I wondered. A rope?

"Nigger, nigger on the wall, who's the deadest of them all," Andy shouted as he hesitated, waiting for his friends. Now, they were only about a quarter of a block away. "Stand still, don't run, 'cause if you do, it'll be worse for you," Andy shouted.

What now? My mind scrambled to figure out what I should do.

"Melba," the blond boy whispered my name, "listen to me. I'm gonna call you nigger—loud. I'm gonna curse at you, but I'm gonna put my keys on the trunk of this car. Get out of here, now. My name is Link, I'll call you later."

"But I can't do that."

"Get the hell out of here.... Andy's gonna kill you."

"But I can't.... I ... uh ..." I stood there gasping for words. He's up to something, I thought. Now I'm surrounded. Why doesn't the car-pool driver come after me now ... right now, please, God.

"You don't have any choice," he whispered. "Go!" I turned to see that Andy and his friends were only a short distance away. I wasn't even sure I could make it to the car.

"If you don't get out of here, you're gonna get us both killed," the blond boy urged.

"Hey, Andy, we're gonna have us some nigger tonight." I heard Link shout as he walked away from the car, toward them. I grabbed the keys and ran around quickly to open the door on the driver's side. I hopped in and locked all the doors. By the time I turned the key in the engine, Andy was clawing at the lock, while the other boys popped off the windshield wipers, and tried to get into the passenger's side. Link stood glaring at me with an anxious look on his face, spewing hate words just like them. I pressed down the clutch, shifted into first gear, and the car jumped forward. Andy was still running alongside, holding on to the door handle, but as I sped up, he had to let go. Even if that boy Link got me later for stealing his car, I was alive and on my way for now.

After a couple of blocks, when I could breathe a little easier, I craned to look around. I couldn't see anybody following me. "Thank you, God," I whispered, as I headed for home. "Thank you for saving me one more time."

6. Alabama Clergy Write an Open Appeal to End the Demonstrations, 1963

APRIL 12, 1963

We the undersigned clergymen are among those who, in January, issued "An Appeal for Law and Order and Common Sense," in dealing with racial problems in Alabama. We expressed understanding that honest convictions in racial matters could properly be pursued in the courts, but urged that decisions of those courts should in the meantime be peacefully obeyed....

However, we are now confronted by a series of demonstrations by some of our Negro citizens, directed and led in part by outsiders. We recognize the natural impatience of people who feel that their hopes are slow in being realized. But we are convinced that these demonstrations are unwise and untimely.

We agree rather with certain local Negro leadership which has called for honest and open negotiation of racial issues in our area. And we believe this

---

From *The Birmingham News*, April 12, 1963.

kind of facing of issues can best be accomplished by citizens of our own metropolitan area, white and Negro, meeting with their knowledge and experience of the local situation. All of us need to face that responsibility and find proper channels for its accomplishment.

Just as we formerly pointed out that "hatred and violence have no sanction in our religious and political traditions," we also point out that such actions as incite to hatred and violence, however technically peaceful those actions may be, have not contributed to the resolution of our local problems. We do not believe that these days of new hope are days when extreme measures are justified in Birmingham.

We commend the community as a whole, and the local news media and law enforcement officials in particular, on the calm manner in which these demonstrations have been handled. We urge the public to continue to show restraint should the demonstrations continue, and the law enforcement officials to remain calm and continue to protect our city from violence.

We further strongly urge our own Negro community to withdraw support from these demonstrations, and to unite locally in working peacefully for a better Birmingham. When rights are consistently denied, a cause should be pressed in the courts and in negotiations among local leaders, and not in the streets. We appeal to both our white and Negro citizenry to observe the principles of law and order and common sense.

C.C.J. Carpenter, D.D., L.L.D., Bishop of Alabama; Joseph A. Durick, D.D., Auxiliary Bishop, Diocese of Mobile-Birmingham; Rabbi Milton L. Grafman, Temple Emanu-El, Birmingham, Alabama; Bishop Paul Hardin, Bishop of the Alabama-West Florida Conference of the Methodist Church; Bishop Nolan B. Harmon, Bishop of the North Alabama Conference of the Methodist Church; George M. Murray, D.D., L.L.D., Bishop Coadjutor, Episcopal Diocese of Alabama; Edward V. Ramage, Moderator, Synod of the Alabama Presbyterian Church in the United States; Earl Stallings, Pastor, First Baptist Church, Birmingham, Alabama.

7. Martin Luther King, Jr. Responds to the Alabama Clergy with "Letter from Birmingham Jail," 1963

My dear Fellow Clergymen,

While confined here in the Birmingham city jail, I came across your recent statement calling our present activities "unwise and untimely." Seldom, if ever, do I pause to answer criticism of my work and ideas. If I sought to answer all of the criticisms that cross my desk, my secretaries would be engaged in little else in the course of the day, and I would have no time for constructive work. But since I feel that you are men of genuine good will and your criticisms are sincerely set forth, I would like to answer your statement in what I hope will be patient and reasonable terms.

I think I should give the reason for my being in Birmingham, since you have been influenced by the argument of "outsiders coming in." I have the honor of serving as president of the Southern Christian Leadership Conference, an organization operating in every southern state, with headquarters in Atlanta, Georgia. We have some eighty-five affiliate organizations all across the South—one being the Alabama Christian Movement for Human Rights. Whenever necessary and possible we share staff, educational and financial resources with our affiliates. Several months ago our local affiliate here in Birmingham invited us to be on call to engage in a nonviolent direct-action program if such were deemed necessary. We readily consented and when the hour came we lived up to our promises. So I am here, along with several members of my staff, because we were invited here. I am here because I have basic organizational ties here.

Beyond this, I am in Birmingham because injustice is here. Just as the eighth century prophets left their little villages and carried their "thus saith the Lord" far beyond the boundaries of their hometowns; and just as the Apostle Paul left his little village of Tarsus and carried the gospel of Jesus Christ to practically every hamlet and city of the Graeco-Roman world, I too am compelled to carry the gospel of freedom beyond my particular hometown. Like Paul, I must constantly respond to the Macedonian call for aid.

Moreover, I am cognizant of the interrelatedness of all communities and states. I cannot sit idly by in Atlanta and not be concerned about what happens in Birmingham. Injustice anywhere is a threat to justice everywhere. We are caught in an inescapable network of mutuality, tied in a single garment of destiny. Whatever affects one directly affects all indirectly. Never again can we afford to live with the narrow, provincial "outside agitator" idea. Anyone who lives in the United States can never be considered an outsider anywhere in this country.

You deplore the demonstrations that are presently taking place in Birmingham. But I am sorry that your statement did not express a similar concern for the conditions that brought the demonstrations into being. I am sure that each of you would want to go beyond the superficial social analyst who looks merely at effects, and does not grapple with underlying causes. I would not hesitate to say that it is unfortunate that so-called demonstrations are taking place in Birmingham at this time, but I would say in more emphatic terms that it is even more unfortunate that the white power structure of this city left the Negro community with no other alternative.

In any nonviolent campaign there are four basic steps: (1) collection of the facts to determine whether injustices are alive, (2) negotiation, (3) self-purification, and (4) direct action. We have gone through all of these steps in Birmingham. There can be no gainsaying of the fact that racial injustice engulfs this community.

Birmingham is probably the most thoroughly segregated city in the United States. Its ugly record of police brutality is known in every section of this country. Its injust treatment of Negroes in the courts is a notorious reality. There have been more unsolved bombings of Negro homes and churches in Birmingham than any city in this nation. These are the hard, brutal and unbelievable facts. On the basis of these conditions Negro leaders sought to negotiate with the city fathers. But the political leaders consistently refused to engage in good faith negotiation.

Then came the opportunity last September to talk with some of the leaders of the economic community. In these negotiating sessions certain promises were made by the merchants—such as the promise to remove the humiliating racial signs from the stores. On the basis of these promises Rev. [Fred] Shuttlesworth and the leaders of the Alabama Christian Movement for Human Rights agreed to call a moratorium on any type of demonstrations. As the weeks and months unfolded we realized that we were the victims of a broken promise. The signs remained. Like so many experiences of the past we were confronted with blasted hopes, and the dark shadow of a deep disappointment settled upon us. So we had no alternative except that of preparing for direct action, whereby we would present our very bodies as a means of laying our case before the conscience of the local and national community. We were not unmindful of the difficulties involved. So we decided to go through a process of self-purification. We started having workshops on nonviolence and repeatedly asked ourselves the questions, "Are you able to accept blows without retaliating?" "Are you able to endure the ordeals of jail?" We decided to set our direct-action program around the Easter season, realizing that with the exception of Christmas, this was the largest shopping period of the year. Knowing that a strong economic withdrawal program would be the by-product of direct action, we felt that this was the best time to bring pressure on the merchants for the needed changes. Then it occurred to us that the March election was ahead and so we speedily decided to postpone action until after election day. When we discovered that Mr. [Eugene "Bull"] Connor [Birmingham's Public Safety Commissioner] was in the run-off, we decided again to postpone action so that the demonstrations could not be used to cloud the issues. At this time we agreed to begin our nonviolent witness the day after the run-off.

This reveals that we did not move irresponsibly into direct action. We too wanted to see Mr. Connor defeated; so we went through postponement after postponement to aid in this community need. After this we felt that direct action could be delayed no longer.

You may well ask, "Why direct action? Why sit-ins, marches, etc.? Isn't negotiation a better path?" You are exactly right in your call for negotiation. Indeed, this is the purpose of direct action. Nonviolent direct action seeks to create such a crisis and establish such creative tension that a community that has constantly refused to negotiate is forced to confront the issue. It seeks so to dramatize the issue that it can no longer be ignored. I just referred to the creation of tension as a part of the work of the nonviolent resister. This may sound rather shocking. But I must confess that I am not afraid of the word tension. I have earnestly worked and preached against violent tension, but there is a type of constructive nonviolent tension that is necessary for growth. Just as Socrates felt that it was necessary to create a tension in the mind so that individuals could rise from the bondage of myths and half-truths to the unfettered realm of creative analysis and objective appraisal, we must see the need of having nonviolent gadflies to create the kind of tension in society that will help men to rise from the dark depths of prejudice and racism to the majestic heights of understanding and brotherhood. So the purpose of the direct action is to create a situation so crisis-packed that it will inevitably open the door to negotiation. We, therefore, concur with you in your call for negotiation. Too long has our beloved Southland been bogged down in the tragic attempt to live in monologue rather than dialogue.

One of the basic points in your statement is that our acts are untimely. Some have asked, "Why didn't you give the new administration time to act?" The only answer that I can give to this inquiry is that the new administration must be prodded about as much as the outgoing one before it acts. We will be sadly mistaken if we feel that the election of Mr. [Albert] Boutwell will bring the millennium to Birmingham. While Mr. Boutwell is much more articulate and gentle than Mr. Connor, they are both segregationists, dedicated to the task of maintaining the status quo. The hope I see in Mr. Boutwell is that he will be reasonable enough to see the futility of massive resistance to desegregation. But he will not see this without pressure from the devotees of civil rights. My friends, I must say to you that we have not made a single gain in civil rights without determined legal and nonviolent pressure. History is the long and tragic story of the fact that privileged groups seldom give up their privileges voluntarily. Individuals may see the moral light and voluntarily give up their unjust posture; but as Reinhold Niebuhr has reminded us, groups are more immoral than individuals.

We know through painful experience that freedom is never voluntarily given by the oppressor; it must be demanded by the oppressed. Frankly, I have never yet engaged in a direct action movement that was "well-timed," according to the timetable of those who have not suffered unduly from the disease of segregation. For years now I have heard the word "Wait!" It rings in the ear of every Negro with a piercing familiarity. This "Wait!" has almost always meant "Never." It has been a tranquilizing thalidomide [a drug that caused birth defects], relieving the emotional stress for a moment, only to give birth to an ill-formed infant of frustration. We must come to see with the distinguished jurist of yesterday that "justice too long delayed is justice denied." We have waited for more than 340 years for our constitutional and God-given rights. The nations of Asia and Africa are moving with jetlike speed toward the goal of political independence, and we still creep at horse and buggy pace toward the gaining of a cup of coffee at a lunch counter. I guess it is easy for those who have never felt the stinging darts of segregation to say, "Wait." But when you have seen vicious mobs lynch your mothers and fathers at will and drown your sisters and brothers at whim; when you have seen hate-filled policemen curse, kick, brutalize and even kill your black brothers and sisters with impunity; when you see the vast majority of your twenty million Negro brothers smothering in an airtight cage of poverty in the midst of an affluent society; … when you take a cross-country drive and find it necessary to sleep night after night in the uncomfortable corners of your automobile because no motel will accept you; when you are humiliated day in and day out by nagging signs reading "white" and "colored"; when your first name becomes "nigger" and your middle name becomes "boy" (however old you are) and your last name becomes "John," and when your wife and mother are never given the respected title "Mrs."; when you are harried by day and haunted by night by the fact that you are a Negro, living constantly at tiptoe stance never quite knowing what to expect next, and plagued with inner fears and outer resentments; when you are forever fighting a degenerating sense of "nobodiness"; then you will understand why we find it difficult to wait. There comes a time when the cup of endurance runs over, and men are no longer willing to be plunged into an abyss of injustice where they experience the blackness of corroding despair. I hope, sirs, you can understand our legitimate and unavoidable impatience.

You express a great deal of anxiety over our willingness to break laws. This is certainly a legitimate concern. Since we so diligently urge people to obey the Supreme Court's decision of 1954 outlawing segregation in the public schools, it is rather strange and paradoxical to find us consciously breaking laws. One may well ask, "How can you advocate breaking some laws and obeying others?" The answer is found in the fact that there are two types of laws: there are *just* and there are *unjust* laws. I would agree with Saint Augustine that "An unjust law is no law at all."

Now what is the difference between the two? How does one determine when a law is just or unjust? A just law is a man-made code that squares with the moral law or the law of God. An unjust law is a code that is out of harmony with the moral law. To put it in the terms of Saint Thomas Aquinas, an unjust law is a human law that is not rooted in eternal and natural law. Any law that uplifts human personality is just. Any law that degrades human personality is unjust. All segregation statutes are unjust because segregation distorts the soul and damages the personality. It gives the segregator a false sense of superiority, and the segregated a false sense of inferiority. To use the words of Martin Buber, the great Jewish philosopher, segregation substitutes an "I-it" relationship for the "I-thou" relationship, and ends up relegating persons to the status of things. So segregation is not only politically, economically and sociologically unsound, but it is morally wrong and sinful. Paul Tillich has said that sin is separation. Isn't segregation an existential expression of man's tragic separation, an expression of his awful estrangement, his terrible sinfulness? So I can urge men to disobey segregation ordinances because they are morally wrong....

Let me give another explanation. An unjust law is a code inflicted upon a minority which that minority had no part in enacting or creating because they did not have the unhampered right to vote. Who can say that the legislature of Alabama which set up the segregation laws was democratically elected? Throughout the state of Alabama all types of conniving methods are used to prevent Negroes from becoming registered voters and there are some counties without a single Negro registered to vote despite the fact that the Negro constitutes a majority of the population. Can any law set up in such a state be considered democratically structured?...

I hope you can see the distinction I am trying to point out. In no sense do I advocate evading or defying the law as the rabid segregationist would do. This would lead to anarchy. One who breaks an unjust law must do it *openly, lovingly* (not hatefully as the white mothers did in New Orleans when they were seen on television screaming, "nigger, nigger, nigger"), and with a willingness to accept the penalty. I submit that an individual who breaks a law that conscience tells him is unjust, and willingly accepts the penalty by staying in jail to arouse the conscience of the community over its injustice, is in reality expressing the very highest respect for law.

Of course, there is nothing new about this kind of civil disobedience. It was seen sublimely in the refusal of Shadrach, Meshach and Abednego to obey the laws of Nebuchadnezzar because a higher moral law was involved. It was practiced superbly by the early Christians who were willing to face hungry lions and the excruciating pain of chopping blocks, before submitting to certain unjust laws of the Roman Empire. To a degree academic freedom is a reality today because Socrates practiced civil disobedience....

First, I must confess that over the last few years I have been gravely disappointed with the white moderate. I have almost reached the regrettable conclusion that the Negro's great stumbling block in the stride toward freedom is not the White Citizen's Counciler or the Ku Klux Klanner, but the white moderate who is more devoted to "order" than to justice; who prefers a negative peace which is the absence of tension to a positive peace which is the presence of justice; who constantly says, "I agree with you in the goal you seek, but I can't agree with your methods of direct action"; who paternalistically feels that he can set the timetable for another man's freedom; who lives by the myth of time and who constantly advised the Negro to wait until a "more convenient season." Shallow understanding from people of good will is more frustrating than absolute misunderstanding from people of ill will. Lukewarm acceptance is much more bewildering than outright rejection....

I wish you had commended the Negro sit-inners and demonstrators of Birmingham for their sublime courage, their willingness to suffer and their amazing discipline in the midst of the most inhuman provocation. One day the South will recognize its real heroes. They will be the James Merediths, courageously and with a majestic sense of purpose facing jeering and hostile mobs and the agonizing loneliness that characterizes the life of the pioneer. They will be old, oppressed, battered Negro women, symbolized in a seventy-two-year-old woman of Montgomery, Alabama, who rose up with a sense of dignity and with her people decided not to ride the segregated buses, and responded to one who inquired about her tiredness with ungrammatical profundity: "My feet is tired, but my soul is rested." They will be the young high school and college students, young ministers of the gospel and a host of their elders courageously and nonviolently sitting in at lunch counters and willingly going to jail for conscience's sake. One day the South will know that when these disinherited children of God sat down at lunch counters they were in reality standing up for the best in the American dream and the most sacred values in our Judeo-Christian heritage, and thusly, carrying our whole nation back to those great wells of democracy which were dug deep by the Founding Fathers in the formulation of the Constitution and the Declaration of Independence....

Let us all hope that the dark clouds of racial prejudice will soon pass away and the deep fog of misunderstanding will be lifted from our fear-drenched communities and in some not too distant tomorrow the radiant stars of love and brotherhood will shine over our great nation with all of their scintillating beauty.

Yours for the cause of Peace and Brotherhood,
Martin Luther King, Jr.

8. Anne Moody Recalls the Sit-In Movement in Jackson, Mississippi, 1963

I had counted on graduating [from Tougaloo College] in the spring of 1963, but as it turned out, I couldn't because some of my credits still had to be cleared with Natchez College.... A year before, this would have seemed like a terrible disaster, but now I hardly even felt disappointed. I had a good excuse to stay on campus for the summer and work with the Movement, and this was what I really wanted to do. I couldn't go home again anyway, and I couldn't go to New Orleans—I didn't have money enough for bus fare.

During my senior year at Tougaloo, my family hadn't sent me one penny. I had only the small amount of money I had earned at Maple Hill. I couldn't afford to eat at school or live in the dorms, so I had gotten permission to move off campus. I had to prove that I could finish school, even if I had to go hungry every day.... But something happened to me as I got more and more involved in the Movement. It no longer seemed important to prove anything. I had found something outside myself that gave meaning to my life.

I had become very friendly with my social science professor, John Salter, who was in charge of NAACP activities on campus. All during the year, while the NAACP conducted a boycott of the downtown stores in Jackson, I had been one of Salter's most faithful canvassers and church speakers. During the last week of school, he told me that sit-in demonstrations were about to start in Jackson and that he wanted me to be the spokesman for a team that would sit-in at Woolworth's lunch counter. The two other demonstrators would be classmates of mine, Memphis and Pearlena. Pearlena was a dedicated NAACP worker, but Memphis had not been very involved in the Movement on campus. It seemed that the organization had had a rough time finding students who were in a position to go to jail. I had nothing to lose one way or the other. Around ten o'clock the morning of the demonstrations, NAACP headquarters alerted the news services. As a result, the police department was also informed, but neither the policemen nor the newsmen knew exactly where or when the demonstrations would start. They stationed themselves along Capitol Street and waited.

To divert attention from the sit-in at Woolworth's, the picketing started at J. C. Penney's a good fifteen minutes before. The pickets were allowed to walk up and down in front of the store three or four times before they were arrested. At exactly 11 A.M., Pearlena, Memphis, and I entered Woolworth's from the rear entrance. We separated as soon as we stepped into the store, and made small purchases from various counters. Pearlena had given Memphis her watch. He was to let us know when it was 11:14. At 11:14 we were to join him near the lunch counter and at exactly 11:15 we were to take seats at it.

Seconds before 11:15 we were occupying three seats at the previously segregated Woolworth's lunch counter. In the beginning the waitresses seemed to ignore us, as if they really didn't know what was going on. Our waitress walked past us a couple of times before she noticed we had started to write our own orders down and realized we wanted service. She asked us what we wanted. We began to read to her from our order slips. She told us that we would be served at the back counter, which was for Negroes.

"We would like to be served here," I said.

The waitress started to repeat what she had said, then stopped in the middle of the sentence. She turned the lights out behind the counter, and she and the other waitresses almost ran to the back of the store, deserting all their white customers. I guess they thought that violence would start immediately after the whites at the counter realized what was going on....

By this time a crowd of cameramen and reporters had gathered around us taking pictures and asking questions, such as Where were we from? Why did we sit-in? What organization sponsored it? Were we students? From what school? How were we classified?

I told them that we were all students at Tougaloo College, that we were represented by no particular organization, and that we planned to stay there even after the store closed. "All we want is service," was my reply to one of them. After they had finished probing for about twenty minutes, they were almost ready to leave.

At noon, students from a nearby white high school started pouring in to Woolworth's. When they first saw us they were sort of surprised. They didn't know how to react. A few started to heckle and the newsmen became interested again. Then the white students started chanting all kinds of anti-Negro slogans. We were called a little bit of everything. The rest of the seats except the three we were occupying had been roped off to prevent others from sitting down. A couple of the boys took one end of the rope and made it into a hangman's noose. Several attempts were made to put it around our necks. The crowds grew as more students and adults came in for lunch.

We kept our eyes straight forward and did not look at the crowd except for occasional glances to see what was going on.... Memphis suggested that we pray. We bowed our heads, and all hell broke loose. A man rushed forward, threw Memphis from his seat, and slapped my face. Then another man who worked in the store threw me against an adjoining counter.

Down on my knees on the floor, I saw Memphis lying near the lunch counter with blood running out of the corners of his mouth. As he tried to protect his face, the man who'd thrown him down kept kicking him against the head. If he had worn hard-soled shoes instead of sneakers, the first kick probably would have killed Memphis. Finally a man dressed in plain clothes identified himself as a police officer and arrested Memphis and his attacker.

Pearlena had been thrown to the floor. She and I got back on our stools after Memphis was arrested. There were some white Tougaloo teachers in the crowd. They asked Pearlena and me if we wanted to leave. They said that things were getting too rough. We didn't know what to do. While we were trying to make up our minds, we were joined by Joan Trumpauer. Now there were three of us and we were integrated. The crowd began to chant, "Communists, Communists, Communists." Some old man in the crowd ordered the students to take us off the stools.

"Which one should I get first?" a big husky boy said.

"That white nigger," the old man said.

The boy lifted Joan from the counter by her waist and carried her out of the store. Simultaneously, I was snatched from my stool by two high school students. I was dragged about thirty feet toward the door by my hair when someone made them turn me loose. As I was getting up off the floor, I saw Joan coming back inside. We started back to the center of the counter to join Pearlena. Lois Chaffee, a white Tougaloo faculty member, was now sitting next to her. So Joan and I just climbed across the rope at the front end of the counter and sat down. There were now four of us, two whites and two Negroes, all women. The mob started smearing us with ketchup, mustard, sugar, pies, and everything on the counter. Soon Joan and I were joined by John Salter, but the moment he sat down he was hit on the jaw with what appeared to be brass knuckles. Blood gushed from his face and someone threw salt into the open wound. Ed King, Tougaloo's chaplain, rushed to him.

At the other end of the counter, Lois and Pearlena were joined by George Raymond, a CORE field worker and a student from Jackson State College. Then a Negro high school boy sat down next to me. The mob took spray paint from the counter and sprayed it on the new demonstrators. The high school student had on a white shirt; the word "nigger" was written on his back with red spray paint.

We sat there for three hours taking a beating when the manager decided to close the store because the mob had begun to go wild with stuff from other counters....

After the sit-in, all I could think of was how sick Mississippi whites were. They believed so much in the segregated Southern way of life, they would kill to preserve it. I sat there in the NAACP office and thought of how many times they had killed when this way of life was threatened. I knew that the killing had just begun. "Many more will die before it is over with," I thought. Before the sit-in, I had always hated the whites in Mississippi. Now I knew it was impossible for me to hate sickness. The whites had a disease, an incurable disease in its final stage. What were our chances against such a disease? I thought of the students, the young Negroes who had just begun to protest, as young interns. When these young interns got older, I thought, they would be the best doctors in the world for social problems.

9. John Salter, Joan Trumpauer, and Anne Moody Sit-In at the Woolworth's in Jackson, 1963

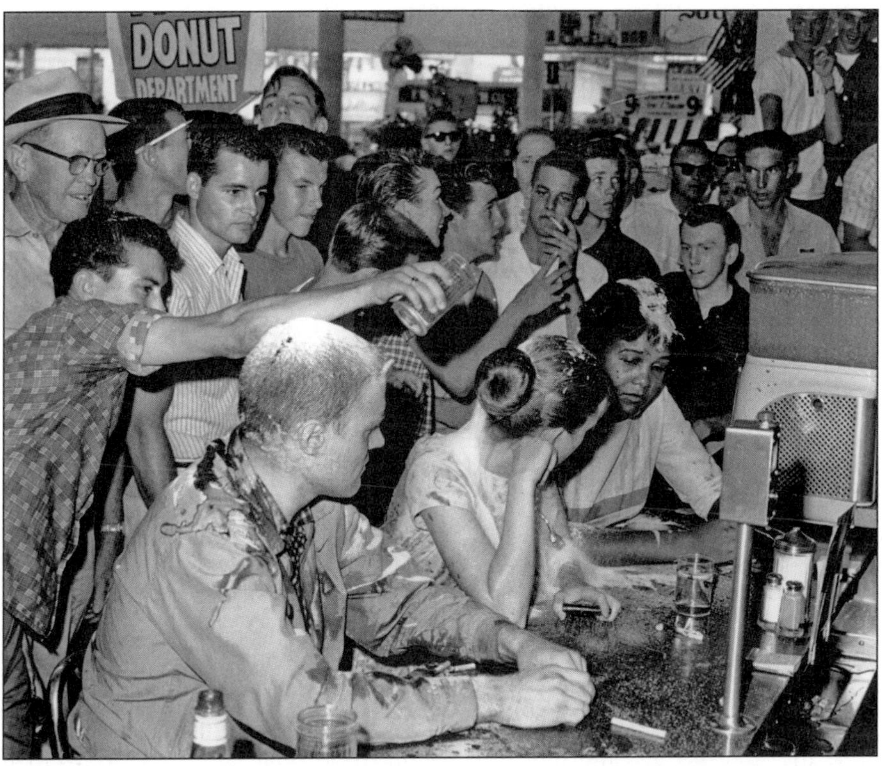

The Woolworth's sit-in in Jackson, May 23, 1963. Seated (left to right) are John Salter, Joan Trumpauer, and Anne Moody. (Fred Blackwell)

10. Results of the 1965 Voting Rights Act, 1986

TABLE 1 Estimated Percentage of Voting-Age Blacks Registered, Eleven Southern States, 1947–1986

State	1947	1956	1964	1968	1976	1986
Alabama	1.2	11.0	23.0	56.7	58.4	68.9
Arkansas	17.3	36.0	49.3	67.5	94.0	57.9
Florida	15.4	32.0	63.8	62.1	61.1	58.2
Georgia	18.8	27.0	44.0	56.1	74.8	52.8
Louisiana	2.6	31.0	32.0	59.3	63.0	60.6
Mississippi	0.9	5.0	6.7	59.4	60.7	70.8
N. Carolina	15.2	24.0	46.8	55.3	54.8	58.4
S. Carolina	13.0	27.0	38.7	50.8	56.5	52.5

(Continued)

TABLE 1 Estimated Percentage of Voting-Age Blacks Registered, Eleven Southern States, 1947–1986 (Continued)

State	1947	1956	1964	1968	1976	1986
Tennessee	25.8	29.0	69.4	72.8	66.4	65.3
Texas	18.5	37.0	57.7	83.1	65.0	68.0
Virginia	13.2	19.0	45.7	58.4	54.7	56.2
TOTAL SOUTH	12.0	24.9	43.1	62.0	63.1	60.8

SOURCE: Data are from *Quiet Revolution in the South: The Impact of the Voting Rights Act, 1965–1990*, by Chandler Davidson and Bernard Grofman, editors (Princeton, N.J.: Princeton University Press, 1994).

ESSAYS

In the first essay, historian Elizabeth Jacoway takes a long look at the inadequate protection provided for all the Little Rock Nine students in 1957 and 1958, but she takes special notice of Minnijean Brown. If the world thought that the students integrating Central High School were safe because of the intervention of federal troops, this essays tells a different story. Almost all involved in desegregation from the U.S Attorney General to the school principal underestimated the determination of white segregationists to thwart integration. What emerges is a picture of a "band of courageous Negro children fighting a long battle while the community waits for them to surrender." Too little was done to counter massive resistance from local officials and the federal government under President Eisenhower's tepid leadership. The result was that Governor Orval Faubus closed all the Little Rock schools the following year and leaned on the argument that it was the state's right to resist a federal law. This encouraged other southern states to follow Arkansas' example, form White Citizens' Councils, and stall integration. In the second essay, historian Barbara Ransby recounts the involvement of many of the civil rights organizations—NAACP, CORE, SNCC, SCLC, and COFO (Council of Federated Organizations)—and their effects on the movement in Mississippi. Her essay, taken from her biography of civil rights activist Ella Baker, turns toward Freedom Summer 1964, the creation of the Mississippi Freedom Democratic Party (FDP), and its success in challenging the established Regular Democratic Party in Mississippi. The showdown came in August 1964 at the National Democratic Convention in Atlantic City, New Jersey, when Lyndon Johnson sought the party's nomination for election and did not want national attention sidetracked to Mississippi's disfranchisement problems. Ransby argues that the experience in Atlantic City taught the civil rights leaders unexpected political realities and "stiffened the resolve" of those who would continue the fight for voting rights and office holding in Mississippi and the South. In the first essay, we see a group of nine students in 1957 who were inadequately supported with a nation reluctant or unwilling to defend their rights. In the second essay support for civil rights activists, the effects of massive organization, the infusion of hundreds of civil rights workers, and the involvement of national organizations all provide evidence of the maturation of the civil rights movement. Seven years after the integration of Central High School in Little Rock, Arkansas, Congress finally involved itself in the freedom struggle by shaping the laws to correspond to the realities of discrimination in states like Mississippi. It was too long for many blacks whose hopes for a better future waited for American justice.

Torments Behind Closed Doors

ELIZABETH JACOWAY

People around the world knew of the Little Rock Nine and drew mental images of them from the many photographs taken outside Central High at the start of the school year. What happened to them later, inside the building, is much less well known, and almost unrelentingly painful. By mid-October, the nine black students had settled in for a long season of torment. Federal, state, and local governments—and school officials—abandoned the young pioneers to the fiendish efforts of a small band of student segregationists, misfits who were committed to forcing the black children's withdrawal from Central High.

Bright, vivacious, emotionally unguarded, and thoroughly adolescent in her need for recognition and acceptance, Minnijean Brown had thought that going to Central High School with her two best friends, Melba Patillo and Thelma Mothershed, would be a lark. She had always been fascinated by the castlelike high school for whites, and she thought it was "true proof that more money was being spent [on whites] so it must have had something in it that was of use to me because otherwise it wouldn't be so big...." A voracious reader and a strong student, Minnijean had no doubt she could compete academically, and her musical gifts made her feel certain that the white kids would like her as soon as they heard her sing. An adventurous girl who had already begun to test the rules of segregation by refusing to ride in the back of the city buses and getting kicked off as a result, Minnie had no way of knowing that her high spirits, her need for peer acceptance, and her unwillingness to identify herself as a social subordinate would lead to the Central High School officials' labeling her a troublemaker, and the segregationists' focusing on her as a target.

Elizabeth Huckaby [vice principal for girls] wrote in her memoir that at the beginning of the year Minnijean had been "too effervescent" as well as a "show-off and braggart." When Richard Boehler tripped Minnie in French class early in the fall, she called him "white trash" and summoned her guard into the classroom, alienating the already-overwhelmed first-year teacher. She challenged her American history teacher about the slim treatment of slavery in the class's textbook. She called a segregationist girl who was verbally persecuting her "a midget." She earned a seat in early-morning detention hall for being tardy to class five times.

The other black students were more guarded in their interactions with whites and their respect for the rules, but they too suffered relentless harassment from a small group of vicious white "hoods," the black-jacketed, blue jeans wearing, James Dean and Elvis wannabes that haunted the nightmares of school officials all over the country. Beginning with what [Superintendent of Schools] Virgil Blossom dismissed as a "campaign of petty harassment"—shoving, name-calling, throwing sharpened pencils and spitballs—in the absence of any significant administrative response these young delinquents graduated to more dangerous, threatening behavior.

The school staff counseled the nine black children repeatedly not to respond to this harassment, as Blossom said, "in the hope it would die out." But it only escalated. On October 28, after a month of unremitting daily attacks, such as kicks to the shins and ankles, assaults with a closed fist, or treacherous shoves down the numerous stairwells, the Nine and their parents met with school officials in Superintendent Blossom's downtown office. Worried about the rapidly diminishing numbers of soldiers inside the school and expecting to hear some plans for the protection of their children, the parents were astonished to hear Blossom counsel the Nine once again not to respond to their attackers. The superintendent also explained that a teacher had to witness and report any instances of abuse, because if the staff started suspending students simply on the word of other students, in no time at all the segregationists could have the black children out of the school. Impatient with this approach, the customarily circumspect Lois Patillo stood up and confronted Blossom, asking what plans school officials had made to provide protection for her daughter. "That's none of your business!" the burly superintendent growled. Mrs. Patillo thought her child's welfare was very much her business, and she and the other parents left the meeting with a renewed sense of unease....

On November 12, with all of the 101st paratroopers removed from the scene and only six National Guardsmen remaining inside the school, Jefferson Thomas stood facing his opened hall locker when Hugh Williams dashed behind him, hit him on the side of the head with some kind of hard object, and knocked him unconscious. Williams later confessed to the incident and was suspended for three days, the customary slap on the wrist for segregationist infractions. Clarence Laws [NAACP Field Secretary] took Jeff to see a doctor, who ascertained that no real damage had been done, and the indomitable Jeff insisted on going back to school the next day. Daisy Bates [State President of the NAACP] took Jeff shopping for running shoes, so he could run away from his attackers in the halls. The resourceful boy also reported to Bates that he had started buttoning the top button of his shirts so no one could drop cigarettes down his back. School authorities called the attack on Jefferson Thomas "nothing to get excited about," and Virgil Blossom later described the incident as "a scuffle."

The afternoon of the attack on Jefferson Thomas, Daisy Bates went to Central High to complain about the escalating harassment of the black students, but she got little satisfaction. The Associated Press quoted her that evening as saying the children "are being bullied and harassed to try to force them to leave. But they're not going to give in." An irritated Army captain called Bates wanting to know "who gave the information to the newspaper about the incident at the school today?" Bates replied with characteristic bite, asking if he was more interested in publicity than in the welfare of the children.

Clarence Laws reported to his superiors in New York that there seemed to be a lackadaisical attitude on the part of Army personnel in Little Rock....

On the morning after the attack on Jefferson Thomas, Daisy Bates and Clarence Laws went to see Virgil Blossom. They asked him "what he intended to do about the continued brutal attacks on the children by the organized gang—attacks that had been reported many times." When Blossom said he was not aware of a large number of offenses, Bates handed him the list she had been keeping based on the children's reports to her. Bates wrote in her memoir, "As he looked at the long list of names and the repeated brutalities against the nine children, his expression lost some of its hardness, and his face seemed to soften." Yet she miscalculated when she admonished him, "If you are really interested in clearing up this trouble, you should expel some of these repeated troublemakers." Blossom bristled at the suggestion and retorted, "You can't tell me how to run my school." Bates dug in, saying "No, I can't ... but it's up to you—not the Army—to maintain discipline inside the school. By not doing so, you are subjecting the children to physical torture that you will have to live with the rest of your life." The feisty Bates knew when she left the superintendent's office that she had lost a potential ally, and she was correct....

Jess Matthews had been a popular principal of Little Rock Central High School for many years, and he took great pride in his school's outstanding academic and athletic records. Described by several former students as a "gentle giant," Matthews was the kind of principal who wanted everyone to be happy, and who wanted everyone to like him. He was unwilling to stir the wrath of the segregationists. Vice principal J. O. Powell, a Little Rock native and a Central High graduate, could hardly contain his dismay over Jess Matthews's unwillingness to intervene aggressively and stop the persecution of the nine black children in his school....

As Powell described Matthews's early counseling sessions with the school's segregationist tormentors, the avuncular principal often counseled the segregationist tormenters by saying, "You're not going to solve this thing by punching niggers. This thing is bigger than you and me and Congress and the Governor and everybody else, and it's not going to be solved any time soon. We don't like it any more than you do. But it's here.... You start thinking about your education and quit worrying about integration and niggers."

Although Superintendent Blossom told him explicitly to weed out the troublemakers, and Powell claimed there were only fifty or so "hard core" offenders, Matthews refused to do it. His explanation was that any time he disciplined a segregationist, that child's parents either asked for a hearing before the School Board or threatened to file a lawsuit, and as Powell wrote, "... the principal was not accustomed to defending his judgment or having his professional posture publicly or privately scrutinized." The predictable effects were that the troublemakers became "more overt and more arrogant" and the teachers became less vigilant, inclined increasingly to believe that reporting infractions was "a waste of time." J. O. Powell had no way of knowing, of course, that a part of Jess Matthews's difficulty sprang from the Little Rock School Board's ambivalence about discipline.

Elizabeth Huckaby wrote that in mid-November Jess Matthews was deeply hurt by a Capital Citizens' Council petition calling for his dismissal for supposedly "selling out to the Virgil Blossom crowd." Blossom was actually the segregationists' primary target. As Blossom wrote, the segregationists described all the school officials, and especially the superintendent, as race-mixers and advocates of communism, and they kept harping "without much imagination" on the theme of miscegenation. A native of Missouri who had little familiarity with the sources and content of southern racism, Blossom failed completely to understand that fears about race-mixing formed the very heart of his community's rejection of his plan and efforts. This was not empty rhetoric designed to mask an intent to exploit blacks economically; this was the vital center of the southern resistance to desegregation....

By mid-November, Blossom and the Little Rock School Board had become completely marginalized, largely abandoned by the erstwhile moderates who were now either struggling with their own values and emotions or working behind the scenes to effect some kind of compromise....

[Governor] Orval Faubus had said on October 9 that the only solution to the Little Rock crisis was for the black children to withdraw from Central High School. On November 17, in a long, relaxed interview with journalist Relman Morin, Faubus reiterated this view, commenting, "I have always believed, and still do, that you have to create a climate of community acceptance before integration can be successful." It was almost an invitation to the hoods to step up the harassment....

On November 19 the Army announced it planned to withdraw the 101st Airborne Division from Little Rock after Thanksgiving, leaving control of affairs at Central High School to the Arkansas National Guard. Governor Faubus said he would not protect the black children if control of the National Guard were turned over to him, and he commented that it was unfair to expect the Arkansas Guardsmen to perform the "distasteful" task of enforcing integration because they did not enlist to do that but instead "to defend their country in time of need."

Elizabeth Huckaby wrote in her memoir that she felt fearful when she heard the Army was leaving, for she knew the situation inside Central High School to be very dangerous....

Secretary of the Army Wilber Brucker had wanted to force local authorities to take responsibility for the situation in Little Rock, but he had never been able to figure out how to make that happen. Since early October his paramount concern had been, "No situation could be allowed to develop in which the Negro students would be forced to withdraw by physical violence." Now he apparently deceived himself into believing that the situation had achieved a level of stability that would allow decreased vigilance inside Central High....

Throughout October and November interested parties on all sides waited expectantly to see what role the Justice Department would play in prosecuting the troublemakers who had been arrested during the rioting at Central High School in September. Virgil Blossom, Harry Ashmore [Editor, *Arkansas Gazette*] Daisy Bates, Senator J. William Fulbright, and many others had expressed their certainty that when the federal government showed its resolve to deal harshly with those who had resorted to violence to oppose integration, then the vocal minority who were willing to defy law and order would be intimidated and silenced. To the shock and dismay of those who were struggling in Little Rock to uphold the law as it had been newly interpreted in the *Brown* decision, on November 20 Justice Department spokesmen announced they had decided not to prosecute the troublemakers at Central High. "U.S. Officials Drop Plans to Prosecute Agitators at School" blared the headline on page one of the *Arkansas Gazette*. News articles suggested that unnamed Little Rock people had given Justice Department officials "assurances" that in the absence of further difficulties, they could handle the situation in their city....

Minnijean's exclusion from the Christmas program was not her first. She had also been left out of the student talent show, and she was bitterly disappointed over not being able to sing "Tammy" in front of the student body. Melba Patillo Beals wrote years later that Minnijean "was beginning to be deeply affected by what was being done to her at Central High," and that Minnie's "sadness over being left out was clouding her view." Mrs. Huckaby reported a poignant episode in the fall when Minnijean wore Central High's school colors, gold and black, on her sweater before a football game and a segregationist girl challenged her right to wear them. Minnijean tore off the colors and stepped on them; about this same time she went sobbing to Mrs. Huckaby that she just wanted to quit.

Melba Patillo was also chafing from the isolation imposed on her, as would any normal teenager. As she wrote in her memoir, "a deep yearning for human contact was growing inside me.... I longed for someone to acknowledge that I was alive by saying something pleasant to me, and allowing me to say something back." The white students treated her as if she were invisible. "Sometimes when a classmate said something funny, I would smile and even laugh out loud, forgetful for just one instant of my predicament. "We weren't talking to you, nigger,' they would say. Jolted back to reality by their cruelty, I would catch myself, neutralize my expression to hide my feelings, and stare straight ahead."...

Isolated inside Central High, the black children also lost their friends from Horace Mann [High School]. Melba Patillo's old friends were afraid to come to her home and resentful of the dislocations in their own lives caused by Melba's and the others' collective decision to integrate Central High.... Nat Griswold heard similar reports ten years later when he was collecting information for a book on the Little Rock crisis. In his words, "Some of the Negro students who early entered Central High reported they received strong social disapproval from some teachers and some students of Horace Mann High, from which they transferred. 'Do you think you are better than we are?' was the question posed and imposed by their critics."...

Blossom's school board struggled to prepare a petition to the federal court asking for a delay of integration. On December 3 J. Edgar Hoover received information from a source "close to the Little Rock School Board" that at the next hearing in federal court, the board would ask for a delay based on two points: (1) Melba

Patillo, Jefferson Thomas, and Minnijean Brown were "unadjusted," and (2) the community was not ready for integration. According to reports turned in to Army analysts, Melba, Jeff, and Minnijean were responsible for the attacks on themselves because they were "antagonistic."...

Minnijean now became the primary target of segregationist torment. Many white students teased her mercilessly about being left out of the Christmas program. One boy reported her for supposedly "shooting the bird," or giving him the finger. Numerous students provoked Minnijean to respond to them verbally. She thought they were trying to "break" her by getting her to cry, and she struggled to maintain her composure—but they were content to get a rise out of her. Melba Patillo recalled that all of the Nine were suffering from "extreme fatigue," and that the taunting whites worked especially hard to get Minnijean to "blow her fuse."

With just one day left before the much-needed rest of Christmas vacation, the segregationists scored a victory. Minnijean went into the cafeteria about 1:30 P.M., during the second lunch period. As she carried her tray toward the table where Melba, Ernie, and the others sat waiting for her, four boys pushed their chairs into the aisle, blocking her passage. She waited a moment, and the boys withdrew the chairs. As soon as she started to move again, the boys pushed the chairs back into her path, then removed them once again. This time, as Minnijean tried to proceed sideways between the tables, Rob Pittard started to get up from his seat, pushing his chair directly in front of her. Minnijean had been provoked previously in the same location and had warned the boys "they might get something on them." Melba could tell that an incident was building, but she knew she could not help without starting a riot; as she wrote, "they outnumbered us two hundred to one."

Melba described the scene in her memoir. "As more and more people realized something was brewing," she wrote, "the chatter in the cafeteria quieted down. I could tell Minnijean was trapped and desperate, and very fast running out of patience. She was talking back to the boys in a loud voice, and there was jostling all around her.... It was as though she were in a trance, fighting within herself." Minnijean stood with her tray poised above the head of Dent Gitchel. Suddenly she just let it fall, covering Pittard and Gitchel with an abundance of chili, milk, fork, and straw. After a moment of complete silence in the cavernous hall, the black cafeteria workers burst into applause. Almost as quickly, the segregationist students became jubilant, realizing they had finally provoked one of the Nine into a response that would get her suspended from school.

Two National Guard soldiers collared Minnijean and the two boys, taking them directly to the principal's office. There Dent Gitchel, still dripping, rushed to Minnijean's defense, saying he "knew she'd been through a lot of strain recently and could be expected to pop off." Gitchel, who had not been involved in previous racial incidents, suggested to Jess Matthews "that maybe this evened things up somewhat and that the matter be dropped." Matthews had other ideas. After interviewing Minnijean and ascertaining that the incident was not entirely accidental, Matthews suspended her from school for an indefinite period. Mrs. Huckaby wrote in her daily report, "Thanks to ... sharp observation on the part of two national guard sergeants in federal service, a possibly riotous incident was prevented. Poor Minnie."

Where were the "good" white students while all of this harassment was going on? Student Body President Ralph Brodie recalled years later that he never saw any incidents, which can probably be explained by his student leader status, his athletic prowess, and his height at 6'5"; few "hoods" would have chosen to ply their trade in his presence. The larger explanation seems to be that those white students making overtures of friendship or assistance to the black children soon found themselves harassed and often threatened by segregationist callers. Their resultant silence mirrored the growing silence of moderate elements in the larger community. Enough of these students reported to Bishop Brown their concerns about the absence of discipline at Central High that he wrote in his memoir, "The other students were resentful of the ability of 'these hoods to get away with it.' However, the opinion became widespread that the matter had reached the point where the school officials themselves should take over the discipline within the school."...

The first day back at school after Christmas vacation set the pattern for a deteriorating situation inside Central High School, presaging what ACHR Executive Director Nat Griswold described as a "reign of terror." An anonymous caller telephoned the school office with the threat of a bomb inside the school; many such threats had come across the wires in the preceding months, and each one necessitated an extensive and costly search of the building. As had all the others, this threat proved to be false.

In the face of what J. O. Powell called a "near total collapse of administrative discipline," the nine black children were alarmed to arrive back at school amid rumors that the Capital Citizens' Council was offering a reward to anyone who could incite them to misbehave and get expelled. Throughout the holidays, the segregationists had been busy scheming, hoping in effect to nullify the federal court order by forcing the removal of the black children.

The lengthening chronicle of harassment of the Nine led *New York Times* reporter Gertrude Samuels to suggest, "The mob has moved inside the school." Darlene Holloway pushed Elizabeth Eckford down the stairs and was suspended for three days. Another student tripped Carlotta Walls as she left her biology class and then followed her briefly to step on her heels. Yet another threatened to kill her while he sharpened his pencil standing close to her desk. Sammie Dean Parker (a female) and Wanda Cole shoved Melba Patillo as she bent over to pick up her books and sent her sprawling spread-eagle on the floor. Sammie Dean Parker and David Sontag squirted ink on Melba Patillo's new pink felt skirt in the cafeteria, as had been done to Thelma and Minnijean in the days immediately preceding....

Minnijean Brown had been admitted back into the school after a conference in Superintendent Blossom's office that included her parents and Mrs. Huckaby, and after she had promised not to retaliate in any future incidents. She returned on January 13 and almost immediately found herself squirted with ink. On the 16th, David Sontag dropped a bowl of soup on her in the cafeteria, claiming that she had always called him "white trash." With David at the time were Sammie

Dean Parker, Wanda Cole, and Darlene Holloway. Minnijean did not respond, other than to turn to Elizabeth Eckford, who was sitting at the table beside her, and say "Oh, well, they got even with me."

At its regularly scheduled January board meeting, the Little Rock School Board finally enunciated a discipline policy, including the timid assertion: "Because of integration, there has been more tension in our school system than usual; therefore, our staff has moved slowly and with restrained mildness in handling all children." On January 20, officials found dynamite at Central High School, and Virgil Blossom told a press conference that a few persons were trying to force the closing of the school. In response to this remark, Citizens' Council President Wesley Pruden called for the resignations of Blossom and all the Central High officials, saying that Blossom and the Little Rock School Board created the problem by volunteering to integrate in the first place. By January 24, Central High School had suffered through bomb scares every school day since the Citizens' Council had held a rally on the 14th.

Nat Griswold's quarterly report to the Southern Regional Council included this assessment: "The school officials and Board neglected rather obvious remedies at hand—recognized methods of discipline of students and a request to the Court for an injunction against interference with school operations.... There were reliable reports of ignoring of many incidents of abuse of the Negro students." Griswold echoed one of J. O. Powell's concerns when he wrote, "By and large the public had little knowledge of the serious breakdown of school discipline...." Powell claimed in his memoir that Jess Matthews and Virgil Blossom routinely censored public reports, and that Matthews crusaded for his staff to "keep quiet" about the internal affairs at Central High School.

On January 20 school authorities found dynamite in the basement at Central High. On January 23 they found a firecracker bomb in a locker. The director of school plant services, O. W. Romine, who had a child in the building, reported constant damage to the school and made arrangements to guard the furnace room around the clock, seven days a week. J. O. Powell wrote, "Over a thousand dollars monthly was paid to civilian security guards to patrol the building and grounds on a twenty-four-hour schedule." Powell also wrote about uncurbed vandalism and locker damage from hoax bomb scares and dynamite threats. Every bomb threat, and there were forty-three during the year, necessitated a check of every student locker in the building, and when officials could not open the combination locks with the codes students had provided, they had to cut off the locks and replace them at school expense. In addition to the locker damage, Powell added that "juvenile racists dug, stained, painted, gouged, and burned unprintable anti-Negro propaganda and segregationist slogans into window-glass, furniture, walls, and any other surface at hand." Vandals started many nuisance fires throughout the winter, and in one particularly creative form of protest they urinated on the steam radiators in the bathrooms, sending fumes throughout the building.

The absence of discipline began to turn into something more dangerous on January 27, when a male student dared a National Guardsman to lay a hand on him. Passing Minnijean Brown in the hall, the boy called her a "nigger-looking bitch." The National Guardsman directly behind him told him to go to the principal's office and he replied, "No, I'm not going, and you can't make me," then threw his books on the floor, squared off with his fists doubled up at his sides, and told the Guardsman he had better not touch him. At length Mrs. Huckaby intervened and persuaded the boy to go to Jess Matthews's office. Matthews called his father, a painter, who came immediately and promised that his son would not get into "any more trouble with niggers." The boy was given a tardy slip and went to his next class.

General Walker was alarmed by this incident and soon asked for a judgment from the Army's judge advocate general regarding what action to take if a similar situation arose again. Walker also suggested the Justice Department should seek an injunction against unruly students inside Central High School. Nothing ever came of this suggestion, although by January 31 Clarence Laws was telling the New York office of the NAACP that he and Mrs. Bates had learned through "a most reliable source" that the National Guardsmen had been given new instructions with regard to handling incidents. "In the future no guard is to place a hand upon any student. If the student has committed an act, the guard may attempt to block him if he should try to leave the school, but no other action is to be taken." Bates and Laws asked what would happen if a Guardsman came upon a student or students assaulting another who would not stop upon his orders. "The reply was we do not have the answer now."...

For some time the parents of the Nine had requested a meeting with school officials to protest the absence of discipline and protection for their children. Finally on Sunday, February 9, they met for over two hours with Virgil Blossom, J. O. Powell, and Elizabeth Huckaby. Jefferson Thomas's father, serving as spokesman for the black parents, urged officials to call a student assembly and "lay down the law" concerning mistreatment of the black children. The school officials vetoed that suggestion. As Elizabeth Huckaby explained in her memoir, "most of our students didn't need scolding, and the others probably would have caused a demonstration." Mr. Thomas read a list of the names of boys and girls who were persecuting the black children. He said he had called and talked to some of these students' parents and had gotten cooperation from some of them. It appears that no school official ever did the same.

On February 12, Virgil Blossom met with Minnijean Brown and her mother, telling them he had decided to recommend to the Little Rock School Board that Minnijean be expelled for the duration of the year, not only from Central High but from all Little Rock schools. Mrs. Brown protested vigorously, but to no avail. As Elizabeth Huckaby wrote in her memoir, school officials had come to the conclusion that "we could no longer run the school if Minnijean was there....

In a lengthy telephone conversation on February 13, Clarence Laws and Daisy Bates spelled out for the New York office of the NAACP their suspicions regarding the absence of discipline inside Central High School. Referring to what he called "a well-laid conspiracy," Laws maintained: "It is stated that there are some important people in business here who are behind this and their plans are for getting the kids out and saying that the community is not ready for integration." Southern Regional Council Assistant Director Fred Routh wrote to Thurgood Marshall on February 12, saying "the school administration may use the disciplinary question to oust the Negro children from the school and ask the court for a delay in compliance. This would play directly into the hands of the segregationist element in the State Legislature. They would then take legislative steps to delay further desegregation in Little Rock." This prediction came to fruition within a matter of months....

Virgil Blossom formally announced the School Board's decision to expel Minnijean Brown. Blossom claimed he had made the decision to expel her, since she had not "adjusted." As Elizabeth Huckaby confessed, Minnijean's expulsion "was an admission of defeat on our part.... It was not volatile, natural Minnijean that was our difficulty. It was just that she and our impossible situation would not mix."

Daisy Bates and her friend Kenneth Clark secured a scholarship for Minnijean to attend the experimental, interracial New Lincoln School in New York City, where she lived with the Clarks. Asked if she was happy that her child had been granted a scholarship, Mrs. Brown commented, "While I am gratified I am not happy. I am not happy that our daughter must go away at this time to attend school. I am not happy that our own hometown is permitting this to happen to us. I am not happy that children of both races are being hurt by selfish and hateful men."

When Minnijean arrived in New York she described her new school as "lovely." With sophistication and diplomacy beyond her years, hard-earned in Little Rock, Minnijean faced the press and said she bore no animosity toward the segregationist students. "They felt as right as I did," Minnijean suggested. "I don't hate them. They felt they were right and I felt I was right." She did, however, predict that the segregationists would "get" another student. "There was a campaign to get everybody out and I was first," the plucky teenager declared, as she turned her back on the torment she had endured and prepared to start a new life....

After Minnijean's expulsion, the segregationists inside Central High School went wild, their cruelty unrestrained. As Melba Patillo Beals wrote in her diary, "I think only the warrior exists in me now. Melba went away to hide. She was too frightened to stay here." She struggled not to be jealous of Minnijean's "escape" and began to feel "kind of numb, as though nothing mattered anymore." Yet she felt pain "stinging my heart every time someone called me a nigger."

Writing to Secretary of the Army Wilber Brucker, Roy Wilkins [NAACP executive director] commented poignantly, "we are confronted with the incredible spectacle of the government of the United States placing the burden of enforcing the orders of its Courts upon the slender shoulders and the young hearts of eight teen-age Negro students." An editorial in the *New York Post* argued that firm disciplinary measures could easily stop the persecutions inside Central High. "Instead the picture that emerges is of a band of courageous Negro children fighting a long battle while the community waits for them to surrender. Will the soldiers 'intervene' in the Washington sense only when the fight becomes a lynching bee? The role played by the U. S. Army in the Battle of Little Rock shames the nation. For gallantry in action, the Negro kids take all the medals."

"Mississippi Goddamn": Fighting for Freedom in the Belly of the Beast

BARBARA RANSBY

Alabama's gotten me so upset
Tennessee made me lose my rest
And everybody knows about Mississippi Goddamn.
Nina Simone, 1963

During the tumultuous and decisive years of the early 1960s, SNCC played a leading role in the Black Freedom Movement in Mississippi. Young field organizers put the principles that Ella Baker had taught them into practice by working alongside poor and working-class black people in rural communities where white supremacy had seemed impossible to challenge. As a result, the organizers found themselves at the center of a mass uprising that overturned old stereotypes of downtrodden, passive, and terrorized black folk. Americans outside the South, both white and black, became aware of Mississippi Freedom Summer, the grassroots voting rights campaign conducted in 1964, only after the revelation that three young workers had been ambushed and brutally murdered by segregationists. By risking their lives for justice in the face of vigilante violence, SNCC's organizers experienced profound change in their lives, but they were sustained by the example of many black people in Mississippi for whom facing such risks had long been the price of defending their dignity. In Freedom Schools that were founded on the radically democratic pedagogy that Baker espoused and exemplified within SNCC, organizers taught literacy skills and academic subjects to young blacks and, in turn, learned about the underlying economic structures of white supremacy from their students. Discovering the enormous power of people acting together to confront injustice and inequality, SNCC volunteers and staff felt reassured of the vision that had drawn them to the organization.

One of the critical organizing principles that Ella Baker taught, and SNCC absorbed, was the meaning of self-determination in the context of grassroots organizing in the South. For Baker, this principle was not an exclusively racial proposition, as it was often deployed, but simply the democratic idea that an oppressed group, class, or community had the right to determine the nature of the fight to end its oppression. Such self-control of the movement's leadership by those it purported to represent was essential in Baker's view. Most of SNCC's Mississippi work in the summer of 1964 was carried out under the auspices of a loose coalition called the Council of Federated Organizations (COFO). So, through COFO and the Mississippi Freedom Democratic Party (MFDP), SNCC worked to advance the right of poor black Mississippians to determine their own future.

The decision by SNCC to conduct a major grassroots voting rights campaign in Mississippi in 1961–64 was audacious. From Baker's long experience in the state and from the local activists with whom she had put them in contact, SNCC activists knew that Mississippi's notorious reputation was well earned. Some within the organization dubbed the project the "Move on Mississippi," as if an invasion of enemy territory were being planned. Some of the most brazen and vicious southern segregationists in the South were at the helm of state government there, and Mississippi had a long history of unchecked, often officially sponsored racial violence toward the black population. Many national civil rights leaders had simply written off the state. As Andrew Young, then an SCLC [Southern Christian Leadership Conference] staff person, put it: "We knew the depths of the depravity of southern racism. We knew better than to try to take on Mississippi."

Baker's perspective on Mississippi was precisely the opposite of Young's. She felt that the movement had to organize within the belly of the beast of southern racism rather than on its safer margins. This viewpoint was an expression of her class politics as well. In her words, "If you were supposed to be interested in bettering the lot of the have nots, where … [would] be a better start [than] … in the rural areas … [where] people had the hardest lives?" Baker taught SNCC activists to look to the rural towns and plantations of Mississippi—"areas of greatest direst need … where people had [the] least"—as their central organizing challenge. This was not a challenge to be undertaken lightly or quickly. The project that burst on the national stage in 1964 as Mississippi Freedom Summer grew out of years of less publicized, but no less arduous, work throughout the state….

When Bob Moses [SNCC organizer] said, "We did for the people of Mississippi what Ella Baker did for us," he meant that SNCC field organizers and volunteers tried to absorb the wisdom of indigenous leaders, to build respectfully on the preexisting strength within the communities where they organized, and to provide whatever was lacking—funds, time, youthful energy, and certain skills. In other words, Moses followed the example that Baker had set within SNCC. She never professed to having created SNCC's ideology; rather, she identified and nourished the radical democratic tendencies apparent in the thinking of many of those who were drawn to the organization.

When Bob Moses returned to Mississippi in the summer of 1961 to lend his services to the fledgling movement there … he settled on McComb, a small town in the hilly southwest corner of the state, to be the headquarters for SNCC's voter registration project. An activist in the town had read about Moses's plans to register voters in Mississippi in *Jet Magazine*; he contacted Amzie Moore [NAACP organizer], who suggested that Moses look to McComb for a more promising start. Moses enthusiastically agreed. This would be his first real attempt at organizing and the first major community-based campaign for SNCC's voting rights initiative.

The McComb campaign proved to be a baptism by fire. Within a few months of Moses's arrival, there were mass arrests, beatings, expulsions from school, and at least one murder—that of Herbert Lee on September 25, 1961. Lee—an illiterate black dairy farmer, the father of nine children, and a longtime member of the local NAACP—had driven Moses around town to meet local people. According to movement observers he was singled out for retribution by local racists and was shot dead on a public street by a local white man, allegedly over a personal dispute. After the controversy and violence of those first few months, the people who had initially welcomed Moses with open arms began to pull away. C. C. Bryant, the person who had invited Moses to McComb, was a railroad worker, part–time barber, NAACP branch leader, local bibliophile. But after arrests, beatings, and confrontational protests, especially the unpopular arrest of some 100 high school students, Bryant took a step back and distanced himself from the organization. Moses and the volunteers who came to work with him in McComb nevertheless persevered, even when support from their initial contacts began to wane.

What kept Moses in McComb was the support that SNCC received from groups that had previously been on the margins of the town's black society and had been largely ignored by its civil rights leaders. Perhaps SNCC's greatest accomplishment in McComb was its ability to recruit local young people into its ranks. Brenda Travis, the intrepid teenager whom Baker protected and guided, was a native of McComb and joined the movement there. Hollis Watkins and Curtis Hayes, two teenagers from just outside McComb, also joined forces with SNCC as a result of the 1961 campaign; they eventually became two of the movement's strongest local organizers. Watkins had grown up on a farm in southwest Mississippi, gone off to California after high school, and returned south after witnessing the Freedom Rides on television. The local teenagers participated in desegregation protests at the local Woolworth's drugstore and the Greyhound bus station, leading to their arrest. Brenda Travis was expelled from school for her participation in the movement, an action that triggered a walk-out by sympathetic classmates. Impressed by the boldness and courage that SNCC organizers demonstrated, impatient youths were inspired to join the movement and soon provided inspiration to others.

Another variable that sustained SNCC during its difficult early campaigns was the unwavering moral and material support of Ella Baker. While one time supporters like C. C. Bryant criticized SNCC for endangering children, Baker obtained financial resources from SCEF, [Southern Christian Education Fund] offered strategic advice and encouragement at meetings, and aided individuals whose personal lives were thrown into turmoil because of their involvement. She also reminded SNCC organizers to involve parents and seek parental permission before working with minors in order to minimize opposition. Time and again, Baker expressed her confidence in SNCC's leaders, encouraging them to go forward despite their inevitable mistakes. Such reassurance from the voice of experience was essential to young visionaries just entering the vicious fray of race politics.

According to [historian] John Dittmer, one of the lessons SNCC learned from the McComb campaign was that "the black middle class was under severe economic constraints and could not be counted on to support the assault against segregated institutions." This observation points to a pivotal factor in the campaign. Although SNCC was initially welcomed by the local black middle class—the people with education, reputations, and clout—as the struggle intensified that support quickly evaporated. Dittmer concludes that during the course of the McComb campaign SNCC "intuitively grasped a vital part of its future mission in Mississippi: developing a sense of worth and leadership among people who had never been held in high regard in their communities."

The SNCC organizers shook hands with sharecroppers who had dirt under their fingernails and sat at the feet of workers with dust on their boots. They sat on the front porches of ramshackle tenant houses not only to teach but also to learn. Their attitude, like Baker's, was based on the understanding that expertise and wisdom could emanate from outside a formally educated cadre of leaders. According to one SNCC activist, Baker taught the young people in the movement who had achieved some level of formal education that they were no smarter, and certainly no better, than the uneducated farmers and workers in the communities where they were organizing. Barbara Jones (Omolade), a black SNCC worker from New York City, saw in Baker an example of how educated black organizers should comport themselves. "There was no room for talking down to anyone," she recalled. "There was never the expressed attitude that a person who was illiterate had something less to offer." Rather, Baker set a tone that said, "you've got your education, now sit and learn … learn what the conditions are that people have around … and it was hip to do that at that time."…

The McComb campaign led SNCC organizers to conclude that the struggle had to be intensified if any meaningful change was going to occur. But how that should be done was the subject of ongoing debate. Those who joined Bob Moses in McComb—including Reggie Robinson, John Hardy, Chuck McDew, Charles Sherrod, Ruby Doris Smith, Travis Britt, and Marion Barry—had varying views on what route the Mississippi movement should take.… One possible scenario was to bring in more outside supporters whose presence would attract … attention. But there was not unanimity on this. Some SNCC staff felt that the initiative should remain with the local people themselves. If SNCC focused on strengthening their skills, confidence, and resolve, they argued, all else would flow from that strength.

SNCC undertook its massive voter registration campaign in Mississippi under the umbrella of the Council of Federated Organizations (COFO), a Mississippi-based coalition that was originally organized by Aaron Henry as an ad hoc group in 1961 and was reconstituted a year later by the new constellation of organizations active in the state. It included SNCC, CORE, a somewhat reluctant NAACP, and an even less active SCLC. Much of the personnel and leadership came from SNCC and CORE. In 1962, COFO received a $14,000 grant through the Voter Education Project (VEP) administered by the Southern Regional Council, with funds provided by the Field and Taconic Foundations. The money helped defray the costs of purchasing supplies, printing literature, and providing subsistence-level stipends (in some cases ten dollars a week) to organizers, who were called field staff. While COFO was most visible to the campaign's northern, white supporters, SNCC and, in some places, CORE represented the campaign to black Mississippians.

Of the nearly two dozen local projects that SNCC initiated in Mississippi during the early 1960s—including ones in Canton, Holly Springs, Natchez, Harmony, Clarksdale, and Jackson—the movement in the Delta community of Greenwood perhaps best reflected the spirit of organizing that Ella Baker advocated. Here, in what would become SNCC's state headquarters, lucrative cotton plantations were thriving while white vigilantes carried out ruthless repression.…

While Greenwood remained a vital center of movement activity throughout the 1960s, SNCC's work in Ruleville, Mississippi, in adjacent Sunflower County, attracted a middle-aged black woman who would come to personify the heart and soul of the Mississippi movement: Fannie Lou Hamer. One of twenty children born to impoverished sharecroppers in Montgomery County, Mississippi, Hamer never had the opportunity to obtain much formal education, but she was acutely aware of the world around her and the injustices that defined it. A woman of deep religious faith, she once remarked that the civil rights movement appealed to her as much as it did because she was simply "sick and tired of being sick and tired." When in August 1962 SNCC's James Forman and SCLC's James Bevel held a meeting about voter registration in Ruleville, Hamer was in attendance and volunteered, along with seventeen others, to travel to nearby Indianola, the closest courthouse, to register to vote. On her return home, she was fired from the plantation she had worked on for eighteen years; later, she was harassed and shot at by local vigilantes. These attacks only steeled her resolve, she allied herself with SNCC and began to work full time for the movement. In 1963, on her way back from a voter registration workshop in Charleston, South Carolina, Hamer and several others were jailed in Winona County and beaten in retaliation for their activism, an experience that Hamer would never forget and would often talk about. Buoyed by her strong religious faith, she was undeterred. What did she have to lose? she reasoned. "The only thing they could do to me was to kill me and it seemed like they'd been trying to do that a little bit at a time ever since I could remember."

The first statewide campaign that SNCC and COFO carried out in Mississippi, and in which Fannie Lou Hamer and Ella Baker were intimately involved, was Freedom Vote. Held in November 1963, this was a mock election campaign meant to prove that the black electorate would cast their ballots if they were not blocked or intimidated from doing so. The campaign was carried out with the aid of student volunteers, most of whom were white, many of them from elite northern universities. Bob Moses, Ella Baker, and Amzie Moore had long understood that bringing outside resources to bear on the situation in Mississippi was necessary if things were ever going to change. Who, when, and on what terms were always in question....

The plan was to have volunteers travel around the state collecting ballots in an unofficial election process free of intimidating and uncooperative registrars and other deterrents that typically thwarted black participation. A successful turn-out would expose the fact that vigilante violence, economic harassment, and blatant corruption, not apathy, were the obstacles that rendered 98 percent of the state's black electorate voteless. Organizers ran an interracial slate in the November election, in part to demonstrate that the campaign was not solely about race but about building a more inclusive democracy in Mississippi. The gubernatorial candidate was Aaron Henry, the black Clarksdale pharmacist and state NAACP president, and Ed King, the antiracist white chaplain of Tougaloo College, ran for lieutenant governor.

While there may have been some rationale for a biracial gubernatorial ticket in 1963, the reason that two men headed a political campaign in which women formed the largest base of local support is more complex. It foreshadowed the intricate gender politics of the late 1960s.

Some men and women in SNCC felt that black men should be the titular heads of black freedom organizations, thus serving as a counter to the racist culture that sought to systematically relegate them to the denigrated status of boys. Some also felt that black women, long denied the "provisions" and "protection" ostensibly afforded to southern white ladies, deserved to be shielded from the harshest aspects of political combat. These sentiments notwithstanding, there were inclinations and ideological influences pulling SNCC and local activists in another, more egalitarian, direction. Passionate new democratic tendencies pushed hard against old patriarchal habits. The determination to allow each individual to make a contribution and play a role in his or her own emancipation; the emphasis on giving voice and space to those who had previously been excluded from leadership; and the desire to "free men's minds" as Charles Sherrod once put it—all of these sentiments (none of which were articulated specifically in terms of gender) informed the creation of a fluid structure in which women's leadership could and did thrive....

While the struggle for political power in Mississippi represented a landmark in the southern-based struggle for black freedom, that forward movement came at a hefty price. Violence, harassment, and intimidation escalated, and movement leaders lived with the constant threat of attack. And women were not spared. Homes and offices were routinely firebombed, and arrests, beatings, and death threats were commonplace. Regular acts of violence directed at so-called uppity or dissident black individuals had kept the old order in place. As the black resistance movement grew, violence was increasingly directed at it.

Ella Baker got a first-hand look at the political terrorism that dominated the local scene when she traveled through the state drumming up support for the Freedom Vote campaign in the fall of 1963. On October 31, Halloween night, Baker and two of her young colleagues had a frightening encounter with a gang of local white thugs. Baker had just delivered a speech to a group of black businessmen in Natchez, Mississippi. The engagement had not been a rousing success. Baker was anxious to move on to her next appointment in Port Gibson, some forty miles away. Two volunteers, George Green, a twenty-year-old African American activist from Greenwood, and Bruce Payne, a twenty-one-year-old white political science graduate student from Yale University, were assigned to escort her from Natchez to her next stop. Even though she virtually lived on the road, Baker had never learned to drive; so she often relied on others to help her get from place to place.

When Payne arrived to pick Baker up at the house where she had been staying, he told her he was being followed. In an obvious gesture of intimidation, the two cars that had been following him circled the house while he was inside. After some hesitation, Baker, Payne, and Green decided to take their chances and travel as planned. When they started off, the cars continued to follow them; and when they stopped for directions at a gas station outside of Natchez, Payne was attacked and brutally beaten. As he got out of the car, the men jumped out of their car and punched and kicked him; they banged his head against the gas pumps before jumping back into their car and speeding off. Although Payne suffered facial lacerations and bruises, he did not need to be hospitalized, and the threesome drove on to Port Gibson, where they immediately filed complaints with the U.S. Attorney General's Office and the FBI. Several days later, Green and Payne, who were both warned to stay out of town, had another run-in with the two same men and were shot at and run off the road.

Ella Baker had seen the ugly face of southern vigilantism many times, yet every encounter was horrifying. The beating she witnessed that Halloween proved to be a preview of the even more deadly violence that awaited SNCC activists as their campaign for racial and economic justice in Mississippi shifted into high gear. Baker was both fearful and determined. Despite harassment and intimidation by local officials, between 80,000 and 85,000 Mississippians cast their ballots for Freedom candidates. The mock election contradicted the myth that blacks in the state were politically apathetic and would not vote even if given the opportunity.

Despite the relative success of Freedom Vote that year, 1963 was marked by escalating violence against the southern-based Black Freedom Movement and in the society in general. The type of assault Baker witnessed outside Natchez was not uncommon. Between February and May 1963, SNCC workers and supporters in Greenwood were under constant threat, enduring shootings, firebombings, beatings, and arrests. In June, protesters in Danville were so brutally beaten by local police after a series of desegregation protests that observers labeled the event "Bloody Monday." Medgar Evers, an NAACP organizer, was shot to death in the driveway of his home that same month. His assassination sent anger and fear ricocheting through movement circles and elevated Evers to the status of a national martyr. Headlines across the country blazoned the brutal force that Birmingham's police chief, Eugene "Bull" Connor, unleashed against young civil rights demonstrators and the racist recalcitrance of Alabama's newly elected governor, George Wallace, who made a personal pledge to block school desegregation in the state. The violence in Alabama peaked in September 1963 with the bombing of Birmingham's 16th Street Baptist Church, resulting in the tragic deaths of four young black children. The year was also punctuated by events that put civil rights on the national political agenda. The widely publicized March on Washington was held in August 1963, and President Kennedy met with key black leaders before the march. Some civil rights leaders were optimistic, while others saw the continued violence as the prelude to a second Civil War. The assassination of President Kennedy in November struck many as a culmination of the crescendo of violence that had been building up the whole year. While the nation mourned the death of the president, movement activists mourned the growing number of those wounded and killed within its own ranks. Civil rights advocates wondered whether the new president, Lyndon B. Johnson, a liberal Texan, would be more or less sympathetic to the growing black freedom struggle and willing to defend it against the attacks it was suffering.

In November 1963, a week after the Freedom Vote, COFO leaders, including members of SNCC, came together for a meeting in Greenville to reflect on their experiences in the voter registration campaign and the events of the year and to make plans for the group's future work. One of the most contentious topics of discussion was the role of white students within COFO, particularly the upper middle-class whites who had been recruited ... to work on the November campaign. It was at the Greenville meeting that the idea for Freedom Summer began to percolate. Even though Bob Moses supported the idea of utilizing white volunteers in the project, there was not unanimous support. John Dittmer reported that "many of the veteran organizers favored, at best, a limited future role for white students," and some were opposed even to that. Ivanhoe Donaldson, a SNCC staff person, made his feelings known: "I came into SNCC and saw Negroes running things and I felt good." Inviting an influx of whites, he concluded, would mean that they would be losing "the one thing where the Negro can stand first." The heated discussion included accusations that the presence of rich white students might reinforce a deferential "slavery mentality" in southern blacks. This meeting was the continuation of a long and layered process of grappling with the movement's internal racial dynamics....

Freedom Summer was the most widely publicized of the SNCC projects in Mississippi, in part because hundreds of student volunteers arrived in Mississippi in several successive waves to aid the ongoing Black Freedom Movement in the state. After a brief but intense orientation in Oxford, Ohio, the summer volunteers—the overwhelming majority of whom were white—were assigned to projects throughout Mississippi with the expectation that they would assist more experienced field staff in voter education and registration campaigns, staffing freedom schools and keeping the offices up and running.

The concept of Freedom Summer was to draw northern white students directly into the battle for racial democracy in the South and give them, their families, and communities—and hopefully the nation—a greater stake in the outcome. The 1963 Freedom Vote campaign had been the trial run. [Historian] Charles Payne explains that the unchecked violence against black Mississippians was one of the principal factors that convinced Bob Moses of the need to pull other forces into the fray. There had been five mysterious murders in the state between December 1963 and February 1964, but few people outside the area seemed to notice or to care. As a white SNCC staff member, Mendy Samstein, put it, before 1964 Mississippi organizers often felt isolated without any "relief from the daily and brutal confrontation they had with the whole local state system. There was no relief from that, there was no outrage ... when Negroes were beaten or killed. Nobody seemed to care about that, nobody seemed to give a damn." Black southerners had been resisting racism, collectively and individually, all along, placing themselves in danger with each challenge to white rule. The new idea was to ask others to take some of the risks and in the process to raise the stakes.

The renewed black freedom struggle had never been a blacks-only affair. Whites had been involved from the beginning. A handful of whites participated in the sit-ins, and a larger number, many of them northerners, had participated in SNCC's founding conference. And Bob Zellner, Bill Hansen, Connie Curry, Jane Stembridge, Mary King, and Casey Hayden had been involved with SNCC for two or three years by 1963. With Charles Sherrod's encouragement, white organizers had begun working in the Southwest Georgia Project in small numbers in the summer of 1963. However, Freedom Summer would bring many unseasoned volunteers into Mississippi to work in communities alongside blacks in all facets of the organizing effort. At the outset, the two principal concerns were whether they would in some way undermine or usurp less confident black leadership and whether their mere presence would provoke local whites to more acts of violence. Baker understood these concerns, but she was a steadfast supporter of the project. In a series of SNCC executive committee meetings, she laid out her reasons.

On June 9–11, 1964, before the summer volunteers descended on Mississippi, SNCC veterans cloistered themselves away for a two-day meeting and retreat to review one last time the politics surrounding the project, examining what they wanted to accomplish and what dangers and obstacles they would likely encounter over the course of the summer. Ella Baker played an active role in the meeting. She began by framing the purpose of the project in this way: "One of the reasons we're going into Mississippi is that the rest of the United States has never felt much responsibility for what happens in the Deep South. The country feels no responsibility and doesn't see that as an indictment. Young people will make the Justice Department move.... If we can simply let the concept that the rest of the nation bears responsibility for what happens in Mississippi sink in, then we will have accomplished something."...

The influx of hundreds of young white students into the small towns and cities of Mississippi produced culture shock on both sides. It was not the southern dialect, the pace of life, or the food that represented the biggest challenge for the new arrivals; it was the sobering intensity of the situation the volunteers found themselves in. For those who might not have been fully aware of what could be in store for them as they trekked down to Dixie, June 20 was a baptism by fire. On that day, local authorities arrested three young civil rights workers—Michael Schwerner, James Chaney, and Andrew Goodman—who had been investigating a church bombing. They were reportedly released from jail and then mysteriously disappeared and were never heard from again. Their disappearance—and the eventual discovery of their brutally murdered bodies—brought a huge amount of public attention to the project and had a chilling effect on all those involved, especially SNCC's newest recruits. The case of the three missing civil rights workers, whose fate remained unknown all that summer, offered a graphic illustration of the dangerous ground SNCC veterans and volunteers were traversing. Still, only a handful of the volunteers withdrew from involvement after the disappearance of Schwerner, Chaney, and Goodman. But another critical question arose: was the movement exploiting the naive young volunteers who had ventured south over the summer? At the summer's end, Baker published a column in the *Southern Patriot* in response to that allegation. While she had feared for the lives of all young civil rights workers, she had hoped that Freedom Summer would enhance and transform their lives. So, it was not just a matter of what the volunteers could do for the movement, but also of what the movement might offer them. "We wanted their coming to mean something creative for each of them personally as well as for the movement," Baker wrote. As always, Baker had faith in people's capacities to learn from the situations in which they placed themselves and from the people with whom they undertook to struggle for justice....

The Mississippi Freedom Democratic Party (MFDP) came into being on April 26, 1964, at a rally of 200 people in the state capital of Jackson. It represented in its humble birth a truly democratic alternative to the whites-only state Democratic Party, and it had a brief moment on the national political stage at the Democratic Party Convention in Atlantic City, New Jersey, in August 1964. The formation of the MFDP was the successful culmination of four years of life-altering, heart-wrenching, awe-inspiring organizing by a determined little band of freedom soldiers advancing county by county throughout the state. Its success was not determined by what would be won at the convention but rather by what had already been achieved by virtue of the delegation's arrival there....

Freedom Summer volunteers and SNCC and COFO staff circulated literature and canvassed rural and urban communities throughout the state to urge Mississippians to participate in the alternative process of electing their own freedom delegates to go to the Democratic National Convention and hold up two Mississippi alternatives to the nation; one racist and backward-looking, the other democratic and forward-looking. Many activists had decided that black political exclusion was the linchpin holding the entire southern system together. Once that was broken, other possibilities would be created, and black Mississippians would be a force to be reckoned with. Baker was not at all convinced of this, but she thought that any militant mobilization that bolstered local nonelite leadership was a good thing; so she was prepared to support it with all the energy she could muster. The MFDP was another attempt by SNCC to give some of the most oppressed sectors of the black community something of their own, an independent political organization run for and by Mississippi blacks. Once this new political tool was firmly in hand, the idea was that it could be used to extract concessions from northern liberals, to confront them in the most direct way possible to acknowledge the legitimacy of the grievances and claims of Mississippi blacks, and to rally and mobilize the collective strength of black Mississippians. Northern liberal Democrats had taken a hands-off policy while professing support in principle for black political rights. The idea of forming an alternative Democratic Party in the state that was based on inclusion rather than exclusion was designed to force the hand of northern liberals and simultaneously empower local blacks and their allies.

While young SNCC field secretaries donned overalls and boots and traveled the back roads of the state to drum up support, Baker put on her respectable gray suit and knocked on the doors of Congress, labor organizations, and civil rights groups to make sure MFDP delegates had the support they needed when they arrived in Atlantic City. Ella Baker was still on the payroll of SCEF, but Jim Dombrowski and the Bradens shared her assessment about the importance of the MFDP campaign; so the focus of her activity from the summer through the fall of 1964 was the MFDP. She agreed to act as director of the MFDP's Washington, D.C., office. Because the fledgling party had such meager funds, it could not have afforded to pay a full-time staff person, which made Baker's volunteer services all the more welcome.

Much of the struggle to guarantee that the MFDP got a hearing at the Atlantic City convention occurred over the five-month period between the founding conference in April and the national convention in August. The MFDP was founded against the backdrop of African nations declaring their independence from European colonialism. Similarly, black Mississippians declared their independence from the prosegregationist state Democratic Party, which of course they had never really been a part of, and invited any whites bold enough to break ranks to join with them. Few did. But the MFDP was not simply trying to make a symbolic gesture; it wanted to test the resolve of northern Democrats, to have them make good on their promise of inclusion, and ultimately to obtain the power to elect politicians more responsive to their needs. The Democratic Party's convention in Atlantic City would become the place where the gauntlet would be thrown down. The MFDP would demand that the all-white delegation, the state party's so-called regulars, be ousted in favor of a "freedom" delegation.

Baker, the SNCC activists, and the members of the MFDP knew that this was not an effort they could undertake without allies. The new faction had to persuade enough delegates to support them if the issue was going to make it to the convention floor. In March 1964, even before the MFDP's founding convention, Ella Baker and Bob Moses attended the United Auto Workers convention, also in Atlantic City, and met at length with Joseph Rauh, a UAW lawyer who was a leading member of Americans for Democratic Action, a liberal organization. Rauh was eager to get involved in the MFDP campaign, after having talked with Moses earlier that year. Also present was Mildred Jeffrey, a Democratic national committeewoman from Michigan and the mother of a Freedom Summer volunteer. Moses and Baker laid out a convincing case, and Rauh and Jeffrey were on board. On May 20, Moses and Baker went to Washington to again rally support. At a conference that had just ended, the Americans for Democratic Action had passed a resolution supporting the MFDP....

Over the course of the spring and summer, thousands of people joined the MFDP. They were overwhelmingly black. While some of the official party leaders were men, the most visible, vocal, and influential leaders were women: Fannie Lou Hamer, the impoverished sharecropper from Ruleville, Mississippi, who had participated in Freedom Vote and who spoke powerfully about her life in struggle; Annie Devine, a one-time schoolteacher, insurance agent, and CORE organizer from Canton, Mississippi; and Victoria Gray, a young mother of three who ran a small cosmetics business in Hattiesburg and resented the middle-class leaders of the local NAACP because they functioned as a "closed social group." The gender composition and dynamics of the MFDP reflected the characteristics of the grassroots movement of the 1950s and 1960s rather than the male domination that prevailed within more hierarchical organizations....

Southern black communities were emboldened and empowered as a result of the MFDP mobilization. The stranglehold of fear had been loosened, and the silence had been broken. And once the world saw the ugly reality of Mississippi's racism, some participants believed, it would be unable simply to look the other way. At least in part, they were right. Throughout the summer of 1964, Freedom Summer volunteers and SNCC/COFO volunteers and staff went door to door in small towns and cities throughout the state spreading the gospel about the MFDP and documenting instances of black voter intimidation and outright obstruction. They were joined by local young people who had been angry and dissatisfied with their lot long before the SNCC and COFO organizers arrived and were happy to finally have allies, resources, and a clear outlet for their pent-up political energies. Young Mississippians like Sam Block, Willie Peacock, Curtis Hayes, Hollis Watkins, June Johnson, and Dorie and Joyce Ladner were among them.

When the MFDP held its nominating convention on August 6 in Jackson to select sixty-eight delegates to travel to Atlantic City as representatives of the party, Baker was once again asked to deliver the keynote address. This speech was different. Only two days before, the risks that the struggle for justice entailed had been dramatically revealed by the discovery of the bodies of the three missing civil rights workers. James Chaney, Andrew Goodman, and Michael Schwerner had been brutally murdered, and their mangled bodies had been buried in a dam near Philadelphia, Mississippi. Ella Baker stood before the grief-stricken crowd of 800 that had gathered in Jackson's Masonic Hall on that hot summer night and delivered a political message full of anger and determination. Sensitive to the agony that the families of the victims must have felt at that moment, Baker was both mournful and militant as she eulogized the three young men, and she urged movement activists to carry on where their three brave young comrades had left off. At the same time, she underscored the lesser value that white society placed on black lives: "Until the killing of black mothers' sons is as important as the killing of white mothers' sons, we who believe in freedom cannot rest."…

When the weary but determined delegation of Mississippi farmers, beauticians, schoolteachers, and one pharmacist arrived in New Jersey in late August, the outcome of their long, arduous journey was still unclear.… The first confrontation after they arrived in New Jersey was with the credentials committee of the national convention. Fannie Lou Hamer, the vice chairperson of the MFDP delegation, made an impassioned plea for recognition. All she had to do to make a compelling case against the blatant oppression and disenfranchisement of Mississippi blacks was to tell her own story. She had been threatened, evicted, and beaten by local police for daring to assert her rights as an American citizen. How could northern liberals who professed their commitment to equality and democracy ignore Hamer's ordeal or fail to recognize the challenge it represented for the Democratic Party? But President Johnson was so fearful that Hamer's remarks would upset his electoral ambitions that he called an emergency press conference just as her speech was going to be aired on network television to deflect attention away from the MFDP's most powerful spokesperson.

Protests outside the convention demanding the Democratic leadership take a stand, coupled with the unbending resolve of the Freedom delegates to be seated at the convention, created a series of crises for Johnson and his supporters. They did not want to give any political ammunition to the Republican candidate, Barry Goldwater, by having disruptions or defections in Atlantic City, nor did they want to appear to be callously insensitive to the compelling grievances of black Mississippians. White liberals such as Allard Lowenstein and Joe Rauh, who operated a bit more on the fringes of the Democratic Party mainstream, also faced a crisis. They wanted to please the Mississippi civil rights activists, with whom they had allied themselves going into the convention, but they wanted to do so without alienating the top leadership of the Democratic Party. The crisis spilled over to high-ranking black leaders, such as King, Wilkins, and Rustin. Northern black elected officials and civil rights leaders in attendance at the convention were lobbied hard by supporters of Hubert Humphrey, the aspiring vice presidential nominee, to try to avert a scene; and not wanting to alienate the man who was likely to be vice president, they did.

Much of the drama in Atlantic City was played out behind closed doors. There were numerous late-night strategy sessions in Martin Luther King's hotel suite, in the MFDP's makeshift office, and in the corridors of the convention hall. There were also impromptu vigils and the singing of freedom songs outside the hall. The top Democratic Party leadership sought, above all, to avoid bad publicity and a messy fight on the convention floor. Humphrey, aided by Walter Mondale and a coterie of aides, pushed for some type of compromise short of an all-out concession. The right-wing position at the convention was summed up by Texas governor John Connally, who blurted out in one discussion that he'd walk out if the MFDP "baboons" were seated. In the face of such racist opposition, MFDP sympathizers groped for a solution. Congresswoman Edith Greene proposed one compromise, which would have likely resulted in seating nearly the entire MFDP delegation, but this proposal somehow got lost in the shuffle. The compromise offer that emerged was that the MFDP would be given two symbolic seats on the convention floor alongside the regular all-white delegation. "We didn't come all this way for no two seats," replied an insulted and adamant Fannie Lou Hamer....

So, what was the MFDP to do? A handful of the delegates initially wanted to accept the compromise. The two official leaders of the delegation, Aaron Henry and Ed King, even argued its merits. And some of those who had been allies throughout the campaign were also advising moderation, compromise, and cooperation with the Democratic Party, even though establishment party leaders were unwilling to fully support the MFDP. It was the practical thing to do, urged King, Rustin, Wilkins, and Rauh. But the majority of activists who had trekked to Atlantic City on their own political pilgrimage were in no mood to compromise. In an all-night meeting at a local church, speaker after speaker pleaded with the MFDP delegates to be reasonable, to think strategically, to remember who their friends were. Baker said nothing. Her sentiments had already been expressed and were no secret. After the speech making, the delegates met alone to confer and opted to reject the compromise. Later that night, there was a vigil on the boardwalk where the group sang freedom songs; some cried, and others expressed anger and disbelief at what had happened—all against the backdrop of three haunting images, those of Chaney, Goodman, and Schwerner. The next day, the MFDP again captured media attention and disrupted the convention by forcibly occupying a row of seats with false credentials given to them by sympathetic delegates from other states. They had no intention of retreating quietly.

The showdown in Atlantic City was a turning point in the movement. Many hopes had been riding on the outcome of the convention. Those hopes had been dashed. Time, energy, dollars, and lives had been invested to obtain this small slice of freedom. Many MFDP activists went away from the 1964 convention feeling cheated and betrayed. Baker had been less optimistic at the outset; so she was less disappointed in the end. She did not view the MFDP campaign as a defeat. Rather, she saw it as a "testing force" and an "alerting process." It had not wrested political power from the hands of the Democratic Party elites, but it had successfully mobilized a solid core of Mississippi activists. The experience had provided a set of political lessons for organizers, as she hoped it would, lessons that could not have been obtained from any book, lecture, or workshop. In Baker's mind, the MFDP experiment had "settled any debate" about "the possibility of functioning through the mainstream of the Democratic Party." It also stiffened the resolve and determination of those who were not wholly alienated and disheartened to fight harder and to fight for more radical kinds of changes.

FURTHER READING

Karen Anderson, *Little Rock: Race and Resistance at Central High School* (2010).

Raymond Arsenault, *Freedom Riders: 1961 and the Struggle for Racial Justice* (2006).

Numan V. Bartley, *The Rise of Massive Resistance: Race and Politics in the South in the 1960s* (1969).

Numan V. Bartley and Hugh D. Graham, *Southern Politics and the Second Reconstruction* (1975).

Jack Bass, *Unlikely Heroes: The Southern Judges Who Made the Civil Rights Revolution* (1981).

Jack Bass and Walter De Vries, *The Transformation of Southern Politics: Social Change and Political Consequences* (1976).

Daisy Bates, *The Long Shadow of Little Rock: A Memoir* (1962).

Mark K. Bauman and Berkley Kalin, *The Quiet Voices: Southern Rabbis and Black Civil Rights 1880s–1990s* (1997).

Earl Black, *Southern Governors and Civil Rights: Racial Segregation as a Campaign Issue in the Second Reconstructions* (1976).

Taylor Branch, *Pillar of Fire, America in the King Years, 1963–65* (1998).

Tomiko Brown Nagin, *Courage to Dissent: Atlanta and the Long History of the Civil Rights Movement* (2011).

Robert Frederick Burk, *The Eisenhower Administration and Black Civil Rights* (1984).

Eric R. Burner, *And Gently He Shall Lead Them: Robert Purris Moses and Civil Rights in Mississippi* (1994).

Stewart Burns, ed., *Daybreak of Freedom: The Montgomery Bus Boycott* (1997).

Clayborne Carson, *In Struggle: SNCC and the Black Awakening of the 1960s* (1981).

Derek Charles Catsam, *Freedom's Main Line: The Journey of Reconciliation and the Freedom Rides* (2009).

William Chafe, *Civilities and Civil Rights: Greensboro, NC, and the Black Struggle for Freedom* (1980).

David Chappell, *Inside Agitators: White Southerners in the Civil Rights Movement* (1994).

———, *A Stone of Hope: Prophetic Religion and the Death of Jim Crow* (2004).

Melinda Chateauvert, *Marching Together: Women of the Brotherhood of Sleeping Car Porters* (1998).

E. Culpepper Clark, *The Schoolhouse Door: Segregation's Last Stand at the University of Alabama* (1993).

Thomas R. Cole, *No Color Is My Kind: The Life of Eldrewey Stearns and the Integration of Houston* (1997).

Robert Coles, *Children of Crisis: A Study in Courage and Fear* (1964).

Bettye Collier-Thomas, *Jesus, Jobs, and Justice: African American Women and Religion.* (2010).

Vicki Crawford et al., eds., *Women in the Civil Rights Movement: Trailblazers and Torchbearers, 1941–1965* (1990).

Emilye Crosby, *A Little Taste of Freedom: The Black Freedom Struggle in Claiborne County, Mississippi* (2005).

Constance Curry, *Silver Rights* (1995).

Pete Daniel, *Lost Revolutions:The South in the 1950s* (2000).

Dennis C. Dickerson, *Militant Mediator: Whitney M. Young Jr.* (1998).

John Dittmer, *Local People: The Struggle for Civil Rights in Mississippi* (1994).

Mary L. Dudziak, *Cold War Civil Rights: Race and the Image of American Democracy* (2000).

Charles W. Eagles, *Outside Agitator: Jon Daniels and the Civil Rights Movement in Alabama* (2000).

———. *The Price of Defiance: James Meredith and the Integration of Ole Miss* (2009).

Glenn Eskew, *But for Birmingham: The Local and National Movements in the Civil Rights Struggle* (1997).

Steve Estes, *I Am a Man! Race, Manhood, and the Civil Rights Movement* (2005).

Sara Evans, "Women's Consciousness and the Southern Black Movement," *Southern Exposure* 4 (1976), 10–17.

Adam Fairclough, *To Redeem the Soul of America: The SCLC and Martin Luther King, Jr.* (1987).

———, *Race and Democracy: The Civil Rights Struggle in Louisiana,1915–1972* (1995).

Cynthia Griggs Fleming, *Soon We Will Not Cry: The Liberation of Ruby Doris Smith Robinson* (1998).

Kari Frederickson, *The Dixiecrat Revolt and the End of the Solid South,1932–1968* (2001).

Tony Freyer, *The Little Rock Crisis: A Constitutional Interpretation* (1984).

David Garrow, *Protest at Selma: Martin Luther King, Jr., and the Voting Rights Act of 1965* (1978).

Tiffany M. Gill, *Beauty Shop Politics: African American Women's Activism in the Beauty Industry* (2010).

David R. Goldfield, *Black, White, and Southern: Race Relations and Southern Culture, 1940 to the Present* (1990).

Christina Greene, *Our Separate Ways: Women and the Black Freedom Movement in Durham, North Carolina* (2005).

Hugh Davis Graham, *The Civil Rights Era: The Origins and Development of National Policy* (1990).

John A. Hardin, *Fifty Years of Segregation* (1997).

Russell J. Henderson, "The 1963 Mississippi State University Basketball Controversy and the Repeal of the Unwritten Law: 'Something More than the Game Will Be Lost,'" *Journal of Southern History* 63 (November 1997), 827–854.

Alton Hornsby Jr., *Black Power in Dixie: A Political History of African Americans in Atlanta* (2009).

Elizabeth Jacoway and David R. Colburn, eds., *Southern Businessmen and Desegregation* (1982).

Elizabeth Jacoway, *Turn Away Thy Son: Little Rock, the Crisis that Shocked the Nation* (2007).

V.O. Key Jr., *Southern Politics in State and Nation* (1949).

Martin Luther King Jr., *Stride Toward Freedom: The Montgomery Story* (1958).

Richard Kluger, *Simple Justice: The History of* Brown v. Board of Education *and Black America's Struggle for Equality* (1976).

Robert Rodgers Korstad, *Civil Rights Unionism: Tobacco Workers and the Struggle for Democracy in the Mid-Twentieth-Century South* (2003).

Steven F. Lawson, *Black Ballots: Voting Rights in the South, 1944–1969* (1976).

———, *In Pursuit of Power: Southern Blacks and Electoral Politics, 1865–1982* (1985).

———, *Running for Freedom: Civil Rights and Black Politics* (1991).

Chana Kai Lee, *For Freedom's Sake: The Life of Fannie Lou Hamer* (1999).

George Lewis, *Massive Resistance: The White Response to the Civil Rights Movement* (2006).

John Lewis, *Walking with the Wind: A Memoir of the Movement* (1998).

Manning Marable, *Race, Reform, and Rebellion: The Second Reconstruction in Black America* (1991).

Doug McAdam, *Freedom Summer* (1988).

Gerald D. McKnight, *The Last Crusade: Martin Luther King, Jr., FBI, and the Poor People's Campaign* (1998).

Danielle McGuire, *At the Dark End of the Street: Black Women, Rape, and Resistance. A New History of the Civil Rights Movement from Rosa Parks to the Rise of the Black Power Movement* (2010).

Neil R. McMillan, *The Citizens' Council: Organized Resistance to the Second Reconstruction* (1971).

August Meier and John H. Bracey Jr., "The NAACP as a Reform Movement, 1909–1965: 'To Reach the Conscience of America,'" *Journal of Southern History* 59 (February 1993), 3–30.

Sherie Mershon and Steven Schlossman, *Foxholes and Color Lines: Desegregating the U.S. Armed Forces* (1998).

Kay Mills, *This Little Light of Mine: The Life of Fannie Lou Hamer* (1993).

Timothy Minchin, *Hiring the Black Worker: The Racial Integration of the Southern Textile Industry, 1960–1980* (1999).

Anne Moody, *Coming of Age in Mississippi* (1968).

Aldon D. Morris, *The Origins of the Civil Rights Movement: Black Communities Organizing for Change* (1984).

J. Todd Moye, *Let the People Decide: Black Freedom and White Resistance Movements in Sunflower County, Mississippi, 1945–1986* (2004).

Gunnar Myrdal, *An American Dilemma* (1944).

Thomas R. Peake, *Keeping the Dream Alive: A History of the Southern Christian Leadership Conference* (1987).

Julie L. Pycior, *LBJ and Mexican Americans: The Paradox of Power* (1997).

Howell Raines, *My Soul Is Rested: Movement Days in the Deep South Remembered* (1977).

Barbara Ransby, *Ella Baker and the Black Freedom Movement: A Radical Democratic Vision* (2003).

William T. Martin Riches, *The Civil Rights Movement: Struggle and Resistance* (1997).

Belinda Robnett, *How Long? How Long? African-American Women in Struggle for Civil Rights* (1997).

Armstead L. Robinson and Patricia Sullivan, eds., *New Directions in Civil Rights Studies* (1991).

James Silver, *Mississippi: The Closed Society* (1964).

Harvard Sitkoff, *The Struggle for Black Equality, 1954–1980* (1980).

Jason Sokol, *There Goes My Everything: White Southerners in the Age of Civil Rights, 1945–1975* (2006).

Patricia Sullivan, *Lift Every Voice: The NAACP and the Making of the Civil Rights Movement* (2009).

J. Mills Thornton III, "Challenge and Response in the Montgomery Bus Boycott of 1955–1956," *Alabama Review* 33 (1980), 163–235.

Timothy B. Tyson, *Radio Free Dixie: Robert F. Williams and the Roots of Black Power* (1999).

Mark V. Tushnet, *The NAACP's Legal Strategy against Segregated Education, 1925–1950* (1987).

Nancy J. Weiss, *Whitney M. Young, Jr., and the Struggle for Civil Rights* (1989).

Nan E. Woodruff, *American Congo: The African American Freedom Struggle in the Delta* (2003).

CHAPTER 13

The Recent South and Its Culture Wars

In the years after the passage of the 1965 Voting Rights Act, millions of formerly disfranchised African Americans became voters. At the same time, however, the major civil rights organizations disintegrated into warring factions, the Vietnam War overwhelmed the domestic mission of the Johnson administration, and the politics of rage, heralded by such flamboyant figures as George Wallace, dominated the news. Richard Nixon and his Republican followers became more interested in appealing to southern whites than in maintaining the gains of the 1960s. In the South, the annealing had occurred, and the healing was beginning. The southern caterpillar was transformed into a Sunbelt butterfly, and the business of business soon overshadowed lingering racial tensions.

Gains for African Americans were most visible in southern politics. By 1975, blacks held more political offices in the South than in any other region. Race baiting virtually disappeared from campaigns, and many leaders who emerged during the 1970s owed their election in great part to the expanding black electorate. The Democratic Party, which had once based its power on white supremacy, came to rely heavily on black votes. In employment, gains for blacks also came, although more slowly, as barriers to jobs, education, and entry to the professions declined.

The Republican Party gained converts among southern white conservatives and retained the allegiance of migrating northerners. As a result, for a time, the era of one-party politics was over. By the 1980s, however, the Republican party, with Ronald Reagan at its head, brought about one of the most powerful political revolutions in American history. The region once more became nearly the Solid South—the solid Republican South. And Newt Gingrich, spokesperson for southern Republicans as well as majority leader in the House, negotiated a "Contract with America." This transformation in party loyalty arose in part because many white southerners were uncomfortable with the advances of the civil rights movement, affirmative action, and women's rights, including abortion. On another front, evangelical religious leaders, such as Jerry Falwell, who in theory eschewed politics, found that their followers favored a conservative political agenda, one that could give power to a growing Religious Right. Because of population growth in the Sunbelt South, especially in the suburbs, the region now greatly influenced national politics, including the rejection of the Equal Rights Amendment (ERA).

*Historians, who normally study issues only after a space of 50 years, are beginning to ask questions related to recent changes in the South. What happened to the civil rights movement? What happened to white supremacy? How significant and lasting are the political and economic advances for African Americans? Why, with the changes brought about by the freedom struggles, does poverty still exist among southerners, especially blacks? How has the rise of the Religious Right influenced southern politics? What happened to the women's rights movement—*Roe *v.* Wade *and the ERA—in the South? What role did Phyllis Schlafly play in southern politics?*

DOCUMENTS

The political shifts that would affect the South during the civil rights years brought the attention of the nation to the region. Freedom struggles and determined intransigence on the part of most white southerners became headline news. Almost silently, however, another movement was taking place. Southern agriculture, as the staple economic base for the region, was in decline between 1955 and 1987 to be replaced by a more diversified economy of trade, services, government, manufacturing, finance, construction, and transportation. Based on a Department of Commerce survey of the numbers of workers in each of these commercial pursuits, nothing short of an economic restructuring occurred during these pivotal years (Document 1). After 1965, the civil rights movement splintered as it began to move away from nonviolence toward self-defense, black power, and women's rights. Casey Hayden and Mary King, committed civil rights activists, wrote a two-page document, "Sex and Caste: A Kind of Memo" (Document 2), outlining the inequality for women in the movement. They showed the document to 40 other women civil rights workers who shared the same concerns: In their struggle against racism, they were themselves the victims of sexism. Historians credit this "Memo," coming as it did out of the South's civil rights movement, as one of the most important documents leading to the late-twentieth-century feminist movement. The civil rights and the women's rights movements left some white southerners with a sense of loss for the culture that they had always known. Jerry Falwell, a white southern preacher and founder of the Moral Majority, capitalized on these feelings and rode the wave of conservative resurgence ushered in by Ronald Reagan in 1980 when he wrote *Listen, America!* (Document 3). Basing his premise on born-again Christian principles, Falwell portrays "a vicious assault upon the American family" that can be remedied by eschewing the "women's liberation movement" and bringing about the defeat of the Equal Rights Amendment. By 1980 the Republican revolution had engulfed the South, and, as the photographs in Document 4 indicate, the Religious Right, led by Jerry Falwell, helped to boost southern support. In 1992, before the Republican National Convention in Houston, George Bush actively courted the Christian Coalition, while the

Religious Right and pro-life advocates such as Phyllis Schlafly and Rush Limbaugh swayed the party in the direction of family values. Document 5 demonstrates the advance of Republican Party strength in the South between 1980 and 1998. In Document 6, two politicians from opposing parties candidly discuss such issues as coded racism (using language that masks the intent to dismantle court mandated busing, food stamp programs, and legal services) on the one hand and balancing the needs of black constituents while continuing to seek support from white conservative voters on the other. The interview, conducted by political scientist Alexander Lamis, shows the racial bifurcation of southern political parties and implies a more subtle but nonetheless important indication of the persistence of race in regional life and politics. In the secession crisis leading to the Civil War, southern Baptists had split away from the national denomination over the issue of slavery, creating their own denomination, the Southern Baptist Convention. One hundred and fifty years later, the SBC, in a Declaration of Repentance, apologized for endorsing slavery and segregation, as indicated in Document 7. Cartoonist Walt Handelsman, two-time Pulitzer Prize winner, gives an ironic touch to the Confederate battle flag debate in Document 8. Often race divides proponents and opponents over displaying the flag, but in this instance Handelsman brings the flag's history into sharp relief. The controversy of flying the Confederate battle flag over the statehouse in Columbia, South Carolina, reached epic proportions in 2000, resulting in a compromise that left the flag on Capitol grounds but raised above a Confederate memorial. Document 9 brings yet another perspective to the political culture wars. According to Bob Moser, writing for *The Nation,* Barack Obama "looked South and saw not stereotypes but—wonder of wonders!—Americans." To win his 2008 presidential campaign, Obama organized Democratic Party offices in southern states, mobilized 20,000 volunteers, and contradicted the notion that only Republicans represent the South.

1. The Department of Commerce Charts the Economic Transformation of the South, 1955–1987

Southeast Economic Structure

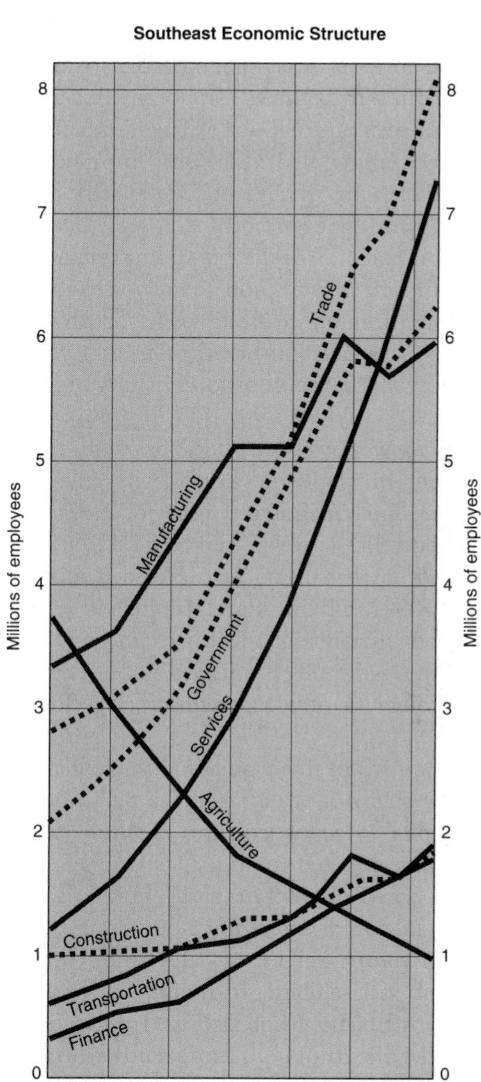

SOURCE: U.S. Department of Commerce, Bureau of Census, *Statistical Abstract of the United States*, 1985, 1988; U.S. Department of Agriculture, Agricultural Statistics, 1980, 1984, 1988.

James W. Clay and Alfred W. Stuart, editors, *Charlotte Metro Region: Hub of the Carolinas* (Charlotte: UNC Charlotte Department of Geography and Earth Sciences, n.d.) [1989 or later].

2. Casey Hayden and Mary King Write "Sex and Caste: A Kind of Memo," 1965

We've talked a lot, to each other and to some of you, about our own and other women's problems in trying to live in our personal lives and in our work as independent and creative people. In these conversations we've found what seem to be recurrent ideas or themes. Maybe we can look at these things many of us perceive, often as a result of insights learned from the movement:

Sex and caste: There seem to be many parallels that can be drawn between treatment of Negroes and treatment of women in our society as a whole. But in particular, women we've talked to who work in the movement seem to be caught up in a common-law caste system that operates, sometimes subtly, forcing them to work around or outside hierarchical structures of power which may exclude them. Women seem to be placed in the same position of assumed subordination in personal situations too. It is a caste system which, at its worst, uses and exploits women. This is complicated by several facts, among them:

1) The caste system is not institutionalized by law (women have the right to vote, to sue for divorce, etc.);
2) Women can't withdraw from the situation (a la nationalism) or overthrow it;
3) There are biological differences (even though those biological differences are usually discussed or accepted without taking present and future technology into account so we probably can't be sure what these differences mean). Many people who are very hip to the implications of the racial caste system, even people in the movement, don't seem to be able to see the sexual caste system and if the question is raised they respond with: "That's the way it's supposed to be. There are biological differences." Or with other statements which recall a white segregationist confronted with integration.

Women and problems of work: The caste system perspective dictates the roles assigned to women in the movement, and certainly even more to women outside the movement. Within the movement, questions arise in situations ranging from relationships of women organizers to men in the community, to who cleans the freedom house, to who holds leadership positions, to who does secretarial work, and who acts as spokesman for groups. Other problems arise between women with varying degrees of awareness of themselves as being as capable as men but held back from full participation, or between women who see themselves as needing more control of their work than other women demand. And there are problems with relationships between white women and black women.

Casey Hayden and Mary King Write "Sex and Caste: A Kind of Memo," 1965. From Mary Elizabeth King, *Freedom Song: A Personal Story of the Civil Rights Movement* (New York: Morrow, 1987), pp. 571–74. Reprinted by permission of the authors.

Women and personal relations with men: Having learned from the movement to think radically about the personal worth and abilities of people whose role in society had gone unchallenged before, a lot of women in the movement have begun trying to apply those lessons to their own relations with men. Each of us probably has her own story of the various results, and of the internal struggle occasioned by trying to break out of very deeply learned fears, needs, and self-perceptions, and of what happens when we try to replace them with concepts of people and freedom learned from the movement and organizing.

Institutions: Nearly everyone has real questions about those institutions which shape perspectives on men and women: marriage, child rearing patterns, women's (and men's) magazines, etc. People are beginning to think about and even to experiment with new forms in these areas.

Men's reactions to the questions raised here: A very few men seem to feel, when they hear conversations involving these problems, that they have a right to be present and participate in them, since they are so deeply involved. At the same time, very few men can respond non-defensively, since the whole idea is either beyond their comprehension or threatens and exposes them. The usual response is laughter. That inability to see the whole issue as serious, as the straitjacketing of both sexes, and as societally determined often shapes our own response so that we learn to think in their terms about ourselves and to feel silly rather than trust our inner feelings. The problems we're listing here, and what others have said about them, are therefore largely drawn from conversations among women only and that difficulty in establishing dialogue with men is a recurring theme among people we've talked to.

Lack of community for discussion: Nobody is writing, or organizing or talking publicly about women, in any way that reflects the problems that various women in the movement come across and which we've tried to touch above. Consider this quote from an article in the centennial issue of *The Nation*:

> However equally we consider men and women, the work plans for husbands and wives cannot be given equal weight. A woman should not aim for "a second-level career" because she is a woman; from girlhood on she should recognize that, if she is also going to be a wife and mother, she will not be able to give as much to her work as she would if single. That is, she should not feel that she cannot aspire to directing the laboratory simply because she is a woman, but rather because she is also a wife and mother....

And that's about as deep as the analysis goes publicly, which is not nearly so deep as we've heard many of you go in chance conversations....

The very fact that the country can't face, much less deal with, the questions we're raising means that the movement is one place to look for some relief. Real efforts at dialogue within the movement and with whatever liberal groups, community women, or students might listen are justified.... To raise questions like those above illustrates very directly that society hasn't dealt with some of its deepest problems and opens discussion of why that is so. (In one sense, it is a radicalizing question that can take people beyond legalistic solutions into areas of personal and institutional change.) The second objective reason we'd like to see discussion begin is that we've learned a great deal in the movement and perhaps this is one area where a determined attempt to apply ideas we've learned there can produce some new alternatives.

3. Jerry Falwell Publishes *Listen, America!*, 1980

Prologue

Shortly after President Reagan had won his very difficult congressional battle for his economic program, a pro-Reagan conservative commented, "I just hope it isn't too late to save the country."...

But the real battle for America's survival lies in her ability to re-arm morally. Solomon, the wisest man who ever lived, once said, "Living by God's principles promotes a nation to greatness; violating God's principles brings a nation to shame" (Proverbs 14:34, paraphrased)....

I believe we not only can, but we must win this race! We have already won some significant battles along the way. These include the virtual burial of the Equal Rights Amendment after its quick ratification by all but three of the required 38 states; the passage of the Hyde Amendment which cut off tax money for welfare abortions and the upholding of the amendment's constitutionality by the Supreme Court; the crushing defeat of the television networks' attempt to denigrate the airwaves with gratuitous sex and violence through the efforts of the Coalition for Better Television; the support of creationism bills in half of the 50 state legislatures requiring that the scientific evidence for creation be taught alongside the scientific evidence for evolution in public schools; and, of course, the mighty effect in the 1980 elections caused by the mobilization of millions of heretofore uninvolved pro-moralists, born-again Christians, and religious people in general.

Now, these same pro-moral forces are coalescing to stop the aborting of one and one-half million babies each year in America. These pro-moral forces are considering a human life amendment, the appointment of personnel to the Supreme Court who might possibly reverse *Roe* vs. *Wade*, and other means to put a stop to America's "national sin."...

Pro-moral Americans are alive. The sleeping giant is standing up. We are awake! ... I have made my decision to speak out and to act....

Family—The Basic Unit

There is a vicious assault upon the American family. More television programs depict homes of divorced or of single parents than depict the traditional family. Nearly every major family-theme TV program openly justifies divorce, homosexuality, and adultery. Some sociologists believe that the family unit, as we know it, could disappear by the year 2000....

In the war against the family today, we find an arsenal of weapons. The first weapon is the cult of the playboy, the attitude that has permeated our society in these last twenty years. This playboy philosophy tells men that they do not have to be committed to their wife and to their children, but that they should be some kind of a "cool, free swinger." Sexual promiscuity has become the life style of America. The cult of the playboy is more that just a revolution of dirty magazines. It represents a life style that ultimately corrupts the family. Men are satisfying their lustful desires at the expense of family.

The second weapon against the family is the feminist revolution. This is the counterreaction to the cult of the playboy. Many women are saying, "Why should I be taken advantage of by chauvinists? I will get out and do my own thing. I will stand up for my rights. I will have my own dirty magazines." Feminists are saying that self-satisfaction is more important than the family. Most of the women who are leaders in the feminist movement promote an immoral life style.

In a drastic departure from the home, more than half of the women in our country are currently employed. Our nation is in serious danger when motherhood is considered a task that is "unrewarding, unfulfilling, and boring." I believe that a woman's call to be a wife and mother is the highest calling in the world....

The Feminist Movement

I believe that at the foundation of the women's liberation movement there is a minority core of women who were once bored with life, whose real problems are spiritual problems. Many women have never accepted their God-given roles. They live in disobedience to God's laws and have promoted their godless philosophy throughout our society. God Almighty created men and women biologically different and with differing needs and roles....

The Equal Rights Amendment is a delusion. I believe that women deserve more than equal rights. And, in families and in nations where the Bible is believed, Christian women are honored above men. Only in places where the Bible is believed and practiced do women receive more than equal rights. Men and women have differing strengths. The Equal Rights Amendment can never do for women what needs to be done for them. Women need to know Jesus Christ as their Lord and Savior and be under His Lordship. They need a man who knows Jesus Christ as his Lord and Savior, and they need to be part of a home where their husband is a godly leader and where there is a Christian family.

The Equal Rights Amendment strikes at the foundation of our entire social structure. If passed, this amendment would accomplish exactly the opposite of its outward claims. By mandating an absolute equality under the law, it will actully take away many of the special rights women now enjoy. ERA is not merely a political issue, but a moral issue as well. A definite violation of holy Scripture, ERA defies the mandate that "the husband is the head of the wife, even as Christ is the head of the church" (Ep. 5:23). In 1 Peter 3:7 we read that husbands are to give their wives honor as unto the weaker vessel, that they are both heirs together of the grace of life. Because a woman is weaker does not mean that she is less important.

I deeply respect Mrs. Phyllis Schlafly. Mrs. Schlafly is a conservative activist. She is a lawyer and has an extensive background in national defense. At services in the Thomas Road Baptist Church, Lynchburg, Virginia, Mrs. Schlafly made these comments: "The more I work with the issue of ERA, the more I realize that the women's liberation movement is antifamily. The proof came in November 1977 when the conference on International Women's Year met in Houston. It passed twenty-five resolutions which show very clearly what the feminists are after. They are for the Equal Rights Amendment, which would take away the marvelous legal rights of a woman to be a full-time wife and mother in the home supported by her husband. They are for abortion on demand, financed by the government and taught in the schools. They are for privileges for lesbians and homosexuals to teach in the schools and to adopt children. They are for the government assuming the main responsibility for child care because they think it is oppressive and unfair that society expects mothers to look after their babies. All their goals and dogmas are antifamily. They believe that God made a mistake when He made two different kinds of people....

The Equal Rights Amendment offers women nothing in the way of rights or benefits that they do not already have. In the areas of employment and education, laws have already been enacted to protect women. The only thing the Equal Rights Amendment would do would be to take away rights and privileges that American women now have in the best country in the world....

4. The Religious Right Joins the Republican Party, 1980–1992

In its first electoral outing, the Religious Right hitched its star to candidate Ronald Reagan. Though Reagan's personal life was not as religiously oriented as Jimmy Carter's, he championed the "family values" agenda that [Jerry] Falwell and others espoused. But when his administration failed to follow through, the Religious Right began learning the compromises of political involvement. (AP Photos)

From: William Martin, *With God on Our Side: The Rise of the Religious Right in America* (New York: Broadway Books, 1996).

Just before the 1992 presidential election, George Bush made a series of last-minute outreach appearances to rally the support of conservative groups. Seen here at the Christian Coalition's Road to Victory Conference in September of that year, he received a standing ovation when he told his audience, "I join with you in committing to uphold the sanctity of Life." (George Bush Presidential Library and Museum)

5. Republican Party Advances in the South, 1980–1998

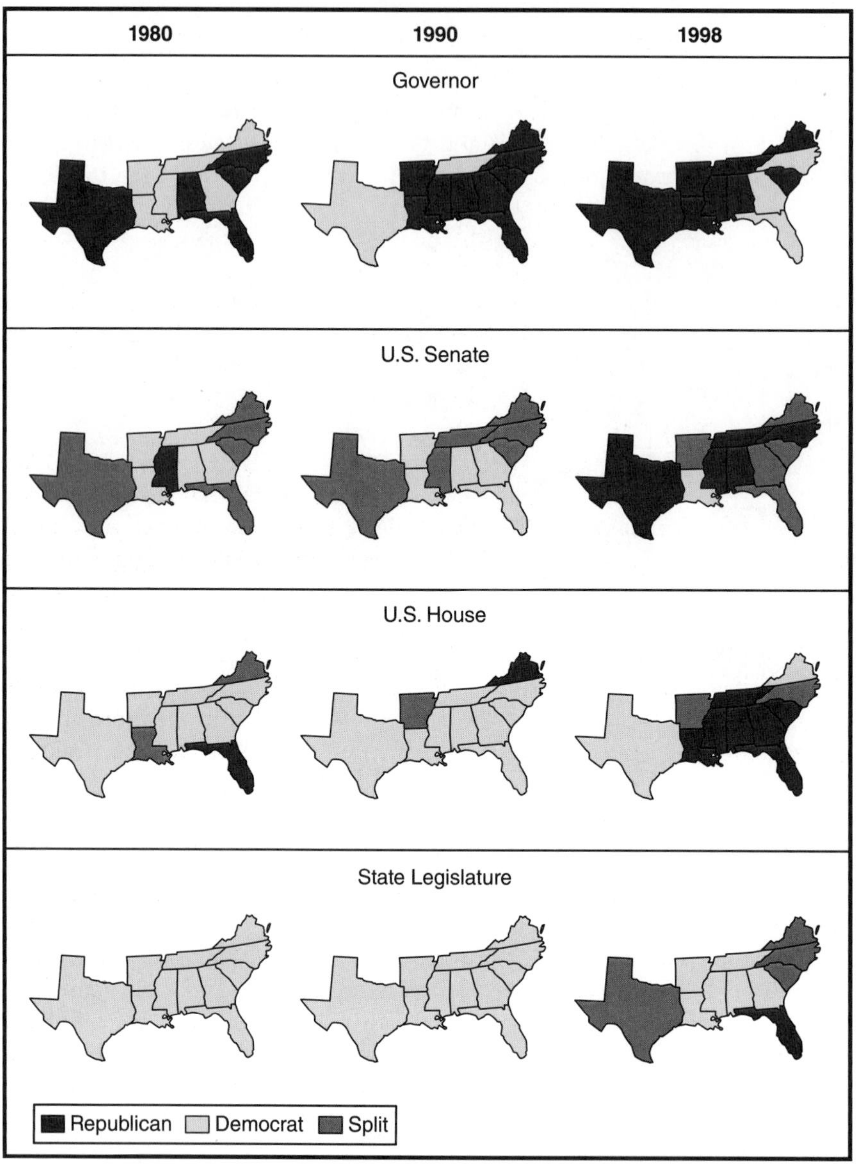

From the National Conference of State Legislators, *Almanac of American Politics*. The *New York Times*, March 16, 1998.

6. Two Southern Politicians, a Republican and a Democrat, Candidly Discuss Politics, 1981, 1982

Interview with Unidentified Republican Official, 1981

Official. As to the whole Southern strategy that Harry Dent [Republican strategist from South Carolina] and others put together in 1968, opposition to the Voting Rights Act would have been a central part of keeping the South. Now [the new Southern strategy] doesn't have to do that. All you have to do to keep the South is for Reagan to run in place on the issues he's campaigned on since 1964 ... and that's fiscal conservatism, balancing the budget, cut taxes, you know, the whole cluster....

Questioner: But the fact is, isn't it, that Reagan does get to the [George] Wallace voter and to the racist side of the Wallace voter by doing away with Legal Services, by cutting down on food stamps...?

[The official answered by pointing to what he said was the abstract nature of the race issue today.]

Official: You start out in 1954 by saying "Nigger, nigger, nigger." By 1968 you can't say "nigger"—that hurts you. Backfires. So you say stuff like forced busing, states' rights, and all that stuff. You're getting so abstract now [that] you're talking about cutting taxes, and all these things you're talking about are totally economic things and a by-product of them is [that] blacks get hurt worse than whites. And subconsciously maybe that is part of it. I'm not saying that. But I'm saying that if it is getting that abstract, and that coded, that we are doing away with the racial problem one way or the other. You follow me—because obviously sitting around saying, "We want to cut this," is much more abstract than even the busing thing *and* a hell of a lot more abstract than "Nigger, nigger."...

Interview with U.S. Representative David R. Bowen (D-Miss.), 1982

Yes, it was a little bit [like walking a tightrope]. Of course, I had a lot of very conservative white people supporting me, a lot of conservative farmers and businessmen, people like that. And at the same time a large bloc of the black community. I think if you don't have a hard-core doctrinaire position on something in which you lock yourself in by saying, "I am a liberal and I believe in a liberal program, which is the following," and therefore you sort of announce that "I am going after labor votes and black votes and that's that and if I can pick up any more on friendship or personal charm or on whatever, well, I'll get a few more someplace else." That's one way.

Or you can go to the other side and say, "I am a conservative and I am going to get business votes and wealthy farmer votes and I am going to pick up any others wherever I can." Obviously, I was not either of those two extremes.... And I had no particular reason to be....

It's easy enough when you are in [the first] campaign to make everybody happy because you never had to vote on anything … but how'd you stay in office for ten years? I think I just didn't do anything to alienate either of those two blocs that I had put together. Obviously, there were a lot of white votes I didn't get. Because if my high-water mark was 70 percent of the votes and I was getting maybe 90 percent of the black votes, there were a lot of white votes I was not getting. But my voting record was often on the conservative side, but it varied across the middle of the board. It was not far right or far left. In all these national organizations that rate you, I might range from 35 to 85.… My ADA [Americans for Democratic Action] and liberal-type votes were usually in the low numbers. The conservative organizations were more often in the high numbers, but usually in the middle ranges somewhere.

So it was not a very doctrinaire sort of pattern. You could look at it and you could say, "I don't know whether it falls under liberal or conservative." That's pretty much the way it was. No one could really stamp me as a liberal or a conservative. I never did anything to alienate the black support that I had. I never did anything to alienate the business support that I had. There were never very many issues that came along which were kind of no-win issues where you would totally outrage half the people whatever you did.…

Take things like food stamps.… Theoretically, a lot of the people who do not receive food stamps are against them. Of course, almost all the black community is for them as well as a lot of the whites. I'm on the Ag[riculture] Committee and I have to write food stamp legislation. Of course, blacks stayed with me because I voted for food stamps. And [to] the whites, I was able to explain that I was tightening up the legislation, improving it. And it would have been a lot more costly and a lot less efficient if I were not in there trying to put amendments in there to improve it—conditions that require recipients to register for work and accept work if it is offered and to make sure that people don't draw food stamps who are able-bodied and unwilling to work. So, generally those conservatives who would cuss and holler about food stamps all the time would say, "Well, David's doing a good job trying to improve the program. They are going to pass the thing … anyhow. He's in there trying to improve it, trying to tighten it up, trying to cut out the fraud, the waste." But I would certainly vote for the program after I got through tightening it up.

So, … what makes good politicians, I guess, is someone who can take whatever his vote is and do a good job of explaining it.… If you can explain it to those who are against it and make them like it, even though you voted for it, and then, of course, let the ones who are for it know that you voted for it … then you are in good shape. And I think that is probably what I did.… It's just kind of a matter of personal skill and packaging what you do and explaining it.

7. Southern Baptists Apologize for Endorsing Slavery, Segregation, and Racism, 1995

Declaration of Repentance

Historical Perspective

Since its founding in 1845, the Southern Baptist Convention has been a leader in missions, evangelism, and social ministry. However, our relation to persons of African descent has been less than ideal. One of the precipitating factors (though not the only factor) in the formation of the Southern Baptist Convention was the desire to appoint missionaries who owned slaves. In later years Southern Baptists, though the dominant Christian denomination in the South, did not take bold initiatives to secure the civil rights of Black people. In recent years progress has been made in the integration of churches and the passage of resolutions on racial reconciliation. While we cannot undo the past, we desire to express our sense of grief for the injustice of our former days.

Definition

We believe racism begins with the unproven theory that one's race is superior to another race in intellectual, spiritual, physical and/or cultural traits, then acts in a discriminatory and prejudicial way toward what one considers an "inferior" race or perpetuates an institutionalized racist system through inaction and/or silence.

Rejection of Racism

We wholeheartedly reject all forms of racism. We join Billy Graham in asserting, "Racism ... in the world and in the church ... is a sin and we need to label it as such ... (it) is a sin precisely because it keeps us from obeying Christ's command to love our neighbor and because it has its roots in pride and arrogance" (*Christianity Today*, October 4, 1993, p. 27).

Repentance

We publicly repent and apologize to all persons of African descent for condoning and perpetuating individual and systematic racism in our lifetime. Though we may not have personally participated in such distant acts of evil (i.e. slavery), we continued to reap the bitter harvest of the resulting inequality. We recognize that the racism which plagues our culture today is inextricably tied to the past and we must be continually willing to confront it anew.

Therefore, we ask for the forgiveness of our brothers and sisters of African descent. In doing so, we acknowledge that our own healing is at stake, that

"Resolution No. 1—On Racial Reconciliation on the 150th Anniversary of the Southern Baptist Convention," from *The Annual of Southern Baptist Convention, 1995.* Reprinted by permission.

racism impedes our own development as a people and discredits the Gospel we proclaim. We believe that racism negates the liberating and reconciling work of Christ. It is therefore our fervent hope and prayer that by acknowledging and repenting of the sins of the past we will be freed to live in justice and peace in the present.

Resolution No. 1: On Racial Reconciliation on the 150th Anniversary of the Southern Baptist Convention

WHEREAS, Since its founding in 1845, the Southern Baptist Convention has been an effective instrument of God in missions, evangelism, and social ministry; and

WHEREAS, The Scriptures teach that Eve is the mother of all living (Genesis 3:20), and that God shows no partiality, but in every nation whoever fears him and works righteousness is accepted by him (Acts 10:34–35), and that God has made from one blood every nation of men to dwell on the face of the earth (Acts 17:26); and

WHEREAS, Our relationship to African-Americans has been hindered from the beginning by the role that slavery played in the formation of the Southern Baptist Convention; and

WHEREAS, Many of our Southern Baptist forbears defended the right to own slaves, and either participated in, supported, or acquiesced in the particularly inhumane nature of American slavery; and

WHEREAS, in later years Southern Baptists failed, in many cases, to support, and in some cases opposed, legitimate initiatives to secure the civil rights of African-Americans; and …

WHEREAS, Many of our congregations have intentionally and/or unintentionally excluded African-Americans from worship, membership, and leadership; and

WHEREAS, Racism profoundly distorts our understanding of Christian morality, leading some Southern Baptists to believe that racial prejudice and discrimination are compatible with the Gospel; and

WHEREAS, Jesus performed the ministry of reconciliation to restore sinners to a right relationship with the Heavenly Father, and to establish right relations among all human beings, especially within the family of faith.

Therefore, be it RESOLVED, that we, the messengers to the Sesquicentennial meeting of the Southern Baptist Convention, assembled in Atlanta, Georgia, June 20–22, 1995, unwaveringly denounce racism, in all its forms, as deplorable sin.…

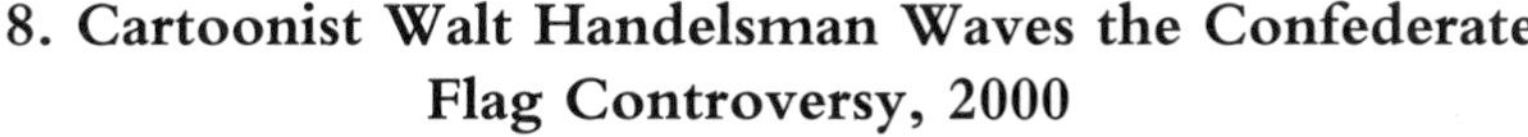

8. Cartoonist Walt Handelsman Waves the Confederate Flag Controversy, 2000

Walt Handelsman

9. Obama Strikes a Southern Strategy for a New, Blue Dixie, 2008

It was hot as Hades on June 5 in the little mountain town of Bristol, Virginia. But that didn't stop hundreds of southwest Virginians—in the most staunchly Republican part of a state that hadn't voted Democratic for president since 1964—from streaming into the local high school gym to whoop it up for a liberal, mixed-race fellow from Chicago with a mighty suspicious moniker. Fresh off his lopsided, nomination-clinching primary victory in North Carolina, Barack Obama had chosen—to the mystification of political experts—to launch his general election campaign not in the "battlegrounds" of Pennsylvania or Ohio but in a remote Southern backwater containing 17,000 souls who'd given George W. Bush 64 percent of their vote in 2004.

Strangest of all, he spoke to these people in exactly the same way he had addressed stadiums full of urbanites in Philadelphia or Cleveland. "It's not just struggles overseas. It's also struggles here at home that are causing so much anxiety," he declared without the merest hint of a drawl. "Everywhere I go, I meet people. They are struggling to get by. We just went through an economic expansion period … where corporate profits were up, the stock market was up … and the average family income went down by a thousand dollars. The

Walt Handelsman, *The New Orleans Picayune.*

first time it had ever happened since World War II where the economy's growing, but you have less money in your pocket."

The folks in Bristol cheered at that, and they listened attentively as Obama detailed his healthcare plan. But what brought them to their feet was this: "When I announced [my candidacy] I was convinced the American people were tired of being divided—divided by race, divided by religion, divided by region."

From the start of his campaign, when he brashly promised to compete and win in Southern states, Obama grasped something that only Howard Dean, among Democratic heavyweights, had recognized: not only was the South changing fast, demographically and culturally, but nobody had more reason to be sick to death of all those artificial divisions than Southerners themselves. For forty years, the South had been shunned and denigrated by national Democrats who looked at the country's largest chunk of voters and saw nothing but a uniform sea of racist, fundamentalist, xenophobic dimwits.

Efforts to appeal to these mental and moral midgets, Democratic pundit Tom Schaller argued in his much-cited 2006 book, *Whistling Past Dixie*, had only watered down the party's progressive message. "When Democrats give the president authority to start a preemptive war in Iraq, they accede to Southern bellicosity," Schaller wrote. "When Democrats go soft on defending social policies, they lend credence to the Southernized, 'starve the beast' mentality of governance. When Democrats scramble around to declare that they, too, have moral values, they kneel in the pews of southern evangelism. This absurdist catering to the worst fitting, least supportive component of the Democratic coalition must cease."

"Everybody always makes the mistake of looking South," John Kerry repeatedly huffed during the 2004 primaries. Like Al Gore before him, Kerry avoided that "mistake" with a vengeance, shutting down his campaign efforts in every Southern state but Florida before Labor Day and refusing to set foot, even once, in Democratic-trending states like Virginia during the general election campaign. The South? Republicans could have it.

Obama begged to differ. Conventional wisdom advised Democratic presidential candidates to bend over backward to look like "regular" Southern guys–tote a gun, adopt an accent, pretend to be a NASCAR freak, run around with a Holy Bible tucked under each arm and, if all else failed, campaign atop a hay bale (as Michael Dukakis once did in North Carolina). Obama, precisely the kind of Democrat who was supposed to be an impossible sell in the South, eschewed such fakery. He looked South and saw not stereotypes but—wonder of wonders!—Americans.

The Senator from Illinois showed up to campaign not just in exploding urban and suburban areas (where he won big) but also in towns like Bristol. He talked—seriously, soberly, in detail—about healthcare, the climate crisis, education and kitchen-table economics. He understood that while most Southerners remain cultural traditionalists, they are also increasingly progressive on economic and environmental issues. That insight best explains why Obama won three of the region's five largest states (Virginia, North Carolina and Florida), and earned the fifty-five electoral votes that lifted him from a narrow victory to a landslide.

And voilà! The wedge issues that had fueled the GOP's Southern successes ever since Richard Nixon became afterthoughts, not obsessions—try as the Republicans did to stoke the same old fires. It was in Guilford County, North Carolina, where Sarah Palin made her controversial proclamation that she was happy to be in "Real America." On election day, Guilford County went 59 to 41 percent for Obama, a nine-point swing from 2004.

As soon as the incongruous results from Dixie came in, the pundits and pols began scrambling to explain them away. Surely something fluky had happened. Obama had won, some said, on the strength of record black turnout and support—eliding the fact that he'd won considerably more white votes in the region than Kerry, and that the most heavily black states in the South had remained Republican. It had been such a historically lousy year for Republicans, others insisted, that they were bound to lose even some Southern turf—ignoring the fact that Obama made his gains by out-organizing Southern Republicans for the first time in modern history. (In North Carolina alone, the campaign had fifty field offices and more than 20,000 volunteers.)

Regionwide, Obama won the majority of the under-35 vote from all races. He doubled Kerry's vote among young white evangelicals. He blew McCain away among Latinos—the South's swing vote of the future. And he did it with the same message and same organizing that fueled his victory in the rest of the country. America, he said shortly before the election in another Virginia town, Roanoke, "will rise or fall as one nation."

As we say in the South, it's about damn time.

ESSAYS

In the first essay historian Dan T. Carter examines the southern strategy employed by Richard Nixon to win the presidency in 1968. Bringing in Strom Thurmond as his political ally, Nixon, with the help of his vice presidential candidate Spiro Agnew, emulated the techniques of his most important opponent in the primaries, George Wallace of Alabama. Carter argues that issues of race led to the rise of the Conservative Right in southern politics and, following Wallace's example, Nixon used this rising tide of conservative opposition to federal activism but without mentioning race. It was Wallace, Carter argues, whose ideas shaped the Republican agenda from then on; this essay helps to explain how the Republican party triumphed in 1968 and why it continued to veer to the right for decades afterward. In the second essay, history professors Matthew D. Lassiter and Kevin M. Kruse tie the increasing suburbanization of southern cities to the political alignment of Republican voters. Suburbs with their low crime rates, mostly independent school districts, and homogeneous neighborhoods provided the setting for a conservative voting bloc. "Southern Republicanism… thrived in the region's new suburbs," and, as shown in the previous essay, Nixon won his 1968 bid for the presidency via his southern strategy. Lassiter and Kruse argue that Nixon built his base from the middle-class suburbs of large cities across the South. In recent decades the suburbs have become more ethnically diverse. The results of the 2008 election suggest that another political realignment may have taken place in suburbia, one that gave rise to Bill Clinton, Al Gore, and Barack Obama. The last essay by historian Marjorie Julian Spruill speaks both to the region's rising feminism and to its conservative counterpart, which thrived in the suburbs described by Lassiter and Kruse. Congress established the International Women's Year with a $5 million appropriation for a conference scheduled to take place in Houston, Texas, in 1977. Conservative Mississippi women, fearing that the Equal Rights Amendment and legalized abortion would destroy traditional family values, made plans to attend the conference in Houston and vote against the "feminist agenda." The civil rights movement was a force in creating a feminine backlash. Mississippi conservatives saw federal intervention in any form as anathema and took their views to the Houston Conference. Professor Spruill argues that the Mississippi delegation's issues eventually became the Republican Party's issues as well. Yet, she notes, "the IWY experience solidified coalitions and networks for both conservatives and feminists."

Richard Nixon, George Wallace, and the Rise of the Conservative Right

DAN T. CARTER

After his hairbreadth loss to John Kennedy in 1960, Richard Nixon had played the role of the magnanimous loser, congratulating Kennedy and discouraging supporters who wanted to challenge questionable election returns from precincts in Mayor Daley's Chicago. Two years later, faced with another heartbreaking loss to California governor Pat Brown, his mask of control slipped; exhausted, hung over, and trembling with rage, he had stalked into the press room of his campaign headquarters and lashed out at assembled newsmen in rambling remarks so incoherent that reporters—who are not noted for their empathy for wounded politicians—sat in silent embarrassment. For ten minutes (though it seemed like hours to his staff) the former vice president alternated between mawkish self-pity and bitter attacks on the press, which he blamed for his defeat. He closed with the line memorable for its unintended irony: "Well, you won't have Nixon to kick around anymore, because, gentlemen, this is my last press conference...." As stunned aids Herbert Klein and H. R. Haldeman pulled him from the room, the defeated candidate was unrepentant. "I finally told those bastards off, and every Goddamned thing I said was true."

From Dan T. Carter, *The Politics of Rage: George Wallace, the Origins of the New Conservatism, and the Transformation of American Politics* (Baton Rouge: Louisiana State University Press. Revised edition, 2000), pp. 324–334, 337–338, 345, 347–349, 362–367, and 465–468. Reprinted by permission of the author.

By December 1967, memories of his losses had faded. With the determination that had led his Duke Law School classmates to dub him Richard the Grind, Nixon fought his way back to political center stage....

If there was a turning point in the political recovery of Richard Nixon, it had come in 1964. Faced with the likelihood that his party would nominate conservative standard-bearer Barry Goldwater (and the certainty he would suffer a smashing defeat), the former vice president introduced the Arizona senator at the convention and then dutifully delivered more than one hundred and fifty speeches for Republican candidates in thirty-six states, always emphasizing his support for Goldwater even as he distanced himself from the nominee's more extreme positions. By the time the votes were counted in the Johnson landslide, Nixon had compiled a staggering number of chits from conservative and moderate Republicans. When he embarked on an equally aggressive speaking schedule for party candidates in the 1966 off-year elections, he became the odds-on favorite for the GOP nomination in 1968. And the long-coveted prize—the presidency—appeared within reach as the Democratic Party seemed to implode....

In the two years after the 1964 election, Nixon traveled 127,000 miles, visited forty states, and spoke to four hundred groups, nearly half of them in the South. On his southern swings, he was conservative, but not too conservative; a defender of civil rights, but always solicitous of white southerners' "concerns." He often prefaced his remarks with a reminder that he had supported the Supreme Court's decision in 1954 as well as the Civil Rights Acts of 1964 and the Voting Rights Act of 1965. His bona fides established, he would then launch into a stern lecture on the problem of "riots, violence in the streets and mob rule," or he would take a few swings at the "unconscionable boondoggles" in Johnson's poverty program or at the federal courts' excessive concern for the rights of criminals. The real culprits in the nation's racial conflicts were the "extremists of both races," he kept saying....

During one of those southern forays in the spring of 1966, Nixon traveled to Columbia, South Carolina, for a fund-raising dinner for the South Carolina GOP. Senator Strom Thurmond had easily assumed command of the state's fledgling Republican Party when he officially switched to the GOP during the Goldwater campaign. In the years after his 1948 presidential run, he modulated his rhetoric and shifted the focus of his grim maledictions to the "eternal menace of godless, atheistic Communism." He had even learned (when pressed) to pronounce the word "Negro" without eliciting grimaces from his northern fellow Republicans. But race remained his subtext; he continued to Red-bait every spokesman for civil rights from Whitney Young of the Urban League to Stokely Carmichael of the Black Panthers. For the traditional southern campaign chorus of "Nigger-nigger-nigger," he substituted the Cold War battle cry: "Commie-Commie-Commie." On the eve of Nixon's visit, Thurmond was still attacking the civil rights movement, still accusing the Supreme Court of fostering "crime in the streets" and of promoting "a free rein for communism, riots, agitation, collectivism and the breakdown of moral codes."

The senator assigned Harry Dent to act as the vice president's host. Despite Nixon's reputation as wooden and aloof, he charmed Thurmond's aide by bluntly acknowledging his presidential aspirations and soliciting advice. He had no illusions about the difficulties of getting the nomination and defeating Lyndon Johnson, he told Dent. But the man he feared most was George Wallace.

In his public statements, Nixon always professed to be unconcerned about the Alabama governor. As a third-party candidate, Wallace might hurt the GOP in the South, argued Nixon, but he would draw an equal number of votes from normally Democratic blue-collar voters in the North. "I don't think he'll get four million votes," said Nixon, who pointed to the dismal past experience of third-party candidates. Four million votes would translate into less than six percent of the expected turnout.

He was considerably more frank in his conversation with Dent.... If Wallace should "take most of the South," Nixon told Dent, as the Republican candidate he might be "unable to win enough votes in the rest of the country to gain a clear majority." Once the election went to the Democratic-controlled House of Representatives, the game was over.

Dent argued that Thurmond was the key to gaining the support of southern Republicans. Conservatives might privately deride the South Carolina senator as an egotistical fanatic, but his very estrangement from the traditional political process—his refusal to cooperate or compromise with fellow senators—made him the ideological measuring stick for southern GOP leaders baptized in the ideologically pure waters of Goldwater Republicanism.

At an afternoon press conference, Richard Nixon went out of his way to praise the former Dixiecrat. "Strom is no racist," he told reporters; "Strom is a man of courage and integrity." To Thurmond, laboring under the burden of his past as the "Dr. No" of American race relations, it was like being granted absolution from purgatory by the pope of American politics. Almost pathetically grateful, the senator seldom wavered in his support for Nixon in the years that followed.

Nixon's careful cultivation of southern white sensibilities and of power brokers like Thurmond paid off at the 1968 Republican convention....

Flanked by his impassioned sidekick, Strom Thurmond, Nixon summoned the southern delegations to his suite at the Hilton Plaza for a virtuoso performance. (The meeting was captured on tape by an enterprising *Miami Herald* reporter who persuaded a Florida delegate to carry a concealed recorder into Nixon's suite.) Nixon first reaffirmed his commitment to economic conservatism and a foreign policy resting upon equal parts of anticommunism and military jingoism. Still, the issue of race preoccupied the group. Once again, Nixon showed that he was the master of the wink, the nudge, the implied commitment. Without ever explicitly renouncing his own past support for desegregation, he managed to convey to his listeners the sense that, as President, he would do the absolute minimum required to carry out the mandates of the federal courts. In a Nixon administration, there would be no rush to "satisfy some professional civil-rights group, or something like that."

Although some members of his audience believed that George Wallace had the right solution ("take those bearded bureaucrats and throw them in the

Potomac") or that the golden-tongued Reagan was the more authentic conservative, the bitter memories of the Goldwater debacle made them pause and listen to Thurmond. "We have no choice, if we want to win, except to vote for Nixon," he insisted. "We must quit using our hearts and start using our heads." Believe me, he said, "I love Reagan, but Nixon's the one."

After the convention, Texas Republican senator John Tower described Nixon's southern brigade as the "thin gray line which never broke."...

They received their first reward with Nixon's announcement that Spiro Agnew would be his running mate.

A few weeks before the convention, the candidate had accompanied his old law partner, John Mitchell, to an Annapolis restaurant to meet Maryland's governor. Afterward, Nixon told an aide: "That guy Agnew is really an impressive fellow. He's got guts. He's got a good attitude." Although he concealed his decision to the last to gain maximum leverage, it was a done deal....

The former Maryland governor seemed perfectly suited for the job....

What really sold Nixon, however, was the Maryland governor's performance during the five-day Baltimore race riot that followed Martin Luther King's assassination in April 1968. As the city returned to some degree of normality, Agnew summoned one hundred mainstream black city leaders—respected community organizers, middle-class preachers, lawyers, businessmen, and politicians—to a conference in Annapolis. Instead of holding a joint discussion, the governor lashed out at his audience's failure to condemn the "circuit-riding Hanoi-visiting ... cater-wauling, riot-inciting, burn-American-down type of leader[s]" who, he said, had caused the rioting in the city. Pointing his finger for emphasis, he accused the moderates of "breaking and running" when faced with the taunts of "Uncle Tom" from black radicals like Stokely Carmichael and H. Rap Brown. Three fourths of his audience—many still exhausted from long days and nights on the street trying to calm the rioters—angrily walked out of the meeting. These were the "very people who were trying to end the riots," pointed out the executive director of the city's Community Relations Commission, but Baltimore's television stations reported a flood of telephone calls supporting the governor....

By the end of August, George Wallace held a commanding lead in the Deep South and trailed Nixon narrowly in much of the remainder of the region. In the long run, Nixon believed, Dixie's heartland—Mississippi, Alabama, Louisiana, and Georgia—would come home to the Republican Party because the national Democrats, sensitive to their black constituency, could not appeal to the region's racially conservative white voters. In the meantime, the GOP nominee abandoned his original goal of a southern sweep and adopted a modified Southern Strategy. Thurmond would give him South Carolina; he would work to carry the border South. His main weapon would be Spiro Agnew, who soon began sounding like a rather dignified clone of George Wallace....

A Chattanooga Baptist preacher heralded Wallace's reemergence on the campaign trail with an apocalyptic invocation: "Outside the visible return of Jesus Christ," shouted the Reverend John S. Lanham, "the only salvation of the country is the election of George Wallace." In the city's ramshackle municipal auditorium six thousand Tennessee farmers, factory employees and white-collar workers, small businessmen and retirees gave the Alabamian eleven standing ovations as he laid out his lambasted back-alley muggers, urban rioters, HEW bureaucrats, federal judges, and—most of all—the "out-of-touch politicians" who led the Democratic and Republican parties. "You could put them all in an Alabama cotton picker's sack, shake them up and dump them out; take the first one to slide out and put him right back into power and there would be no change."...

At least a dozen articles that appeared during the 1968 campaign compared Wallace to Louisiana's "Kingfish," Huey Long. Both were authoritarian, but the Kingfish rejected the politics of race. In speech after speech Wallace knit together the strands of racism with those of a deeply rooted xenophobic "plain folk" cultural outlook which equated social change with moral corruption. The creators of public policy—the elite—were out of touch with hardworking taxpayers who footed the bill for their visionary social engineering at home and weak-minded defense of American interests abroad. The apocalyptic rhetoric of anticommunism allowed Wallace to bridge the gap between theocratic and "moral" concerns and the secular issues of government economic policy, civil rights, and foreign policy....

The trick, for candidates who hoped to benefit from the "Wallace factor," was to exploit the grievances he had unleashed while disentangling themselves from the more tawdry trappings of his message. The Republican number-crunchers knew the figures by heart: eighty percent of southern Wallace voters preferred Nixon to [Democratic presidential candidate Hubert] Humphrey; by a much narrower margin, northern Wallace voters preferred Humphrey to Nixon. How could they drive the southern Wallace voters into the GOP without disturbing those in the North? That balancing act was proving more difficult than Nixon had imagined, particularly since he wanted to run a nondivisive campaign.

The counterattack against the Wallace threat to the Southern Strategy was executed by Strom Thurmond's assistant Harry Dent....

Dent repeatedly insisted that neither the Southern Strategy nor Nixon's generally conservative emphasis in 1968 was racist. And, in fact, he (like other members of the Nixon team) scrupulously avoided explicit references to race. The problem with the liberalism of the Democrats, Dent charged, was not that it was too problack, but that it had created an America in which the streets were "filled with radical dissenters, cities were literally burning down, crime seemed uncontrollable," and the vast social programs of the Democrats were creating an army of the permanently dependent even as they bankrupted the middle class. The rising tide of economic and social conservatism clearly complemented opposition to federal activism, north and south.

But the political driving force of Nixon's policies toward the South was *not* an abstract notion about the "preservation of individual freedom"; almost every aspect of the 1968 campaign was tightly interwoven with issues of race....

In much the same way, racial fears were linked to concerns over social disorder in American streets. The threat of crime was real; every index of criminality showed an increase in the number of crimes against property and in crimes of violence. Americans were still more likely to be maimed or killed by their friends and relatives than by strangers, but the growth of random, brutal urban violence—an escalation of black-on-white violence attracted the most attention—made law and order an inevitable issue in the 1960s.

And Wallace simply erased the line between antiwar and civil rights protests, between heckling protesters and street muggers. By the fall, Nixon and even Humphrey were attempting to play catch-up with the crime issue, although both went to great lengths to insist that the issue was nonracial. (As the former vice president pointed out on several occasions, blacks were far more likely to be the victims of crime than whites were.) Occasionally, the façade slipped. Early in the campaign Nixon had taped a television commercial attacking the decline of "law and order" in American cities. As he reviewed it with his staff, he became expansive. That "hits it right on the nose," he said enthusiastically. "It's all about law and order and the damn Negro-Puerto Rican groups out there." Nixon did not have to make the racial connection any more than would Ronald Reagan when he began one of his famous discourses on welfare queens using food stamps to buy porterhouse steaks. His audience was already primed to make that connection.

For nearly a hundred years after the Civil War, politicians had manipulated the racial phobias of whites below the Mason-Dixon line to maintain a solidly Democratic South. To Nixon it seemed only poetic justice that the tables should be turned. The challenge lay in appealing to the fears of angry whites without appearing to become an extremist and driving away moderates....

Ultimately, an enormous gender gap emerged: women—particularly non-southern women—proved far less willing than men to vote for the Alabama politician. In the eleven states of the old Confederacy, half of the men and forty percent of the women were ready to vote for Wallace in late September, at the high-water mark of his campaign. In the North, one-fifth of white males claimed he had their vote, but less than half that number of women supported him.

Cultural and regional differences undoubtedly played a role, but the reason women most often volunteered for opposing Wallace was that he was "dangerous." In his public performances—the speeches and rallies—Wallace often teetered along a razor's edge of violence. Where Nixon and Humphrey hated the hecklers and demonstrators, particularly the antiwar demonstrators, who appeared on the campaign trail, Wallace welcomed them, and had become a master at manipulating them....

And in one rally after another, Wallace's angry rhetoric ignited fist-swinging, chair-throwing confrontations between these hardcore followers and antiwar and civil rights demonstrators, who on occasion pelted the candidate with various objects. Wallace was hit by rocks, eggs, tomatoes, pennies, a peace medallion, Tootsie Rolls, a sandal, and a miniature whiskey bottle. By October, television crews always set up two cameras: one to focus on the stage, the other to capture the mêlées and bloodied demonstrators in the audience.

Wallace's troubles gave Nixon the opening he needed....

During the last two weeks of the campaign, Nixon took to the air himself in advertisements specifically tailored to white southern voters: "There's been a lot of double-talk about the role of the South"—by which he meant the white people of the South—"in the campaign of nineteen sixty-eight, and I think it's time for some straight talk," he told his listeners. Without mentioning Wallace by name, Nixon warned that a "divided vote" would play into the hands of the Humphrey Democrats. "And so I say, don't play their game. Don't divide your vote. Vote for ... the only team that can provide the new leadership that America needs, the Nixon-Agnew team. And I pledge to you we will restore law and order in this country...."

October 24, 1968, was overcast and drizzly, but unseasonably warm for New York City. More than a thousand police—a hundred of them on horseback—lined up on Seventh Avenue between West Thirty-first and West Thirty-third streets as the crowds began to pour into Madison Square Garden. Twenty thousand of the faithful packed the arena by eight P.M. for the largest political rally held in New York City since Franklin Roosevelt had denounced the forces of "organized money" from the same stage in 1936. At eight-twenty, George Wallace stepped out into the lights and the audience erupted. Although the campaign had another week to run, for Wallace, the evening was the emotional climax of his race for the presidency....

Inside the Garden, while a brass band played a medley of patriotic songs, Wallace strode back and forth across the stage, saluting the crowd, which roared his name again and again in a chant that could be heard by the demonstrators half a block away. Soon he was joined by Curtis LeMay and his wife, Helen.

After more than fifteen minutes, Wallace finally brought his followers to order by having a country singer perform "God Bless America." Apparently overwhelmed by the fervor of the crowd, he began his speech awkwardly. In the southwest balcony of the Garden, a squarely built black man stood and held up a poster proclaiming "Law and Order—Wallace Style." Underneath the slogan was the outline of a Ku Klux Klansman holding a noose. Another demonstrator at his side suddenly turned on a portable bullhorn and began shouting: "Wallace talks about law and order! Ask him what state has the highest murder rate! The most rapes! The most armed robberies." The overwhelmingly pro-Wallace crowd exploded in rage, and police hurried to rescue three suddenly silent black demonstrators who were surrounded by a dozen Wallace followers shouting "Kill 'em, kill 'em, kill 'em."

The heckling seemed to ignite the Alabama governor: "Why do the leaders of the two national parties kowtow to these anarchists?" he demanded, gesturing toward the protesters in the balcony. "One of 'em laid down in front of President Johnson's limousine last year," said Wallace with a snarl. "I tell you when November comes, the first time they lie down in front of my limousine it'll be the last one they'll ever lay down in front of; their day is *over*!"

The crowd was on its feet for the first of more than a dozen standing ovations.

"We don't have a sick society, we have a sick Supreme Court," he continued, as he scornfully described "perverted" decisions that disallowed prayer in the classrooms even as they defended the right to distribute "obscene pornography."

Fifteen minutes into his talk, he shed his jacket as he weaved and bobbed across the stage, his right fist clenched, his left jabbing out and down as if he were in the midst of one of his youthful bantamweight Golden Gloves bouts. "We don't have riots in Alabama," shouted Wallace. "They start a riot down there, first one of 'em to pick up a brick gets a bullet in the brain, that's all. And then you walk over to the next one and say, 'All right, pick up a brick. We just want to see you pick up one of them bricks, now!'"...

Richard Nixon always saw the Alabama governor as the key to understanding the reshaping of American politics. Nearly twenty years after the former President left office in disgrace, historian Herbert Parmet interviewed him for a biography, *Richard Nixon and His America.* At the end of his fourth and last question-and-answer session, Parmet methodically outlined the conservative shifts Nixon had made after 1970 to placate the Wallace constituency.

"Your point is that we had to move to the right in order to cut Wallace off at the pass?" asked Nixon.

"Absolutely," replied Parmet.

"Foreign policy was my major concern. You start with that," said Nixon. "To the extent that we thought of it [the Wallace movement] at all—maybe subconsciously—anything that might weaken my base because of domestic policy reasons had to give way to the foreign policy priorities." There was "no question that all these things must have been there.... I think," he added, "it's a pretty clear-headed analysis." It was as close as the proud Nixon would ever come to admitting that, when George Wallace had played his fiddle, the President of the United States had danced Jim Crow.

In the decorous landscape of upscale malls, suburban neighborhoods, and prosperous megachurches that has become the heartland of the new conservatism, Ronald Reagan, not George Wallace, is the spiritual godfather of the nineties. During such moments of racial crisis as the spectre of cross-district busing, surburbanites occasionally turned to George Wallace in the 1960s and early 1970s to voice their protest, but he was always too unsettling, too vulgar, too overtly southern. With the exception of a few hard-line right-wingers like Patrick Buchanan, the former Alabama governor has been a prophet without honor, remembered (if at all) for his late-life renunciation of racism....

But two decades after his disappearance from national politics, the Alabama governor seems vindicated by history. If he did not create the conservative groundswell that transformed American politics in the 1980s, he anticipated most of its themes. It was Wallace who sensed and gave voice to a growing national white backlash in the mid-1960s; it was Wallace who warned of the danger to the American soul posed by the "intellectual snobs who don't know the difference between smut and great literature"; it was Wallace who railed against federal bureaucrats who not only wasted the tax dollars of hardworking Americans, but lacked the common sense to "park their bicycles straight." Not surprisingly, his rise to national prominence coincided with a growing loss of faith in the federal government. In 1964, nearly 80 percent of the American people told George Gallup's pollsters that they could trust Washington to "do what is right all or most of the time." Thirty years later, that number had declined to less than 20 percent.

If George Wallace did not create this mode of national skepticism, he anticipated and exploited the political transformation it precipitated. His attacks on the federal government have become the gospel of modern conservatism; his angry rhetoric, the foundation for the new ground rules of political warfare. In 1984, a young Republican Congressman from Georgia explained the facts of life to a group of young conservative activists. "The number one fact about the news media," said Newt Gingrich, "is they love fights. You have to give them confrontations." And they had to be confrontations in a bipolar political system of good and evil, right and wrong. The greatest hope for political victory was to replace the traditional give-and-take of American politics with a "battleground" between godly Republicans and the "secular anti-religious view of the left" embodied in the Democratic Party.

The notion of politics as a struggle between good and evil is as old as the Republic; that moral critique of American society lay at the very core of populism in the late nineteenth century. But angry reformers of an earlier generation had usually railed against the rich and powerful; Wallace turned the process on its head. He may have singled out "elitist" bureaucrats as symbols of some malevolent abstraction called "Washington," but everyone knew that his real enemies were the constituencies those federal officials represented; the marginal beneficiaries of the welfare state....

Much has changed in southern and American politics in the years since 1958 when George Wallace promised his friends that he would "never be out-niggered again." Middle- and upper-income suburbanites have fled the unruly public spaces of decaying central cities and created (or tried to create) a secure and controlled environment. Isolated from the expensive and frustrating demands of the growing urban underclass, suburbanites could control their own local government; they could buy good schools and safe streets—or at least better schools and safer streets than the inner city. "Big" government—the federal government—they complained, spent *their* hard-earned taxes for programs that were wasteful and inefficient and did nothing to help them....

George Wallace had recognized the political capital to be made in a society shaken by social upheaval and economic uncertainty. As the conservative revolution reached high tide, it was no accident that the groups singled out for relentless abuse and condemnation were welfare mothers and aliens, groups that are both powerless and, by virtue of color and nationality, outsiders. The politics of rage that George Wallace made his own had moved from the fringes of our society to center stage.

He was the most influential loser in twentieth-century American politics.

The Bulldozer Revolution: Suburbs and Southern History

MATTHEW D. LASSITER AND KEVIN M. KRUSE

A generation ago, a state-of-the-field forum on southern history would have included an entry on cities rather than suburbs. Ever since the World War II era, southern historians have followed the lead of V. O. Key Jr., who in 1949 predicted, "The growth of cities contains the seeds of political change for the South." Key and other contemporaries assumed that urban development would not only modernize but also liberalize southern politics, especially by shifting the balance of power away from "the black-belt whites [who had] succeeded in imposing their will on their states and thereby presented a solid regional front in national politics on the race issue." Before long, however, analysts recognized that "the first fruits of increasing industrialism" ... had not liberalized the South by empowering the labor movement but were instead fostering "a rising urban middle class, which is virtually Republican in political sympathies."...

Until quite recently, the suburbs had not played a central or often even an explicit role in the historical analysis of southern politics and society since World War II....

The suburbs of the postwar South, however, were home to many of the most dynamic and cutting-edge forces anywhere in the region. The suburbs provided the main locations for cold war military-industrial complexes and the power base of new Republican voters in the 1950s and 1960s. They became pivotal sites for the national battles over court-ordered busing in the 1970s and the mobilization of the Religious Right in the 1980s and 1990s. Southern suburbia also has long been the national pacesetter in the expansion of middle-class black communities and, since the 1980s, has emerged as the primary destination for Latino and Asian immigrants, who are radically altering the region's traditional biracial structure.

Despite the significance of suburban growth to the political culture and economy of the modern South, it was not until the so-called Gingrich Revolution of 1994 that the suburbs became a principal focus of efforts to explain regional change and electoral realignment. "Southern Republicanism especially thrived in the region's new suburbs," Earl Black and Merle Black clarified in 2002, most notably since the GOP's three most important leaders in the mid-1990s—Newt Gingrich of Georgia and Tom DeLay and Dick Armey of Texas—each "represented overwhelmingly white, suburban, middle-class districts in key southern metropolitan areas." Journalists Dan Balz and Ronald Brownstein highlighted the in-migration of white-collar voters from the North and Midwest in another study of the Republican breakthrough, arguing, "Almost every new housing development rising in the suburban and exurban counties of the South represented another potential Republican enclave and a further nail in the Democrats'

Matthew D. Lassiter and Kevin M. Kruse, "The Bulldozer Revolution: Suburbs and Southern History since World War II," *The Journal of Southern History,* LXXV (August 2009), pp. 691–706.

coffin." Reports from the U.S. Census Bureau confirmed the explosive growth of the suburban South and the parallels with booming areas in the suburban West, as the top four states for total population increase in the 1990s were California, Texas, Florida, and Georgia. During the same decade, seventy-six of the eighty-six fastest-growing counties in the nation were located in the South and West, with Atlanta second only to Phoenix among large metropolitan areas for the highest percentage increase in population. Between 2000 and 2005, seven of the top ten counties for rate of population expansion were in the South: four exurban counties outside Atlanta, Flagler County north of Daytona Beach, Rockwall County near Dallas, and Loudoun County in the northern Virginia suburbs. Across the South, as throughout the nation, the suburbs are increasingly the places to find leading political, economic, and social trends—including answers to the debate over partisan realignment that has long consumed southern historians.

In his famous 1958 essay "The Search for Southern Identity," C. Vann Woodward observed that a "Bulldozer Revolution" had "already leveled many of the old monuments of regional distinctiveness and may end eventually by erasing the very consciousness of a distinctive tradition along with the will to sustain it." In Woodward's view, the postwar South was rushing headlong into a complacent and conformist "pursuit of the American Way and the American Standard of Living" as the region underwent the fastest rate of metropolitan growth in the nation and experienced the swift triumph of a suburban-corporate value system....

The Bulldozer Revolution described by Woodward ... was a fully national phenomenon. During the postwar decades, federal programs played the most critical role in building the suburban South and simultaneously standardizing patterns of residential development and housing segregation across the nation. The Federal Housing Administration subsidized the private construction of all-white subdivisions and permitted open racial discrimination in the sale and rental of federally supported housing well into the 1960s. The interstate highway system promoted the sprawl of a horizontal metropolis designed around accommodation of the automobile, with easy downtown access for suburban commuters and the decentralization of office complexes and shopping malls near large-scale residential developments located on the fringe....

The insights of urban and suburban history provide a national framework for interpreting the "long civil rights movement" that emphasizes the importance of federal policies and grassroots struggles over race and space in southern cities and suburbs more than the traditional focus on the state-level politics of massive resistance. Dramatic stories about the so-called Second Reconstruction—when white southern defiance and segregationist violence forced federal intervention in a region that seemed once again to have seceded from American norms—have obscured the many ways in which racial conflicts in the metropolitan South mirrored those in other parts of the nation. When Little Rock, Greensboro, and Birmingham entered the national spotlight during the late 1950s and early 1960s, the cities themselves served mainly as the backdrops for a regional story about the collapse of Jim Crow. But as recent case studies have shown, the long-term battles in the cities and suburbs of the South involved the same issues that shaped the civil rights era in Chicago, Detroit, and Los Angeles—challenges to segregated housing patterns and "neighborhood schools," municipal planning for urban renewal and highway construction, and control over antipoverty programs and the distribution of low-income housing. At the same time, white flight to the suburbs represented the most successful form of resistance to the civil rights revolution, a "politics of suburban secession" evident across the nation." The rise of massive resistance in the South also reflected the widespread political malapportionment that enabled rural interests to dominate many state governments by effectively disenfranchising urban and suburban residents, until the U.S. Supreme Court established the principle of "one person, one vote" in the early 1960s. Reformers believed that reapportionment would finally shift power from the countryside to the cities, but the real winners in the long run turned out to be the fast-growing suburbs in the South and elsewhere across the nation.

For many southern and western cities, however, the ability to annex adjacent suburbs meant that metropolitan fragmentation proved less debilitating in the emerging Sun Belt than in the older urban centers of the North and Midwest. During the 1950s and 1960s, a remarkable 93 percent of population growth in the metropolitan South initially took place in suburbs, but only 55 to 60 percent of these new developments remained "suburban" (as a census category) because of the prompt annexation of the rest. Few cities in the nation spread as dramatically as Jacksonville, Florida, which expanded from 26 to 827 square miles between 1930 and 1968, when it consolidated with surrounding Duval County. The city of Miami's 1957 merger with suburban Dade County established the model for metropolitan consolidation in Florida, where each public school system operates at the countywide level. The major metropolises in Texas—Houston, Dallas, and San Antonio—each swallowed much of their suburban populations and grew in land area by a range of five to seven times as large during the 1930–1970 period.... Annexation fortified the central city tax base and limited the consequences of white flight by turning many southern suburbs into nominally urban neighborhoods, but middle-class areas increasingly mobilized to defend their political autonomy after issues such as racial integration and property taxation moved to center stage in the 1960s. The almost all-white suburban municipalities of Virginia Beach and Chesapeake, Virginia, were incorporated in 1963 to preempt involuntary annexation by Norfolk, and a few years later a grassroots suburban revolt ended annexation for good in metropolitan Atlanta. This strategy of suburban secession soon spread to other parts of the South, and regional growth trends since the late 1960s have corresponded more closely than ever to the northern model of metropolitan fragmentation.

Many of the vibrant suburbs that resisted annexation were prime examples of what social scientists later labeled the "rise of the gunbelt," the national growth of the military-industrial complex during World War II and the cold war. In sites throughout the South, from strategic coastal locations to the suburbs in congressional districts of powerful politicians, military bases and federal defense spending transformed the physical landscape, powered the local economy, and served as a magnet for additional high-tech industries and white-collar migrants. In Virginia's Norfolk/Hampton Roads area, federally financed suburban development accompanied the expansion of bases and shipyards during World War II and then grew explosively with the cold war arrival of the Atlantic commands for the U.S. Navy and NATO. Ripple effects from the construction of the Pentagon and the CIA headquarters likewise accelerated suburban growth and economic prosperity in the northern Virginia counties outside Washington, D.C.....

A suburban-centered vision reveals that demographic change played a more important role than racial demagoguery in the emergence of a two-party system in the American South. This analysis runs contrary to both the conventional wisdom and a popular strain in the scholarly literature: the claim that the GOP came to dominate a new Solid South by repackaging the segregationist platform of George C. Wallace and capitalizing on a racial backlash that originated in the Deep South and the countryside. According to *Whistling Past Dixie* (2006), a widely cited book by political scientist Thomas F. Schaller, Republican presidential candidates from Barry Goldwater through Ronald Reagan implemented a "southern strategy" with "initial appeal to rural southerners [that] has expanded to the suburbs and exurbs, and to states outside the South." This interpretation essentially reverses the actual process of realignment in the South and misleadingly attributes racial backlash nationwide to the effects of "southernization" rather than to the dynamics of suburbanization itself. The GOP's first southern beachheads clearly came in the high-growth and highly suburbanized states of Texas and Florida, as well as in middle-class suburban counties outside cities such as Atlanta, Charlotte, Nashville, and Washington, D.C..... In 1968 Richard M. Nixon won ... the outer South states by conceding the Deep South to the third-party Wallace campaign and building instead on Eisenhower's middle-class base, with large margins in the GOP's grassroots suburban strongholds. Resistance to the civil rights movement certainly motivated many of these white voters, but in ways similar to their Republican counterparts who lived in equally segregated suburbs outside the South....

Nixon won in 1968 and 1972 on the basis of a national suburban strategy framed by populist appeals to the "silent majority" and pledges to protect white middle-class neighborhoods from court-ordered busing, low-income housing, urban crime, and liberal welfare programs that allegedly sent their tax dollars to the inner-city poor. President Nixon made the same promises in the suburbs of Atlanta and Charlotte that he did outside Los Angeles and Detroit: his administration would enforce "color-blind" policies that guaranteed equal opportunity to individuals but would also defend "neighborhood schools" and exclusionary residential zoning because "forced integration of the suburbs is not in the national interest." During the 1970s, each of these metropolitan regions faced a civil rights lawsuit to integrate public schools by transporting students between the central city and the surrounding suburbs, part of a national conflict over court-ordered busing that set off an explosive grassroots backlash by the so-called silent majority. Of the four metropolises, only Charlotte ultimately implemented a two-way busing plan that included white neighborhoods in the suburbs because of the prior consolidation of the city schools with the surrounding system of Mecklenburg County. By the mid-1970s, public schools in the South had achieved the highest degree of racial integration of any section of the country, in part because the suburbs could not escape busing plans in the county wide districts common in North Carolina, Tennessee, and Florida. But the Supreme Court's refusal to order busing through the merger of urban and suburban systems exacerbated patterns of racial fragmentation in southern metropolises such as Atlanta and Richmond, with similar results in Boston, Detroit, and Los Angeles. In 1972 Nixon affirmed the national efficacy of this politics of suburban secession when he informed a Republican audience in Atlanta that his platform was "not a Southern strategy; it is an American strategy." He insisted that "the so-called Southern issues .... are the same here as they are in America."

With the discovery of the Sun Belt region in the 1970s, scholars and journalists alike began to recognize that the suburban South had become a leading indicator of national trends rather than simply part of an aberrant region that was slowly in the process of being "northernized" or "Americanized." Political strategist Kevin P. Phillips coined the term *Sun Belt* in *The Emerging Republican Majority* (1969), which credited Nixon's election in 1968 and the broader forces of conservative realignment to factors including "the rising insurgency of the South, the West, ... and middle-class suburbia." Phillips predicted an era of GOP dominance based on urban and especially suburban expansion in states such as Florida and Texas, where "the new white residential stretches are growing with a speed unmatched east of Southern California and Arizona."... In the presidential elections of 1980 and 1984, a large majority of white southerners joined a substantial majority of other white Americans in voting for the Reagan realignment, powered by the GOP's regional and national strength in the suburbs.

The rapid growth of the suburban South has opened up many new possibilities for research.... Among the most exciting recent developments are studies that evaluate the grassroots mobilization of the Religious Right as a specifically suburban and exurban phenomenon.... [T]he combination of militarization, massive white-collar in-migration, Protestant megachurches, and decentralized civic life also created fertile ground for conservative politics in similar Sun Belt suburbs in metropolitan Phoenix, Colorado Springs, Dallas-Fort Worth, and Atlanta. While the origins of the Religious Right can be traced to the rise of an ecumenical brand of Christian nationalism during the early cold war, a large number of the organizations founded to fight the "culture wars" of the 1970s and beyond emerged from Sun Belt boomtowns. Televangelist Jerry Falwell began his ministry in Lynchburg, Virginia, a southern mill village that evolved into a middle-class suburban city after General Electric and Babcock & Wilcox (a nuclear reactor manufacturer) opened plants in the 1950s. Falwell cofounded the Moral Majority in 1979 along with prominent pastors of megachurches in Atlanta, Fort Lauderdale, and San Diego that each drew members largely from the white upper-middle-class suburbs. That same year, televangelists James Robison of Fort Worth and Pat Robertson of Virginia Beach helped start the Religious Roundtable, and a decade later Robertson headquartered the Christian Coalition in the Norfolk suburbs. In the mid-to-late 1970s, the suburban Sun Belt also provided the base for Anita Bryant's grassroots campaign against gay rights in Miami-Dade County....

At the time of the GOP's takeover of Congress in 1994, when Gingrich and other Sun Belt conservatives promised to cut middle-class taxes and slash urban welfare programs, Cobb [County] was receiving more federal dollars per capita than any other suburban county in the nation except Arlington County in northern Virginia (home of the Pentagon and the CIA) and Brevard County in Florida (Kennedy Space Center). The latest trends have shown Democratic inroads in Cobb, however; Barack Obama won 44 percent of the 2008 vote, largely because the county's white population has declined to 64 percent, which points to another set of significant developments in the region's suburbs.

The racial and ethnic diversity of the suburban South has skyrocketed in recent decades, driven by spillover migration from central cities, a reverse "great migration" of black professionals from the North and Midwest, and the spread of Latino immigration beyond established gateways in Texas and Florida. The 2000 U.S. Census revealed the increasing heterogeneity of American suburbia, which had become home to 54 percent of Asian Americans, 49 percent of Hispanics, and 39 percent of African Americans. Seventeen of the twenty largest "melting pot metros," those with high minority populations in the suburbs, were located in the Sun Belt, with western states displaying the highest rates of Asian and Latino suburbanization and southern states home to more than half of the nation's African American suburbanites (6.8 of 11.9 million). Black suburbanization has a long history in the modern South, … including politically negotiated "Negro expansion" in the 1940s and 1950s through construction of middle-class subdivisions on the fringes of cities such as Atlanta and Dallas. A much greater number of African Americans moved into inner-ring suburbs in the 1960s, 1970s, and 1980s, part of a national pattern of racial turnover that did not substantially diminish patterns of residential segregation because many white families soon relocated to outer-ring suburbs and exurbs. Metropolitan Atlanta has remained at the cutting edge of these trends, with 68 percent of its black population residing in the suburbs by the end of the century, led by the transformation of DeKalb County from almost all white in the late 1960s to its current majority-black population (along with major Asian and Latino clusters).… African American and Latino migration … are each transforming the suburbs of Houston, Dallas, Miami-Fort Lauderdale, Orlando, Charlotte, Raleigh, and Washington, D.C.….

Important recent work on the globalization of the South has highlighted the boom in foreign investment that brought exurban manufacturing sites for Japanese and German automakers to the Piedmont's former textile belt, while Wal-Mart's homegrown style of capitalist development continues to remake international markets and transform suburbs and small towns into the homogenized strip-mall wastelands of C. Vann Woodward's nightmares. Although environmental historians often concentrate more on rural places and wilderness issues than on metropolitan development, a closer focus on the suburbs would reveal that the same forces that generated unrestrained sprawl also inspired middle-class campaigns for open-space preservation and slow-growth policies. Public policy scholars also have redefined environmentalism as a civil rights issue, charting the ways in which air and water pollution have combined with suburban exclusionary zoning to exacerbate racial and class inequalities....

The results of the 2008 presidential election, when Democratic candidate Barack Obama carried the large outer South states of Virginia, North Carolina, and Florida, offer another golden opportunity to move beyond the regional clichés of red-blue polarization and reconsider the declarations of a Republican Solid South that have distorted political analysis of late. In 2002, a little more than three decades after Kevin Phillips forecast a Republican realignment based in the suburbs and the Sun Belt, two liberal strategists predicted an "emerging Democratic majority" that would be driven by demographic changes in many of the very same high-growth and high-tech areas. "[A]s long as the Democrats maintain a fiscally moderate, socially liberal, reformist, and egalitarian outlook," John B. Judis and Ruy Teixeira proclaimed, "America's future lies in places like Silicon Valley and North Carolina's Research Triangle." Political scientists and historians have spent a lot of energy explaining how the New Right of Nixon, Reagan, and Gingrich emerged from the confluence of Sun Belt growth and civil rights backlash between the 1960s and the 1990s, but further exploration is needed to trace how the same conditions produced the "New Democratic" movement of Jimmy Carter, Bill Clinton, and Al Gore Jr. as well. In Sun Belt states such as Virginia and North Carolina, the Democratic Party has attracted white-collar suburban professionals who reject the social conservatism of the Religious Right, and it has capitalized on the votes of Latino and Asian migrants who are redrawing the region's electoral map once again. In northern Virginia's suburbs, which formed an early pillar of the Republican South in the 1950s and 1960s, minorities now make up 40 percent of the total in the most populous counties of Arlington and Fairfax and more than 30 percent in the fast-growing exurbs of Loudoun County. The Democrats are surging there, according to current governor Tim Kaine, because the party is newly attuned to "'quality of life' issues" such as "[o]vercrowded schools, highway congestion, sprawl, housing prices, and property taxes." In short, Kaine concludes, these voters are primarily concerned with "[h]ow to preserve the lifestyle they sought by moving to the suburbs."

The Mississippi 'Takeover': Feminists, Social Conservatives, and the International Women's Year Conference of 1977

MARJORIE JULIAN SPRUILL

In 1977, the eyes of the nation, which had focused on Mississippi during the civil rights movement, were again focused on the state. Advocates for change and defenders of tradition were again embattled, but this time the conflict was over women's rights. A series of federally-funded conferences in observance of

---

Marjorie Julian Spruill, "The Mississippi 'Takeover': Feminists, Social Conservatives, and the International Women's Year Conference of 1977" in *Mississippi Women: Their Histories, Their Lives* (Athens: University of Georgia Press, 2010), pp. 287–308.

International Women's Year (IWY) set the stage for the conflict which polarized and politicized Mississippi women.

The IWY conferences, convened in each state and territory and culminating in a National Women's Conference in Houston, Texas, were mandated by Congress in 1975 at the behest of the United Nations and leading feminists including Congresswoman Bella Abzug of New York. The goal was to involve a broad spectrum of American women in formulating a National Plan of Action to guide the federal government on policy regarding women: the congressional guidelines stipulated that the delegates elected to participate in the national IWY conference reflect the full diversity of the state's population. The National Commission on the Observance of International Women's Year, appointed by President Gerald Ford and (subsequently, President Jimmy Carter), was a predominantly feminist group that hoped the conferences would unite and expand the women's movement and move it beyond its white, middle-class base. In this the IWY was highly successful. However, the conferences also mobilized social conservatives across the United States who organized to challenge feminists for the right to speak for American women. And nowhere was the conservatives' challenge to feminists as dramatic as in Mississippi. At the July 8–9, 1977 IWY conference in Mississippi, conservatives managed to achieve a complete "takeover" which would have enduring consequences for Mississippi women and for state politics.

The modern women's rights movement, inspired and informed by the civil rights movement, was strongest outside the South, but it had considerable support in the region. In Mississippi, support was strongest in larger cities and university towns. It came from women's organizations, the press, and a number of prominent politicians including Lt. Governor Evelyn Gandy of Hattiesburg, elected in 1975, and William Winter of Grenada, who would be elected governor in 1979. Since 1972, when the Equal Rights Amendment (ERA)—a proposed amendment to the U.S. Constitution and a key feminist goal—was approved in Congress and sent to the states for ratification, it had been introduced repeatedly in the Mississippi legislature. Yet there was little chance it would be ratified in this conservative state. As a result women's rights advocates were far more vocal and visible in Mississippi than social conservatives who opposed their ideas generally and the ERA in particular. Until 1977, the conservatives saw little need to organize. This situation changed as a strong antifeminist movement emerged in the state in response to the IWY conferences.

At the national level the conflict between feminists and social conservatives developed gradually. In the late 1960s and early 1970s, the modern women's rights movement experienced phenomenal success. While internal divisions and militant participants played disproportionately and negatively in the media, the movement enjoyed widespread support. National politicians responded positively to many of demands of the feminists and seemed to accept them (at least, the more moderate feminists) as speaking for American women. For the most part, socially conservative women focused on other causes or were apolitical. As President Richard Nixon developed his "southern strategy," he focused on race rather than gender as he wooed white conservatives in the region.

To a limited degree, social conservatives, especially Catholics, began to mobilize as several states legalized abortion ... in the late 1960s. The major backlash against the women's rights movement came later, however, as a growing number of conservatives came to believe that the women's movement had moved beyond pursuit of equality and was offering too drastic a challenge to traditional gender roles. In 1972, feminists proposed the Equal Rights Amendment as a means of guaranteeing women's constitutional equality, rendering unconstitutional all laws that discriminated against women, and precluding future passage of such laws. The ERA was approved overwhelmingly by Congress and sent to the states and many rushed to ratify. But conservative women—fearing that the vaguely worded amendment would usher in unwanted changes—found their voices and their leader—Phyllis Schlafly—and began an organized challenge to the ERA and feminism. Their ranks swelled further after the Supreme Court in 1973 announced its decision in *Roe v. Wade* which made abortion legal nationwide. Opinion polls continued to show strong support for the ERA throughout the decade, but as its opponents raised doubts about its impact, the ERA lost its forward momentum. By 1975, the year the IWY program was established, 34 of the necessary 38 states had ratified: only one more state would ratify and several others would try to rescind ratification.

Conservatives, elated by their success, were therefore appalled when Congress established the International Women's Year (IWY) program with a $5 million appropriation and the feminists appointed to lead it declared their intent to promote the ERA as well as many additional feminist goals. Many of these goals were anathema to social conservatives who believed in social hierarchy and "traditional family values."...

Thus, while feminist leaders looked to the IWY to involve greater numbers of women in establishing an agenda to improve their lives, conservatives saw it as a U.N.-conceived, federally-funded effort to force unwanted changes on those Americans just starting to rise up against the ERA and the legalization of abortion. They insisted that the federal government had given $5 million to fund one side of a national debate. Between 1975 and 1977 they sought to halt the IWY program through Congress and the courts. When it was clear that the conferences were going forward, they resolved to challenge the feminists for control of them. In 1975 Schlafly created ... the Eagle Forum, "an alternative to women's lib," whose ranks would expand dramatically during the IWY controversy.

As the state IWY conferences got under way in February 1977, conservatives were alarmed when participants at the first one, held in Vermont, approved staunchly feminist resolutions and delegations to the national conference. The resolutions supported the ERA, "choice" on abortion, and what conservatives called "an additional anti-family goal—gay rights." Then, in March, the newly elected president Jimmy Carter appointed Bella Abzug, regarded by conservatives as radical, as chair of the National IWY Commission. The last straw was the commission's sending to state IWY organizers a list of feminist-inspired "core recommendations" for consideration at the state conferences. At that point, conservatives created a formal organization, the IWY Citizen's Review Committee, to coordinate their challenge....

In May 1977 Schlafly urged readers of the newsletter the *Phyllis Schlafly Report* to turn out en masse for the state IWY conferences. A devout Catholic, she was remarkably successful at uniting varied religious groups that had in the past been hostile to one another, including Catholics, Mormons, and previously apolitical evangelical and fundamentalist Protestants. Led by ministers, including the Reverend Jerry Falwell, who had criticized African-American ministers for mixing politics and religion during the civil rights movement, conservative Protestants proved surprisingly responsive to a northern Catholic woman's appeal for "Christian soldiers" to defend traditional values. Members of Congress were soon deluged with letters protesting IWY and coalitions of social conservatives varying in composition from state to state made their presence felt at the state conferences....

The National IWY Commission notified state IWY organizers about the unexpectedly large conservative turnout but did little more. They *wanted* women of all points of view to participate in the IWY state conferences and the workshops where women's issues would be debated, hoping they would respond positively to feminist ideas. Mississippi IWY leaders, busy planning the state IWY conference to be held in July, remained unaware of the systematic challenge conservatives were organizing nationally and in Mississippi. IWY committee members later noted that information about the surprise tactics employed elsewhere would have been quite welcome as they planned the conference they ironically chose to call "Mississippi Women: Awake and Aware."

The IWY Coordinating Committee for Mississippi began its work on February 26, 1977 at a meeting hosted in Oxford by Dr. Katherine Rea of the University of Mississippi. This was a racially diverse group of women, moderate to liberal in political leanings, and active in a variety of organizations including churches. Few had known one another previously. As in other states, the members were selected by the national IWY organizers (who had decided not to rely on state governors to appoint progressive and diverse commissions) on the basis of years of leadership in women's advocacy organizations including the American Association of University Women (AAUW), the League of Women Voters (LWV), the National Council of Negro Women (NACW), the Mississippi State Federation of Colored Women's Clubs, the National Organization for Women (NOW), and the Business and Professional Women's Federation (BPW). There were committee members active in the American Civil Liberties Union (ACLU), the Democratic Party, arts commissions, chambers of commerce, the American Cancer Society, the Afro-American Historical Society, and the Mississippi Humanities Council. Many were involved in religious organization including the Young Women's Christian Association (YWCA), Church Women United, the National Council of Jewish Women, and other church groups and some were wives of clergymen. The group included university professors, a dean, a hairdresser, lawyers and law students, homemakers, bankers, mental health and social workers, and the head of a displaced homemakers aid organization. There were advisors to the U.S. Civil Rights Commission, members of the NAACP, and officeholders whose elections had been made possible by the Voting Rights Act of 1965 (Mayor Unita Blackwell of Mayersville and City Councilwoman Sarah

Johnson of Greenville). Natalie Mason's husband had led the "wadeins" that desegregated Gulf Coast beaches, and Dr. Jessie B. Mosley had been active in "Wednesdays in Mississippi," an interracial women's group that quietly promoted interracial understanding.

At the opening meeting the group heard from a representative of the National Commission on the Observance of IWY and elected Dr. Mosley as their chair. Mosley, a leader among African Americans in Jackson, had held national and state offices in the National Council of Negro Women....

The committee's choices coincided often but not always with the national commission's suggestions. With years of experience operating in a conservative social climate, they knew that some of national's ideas "did not have enough Mississippi in them" to be palatable to people in the state....

That the organizers were bent on planning a program palatable to Mississippians and ... despite strenuous efforts to publicize a conference open to all, they expected only progressive-minded Mississippians to participate.... Perhaps they were living in "a fool's paradise," [Alison] Steiner observed years later, but "it never occurred to us that there would be an organized right-wing." Women's political activism seemed contradictory to the ideas Mississippi conservatives espoused. Thus supporters of women's rights believed, she said, "that we had fertile ground for organizing women who had not previously been involved" in public discussion of women's issues....

The word circulated among the conservatives was that a group of feminist radicals planned to hold a meeting in Jackson and promote resolutions supporting the ERA, gay rights, federally controlled day care, and other issues abhorrent to social conservatives. In addition, they would elect delegates to a national conference that would then advise Congress on what American women wanted. Conservatives, they said, must turn out to challenge the feminists' "pre-packaged" slates they and resolutions.... [T]hey pursued a stealth strategy: feminists later concluded that [they] carefully planned a takeover and believed their success depended upon keeping IWY organizers ignorant of their plans....

According to both sides, an atmosphere of hostility between feminists and conservatives prevailed. Conservatives claimed that feminist organizers treated them like interlopers or spoilers. Eddie Myrtle Moore said they had to fight to be heard and to oversee ballot counting by the distrusted feminists. The organizers—most of them married women with children; from strong religious backgrounds; and with extensive service to their state, nation, and churches were shocked and dismayed to be called "godless communists" as well as "anti-family," "immoral," and advocates of promiscuity and perversion by members of the conservative coalition calling itself "Mississippians for God, Country, and Family." Such accusations from persons who had known them for years—and certainly knew better—flabbergasted Cora Norman and others on the coordinating committee.

"Mississippians for God, Country, and Family," making good use of the prerogatives of a majority, passed substitute recommendations and a slate of delegates that reflected their own values and ideas about women and public policy. The well-organized conservatives, including a group of male "controllers" using the hand-held radios then called "walkie-talkies," often instructed the conservative women on how to vote. Linda Williams, a reporter for the *South Mississippi Sun,* observed that the "group that wielded the most power … was a group of Pentecostal ministers who bused in entire congregations and controlled their every move."

The adopted resolutions underscored the fundamental differences the conservatives had with feminists. Beyond "equal pay for equal work" they agreed on very little. Though most in each group were religious, their religion spoke to them quite differently on women's issues. To the conservatives, denying gender differences and roles was not only socially destructive but sacrilegious. Many believed that God had created woman to be honored by, but obedient to, man; that her highest calling was wife and mother; that feminists disdained that role, and that feminism held forth false promises about the benefits and satisfactions of work outside the home….

The conservatives' resolutions reflected their convictions that families suffered, children were poorly reared, and the nation was weakened when women left traditional roles. They approved only one plank suggested by the organizers—one supporting improvements in public education—but only after omitting endorsement of public kindergarten. Conservatives saw federal programs to assist women and children as wasteful, indeed "communistic," and their own resolutions called for major spending cutbacks. Many were convinced that programs favored by the feminists, including social security benefits for homemakers, would lead to higher taxes and would drive even more women into the paid labor force. Their resolutions opposed all affirmative action (which they called "reverse discrimination") and programs, including Title IX, that required equal opportunities for women in educational institutions. They opposed proposals for gender equality in the military and international cooperation to promote women's rights and world peace. These ideas were anathema to many conservatives who were ardent nationalists and isolationists, opposed to the United Nations and taxes to support foreign aid, and advocates of a strong military—with no women in combat—that was able to withstand the threat of communism….

A sweeping resolution proposed and adopted by the conservative summed up their position: "BE IT RESOLVED that the IWY conference declare itself opposed to sin and injustice in all their forms." It was then amended to read: "BE IT RESOLVED that sin and injustice be defined as that which is condemned in the Holy Bible."…

With the civil rights movement in Mississippi still fresh in their minds, many conservatives remained angry over what they viewed as ill advised and unwanted federal intervention in the form of court decisions and federal legislation. To white Mississippians who had opposed civil rights for African Americans, further expansion of federal power—especially in the sensitive arena of gender relations—must be opposed to the last ditch, just as many white southerners had opposed the woman suffrage amendment earlier in the century. Perhaps, with white supremacy legally overturned, preserving traditional gender hierarchies and the protection of women seemed to them more important than ever….

"Mississippians for God, Country, and Family" elected a solidly conservative group of delegates to the National Women's Conference…. The men in the group would be the only men elected from any state as delegates to the Houston conference. Two of them, Curtis Caine and Homer Morgan, were elected in absentia.... The delegates elected included three married couples and only one African American, Willie Mae Latham Taylor, who promptly declined and was replaced by a white alternate.

The election of Dallas Higgins, a Klan leader's wife, shocked the nation and embarrassed most of the conservatives. Eddie Myrtle Moore denied adamantly that there were any Klan members in the delegation, insisting "there's been a smear on the Mississippi delegates." "As chairman I can assure you that not one member is a Klansman." She had the delegates sign affidavits to that effect, but Dallas Higgins revealed that, though not an official member, she had attended Klan rallies "as a concerned citizen."...

[T]he fact that a state with a 36 percent black population was sending an all-white delegation to Houston was the news that stuck, and it was roundly condemned by IWY leaders nationwide. Unita Blackwell said, "Even if they say they are for God, country, and family, they're the same group of people that have always oppressed black people" in the state.

After the Mississippi conference, Richard Barrett boasted of the conservatives' triumph and denounced the defeated feminists' "core recommendations" for seeking "to set men against women and to increase federal power," adding "Women don't want quotas, men don't want quotas." He bragged about the passage of resolutions against gay rights legislation, saying "when you talk about legalizing homosexuality, when you talk about legalizing perversion, you're touching the soul of America." The conservative takeover in Mississippi, he proclaimed, was of utmost importance: "It's undisputed and undoubted that we have sent a mandate to the nation. That the ERA is dead, and that the moral womanly woman is alive and well in Mississippi, and that she will win this battle."...

Columnist Bill Minor, a leading analyst of Mississippi politics, ... predicted a lasting influence. The state, he wrote, had just gotten "a look-see" at "a new form of militant conservatism" which had "emerged to replace the old-time anti-black militancy of the White Citizens' Councils and the Ku Klux Klan." Though "ostensibly not racist" it "comes out of a strong reactionary backlash led by religious fundamentalism, self-acclaimed patriotic organizations and some old-time staunchly conservative political groups. Their overall enemy now is not the black man but 'liberalism' in any form, as they see it." In place of opposition to civil rights and voting rights bills, wrote Minor, they are now focusing on "such issues as ERA, gay rights, and abortion." Stating that "once state legislators were afraid to move without getting approval from the Citizens' Council hierarchy," he asked, "Is it possible a new fear of the right may emerge in the halls of the legislature?"

When viewed in a national context, Mississippi's takeover was as unusual as it was thorough. When the last of the state conferences ended, it was clear that feminists prevailed at most IWY conferences. Eighty percent of the delegates elected to participate in the Houston IWY conference supported the feminist movement.

In thirty states, participants adopted all of the "core recommendations" and in eleven states approved most of them. But a new a round of controversy over the IWY followed the state conferences and lasted until the national conference in November. Conservatives nationwide filed challenges with the national commission, accusing IWY state coordinators of trying to exclude or silence them. The charges received national attention when Senator Jesse Helms (R-N.C.), working with the IWY Citizens Review Committee, organized congressional hearings at which conservative women from many states testified. Letters protesting the conferences poured in, and many politicians began to wonder which group of women they should appease. Schlafly denounced the conferences for "rigging, ruthlessness, and railroading" and "lesbian aggressiveness" and urged conservatives to save American society from "the libs" who "will replace it with a society that does not respect gender differences, moral values, church, or family."

Feminists fought back, alarmed by the attention the conservatives commanded from politicians and from the press—that developed a strong interest in the IWY conferences only after the battles among women began. Feminists accused Schlafly of "seeking a resurgence of the far right by exploiting the women's movement," and led by the AAUW [American Association of University Women], forty women's organizations formed "Truth Squads" to "rebut the false or exaggerated charges anti-change groups had been making to the press and even in Congress."

As conservatives elsewhere were challenging the legitimacy of the delegates elected to attend the Houston conference, in Mississippi it was the feminists who challenged the legitimacy of their state's delegation. Calling themselves the "Minority Caucus," they protested the methods used by conservatives in taking over the state IWY conference, denounced the conservative resolutions as racist as well as antifeminist, and charged that the election of an all-white delegation violated the letter as well as the spirit of IWY's congressional mandate. National IWY leaders, while "shocked" by the all-white delegation, nonetheless denied the Mississippi feminists' challenge along with the conservative challenges from other states. Instead, they decided to appoint "at-large delegates" in states where the elected delegation did not meet the diversity requirement. They appointed nine at-large delegates from Mississippi including eight black women....

When the long-awaited National Women's Conference got underway, television audiences around the world watched as the celebrities arrived in Houston, including feminist leaders Bella Azbug, Gloria Steinem, and Betty Friedan; actress Jean Stapleton, then famous as Edith Bunker on the hit television sitcom "All in the Family"; civil rights leader Coretta Scott King; poet Maya Angelou; scholar Margaret Mead; former First Ladies Lady Bird Johnson and Betty Ford, and the current First Lady, Rosalynn Carter. But the press also swarmed the elected delegates from Mississippi, especially Dallas Higgins, who expressed concerns that IWY organizers were going to harass conservatives by assigning them black lesbians as roommates. She was accompanied by her husband George; KKK Imperial Wizard Robert Shelton of Alabama had announced that Klansmen would be going to Houston "to protect our women from all the militant lesbians."...

Both groups of Mississippi delegates, elected and at-large, participated in the conference. The 20 percent conservatives were outvoted as 80 percent feminist majority adopted all but one plank—that calling for a cabinet-level women's department—of the proposed National Plan of Action....

After the Houston conference, feminists celebrated their victory. But they were soon in conflict with President Carter who in their eyes did not do enough to implement the National Plan of Action and fired Abzug as head of the IWY continuing committee when she criticized him to the press. Over the next decade the women's movement continued to pursue the Houston objectives but with little federal support and considerable opposition as the nation turned politically and culturally to the right. It appeared that the rest of the nation was catching up with Mississippi in defense of tradition against change. When in 1979 Congress extended the deadline for ERA ratification over the bitter protests of opponents, Mississippi senator John Stennis—one of the few senators who had voted against the ERA back in 1972—was one of those protesting most forcefully. Jimmy Carter continued to work hard for the amendment, but his influence was waning. Meanwhile, Ronald Reagan—who launched his post-convention campaign at the Neshoba County Fair near Philadelphia, Mississippi, to a mostly-white throng of around ten thousand—captured the Republican nomination and led the party to reverse its forty-year history of support for the ERA....

The IWY experience solidified coalitions and networks for both conservatives and feminists in Mississippi, and after the 1977 conference both sides remained politically active. After Houston, Mississippi conservatives celebrated their victory and vowed to continue their work....

For women's rights supporters, the most important legacy of the IWY in Mississippi was the additional strength they drew from newly created alliances across racial and class lines. Black and white feminists who had been gathered together on the coordinating committee and others who had experienced the Mississippi takeover of July 1977 would never forget the experience or the sense of being connected in a common cause against a common foe. Jessie Mosley told a reporter, "We sincerely feel that something has been started here. Just working together as a committee, we have discovered a feeling of oneness that one would not expect to find between black and white women of all strata in Mississippi."...

The Mississippi IWY conference of 1977 was deeply disturbing to all involved but it was also an awakening. The IWY conferences brought the state's women—many of whom had little previous awareness of current debates on women's issues taking place elsewhere in the United States and abroad—into the discussion and into politics. The experience also made Mississippi women, feminist and conservative alike, more aware of one another and of their profound differences. If, as it seems, Mississippi women had not been "Awake and Aware" before July 1977, after the state's IWY conference they surely were. And both sides would remain awake, aware, deeply polarized, and very active in the years ahead.

FURTHER READING

Carl Abbott, *The New Urban America: Growth and Politics in Sunbelt Cities* (1981).

Peter Applebome, *Dixie Rising: How the South Is Shaping American Values, Politics, and Culture* (1997).

Howard Ball et al., *Compromised Compliance: Implementation of the 1965 Voting Rights Act* (1982).

Numan V. Bartley, "Another New South?" *Georgia Historical Quarterly* 65 (1981) 119–137.

Jack Bass and Walter De Vries, *The Transformation of Southern Politics: Social Change and Political Consequences since 1945* (1976).

Joan Turner Beifuss, *At the River I Stand: Memphis, the 1968 Strike, and Martin Luther King* (1985).

William C. Berman, *America's Right Turn: From Nixon to Bush* (1994).

Earl Black, *Southern Governors and Civil Rights: Racial Segregation as a Campaign Issue in the Second Reconstruction* (1976).

Earl Black and Merle Black, *Politics and Society in the South* (1987).

———, *The Rise of Southern Republicans* (2002).

———, *The Vital South: How Presidents Are Elected* (1992).

Peter G. Bourne, *Jimmy Carter: A Comprehensive Biography* (1997).

Dan T. Carter, *From George Wallace to Newt Gingrich: Race in the Conservative Counterrevolution, 1963–1994* (1996).

———, *The Politics of Rage: George Wallace, the Origins of the New Conservatism, and the Transformation of American Politics* (1995).

Joseph Crespino, *In Search of Another Country: Mississippi and the Conservative Counterrevolution* (2009).

Robert Dallek, *Flawed Giant: Lyndon Johnson and His Times, 1961–1973* (1998).

Chandler Davidson, ed., *Minority Vote Dilution* (1984).

Chandler Davidson and Bernard Grofman, *Quiet Revolution: The Impact of the Voting Rights Act in the South* (1994).

Jane Sherron De Hart, "Second Wave Feminism(s) and the South: The Difference That Differences Make," in Christie Anne Farnham, ed., *Women of the American South* (1997), 276–292.

Paul Delaney, "A New South for Blacks?" in John B. Boles, ed., *Dixie Dateline: A Journalistic Portrait of the Contemporary South* (1983).

Marvin Dunn, *Black Miami in the Twentieth Century* (1997).

Gary M. Fink, *Prelude to the Presidency: The Political Career and Legislative Leadership Style of Governor Jimmy Carter* (1980).

Frye Gaillard, *The Dream Long Deferred: The Landmark Struggle for Desegregation in Charlotte, North Carolina* (2006).

David R. Goldfield, *Region, Race, and Cities: Interpreting the Urban South* (1997).

Carl Grafton and Anne Permaloff, *Big Mules and Branchheads: James E. Folsom and Political Power in Alabama* (1985).

Dewey W. Grantham, *The Life and Death of the Solid South: A Political History* (1988).

———, *The South in Modern America: A Region at Odds* (1994).

Melissa Fay Greene, *Praying for Sheetrock: A Work of Nonfiction* (1991).

Edward R. Haas, *De Lesseps S. Morrison and the Image of Reform: New Orleans Politics, 1946–1961* (1974).

William C. Havard, ed., *The Changing Politics of the South* (1972).

Alexander Heard, *A Two-Party South?* (1952).

Samuel S. Hill, *The New Religious-Political Right in America* (1982).

John Howard, ed., *Carryin' On in the Lesbian and Gay South* (1997).

Burton Ira Kaufman, *The Presidency of James Earl Carter, Jr.* (1993).

Martin Luther King Jr., *Where Do We Go from Here: Chaos or Community* (1967).

Kevin Michael Kruse, *White Flight: Atlanta and the Making of Modern Conservatism* (2005).

Alexander P. Lamis, *The Two-Party South* (1984).

Matthew D. Lassiter, *The Silent Majority: Suburban Politics in the Sunbelt South* (2006).

Harold H. Martin, *William Berry Hartsfield: Mayor of Atlanta* (1978).

William Martin, *With God on Our Side: The Rise of the Religious Right in America* (1996).

Donald Mathews and Jane S. DeHart, *Sex, Gender, and the Politics of ERA: A State and the Nation* (1990).

Kevin E. McHigh, "Black Migration Reversal in the United States," *Geographical Review* 77 (1987), 171–182.

Stevan P. Miller, *Billy Graham and the Rise of the Republican South* (2009).

Frank R. Parker, *Black Votes Count: Political Empowerment in Mississippi* (1990).

Richard A. Pride and J. David Woodard, *The Burden of Busing: The Politics of Desegregation in Nashville, Tennessee* (1985).

John Shelton Reed, "Up from Segregation," *Virginia Quarterly Review* 60 (1984), 377–393.

John Rozier, *Black Boss: Political Revolution in a Georgia County* (1982).

Thomas F. Schallar, *Whistling past Dixie: How Domocrats Can Win without the South* (2006).

Robert Sherrill, *Gothic Politics in the Deep South: Stars of the New Confederacy* (1968).

Bruce Shulman, *From Cotton Belt to Sunbelt: Federal Policy, Economic Development, and the Transformation of the South, 1938–1980* (1991).

Robert P. Steed et al., *Party Organization and Activism in the American South* (1998).

David M. Tucker, *Memphis Since Crump: Bossism, Blacks, and Civic Reformers, 1948–1968* (1980).

Trent Watts, ed., *White Masculinity in the Recent South* (2008).

Amy Wells and Robert Crain, *Stepping Over the Color Line: African American Students in White Suburban Schools* (1997).

CHAPTER 14

The South in America

As others have wisely noted, there are many Souths and, one could add, many facets to the South. In this final chapter we have chosen several essays that speak to the many-sidedness of southern culture, life, and history. The importance of the South to the nation is unquestioned today. Its economic growth has offered employment to millions, especially immigrants, who have come to work and once there to stay. This has led to diversity beyond the black-white cultural milieu normally associated with the region. In North Carolina, Latino Catholics celebrate mass in Spanish-speaking parishes. In downtown Houston, the street signs are printed in Vietnamese and English. In Miami, Cuban festivals with food and music bring to the city the flavor of Havana. In terms of population, the South is one of the fastest growing regions in the nation. Politically, Dixie has proven vital to presidential elections. Since 1963 half the presidents of the United States have come from the South (four out of eight). There are other manifestations of southern influence on America—music, food, patterns of speech (Hi, y'all), religion, family life, and history, to name a few.

This does not mean that the South as a distinctive entity has vanished. The South and the rest of the nation have at last reached a compromise. With so many northerners and westerners moving south and so many shopping malls and skyscrapers going up, southern metropolitan areas could be mistaken for any other place in the country. Yet regional differences abound, and as C. Vann Woodward wrote, "Is there nothing about the South that is immune from the disintegrating effect of nationalism ...? There is only one thing that I can think of, and that is its history."

ESSAYS

Historian Raymond Arsenault, in the first essay, points to one technical dimension of southern life that has made the region a great deal more attractive to Americans since the 1930s—air conditioning. Climate control has not only brought newcomers to the South, it has also brought about a decline in mortality rates, an increase in industrialization and urbanization, and changes in family life, architecture, and the incidence of violence. On the cultural side, in "Rhythms of the Land," historian Pete Daniel speaks of the "unlikely renaissance" that "swept through southern society. Black and white musicians were part of a vibrant cultural exchange." In noting the influx of white and black southerners to cities such as Memphis after World War II, Daniel found that "musicians and athletes did more to undermine segregation than community leaders." Such luminaries as B. B. King and Elvis Presley represent an interracial camaraderie and a musical rock 'n' roll revolution that brought the South to the consciousness of America. Historian Jack Temple Kirby, in the third essay, brings to this chapter a reflective look at the environmental South, particularly Appalachia, the coastal regions, the piney woods, and the plantation heartlands. When post–World War II industries came to the South, they brought with them not only economic advances for corporations and workers but also the makings of severe ecological damage. The South, once an industrially undeveloped region, has become another area of America as polluted as the cities of the Northeast or as redolent with pesticides as the Far West. Kirby asks the question suitable for the South in America, "When ... will we have had enough of tampering with nature ...?" In the last essay, journalist John Egerton brings into focus the South in America. It is a capstone of sorts, recounting much of the history the region has experienced in its years since the Civil War. Two pivotal events in the more recent civil rights history of the South stand out in his essay: Martin Luther King Jr.'s "I Have a Dream" speech before the Lincoln Memorial, and President Lyndon B. Johnson's repetition of these words from a civil rights anthem—"We Shall Overcome." But can it be truly affirmed that "the South has cast off the fetters of racial and regional inferiority and taken its rightful place in the national circle of citizenship"? Let us hope so.

The Air Conditioner and Southern Culture

RAYMOND ARSENAULT

In 1979 *Time* magazine columnist Frank Trippett took the American intellectual community to task for ignoring the social and cultural significance of air conditioning. Scholars and pop sociologists have been keenly aware of "the social implications of the automobile and television," he observed, but for some reason they have not gotten around "to charting and diagnosing all the changes brought about by air conditioning." Trippett's complaint is valid, and strange as it may seem, nowhere is this more evident than in the field of southern history. When the journalist Pat Watters called the air conditioner the "unsung hero" of the modern South in 1963, he knew what he was talking about. With few exceptions, historical works on the twentieth-century South published during the last forty years make no mention of air conditioning or, for that matter, of anything related to climate or climate control. The recently published *The*

Raymond Arsenault, "The End of the Long Hot Summer: The Air Conditioner and Southern Culture," *Journal of Southern History*, L (November 1984), pp. 597–628.

Encyclopedia of Southern History contains 2,900 articles, covering everything from "Abbeville" to "Zwaanendael," but incredibly it has no article on "air conditioning." Even the broader subject of southern climate is dismissed in three paragraphs—less space than is devoted to "reptiles and amphibians."

This scholarly neglect is surprising because it goes against the grain of common sense and popular culture. Ask any southerner over thirty years of age to explain why the South has changed in recent decades, and he may begin with the civil rights movement or industrialization. But sooner or later he will come around to the subject of air conditioning. For better or worse, he will tell you, the air conditioner has changed the nature of southern life. Some southerners will praise air conditioning and wonder out loud how they ever lived without it. Others will argue that the South is going to hell, not in a hand basket, but in an air-conditioned Chevy. As one Florida woman recently remarked, "I hate air conditioning; it's a damnfool invention of the Yankees. If they don't like it hot, they can move back up North where they belong."...

The so-called "air conditioning revolution" ... was actually an evolution—a long, slow, uneven process stretching over seven decades. The air conditioner came to the South in a series of waves, and only with the wave of the 1950s was the region truly engulfed. What had been largely a curiosity in the pre–World War II South became an immutable part of southern life in the postwar era. After the air conditioner invaded the home and the automobile, there was no turning back. By the mid-1970s air conditioning had made its way into more than 90 percent of the South's high-rise office buildings, banks, apartments, and railroad passenger coaches; more than 80 percent of its automobiles, government buildings, and hotels; approximately two-thirds of its homes, stores, trucks, and hospital rooms; roughly half of its classrooms; and at least a third of its tractors. Virtually all of the region's newer buildings, regardless of type or function, were equipped with air conditioning. The South of the 1970s could claim air-conditioned shopping malls, domed stadiums, dugouts, green-houses, grain elevators, chicken coops, aircraft hangars, crane cabs, off-shore oil rigs, cattle barns, steel mills, and drive-in movies and restaurants.... Predictably, the South's most air-conditioned state was Texas, where even the Alamo had central air. In Houston alone the annual cost ($666 million) of air conditioning exceeded the annual gross national product of several Third-World nations in 1980....

In varying degrees virtually all southerners have been affected, directly or indirectly, by the technology of climate control. Air conditioning has changed the southern way of life, influencing everything from architecture to sleeping habits. Most important, it has contributed to the erosion of several regional traditions: cultural isolation, agrarianism, poverty, romanticism, historical consciousness, an orientation towards nontechnological folk culture, a preoccupation with kinship, neighborliness, a strong sense of place, and a relatively slow pace of life. The net result has been a dramatic decline in regional distinctiveness. In combination with other historical forces—such as the civil rights movement, advances in communication and transportation technology, and economic and political change—the air conditioner has greatly accelerated what John Egerton has called "the Americanization of Dixie."

Perhaps most obviously, air conditioning has had a major impact on southern population growth. The population density of the South (86.3 persons per square mile in 1980) has doubled since 1930. Some of this growth can be attributed to a high birth rate, some to a declining death rate, and some to migration. For the most part, the demographic impact of air conditioning has been limited to the latter two phenomena....

The link between air conditioning and declining mortality is much more substantial. Prior to the twentieth century the nonmountain South was a relatively unhealthy place. Generally speaking, southern mortality rates were much higher than those of other areas of the United States. And as David Hackett Fischer has recently pointed out, the southern climate, which fostered yellow fever, malaria, and other semi-tropical diseases, was a primary determinant of the region's high mortality. Significantly, since the beginning of the twentieth century regional mortality rates have converged, and the southern population is much healthier today than it was a century ago. The proliferation of air conditioning is one of the reasons. In addition to making millions of hospital patients more comfortable, air conditioning has reduced fetal and infant mortality, prolonged the lives of thousands of patients suffering from heart disease and respiratory disorders, increased the reliability and sophistication of micro-surgery, facilitated the institutionalization of public health, and aided the production of modern drugs such as penicillin. On the other side of the ledger, critics of air conditioning claim that it causes allergies and that it is partially responsible for the pervasiveness of the common cold. Nevertheless ... the net effect of air conditioning on southern health and life expectancy has been positive.

Climate control has had an even greater impact on migration patterns. In a variety of ways the air conditioner has helped to reverse an almost century-long southern tradition of net out-migration. Between 1910 and 1950 alone, the South's net loss was more than 10 million people. It is more than a coincidence that in the 1950s, the decade when air conditioning first engulfed the South, the region's net out-migration was much smaller than in previous decades and that in the 1960s, for the first time since the Civil War, the South experienced more in-migration than out-migration....

Because of air conditioning an undetermined but clearly substantial number of southerners who might otherwise have left the South have remained in the region. Insofar as it has promoted personal contentment, employment opportunities, and improved working conditions, the air conditioner has helped to stem the tide of out-migration. This reduction in out-migration has influenced southern political and economic life. But its qualitative impact on regional culture has been somewhat limited. The cultural transformation that has rocked the South in recent years is essentially an outgrowth of the other side of the migration equation. Abetted by millions of tourists, northern migrants have brought new ideas and new lifestyles to the South, disrupting the region's long-standing cultural isolation....

Air conditioning also has played a key role in the industrialization of the modern South. After decades of false starts and inflated promises, industry came to the South in a rush after World War II. The number of southerners employed in manufacturing exceeded those in agriculture for the first time in 1958, and by

1980 the region's manufacturing work force was more than three times as large as its agricultural work force.... Climate control has not only brought new factories and businesses to the region. It has also brought improved working conditions, greater efficiency, and increased productivity. As numerous controlled studies have demonstrated, an air-conditioned workplace invariably means higher productivity and greater job satisfaction. One of air conditioning's most telling effects has been its positive influence on southern economic growth.

This economic growth has led in turn to a rising standard of living for many southern families. Real wages have increased substantially during the postwar era, and per capita income in the South has risen from 52 percent of the national average in 1930 to almost 90 percent today. Although this increased income has been unevenly distributed across the region—Texas, Florida, and Virginia registered the biggest gains—few areas have been left unaffected. Maldistribution of wealth remains a serious regional problem, but the proportion of southerners living in Tobacco Road–style poverty has declined significantly in recent decades. Thus, in an indirect way, air conditioning has helped to ameliorate one of the post–Civil War South's most distressing characteristics. The social and cultural implications of the decline in southern poverty are immense, because, as C. Vann Woodward noted in 1958, "Generations of scarcity and want constitute one of the distinctive historical experiences of the Southern people...."

Air conditioning has also fostered the urbanization of the South. Since 1940 the South "has been the most rapidly urbanizing section of the country." During this period the proportion of southerners living in urban areas has nearly doubled, from 36.7 percent in 1940 to almost 70 percent today. Although the South remains the most rural area of the United States, the gap between the region and the rest of the nation is closing fast. How much of this recent urbanization can be attributed to air conditioning is difficult to say. But a number of observers have credited the air conditioner with being a major factor behind the rise of the urban South. According to the journalist Wade Greene, " Two of the country's fastest growing cities, Houston and Dallas, would probably be provincial backwaters today without air conditioning...."

Air conditioning has promoted the growth of the urban South in a variety of ways: by encouraging industrialization and population growth; by accelerating the development of large public institutions, such as universities, museums, hospitals, sports arenas, and military bases; by facilitating the efficient use of urban space and opening the city to vertical, high-rise development; and by influencing the development of distinctively urban forms of architecture Without air conditioning, skyscrapers and high-rise apartments would be less prevalent (indeed, they would not exist in their present form); urban populations would be smaller; cities would be more spread out; and the physical and architectural differences between inner cities and suburbs would be less striking (even though as an integral component of enclosed shopping malls, air conditioning has contributed to urban sprawl). In sum, the size, shape, and character of urban centers would be vastly different....

The locus of power and activity in the South has moved to Main Street, and air conditioning is one of the reasons why.

In a related development, climate control has altered southern attitudes toward nature and technology....

To confirm this point, one has only to walk down almost any southern street on a hot summer afternoon, listen to the whir of compressors, and look in vain for open windows or human faces. As Frank Trippett put it, air conditioning has "seduced families into retreating into houses with closed doors and shut windows, reducing the commonality of neighborhood life and all but obsoleting the front-porch society whose open casual folkways were an appealing hallmark of a sweatier America."

In many cases the porch is not simply empty, it's not even there. To the dismay of many southerners, air conditioning has impinged upon a rich tradition of vernacular architecture. From the "dogtrot cabin" with its central breezeway to the grand plantation house with its wrap-around porch, to the tin-roofed "cracker" house up on blocks, traditional southern architecture has been an ingenious conspiracy of passive cooling and cross-ventilation.... Historically, these techniques have been an important element of an aesthetic and social milieu that is distinctively southern....

Residential air conditioning has not only affected architectural form; it has also influenced the character of southern family life. Since strong family ties have long been recognized as an integral characteristic of southern culture, this is a matter of some importance. During the 1950s and 1960s the air conditioner was often portrayed as the savior of the American family. In 1955, for example, one observer claimed that residential air conditioning was changing "the family living pattern back to the days before the automobile took Americans out of their homes." "With comfort in its own living room," he argued, "the family tends to stay home and enjoy each other's society in relaxed evenings of reading, sewing, television, or card-playing."...

The alleged benefits of residential air conditioning ranged from better dispositions to increased family privacy. In retrospect, such expansive claims seem naive and misleading. Air-conditioned living may have made many individual family members happier, but it does not necessarily follow that the family unit was strengthened in the process. As numerous social critics eventually pointed out, endless hours of television watching often detracts from meaningful family life. In any event, the popularity of the air-conditioned living room was soon counterbalanced by the lure of air-conditioned shopping malls, bowling alleys, and other amusements. Of course, even if, on balance, residential air conditioning strengthened the nuclear family, the impact on wider kinship networks probably went in the opposite direction.... As more than one observer has noted, the vaunted southern tradition of "visiting" has fallen on hard times in recent years. This is an important point, because the essence of southern family life has always been its semi-extended nature. Thus, the overall effect of chilled air on traditional ties of blood and kin has been, at best, contradictory.

The same could probably be said for air conditioning's effect on patterns of aggression and violence. Throughout much of its history, the South has been the most violent section of the United States. In 1934 H. C. Brearley aptly described the South as "that part of the United States lying below the Smith and Wesson line." More recently, Sheldon Hackney and Raymond D. Gastil have used homicide and suicide rates to document the South's "regional culture of violence." Interestingly, few students of southern violence have paid much attention to climatic forces. Instead, they have concentrated on such factors as a lingering frontier tradition, adherence to an aristocratic code of honor, white supremacist ideology, racial demography, rurality, poverty, and an endemic "siege mentality" related to the nature of southern history. On occasion, however, climate has been cited as an important determinant of southern violence. In 1969 the historian Albro Martin insisted that the region's propensity for violence was largely a function of climate. And in 1977 Joseph C. Carroll's statistical analysis of homicide and suicide rates in 100 American cities uncovered a strong positive correlation between heat and humidity and both homicide and suicide. If these assessments are accurate, what does one make of the fact that southern homicide rates have increased since the advent of air conditioning? Would the rates have increased even more rapidly in a non-air-conditioned South? Unfortunately, the answers to these questions await further study. Proponents of indoor cooling have often argued that air conditioning invariably makes people less irritable and hence less violent....

A more immediate threat is the air conditioner's assault on the South's strong "sense of place." Southerners, more than most other Americans, have tied themselves to local geography. Their lives and identities have been rooted in a particular piece of turf—a county, a town, a neighborhood, a homestead, a family graveyard. Yet in recent year, thanks in part to air conditioning, southern particularism has been overwhelmed by an almost endless string of look-alike chain stores, tract houses, glassed-in high-rises, and, perhaps most important, enclosed shopping malls. The modern shopping mall is the cathedral of air-conditioned culture, and it symbolizes the placelessness of the New South. As William S. Kowinski recently observed, "these climate-controlled bubbles" are designed "to create timeless space. Removed from everything else and existing in a world of its own, a mall ... is a placeless space." As such, it is the antithesis of traditional southern culture. To quote Kowinski, "can you imagine William Faulkner writing about the Yoknapatawpha Mall?"

At one level or another, air conditioning has affected nearly every aspect of southern life. But it has not changed everything. Although climate control has done its best to homogenize the nation and eliminate regional consciousness, the South remains a land apart—a land that still owes much of its distinctiveness to climatic forces. Of course, how long this will remain so is an open question. Perhaps, as it has done so often in the past, the southerner's special devotion to regional and local traditions will ensure the survival of southern folk culture. But this time it will not be easy: General Electric has proved a more devastating invader than General Sherman. As long as air conditioning, abetted by immigration, urbanization, and broad technological change, continues to make inroads, the South's distinctive character will continue to diminish, never to rise again.

Rhythms of the Land: A Look at Southern Culture

PETE DANIEL

Southern rural music—blues, country, gospel, work songs, and field hollers—evolved from the everyday trials, tribulations, and hopes of southern farmers. Country people often spent their lives within a community, but their cultural landscape extended beyond county and state lines. Even before Victrolas and radios became commonplace, traveling musicians transmitted the latest popular music to the most isolated crossroads. They traveled along an invisible network composed of the shifting and overlapping itineraries of minstrel and vaudeville shows, one-night stands in small towns, street corners, brothels, juke joints, and honky-tonks far removed from any tracking system.

Whether it was blues, country, or gospel, rural music was dynamic and evolving. The younger generation of musicians might well have learned how their ancestors played, but its presentation addressed contemporary concerns and provided a commentary on family, love, tragedy, and frustration. When farming failed, rural refugees gathered their earthly belongings and moved to towns and cities, where their music became the seed of a mid-century revolution. Rural African American music, sacred and secular, urbanized and electrified, ripened into rhythm and blues. At almost the same time, a faster beat infected hillbilly music and, drawing on African American sources and its own vitality, flowered into rock 'n' roll. Although spirited debate over the origins of these musical genres continues, blues, black and white gospel music, and hillbilly music all had rural roots. Much of the music of the latter twentieth century thus goes back to rhythms of the land and embodies the essence of rural life and memory....

During the middle decades of the twentieth century, an unlikely renaissance swept through southern society. Black and white musicians were part of a vibrant cultural exchange that produced jazz, blues, country, gospel, rhythm and blues, rock 'n' roll, and soul music.

Memphis and its surrounding countryside cultivated a disproportionate number of musicians, and their experiences suggest that they shared a compulsion to travel, an ambition to master all forms of popular music, and an eagerness to perform and record despite receiving little compensation for their creative work. Ashley Thompson, for example, grew up at the turn of the century near Ripley, Tennessee, and performed with whites and blacks throughout the South. In 1928, Thompson and his friend Noah Lewis joined their old acquaintance Gus Cannon in Memphis to make a record. In this session, Thompson sang "Minglewood Blues" and "Big Railroad Blues" for Cannon's Jug Stompers. They performed on a work-for-hire basis, waiving royalties and copyright protection. "I got $7.50 a song," Thompson remembered; he took home $30 for the four-song session. Sam Chatmon, who lived near Bolton, Mississippi, formed the Mississippi Sheiks along with members of his extended family. Their songs "Sitting on Top of the

World" and "Corinna" sold millions of copies, he recalled, but "I ain't got a penny, not nairn." He received a lump sum at the recording session. "Wasn't no royalties in them days," he noted. "He give you $20 and you'd go on back home and forget it." As members of the black working class, Thompson and Chatmon measured their payments against assumed corporate profits.

Arthur Crudup personified the tribulations of a poor creative artist. Born in Forrest, Mississippi, in 1905, Crudup wrote, performed, and recorded songs while working day jobs in Indianapolis, Chicago, and the Mississippi Delta. In 1949, while farming in Mississippi, he insisted that the landlord cheated him out of over $1,500. In 1954, when Elvis Presley launched his career by recording one of Crudup's songs, "That's All Right, Mama," Crudup was headed for Florida to join the migrant labor stream. When he died in 1974, Crudup was still claiming $60,000 in back royalties. Such musicians as Thompson, Chatmon, and Crudup, along with hundreds of others who came from the Memphis countryside, made significant contributions to the musical revolution that swept Memphis in the mid-1950s. If a complete list of musicians from the 150-mile radius around Memphis could be compiled, it would be enormous.

The vitality of fifties Memphis owed a huge debt to the city's rural refugees. When rural options were exhausted, farmers turned to what they deigned public work, and Memphis was the largest mid-South city. Rural people did not move because they yearned to live in northern or southern towns and cities. They moved because of the depression, because landlords evicted them in order to pocket their share of New Deal payments. They moved when the defense industry boomed during World War II, when draft notices arrived, and when tractors, picking machines, and herbicides replaced them. The collapse of labor-intensive agriculture triggered not only the spread of southern music but also its transformation. Something significant happened in the 1940s and 1950s when the last generation of sharecroppers arrived in towns and cities. Although many parents viewed public work and dense urban housing with distaste, their children arrived in Memphis and other cities immensely excited about their prospects. To young refugees, cities and towns offered a lifeline. As they matured, many found security in day jobs, but they dreamed of creating music....

In Memphis, as in other places, musicians and athletes often did more to undermine segregation than community leaders. Musician Jim Dickinson credited 220-pound Louisiana wrestler Sputnik Monroe—who had a white skunk line in his hair, "hot" and "cold" tattooed above his nipples, and arms like Popeye—with integrating Memphis public arenas. Many whites considered Monroe white trash and cheered his opponents. Monroe challenged the color line with impunity and drew an enthusiastic African American following. He often strutted down Beale Street preening for his fans. When he performed in Ellis Auditorium, segregation laws dictated that whites sit downstairs and blacks in the balcony, and management insisted that whites compose 50 percent of the audience. Dickinson reported that segregation dissolved at Monroe's matches, however; "greed took over and they had to let more blacks in to where eventually the audience was integrated. They had to let them come downstairs." In Dickinson's opinion, Monroe "had more to do with integrating the Memphis audience than anything that was litigated by the city fathers."

Whereas Sputnik Monroe blatantly challenged segregation, the radio encouraged what amounted to invisible integration. Some radio stations, immune to segregation laws, carried all types of music. "If some Southerners could have segregated the airwaves," blues musician B. B. King wrote, "they would have." In October 1948, white-owned WDIA became the first radio station to feature an all-black team of disc jockeys. High school teacher Nat D. Williams became the dean of African American DJs, joined by Rufus Thomas, Ford Nelson, A. C. "Moohah" Williams, B. B. King, and others. They mixed blues and gospel and included live music, WDIA became more than a radio station; it was also a community institution that promoted racial goodwill. By 1956, twenty-eight stations in the country had all-black programming, and most were in the South. As late as 1960, blacks owned only four radio stations.

At night after WDIA signed off, white disc jockey Dewey Phillips, who joined WHBQ in October 1949, symbolically desegregated white programming from nine to midnight. He mixed country, rhythm and blues, gospel, and later rock 'n' roll on his *Red, Hot, and Blue* program. Phillips understood both the city's unique musical endowment and the communications revolution that would spread it. He spoke in a frantic blur, mixing metaphors, commercials, and nonsense. Phillips ignored categories and played what he considered the best contemporary music, which strayed far beyond conventional white tastes. In 1956, thirty-year-old Phillips went on television with his *Phillips' Pop Shop* program, which took improvisation to a new level. For six months, he rode a wave of popularity before the station syndicated the less spontaneous and more mainstream *American Bandstand*. Radio, recordings, television, and live performance allowed music to flow almost unimpeded through the city. White teenagers in particular felt an almost illicit thrill when they heard African American music on the radio or in some cases at black clubs.

Rigid segregation could not silence radio stations or jukeboxes or prevent record stores from stocking all types of music. In July 1946, John Novarese, Joe Coughi, and Frank Berretta opened a record store on Poplar Avenue named Poplar Tunes. It became a "one-stop" shop for jukebox distributors, who formerly had been forced to call on each label outlet in the city. Disc jockeys such as Dewey Phillips would drop by almost daily to chat and look for new material. Record producers, aspiring musicians, and music-savvy consumers, nearly all white males, moiled around Poplar Tunes, making it not only a regional information exchange but also a powerful force in shaping the musical tastes of the mid-South. Eventually Coughi was instrumental in founding Hi Records and bringing in black band leader Willie Mitchell to arrange and produce records. Novarese and Coughi also booked concerts. As independent labels declined, Novarese judged, music's "zeal" died. The hungry independents had been the ones to take the chances. As with auto racing, increasing popularity and commercialization in the music business tamed creativity....

Memphians enthusiastically supported live music. Across the Mississippi River in West Memphis, the Plantation Inn employed the cream of Memphis's black musicians. The Cotton Club and Danny's attracted a wilder clientele. Lax, or at least selective, law enforcement in West Memphis opened the fleshpots to young whites who flocked over the bridge from Memphis. For twenty years after World War II, Plantation Inn owner Morris Berger cultivated a diverse clientele that varied from underage thrill-seekers to movie stars. All the patrons were white; all the musicians black. If transgressions occurred at the Plantation Inn, they comprised underage drinking, stimulating dancing, and the thrill of hearing an excellent black band. A high school girl would arrive from a prom with perfect hair and wearing a formal dress, a corsage, and white gloves and, according to Morris Berger's daughter-in-law Bettye Berger, leave disheveled, barefoot, corsageless, "perspired, and probably smooched." The Plantation Inn set the standard for dance music, and the bands that played there in the late 1940s and 1950s—the Phinas Newborn Sr. Band, Willie Mitchell and the Four Kings, and the Ben Branch Band—had a significant influence on musicians, black and white....

Nearly all musicians, black and white, shared a knowledge of church music and a love of gospel singing. Churches varied enormously in their choice of music, which ranged from unaccompanied quartets to various combinations of organs, guitars, drums, and cymbals. A variation of what pleased the Lord on Sunday morning had pleased the Lord's followers the night before, for religious music's cadence and beat, under a different guise, praised the devil on Saturday night. As historian Martha Bayles has pointed out, Elvis Presley, Jerry Lee Lewis, and Little Richard Penniman all grew up in the Pentecostal faith. Presley's fondness for gospel music is better known than the fierce struggles of conscience that both Lewis and Penniman endured in singing the devil's music. White and black southerners had a similar affinity for religious music....

At mid-century, then, Memphis contained an explosive diversity of musicians. The air was filled with sounds ranging from nationally popular music to rhythm and blues, upbeat country, and gospel. Despite some DJs' propensity to mix black and white music, a distinct musical color line segregated country and much popular music from blues and rhythm and blues.

Samuel Cornelius Phillips, who would go on to found Sun Studio and record a stunning array of blues and rock 'n' roll performers, attempted to erase the musical color line. Born in 1923 near Florence, Alabama, Sam Phillips was one of seven children. After dropping out of school, he became a local radio announcer, moved to WLAC in Nashville, and in 1945 arrived in Memphis. Although he was not a musician in the formal sense, Phillips had a keen ear for music and heard it changing. He became a Memphis radio announcer and technician and engineered national hookups of big band music from the Skyway at the Peabody Hotel. But his ear was attuned to a different sound, for all his life he "had heard the innate rhythms of people that had absolutely no formal training in music, didn't know one note from the other."

In 1950, Phillips opened a recording studio at 706 Union Avenue. He sensed that underneath the Beale Street beat and the club music, something revolutionary pulsed. He recorded African American blues and rhythm and blues artists such as B. B. King, Joe Hill Louis, Rufus Thomas, the Prisonaires, Junior Parker, Roscoe Gordon, Jackie Brensten, Ike Turner, James Cotton, and Howlin' Wolf—a virtual who's who of African American performers, most of whom had grown up within a 150-mile radius of Memphis. Whites often taunted Phillips about his association with black performers. He sold his recordings to other labels such as Chess and RPM until 1952, when he started his own label, Sun Records.

In 1953, Rufus Thomas gave Phillips his first Sun Records hit with "Beat Cat." Born in 1917, Thomas took advantage of the diverse musical opportunities in and around Memphis. In high school, he joined the Brown Brevities, a vaudeville group. In the 1930s, he toured with F. S. Wolcott's Rabbit Foot minstrel troupe out on Port Gibson. Mississippi, and, like other black performers, remembered having to stay in private homes because he was barred from white hotels. Entertainment jobs did not pay the bills, however, and for twenty-two years, Thomas held a day job at the American Finishing Company, a textile mill. When he started there in 1941, he recalled, "they had that colored water and the white water." He condemned the notion that "white and black can't work together" as "one of the biggest lies ever told." Thomas's enormous love of Memphis was edged with bitterness over the destruction of Beale Street, which he described as "the black man's haven."

B. B. King, another of Phillips's artists, was born in rural Mississippi in 1925 near Itta Bena and brought country blues to the city. As a youngster, King eagerly listened to blues records on his aunt's Victrola. "As a little kid," he recalled, "blues meant hope, excitement, pure emotion. Blues were about feelings." ... "I found Beale Street to be a city unto itself." he marveled. In 1948, he brazenly introduced himself to Sonny Boy Williamson, auditioned, and appeared on his *King Biscuit Time* radio show. King recalled the late 1940s as a time when "black music was on fire." He had grown up with country blues but was also influenced by T-Bone Walker, Louis Jordan, and Wynonie Harris. He appeared on WDIA and played extensively in the countryside around Memphis. In 1952, the twenty-six-year-old King recorded "Three O'Clock Blues," which hit the top of the *Billboard* rhythm and blues chart. This hit launched a career that for nearly a half century kept King on the road doing as many as 330 shows a year, "a commitment," he declared, "that's serious, solitary, and damaging to the idea of a full-time love."

Although Sam Phillips was not known for being overly generous with royalties, he did give aspiring musicians such as Rufus Thomas and B. B. King an opportunity to record....

Phillips focused on rhythm and blues performers because he recognized that the faster beat captured the ongoing evolution of blues. He heard other hints of change in upbeat country tunes. Blues and country music reflected the cadences and experiences of rural life, whereas rhythm and blues and upbeat country suggested the more rapid pace of urban life. Young white musicians, in particular, were drawn to upbeat Hank Williams and Bob Wills songs. In Phillips's mind, country performers were, in their own way, edging toward rhythm and blues. He suspected that a white crossover musician was waiting to be discovered.

Phillips searched among the last generation of sharecroppers and their urban cousins, rebellious high school students and young working-class musicians who were adventurous and hungry....

Sam Phillips listened to the hopefuls who dropped by Sun Studio. He cut acetate records for self-conscious young musicians who were willing to pay to hear themselves. In the summer of 1953, a bashful Elvis Presley paid $3.98 to Sun receptionist Marion Keisker to record two ballads. Phillips dropped a passing compliment, and Keisker noted his name and phone number. In January 1954, while working as a truck driver, Presley recorded two more tunes, and on June

26, Phillips called Presley to tell him he had arranged a session with guitarist Scotty Moore and bass player Bill Black....

The next day, the trio arrived at Sun Studio at seven in the evening to record. Either relieved to finish the uninspiring session or desperate to catch Phillips's attention, Presley started clowning around with "That's All Right, Mama," the song Arthur Crudup had recorded for RCA seven years earlier. Black and Moore joined in the fun, and an incredulous Phillips emerged from the control room, he later recalled, feeling "like someone stuck me in the rear end with a brand new supersharp pitch fork." In that moment, Elvis Presley transcended his musical inhibitions; he crossed the line.

WDIA disc jockey Dewey Phillips dropped by Sun Studio the next day, and Sam Phillips played the tape of "That's All Right, Mama." After both men listened, lost in thought, Dewey Phillips agreed to play the song. Presley was at the movies when Phillips queued up the record around 9:30 or 10:00 P.M. Telegrams and phone calls began flooding the studio as soon as the song ended. Phillips called the Presley house and told Gladys Presley to get her son out of the movie theater and send him to the studio. Although listeners were unsure whether Presley was white or black until he revealed his Humes High School background on the air that evening, they knew immediately that they liked this music.

Presley's first record epitomized the union of black and white music: Crudup's rhythm and blues song was on one side and Bill Monroe's country "Blue Moon of Kentucky" was on the other. But Presley's record was neither black nor white, neither rhythm and blues nor country. Presley tried to explain this to Marion Keisker when she asked him who he sang like; he told her, "I don't sound like nobody." Sam Phillips had found what he was searching for—"the blues with a mania." Such alterations in musical style were not unique to Memphis. Wherever rural southerners settled across the country, a spontaneous invention of music akin to rock 'n' roll occurred.

After recording five singles, Phillips sold Presley's contract to RCA. Phillips then devoted his resources to molding the talents of an improbable group of young white men and women who walked into Sun Studio, including Carl Perkins, Jerry Lee Lewis, Johnny Cash, the Miller Sisters, Charlie Rich, Barbara Pittman, Sonny Burgess, Roy Orbison, Billy Lee Riley, and Stan Kesler. Many of the Sun performers who followed Presley had strong rural roots. The white artists who recorded at Sun brought not only the musical heritage of the rural South but also the influence of radio, recordings, and film....

Over time, Phillips and these country boys became a cult, and they have been elevated—Elvis Presley above all—to a hallowed place in American music. The shared rural heritage was the core of Sun, whose label featured a rooster crowing at the morning sun. Phillips's genius in provoking several dozen black and white musicians to record songs that changed national, even international, musical tastes made him one of the most significant music producers of the mid-twentieth century....

The musical revolution that seized Memphis and then the nation had its roots in the surrounding countryside. It was conducted by creative but often uneducated people who were not constrained by elite taste. Other cities experienced similar musical revolutions, but Memphis was unique. Something in migrants' musical heritage, their spirit, and their abrupt flight from the countryside disposed them to explore Beale Street, listen to radio stations, inspect freelance studios, patronize clubs, and haunt music stores. They hungered to make music. During the 1950s and 1960s, there was enormous pressure to conform, but Sam Phillips and Jim Stewart nurtured young musicians' untamed streak and encouraged them to take risks. "Sam was after the unknown," guitarist Scotty Moore declared. At Sun Studio, the rhythms of the land collided with the beat of the city, and at Stax Studio, blacks and whites joined forces, and the energy redefined American music. A surprising number of the performers recognized immediately anywhere in the world came from Memphis and its environs. For a moment at mid-century, lowdown southerners rewrote popular culture. It was a time many people look back on as the Golden Age.

Postmodern Landscapes: A Look at Southern Ecology

JACK TEMPLE KIRBY

Consider first southern Appalachia. Never a great agricultural commodities empire like the South's piedmonts and deltas, the mountains nonetheless were home to many farmers for a long time, many of them participating in remote markets. Deep Appalachian farmland (i.e., not on plateaus and broad river valleys) was typically "cove land," narrow, fertile streamside settlements. Hardly anyone lived on heavily forested ridges and peaks. This land held rains, filtered water, and provided fuel, building materials, and selectively cut timber for downriver markets. Then came railroads and timber and coal corporations. Forests were clear-cut, and mines, whether "slope" or "deep," brought forth not only coal but slag wastes including toxic minerals that tumbled down ridges onto farms and into streams. Farmers went to work in the mines or left for the Midwest, and by 1960, agricultural census takers designated most of the subregion as either "industrial" or some rural-undeveloped descriptor.

Then appeared a quantum leap in mining technology: giant machines that could strip away vegetation, dirt, and rock to reach seams of coal approximately parallel to horizon or slope. Federal and state legislation during the 1970s required operators to "restore" landscapes once coal seams were depleted, but legislators did not intend replication of original morphology and ground cover. Instead they insisted that mined landscapes be returned to some economically useful form, and this usually meant near-flat, grassy (i.e., treeless), would-be beef pastures. What is called "restoration ecology" bears little or no resemblance, in any of its forms, to preservation, anyway. And so the literal leveling of the South was under way.

Now, after four decades of eastern strip-mining and "restoration," coal operators have engineered ever-larger machines and a new (during the 1990s) method called 'mountaintop removal." Actually, miners now refer to mountaintops as "overlays,"

From *Mockingbird Song: Ecological Landscapes of the South* by Jack Temple Kirby.

since peaks and ridges cover seams of low-sulfur coal; so "overlay removal" is the interchangeable term. The removal procedure begins with blowing up mountaintops; then teams of towering machines, each twenty stories high, manipulate monster draglines to dump millions of tons of rubble into valleys, most with streams. People living below such overlays are typically bought out, their villages to become "valley fill." The Army Corps of Engineers, which issues permits for filling watersheds in coal country, concedes that about 1,000 miles of Appalachian streams have disappeared as a result of landscape leveling. The concession may be too modest, and destructive flooding in southern West Virginia during the spring of 2002 suggested to many a causative relationship with wholesale obliteration of forests. In 1999 and again during the floods of 2002, the chief judge of the federal district court of southern West Virginia condemned government permits for valley filling as an "obvious perversity" of the Clean Water Act. The judge's first ruling was overturned on appeal, and King Coal marched on, imperiously confident in a cozy consensus with the rest of the federal judiciary, not to mention the entire executive branch.

Now consider the coastal South. Here a much older and pervasive perversity of several clean water acts is evident everywhere, from Chesapeake Bay and the Delmarva Peninsula to Key West to Padre Island. Mile after mile, as any beachgoer or gliding pelican has observed, any patch of land, dry or soggy, not already built upon is for sale and development. Since World War II, but explosively since the 1960s, the eastern riviera has risen, quite literally (even as parts of the mountains have fallen). Most of this low landscape consisted of wetlands of one sort or another: floodplain pine barrens, pocosins, tidal marshes, and estuarial swamps. Ocean and Gulf beaches themselves are deserts, of course, delicate, shifting, and windblown. Yet ironically, even as wetlands' ecological functions and beaches' impermanence became generally understood—during the 1960s—Americans herded to the coasts to live, permanently or on regular or extended holidays. Private developers and eager local and state governments obliged private landowners, but it was the Army Corps of Engineers (again) that sanctioned the dredging and straightening of creeks, the digging of canals, and the draining of thousands of acres of wetlands, using spill from massive excavations to build (relatively) high and dry landscapes for safe home-sites and convenient business districts. When environmentalists recoiled in horror at losses of wildlife habitat, natural fish hatcheries, and estuarial function—as early as the mid-1960s—the corps resisted or ignored checks by Congress, the Fish and Wildlife Service, and private conservationist groups.

Florida, the lowest southern state with the longest coastline, was (and remains) the epicenter of reengineered hydrology and runaway development. During the late 1960s and early 1970s, however, in a move astounding in its secrecy and state-corporate collusion, the Walt Disney company bought miles of orange groves and wetlands near Orlando, established a private government for its domain, and built Disney World, transforming a low, pastoral landscape into a soaring tourist attraction, the biggest in the East, that supports a year-round population in sprawling suburbs. Northeast of Orlando, along the I-95 corridor from Jacksonville toward Daytona Beach, good well-drained farmland is now under wholesale conversion to gated golf course community developments. This despite the shocking news, in 2001, that Florida's water supply is compromised by pollution and limited in relation to population growth, which passed 15 million in the 2000 census, heading for at least 20 million by 2010.

It is South Florida, however, that has become the most elevated of all southern coastal places. Limestone foundations support impressive skylines of office towers and multistory condominiums, from Palm Beach to Miami and from Tampa—St. Petersburg to Naples. Canalization sanctioned by the Army Corps of Engineers yields more and more (and more expensive) "waterfront" property, which is essentially fill from canal digging. Truck and auto traffic—and air pollution—renders life hectic and dangerous to all but the sequestered wealthy....

Now move a short distance inland, to the Atlantic and Gulf coastal plains, to the piney woods of legend and fact, an enormous southern subregion always rivaling Appalachia in rustic poverty. With a few notable exceptions, little of this tidewater landscape was under cultivation before the Civil War. Instead, entrepreneurs established naval stores industries, especially turpentining, among towering stands of longleaf pines. Then came rolling destruction, as we have noticed, which began in North Carolina about 1850 and then moved down through Georgia, into northern Florida, and across into Texas's big woods. Next came tobacco, sometimes peanut farming, and, later, short-lived assembly plants. The young, able, and ambitious (or desperate)—always at the forefront of migration—fled. The next big thing, beginning in West Point, Virginia, early in the twentieth century, was pulp and paper mills. They persist.... Then came the industrialization of chicken and pork production, a disaster for workers and for watercourses, land, and air. The tidewaters are cursed, their people—recalling Linda Flowers's eastern Carolina-ism—"throwed away."

Meanwhile, in these same sandy, piney landscapes—and indeed, into the piedmonts here and there—piney-ness itself was transformed after about 1960, as an enormous and economically powerful paper complex took shape. Denizens of (say) West Point and Franklin, Virginia; Plymouth, North Carolina; Georgetown, South Carolina; Savannah and St. Marys, Georgia; Jacksonville and Palatka, Florida; or Bogalusa, Louisiana, needed no reminders of the complex's existence. They see and smell the smoke from the mills, and they live in the physical monotony of loblolly culture, where sometimes for miles all plants are one species and all the same size—unless they drive past the ugly remains of a recent harvest. Nearly everyone else, I suspect, especially drivers on I-95 (all the way from Fredericksburg, Virginia, to Jacksonville) or I-75 below Atlanta to Lake City, Florida, or I-10 from Jacksonville to Beaumont, assumes they travel through forests. Not so. Forests—even predominantly coniferous ones—are complex ecosystems including many plant and animal species. Plantations are single-plant constructions; they are effective deserts—except (again) my allusion gives deserts an undeserved bad name. Even after the banning of the notorious pesticide DDT and the harsh herbicide 2-4-D during the early 1970s, the paper complex's vast loblolly plantations remain absolutely chemically dependent. Other pesticides assault pine pests, and Roundup—the same ubiquitous weed-killer of the suburbs—eliminates deciduous competition with conifers. A pine plantation, then, is nature grotesquely simplified, a monochromatic grid bearing little similarity to original landscapes—unless the original were (somehow) a corn or cotton field. White oaks, for instance, are not permitted, and neither is the stately longleaf, which is nearly gone. Animal life is also impoverished. Woodpeckers that normally feed on insects that damage trees have been reduced if not nearly eliminated by pesticides, along with dozens of species of ground animals, worms, fish....

Finally we come to the old plantation heartlands: the red clay piedmonts, the blackland prairies, and the deltas. It was here, during the 1960s, that sharecropping ended and that plantations, after generations of functional subdivision, were recentralized in a new regime of mechanization closely resembling big agriculture in the West. Then, during the 1980s, cotton culture suddenly returned to many parts of the South, from southeastern Virginia out to Texas, following introduction of an effective new boll weevil pesticide. Cotton had been abandoned for so long in the northeasternmost sectors of its renewed domain that no one alive during the 1980s could remember what a harvesttime field looked like....

A few folks in revived cotton country worried about the new pesticide, which is applied aerially. Mostly they were relieved to have a substitute for tobacco, which had come upon hard times, and peanuts, which had failed too often. The earth seemed peaceful again, especially around Thanksgiving. The cotton is in and there are traces of "snow" along roadsides and in the fields. It is really cotton, of course—the debris that escaped from the harvesters or blew from trucks—but festive in a way, if one can forget the pesticide residues.

More typically, however, the former plantation South is no longer recognizable as such. In the sprawling Georgia lower piedmont, the old Natchez district, much of central and northern Louisiana, and other stretches, commodity agriculture of any specialty is largely abandoned. Pine plantations and (more likely) suburbs sprawl over thousands of disappeared Taras. Within the paper complex's conifers it is often possible to find, between the straight rows of loblollies, the remains of other straight rows, where corn and cotton once grew for generations of men and women. And the suburbs' shade-making ornamentals flourish where trees were prohibited for eons of extensive agriculture. Out in the Yazoo-Mississippi Delta, where cotton but especially corn, soybeans, and rice cultures survive, remnants of a formerly large but scattered farmworker population are now recentralized, like the plantations themselves, in housing proximate to machinery sheds. Yet even in the Delta most people are no longer employed in farming but in a variety of industrial and service jobs, and they live in along-the-highway hamlets (as the geographer Charles Aiken terms such settlements) close to churches in clean country air.

Yet is there such a thing as clean country air in any part of the contemporary South? Actually, not much. For many decades the tall stacks of midwestern electrical power plants have sent sulfates, nitrates, mercury, and other particulate matter to the Northeast, not only poisoning trees and water in the Adirondacks but penetrating the lungs of Pennsylvania farmers and Brooklyn pedestrians. More recently the vast expansion of power capacity in the South itself (as well as in the lower Midwest) has conferred on a large subregion called the mid-South the dubious distinction of having the worst air in the nation. The atmosphere over central and western Kentucky, middle and eastern Tennessee, most of western North Carolina, and most of the upper halves of Alabama and Georgia commonly contains more than six micrograms per cubic meter of particulate matter from power plants—compared with, say, zero to one microgram on average in the western half of the United States. (We do not address air pollution from autos and trucks here.) So now trees and water in southern Appalachia suffer the same grim fate as those resources in the Adirondacks. There have been massive tree die-offs in the mountains before, from disease epidemics, and there is now an epidemic of human denial that TVA smokestacks might cause tree deaths in the Great Smokies and the Black Mountains in North Carolina. There, and along the Skyline Drive in Virginia, the Park Service conspires to present evidence. Most effective, I think, are glassed-in displays at pull-offs that used to present grand vistas. Dated photographs demonstrate clear, thin air revealing those grand vistas, back in the day, alongside recent pictures that usually replicate what tourists can see for themselves: gloomy shrouds, more of the stuff of "eco-pessimism."...

When, one must ask, will we have had enough of tampering with nature, especially for our comfort, convenience, and monetary enrichment, as opposed to elemental necessities of life?

The End of the South as an American Problem

JOHN EGERTON

For as long as the lower reaches of the North American continent have been commonly referred to as "the South"—which is to say, since the reigning white overlords of the region started rallying their forces in defiance of the national will about 150 years ago—this obstreperous section of the United States has been a puzzle, a preoccupation, and a problem to the nation and to itself....

What was to become our South got its identity and its cohesion in the first half of the nineteenth century as the young nation fell into deepening internal conflict over the economic, political, social, and moral questions surrounding slavery. Many other distinctions contributed to the cultural divergence of the region; climate and geography ordained a society more rural and agricultural than urban and industrial, and its ethnic makeup, its class structure, and its political, educational, and religious institutions all developed a character and personality quite unlike those in the North. But these were minor and inconsequential differences compared with those that had to do with race—with white and black, European and African, free and slave.

In the early decades of the nineteenth century, as the slave trade was curtailed and slavery was abolished in the North, the white leaders of the southern states drew ever closer to one another in their defense of this social system and their determination to extend it into the western states and territories. It was then, in the 1840s and beyond, that the South became an American problem, a problem so grave and threatening that 250 years of shared history would not be enough to prevent a shattering civil war.

Far from resolving the animosities and smoothing over the differences that separated the North and the South, the War between the States set into stone a

---

John Egerton, "The End of the South as an American Problem," in Larry J. Griffin and Don H. Doyle, eds., *The South as an American Problem* (Athens: The University of Georgia Press, 1995), pp. 259–262, 264–271, 273–274.

pattern of conflict and invidious comparison that would not be worn away by another century of passing time. The victors followed conquest with economic and political domination, as victors invariably do, but they lacked the wisdom, the patience and the vision to bring about genuine democratic reform. When their misguided self-righteousness could produce no model for the attainment of racial and social equality in a vanquished population not far from being half white and half black, the forces of occupation withdrew, leaving the remnant confederacy of reactionary Bourbons to resume their old way of life.

The bargain that ended Reconstruction left economic power in the hands of the northern victors but returned political and social power to the southern white men who had held it previously or to their successors in privilege. In short order, they disfranchised the black minority and systematically imposed segregation and inequality by law. The myth of "separate but equal" development not only assured the general disadvantage of black citizens but also perpetuated the inferiority of the South in the national scheme of things. In continuation of this well-established pattern, the South would remain an American problem right on into the twentieth century. When the Great Depression laid the United States low and ushered in Franklin D. Roosevelt and his New Deal recovery programs in the 1930s, the South was flat on the bottom of the national economic heap....

As time went on, a sense of permanent estrangement came to characterize the relationship between the region and the nation; long after the wounds of war had scarred over, there remained this separation, this distance. White men of power and privilege, in the North as well as the South, apparently perceived their self-interest to be best served by a certain arm's-length coolness. Each side saw itself as different/better and the other as different/worse. But if there was mutuality in the arrangement, there was also one-sided advantage; the South had blindly played into the North's hands, accepting continued isolation and bottom-rung inferiority as the price it would willingly pay for a free hand in perpetuating Jim Crow segregation and white supremacy....

The depression still had not ended when World War II began; in fact, it was the economic and social stimulus of the war itself, more than any other force, that jolted the South and the nation into a volatile new world of peril and promise. But in the postwar era, the South once again missed a golden opportunity to begin a self-prescribed process of healing and reform, and it was thus unprepared when its own black minority, inspired by religious leaders and legal experts devoted to the biblical and constitutional promises of justice and equality, finally demanded redress in the courts and in the streets.

And so the much criticized and still rebellious region continued to be pictured as something of an embarrassment to the United States until the mid-1960s, when new federal laws and court decisions finally destroyed the "separate but equal" myth. The scene of domestic conflict then began to shift to various stages elsewhere in the country, and the scourge of injustice and inequality that had for so long been interpreted as the South's affliction inexorably came to be seen as the nation's.

Throughout two and a half centuries of slavery and another of segregation, the nonsouthern people of the United States were conditioned to assume moral high ground, from whence to gaze down judgmentally upon the backward South as a benighted nether region of pervasive inferiority. But since the mid-1960s, that air of superiority has almost completely evaporated. Now, with the country as a whole beset by racial, ethnic, social, and cultural conflict, it may be more accurate to say that *America* is an American problem—and the South could turn out to be not so much the perpetual source of the trouble as a contemporary key to the solution....

[T]he contrast between life in Dixie and life in other regions of the country [after the Civil War] was conspicuous, accentuated by bad attitudes on both sides—by brash, haughty Yankees and proud, resentful rebels. There were a few creative endeavors at which southerners did often excel (talking, writing, cooking, and music making come quickly to mind), but the lingering stereotypes that seemed to cling to southern people of both races like ticks on a hound were devoid of any positive elements. The derogatory images could be painful and infuriating, but the harsh reality was torment enough: six or seven decades after the Civil War, the South still had the look and feel of an antebellum peasant society—an isolated, race-obsessed, class-riven, violent, intolerant, educationally deficient, hand-to-mouth society that was rapidly losing its best and brightest citizens in the north-bound migration stream.

It was virtually mandatory in southern white society in those days to celebrate the Lost Cause of the Confederacy and to ignore or deny altogether the manifest consequences of insistent and persistent white supremacy. Native sons and daughters courted the wrath and rejection of their peers if they dared to point out that segregation imposed a competitive disadvantage on almost all southerners vis-à-vis other Americans. Not until the New Deal days was there the remotest prospect of reform—and even then, the issue of racial discrimination was cautiously averted, and measurable improvements in the lives of the South's poverty-stricken majority were painfully slow in coming.

Finally, in 1938, the National Emergency Council issued its "Report to the President on Economic Conditions of the South," downplaying the fact that a committee of white southerners had actually drafted and refined the document. In a letter to that committee before it began its deliberations, President Roosevelt subscribed to a point of view that was widely shared outside the South and would be quoted frequently in the years to come. "It is my conviction," he declared, "that the South presents right now the Nation's No. 1 economic problem—the Nation's problem, not merely the South's." (Almost no one knew, then or later, that the president's letter, including that explicit assessment, had been drafted for him by a white southerner, New Deal attorney Clifford Durr of Montgomery, Alabama.)

The white South in 1938 was not ready for social change, to say nothing of racial equality. That very report on economic conditions spelled out all sorts of disparities between southern and nonsouthern peoples, but it studiously avoided all but the most oblique references to race and had absolutely nothing to say about discrimination per se. In Birmingham that fall, some fifteen hundred delegates—progressive whites and blacks of every economic class—organized the Southern Conference for Human Welfare to address the social problems southerners faced, but they were soon assailed as left-wing radicals and Communist fellow travelers by the reactionary ruling class, and the reformers would never attract enough committed allies to be seen as a mass movement.

It was also in the fall of 1938 that Roosevelt got a strong dose of conservative reality at the polls. In the national elections midway through his second term in the

White House, the president could not prevent the progressive wing of the Democratic Party from sustaining heavy losses, as the Republicans captured more than seventy seats in both houses of Congress. Ironically, the housecleaning was energized by a reactionary revolt among southern Democrats who had become implacable enemies of FDR and his reformist New Deal philosophy. World War II may have been all that saved Roosevelt himself from defeat in 1940 and again in 1944....

The South's political, economic, spiritual, and intellectual leaders rarely spoke or acted, even in private, against the prevailing laws and customs of segregation and white supremacy. All the more conspicuous and admirable, therefore, were the notable exceptions to this pattern—a relative handful of men and women, black and white, who tried all through the thirties, forties, and fifties to introduce positive reforms into the region. Their collective biography is an inspiring story in its own right. Different though they were from one another, they all ended up on the side of progressive social change, opposite the reactionary men and women who were willing to pursue any course, no matter how extreme, in order to keep the South from surrendering its undemocratic claim to segregation and white supremacy....

From the beginning of the thirties, and even earlier, a few organizations managed to generate an interest in southern social problems by engaging in activities that raised questions about racial and socioeconomic inequality. Some, such as the Commission on Interracial Cooperation in Atlanta and the Southern Tenant Farmers Union in rural Arkansas, were founded and based in the region; others, such as the National Association for the Advancement of Colored People and the Julius Rosenwald Fund, were headquartered in the North. All of these groups were led either by native southerners or by people whose experiences had given them an intimate knowledge of social problems in the southern and border states.

In this early scattering of activists and reformers was a mixture of well-known and little-known individuals: James Weldon Johnson, Howard A. Kester, Walter White, H. L. Mitchell, W. E. B. Du Bois, Will Alexander, Charlotte Hawkins Brown, Myles Horton, Charles H. Houston, Edwin Embree, Thurgood Marshall, Don West, Mary McLeod Bethune, Claude Williams, Charles S. Johnson, Jessie Daniel Ames, Langston Hughes, James Dombrowski, and others.

The Southern Conference for Human Welfare in 1938 and the Southern Regional Council in 1944 brought more progressives to the fore as the South gradually awakened from its long post-Civil War slumber. Frank Porter Graham, Benjamin Mays, Lucy Randolph Mason, Grace T. Hamilton, Aubrey Williams, Gordon B. Hancock, Clark Foreman, Horace Mann Bond, Virginia F. Durr, Osceola McKaine, Guy B. Johnson, Rufus Clement, Witherspoon Dodge, Albert Dent, and Dorothy Rogers Tilly were among the most visible of these.

All through the thirties and forties and into the fifties, there were southern-born novelists and journalists living in and outside the region who used the power of the written word to nudge the South toward reform. Richard Wright, Erskine Caldwell, Zora Neale Hurston, Lillian Smith, John H. McCray, W. J. Cash, J. Saunders Redding, James Agee, Robert L. Vann, Stetson Kennedy, Robert S. Abbott, William Faulkner, Roscoe Dunjee, Thomas Sancton, Ted Poston, Ralph McGill, Ralph Ellison, Hodding Carter,

P. B. Young, Virginius Dabney, Arna Bontemps, and Jonathan Daniels all contributed in greater or lesser degree to this effort.

As it happens, these short rosters include roughly equal numbers of whites and blacks; the parity is symbolic of the stake both races have had in progressive social reform throughout southern history. Richard Wright said it succinctly for all African Americans in 1941: "If we perish, America will perish." And as Martin Luther King Jr. and others, black and white, would declare a quarter century later, the freedom of black southerners was inseparably linked with the liberation of every American, for segregation and inequality held us all in bondage.

A few southern public servants, elected and appointed, could be counted with these others on the side of favoring a reformation in the states of the Old South. The rules of segregation assured that this list at first would be made up almost exclusively of white males: Congressman Maury Maverick of Texas, Senator Claude Pepper of Florida, Supreme Court justice Hugo L. Black of Alabama, federal district judge J. Waties Waring of South Carolina, Governors Ellis Arnall of Georgia and James E. Folsom of Alabama, Virginia state assemblyman Francis Pickens Miller, and a few others. Federal appeals court judge William H. Hastie became the first African American to join this small circle when he was appointed to the bench by President Roosevelt in 1937. (FDR also named black "advisers" to a number of administrative posts in the New Deal and chose Benjamin O. Davis Sr., a career soldier, to be the first black general in the U.S. Armed Forces.)

Academia contributed indirectly to the cadre of reformers. Howard University in Washington, under its longtime president Mordecai Johnson, was by most assessments the premier model of both scholarship and social responsibility among black institutions; on its standout faculty were such respected activist-scholars as historian Rayford W. Logan, political scientist Ralph J. Bunche, sociologist E. Franklin Frazier, and poet Sterling Brown. The University of North Carolina was a similar beacon on the white side, with playwright Paul Green, the university press under W. T. Couch, and the social science faculty under Howard W. Odum getting the most attention—they and the university's liberal president, Frank Porter Graham.

The great black exodus from Dixie in the depression and war years robbed the South of an abundance of talent, from major league baseball star Jackie Robinson and all the professional athletes who came after him to Louis Armstrong and the scores of musicians who made jazz and swing the most popular music of the thirties and forties. The South spawned other noted northern black leaders, too: labor activist A. Philip Randolph was from Florida, singer-actor Paul Robeson had ancestral roots in North Carolina, District of Columbia human rights advocate Mary Church Terrell was born in Memphis, and Channing Tobias, a native of Georgia, was a respected figure in the YMCA and other public-interest organizations. Florida native James Weldon Johnson was the first black executive director of the NAACP....

All these people with southern origins and with visions of a southern reformation held out the promise of change even in the somber days of rigid segregation that filled the entire first half of the twentieth century. Because their views were consonant with the democratic ideals so deeply embedded in American history—and because fortune has thus far looked kindly on this imperfect nation—the progressive southerners ended up on the "right" side of that history, on the side of the one nation indivisible, with liberty and justice for all....

In many ways, the South and its people, black and white, still suffer from their long history of racial discrimination. But the tide of legalized segregation was turned between 1954 and 1965, and since then the region has made significant social and economic strides. Two profoundly symbolic events in the 1960s indelibly marked the turning. The first was on August 28, 1963, when a quarter of a million people at the Lincoln Memorial in Washington—and millions more on television—heard the Reverend Martin Luther King Jr., a black native of Georgia, deliver his spellbinding "I Have a Dream" oration. The second was on March 15, 1965, when a joint session of the United States Congress and a vast television audience heard President Lyndon B. Johnson, a white native of Texas, invoke the words of the civil rights anthem "We Shall Overcome" in putting the full weight of his office behind passage of the 1965 Voting Rights Act.

With quickening speed over the past thirty years, the South has cast off the fetters of racial and regional inferiority and taken its rightful place in the national circle of citizenship. Economic and racial problems that once were considered paramount have diminished to such an extent that many people of both races in and outside the region now see the South as a more appealing place to live than any other part of the country. The so-called Sunbelt—an image-conscious, quasi-mythical new Promised Land—now beckons investors, young fortune seekers, retirees, and even many of the migrants and exiles who left in anger years ago. This is no longer a shunned address, a dreaded destination; in fact, the very term *Sunbelt* has an intentional glow, an enticing sheen, in favorable contrast to the new and negative tag that clings to some parts of the North: the "rust belt."

The extent of some changes is simply astonishing. In 1940, most of the southern states effectively denied the ballot to all except a token few black citizens, but now, blacks in the South register and vote in percentages that closely parallel those of whites. Fifty years ago, there were virtually no black elected public officials in the South at any level, and fewer than a hundred nationwide, but by 1994 there were more than eight thousand in the country, and seven of every ten—more than fifty-five hundred—were the chosen representatives of voters in the southern and border states. Those same states elected more than half of the forty African-American members (thirty-nine Democrats, one Republican) of the 103d Congress, which took office in 1993—and not a single one of them perished in the 1994 midterm-election landslide that gave the Republicans controlling majorities in both houses. (Some were jeopardized, however, by pending lawsuits challenging the configuration of the majority-black districts from which they come.) Blacks have also been elected in recent years to serve as mayors of many of the South's largest cities, and one, Douglas Wilder, was voted in as governor of Virginia in 1989.

The South's public schools were completely segregated by law until the Supreme Court declared such statutes unconstitutional in 1954; forty years later, biracial or multiracial enrollment was a more commonplace characteristic of the schools in this region than it was in most other parts of the nation. And in the categories of employment and housing, two more fundamental indicators of societal stability, southerners in general and black southerners in particular could look back on a fairly consistent pattern of both relative and absolute progress since segregation was outlawed.

These four factors—politics, education, employment, and housing—are like the legs that support a solid table; when properly constructed, they should bring about stability, balance, and equity. Without in any way suggesting that the South has built a perfect table, it seems fair to say that it has strengthened every leg for all its citizens over the past fifty years. The beleaguered South that Franklin Roosevelt saw as the nation's most pressing domestic problem in 1938 is now at least as functional as the other regions; indeed, the condition of its economic and social health elicits a certain note of envy in many states from New England to the West Coast....

All of which begs another question: Does the South have collective qualities of character and personality arising from its history that might now be summoned to point the nation toward higher ground? It seems prudent not to overstate such a claim. After all, this is the same South that in the past so vigorously defended slavery, that invented segregation, that resisted even the most modest attempts to nourish simple justice. Furthermore, the South traditionally has been identified with political, religious, economic, and social conservatism—and conservatism by definition has more to do with resisting change than with stimulating it. The conservative Republican avalanche of 1994 was nowhere more powerful than in the South, and southern members of Congress were among the principal instigators of it.

As the United States gropes for a central path to unity within the broad landscape of diversity, however, it is worth remembering that the social and ideological bomb that blew the South and the nation apart in the first place was triggered by a misguided faith in racial chauvinism, in white supremacy—and that is a subject that southerners white and black have been compelled existentially to face.

Their common history has linked them inseparably; whether friend or foe, they are kinfolk—spiritual and cultural first cousins, if not brothers and sisters, husbands and wives. Southern whites assumed advantage over southern blacks, but neither race was shielded from the consequences of poverty, oppression, discrimination, and defeat. They endured and survived a history that set them apart together on a tributary of the American mainstream, and there their lives were similarly shaped by proximity. Their speech, their music, their food and drink, their work, their entertainment, their religion, their rites of passage into birth and marriage and death—all these were recognizably alike, albeit not identical.

Racially different southerners were not strangers; they knew one another on sight and often by name. Whether or not they could acknowledge it comfortably, they shared a place, an identity, a culture. In the best of circumstances, a measure of affection and trust developed between them—and in that slender reed of caring and knowing there is an element of hope, a seed of possibility that could transcend the limits of liberal and conservative ideology.

The end of the South as an American problem does not signal the end of social and cultural conflict in the United States. It could mean, however, that this region, with its long history of internal conflict, is now in a better position to steer the country closer to its ideals, if only because the people of the South know from bitter experience how disastrous the policy of segregation and enforced inequality was—for whites as well as blacks, for men and women of every station, and for the entire nation no less than its once rebellious southern states.

FURTHER READING

Peter Applebome, *Dixie Rising: How the South Is Shaping American Values, Politics, and Culture* (1997).

Harry S. Ashmore, *An Epitaph for Dixie* (1958).

Nelson M. Blake, *Land into Water—Water into Land: A History of Water Management in Florida* (1980).

James C. Cobb, *Away Down South: A History of Southern Identity* (2005).

Albert E. Cowdrey, *This Land, This South: An Environmental History* (1983).

Fifteen Southerners, *Why the South Will Survive* (1981).

Joel Garreau, *The Nine Nations of North America* (1981).

Larry J. Griffin and Don H. Doyle, eds., *The South as an American Problem* (1995).

Robert L. Hall and Carol B. Stack, eds., *Holding on to the Land and the Lord: Kinship, Ritual, Land Tenure, and Social Policy in the Rural South* (1982).

Robert G. Healy, *Competition for Land in the American South: Agriculture, Human Settlement, and the Environment* (1985).

Florence King, *Southern Ladies and Gentlemen* (1975).

E. Blaine Liner and Lawrence K. Lynch, eds., *The Economics of Southern Growth* (1977).

Tara McPherson, *Reconstructing Dixie: Race, Gender, and Nostalgia in the Imagined South* (2003).

Randall M. Miller and George E. Pozzetta, eds., *Shades of the Sunbelt: Essays on Ethnicity, Race, and the Urban South* (1988).

Raymond A. Mohl, ed., *Searching for the Sunbelt: Historical Perspectives on a Region* (1989).

William Least Heat Moon, *Blue Highways: A Journey into America* (1982).

Bethany Moreton, *To Serve God and Wal-Mart: The Making of Christian Free Enterprise* (2009).

Thomas H. Naylor and James Clotfelter, *Strategies for Change in the South* (1975).

John Shelton Reed, *The Enduring South: Subcultural Persistence in Mass Society* (1972).

———, *One South: An Ethnic Approach to Regional Culture* (1982).

Charles P. Roland, "The Ever-Vanishing South," *Journal of Southern History* 48 (1982), 3–20.

John David Smith and Tom Appleton, eds., *A Mythic Land Apart: Reassessing Southerners and Their History* (1997).

Carol Stack, *Call to Home: African Americans Reclaim the Rural South* (1996).

Rupert B. Vance and Nicholas J. Demerath, eds., *The Urban South* (1954).

Sandra Vance and Roy Scott, "Sam Walton and Wal-Mart Stores, Inc.: A Study in Modern Southern Entrepreneurship," *Journal of Southern History* 58 (May 1992), 231–252.

Bernard L. Weinstein and Robert E. Firestine, *Regional Growth and Decline in the United States: The Rise of the Sunbelt and the Decline of the Northeast* (1978).

David E. Whisnant, *All That Is Native and Fine: The Politics of Culture in an American Region* (1983).

———, *Modernizing the Mountaineer: People, Power, and Planning in Appalachia* (1980).